EKTRON DEVELOPER'S

INTRODUCTION xxiii

▶ PART I GETTING STARTED

CHAPTER 1	Introducing Ektron 3
CHAPTER 2	The Ektron Web Project Methodology 17
CHAPTER 3	The Implementation Guide 29
CHAPTER 4	Configuring Your Development Environment 45

▶ PART II BUILDING THE TECHPOINT SITE

CHAPTER 5	Understanding Content Management Fundamentals 53
CHAPTER 6	Configuring Commonly Used Components 107
CHAPTER 7	The Homepage 147
CHAPTER 8	Reaching Prospects 225
CHAPTER 9	Generating Leads Through Campaign Optimization 265
CHAPTER 10	Supporting Customers 333
CHAPTER 11	Implementing the OnTrek Social Network 389
CHAPTER 12	Creating the Catalog of Products for the eCommerce Storefront . . . 441
CHAPTER 13	Constructing the Online Storefront with eCommerce 491

▶ PART III DEPLOYING THE TECHPOINT SITE

CHAPTER 14	Deploying Your Website 547
CHAPTER 15	Maintaining Your Website 571
CHAPTER 16	Next Steps 587

▶ PART IV APPENDIXES

APPENDIX A	CMS Extensions 599
APPENDIX B	Framework API 605
APPENDIX C	Performance Checklist 611

GLOSSARY 615

INDEX 625

Ektron Developer's Guide

Ektron Developer's Guide
BUILDING AN EKTRON POWERED WEBSITE

Bill Cava
Bill Rogers
Aniel Sud

Wiley Publishing, Inc.

Ektron Developer's Guide: Building an Ektron Powered Website

Published by
Wiley Publishing, Inc.
10475 Crosspoint Boulevard
Indianapolis, IN 46256
www.wiley.com

Copyright © 2011 by Wiley Publishing, Inc., Indianapolis, Indiana

Published simultaneously in Canada

ISBN: 978-0-470-88569-7
ISBN: 978-1-118-05800-8 (ebk)
ISBN: 978-1-118-05801-5 (ebk)
ISBN: 978-1-118-05802-2 (ebk)

Manufactured in the United States of America

10 9 8 7 6 5 4 3 2 1

No part of this publication may be reproduced, stored in a retrieval system or transmitted in any form or by any means, electronic, mechanical, photocopying, recording, scanning or otherwise, except as permitted under Sections 107 or 108 of the 1976 United States Copyright Act, without either the prior written permission of the Publisher, or authorization through payment of the appropriate per-copy fee to the Copyright Clearance Center, 222 Rosewood Drive, Danvers, MA 01923, (978) 750-8400, fax (978) 646-8600. Requests to the Publisher for permission should be addressed to the Permissions Department, John Wiley & Sons, Inc., 111 River Street, Hoboken, NJ 07030, (201) 748-6011, fax (201) 748-6008, or online at http://www.wiley.com/go/permissions.

Limit of Liability/Disclaimer of Warranty: The publisher and the author make no representations or warranties with respect to the accuracy or completeness of the contents of this work and specifically disclaim all warranties, including without limitation warranties of fitness for a particular purpose. No warranty may be created or extended by sales or promotional materials. The advice and strategies contained herein may not be suitable for every situation. This work is sold with the understanding that the publisher is not engaged in rendering legal, accounting, or other professional services. If professional assistance is required, the services of a competent professional person should be sought. Neither the publisher nor the author shall be liable for damages arising herefrom. The fact that an organization or Web site is referred to in this work as a citation and/or a potential source of further information does not mean that the author or the publisher endorses the information the organization or Web site may provide or recommendations it may make. Further, readers should be aware that Internet Web sites listed in this work may have changed or disappeared between when this work was written and when it is read.

For general information on our other products and services please contact our Customer Care Department within the United States at (877) 762-2974, outside the United States at (317) 572-3993 or fax (317) 572-4002.

Wiley also publishes its books in a variety of electronic formats. Some content that appears in print may not be available in electronic books.

Library of Congress Control Number: 2010941222

Trademarks: Wiley, the Wiley logo, Wrox, the Wrox logo, Programmer to Programmer, and related trade dress are trademarks or registered trademarks of John Wiley & Sons, Inc. and/or its affiliates, in the United States and other countries, and may not be used without written permission. Ektron, the Ektron logo and eIntranet, are registered trademarks of Ektron, Inc. All other trademarks are the property of their respective owners. Wiley Publishing, Inc., is not associated with any product or vendor mentioned in this book.

Dedicated to the Ektron team, each and every person makes a significant difference.

CREDITS

ACQUISITIONS EDITOR
Paul Reese

PROJECT EDITOR
Maureen Spears

TECHNICAL EDITORS
Jason Arden
Joseph Cicchetto

PRODUCTION EDITOR
Kathleen Wisor

COPY EDITOR
Kezia Endsley

EDITORIAL DIRECTOR
Robyn B. Siesky

EDITORIAL MANAGER
Mary Beth Wakefield

FREELANCER EDITORIAL MANAGER
Rosemarie Graham

ASSOCIATE DIRECTOR OF MARKETING
David Mayhew

PRODUCTION MANAGER
Tim Tate

VICE PRESIDENT AND EXECUTIVE GROUP PUBLISHER
Richard Swadley

VICE PRESIDENT AND EXECUTIVE PUBLISHER
Barry Pruett

ASSOCIATE PUBLISHER
Jim Minatel

PROJECT COORDINATOR, COVER
Katie Crocker

PROOFREADER
Nancy Carrasco

INDEXER
Johnna VanHoose Dinse

COVER DESIGNER
Michael E. Trent

COVER IMAGE
© Petr Novotny/istockphoto.com

ABOUT THE AUTHORS

BILL CAVA is a six-year veteran of Ektron. As Chief Evangelist, Bill channels his passion for internet technology, WCM, and software development into the Ektron Developer Community. Prior to this role, Bill served as Chief Technologist responsible for guiding the company's technology direction, product strategy, new product development and engineering practices. Before joining Ektron, Bill was a principal engineer at Lycos, one of the Internet's first search engines. Earlier in his career he worked at the Center for Intelligent Information Retrieval as a research engineer. He holds patents on Information Retrieval and is a technology advisor for a number of internet companies. As an undergraduate at the University of Massachusetts Amherst, Bill studied Italian Literature, Fine Art and Computer Science, and continued his Computer Science studies as a graduate student at Worcester Polytechnical Institute (WPI).

BILL ROGERS founded Ektron in 1998 with a simple vision: enable business users to easily author and publish content on websites. Today, Rogers has sparked a revolution in the way organizations create and manage interactive Web, intranet and extranet sites. He recognized early on how important websites would become to companies' business models, and guided Ektron in creating a Web content management software platform that provides all the functionality Webmasters, designers and developers want in a single application, while still minimizing the complexity to which the non-technical users are exposed.

In his role as a hands-on chief executive officer, Rogers is actively engaged in keeping Ektron a Web content management market and technology leader. He sets the company's strategic direction, aligns product development with his forward-looking vision for website technology and is involved in all aspects of Ektron's operations. In addition, he frequently participates in industry events and solicits feedback from Ektron's customers and partners to stay on the leading edge of Web technology development. Rogers received a Bachelor of Science degree in Electrical Engineering from Boston University.

ANIEL SUD has been in the WCM industry since 2002 and with Ektron for four years. Serving Ektron as CMS Architect, he envisions new features like Ektron's PageBuilder and brings them to reality. Before becoming CMS Architect, Aniel served as Ektron's Technical Evangelist, a role where he helped customers, through trade show talks, local user groups, and one-on-one consultation, to understand methods of enabling Ektron to make their lives easier. Prior to joining Ektron, Aniel co-founded Firefall Pro, a boutique Web development firm, specializing in marketing and content management systems. He received his Bachelors from Drexel where he studied Computer Engineering.

ABOUT THE TECHNICAL EDITORS

JASON ARDEN joined Ektron in 2006, and currently serves as Director of Partner Engineering. The Partner Engineering Team is a key part of the complete set of services and support options that allows Ektron to ensure that their Partners succeed in deploying Ektron solutions. Prior to heading up the Partner Engineering Team, Mr. Arden served as a Lead Consulting Sales Engineer working with Ektron Partners and prospects during the pre-sales lifecycle. Prior to joining Ektron, Jason was part of the IT staff at the Radiological Society of North America. He holds a BS in Networking and Telecommunications Management from DeVry University.

JOSEPH CICCHETTO is a Sr. CMS Architect at Ektron, overseeing the corporate architecture team for the Professional Services Group. In this role, Joe is responsible for setting architecture standards, and acting as lead architect on enterprise solutions. Prior to joining Ektron, Joe was Director of Engineering for Softmedia and has a broad background in software development and project management. Joe studied Computer Science as an undergraduate student at Boston University.

ACKNOWLEDGMENTS

WE'D LIKE TO THANK the Wrox staff, especially Paul Reese, Maureen Spears, and Kezia Endsley. Maureen and Kezia were instrumental in their editing efforts, and without them, the process of writing this book would have been infinitely more painful. Behind the scenes, Anna Jeon and Fred Bals worked very hard to help us to maintain standards and made sure to berate Aniel every time he ended a sentence with a preposition.

Our technical editors — Jason Arden and Joe Cicchetto — were also key to the process of getting the content into a publishable format. Without them, the code samples in this book probably wouldn't even compile. Ted Henry and Keith Pepin also played essential roles in working with the authors to ensure that the content was sound and correct. Brian Fanny also provided substantial input, giving us technical feedback and general knowledge relating to support issues, including deployment and maintenance.

Brian Browning went above and beyond, creating large portions of the content for Chapters 2 and 3. As the Senior Director of Client Services at Ektron, he is uniquely poised to create content outlining Ektron's Professional Services process.

Chris Banner, Bob Bolt, Bruce Bourdon, Doug Domeny, Steve Mann, Alpesh Patel and Justin West all played central roles in helping the authors to understand various technical approaches to individual issues, and their input is greatly appreciated. Scott Kearney provided valuable insight into the eCommerce related content, and Joe Chestnut, Justin Ryan, and Sanela Suljic all assisted by giving us feedback on Deployment and Maintenance.

CONTENTS

INTRODUCTION *xxiii*

PART I: GETTING STARTED

CHAPTER 1: INTRODUCING EKTRON — 3

- **Ektron: The Company** — 3
- **Ektron's Community, Support, and Services** — 4
  - Ektron's Online Community — 4
  - Ektron Technical Support — 5
  - Ektron's Best Practices and Professional Services — 6
  - Ektron Training — 7
- **Ektron, the Framework** — 7
  - All-in-One versus Best-of-Breed — 8
  - Developing with the Ektron Framework — 9
  - System Requirements — 13
- **Who Uses Ektron?** — 15
- **Take Home Points** — 16

CHAPTER 2: THE EKTRON WEB PROJECT METHODOLOGY — 17

- **Iterative/Waterfall versus Agile Approaches** — 18
- **The Business Case: Where It All Starts** — 18
- **Understanding the Implementation Process** — 19
- **The Discovery Phase** — 19
  - Kicking Off the Project — 20
  - Developing a Project Plan — 20
- **The Implementation Phase** — 24
  - Starting Development — 24
  - Content Migration — 25
- **The Quality Assurance Phase** — 26
  - System Testing — 26
  - User Acceptance Testing — 27
- **Take Home Points** — 28

CONTENTS

CHAPTER 3: THE IMPLEMENTATION GUIDE — 29

The Ektron Approach — 30
Implementation Guide — 31
The OnTrek Implementation Guide — 32
    The Homepage — 33
    Product Page — 35
    User Dashboard Page — 39
Take Home Points: Best Practices for Creating an Implementation Guide — 42

CHAPTER 4: CONFIGURING YOUR DEVELOPMENT ENVIRONMENT — 45

What You Need to Configure Your Machine — 45
Installing the Framework — 46
    Development Scenarios — 47
    Source Control — 47
    Data Synchronization — 47
Further Tips — 49
Take Home Points — 49

PART II: BUILDING THE TECHPOINT SITE

CHAPTER 5: UNDERSTANDING CONTENT MANAGEMENT FUNDAMENTALS — 53

Login and Workarea — 54
    Logging In and Creating a User — 55
    Exploring the Workarea — 59
Content Entry and Display — 62
    Content Storage and Status — 62
    Adding and Managing Content — 64
    Using the Content Block Server Control — 82
Folders and the Library — 85
    Implementation: Adding a Folder and Managing Library Items — 85
    Under the Hood: Folders and Libraries — 95
    Folders and Library in Brief — 95
Permissions, Approvals, and Roles — 95
    Understanding Permissions — 95
    Understanding Approval Chain Workflows — 96

Understanding Roles	96
Managing Permissions and Workflow	96
Under the Hood	102
Take Home Points	**105**

CHAPTER 6: CONFIGURING COMMONLY USED COMPONENTS — 107

Understanding the Technology	**108**
Smart Forms	**109**
The Difference between Smart Forms and HTML Forms	110
Understanding Smart Form Design	110
Creating Smart Form Designs	111
Retrieving, Manipulating, and Rendering Structured Data	113
Implementation	117
Under the Hood	122
Taxonomy	**124**
Implementation	125
Under the Hood	128
Aliasing	**130**
Taxonomy Based Aliasing	131
Folder Based Aliasing	131
RegEx Based Aliasing	131
Community Aliasing	131
Manual Aliasing	132
Implementation	132
Under the Hood	135
Multilingual Sites	**136**
Designing an Ektron Multilingual Website	137
Managing the Displayed Content Language	141
Implementation	142
Under the Hood	144
Take Home Points	**145**

CHAPTER 7: THE HOMEPAGE — 147

Use Case	**148**
Technology	**150**
Using Rotating Graphics	150
Adding Navigation	150
Rich Interaction Using jQuery, Smart Forms, and Handlers	**151**

Types of Interaction	151
Homepage Image Rotator Using Serialization	153
Homepage Image Rotator Using XSLT	162
Web Service Creation and Consumption	169
Using Menus for Navigation	**185**
Ektron Menu Basics	185
Implementing the Global Navigation Menu	191
Under the Hood	195
Using Search for Navigation	**197**
Defining Your SiteSearch Strategy	198
Adding Search to the Global Navigation	203
Under the Hood	205
Sitemap and Breadcrumbs	**209**
Creating Breadcrumbs for the Products Folder	210
Implementing the BreadCrumb Server Control	212
Creating a Sitemap Page	213
Registration	**215**
Allowing a User to Register on the Site	215
Allowing Users to Modify Their Properties	218
Implementing a Password Reset Feature	219
Implementing Facebook Registration	220
Take Home Points	**223**

CHAPTER 8: REACHING PROSPECTS — 225

Use Case	**225**
Technology	**227**
ListSummary	**228**
Implementing a Basic ListSummary	229
Changing the HTML Markup Using XSLT	232
Changing the Markup Using EKML	236
Calendars	**239**
Creating a System Calendar, User Calendar, and Group Calendar	240
Displaying Events Using a WebCalendar Server Control	246
Displaying Events Using a ListSummary Server Control	250
Displaying Events Using a Content Block Server Control	250
Display a List of Upcoming Events	253
Outputting iCal Feeds	256
Video/Customer Testimonials	**257**

Adding an Object to the DMS	257
Modifying Settings on Managed Objects	259
Displaying the Managed Object	261
Alternatives to Using the Ektron Framework	262
Take Home Points	**263**

CHAPTER 9: GENERATING LEADS THROUGH CAMPAIGN OPTIMIZATION — 265

Use Case	**266**
Understanding the Technology	**268**
Implementation Using Collections	**270**
Creating a Collection	271
Adding to the Collection	272
Putting the Collection on the Landing Page	273
Customizing the Presentation of the Collection Widget	275
Under the Hood: Collection Data Model	280
PageBuilder	**282**
Creating the Wireframe	283
Associating the Wireframe to a Folder	286
Creating a Layout Based on the Wireframe	286
Under the Hood	292
Widgets	**297**
Creating the Widget	299
Under the Hood: Widgets	307
HTML Forms	**310**
Creating a Form	310
Implementation: The "Request a Demo" Form	311
Under the Hood: HTML Form Data Model	315
Multivariate Testing	317
Under the Hood: Multivariate	323
Multivariate Brief	324
Web Analytics	**324**
Traffic Analytics versus Business Analytics	324
Analytics Reports	325
Setting Up Site Wide Traffic Analytics	326
Measuring Effectiveness of the Campaign Using Traffic Analytics	328
Under the Hood: Analytics	329
Take Home Points	**330**
Additional Practice Steps	**331**

CHAPTER 10: SUPPORTING CUSTOMERS — 333

- **Understanding the Technology** — 334
  - Forums — 334
  - Blogs — 334
  - Wiki — 335
- **Use Case** — 336
- **Building Forums** — 338
  - Creating Forums in the Workarea — 339
- **Blogs** — 353
  - Create a Blog in the Workarea — 354
  - Create a Template with a Blog Server Control — 358
- **Wikis** — 363
  - Creating a Wiki in the Workarea — 364
  - Using the Wiki Feature in the Site — 364
  - Creating a New PageBuilder Page — 365
  - Using the Wiki and Creating Links — 367
  - Editing Existing Content — 369
- **The SocialBar Server Control** — 369
  - Implementing the SocialBar Widget — 370
- **Content Flagging and Content Review** — 378
  - Setting Up Flagging Definitions — 378
  - Implementing the ContentFlagging and ContentReview Server Controls — 379
  - Running Flagging and Review Reports, and Moderating Reviews — 383
- **Take Home Points** — 387

CHAPTER 11: IMPLEMENTING THE ONTREK SOCIAL NETWORK — 389

- **The Importance of Social Networking** — 390
- **Technology** — 391
- **Users, Friends, and Profiles** — 392
  - Understanding the Friending Process — 392
  - Understanding User Profile Functionality — 393
  - Configuring Community Member Templates — 396
  - OnTrek's User Profile User Control — 397
  - Under the Hood — 404
- **Community Groups** — 408
  - How Users Discover Community Groups — 409
  - Creating a Community Group — 409
  - Configuring Community Group Templates — 411

OnTrek's Group Profile User Control	412
Under the Hood	416
Dashboards	**419**
What's on the Dashboard?	419
Using the Dashbard Components and Widget Spaces	420
Activity Streams	**422**
Using Activity Streams to Your Advantage	422
Under the Hood	428
Micro-Messaging	**433**
Micro-Messaging Strategies	433
Adding Micro-Messaging to the User Profile	435
Under the Hood	437
Take Home Points	**438**

CHAPTER 12: CREATING THE CATALOG OF PRODUCTS FOR THE ECOMMERCE STOREFRONT — 441

Use Case	**442**
Understanding the Technology	**444**
Configuring eCommerce	**444**
Managing Major Configuration Options	445
Configuring the Settings for Shipping and Taxes	461
Creating a Catalog and Product	**467**
Creating Product Types	468
Creating a Catalog	471
Creating a Product	473
Coupons	**481**
Product Reports and Order Management	**485**
Reports	485
Order Management	488
Take Home Points	**489**

CHAPTER 13: CONSTRUCTING THE ONLINE STOREFRONT WITH ECOMMERCE — 491

Use Case	**492**
eCommerce Server Controls and Implementation	**494**
Browsing Experience Controls	495
Purchase and Maintenance Controls	506
OnTrek eCommerce Implementation	516
Custom Order Workflow	**525**
Windows Workflow Foundation Basics	526
Creating a Custom Activity	527

Building a Workflow	531
Using a Custom Workflow in an Ektron Site	535
Building a Payment Gateway Provider	**536**
Brief Overview of Payment Gateways	537
Creating a Gateway Provider	538
Installing the Gateway Provider into the OnTrek Website	543
Take Home Points	**544**

PART III: DEPLOYING THE TECHPOINT SITE

CHAPTER 14: DEPLOYING YOUR WEBSITE — 547

Pre-Conditions for a Successful Deployment	**548**
Creating the Discovery Collateral	548
Completion of the Development Process	549
Creating the Staging Environment	549
Content Is in a Staged Environment	550
Completion of System Testing	551
Understanding the Different Deployment Scenarios	**554**
Understanding the Basic Terminology	554
Determining the Content Flow	555
Moving Content with or without eSync	**558**
Moving Content with eSync	558
Moving Content without eSync	561
The Deployment	**563**
Installing Your Website on Another Server	563
Securing the Server	567
Take Home Points	**568**

CHAPTER 15: MAINTAINING YOUR WEBSITE — 571

Creating an Effective Maintenance Plan	**571**
Capturing Data	572
Analyzing Data	572
Acting upon Data	573
Maintaining Content Freshness	**573**
Running Content Reports	574
Performing "Spot Checks"	576
Maintaining Availability	**577**
Maintaining Performance	**579**
Maintaining Usability	**581**

Maintaining (and Building) Reach	582
Maintaining Calm During Disaster Recovery	584
Take Home Points	585

CHAPTER 16: NEXT STEPS — 587

Reviewing What You Learned	587
Connecting with Ektron and the Online Community	588
A Quick Review of Ektron's Technical Support	589
Don't Forget Your Account Manager	589
Utilizing Ektron's Professional Services and Training Packages	590
Leveraging Online Developer Resources	590
The Framework API	591
CMS Extensions	591
Integrating Ektron with a Content Delivery Network	591
Building Your First Ektron eCommerce Site	592
Utilizing the Ektron eCommerce APIs	592
Introduction to the Ektron eCommerce Workflow Engine	592
Creating Your Own eCommerce Payment Gateway Provider	593
Hands On with the Content Targeting Widget	593
Introduction to Ektron eSync	593
Introduction to the Ektron Marketing Optimization Suite	594
Ektron Widgets in Version 8	594
Writing an RIA Application with Ektron	594
Take Home Points	595

PART IV: APPENDIXES

APPENDIX A: CMS EXTENSIONS — 599

Benefits of Ektron Framework, Version 8	599
Building Your Extension	600
Available Strategies and Overrides	600
The Completed Extension	602
Registering Your Extension	603

APPENDIX B: FRAMEWORK API — 605

Working with the Framework API	605
Framework Object Constructors	605

Where to Find the Framework API	606
CRUD Operations on Content	**607**
Create	607
Retrieve	607
Retrieving a List of Data	608
Update	609
Delete	609
Take Home Points	**609**

APPENDIX C: PERFORMANCE CHECKLIST — 611

Hardware Requirements	611
Appropriate SQL Server Deployment	611
Appropriate and Judicious Caching	612
Code Profiling	613
Compiled Site	613
Event Error Maintenance	613
Gzip Response Compression	613
Externalize Resources and Use CDNs Where Applicable	613
Request Minimization	614
Glossary	615

INDEX — **625**

INTRODUCTION

GIVEN THAT YOU'RE READING the introduction to a Wrox book about Ektron, you likely have (or will soon have) some level of technical responsibility for a website powered by the Ektron Framework. Maybe you're tasked with the duty of maintaining an existing site and are looking for information to help make that process more efficient; or maybe you're developing a new site and are in need of deep technical information, best practices, and step-by-step guidance showing how to build a website from the ground-up using the Ektron framework. Whichever it is, you are involved in a Web project of some form, and you've most likely picked up this book to gain some level of technical competency with the Ektron Framework.

This book will cover the Ektron Framework in great technical depth, covering step-by-step instructions, best practices, and tips and tricks, in a way that is useful for someone needing to build a new website, maintain an existing one, or something in the middle. The book goes beyond the basics of technical competency with the Ektron platform, however, and helps you gain a solid understanding of how to achieve success with your Ektron Web projects. From a developer's standpoint, becoming technically proficient in Ektron is a prerequisite for this success; but when all is said and done, your project's success depends on more than just your knowledge of how to get the latest gadget on your website.

What makes a Web project successful? Far too often, Web projects begin without the proper preparation work in place to ensure their success. Web projects can fail for a great number of reasons, but most often, they break down when they fail to follow a standardized and proven methodology. A methodology is a defined set of repeatable steps that can better guarantee a successful outcome. Following a methodology ensures that the result of your project is aligned to the needs of the business, addresses all of the components of the site's user experience and is a technically solid solution, able to scale and perform in a way that supports your organization's objectives. It also helps the team to understand whether or not success has been achieved because it compares the project's progress against the milestones and success metrics established during project planning.

Although this type of planning may sound unimportant to a developer "just" trying to build a website, it's important to understand what makes a Web project successful; even if some of the responsibilities aren't a part of your day-to-day job description, the ultimate responsibility for a Web project's success typically falls on the laps of those closest to it. This book was written to provide Web developers and technical project managers with the overarching knowledge needed to achieve success with their Ektron Web projects — including information on both technology and methodology.

The approach taken in this book is to first cover Ektron's recommended project discovery process, discussing the methodology employed by Ektron Professional Services, and learning about the documentation generated as part of this process, all of which ensures a successful Web project. This process stems from ten years of experience during which the Ektron professional services team developed over 1,000 successful websites for its customers. Over this time, the team not only developed a comprehensive website design methodology, but also enhanced and optimized that methodology to service the specific considerations unique to implementing an Ektron powered website.

This book also has documentation in each chapter so you can implement specific portions and functionalities of an example site. You can install this site locally and use it to follow as you read the book. Chapters focus on the technical material you'll need to master the Ektron Framework. Each technical chapter follows a similar pattern in that it focuses on the implementation of a subsection of a website for a fictional software company called OnTrek, and then creates a meaningful context for instruction centered around business-driven use cases.

WHO THIS BOOK IS FOR

The target audience for this book is ASP.NET developers and technical project managers who want to learn how to achieve success with Ektron Web projects. The value of the methodology chapter will be apparent to Technical Project Managers, but is written in such a way as to appeal to technical developers as well. Developers will appreciate the best practices, tips and tricks, step-by-step instruction, and deep-dive "under the hood" explanations of the Ektron Framework.

Whether you're just starting out with the Ektron Platform or have used it in the past, this book covers the latest Ektron technology in a way that will benefit both audiences. Readers do not need to have experience with Ektron, but they should have experience with current ASP.NET development practices using Visual Studio and C#.

WHAT THIS BOOK COVERS

This book covers the theory and practice for building and managing a successful website with Ektron CMS400.NET version 8.0.2. The book is divided into three primary parts, with the first covering the Ektron development methodology, development environment considerations, and other items of interest in the process leading up to actual development.

The second part discusses the actual buildout of a site on the Ektron Framework. In this part, you touch on content management principles and concepts as they apply to the Ektron Framework, and then see each major feature of the framework. These discussions focus on using a combination of codebehind, server controls, and PageBuilder to achieve various goals. Each chapter discusses a real-world use case from the OnTrek starter site, and then either implements that functionality within the OnTrek site or analyzes how it was previously implemented in the site.

The bulk of the discussions in this book pertains specifically to version 8.0.2 of the Ektron Framework, but in most cases will also apply to other recent versions. In some cases, the authors discuss previous iterations of a given piece of the framework, to help you better understand how the technology works today. In other cases, they discuss where the technology is heading next.

HOW THIS BOOK IS STRUCTURED

This book will walk you through the process of creating a website using the Ektron CMS Framework. It is divided into three main sections.

Part I: Getting Started

This part covers background material relating to Ektron, the Ektron Framework, and the methodology employed for Ektron projects. This methodology is then used in Part II.

- **Chapter 1: Introducing Ektron** — This chapter provides an introduction to Ektron the company, and the Ektron Framework. It gives readers an understanding of why the book was written as well as the target audience. It also covers the general structure of the book, introducing the OnTrek site, business drivers, and overview of use cases

- **Chapter 2: The Ektron Web Project Methodology** — This chapter introduces the methodology recommended by Ektron and followed by its own Professional Service teams. It will discuss the pros and cons of its approach and guide you through the process of adapting this process to meet the needs of your project.

- **Chapter 3: The Implementation Guide** — This chapter introduces the website of a fictitious software company that is used in each of the technical sections throughout the book. It also presents the implementation guide.

- **Chapter 4: Configuring Your Development Environment** — This chapter introduces the software configuration needed to start developing on the Ektron Framework.

Part II: Building the TechPoint Site

Part II builds on the methodology discussed in Part I (to create an implementation guide), which is used as a specification guide throughout the implementation process. Each chapter covers a specific area of the site, implementing features against the implementation guide.

The implementation sections of the Part II chapters follow a pattern in that they outline a portion of the implementation guide, starting with a use case that is the jumping point to the particular area of the site under development. This is followed by an overview of the features used in the chapter. Each individual technology is then discussed in depth. The chapters close with a summary of the lessons learned in the chapter.

- **Chapter 5: Understanding Content Management Fundamentals** — This chapter discusses core Web Content Management concepts within the context of the OnTrek site.

- **Chapter 6: Configuring Commonly Used Components** — This chapter goes a step further in the core technologies, and helps you to configure items like URL aliasing, structured content, and multilingual content.

- **Chapter 7: The Homepage** — This chapter discusses the main elements of the most visited part of the OnTrek site, the homepage. The technologies here include rich interfaces, user registrations, and many navigational items.

- **Chapter 8: Reaching Prospects** — This discusses the area of the site dedicated to educating prospects about TechPoint's products and services. This includes delivering video, implementing calendars, and core technology items like ListSummaries.

- Chapter 9: Generating Leads through Campaign Optimization — This chapter discusses PageBuilder in depth, and how it can be paired with abilities like multivariate testing and analytics.
- Chapter 10: Supporting Customers — This chapter discusses the technology that creates a successful customer support portal. It focuses on the roll of community generated content as well as editorial managed information.
- Chapter 11: Implementing the OnTrek Social Network — Social Software has become an essential part of modern websites. This chapter introduces the Ektron CMS Framework's social software and works through the process of building the Community Network.
- Chapter 12: Creating the Catalog of Products for the eCommerce Storefront — This chapter discusses how to create the product catalog for the OnTrek storefront using Ektron's eCommerce. It focuses primarily on configuring software options rather than development.
- Chapter 13: Constructing the Online Storefront with eCommerce — This chapter discusses how to implement OnTrek's online storefront using Ektron's eCommerce. It focuses on the available server controls and how to combine them to create a meaningful shopping experience.

Part 3: Deploying the TechPoint Site

Once implementation has finished, the process of bringing the website live begins — along with maintenance and reporting. These chapters give you hints and tips on how to continue to achieve the goals that were originally set for your website.

- Chapter 14: Deploying Your Website — This chapter discusses the process for deploying a fully developed and tested site.
- Chapter 15: Maintaining Your Website — A site is dynamic — once it is live, ongoing work is needed to ensure that the content remains relevant and that it meets and continues to meet the business objectives.
- Chapter 16: Next Steps — This chapter provides a review of the information covered and provides the reader with direction to learn more about Ektron.

WHAT YOU NEED TO USE THIS BOOK

You need to have the following software installed on your computer to run the examples in this book:

- Ektron Framework 8.0.2: The current version as of this writing is 8.0.2 and all of the code samples, screenshots, and instructions will be written against it. If you're using an earlier or later version, you might have to adjust the information slightly to accommodate modifications provided in newer versions of the software.
- OnTrek Starter Site: Ektron makes several starter sites available for free to developers using the Ektron Framework. OnTrek is one of these starter sites, and this book uses it to discuss the various capabilities made available by the framework. It is recommended that you have this installed if you want to work through the examples in the book.

- **Microsoft Visual Studio:** There are many different flavors of Microsoft Visual Studio these days — Visual Studio Web Developer Express Edition, Visual Studio Professional Edition, and Visual Studio for Architects, to name just a few. You will need at least Microsoft Visual Studio 2005 or later and it's recommended that you use the paid Professional Edition, but the free Web Developer Express Edition will work for most examples as well. Because you're creating Web projects, you cannot use Visual Studio Visual C# Express Edition or Visual Studio Visual Basic because they lack the ability to create Web projects, templates and resources.
- **ASP.NET 3.5 or Later:** The Ektron Framework requires at least ASP.NET 3.5 but you can run it and all the code samples found in this book on the latest .NET 4.0 Runtime.

CONVENTIONS

To help you get the most from the text and keep track of what's happening, we've used a number of conventions throughout the book.

> *Boxes with a warning icon like this one hold important, not-to-be forgotten information that is directly relevant to the surrounding text.*

> *The pencil icon indicates notes, tips, hints, tricks, and asides to the current discussion.*

USE CASE TITLE

We place Use Case examples in this format. Use Cases present the potential users of the Ektron site and illustrate how a user may approach and/or interact with the site.

As for styles in the text:

- We *highlight* new terms and important words when we introduce them.
- We show keyboard strokes like this: Ctrl+A.
- We show file names, URLs, and code within the text like so: `persistence.properties`.
- We present code in two different ways:

```
We use a monofont type with no highlighting for most code examples.
We use bold to emphasize code that's particularly important in the present context.
```

SOURCE CODE

As you work through the examples in this book, you may choose either to type in all the code manually or to use the source code files that accompany the book. All of the source code used in this book is available for download at www.wrox.com. You will find that the code snippets from the source code are accompanied by a download icon and note indicating the name of the program so you know it's available for download and can easily locate it in the download file. Once at the site, simply locate the book's title (either by using the Search box or by using one of the title lists) and click the Download Code link on the book's detail page to obtain all the source code for the book.

Available for download on Wrox.com

Listings include the filename in the title. If it is just a code snippet, you'll find the filename in a code note such as this:

code snippet filename

Because many books have similar titles, you may find it easiest to search by ISBN; this book's ISBN is 978-0-470-88569-7.

Once you download the code, just decompress it with your favorite compression tool. Alternately, you can go to the main Wrox code download page at www.wrox.com/dynamic/books/download.aspx to see the code available for this book and all other Wrox books.

ERRATA

We make every effort to ensure that there are no errors in the text or in the code. However, no one is perfect, and mistakes do occur. If you find an error in one of our books, like a spelling mistake or faulty piece of code, we would be very grateful for your feedback. By sending in errata you may save another reader hours of frustration and at the same time you will be helping us provide even higher quality information.

To find the errata page for this book, go to www.wrox.com and locate the title using the Search box or one of the title lists. Then, on the book details page, click the Book Errata link. On this page you can view all errata that has been submitted for this book and posted by Wrox editors.

A complete book list including links to each book's errata is also available at www.wrox.com/misc-pages/booklist.shtml.

INTRODUCTION

If you don't spot "your" error on the Book Errata page, go to www.wrox.com/contact/techsupport.shtml and complete the form there to send us the error you have found. We'll check the information and, if appropriate, post a message to the book's errata page and fix the problem in subsequent editions of the book.

P2P.WROX.COM

For author and peer discussion, join the P2P forums at p2p.wrox.com. The forums are a Web-based system for you to post messages relating to Wrox books and related technologies and interact with other readers and technology users. The forums offer a subscription feature to e-mail you topics of interest of your choosing when new posts are made to the forums. Wrox authors, editors, other industry experts, and your fellow readers are present on these forums.

At p2p.wrox.com you will find a number of different forums that will help you not only as you read this book, but also as you develop your own applications. To join the forums, just follow these steps:

1. Go to p2p.wrox.com and click the Register link.
2. Read the terms of use and click Agree.
3. Complete the required information to join as well as any optional information you wish to provide and click Submit.
4. You will receive an e-mail with information describing how to verify your account and complete the joining process.

You can read messages in the forums without joining P2P but in order to post your own messages, you must join.

Once you join, you can post new messages and respond to messages other users post. You can read messages at any time on the Web. If you would like to have new messages from a particular forum e-mailed to you, click the Subscribe to this Forum icon by the forum name in the forum listing.

For more information about how to use the Wrox P2P, be sure to read the P2P FAQs for answers to questions about how the forum software works as well as many common questions specific to P2P and Wrox books. To read the FAQs, click the FAQ link on any P2P page.

PART I
Getting Started

- **CHAPTER 1:** Introducing Ektron
- **CHAPTER 2:** The Ektron Web Project Methodology
- **CHAPTER 3:** The Implementation Guide
- **CHAPTER 4:** Configuring Your Development Environment

Introducing Ektron

- What is Ektron?
- What support and services does Ektron provide?
- What makes the Ektron Framework unique?
- Who uses Ektron?

Welcome to the first ever Ektron book. As explained in the Introduction, the ultimate goal of this book is to give you a solid understanding of how to achieve success with your Ektron Web projects. As a developer using the Ektron Framework, you not only have access to its full suite of software components designed to help you build compelling and engaging websites, but you also have an entire array of services and support available at your fingertips from the online developer community, Ektron's Global Partner Network, Ektron's own Best Practices, Professional Services, and Training teams. Understanding that Ektron provides not just a framework, but also a complete solution, is the first step to achieving success with Ektron. This chapter offers a high-level introduction to both Ektron as a company (Ektron, Inc.) and the Ektron Framework to give you an understanding of what that complete solution looks like.

EKTRON: THE COMPANY

Ektron is a global Web solutions leader, providing a Web content management, marketing optimization, and social software platform, founded in 1998 and headquartered in Nashua, New Hampshire.

Ektron's founders, Bill and Ed Rogers, are the driving force behind the company, setting strategic direction and aligning product development with their forward-looking vision for website technology. They founded Ektron ten years ago with a simple and clear vision: enable non-technical people to author and publish content easily on the Web. As an integrated solutions company, Ektron is dedicated to the success of its customers' and partners' Web projects as well as the entire lifecycle of their websites. In addition to software offerings, Ektron has built the services infrastructure to ensure the success of its clients' and partners' Web projects.

From building a software platform capable of supporting the benefits of an active virtual community to building relationships that benefit their customers and company alike, Bill and Ed believe in the power of community. The Ektron community spans the online world and in-person interactive opportunities such as Ektron's local user group tour and worldwide user conference. The members of this community have become trusted resources both inside and outside of Ektron, driving product innovation and contributing to the success of each other's projects.

EKTRON'S COMMUNITY, SUPPORT, AND SERVICES

Ektron's approach to enabling customer success revolves around maintaining an ongoing conversation through many mediums, ensuring that developers and content managers can reach people in the know through whatever format is most useful to them. Through the use of online peer-to-peer interaction, a multilevel support infrastructure, and the availability of professional services staff, Ektron has made finding help on a given issue quick and easy.

Ektron's Online Community

Ektron has demonstrated that it understands the importance of engaging social networks such as Twitter and Facebook in order to connect with its current and potential customers. On Twitter, Ektron can be seen interacting with customers, partners, and analysts, engaging potential customers, and sharing information on topics concerning CMS and Web technology. Technical support plays an important role on Twitter as well, as Ektron engages with customers to promote the *Dev Center*, a peer-to-peer support area for clients to assist one another with problems and ask general questions, with input from Ektron technical support and engineering staff.

On Facebook, Ektron promotes current events and webinars and takes the time to engage with fans. The company runs promotions and contests as a way to engage with the audience, making it fun and putting a personality behind the corporate brand.

An extension of the Dev Center is the *Ektron Exchange Community*. Developers can upload and showcase their code, add-ons, and widgets with others. The community can download, rate the code, and follow favorite developers.

The Ektron community is a vibrant and active one whose members are gathered around common interests. The energy of the community is evidence of the eagerness of its members to participate and help each other. The commitment Ektron has made to supporting, joining, and taking an active part in community activities plays an important role as well.

Here's a quick reference guide to where to find the Ektron Community online:

- **Dev Center:** http://dev.ektron.com/
- **Facebook:** http://facebook.com/ektron
- **Homepage:** http://www.ektron.com/
- **The Exchange:** http://dev.ektron.com/exchange/
- **Twitter:** http://twitter.com/ektron

Ektron Technical Support

When you find yourself in need of more support than what's available through the online community, it is good to remember that Ektron offers full technical support to all customers with an active maintenance agreement. When customers purchase the product, the first year of maintenance is included in the initial license agreement. To keep the maintenance agreement active, the maintenance agreement must be renewed annually. Doing so is an extremely smart idea, as it not only includes access to Ektron Technical Support but gives customers the access to download all current and future software releases, both minor (Service Packs, maintenance releases) and major product releases (8.0, 9.0, and so on). Considering that Ektron has a track record of releasing a new major version of the software at least once a year, keeping the maintenance agreement active is a cost-effective decision as well. Ektron's Technical Support hours are Monday through Friday from 8 a.m. EST to 8 p.m. EST. There are a number of ways to access support services listed here.

Phone Support

Phone calls made to Ektron Technical Support will be answered almost immediately. All calls are routed to a dispatcher responsible for compiling the case information (version information, symptoms, logs, and so on), verifying an active maintenance agreement, and providing a case number. Once this dispatch call is complete, the information is reviewed by the support team and a Technical Support Engineer is assigned to the case and must return the call within two hours. In cases where there is a critical issue requiring a quick response time, phone support should be used. Issues submitted after 7 p.m. EST may not get a response before 8 a.m., but will be handled first thing the following business day. The telephone numbers to initiate support cases are:

United States: 1-866-4-EKTRON x7002

United Kingdom: +44 1628 509 040

Australia: +61 2 9248 7222

Check the Ektron website for the latest contact information at `http://www.ektron.com/contact/`.

Web Form Support

Technical Support cases may also be initiated using the following Web form: `http://dev.ektron.com/requestsupport`.

Ektron's Support Service Level Agreement (SLA) states that the Technical Support Engineer assigned to a case initiated through the Support Web Form must respond to the customer within four to six hours. Once the form is submitted, a case number is assigned and immediately returned.

E-mail Support

Sending an e-mail to `support@ektron.com` is useful when you have a technical support issue that requires resolution but lacks the need for a quick response. The Technical Support Engineer assigned to the case must respond to the customer within 24 hours.

Chat Support

Live chat is available through the Ektron website for basic questions from 8:30 a.m. to 5:30 p.m. EST. In the event that a case cannot be resolved immediately in the chat session, a case will be created by the Technical Support Engineer, and then follows the same process as if it were submitted through the Web Form.

Ektron Contact Method Summary

Table 1-1 includes a list of contact methods.

TABLE 1-1: Ektron Contact Methods

CONTACT METHOD	RESPONSE TIME	CONTACT
Phone Case	1–2 hrs	1-866-4-EKTRON x7002 or 1-603-816-2048
Web Form	Half a day	http://dev.ektron.com/requestsupport
E-mail	Within 24 hrs	support@ektron.com
Chat	Immediately	http://dev.ektron.com/support

Ektron's Technical Support Department is committed to achieving the highest level of customer satisfaction and has many quality-focused programs and processes to ensure that the support it provides exceeds customer expectations. However, there may be cases where your project requires assistance that falls outside of the level of support provided through the Standard Maintenance package. In these situations, you should consider Ektron's Best Practice Services.

Ektron's Best Practices and Professional Services

There are three main groups of technical services that Ektron provides to customers. Depending on your in-house skill level, you may be interested in some combination of these services to help ensure the success of your project. These services can make the difference by bringing Ektron application engineers in who bring years of experience on the Ektron platform with them and who work closely with the platform engineering staff at Ektron.

- ➤ **Best Practice Services:** This service gives you access to a dedicated on-call solution engineer at low cost. It serves as a king of advanced support system, where you might need faster turn-around times than normal support can provide, or where you want the assurance of having someone who knows your project and has been involved with it to be available at any time. These solution engineers can help you align your functionality with the Ektron Framework throughout the lifecycle of your project, and can continue to support your needs as your project moves towards maintenance and support.
- ➤ **Application Engineering:** This service is designed to fill in the blanks on your project, whatever they may be. The Application Engineering group is set up to handle your project from start to finish, moving from the requirements phase all the way to delivering the completed site. They can also be contracted to augment your staff on a temporary basis. This option is useful when you need either a turn-key solution, or when you've hit a rough spot and your deadlines are looming.

➤ **Hosting Solutions:** This service can range from a shared environment all the way to full co-located servers.

Ektron Training

Ektron provides several distinct packages to provide the appropriate level of training for the different stages of your Web project. Given on site at your organization, or at one of Ektron's Educational Facilities around the world (Nashua, NH; San Francisco, CA; Toronto, Canada; London, England and Sydney, Australia), an Ektron trainer works with you on all aspects of a Web project. They can assist with issues throughout the lifecycle of your implementation, from installing the software to overseeing your project requirements and matching CMS features and best practices to the project goals. They also offer in-depth developer training on how to use and implement CMS features, and cover Ektron's Web Project Methodology on building successful websites (Ektron's methodology is covered in Chapter 2).

The types of training offered by Ektron are as follows:

➤ **Ektron Quick Start Consulting:** A fast-paced training that covers the essentials to get you up to speed and running with Ektron.

➤ **Ektron Certified Developer Training:** In depth, hands-on, technical training covering best practices, development, deployment, and methodology.

➤ **Ektron Certified System Administrator Training:** A training that any Webmaster, Web administrator, or IT staff responsible for the ongoing website management and maintenance will benefit from.

➤ **Ektron End User Training:** While the other training types are geared toward people who administer your site, the end user training is geared to help your users understand the system and to facilitate end user adoption.

➤ **Ektron Custom End User or Administrator Training:** By opting for a customized training, Ektron trainers will work to develop a custom curriculum covering any specific business processes related to the administration or content management of your site, in addition to the core skill set offered through the standard training options.

More information on Ektron's Training options are available on the Ektron website at http://www.ektron.com/training.

EKTRON, THE FRAMEWORK

The *Ektron Framework*, which began as a simple Web content management system (WCMS), has long since outgrown the limiting WCMS label. The feature cloud shown in Figure 1-1 highlights the breadth of the version 8.0 platform. With today's framework you have access to a vast collection of components that assist you in developing a site complete with the compelling features demanded by modern site visitors. It is clear the product has come a long way from its original early functionality of simple WYSIWYG content authoring and publishing.

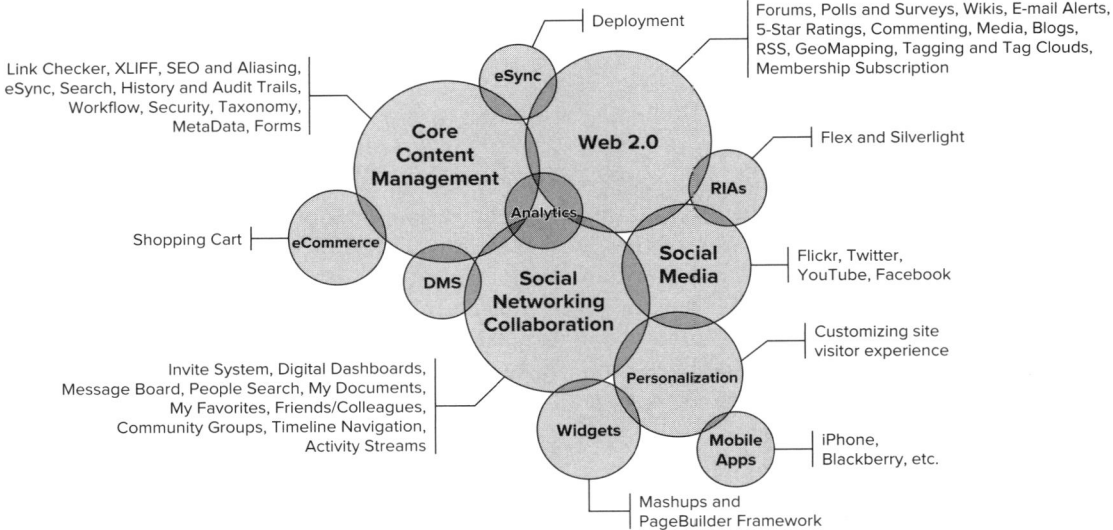

FIGURE 1-1

All-in-One versus Best-of-Breed

In general, Web CMS platforms adopt one of two product architecture paradigms: *All-in-One* (also sometimes called Software Suites) or *Best-of-Breed*.

The goal of the All-In-One approach is to provide all features and functionality "out-of-the-box" without requiring integration with other third-party systems. In a general sense, the benefits of the All-In-One architecture stem from the fact that they are single systems requiring few if any external dependencies to operate. They provide many integrated applications that share a common database, development framework, and consistent user interface so all components have a coherent user experience. From a WCM standpoint, specific benefits of this approach are several:

> ➤ **Cost:** In most cases, All-in-One Software Suites cost less. To achieve a comparable feature set, Best-of-Breed applications must integrate many specialized and individually licensed software components and services.

> ➤ **IT:** Developers need to learn and develop against the single development framework offered by the All-in-One Software Suite and do not need to spend time integrating various frameworks or applications. From an operations standpoint, deployment is simplified since there are fewer disparate systems to manage and configure.

> ➤ **Training:** The interface of an All-in-One system offers a single application for site management and presents administration, IT staff, marketers, and content editors with a single user interface, decreasing the amount of time needed to spend on training to use, manage, and support the system.

The primary drawback to the All-in-One approach also stems from the fact that it is a single framework — you get what you get — and unless it specifically offers external integration points, an extensibility architecture, and open API, you are strictly limited to using what is there.

Standing in contrast to the broad capabilities of All-In-One Software Suites are Best-of-Breed systems. Best-of-Breed systems are specialized tools useful for a singular purpose. What Best-of-Breed systems lack in breadth, they make up for in depth. Since Best-of-Breed systems provide narrow but deep feature sets, many such systems need to be pieced together to offer a comprehensive solution. The single most compelling benefit to this type of product is *rich functionality*. Sometimes a specialized tool is exactly what you need. You might be able to use a Swiss Army Knife's scissors to cut through a piece of thick cardboard, but they certainly won't perform as well as heavy duty office scissors nor will they be as comfortable to use.

The drawback of using Best-of-Breed WCM systems is the complexity of system integration. Consider the various user models and registration systems used by software systems within the enterprise. In order to properly integrate third-party applications, data structures and APIs need to be available. Some notable open source Web CMS platforms follow this approach and therefore require third-party modules to achieve support for such things as LDAP or Active Directory, for example.

The Ektron Framework is unique in that it provides a hybrid approach, offering the breadth of functionality afforded by an All-in-One Software Suite but also providing Best-of-Breed integration judiciously where it makes sense. A perfect example of this type of smart integration is Ektron's choice to integrate with the leading Web Analytics providers such as Google, and Omniture in version 8.5 of the Ektron Framework (see Web Analytics in Chapter 9). Like WCM, Web Analytics is an industry that matured significantly over the past decade, and with the advances made by companies such as Google and Omniture, it makes little sense for Ektron to play catch up and re-invent the wheel at best. Ektron's choice to provide Best-of-Breed integration with such providers means you get the power of the Ektron Framework coupled with the strength of offerings of Google and Omniture, the established leaders in Web Analytics.

Developing with the Ektron Framework

From an ASP.NET developer's perspective, the Ektron Framework can be considered to be a toolkit that contains three general types of components: *.NET Server Controls*, *Ektron Widgets* (.NET User Controls), and *APIs*. With the exception of Ektron Widgets (more on this in Chapter 9), these components are used to assemble ASPX Templates and Master Pages just as you would any ASP.NET website. One of the primary design goals of the Ektron Framework is to make working with it feel very familiar to developers who have experience building ASP.NET websites. This applies to whichever one of the three general types of components you use to build your website depends on your skill set, what you're trying to accomplish, or the level of functionality exposed by it. The following sections contain guidelines that will help you to decide which component to choose.

Server Controls

The Ektron Framework provides more than 80 server controls out-of-the-box, ranging from simple controls such as the Poll Server Control to compound controls such as the Blog Server Controls. All Ektron Server Controls encapsulate complex functionality, making it relatively straightforward for developers to quickly assemble Web pages by dragging and dropping controls from Visual Studio's Toolbox onto your ASPX Template, and then defining their behavior by setting properties either in code or by using Visual Studio's Property dialog box.

The primary reason you'd want to use the Ektron Server Controls over writing code with the APIs directly is the functionality it offers. Each control provides rich functionality that has been developed and tested thoroughly. This means each control has been designed to consider things such as:

- **Permissions:** Does the current visitor have the authorization to read or edit?
- **Approval processes:** Has the item been approved to display?
- **Performance:** Will it handle the heavy demands of a high traffic site?
- **Authoring:** Should content authoring options be displayed for the current user?

While the APIs give you the ability to achieve the same ends, the amount of code required to do this is not always trivial. Take a good look at the server controls before you decide to pursue other options.

Once you've chosen to use the server controls and have started to develop with them, you will find that you need to style the presentation to match the user experience of your site and tweak the markup. These server controls have traditionally offered a few ways to customize the default style and markup it produces:

- **CSS:** The first and most obvious choice for customizing the display is to use Cascading Style Sheets (CSS). Using Firebug (a Web developer add-on for Mozilla Firefox) or something similar, you can inspect the HTML and CSS produced by the control and customize them as you need. Each control typically provides a DisplayCss property that lets you specify the path to your custom CSS file. You override the default presentation once you specify the path to your custom CSS.
- **XSLT:** XML Stylesheet Language for Transformations (XSLT) is an XML grammar for converting an XML document into another format. If it is a language you're familiar with, you will be happy to know that most of the Ektron Server Controls expose data as XML, making the manipulation of the markup straightforward using XSLT. Each control typically provides a DisplayXslt property that lets you specify the path to an XSLT file.
- **EkML:** XSLT is a powerful language for controlling the HTML delivered to the browser, but often times it is overkill when you want to simply tweak an HTML tag or two. EkML was designed for developers needing this level of control. Its simple templating syntax lets you manipulate the markup by inserting and positioning special string tokens that are replaced with data values at runtime. Not all server controls support EkML, so check the documentation before deciding to use EkML on an individual server control.
- **DataBinding:** Many Ektron Server Controls can be used as the data source for data-bindable controls. Because the Ektron Server Control is not used to display results, its visible property is set to false, and a data-bindable control like ASP.NET's ListView or DataGrid control can be used for displaying and controlling the markup instead.

The server controls are a great fit when they closely match the requirements of your project. If you are working under a tight deadline and can trade off any possible feature disparities between your requirements and what is provided by the server control, using the Ektron Server Controls can ultimately save you time. If you're building a website of any serious level of complexity, there are going to be cases where the server controls will not suffice. In these situations, you'll need to peel back a layer of the framework and use Ektron's .NET APIs directly.

The Ektron Framework's .NET APIs, Web Services, and Extensions

The Ektron Framework comes with a full open API, including .NET assemblies, XML Web services, and extensibility architecture. The greatest and most obvious benefit of using the APIs is the level of flexibility and control you have in your site implementation. In fact, you'll later learn how CMS Extensions allow you to override default behavior of the CMS entirely when needed. CMS Extensions can allow you, for example, to control how taxes are calculated in an eCommerce module (Chapter 13), or even to change the very way content is published in the CMS.

Once you've decided that the Ektron APIs are the right fit for your project, you'll then need to determine which API to use. There are currently three central namespaces that you can reference in your Web project: Ektron.CMS.Framework, Ektron.CMS.API, and Ektron.CMS.

- **Ektron.CMS.Framework:** The *Framework API* is the newest member of the Ektron API. It was designed in response to feedback received from developers that the legacy APIs could be cumbersome. Ektron's design goals for the new Framework API focus on discoverability, consistency, and simplicity. An API that is discoverable means that you can guess the namespace, object, and method you need without having to read through a lot of documentation. You can guess your way through a situation using the object names and IntelliSense. A consistent API is one where similar objects function similarly; working with a particular object should feel familiar if you've worked with something similar before. Simplicity refers to the principle that simple things should be easy to do and even difficult things should be possible.

  Since the Framework API is a new addition to the framework, it doesn't yet cover all of the features provided by the CMS. In spite of this disparity, the Framework API has received very positive feedback from the developer community and it should be the first API you look at when using the API. Ektron is working on expanding the Framework API with each release and will continue to do so until it has reached full coverage of the CMS.

- **Ektron.CMS.API:** The *API Namespace* was introduced into the Ektron Framework in Version 6 and provides a collection of APIs that provides programmatic control over a very comprehensive set of Ektron features. This API was introduced for two reasons:

  - To provide programmatic access to the CMS without requiring any type of user authentication information, as customers were looking to perform bulk operations without having to specify an actual system username and password
  - To provide a more logically organized tool for developers than the CMS Namespace

- **Ektron.CMS:** The *CMS Namespace* is the home for all of Ektron's APIs, both the internal ones and the public ones. If you're looking to programmatically access the CMS and cannot find an API to use either in the Framework Namespace or the API Namespace, the CMS Namespace gives you what you need. The benefit of using this API is that it provides an extremely comprehensive API for the Ektron Framework. The drawback is that the API has grown quite large throughout the product's lifecycle. Figure 1-2 depicts the overall architecture of the Ektron Framework.

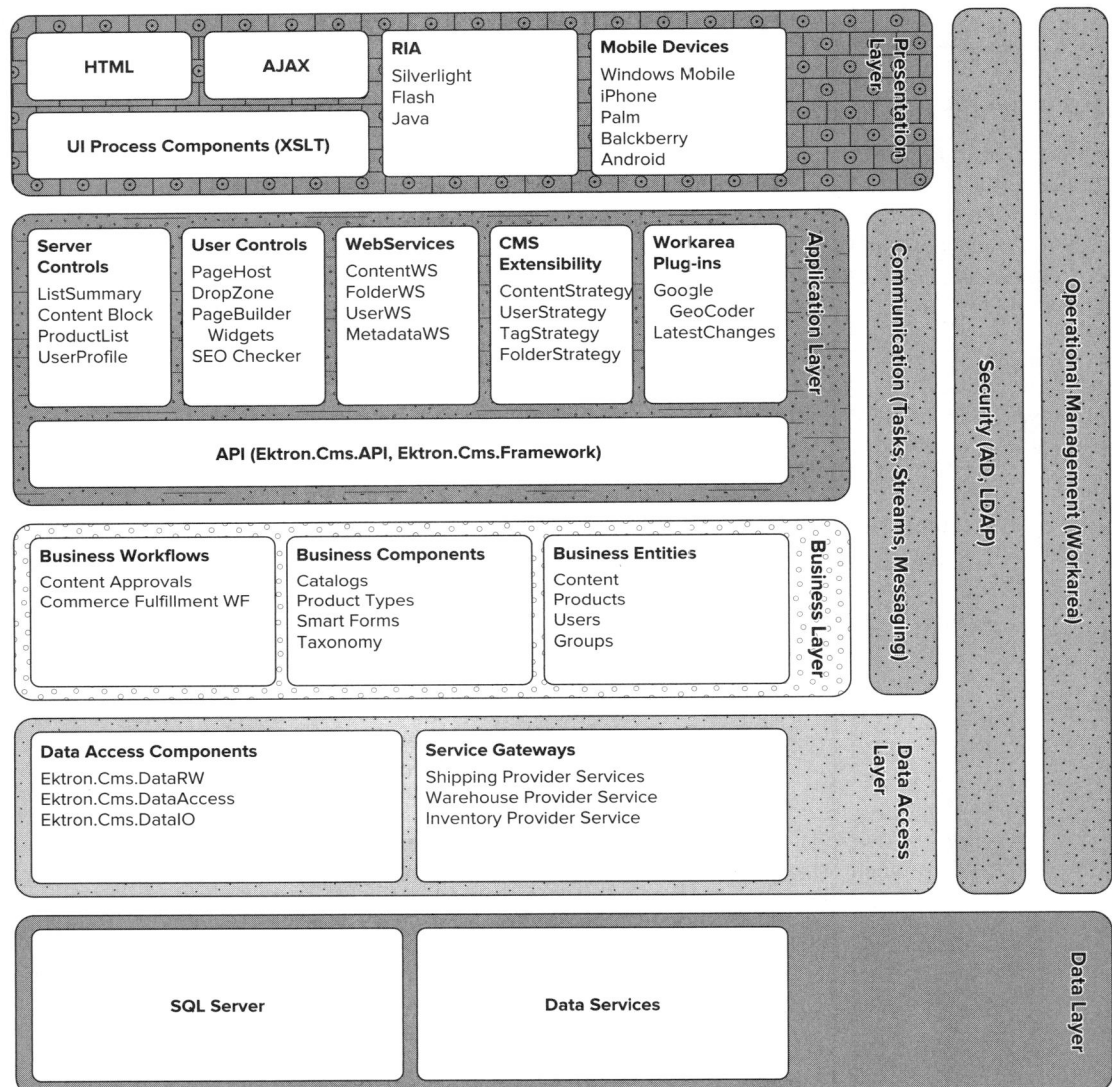

FIGURE 1-2

Ektron PageBuilder and Widgets

User controls are standard ASP.NET components that encapsulate logic, functionality, and user interface, and play a critical role in Ektron's *PageBuilder technology* (PageBuilder is described in detail in Chapter 9). PageBuilder allows Web developers to focus on building repositories of reusable components that non-technical people like marketers use to assemble new Web pages and update existing ones right in the Web browser.

User controls that are designed to work with Ektron's PageBuilder are called *widgets*, and from a developer's perspective, they are simply specialized .NET User Controls. Opening a widget in Visual Studio reveals this clearly — you can see they have an .ASCX extension and extend System.Web .UI.UserControl. So any properties, behaviors, or capabilities of a user control are inherited by a widget.

The Ektron Framework provides over 30 widgets out-of-the-box and even more through the Ektron Exchange (`http://dev.ektron.com/exchange`) a community-based website that lets developers upload and share code with the Ektron developer community. You're free to use the ones provided by Ektron, the developer community, or build your own Ektron widgets using standard .NET technology, Ektron User Controls, and the Ektron APIs.

Data Storage, SQL, and Stored Procedures

Ektron-driven websites store data in relational SQL Server databases, just as any traditional data driven ASP.NET application would. Its database schema is available to developers for debugging purposes. However, Ektron strongly discourages developers from writing SQL statements or stored procedures to directly access the data for any purpose other than debugging in a development environment.

There might be times when you're tempted to write a query to gain quick access to a particular data set, but keep in mind that Ektron has valid reasons for not wanting you to do this. Consider cases where the content you need access to has certain permissions applied to it that prevents it from being displayed, or a workflow process applied. The content must be approved before being displayed, or a "go live" date that is some time in the future. There are so many things to consider in your SQL statement that the statement would be, in most cases, either error-prone or involve too much time to develop. If you need programmatic access to data, stick with the Ektron's APIs.

Framework Summary

Whether you choose to use the .NET APIs, server controls, or widgets depends on the requirements and complexity of your project, your comfort level working with APIs, and your personal preference as a developer. In general, there are few sites that use server controls exclusively. On average, the websites created by Ektron's Professional Services team use the API as much as they use server controls, and choose to use the API in place of server controls when customers have specialized requirements for behavior and layout. The introduction of PageBuilder has not changed this balance. Widgets typically encapsulate the business logic and user interface for what would have been otherwise done in a user control or the page template.

System Requirements

Table 1-2 describes the server, client, and optional requirements for the respective systems.

TABLE 1-2: System Requirements for Servers and Clients

REQUIREMENT GROUP	REQUIREMENT TYPE	REQUIREMENT
Server Requirements	Recommended Minimum Hardware Configuration	Intel Core 2 or greater 4GB RAM or higher RAID Array for hard drives
	Operating System	Microsoft Windows Server 2008 32-bit Microsoft Windows Server 2008 64-bit Microsoft Windows Server 2003 32-bit Microsoft Windows Server 2003 64-bit XP Professional[1] Microsoft Windows Vista Business/Ultimate Microsoft Windows 7

continues

TABLE 1-2 *(continued)*

REQUIREMENT GROUP	REQUIREMENT TYPE	REQUIREMENT
	Web Application Server	Microsoft ASP.NET Framework 3.5 SP1
	Web Server	Microsoft IIS 6.0 or higher
	File System	NTFS (FAT 32 is not supported)
	Database	Microsoft SQL Server 2005 SP2 and higher (including Express version) Microsoft SQL Server 2008[2]
Client Requirements	Operating System	Any IBM-PC compatible system with a Windows OS, including Vista Ultimate or Vista Business. Minimum: 166MHz or faster with at least 64MB RAM Windows 7 MAC OS X
	Browser for Editing	Mozilla Firefox (see Firefox Support Summary)[3] Microsoft Internet Explorer 7.0 or higher *Released versions only*[4]
	Browser for Viewing	All major browsers including: Microsoft Internet Explorer 6.0 and higher, Mozilla Firefox, Apple Safari, and Google Chrome.
Optional Requirements	Web Development Tools	Visual Studio 2005/2008 *For website development:* Visual Web Developer 2005/2008 Express *For plug-in extensions creation:* Visual C# 2005/2008 Express and Visual VB 2005 Express

[1] XP Professional should not be used in production environments, only for testing and development.
[2] Ektron CMS400.Net does not support case-sensitive databases. Virtual Servers are not recommended for database server environments.
[3] http://dev.ektron.com/kb_article.aspx?id=7076.
[4] If a client computer is 64-bit, you cannot use eWebEditPro to create Smart Forms. To create Smart Forms on a 64-bit machine, you must use Release 8.0 or higher and the eWebedit400 editor.

WHO USES EKTRON?

Here is a small sample of some of the award-winning sites that have been deployed using the Ektron Framework, spanning such diverse industries as education, healthcare, and government. The Ektron website lists more sites in additional industries at `http://www.ektron.com/solutions/industry/`.

Associations:

- American Heart Association
- American Speech, Language & Hearing Assoc.
- Association of American Universities
- U.S. Golf Association (USGA)
- USA Hockey Association

Automotive:

- BMW
- Chrysler
- FIAT
- Goodyear
- Mitsubishi

Education: Colleges and Universities:

- Johnson and Wales University
- Rice University
- Seattle University
- University of Notre Dame
- University of Virginia

Education: K–12:

- The Bishop's School
- Jefferson Parish Public Schools
- Learn360
- New Trier High School
- Richland School District Two

Non-Profit Groups:
- The California Endowment
- Juvenile Diabetes Research Foundation
- Special Olympics
- Susan G. Komen for the Cure

TAKE HOME POINTS

This chapter shows how Ektron is more than a technology framework. Rather, it is a complete solution designed to support the success of its customers' Web projects. Some things to remember:

- **About Ektron:** Since Ektron was founded in 1998, their product base has been focused on allowing non-technical users to actively manage content on websites, and on allowing developers to build out complex functionality including online community support.

- **Ektron's Technical Support:** To support Ektron's active and sizable user community, and to support their efforts in developing increasingly sophisticated websites, Ektron has expanded the services offered by its technical support. Ektron has created a professional services department with wide-ranging services including Best Practice Guidance and application development.

- **Ektron Training:** Ektron offers a series of training programs, and participates heavily in the online community on its website and on popular sites such as Facebook and Twitter.

- **The Ektron Framework:** The Ektron Framework comes with fully documented and open .NET architecture, which includes server controls, user controls, .NET assemblies, and XML Web services. These all provide a Web development experience familiar to ASP.NET developers, accustomed to using tools like Visual Studio and programming in languages such as C# and VB.NET for building websites.

The Ektron Web Project Methodology

- What is the difference between Interative/Waterfall and Agile Approaches?
- What are the phases of the Implementation Process?
- What are the steps of the Discovery Phase and how are they important to your project's success?
- How do you successfully implement against your specifications and migrate content?
- How do you effectively test the deliverables?

This chapter begins by asking a fundamental question: Why do so many website projects fail? Projects fail for any number of reasons, but most commonly, they fail because they didn't follow a standardized methodology. A Web development methodology is the system used to control the process of developing a website. Following a process ensures that the result of your project aligns to the needs of the business, that it addresses all of the components of the site's user experience and that it is a technically solid solution, able to scale and perform in a way that supports your organization's objectives.

This chapter is intended for use by project managers and technical developers who are charged with the responsibility of ensuring that their website development project is a success. It is not intended to be a comprehensive guide to project management. It introduces the Ektron methodology and provides advice and recommendations that help ensure you involve the right people in your website-development project, that they have an understanding of what exactly has to be built, and that you have a solid plan for attaining your goals.

ITERATIVE/WATERFALL VERSUS AGILE APPROACHES

Over the years, a number of development methodologies have been created, including waterfall, iterative, and agile. *Waterfall-based methodologies* start with the assumption that requirements must be well defined and documented before proceeding into the actual development effort. With a waterfall approach, the project begins with a comprehensive discovery effort, consisting of stakeholder interviews, functional requirements gathering, technical solution development, and the creation of user experience components. In some cases, deliverables may go through a series of iterations before being considered complete. At the end of the discovery process, the business, technical, and creative components of the project are documented, agreed-upon by the appropriate stakeholders, and used as a baseline to measure the progress of the project.

Agile methodologies typically approach the project from the perspective of defining requirements while the development effort is ongoing. Instead of defining all aspects of the project requirements up front, agile approaches prefer to divide the project into a series of segments or *sprints*. As each sprint is completed, the development effort is presented to the customer and requirements are refined based on direct feedback from the appropriate stakeholders. Clearly, the first several sprints are intended to focus on the core functionality of the website. As feedback is incorporated into subsequent sprints, the website increasingly nears a final format until all sprints are completed and the project is ready to be deployed to the public at large.

There are pros and cons of both approaches. This chapter focuses exclusively on the waterfall approach to website development, as it reflects Ektron's direct experience.

THE BUSINESS CASE: WHERE IT ALL STARTS

Many people think that website projects begin at the kickoff meeting. However, the truth is that most website projects start well before the actual kickoff. As an example, a business owner makes the decision about starting a new website design project. Depending on the size of the organization, the business owner may be in charge of a line of business or of the entire enterprise. Once the need has been identified, the business owner builds a business case that justifies and articulates the business value of the website property. Typically, this business case is then presented to other members of the management team who can provide funding and approval to move forward with the project.

So, what does a business case consist of? Most business cases document the problems to be solved by a website property. For example, it may be to sell more widgets online. Others may find value in developing a community that can be marketed to. Still other businesses can drive results by reducing service calls to their call centers and moving service questions and issues online. Defining the business side of the website property is at the heart of the business case. Just as no two companies are alike, business cases are extremely personalized to the unique circumstances of the particular business or market.

It can't be stressed enough how important it is for the business case to align to the larger enterprise strategy that drives the overall business. This enterprise strategy may be as generic as "being perceived as the industry expert" or "improving our customer service" or even "leading our marketplace." In these examples, developing a website that allows members of an industry to interact in an industry-specific community or offering customers a personalized customer service experience can be drawn directly back to the larger enterprise strategy. Even generic statements such as "leading our marketplace" can translate into website properties that sell products while measuring commerce transactions through the use of Web analytics.

Once the business case is aligned to the enterprise strategy, it should document the specific functionality that is expected to be part of the final product. The business case should express and articulate the positive business effects of the website property with specificity. The business case should articulate the key performance indicators, or KPIs, that will be measured to document the business success of the investment in the website. Examples of KPIs may include but are not limited to the number of orders, number of unique visitors, session length, up-sell or cross-sell completion metrics, revenue generated, and effectiveness of pay-per-click campaigns. The business's needs and expectations are clearly defined and shared with all members of the team before initiating the project by defining these KPIs upfront as part of the business case.

The business case should also describe the kind of resources required to implement the project, the technical and security performance metrics to be tracked, the implementation timelines, dependencies, business process impact analysis, and the financial investment required to support the new website property. Once well defined, the business case is presented for approval within the organization. With approval, the business case becomes an input to the discovery process and provides valuable definition as to the governing characteristics of both the site as well as the implementation project itself.

UNDERSTANDING THE IMPLEMENTATION PROCESS

As mentioned, the Ektron Professional Services website development methodology follows a process in which each phase of the project methodology builds upon the previous phase. For example, the discovery phase provides the functional requirements that serve as input to the implementation phase. When completed, the implementation phase leads to the system acceptance testing phase, which in turn, leads to the user acceptance testing phase. Each phase serves as input to the following set of activities. Omitting individual phases or not addressing all aspects of an individual phase can seriously put the project's success at risk. The phases are listed below.

- Discovery Phase
- Implementation Phase
- Quality Assurance Phase

If you were to compare the building of the website to the building of a house — say a cliff-top mansion — the discovery phase is the series of activities that involve you meeting with an architect, interior designer, and landscape planner to prototype your ultimate dream home. The implementation phase, by contrast, is where you clear the land, lay the foundation, and actually build the home. The quality assurance phase then, would be getting the home inspected.

THE DISCOVERY PHASE

The *discovery phase* of the website development methodology is designed to capture the detail level view of requirements from the perspective of business, creative, and technical stakeholders. Fundamentally, the discovery phase is focused on answering the question: "What do you want your website to do?" In an ideal situation, a business case has been developed and approved that can provide a guide to the entire discovery phase. Of course, we know we don't always live in an ideal world. To that end, the discovery process is flexible enough to help define business requirements, if necessary. Recall, this phase would be like drawing up all your blueprints if you were building a dream house.

Kicking Off the Project

To begin the actual project, Ektron recommends conducting a formal kickoff meeting. Prior to the kickoff meeting, you should develop an agenda that describes who should be involved in the meeting, what topics will be discussed, and what anticipated next steps look like. Traditionally speaking, the kickoff meeting is focused on introducing team members to one another from across the business, defining specific roles and responsibilities for the team, and reviewing the formal scope of work that covers the entire project. In most project kickoff meetings, one single point of contact — a project manager — is appointed. The role of the project manager is to ensure the scope of work is managed, budget and timeline requirements are met, and risk items are identified and mitigated throughout the implementation process.

In addition to the project manager, many organizations designate a business stakeholder who can speak to the concerns of the business, a marketing or creative stakeholder who can speak to the user experience components of the project, and a technical stakeholder who can speak to the performance and security components of the new website. In many cases, these stakeholders may represent larger teams of subject matter experts who exist throughout the business itself. These key stakeholders will bring other subject matter experts from the business into the project at appropriate times to provide feedback, insight, and other value.

Developing a Project Plan

Once individual responsibilities for the team are well defined, the project manager should develop a final, baseline project plan that illustrates and documents the work activity tasks, dependencies, resources, and timelines for the individual project elements. The project plan should take into consideration the time required for signoff and approval of project deliverables, as well as the schedules of people who must provide input throughout the project.

Gathering Business Requirements through Stakeholder Interviews

For most projects, detailed business, user experience and technical requirements are not well defined at this stage of the project. To ensure that you have a comprehensive view of the requirements at the outset of the project, each component of the website should be further defined through a series of requirement gathering activities. To address the needs of the business and functional requirements of the website, you should conduct a series of business stakeholder interviews with a variety of stakeholders across the organization. It is especially important to interview all stakeholders who represent the various functions or departments within the organization that the website will affect. Leaving out an important business segment can lead to real problems, so be expansive in your targeting of stakeholders to participate in the sessions.

To make sure the stakeholders are well prepared in advance of the interviews, Ektron recommends that you develop the interview questions and share these questions with the interviewees before actually conducting the interview. Using this method, business stakeholders have the opportunity to research and discuss the questions with other colleagues before answering your questions. The interview format typically lasts between one and two hours and should be conducted in an informal setting.

The interview questions should be focused purely around the business aspects of the website property. You may want to ask about KPI tracking, business goals for the website, and business processes the website will be expected to interact with. Make sure to ask questions that help to define metrics. These metrics can be tracked and measured at the completion of the project to demonstrate the success of the investment. Also be sure to use plain language and avoid any technical jargon or other confusing terms. As you ask the interview questions, make sure you write the answers exactly as the interviewee provides them. It may also be necessary to educate participants about the questions you're asking so they better understand how to respond. These interview questions and responses will be used later to develop a functional requirements document.

Ektron recommends the interview questions be conducted initially in a one-on-one format. Participants are typically more candid and direct in one-on-one scenarios. As you conduct a series of interviews, you will sometimes hear conflicting responses from various participants. In these cases, identify responses that are common across the interviews and use those as the basis for the core functional requirements. You may also hear great ideas or requirements that are outside the scope of the current website project. Make sure to capture these ideas, because they often serve as the basis for future project activities. In this way, you can make sure that each stakeholder feels as though he or she were heard while also maintaining the scope of the project.

In some cases, conflicting requirements can't easily be resolved in a one-on-one format. To address these kinds of situations, it is best to conduct a follow-up consensus-building session. In this scenario, bring together the stakeholders who participated in the interview sessions into a larger meeting. Share with them the elements of the interview responses that were common across stakeholders and diplomatically bring up areas where requirements conflicted. Stakeholders will often work together to resolve conflicting requirements in a group setting.

Gathering Technical Requirements

With the core business requirements having been defined, the next area of focus is the technical aspect of the website. Leveraging the input from the business, identify third-party tools, systems, and applications that might be affected by the new website project.

Next, focus on performance and security standards requirements related to the website. Conduct research and analysis of the current hosting infrastructure to determine whether new hardware is appropriate or if existing IT infrastructure can be leveraged.

Security is another important component of any technical implementation. With respect to user authentication, identify appropriate active directory or LDAP-based authentication repositories. Leveraging the previously captured input from the business, develop flow maps that explain how users can log in, be assigned permission levels, and manage changing contact information. It may be necessary to review any internal IT policies that have been documented relating to security standards.

Finally, consider the implications of your technical infrastructure with respect to Ektron's licensing policies. For example, Ektron offers special pricing designed for implementation into disaster recovery environments. Ektron also offers a wide variety of licensing options that enable multiple data centers, load balanced server farms, and provide other approaches to the hosting infrastructure that powers your website. Remember to consider the development, staging, and production environments as they relate to licensing and hardware-procurement needs.

Gathering User Experience Requirements

The next area to focus on during the discovery process is to define the user experience. Typically, this is accomplished in a series of creative deliverables, which includes site maps, Wireframes, and user interface prototypes. To begin, check with your marketing department to determine whether your organization has documented Web or style standards. In the event that the standards exist, it is important to align creative deliverables within these requirements. Determine whether any Web-specific standards exist. For example, your marketing or design team may have specific browsers that they want to support, a preference for fixed width versus fluid design approaches, a list of specific plug-ins that are approved or guidelines for color palette, appropriate imagery, and the use of company logos. It's best to understand these guidelines upfront.

Although many people think the user experience consists of purely graphic design, the truth is that the field of information architecture (IA) is equally important. Information architecture refers to the logical grouping of information in a way that serves specific audiences by being uniquely relevant to those audiences. IA affects the overall hierarchy and organization of information on the website, drives the navigational model for the site, and provides a consistent labeling scheme that aids in clarity for the users. The steps are as follows:

1. To leverage the input previously provided by the business stakeholder interviews, you develop a site map that graphically illustrates how information is fundamentally structured on the website. The site map should focus on the top three layers of information on your website. It should provide final naming conventions for each major section of navigation found on the site and should guide the development of the folder structure within Ektron's Workarea.

2. Create a series of Wireframes. Wireframes are intended to serve two purposes.

    ➤ Organize and define the priorities of the key elements of each page. For example, how wide should the body area be? What kind of navigation scheme should be employed?

    ➤ Define interaction design. For process-based web pages, it is important to document where information is captured and how to walk the users through Web-based tasks. Wireframes can be used to prototype these interactions. For example, users must register for membership on your website.

3. Consider graphic design. Develop and design a series of user interface prototypes that represent the major components of your website. Examples include home page, interior sectional page, search page, and any other major sections of the site considered important to the overall user experience.

 Ektron recommends that multiple sets of user interface prototypes be developed at this stage of the project. Each user interface prototype should include the exact same sample pages, but have entirely different design treatments applied to them. In this way, user interface prototypes can be presented to business and marketing stakeholders and their feedback can be focused exclusively on the aesthetic treatment of each design set.

Typically, in a website redesign project, at least three sets of user interface prototypes are presented in the initial round of design comps. When presenting the three designs, make sure to educate the stakeholders that they are not to evaluate the actual content of any of the user interface prototypes. Instead these should focus on the color scheme, use of typography, and general layout. Ask the stakeholders to select one of the three design prototype sets and provide feedback for further evolution of the selected design set.

Creating the Discovery Phase Deliverables

Now that you've completed the requirements-gathering activities related to the business and evaluated the technical and user experience components of the project, you are ready to produce the final deliverables associated with the discovery phase. The Ektron website development methodology calls for the creation of the following:

- **The functional requirements document:** Using the feedback captured during the business stakeholder interviews and any subsequent prioritization sessions, document the specific functional and business requirements of the website. Be as specific as possible when developing these requirements and avoid the natural tendency to try to architect a specific solution.

- **The information architecture document:** Leveraging the site map, develop an information architecture document that captures and documents the higher structure of information on the site. This document defines the types of information you'll find on the site, as well as the structure of the information and how the content items relate to one another through *metadata* and *taxonomy*. Comparing it to non-platform projects, this would be similar to an object-relationship map. The combination of these materials should be documented in the information architecture document and will inform the configuration of the Ektron CMS as you enter the implementation phase.

- **The CMS implementation guide:** Leverage the Wireframes and user interface prototypes to create a CMS implementation guide. For each component defined in the Wireframes and or user interface prototypes, define which Ektron Server Controls should be used to address each component of functionality. The CMS implementation guide is Ektron-specific, in that it defines which server controls, which API calls, and which elements of customization are required to meet the business, user experience, and technical requirements for the project. Typically, a technical developer who is already familiar with the Ektron Server Controls and APIs develops the CMS implementation guide.

Please note that it may be necessary, based on the feedback and input captured throughout the discovery process, to revise the project plan that governs the overall implementation effort. When website requirements are poorly understood, projects are structured so that the discovery phase is addressed as a separate project before the implementation phase. In these cases, it is important to develop a comprehensive project plan that governs the remainder of the implementation and testing.

One final note about the discovery process: remember it is intended as a guide. Feel free to scale the discovery methodology up or down to meet your individual needs. For example, some customers may want to include processes such as usability testing as part of the discovery process. Other customers may not be redesigning a website and should bypass the user interface prototyping phase of the discovery process. What's important to remember is that the methodology is as flexible as your unique environment.

THE IMPLEMENTATION PHASE

The implementation phase is where you start building to the specifications you have been developing. If you follow the project development methodology accurately, the implementation phase should be as straightforward as possible. Returning to the dream house analogy mentioned earlier, the blueprints for the cliff-top mansion would be finished and you would be ready to clear the ground and start construction.

Starting Development

To begin the implementation phase, focus first on the initial setup and configuration of the three environments: development, staging, and production hosting environments, following these steps:

1. Beginning with the development environment set up and install the hardware.
2. Install and configure the operating system and IIS Web server.
3. In a separate environment, and depending on your unique hosting configuration, install, configure, and set up the SQL Server database. Connect the SQL Server and IIS Web servers so that they can communicate.
4. Download and install the latest version of the Ektron CMS400.NET software. Following the instructions provided with the Ektron software, install a CMS Min environment. This ensures that you are prepared to begin the development effort.
5. With the steps being completed, repeat them in the staging and production environments as well.
6. With the three environments now set up and configured, install the Ektron eSync software and configure it to move file system assets and databases from development to staging and finally, to the production hosting environment.

> *There are a number of ways in which Ektron can be configured. Although this chapter describes a traditional three-tier hosting environment, each hosting topology is different and unique to each customer's specific environment. Even though Ektron provides extensive documentation as to the different configuration choices available, you may benefit from a brief consultation with an Ektron Best Practices Engineer, who can advise you on the optimal way in which your hosting environment can be configured. Also remember to use the Ektron Dev Center website* (http://dev.ektron.com) *to run ideas by other community members who have Ektron experience.*

7. You now want to develop actual .ASPX templates. Begin this activity by converting the final user interface prototype designs into a series of XHTML and CSS pages.
8. Before continuing, make sure to conduct browser compliance testing and ensure that the XHTML templates and the user interface will display and function as intended. Making changes to the design and layout of these templates after they have been converted into

.ASPX templates is more involved than making the changes earlier in the process. For the presentation layer, using a CSS-driven design and layout will provide you with greater flexibility while also aligning to industry best practice standards.

9. With the XHTML templates completed, convert the bare XHTML into .NET master pages. Master pages should contain elements of the design that are shared throughout the website. For example, it is often a best practice to have the Search field presented in the upper-right corner of the design. Accordingly, the master page should contain the Search field so it is consistently displayed to the users throughout the website.

10. Next, leverage the master pages to develop specific .ASPX templates that contain the individual functionality that is not common to many pages. These pages were documented and defined in your CMS implementation guide. If you develop these templates, remember to develop the corresponding folder structure and content within the Ektron Workarea. As you add server controls to the .ASPX pages, remember you must also style the output of these controls to match the user interface prototypes. This is when the CSS you developed to support the templates comes in handy. Sometimes it is important to transform the output of the server control as well as style it. In these cases, leverage XSLT to transform server control output and CSS to define the presentation elements of that output. Wherever possible, standardize and leverage common approaches to both XSLT and CSS standards.

Content Migration

When you are done with these steps, you essentially have a skeleton, or framework, of the website. The next step is to begin loading content into the CMS. Depending on whether the project relates to a new website property or a redesign of an existing website, your approach to content migration and loading may differ.

- **New website properties:** Content is typically developed in the form of Microsoft Word documents. Taking the content from these documents and loading it into the CMS is a process that entails copying and pasting content into individual content blocks.

- **Redesign projects:** If the site being redesigned is already on Ektron, the migration process is very straightforward. Using direct APIs, you can migrate content blocks directly from the previous installation into your new development environment. A similar approach may work if you are migrating content from a site that uses a structured database. However, in these cases, it may be necessary to transform the data structures to align with the Ektron objects. If you are migrating from a site that doesn't have a backend database, you may have to consider a manual approach to content migration. One often overlooked aspect of any content loading or migration process is the need to transform the content to align with the style standards of the new site.

- **Large-scale content migration projects:** It may be necessary to use an automated tool to assist in the extraction, transformation, and loading of migrating content. This is another area where Ektron Professional Services may be of some assistance to you.

Regardless of the method you employed to load the content, make sure to plan for the need to revisit the content to freshen its relevance, update CSS style standards, and fix broken links.

Also when considering content loading or migration efforts, remember you might want to use the following tools to build content for structured versus non-structured data:

- **Ektron Smart Form:** Press releases often follow a very structured format. They consist of a headline, summary, contact information for the PR representative, and the body of the press release. Using an Ektron Smart Form is an ideal way to handle such content.
- **Traditional Ektron content block:** Other aspects of the website may require a more free-form approach to content. For example, the About Us section of the website typically provides basic information about the company, its employees, and its mission. This is an opportunity to use traditional Ektron content blocks to provide freedom and flexibility for the design and layout of the content. These considerations should have been initially addressed during the discovery phase and those deliverables should be used to guide this effort.
- **PageBuilder Wireframes:** These are different from traditional CMS templates in that they define specific zones where content and widgets are placed. With this basic framework in place, content authors can drag and drop pre-built pieces of functionality or content into the zones defined by the PageBuilder Wireframe. PageBuilder Wireframes are typically built using a column-based metaphor. For example, you may have two-, three-, and four-column PageBuilder Wireframes available to your users. With PageBuilder Wireframes in place, your content authors will create the content as well as define the individual layout of PageBuilder pages.

Now that the implementation phase is coming to a close, the next areas you'll explore are the testing and deployment steps.

THE QUALITY ASSURANCE PHASE

The testing phase of the project methodology is intended to capture and resolve any issues, bugs, or problems with the website. Revisiting the analogy about the construction of your dream house, the cliff-top mansion, this phase is where you bring in an inspector to ensure the building is up to code, and that the attic light doesn't turn on when you flip the garbage disposal switch.

System Testing

Using your own internal resources, you begin the system testing phase by documenting specific test cases created using the business and functional requirements obtained during the Discovery Phase. Use cases are intended to describe specific tasks or activities that users are expected to perform using the website. They typically are task-based and verifiable. This means that through testing you should be able to determine whether the site behaved as expected after testing. If not, the use case needs to be refined and clarified. For example, a verifiable use case would be to "enter in the search term `<HR Form>` and see five results listed in the search results." A non-verifiable use case would be to "provide search functionality."

If there is one overlooked aspect of website development, it is typically in the testing processes. As you develop your use cases, be expansive and remember to not only cover just the tasks described in the business requirements, but also commonly used website functions, such as search and contact forms. Once your use cases have been fully developed, follow them throughout your testing process.

As you identify issues during the use case testing, document the URL, the expected behavior, and the actual results you encounter during the testing.

It is common to conduct multiple rounds of system testing before moving into user acceptance testing. Remember also to test all aspects of the website. For example, if your website has integration with a third-party tool or application, make sure to test that the information captured in the CMS is accurately migrated to the other system or tool.

As you identify specific issues, document them in a testing spreadsheet or defect tracking tool. Use this defect tracking system with your development team to research, analyze, and resolve each individual issue. As you resolve issues, document the response to the reported issue in the same tool. This provides you with a detailed record of both testing issues documented as well as issue resolution. You can use the same format as you enter the next, and final, phase of testing.

User Acceptance Testing

The final phase of activity before completing and deploying the new website is to conduct user acceptance testing. With the previous testing phase, you used IT developers and QA staff to do the testing and issue resolution activities. In this phase, you use actual end users to complete the testing.

Before user acceptance testing can begin, however, it is important to ensure that the actual end users of the CMS powered website have been trained and know how to manage the site and its functionality. Ektron provides detailed system documentation as well as training materials to all of its customers. However, you may find developing custom author or administrator training materials to be helpful as you educate your end users. It has been Ektron's experience that delivering custom training in an instructor-led, hands-on format is the most effective way to empower the author and administrator audiences.

As before, the use cases will drive the testing effort. Ask your end users to follow the use cases and report any identified issues in the same testing spreadsheet format that you used in the earlier phase of testing. Again, you may decide to do multiple rounds of user acceptance testing before you decide that the site is ready for an appointment. As issues are identified by your end users, involve your IT staff in researching and resolving the reported issues.

When the testing process is complete, training delivered, and a final check of system functionality, you are ready to deploy the new Ektron-powered website to the public at large. Using Ektron's eSync technology, you can quickly deploy content and file system assets from your development to staging and, ultimately, your production hosting environments. Once the site is deployed to the production hosting environment, update the DNS entry for the website point to the production servers. Within 24 to 48 hours, the site will be available to the public at large and you will have your most visible demonstration of the success of the project.

However, this is not necessarily the end of the project. Now that the site has been launched, it is time to enter the ongoing maintenance mode that governs the website until the next major enhancement or release. It is critically important that at this stage of the project, you begin the detailed tracking and reporting of the KPI metrics you defined in the discovery phase of activities. If the initial investment in the website was based on demonstrable business impact, these KPI measurements help to prove that the expected result has, in fact, been attained.

Remember, once the website is launched, you still have ample opportunities to tweak, modify, and enhance the content, layout, and functionality of the website. Use this capability to measure your expected results and make changes as appropriate. No other medium can allow you to quickly change your mind and react to how your customers perceive and interact with your website property. So many projects count success as the mirror launching of a new website. Real success, however, is measured over time and in your newfound abilities to react to the marketplace.

TAKE HOME POINTS

Before this chapter on the Ektron website development methodology ends, the authors want to share a couple of final thoughts and important points to keep in mind:

- **Carefully manage the scope of the project.** If you do not do this, you are almost guaranteed to miss your budgetary and timeline constraints. This is a problem that every website development project faces. However, leveraging an effective change-management process can mitigate scope creep by using the discovery deliverables as a baseline to measure against.

  For example, during the testing process, it is almost inevitable that business users will come up with new ideas and ask for changes. As this occurs, make sure to document the request and assess the impact of the change in both financial and timeline views. Many times, when presented with a specific dollar number and timeline change, business stakeholders will reevaluate the request and either provide additional funding and time to complete the change or decide that the change is something that can wait until the next phase. Effectively managing change requests can be the difference between a project that launches on time and on budget versus a project that never seems to launch and misses the budget wildly.

- **Remember that a website is really never fully completed.** Instead, websites live in specific time frames, constantly evolving and changing to meet the expanding expectations and needs of your customer audiences. Remember to revisit the functional requirements for the website often, paying special attention to those items that were deemed appropriate for future expansion and Ektron features that you may not have used during your initial development effort.

- **Making simple changes to the website that adds functionality will extend the life and business value of the website investment.** A great example of this is an organization that decides to implement Ektron's core website analytics package, and later decides to extend the feedback loop through the use of multivariate testing in a PageBuilder interface. For an established site, this is an easy expansion that can significantly help with KPIs. These types of small enhancements increase the effectiveness of the original business investment in the project and also serve to provide constant "little wins" related to the website that reminds people of the value of both the site as well as the platform it's built upon.

The Implementation Guide

- What is Ektron's approach to the Development Lifecycle?
- What is an implementation guide?
- What is in the OnTrek implementation guide?
- What Best Practices do you use when creating an implementation guide?

The implementation guide is an important step in building any website. It defines a set of expectations that the development team can follow to produce a fully functioning website that meets the needs of the business for which the site is being built. Ektron implementation guides may differ slightly from what you are familiar with on other ASP.NET projects, just as the way developers approach Ektron projects differs from standard ASP.NET projects. These differences are discussed in the first section of this chapter.

Following the discussion on the Ektron approach, this chapter describes the implementation guide in detail, and discusses the OnTrek implementation guide in particular. These sections describe the content of the guide, and walk through some example components of the document. You'll also walk through the steps for creating an implementation guide; each section is fully discussed so that in the future you can document your projects ahead of time.

The full implementation guide for the OnTrek site is available for download at p2p.wrox.com: *this chapter will only cover a small subset of the functionality in the implementation guide. Also note that the document is designed to convey the minimal information necessary for a developer to implement against.*

Finally, this chapter discusses some best practices and notes to keep in mind as you develop an implementation guide for your project. Creating an effective implementation guide is the key to minimizing the risk of scope creep and underestimation of initial scope.

THE EKTRON APPROACH

Before you dig into the implementation guide, a quick review of the Ektron Framework and how you should approach it is in order. While the Ektron Framework is built on ASP.NET and utilizes the component-based architecture inherent in the platform, Ektron takes it a step further through a technology called PageBuilder.

PageBuilder is a feature that takes the concept of ASP.NET User Controls and moves it one step further. In a normal ASP.NET implementation, the typical workflow is for designers to come up with a site layout, and for developers to break that down into components called *user controls*, which are then declaratively placed onto templates. This approach makes it easy and straightforward for developers to maintain the site because it encapsulates features and layout elements into easily reusable pieces of code.

PageBuilder takes .NET User Controls to the next level, providing controls that allow non-developers to add components to pages and modify component settings. It eschews the need for a developer to intervene, and entirely drops the requirement for Visual Studio from the page layout update cycle.

The basic Ektron implementation lifecycle approach is to remove the dependency on developers as early in the website management cycle as possible. To this end, it is best to group the user interaction requirements into three camps.

> ➤ **Developer:** The developer serves the same function as in a normal ASP.NET implementation, working with designers to stabilize the styles used, as well as developing templates and components. Where the exercise differs is that the components in this case are mostly PageBuilder Widgets, which you can then place onto pages by the website production manager.

> ➤ **Messaging Expert:** This role is to manage the raw content elements that are used in the website. Beyond a bare minimum, messaging experts do not need to know how content is used on the site, and they do not need to worry about styling or functionality of the site. They simply generate the content that is then used by the website's production manager.

> ➤ **Web Production Manager:** This is the key role that differentiates an Ektron implementation using PageBuilder from a standard ASP.NET implementation. The website production manager takes the content developed by the messaging expert, and the components and templates created by the developers, and combines them through a drag-and-drop WYSIWYG layout management process.

The addition of a website production manager role alleviates the need to have developers continually returning to existing templates to add a small piece of functionality, or move an element from one location on the page to another. Those requirements can, with the addition of PageBuilder, be moved to a non-technical role filled by someone much closer to the business requirements side of the project. PageBuilder is covered in greater detail in Chapter 9.

IMPLEMENTATION GUIDE

One of the most important deliverables that comes out of the discovery phase of the Ektron website development methodology is the CMS implementation guide. Put simply, the CMS implementation guide provides a technical blueprint for exactly how the Ektron website will be constructed. It defines, on a component-by-component basis, which server controls, widgets, user controls, or other pieces of functionality are required to produce a given Web page. CMS implementation guides are fairly technical documents and are not typically well-suited for presentation to non-technical audiences.

Before proceeding, let's review the discovery phase of Ektron's site development methodology. The discovery phase is intended to capture the requirements and design for the solution. It collects the unique perspectives of business owners, marketing and user experience specialists, and technical or engineering resources. Among the core deliverables that are produced during the discovery process are:

- **The functional requirements guide:** Captures, from a business perspective, how the site should operate.
- **The information architecture guide:** Defines the structure of content in the Ektron Workarea and the use of metadata and taxonomy.
- **The CMS implementation guide:** Builds upon both the functional requirements and information architecture documents, including screenshots of user interface prototypes or Wireframes. It explains step-by-step which components are necessary in order to produce the desired functionality.

For a full discussion of the Implementation Process, which includes the discovery phase, see Chapter 2.

Oftentimes, the construction of a website is compared to the construction of a building. Following this analogy, you could compare the CMS implementation guide to the blueprints that construction workers use as they assemble the structure. Similarly, application engineers and CMS architects use the CMS implementation guide to guide the development of the actual Web pages and the components that are required to create them. Done properly, the CMS implementation guide provides enough detail and direction to the programming team so that they clearly understand all aspects of what is to be produced.

From the perspective of document formatting, the CMS implementation guide consists of several elements:

- **Sitemap:** This is included in the implementation guide merely as a reference to the overall information architecture of the website. It is helpful to refer to the sitemap while constructing the CMS implementation guide to ensure that all pages are properly documented.
- **Page layouts, in Wireframe or screenshot formats:** These provide a visual reference for each page type that will be found in the website. Page layouts should include either screenshots of

approved Wireframes or actual screenshots of the final user interface. By providing a visual reference, application engineers and CMS architects can understand the visual aspects of the programming tasks.

- **Object tables that describe the components in each Wireframe or screenshot:** The role of the object tables is to provide an appropriate label, description, and documentation around expected interactions on a component-by-component basis for each page layout type.
- **Widget listing:** As mentioned in the first section of this chapter, PageBuilder is an important part of building an Ektron-based website. It allows developers to encapsulate pieces of functionality into widgets, which are user controls with additional functionality. These widgets can then be placed onto pages by website production managers, reducing the need for developers in the maintenance stage. The widget listing describes these page components as standalone elements.
- **Object tables specific to widgets:** These describe the elements of a widget, so that a developer can understand the functionality of that widget.

THE ONTREK IMPLEMENTATION GUIDE

The best way to understand how to construct the CMS implementation guide is to review an existing document. To that end, Ektron has provided a copy of the OnTrek implementation guide with this book, available at www.wrox.com. We encourage you to review this guide and to use it as a template for your own projects. The OnTrek CMS implementation guide is based on a website that, following Ektron best practices, heavily utilizes PageBuilder technology. As such, the CMS implementation guide contains sections devoted to both the pages in the site and the widgets available for use on the site.

In the pages section, all aspects of the website are detailed, including a breakdown of product displays, search and detailed product information, the checkout process, event information, content areas, careers and job postings, maps related to locations, a contact form, and much more. Because the OnTrek site also includes social networking community functionality, the pages section also includes overviews of community functionality, personal profile information, friends, activity feeds, blogs, photos, and other group-related functionality. Of course, common elements to all websites are addressed, including search functionality, terms of use, and sitemaps.

The widgets section then documents the full list of widgets available on the site, with details about functionality and the user interface, along with editing options and technical notes. Examples of the kinds of widgets that are documented include most popular products, highest rated, tabbed interfaces, recent posts, discussion forum topics and search functionality, social networking functionality, career searches, search filters, e-commerce discounting rules, event registration, product cross-selling, and accordion menus, among others. These widgets can then be incorporated into any other part of the site by content managers.

For each section, object tables are included that describe the expected interaction and functionality of each element of the page.

In this exploration of the OnTrek CMS implementation guide, you will review three representative pages, and their related object tables. You will also look at the wireframes for the widgets that appear on those pages, followed by their object tables. The discussion begins with the homepage.

The Homepage

The user interface for the homepage, shown in Figure 3-1, is really just a screenshot of the Wireframe.

 Throughout the interface Wireframe, there are specific footnote references embedded in the image. The placement of these footnote references indicates the component that the reference is documenting and is cross-referenced in the page object table.

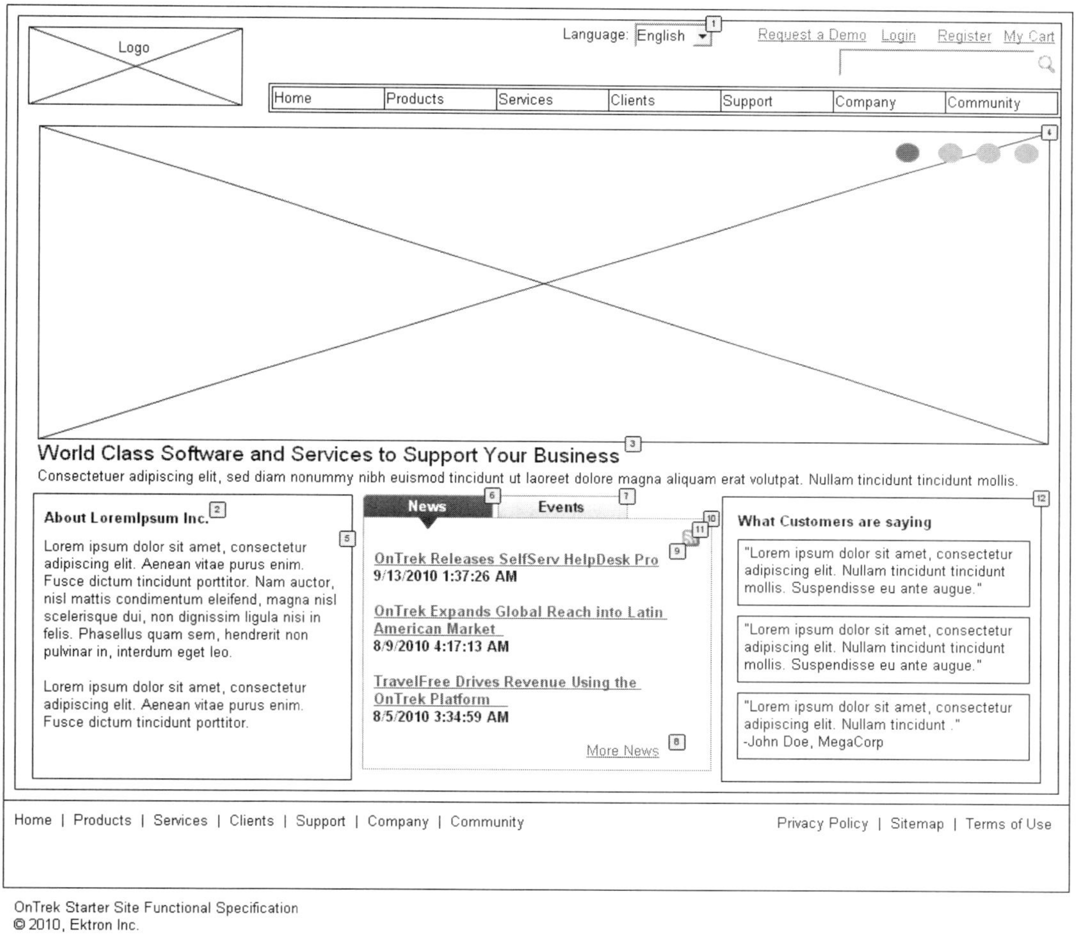

FIGURE 3-1

For each footnote defined in the user interface, the object table, reproduced in Table 3-1, provides a label, expected interaction for the component, and a description of how the component should be constructed. For example, many of the components on the homepage are actually widgets. When looking at the language selector, footnote number one, you'll notice that the description of the object table indicates its expected functionality, including the need for the language selector control content languages for all components found on the page, including menus. As you review the remainder of the objects defined in this specific page, you'll notice that the majority of the remaining components are in fact, widgets.

TABLE 3-1: Object Table for the Homepage

FOOTNOTE	LABEL	INTERACTIONS	DESCRIPTION
1	Language Selector		Language Selector is only shown on the homepage. Should translate everything on this page, including menus.
2	Header Widget		Enter a custom header in the header widget.
3	Banner Text		Intro text for the site.
4	Banner Slider		Banner with sliding images and text that are managable through the CMS.
5	Content Block		Display a content block.
6	News Tab	**OnClick:** **Case 1**: Set Panel state to News State	Lists recent News items.
7	Events Tab	**OnClick:** **Case 1**: Set Panel state to Events State	Lists the upcoming events. Configuarble for the calendar to pull events from and for how many to display.
8	More News Link	**OnClick:** **Case 1**: Open News in Current Window	Link to News page.
9	News List	**OnClick:** **Case 1**: Open News Article Page in Current Window	Lists the latest news item. Can be configured to show X number of items.
10	News Widget		Display item's title, date published, and summary. Link to article page. **Widget Settings:** choose what folder to pull from, how many to show, enable subscription, enable paging, how many per page.

FOOTNOTE	LABEL	INTERACTIONS	DESCRIPTION
11	RSS Feed		User can get the list in an RSS format, or add the RSS feed to an RSS Reader (eg Google Reader).
12	What Customers Are Saying Widget		This display shows what multiple comments enabled would look like. Should allow user to choose which comments to show, change the header text, how many to show, enable paging, how many per page, and whether or not to rotate them on page refresh.

For each widget defined within the page, a similar screenshot and object table are required. This example uses the What Customers Are Saying Widget. Similar to the page interface, the interface for the widget is separately documented in the CMS implementation guide. As before, the separate object table, related specifically to this widget, is also included. The User Interface for the What Customers Are Saying Widget is shown in Figure 3-2.

For the What Customers Are Saying Widget, the object table provides detailed references to the desired functionality of the widget, including how the functionality changes based on whether a user is currently editing the page. The object table for the What Customers Are Saying Widget is reproduced in Table 3-2.

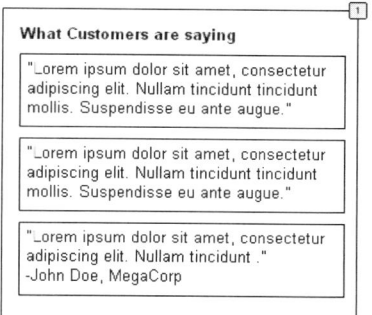

FIGURE 3-2

TABLE 3-2: Object Table for the What Customers Are Saying Widget

FOOTNOTE	LABEL	INTERACTIONS	DESCRIPTION
1	What Customers Are Saying Widget		This display shows what one comment would look like. **Widget Settings:** Widget should allow user to choose which comments to show (collections? content list?), change the header text, how many to show, enable paging, how many per page, and whether or not to rotate them on page refresh.

Product Page

The layout for the products page user interface, as shown in Figure 3-3, is different from the homepage example in the last section. While maintaining the global navigation and company logo across the top of the page, this page produces a new layout and function in the left column. Based on this wireframe, the product details are shown. In the right column, widgets display similar products, items listed as upgrades for the current product, and products other customers have purchased.

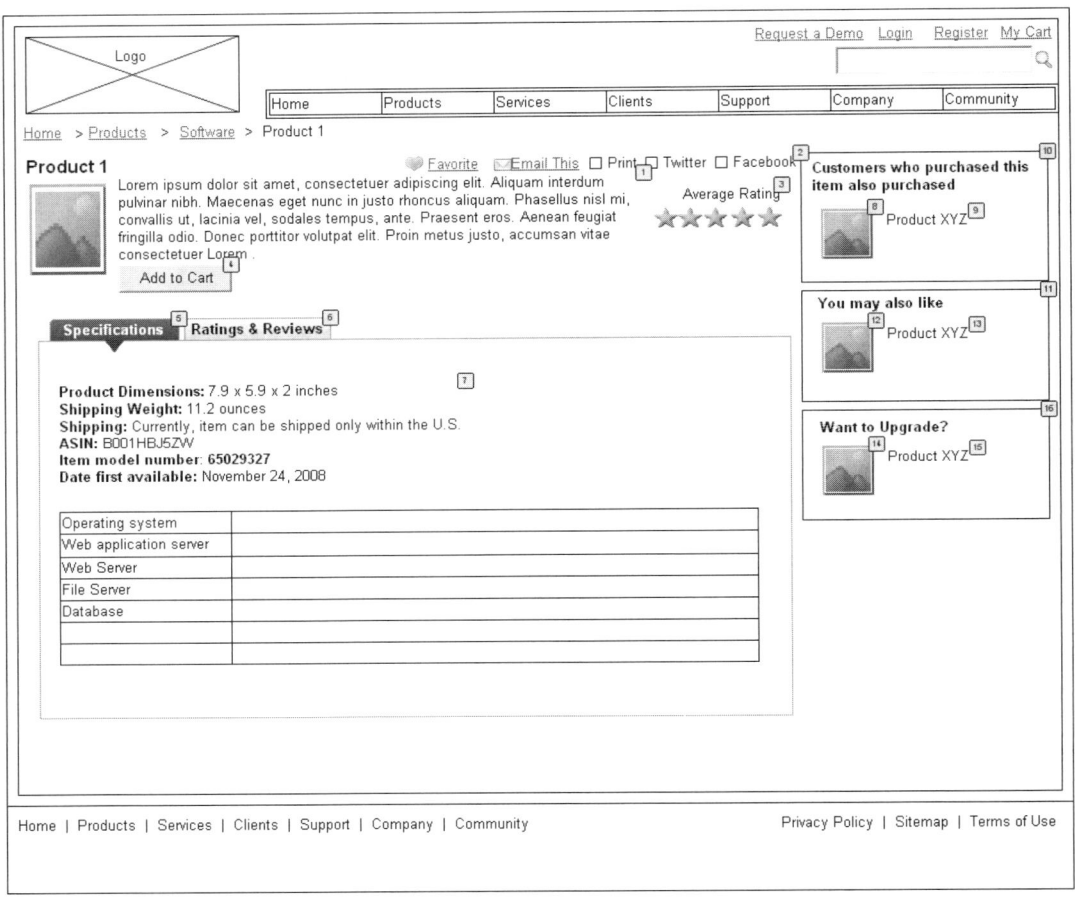

OnTrek Starter Site Functional Specification
© 2010, Ektron Inc.

FIGURE 3-3

The object table for the products page is more complicated than the first example. As before, footnotes make visual references to individual components found in the page. Based on this example, the CMS architect has created this layout leveraging a combination of Ektron Server Controls and widgets. Notice also that in this section, the architect has defined specific interactions for certain components. For example, several items contain an OnClick interaction. This signifies that when the user clicks on the item, the interface will respond by performing the action listed. The object table for this page is reproduced in Table 3-3.

TABLE 3-3: Object Table for the Products Page

FOOTNOTE	LABEL	INTERACTIONS	DESCRIPTION
1	Product details	**Case 1:** Open Product Page in Current Window	Display the product title, image, details, average rating, and add to cart button.
2	Social Bar Widget		Social Bar Widget allowing users to add to favorites (visible when logged in), E-mail link to someone, print the page, tweet the URL, or facebook the URL.
3	Average rating		Display stars showing the average rating for the product. If not yet rated, display "Not yet rated."
4	Add to Cart		Add the item to the user's cart.
5	Specifications Tab	**OnClick:** **Case 1**: Set Panel state to Specifications State	Displays detailed specifications of the product.
6	Ratings & Reviews Tab	**OnClick:** **Case 1:** Set Panel state to Ratings State	Displays ratings and reviews entered by customers for the current product.
7	Product Specs		Display product specifications (size, weight, etc).
8	Product Image	**OnClick:** **Case 1**: Open Product Page in Current Window	Image displayed inside the Product Customer Sell Widget.
9	Product Name	**OnClick:** **Case 1**: Open Product Page in Current Window	Name of product shown in 8.
10	Product Customer Sell Widget		Show products that customers have also purchased when they purchased this item. If none are available, do not display.

continues

TABLE 3-3 *(continued)*

FOOTNOTE	LABEL	INTERACTIONS	DESCRIPTION
11	Product Cross Sell Widget		Recommends products to the user. Displays products associated to the product being displayed on the page using the Recommendation server control. If there are no associated products, this should not display.
12	Product Image	**OnClick:** **Case 1:** Open Product Page in Current Window	Image for product displayed in 11.
13	Product Name	**OnClick:** **Case 1:** Open Product Page in Current Window	Name of product displayed in 11.
14	Product Image	**OnClick:** **Case 1:** Open Product Page in Current Window	Image for product displayed in 16.
15	Product Name	**OnClick:** **Case 1:** Open Product Page in Current Window	Name of product displayed in 16.
16	Product Upsell Widget		Display product upgrade(s) for the product displayed on the page. If no upgrade available, do not display.

As before, certain elements of the page interface are comprised of widgets. An object table and widget screenshots are required for each specified widget. The user interface for the Product Cross Sell Widget is shown in Figure 3-4.

The object table for the Product Cross Sell Widget is reproduced in Table 3-4. This object table defines the display and available widget settings that content managers can customize, as well as the link action for the displayed event.

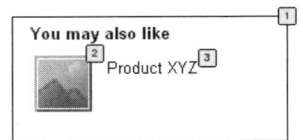

FIGURE 3-4

TABLE 3-4: Object Table for the Product Cross Sell Widget

FOOTNOTE	LABEL	INTERACTIONS	DESCRIPTION
1	Product Cross Sell Widget		Recommends products to the user. Displays products associated to the product being displayed on the page using the Recommendation server control. **Widget Settings:** Header text. How many items to display. Set which product to make recommendations from.
2	Product Image	**OnClick:** **Case 1:** Open Product Page in Current Window	Image for the product being cross sold.
3	Product Name	**OnClick:** **Case 1:** Open Product Page in Current Window	Name of the product being cross sold.

User Dashboard Page

The final example that you see in this section is related to the user's personalized dashboard page. Compared to the previous pages you've reviewed, the user dashboard is fairly complex. Consisting of many server controls and a large amount of custom code, the user dashboard is a very powerful and highly functional element of the OnTrek website. As before, the user interface relies upon a consistent placement of the OnTrek logo and global navigational components across the top of the page. In the left column, an accordion menu is presented that offers links to the user's profile, groups, friends, favorites, a calendar, a blog, documents, and photos.

The right column of the dashboard page is devoted to the display of a user's individual widgets. These widgets are personalization controls that site visitors can add, modify, or remove. Thus, you must define those interactions in the implementation guide. Across the top of the right side of the page, a status bar allows the users to update their friends with activity statuses. Below the status bar, a scrolling list of widgets is displayed. Finally, below the scrolling tray of widgets are the actual widgets that the users have selected for their individual dashboard. The user interface for the user dashboard is shown in Figure 3-5.

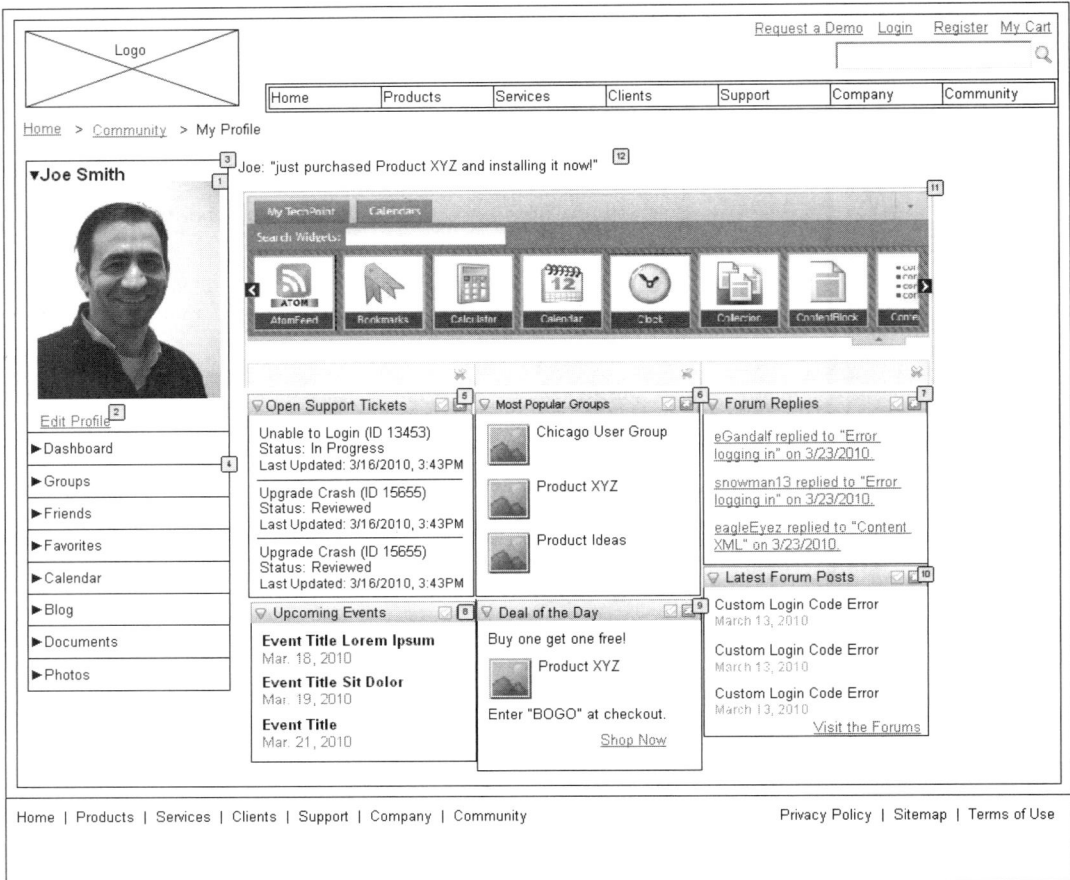

OnTrek Starter Site Functional Specification
© 2010, Ektron Inc.

FIGURE 3-5

The object table for the dashboard is similarly complex. However, in the page view, most of the references point to individual widgets and as such, are defined in the widget object table. Please note that the object table also includes guidance related to business rules that drive the functionality of individual components. The object table for the user dashboard is reproduced in Table 3-5.

TABLE 3-5: Object Table for the User Dashboard Page

FOOTNOTE	LABEL	INTERACTIONS	DESCRIPTION
1	Profile Avatar		User profile image uploaded by user.
2	Edit profile	**OnClick:** **Case 1:** Open Link in Current Window	Edit profile brings user to edit profile screen.

FOOTNOTE	LABEL	INTERACTIONS	DESCRIPTION
3	My profile		Shows the user profile basics. Uses profile format from Eintranet, an earlier project.
4	Left Nav Tabs		Tabs are prioritized in this order for the profile.
5	Status Bar		This should be updated from the current view on the Eintranet to use this format.
6	Open Support Tickets Dashboard Widget		See Dashboard Widget specs. (download the full Implementation Guide for this section).
7	Most Popular Groups Dashboard Widget		See Dashboard Widget specs.
8	Forum Replies Dashboard Widget		See Dashboard Widget specs.
9	Upcoming Events Dashboard Widget		See Dashboard Widget specs.
10	Deal of the Day Dashboard Widget		See Dashboard Widget specs.
11	Latest Forum Posts Dashboard Widget		See Dashboard Widget specs.
12	Personalization Dashboard		User's personalized dashboard. Can include any out-of-the-box widget, plus the widgets shown here. This view shows a proposed search widget box that should function the same as the PageBuilder Widget search.

We have selected the Most Popular Groups Dashboard Widget as an example of the many widgets that make up the dashboard page. Note the default settings are specified in the widget object table and even performance concerns are documented at this stage. The user interface is shown in Figure 3-6, and the object table for the widget is reproduced in Table 3-6.

FIGURE 3-6

TABLE 3-6: Object Table for the Most Popular Groups Dashboard Widget

FOOTNOTE	LABEL	INTERACTIONS	DESCRIPTION
1	Most Popular Groups Dashboard Widget		Widget for Personalization Dashboard. Avatar and text link to the group profile. **Widget Settings**: Set how many groups to display. Default is 5. (Set a max of 25 for performance.)

TAKE HOME POINTS: BEST PRACTICES FOR CREATING AN IMPLEMENTATION GUIDE

Now that you have seen a detailed view of what a content management system implementation guide looks like, this chapter will wrap up by sharing some best practice ideas to guide you as you create your own implementation guides. See Table 3-7.

TABLE 3-7: Best Practice Ideas for Creating an Implementation Guide

IDEA	DESCRIPTION
Be thorough.	If there's one area where CMS implementation guides are not successful, it's generally in their lack of thoroughness in capturing all requirements. The amount of effort you spend planning up front is returned to you many times over because doing so streamlines the development process. Before finalizing your implementation guide, cross-reference all aspects of the guide to existing functional requirements and information architecture standards.
Don't cut corners.	Make sure that you have an extensive set of Wireframes or user interface prototypes to include in your implementation guide. Ensure that your functional requirements and information architecture documents are complete and thorough before beginning work on the implementation guide.
Think strategically.	With the Ektron Framework, you often have many different methods, controls, or components that accomplish similar tasks. When considering different options, always think long-term. The goal of the implementation guide is not just to define how to build this current version of the website, but also to provide the flexibility that you need as the site evolves and grows in the future. If you have questions about which control to use, take advantage of the Ektron devCenter at http://dev.ektron.com, where other Ektron developers can share their thoughts and experiences with you.

IDEA	DESCRIPTION
Develop your implementation guide in multiple passes.	Involve other members of the development team in reviewing your implementation guide to get their input and advice.
Remember to consider the various contexts in which your pages will be rendered.	For example, think about how the page performs for a general website visitor, for a user who has login access, or for a user who is a CMS account holder.
Remember to plan for user interaction.	Keep in mind the flow of specific components of functionality. For example, consider a login process. The interaction design of this process is that users click a login button that opens a new window. In the new window, users enter their usernames and passwords and press the login button in the pop-up. If successful, the login window closes and the page refreshes. If not, an error message displays in the pop-up window and the users have the opportunity to enter the user password again.
Wherever possible, reiterate the business rules that govern functionality.	As seen previously in this chapter, it is always helpful to document relevant business rules in the context of individual components. For example, keeping performance in mind while developing business rules related to taxonomy-driven lists can have a major impact in the overall performance of your website. Including rules like "display only 10 matches" in the context of the implementation guide ensures that your development team will actually implement code in a way that optimizes performance.
Remember that the implementation guide is a living document.	In addition to providing documentation to the development team that is initially building out the site, the implementation guide is also used as a form of ongoing documentation about the functionality the site contains and the key elements of that functionality. Maintaining the implementation guide allows you to bring new team members up to speed quickly, helps alleviate duplicate code, and helps to keep new development exercises in line with existing functionality.

Configuring Your Development Environment

- What do you need to configure your machine to use the Ektron Framework?
- How do you install the Ektron Framework?
- What else do you need to know when you install?

In order to follow along with this book's development samples, you'll need a few programs installed on your computer. This chapter covers the basic software requirements to develop for the Ektron Framework, followed by instructions on setting up the OnTrek starter site on your development machine, followed by a discussion about approaches for team development.

WHAT YOU NEED TO CONFIGURE YOUR MACHINE

Once your system is configured with the required software, you can install the Ektron Framework. The list of required software to run Ektron locally as a developer is not too long. You must have a copy of the following:

- Windows with IIS 6.0 or greater and .NET Framework 3.5 or greater, along with a SQL Server 2005 or later instance available.
- Visual Studio 2005 or later. Any text editor will work for developing .NET code, but Visual Studio provides IntelliSense and other features that are invaluable when working with code you are not familiar with.
- Beyond that, you'll simply need a recent browser — Internet Explorer 7 or greater, or Firefox 2 or greater — and any Webkit browser such as Apple Safari or Google Chrome, supported by the Ektron Framework.

> Visual Studio 2005 or later. Any text editor will work for developing .NET code, but Visual Studio provides IntelliSense and other features that are invaluable when working with code you are not familiar with. Visual Web Developer is also an option that will work for most developers, but keep in mind that it is limited in its debugging capabilities. For example, Visual Web Developer cannot attach to a process, which is the recommended method of debugging a site. Also, Visual Web Developer cannot be used to build Ektron Extensions.

INSTALLING THE FRAMEWORK

The installer for the Ektron Framework can be found at http://www.ektron.com/download_center/. The installer will set up the support files and Windows Service. It presents you with the option of installing one of the included starter sites, which can be used either as examples or as the basis of your final site, to the local machine. Finally, it offers to install the SDK. This allows for building Ektron Extensions. These expose system events like AddUser and OnPublish to the developer.

The installer asks you at one point for a license key. For a local installation, it is easiest to just leave the box blank — this sets the framework to work only when accessed through localhost. In a distributed development environment with a central server, or when you are ready to move to a staging or production server accessed through another URL, you need a license key for the URL. Trial license keys can be requested through http://www.ektron.com/download_center/. To get a non-time-limited license, speak to your account manager or sales engineer at Ektron.

You can install by doing the following:

1. Start your installation by running CMS400Basev80.exe. This installer guides you through installing the core files and the Ektron Windows Service. Once completed, it asks you if you would like to install a site. Select No, since you want to install a starter site.

2. Go to http://www.ektron.com/cms400-starter-sites.aspx and download the OnTrek Starter Site. Running the installer adds the information needed to create an instance of the site to your Program Files directory.

3. Once complete, go to Start ➪ All Programs ➪ Ektron ➪ CMS400v80 ➪ Utilities ➪ CMS400 Site Setup. In the Wizard that appears, select Full Installation and continue. Since you are developing on a localhost, leave the license-key field blank. From the dropdown list of sites to install, select OnTrek.

4. You are asked what site and host you want to install to — leave these as the defaults.

5. You need to specify where the site files will reside; the default here is fine, unless you need to install somewhere else, for instance if you have multiple site roots defined in IIS. The Wizard will now install the site files.

6. Once the installation completes, you will have a live site, but the site won't do anything since you haven't set up the database yet. That database setup is the next thing the Wizard will ask for. Specify the connection parameters to your SQL instance, and it will configure the site to connect to the instance and create the database for the site.

When this Wizard completes, you can go to `http://localhost/OnTrek/`, and the example site for this book will be there.

Development Scenarios

When acting as a single developer, the requirement to manage the source and assets is easily fulfilled. In this scenario, all development is done locally. When the developers are ready to push the site live, they can copy all the files to the production home and perform a backup of the database followed by a restore at the destination. However, when working with a team of developers, a number of additional requirements may present themselves.

Source Control

The first item typically required when multiple developers need to collaborate is a source control system. Almost any versioning system works — Subversion, Git, Perforce, and Visual SourceSafe are all fine. Only the folders under development should be maintained in the repository. This means it is typically safe to leave the Workarea unmanaged. It is also usually best to leave the .config files in the root of the site unmanaged, as the configuration from one machine to another is likely to change.

A typical setup for managing source is to use Subversion to manage the source code. A single server is set up to view the current head revision of the source, and the database is set up on that server. The process to set up this portion is as follows:

1. Install either a min site or a starter site to that machine, and then perform an `svn import` on the directory. Make sure to exclude all .config files, as well as the Workarea, bin, uploadedfiles, and uploadedimages directories.

2. Once the import is complete, use `svn checkout` to turn the site directory into a working copy.

3. From here on, you can just run `svn update` to bring the machine to the head revision. Depending on your source control platform choice, this can usually be automated. For instance, Subversion has a folder that contains executable scripts, so it is straightforward to attach to the post-commit event hook, and force a refresh of the server at that time. Likewise, when using the Perforce daemon, it is possible to configure the daemon so that the working directory is updated at a regular interval.

4. Every developer should then have their own copy of the site installed locally on their machine, where changes are made through the development cycle. To initially set this up, install a min site to each machine, and then perform an `svn checkout` to bring the site up to the same file base as the other machines.

At this point the typical setup has each developer machine connect to the master database on the review server, by modifying the web.config. Through the use of load balancing, the associated assets are kept up-to-date across the machines.

Data Synchronization

There are two main options for managing content across a team of developers. The two options rely on different configurations of client server architectures. The one you choose for your project will depend on your license, your team size, and your requirements. The main difference between the two choices is whether you utilize a single shared database for all developers, or whether each developer has a local database, where each database is synchronized to each other.

In both situations, it is advised that each developer have his/her own ASP.NET instance. This allows for developers to feel free to use breakpoints, and debug output without interrupting the other developers on the project. Whether you share the database or use separate instances is determined by personal preference.

The two options are:

➤ **To use separate databases, one per development instance:** If you want to use this method, you should make sure you have eSync configured. eSync manages updating the database on both sides through the use of the Microsoft Sync Framework. It can also optionally update the templates and other files on the file system, but it is usually more straightforward to use your source control software. eSync is included with an Enterprise license, and is available as an addon with a Professional license.

➤ **To have one shared database that's used with many development servers:** The benefit with this configuration is there is no wait time for the database to be synchronized between the servers. The only caveat is that you should use load balancing to make sure that assets are updated on each of the development servers. *Load balancing* is a feature of the Ektron Framework which allows multiple servers to keep assets including library items and search summaries synchronized. If load balancing is not set up, any assets uploaded are not copied to the other sites. This prevents features such as Search from functioning properly, and may cause content to appear incorrectly. Figure 4-1 depicts the differences between the two options:

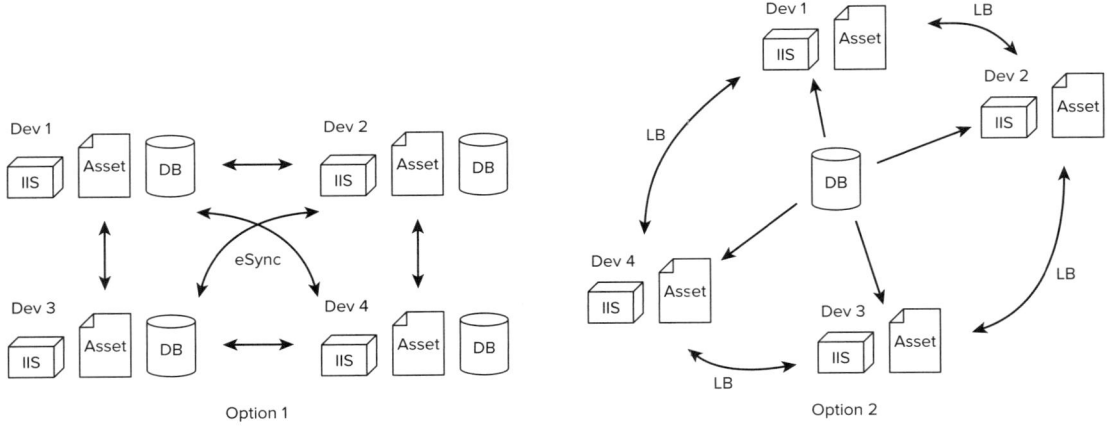

FIGURE 4-1

More information on each of these methods can be found in the CMS400.NET Manual, installed with the Ektron Framework. Chapter 18 in the manual covers eSync in depth, while Chapter 22 in the manual has a section dedicated to load balancing.

FURTHER TIPS

There are a few tips to help you streamline your development process. Some of the items in this section are performance tips that can help your team develop faster, and some are quirks to keep in mind that make working with the Ektron Framework slightly different from working with other ASP.NET sites.

- **Speed:** One of the issues developers run into is not a problem, but rather a question of speed. The typical development server is configured to build on demand by having all the source in the website directory. When the ASP.NET worker process receives a request for a given page, it ensures the files have not been modified since the last time the site was compiled. If they made changes, however, the ASP.NET worker process compiles the relevant files at that time. This makes development straightforward, because there is no build process that must happen after each edit, making it easier to modify code and test the modifications.

- **Time:** Many development teams are accustomed to building the site from Visual Studio in order to debug the code they are writing. A frequent complaint is the amount of time required to build the Workarea folder in the site folder. In a normal project, you can simply right-click a particular folder and select Exclude from Project. However, in an Ektron project, since there is mixed language, there can be no .csproj or .vbproj configuration file, so there is no way to mark a folder as excluded. The workaround for the inability to exclude files is to simply mark the Workarea folder as hidden in Windows Explorer. This typically reduces the build process by several minutes. This is necessary only in a project that is built from Visual Studio — a compiled on-demand site will only compile the required files, which rarely includes much of the Workarea.

- **Debugging:** Part of the reason teams sometimes decide to compile their project from Visual Studio is a lack of clarity on how to enter into debug mode without pressing F5, which initiates a build. However, debugging without precompiling is actually pretty straightforward, and is, within Ektron, the preferred method of day-to-day development. To debug your site in Visual Studio without compiling, first make sure your web.config is set to debug mode. This setting is stored as an attribute (`'debug="true"'`) in the Compilation tag in the System.Web section. Now, in Visual Studio, select Debug ➪ Attach to Process. In the dialog box that appears, find the ASP.NET worker process (either aspnet_wp.exe or w3wp.exe, depending on your version of IIS and Windows) and attach to the process. Visual Studio will load the debug DLLs, and you will be able to set breakpoints and debug your site live.

TAKE HOME POINTS

Setting up an Ektron development instance is fairly straightforward, but here are some take away points:

- All the elements of the Ektron Framework are bundled into an intuitive installer, which takes most of the headache out of the operation.

- There are also several open source starter sites provided by Ektron that can be great jumping off points for your own development efforts.

- Beyond single-server development, there are also several options that allow for rich collaboration between developers, shortening the lifecycle of synchronization so that less time is spent keeping everyone up-to-date, and more time is spent developing new features.
- By choosing an appropriate development practice early on, you can help ensure the success of your project by keeping everything moving smoothly as you move towards completion of your project.

PART II
Building the TechPoint Site

- **CHAPTER 5:** Understanding Content Management Fundamentals
- **CHAPTER 6:** Configure Commonly Used Components
- **CHAPTER 7:** The Homepage
- **CHAPTER 8:** Reaching Prospects
- **CHAPTER 9:** Generating Leads through Campaign Optimization
- **CHAPTER 10:** Supporting Customers
- **CHAPTER 11:** Implementing the OnTrek Social Network
- **CHAPTER 12:** Creating the Catalog of Products for the eCommerce Storefront
- **CHAPTER 13:** Constructing the Online Storefront with eCommerce

Understanding Content Management Fundamentals

- How do you log into the CMS and use the Workarea?
- How do you work with content in the Ektron Framework?
- How can you organize content and assets using folders and the library?
- How do you manage permission structures and create approval chains?

Learning a new framework can be very confusing. You need to figure out what is most central to the framework and what the overall stack looks like. This type of 30,000-ft. view can be difficult, which is why the book addresses these fundamentals.

In the Ektron Framework, the most important concept to grasp is that of content. Almost everything in the system is designed either as an extension of content, such as Calendar Events and PageBuilder pages, or as an organizational tool for content, such as collections and taxonomy. This densely knotted structure is, in many ways, a unique aspect of the Ektron Framework. In most content management systems and portals there is a concept of content, but content is not the basis for other things in those systems.

This chapter starts with the Workarea, which is a browser-based application installed into your site. The Workarea is where the vast majority of management of your site happens. This chapter covers how to log in to the system, and takes you on a tour to get a feel for navigation in the Workarea.

The next section covers how to create, work with, and display content. The interaction with content covered here will be expounded upon in later chapters as you cover other features based on core content such as HTML forms and PageBuilder pages.

You'll also explore some concepts closely related to content, such as permissions, approval chains, and history. These tools allow you as a developer to understand the features content authors will need to interact with regularly, and how those features can impact your overall site design.

One of the largest things that impact site design is the overall site infrastructure, and you will cover the concepts of folders and the library in this chapter as well. When you complete this chapter you will understand how to address the information architecture of your site so that content authors can manage the information of your site on an ongoing basis.

LOGIN AND WORKAREA

Almost all interaction with the Ektron CMS occurs from an application inside your site called the Workarea. The *Workarea* provides an interface to manage your folder structure, content, menu system and metadata, system setup — just about anything that is configurable and manageable for your site. In this chapter, you'll go through some of the basics of interacting with the Workarea application, and learn how the features are organized.

The Workarea is the primary interaction point for content managers in an Ektron installation. It is installed in the directory ~/Workarea. The Workarea is not precompiled or obfuscated, meaning you can look at the code to see how it performs any action. It can also be customized to add functionality, but this is only recommended for advanced users.

Before you dig into the Workarea itself, you'll learn how to log into a freshly installed CMS400Min site. Once you've logged in, you'll learn the process of adding a user to the site and to a group. Then you'll do a run through of the Workarea, which is where all content customizations happen from here on out.

The Ektron Framework has two primary types of users: membership users and content authors. The Workarea is usable only by content authors and is available only if a correct license key is used. This means no key is necessary for localhost operations, but a non-expired license key is required for any domain access. The special user *builtin*, can always access the Workarea, which allows the license key to be updated for a live site. The account types can be found in Table 5-1.

TABLE 5-1: Special Users in the Ektron Framework

USERNAME	PASSWORD	DESCRIPTION
Admin	admin	Automatically granted all permissions.
Builtin	builtin	An emergency account that can be used if all admin accounts are accidentally disabled or locked out. Builtin can log in even if the license key is invalid. The account is only able to access particular areas of the CMS — particularly the user management and setup screens.
InternalAdmin	n/a	Only used for programmatic access. It automatically passes all permission checks.
Vs	vs	Used if data services for Visual Studio are enabled. It connects to the server from the Ektron Framework Server Controls in Visual Studio via Web services, and allows you to select hardcoded values such as Content Block IDs.

The password for the admin, builtin, and vs accounts should always be changed on any production site. Until the site goes live, however, it is fine to leave these accounts with the stock information. In addition to these special users, there are also two special user groups defined in Table 5-2.

TABLE 5-2: Special Groups in the Ektron Framework

GROUP NAME	DESCRIPTION
Everyone	Every user in the system is automatically in this group.
Administrators	Members of this group automatically pass all permission and role tests.

Members of the Administrators group have powerful privileges and can modify anything in the framework, at will. Be careful who you grant this membership to in a production site.

Since you are working with a freshly installed copy of the OnTrek site, log in with the admin user and create an administrator account for use by a developer.

Logging In and Creating a User

To log into the site you follow these steps:

1. Simply go to the home page. Visit the freshly installed site at http://localhost/ontrek/default.aspx unless you installed to a different location. On the home page, you'll see a link in the toolbar, shown in Figure 5-1, to log into the site.

2. Click the Login button and login as admin/admin. Once you're logged in as a CMS user, the Login button will be replaced by a link to the Workarea. If you are starting with a min site, the process is slightly different. The min site ships with a simple template called login.aspx (http://localhost/cms400min/cmslogin.aspx.), and doesn't have the login in the aforementioned toolbar. When you visit this template, you'll see Figure 5-2 on the page.

    This image is produced by the Login Server Control. The login server has the same functionality as the toolbar on the homepage of the OnTrek site, but with a less form-fitting layout.

3. You may find that there is no login available on the front end. If worse comes to worst, the login functionality is available at http://localhost/OnTrek/workarea/login.aspx. Once logged into the site, the Workarea can be launched by visiting http://localhost/OnTrek/workarea/workarea.aspx.

4. Once logged in, you should create an account for use on the development site. This is especially important when you are sharing a demo site, because each login supports only one session at a time. If you were to log in on another browser, the system would invalidate your first session.

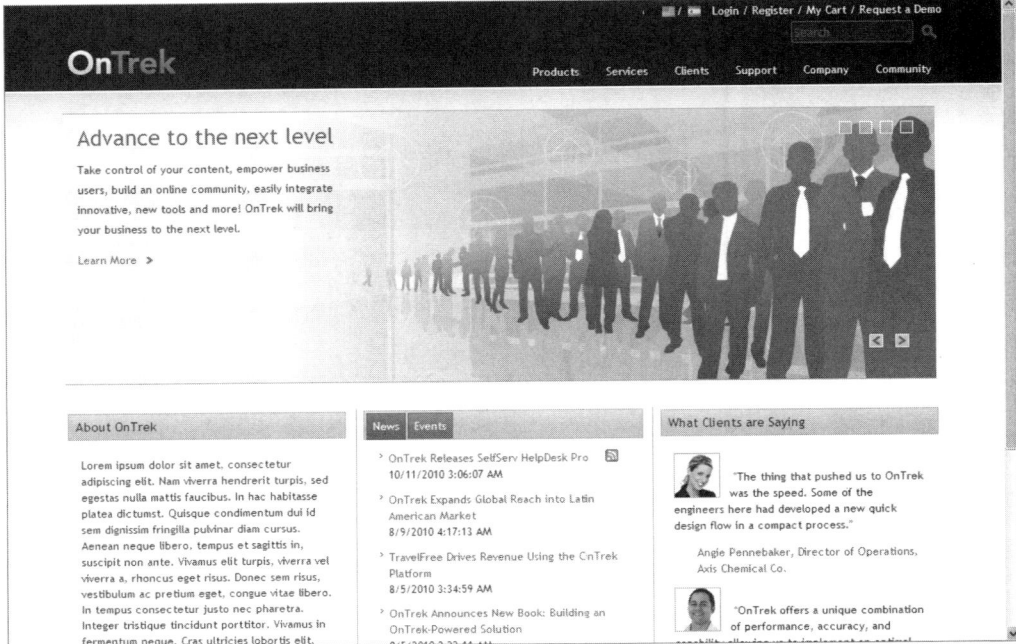

FIGURE 5-1

5. Launch the Workarea now by clicking the Workarea link. When you enter the Workarea, the first thing you see is the Dashboard, pictured in Figure 5-3. This chapter will walk through the tabs one-by-one after you've created your development user.

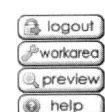

FIGURE 5-2

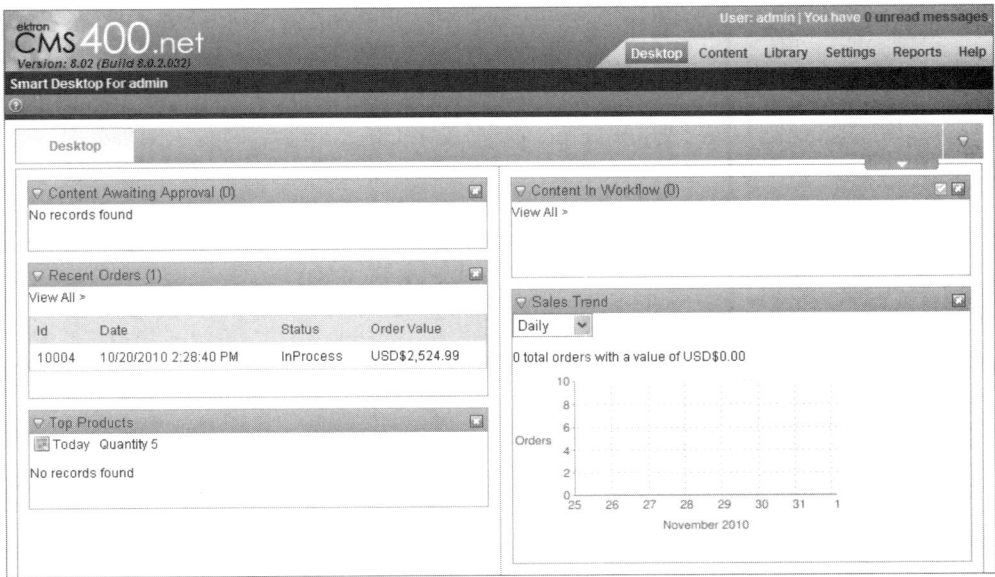

FIGURE 5-3

6. On the top right, select the Settings tab. Once you're viewing the Settings tree, select Users from it. In Figure 5-4, you'll find the Settings tree on the left and a list of users defined in the system on the right.

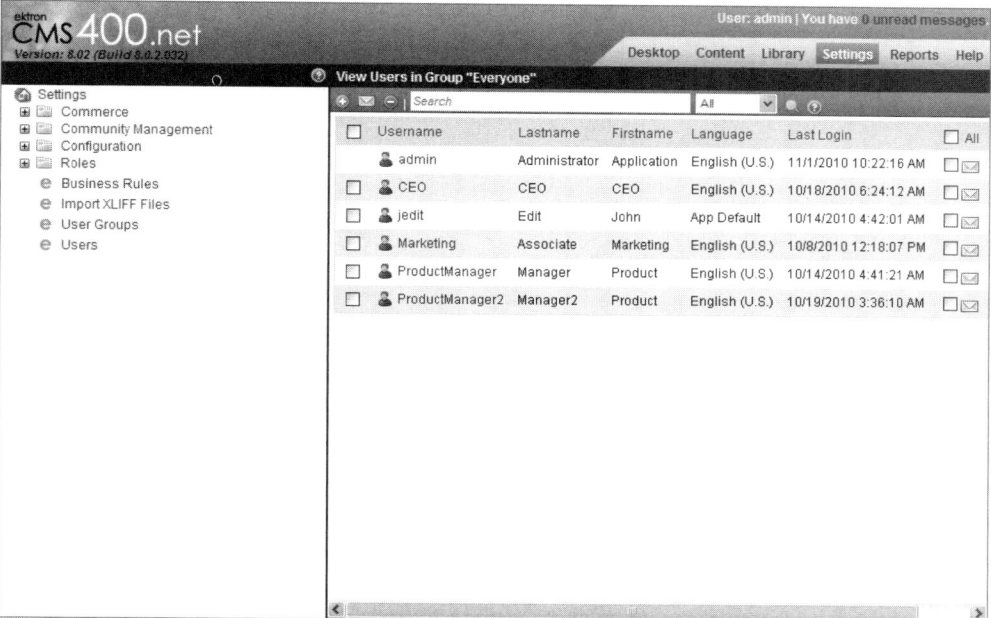

FIGURE 5-4

7. Create a new user by clicking the Add icon just above the list of users. The Add a New User to the System form has a list of fields that must be entered, as pictured in Figure 5-5.
8. Enter the username, first and last name, display name, password, confirm password, and e-mail. Clicking the Save icon throws an error.
9. Click over to the Custom Properties tab and select a time zone for the user to correct the error. Select your time zone, and click the Save icon.

 Custom properties can be created that apply to all users at any time. These properties will appear under the Custom Properties tab on the user registration and modification screen, and can be used for programmatic purposes.

10. This user is now ready for use, except that as a developer, you will likely need administrator privileges on your account. To add the newly created user to the administrator group, select the User Groups node on the Settings tree.
11. You can see the two built-in groups shown in Figure 5-6. Click Administrators, and the page will instead list the users in the Administrators group. The add icon on this screen allows you to add your user to the group.

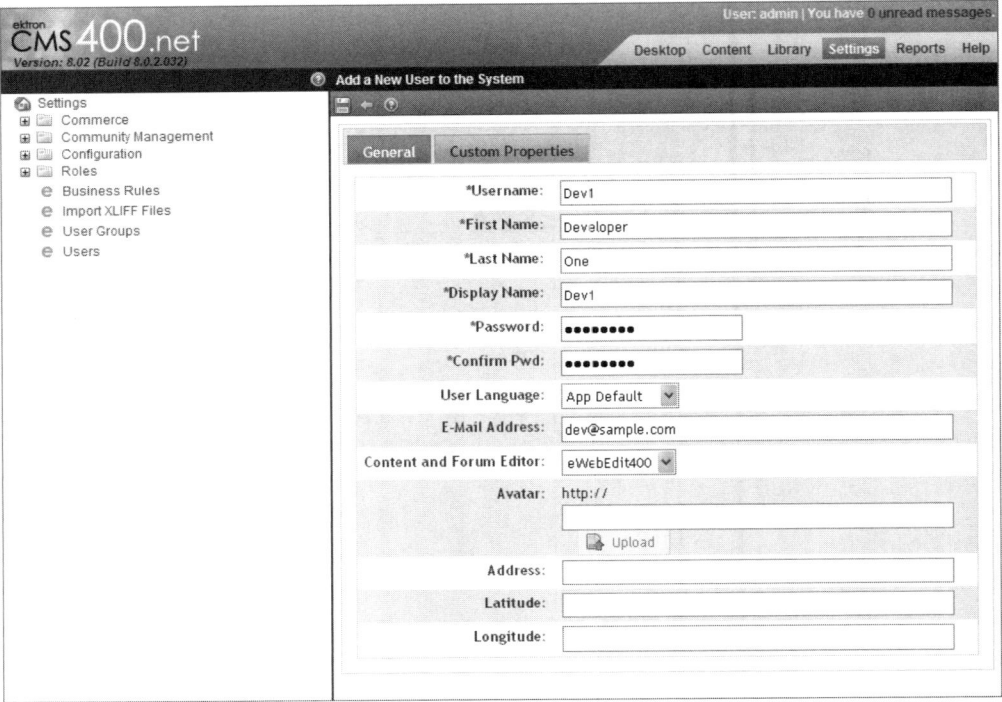

FIGURE 5-5

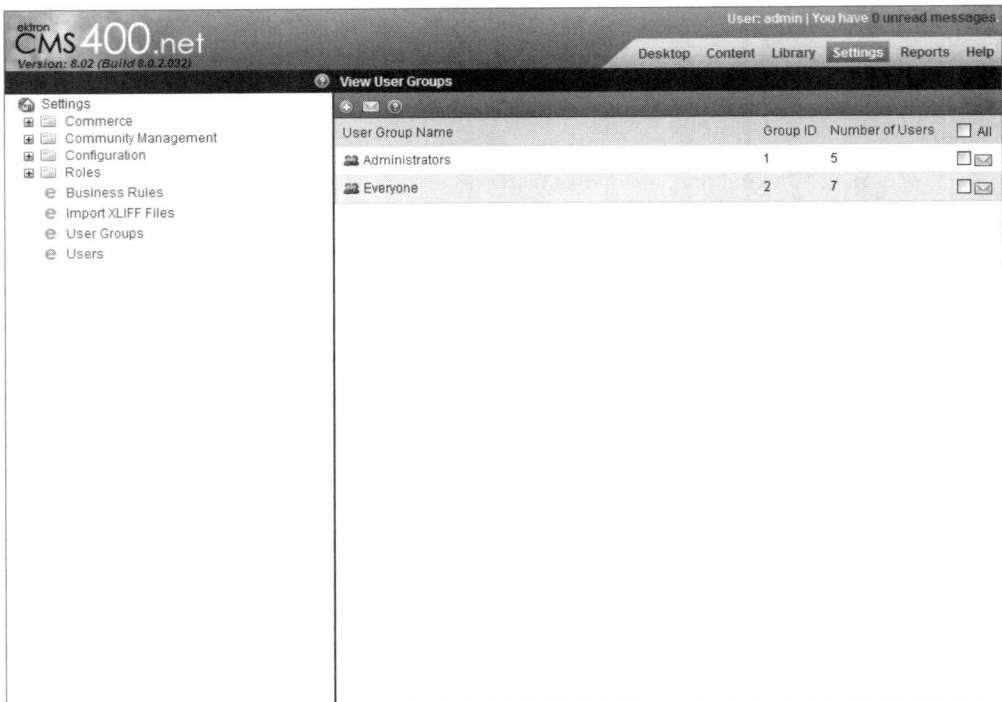

FIGURE 5-6

12. Select the Dev1 checkbox in the list, shown in Figure 5-7, and click the Floppy icon to save, then click OK on the confirmation dialog. Now that Dev1 is a member of the administrator group, Dev1 now has all privileges in the system. You can now close the Workarea browser window, click Logout on the toolbar on the front page of the site, and then log back in as Dev1.

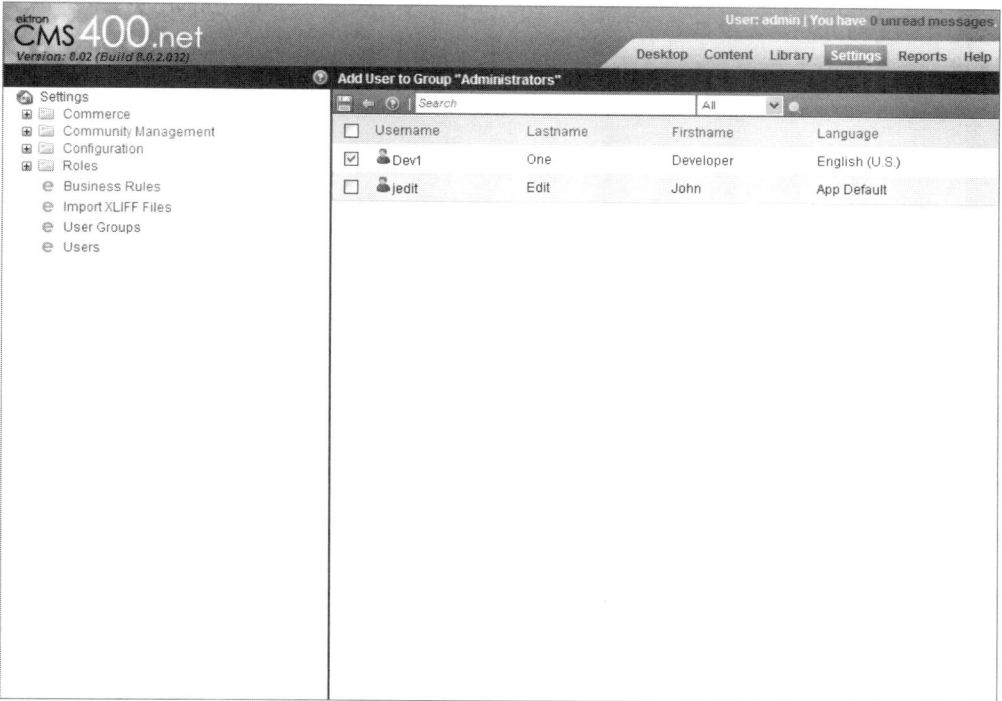

FIGURE 5-7

Exploring the Workarea

Upon launching the Workarea, the first view that comes up is the Dashboard, also known as the Smart Desktop. The Dashboard is a personalized view into the CMS. It allows each user to add widgets to the display and manage the layout of those widgets. The preloaded widgets can display reports on content in certain states, eCommerce trends and orders, and analytics information. The Workarea Dashboard uses the same personalization engine as Member User Dashboards, which are covered in Chapter 11.

After the Dashboard tab comes the Content, Library, Settings, and Reports tabs. These tabs follow a common layout. They are divided into two parts: one on the left and one on the right. The right side, called the "display pane," is used to show the interface of the particular option or content you are currently modifying. The left side is called the "navigation pane," and allows you to select the particular feature you want to interact with in the display pane.

The Settings tab of the Workarea is the key to managing options on the Ektron Framework. This area is where everything that isn't managed content is configured. This includes users and groups, and also more fundamental elements such as aliasing options and system templates.

The Dashboard Tab

The Desktop is the first tab to appear because it is helpful to see what workflows require a user's interaction, as pictured in Figure 5-8.

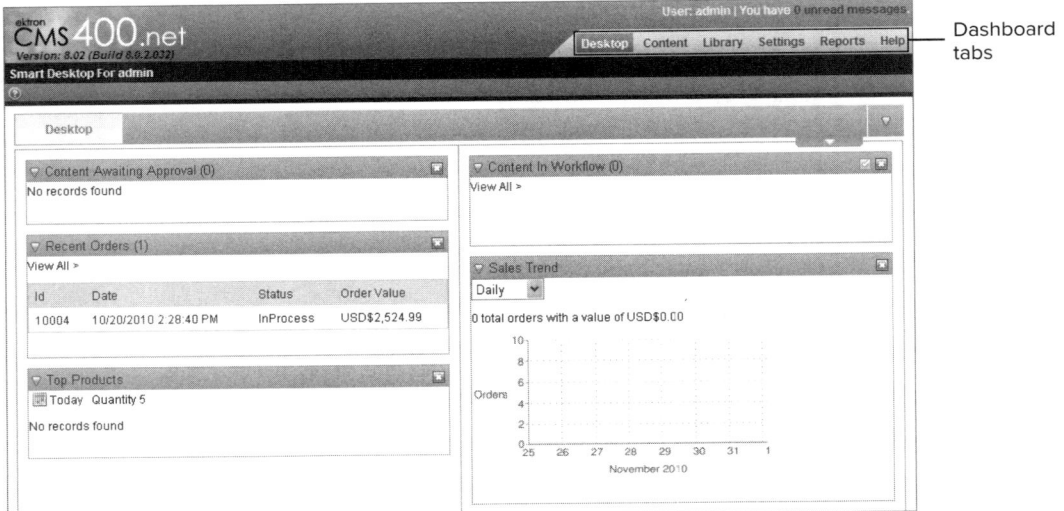

Dashboard tabs

FIGURE 5-8

This makes ongoing management of the content and components of the website easier. However, this tab provides only a brief overview of the state of the system. To see the system in more depth, it is necessary to switch tabs to other views. The tabs are at the top right of the Workarea, the second tab being Content.

The Content Tab

The Content tab is where interaction with the primary elements of the CMS occurs. This Content tab, as mentioned in the general discussion, is comprised of a navigation pane on the left and a display pane on the right. This is shown below in Figure 5-9.

In the navigation pane on the content tab, there are four accordions — Folders, Taxonomies, Collections and Menus. Each accordion contains a "navigation tree," which displays the respective elements associated with that type. For example, in the folders accordion, the navigation tree shows the folders at each level. Selecting a folder from the navigation tree updates the display pane to show the details for that folder — in this case the detail view is the list of content within that folder.

It may seem unusual that all four accordions in the navigation pane of the Content tab do not display content. This is completely normal, since all four accordions are methods of organizing the content. For instance, when showing the Collections accordion, the navigation tree lists each of the collections defined in the site. Selecting one of the collections updates the display pane to show the content associated with that collection.

Interactions with content items also occur through the Content tab. Selecting one of the content items listed in the display pane when navigating the folders tree brings you to the content display page. This page lists all the details for a particular piece of content, and by interacting with the display pane toolbar, shown in Figure 5-10, a content author can manage all aspects of the content.

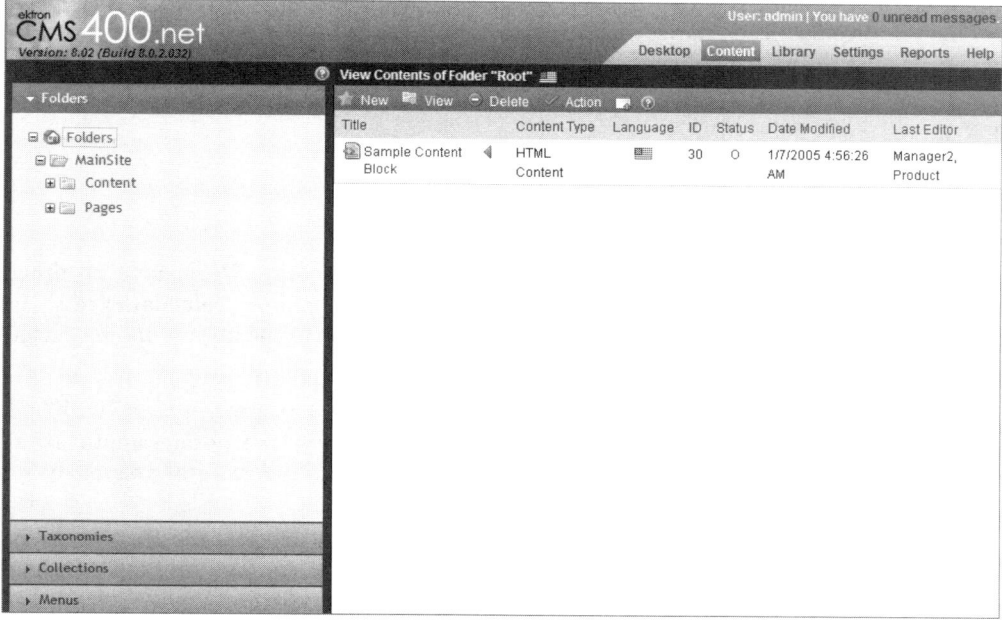

FIGURE 5-9

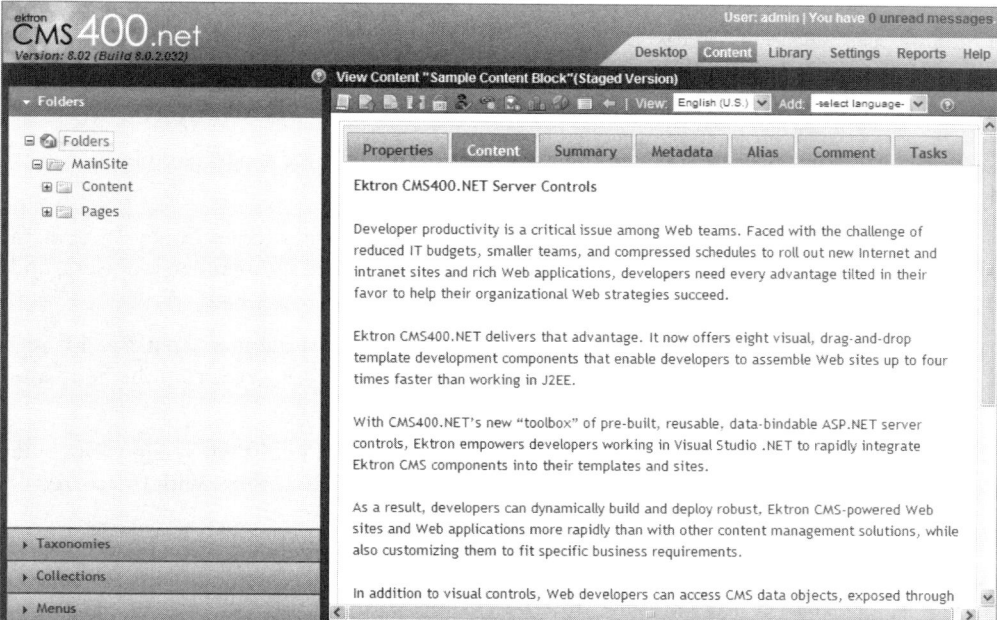

FIGURE 5-10

The Settings and Reports Tabs

The two last tabs oriented towards system management are the Settings tab and the Reports tab. The Settings tab is where non-content oriented options are managed. This includes system wide configuration options like license keys, user and community management, as well as eCommerce management. One of the most important items available in the Settings tab is the Setup pane, accessible through Settings ⇨ Configuration ⇨ Setup on the navigation tree. This is where the license key is entered, among other things.

CONTENT ENTRY AND DISPLAY

Content is the fundamental unit of information displayed on your website. While not everything in the Ektron Framework is based on content, most things are. For example, calendar events, PageBuilder pages, and HTML forms are all based on content, whereas menus, taxonomy categories, and collections are not.

Content in the Ektron Framework follows a predetermined process. This process starts with its addition to the site and ends with its eventual publication. The process incorporates approval chains and permissions to ensure each piece of content has been approved by the necessary people before going live to the site.

In addition to basic properties, such as creation dates, content items also have extensive roots throughout the framework. For instance, content items can belong to taxonomy nodes, collections, and appear on menus. They can have metadata associated with them, support multilingual representations, and can be associated with URL aliases. This section won't cover every connection that content has, but will focus on the process of entering content, how to move it through publication stages, and how, as a developer, to display it.

Content Storage and Status

Depending on the current version state, content is stored in one of three separate tables in the database:

- ➤ `content`: The current live version of a piece of content is always found in the `content` table. This is the version that is accessible to users who aren't logged in, membership users, and anyone not previewing the site.
- ➤ `content_edit`: This table stores the most current version of the content that has not yet been published. Once the changes have been published, the row is removed from the `content_edit` table and moved to the `content` table.
- ➤ `content_history`: This is where all previous checked in and published versions of content go. Content can be restored from the `content_history` table by users with the correct permissions.

Each version of content has a status associated with it. The possible content states are listed in Table 5-3 and as a piece of content moves through the states, only certain actions can be taken. The end goal in each case is to reach the A state, which means that content is viewable to users with the correct permissions.

TABLE 5-3: Content States

LETTER	MEANING	DESCRIPTION	POSSIBLE NEXT STATES
A	Approved	Content has been through the entire workflow and is published and available on the site.	O, M
O	Checked Out	Content is currently checked out to a user. This means the item is currently being edited. It cannot be edited by another user until it has been checked in.	I, S
I	Checked In	Content checked in for other users to edit. Has not yet been published, so it not visible on the site.	A, O, S, M, P, T
S	Submitted for Approval	Content will enter this state only if it has an approval chain it needs to complete. This state is entered when the author submits the content into the chain after making edits.	A, O, S, M, P, T
M	Marked for Deletion	The equivalent of the S state, but for deleting content. When a user attempts to delete content from a folder with an approval chain, the content will remain in the M state until the request is approved or declined.	A, Deleted
P	Pending Go Live Date	The content has been approved and is ready to appear on the site, but it has been marked with a go live date. The content will remain in the P state until the go live data occurs, at which point the content transitions to A and is visible on the site.	A, O, M
T	Awaiting Completion of Tasks	Tasks are items associated to a piece of content and assigned to a person. A piece of content will not be visible on the website until all tasks associated with it have been completed. If there is nothing stopping a piece of content from being displayed except for the completion of tasks, it is in the T state. When the necessary tasks are completed, it will move automatically to A state and become visible on the site.	A, O, M

The movement from one state to the next is limited by the permissions of the current user, as well as any applied approval chains and tasks associated with the content. For instance, the T state will be reached only when attempting to publish a piece of content that has tasks associated with it. Additionally, the S and M states will be reached only if an approval chain has been applied to the folder. If the folder does not have an approval chain, the content moves directly to the A state or is deleted, respectively.

Content in the Ektron Framework is managed through *a lock model*, which means that when one user is editing content, no other user can edit at the same time. It's very similar to a source control model, in that content can only be checked out to one user at a time, and the next user must wait until the content has been checked back in before he or she in turn can check it out to edit it. Publishing content to bring it live on the site can then be done with any version that has been checked in. Each time the content is checked in or published, an additional record is made in the history table that contains that version of the content.

Adding and Managing Content

This section covers some fundamental tasks associated with managing content in the Ektron Framework.

- Creating a content item
- Viewing the content in the Workarea
- Interacting with the Document Management System (DMS) menu and editing in context
- Using the Content Block Server Control

Creating a Content Item

To create a content block in the installed site, open the Workarea and navigate to Root ⇨ Content in the folder tree. The display pane will update a list of all the content in that folder. Hover over New in the display pane toolbar to access the creation menu, and then select HTML content. See Figure 5-11.

The page that appears to collect information about your new content has several tabs, each of which has inputs associated with a particular aspect of the content. In many cases, the tab is prepopulated with information inherited from the folder. However, in some cases the tab is blank and information must be entered at this time. This section first covers the universally available fields in this form, then iterates over the tabs, and finally looks at the available options on the toolbar.

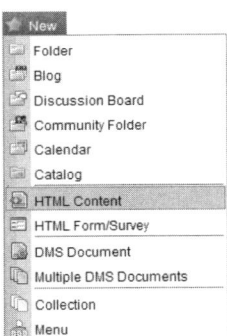

FIGURE 5-11

There are only two options on the form that aren't included in a tab:

- **The title of the content:** The title must be unique within the folder. If it is not, then a number in parentheses will be appended to the end of the name, per Microsoft naming conventions.
- **The Content Searchable field:** This determines whether the content item will be returned in content searches on the site. This only affects the Ektron built-in search results, not external search engines such as Bing or Google.

Using the Content Pane Tabs

Let's now move on to the tabs that are used to manage all other aspects of the content. Figure 5-12 displays the various tabs.

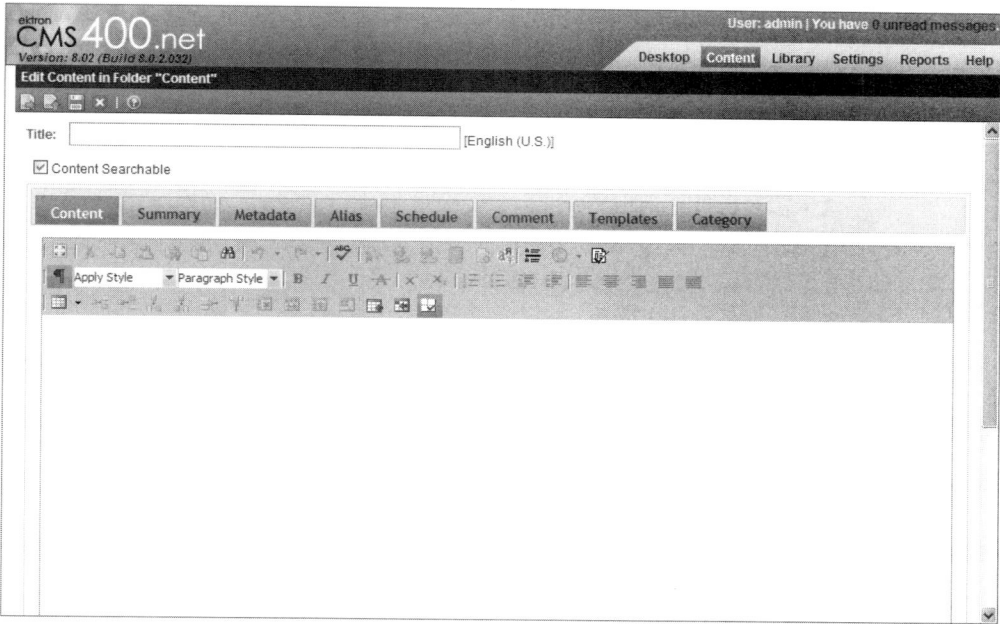

FIGURE 5-12

➤ **Content:** The first tab, Content, is where the actual content is entered. The Ektron eWebEdit400 editor is displayed inside the tab. eWebEdit400 is a full-featured JavaScript-based HTML editor, and is compatible with any recent release of all the major browsers. The discussion of the functionality in eWebEdit400 is outside the scope of this book. This editor displays the content that will actually be displayed to users browsing on the site.

➤ **Summary:** The Summary tab also has an instance of eWebEdit400. This instance is used to enter the summary for the content. The summary can be displayed optionally in many locations that would display a link to this content. For example, the summary can be displayed alongside the link in search results, in folder listings using the ListSummary Server Control, and in collection listings using the Collection Server Control. If you know that the summary won't be displayed on the site, it is not necessary to fill it out, but it is considered Best Practice to enter a summary here.

➤ **Metadata:** *Metadata* is additional information associated to the content. This can be in two forms:

   ➤ Traditional, SEO-style metadata that would be rendered into the document such as the description and keywords.

   ➤ Metadata in the Ektron Framework. That is data that associates this content to other content, or stores settings for display or content tags.

The metadata definitions that apply to a given piece of content are inherited from the folder where the content resides, and the values for the metadata may have defaults associated with the definitions for the metadata. The values you want to use for this particular piece of content, however, should be entered in the area displayed in Figure 5-13.

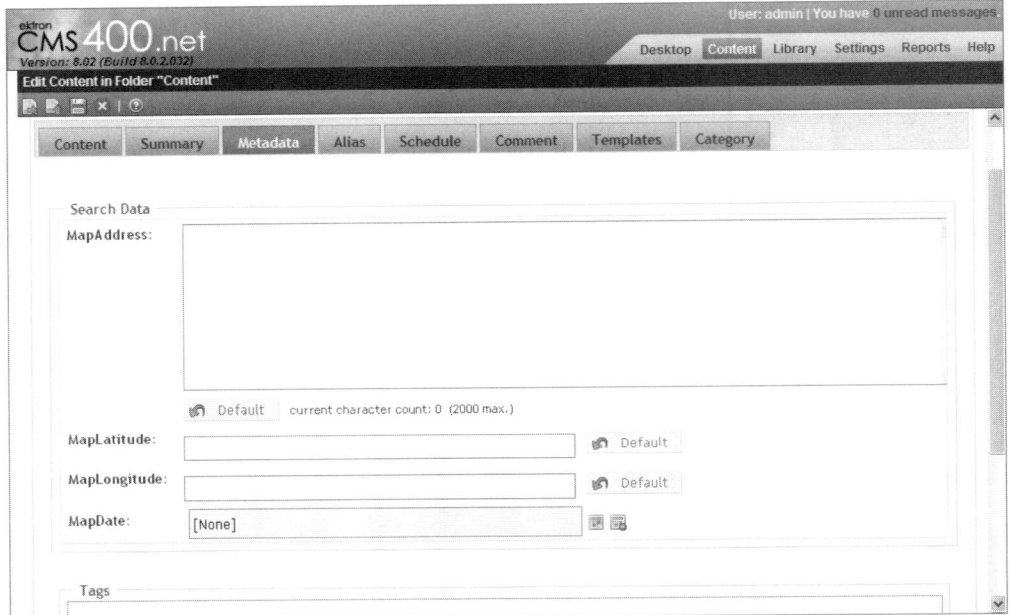

FIGURE 5-13

➤ **Alias:** Aliases are alternative URLs that can be used to access the content in addition to the quicklink for a given piece of content. This allows content managers to manage the SEO needs for a given piece of content. The alias tab allows you to manage a manual alias for the content, which is user entered, and also shows a list of the automatic aliases available for the content.

➤ **Schedule:** Pictured in Figure 5-14, this tab allows the content manager to set when the new published version should go live, and when a piece of content should expire. It also allows you to set the action to take upon expiration. These options can all be left blank, in which case the content remains in its normal state indefinitely. By setting a Start date for the content, however, you can control exactly when the content becomes visible. There are three options for the action to take on expiration:

  ➤ **Archive and remove from site:** Changes the content to be archived. The content is still visible in the Workarea by setting the filter to Archived Content, but is not visible on the site.

  ➤ **Archive and remain on site:** Removes the content from active navigation elements such as ListSummaries, but is still located by search and by direct navigation such as bookmarks. This option also archives the content.

➤ **Add to the CMS Refresh Report:** This adds an entry to a list of items that need to be reviewed by an author. However, the content is still completely normal in terms of front-end navigation and display, as well as with Workarea interaction.

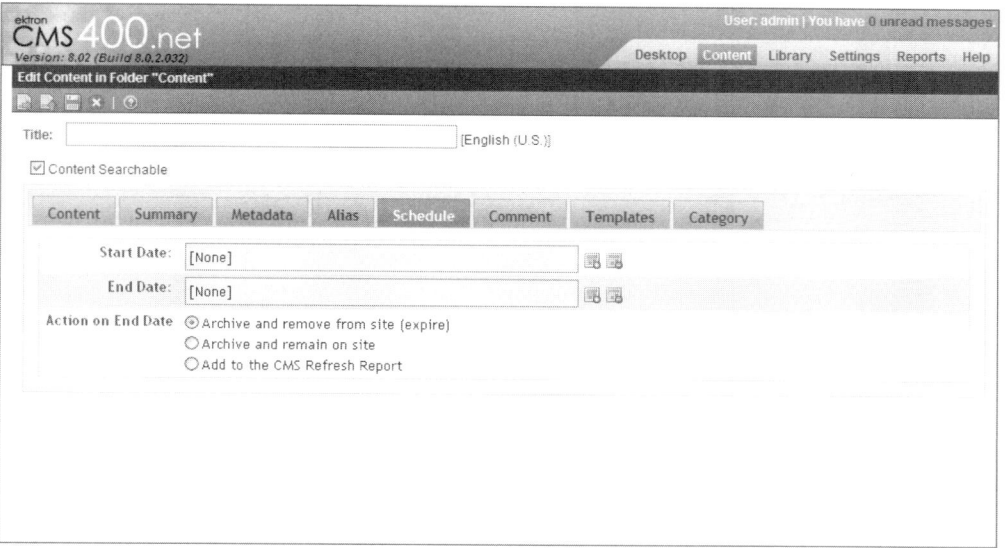

FIGURE 5-14

➤ **Comment:** Comments are internal-only notes that can be entered for each piece of content. These are not displayed anywhere on the front end. Instead, they are used to store information that may be useful to a future editor of the content.

➤ **Templates:** The Templates tab, pictured in Figure 5-15, allows users to select the template for this particular piece of content. The only allowed templates are the ones that the parent folder is configured to use. This controls the template the content is rendered on when a user follows a system-generated link to the content. However, any Content Block Server Control on any template has the ability to display the content item if the controls `DefaultContentID` property is set to the ID of the content item.

➤ **Category:** The Category tab, pictured in Figure 5-16, allows the content author to associate the content item to any applicable taxonomy nodes. Only nodes that have been associated with the parent folder are available for selection on this screen. Also remember that when a piece of content is associated to a taxonomy node, that update happens outside of the normal content workflow. In other words, if an author modifies a piece of content to be associated to a different node, that change happens immediately.

If they have been marked on the parent folder, the only required fields for content are the title, content, metadata, and categories. Enter the following details into those fields now. Table 5-4 provides the fields and corresponding values.

CHAPTER 5 UNDERSTANDING CONTENT MANAGEMENT FUNDAMENTALS

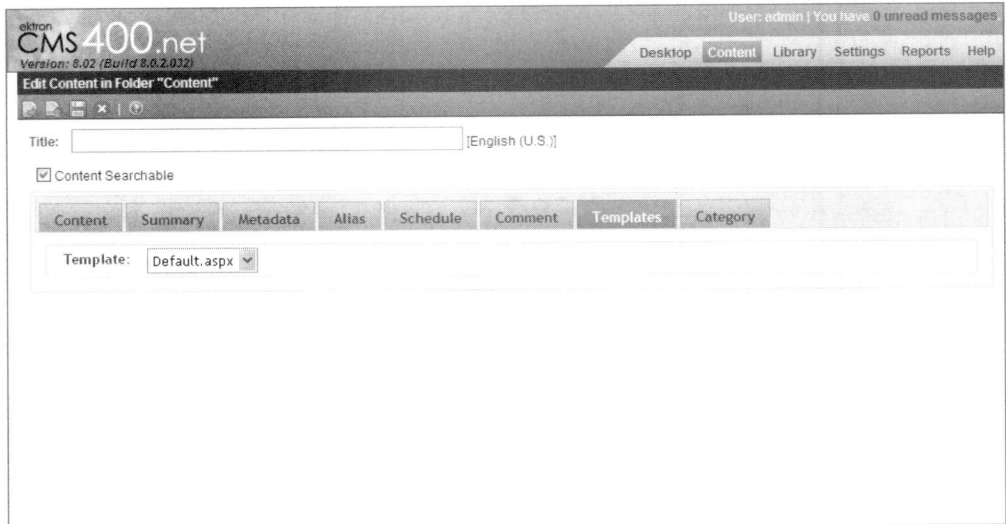

FIGURE 5-15

FIGURE 5-16

TABLE 5-4: Values

FIELD	VALUE
Title	Test Content
Content	This is some test content.
Category	Company

Using the Content Pane Toolbar

Now let's examine the available buttons on the toolbar in the content entry pane. Figure 5-17 displays the toolbar.

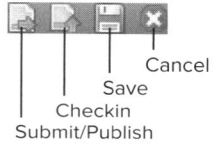

FIGURE 5-17

- **Submit/Publish:** This button will submit the content into the approval chain if configured, and will publish the content immediately if there is no approval chain for the folder.

- **Checkin:** Checks in the content but does not submit it to the approval process or bring it live. Checking in content will allow other authors to begin working on the content.

- **Save:** This keeps the content checked out to the current editor, locking it to other users, while updating the copy in the database so that no changes will be lost.

- **Cancel:** Discards any changes made from the version in the database.

Submit the content now by clicking the first button on the toolbar. This returns you to the View Content screen, where you can see all the details of the content you just created.

Viewing the Content in the Workarea

The View Content screen, shown in Figure 5-18, displays almost the same interface as the Edit Content screen. It has a toolbar with many more options, along with the same tabbed interface from before, and even some of the tabs are the same. This section goes through the screen in the same order as before, first covering the display below the toolbar, and then diving into each item on the toolbar itself.

- **Properties:** Shown in Figure 5-19, this displays everything you need to know at a system level about the content. It displays the title, the ID, language, current content status, action dates, template, system path, and content rating.

- **Content:** Shown in Figure 5-18, this renders the content that will be shown on the site. Content is rendered without any custom stylesheets you may have configured for the folder. This differs from the editor, which does interact with the content with custom stylesheets applied.

- **Summary:** Just like the Content tab, the Summary tab displays the HTML entered into the summary. If nothing is entered for the summary, the summary is automatically generated by the system from the content. Figure 5-20 displays the Summary tab.

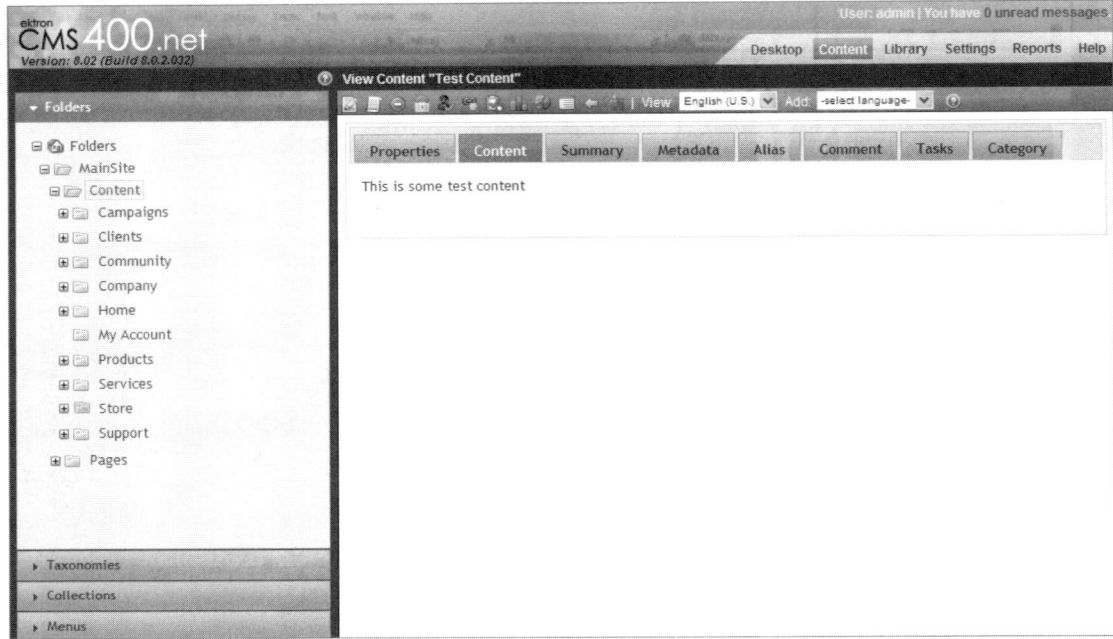

FIGURE 5-18

FIGURE 5-19

Content Entry and Display | 71

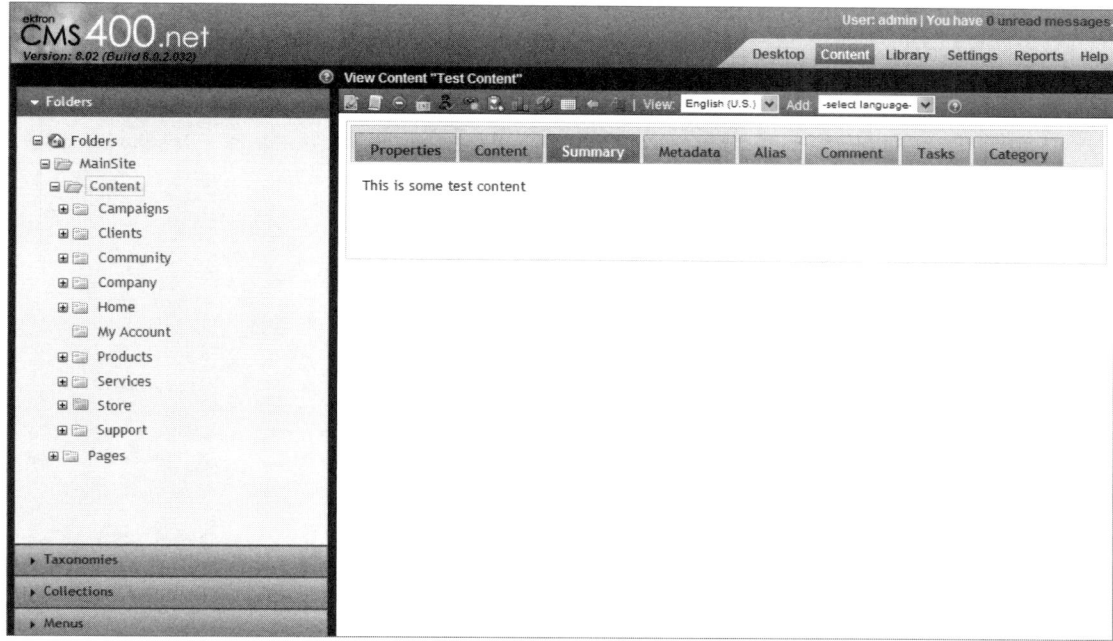

FIGURE 5-20

➤ **Metadata:** The Metadata tab, pictured in Figure 5-21, shows the values stored for each metadata definition for this content item. In some cases this will differ from what was entered on the edit screen. These items, just like all items in the CMS, can be modified by Framework Plugins and Extensions. The reason it is mentioned explicitly here is that one of the extensions shipped with the framework is a GeoMapping Plugin. This reads the data stored in the MapAddress metafield, and converts it to a latitude and longitude, which are stored in the corresponding metafields.

➤ **Alias:** Shown in Figure 5-22, this tab allows you to update the manual alias for the content if aliasing has been enabled on the site, and it will also list any current automatically generated aliases which can come from taxonomy or folder aliasing. For more information on aliasing, see Chapter 6.

➤ **Comment:** This simply displays whatever information was entered into the Comment field on the Edit screen.

➤ **Tasks:** Shown in Figure 5-23, this displays a report of all tasks currently associated with the content. Tasks are notes attached to a piece of content that can be assigned to specific users. If there are any tasks associated with a piece of content, the content will not go live until they have been marked as complete. Administrators can see all tasks associated with a piece of content, but non-administrative users can only see tasks assigned to them.

➤ **Category:** Pictured in Figure 5-24, this simply lists all the taxonomy nodes the content item has been associated with.

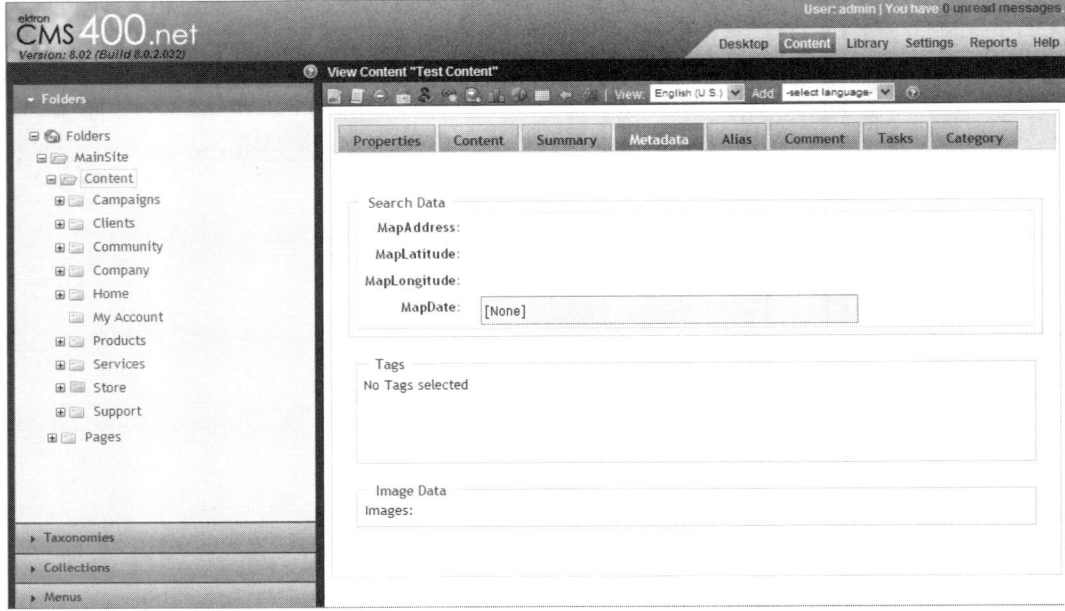

FIGURE 5-21

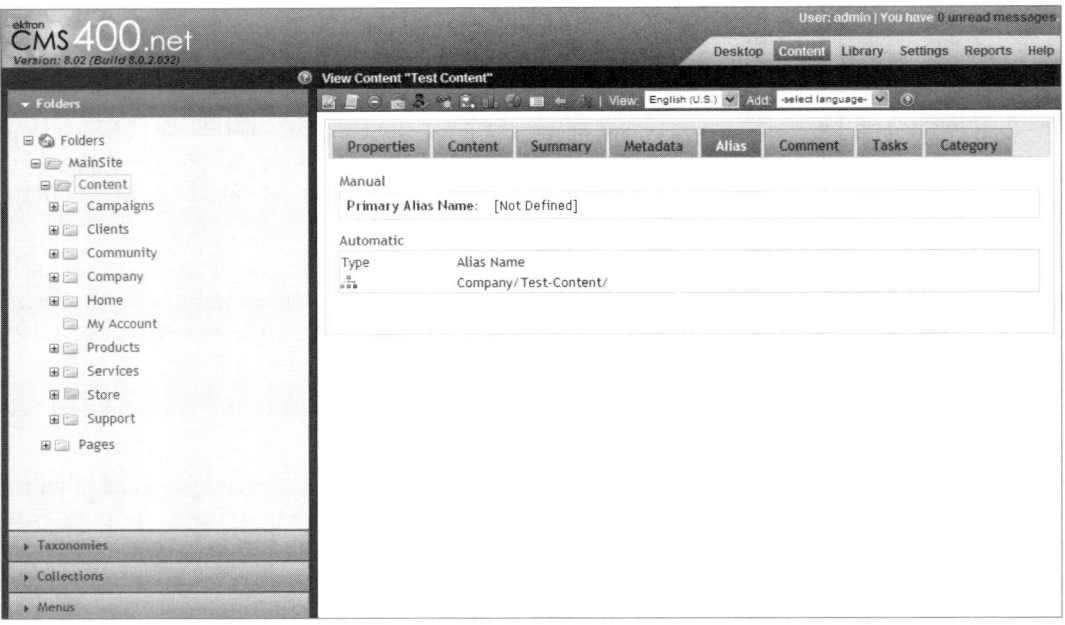

FIGURE 5-22

Content Entry and Display | **73**

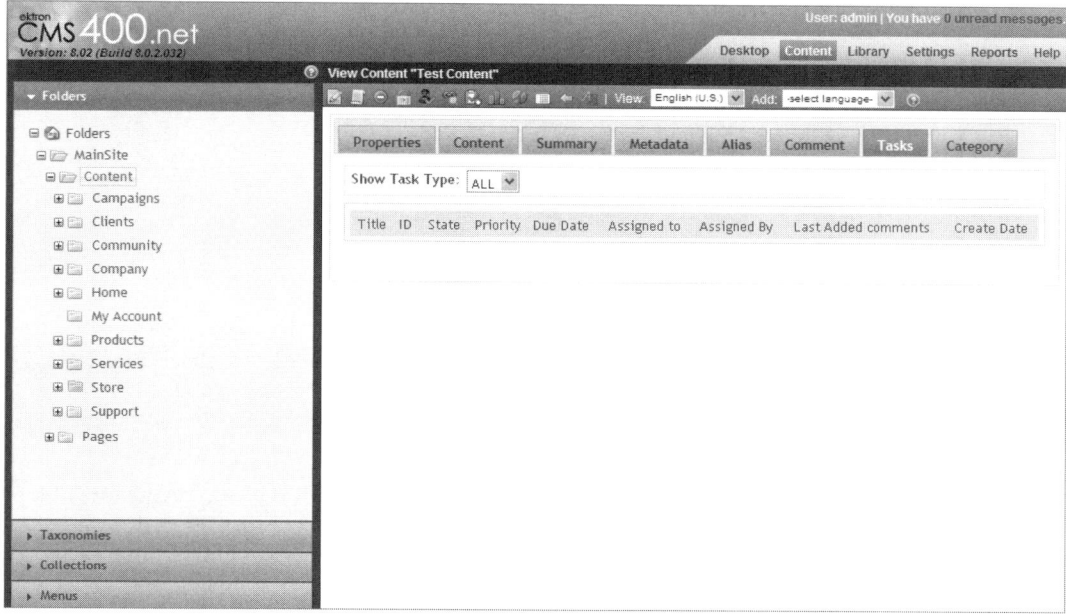

FIGURE 5-23

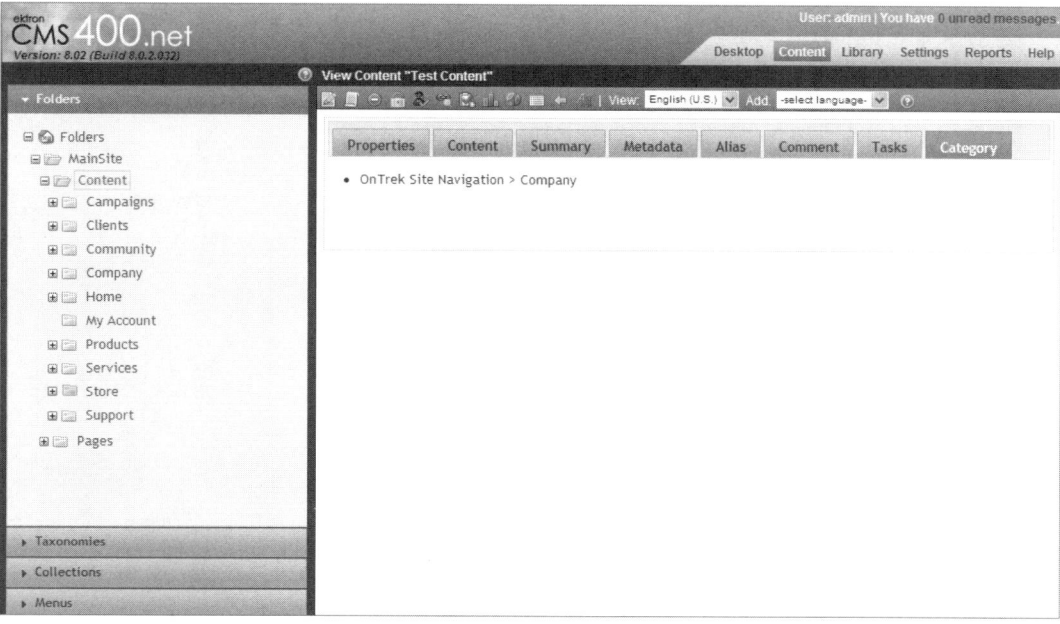

FIGURE 5-24

Using Toolbar Options When Editing Content

As you have seen, the tabs displayed when viewing a piece of content are very closely related to the tabs that are visible when editing content. The toolbar however, is very different, as you'll see in Figure 5-25.

FIGURE 5-25

Let's now look at each item and what it does.

➤ (Edit)

The Edit button allows a user to edit the piece of content. It will first check the content out to the user, preventing other users from making changes at the same time.

➤ (History)

The History screen, shown in Figure 5-26, displays a list of all the stored versions of a piece of content. This includes each time the content has been checked in, and each time it has been published. The History screen allows a user to restore a particular version of the content, as well as view the differences between any two versions of content. The title, content, summary, metadata, and comments are all stored on a version-by-version basis — all other items have no restore capability.

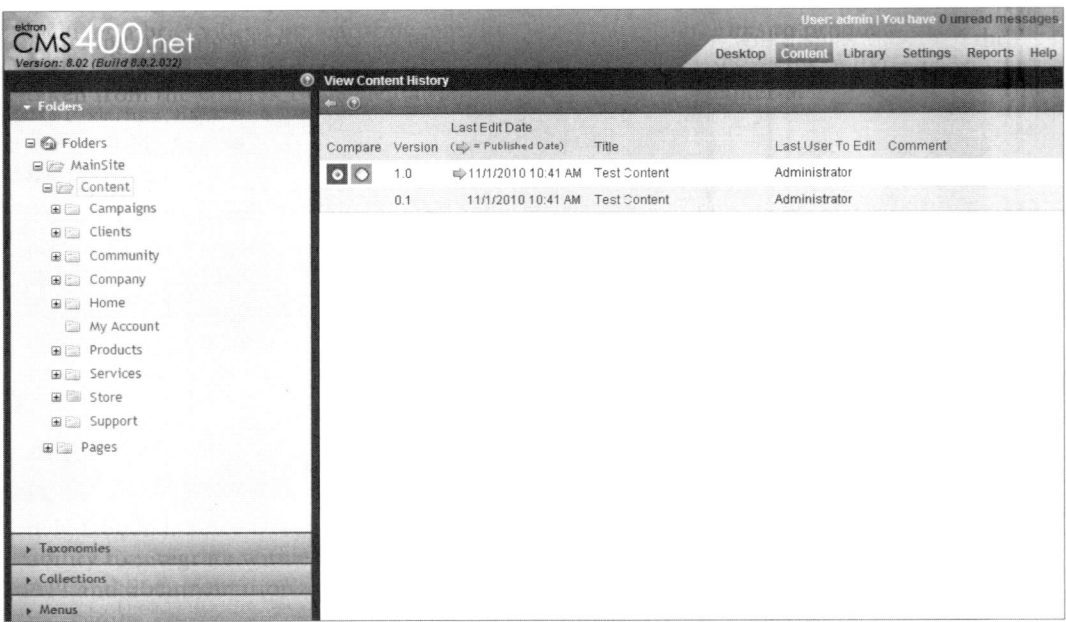

FIGURE 5-26

- ▸ (View Publish)

    View Publish allows you to switch between the version of the content that is currently visible on the site and the version that has not yet been published. This option is available only when there is a version that has been edited since the last time the content was published.

- ▸ (View Diff)

    The View Diff functionality opens a new window that displays any differences between the last published version of the content and the most recent edit of the content. This option appears only when the content has been edited since the last time the content was published.

- ▸ (Delete)

    The Delete button will delete the current content from the website.

- ▸ (View Permissions)

    View Permissions, shown in Figure 5-27, brings up the same permission management screen as is used with folders. Content items inherit permissions from their parent folders by default, but this can be overridden on a per item level. It is recommended that you have the permissions be inherited, and override them only when necessary.

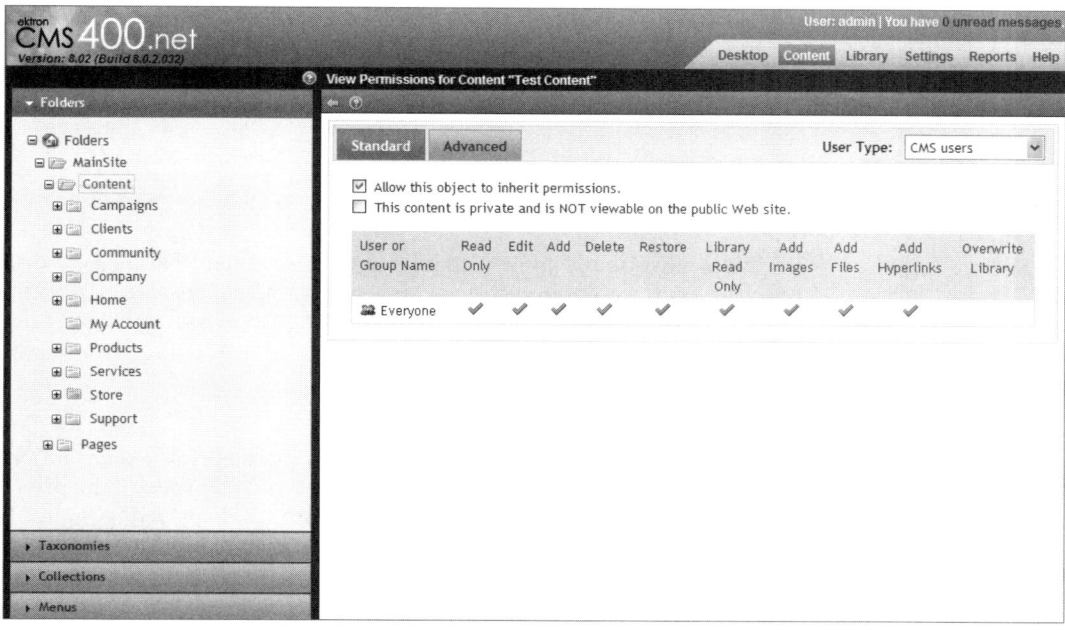

FIGURE 5-27

➤ (View Approvals)

View Approvals, pictured in Figure 5-28, are inherited the same way as permissions. The parent folder settings are applied to the content by default, but can be overridden when necessary.

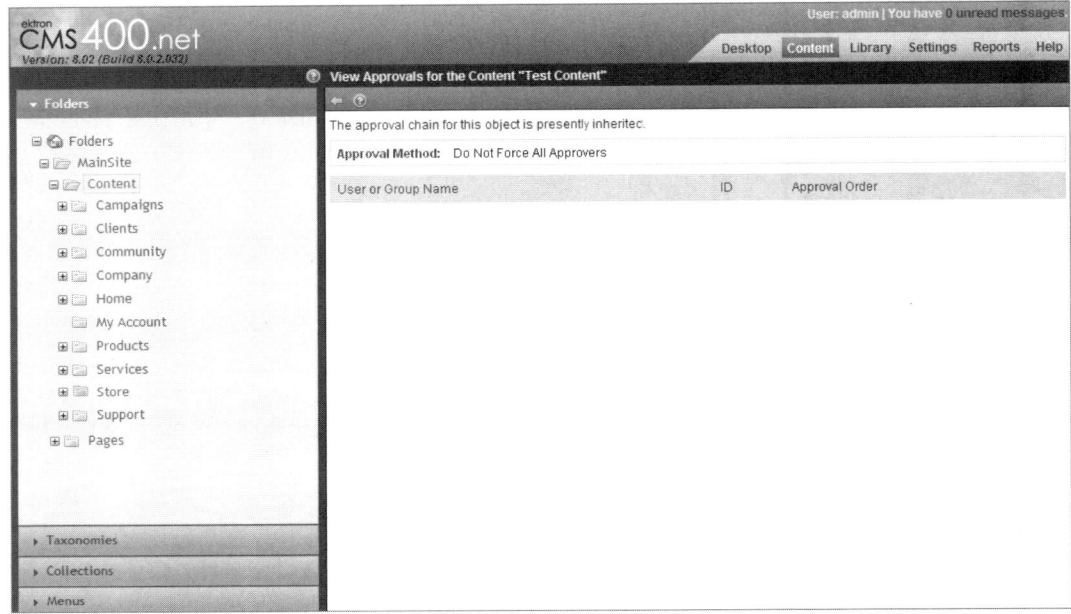

FIGURE 5-28

➤ (Link Search)

Link Search produces a list of any content that links to this content. Figure 5-29 displays the Search Content Folder. This is useful if you are, for example, considering deleting the content item, but need to ensure that nothing relies on the item before doing so. The Broken Link Checker can also help you solve for this scenario.

➤ (Add Task)

This is how you assign a task to users in the system so they can perform some action on the current content item. Add Task produces a form where you can specify the priority, category, type, start and due date, and description. The form is displayed in Figure 5-30. The assigned user then receives a notification to perform the task. Once complete, the item returns to you for approval or rejection.

➤ (Content Reports)

The Content Reports interface shows you feedback for content left by users on your site. It has three tabs, as pictured in Figure 5-31: Rating, Messages, and Flagging. The first tab, Rating, shows the star ratings and comments left by users using the Content Review Server Control. The second tab, Messages, shows comments left by users using the MessageBoard

Server Control. The third tab shows flags selected for the content by users interacting with the ContentFlagging Server Control.

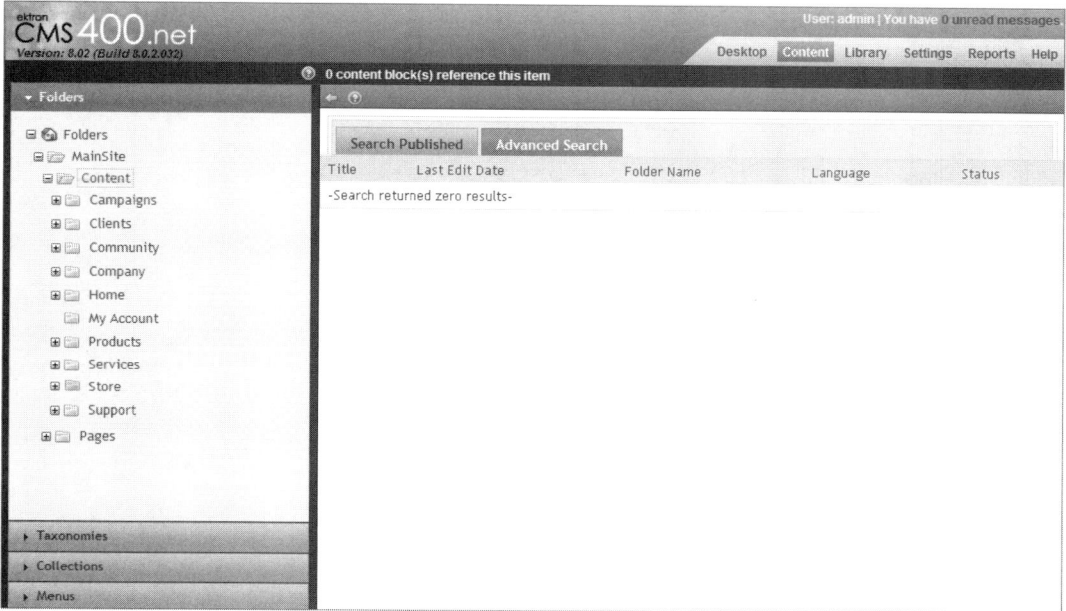

FIGURE 5-29

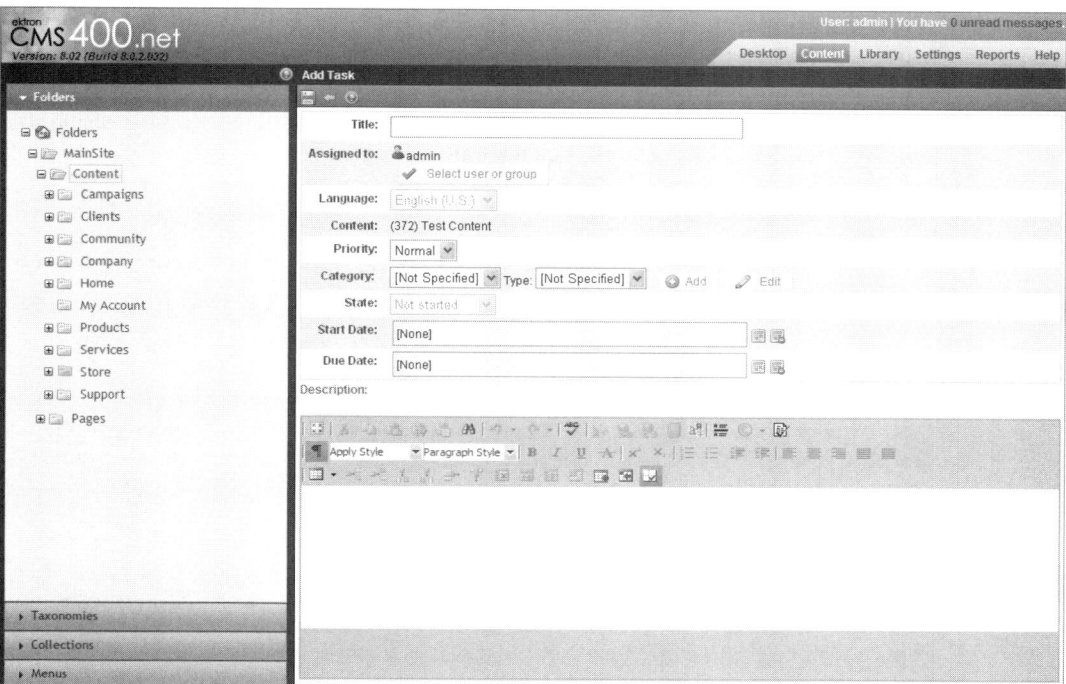

FIGURE 5-30

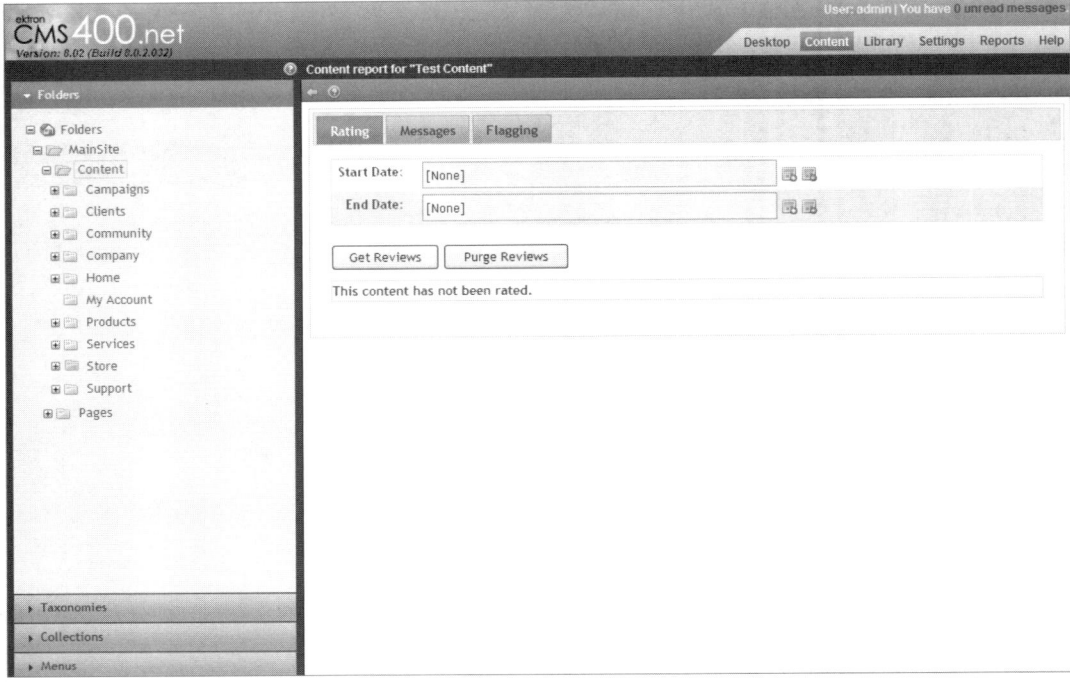

FIGURE 5-31

➤ ![] (Analytics)

When you click Analytics, a new window displays information about the page where the content item appears. It only functions with publically accessible pages, meaning no localhost addresses can be used. It shares information such as an SEO analysis of the page, W3C Validator feedback, Alexa rank, image analysis, and traffic charts.

➤ ![] (Edit Properties)

Edit Properties, shown in Figure 5-32, allows you to select from two options: whether the content is searchable and what flagging definitions to use.

➤ ![] (Export for Translation)

Export for Translation presents you with a list of languages to target for translation, along with a history of translations. The export generates an XLIFF file, which can be directly sent to a translation company. They will then return the file with translated entries, at which point the file can be uploaded into the CMS to enter the data.

➤ ![] (Switch and Add Translation)

The Language Toolbar allows you to select a different language version of the content. Each language can have its own permissions, approval process, and metadata. In fact, everything about the content, including everything that ties it to the rest of the system, can be modified on a language-by-language basis.

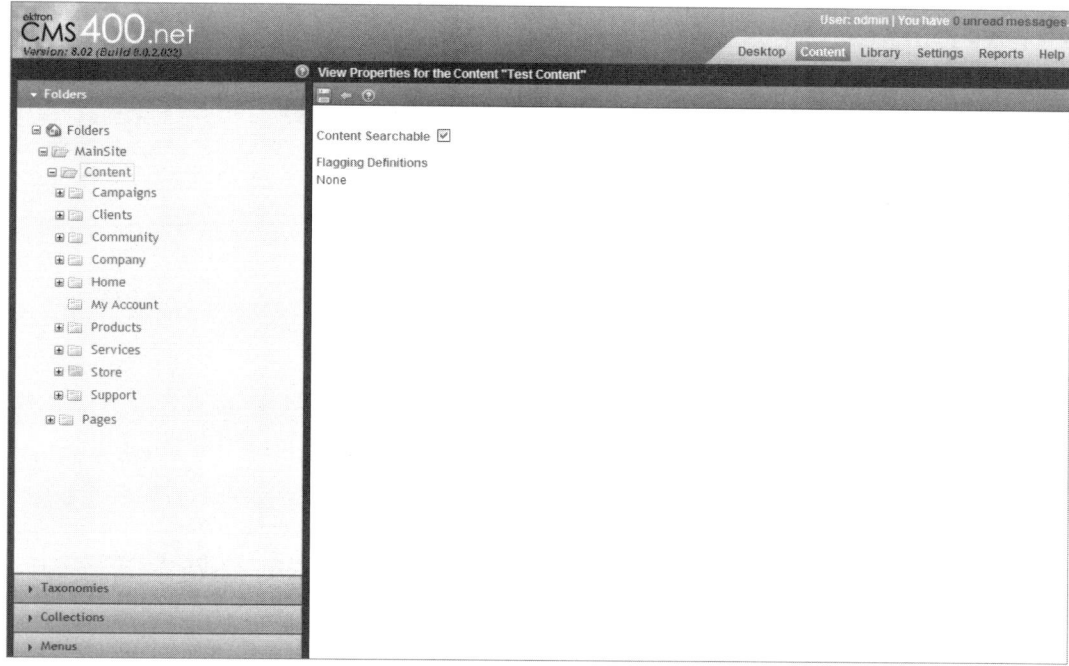

FIGURE 5-32

Interacting with the DMS Menu and Editing in Context

Not all interaction with a piece of content must happen through the content pane in the Workarea. Content can also be managed from a workflow perspective through any content listing on the site and in the Workarea. This interaction is performed through what is called the DMS menu, which is displayed in Figure 5-33.

The DMS menu can be used to access the content pages, with options to view the content page in the Workarea, view the content on the site, interact with the item's properties, and move the item through its workflow. The DMS menu is most useful for bringing these shortcuts to the front end of the site. By combining the DMS menu with the inline editing capabilities of the Content Block Server Control, much of the interaction that would require the user to launch the Workarea can instead be performed on the site itself.

The in-context editing capabilities of the Content Block Server Control simplify the experience of maintaining existing content. Anywhere the Content Block Server Control is used, a logged in author has the ability on the Editors menu (Figure 5-34) to edit in context (Figure 5-35).

Hovering over the Editors menu produces many options. When a content author clicks Edit, it launches the Workarea, allowing the user to edit the properties and the HTML content item in its entirety. However, selecting Edit In Context allows the author to do cursory editing of the content item without launching the Workarea. Editing in context takes place directly on the Web page, meaning the author can see the applied CSS in real time, and see exactly how the content will look when it is published. The drawback is that the inline editor does not have the full range of options that the eWebEdit400 editor in the Workarea supplies to users. Table 5-5 describes the available options and what the options achieve.

CHAPTER 5 UNDERSTANDING CONTENT MANAGEMENT FUNDAMENTALS

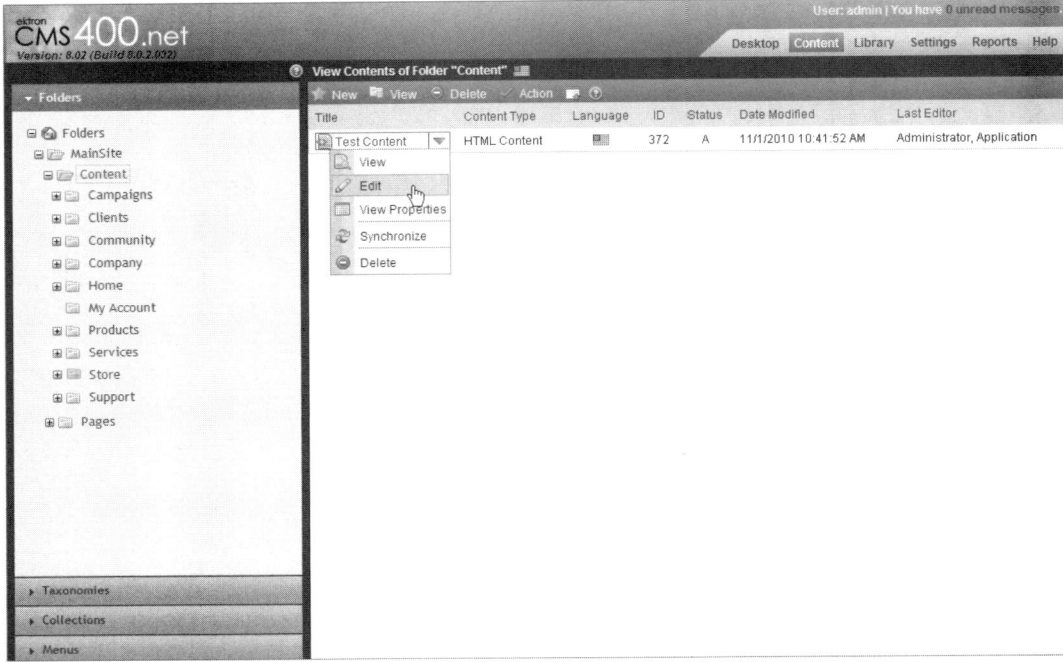

FIGURE 5-33

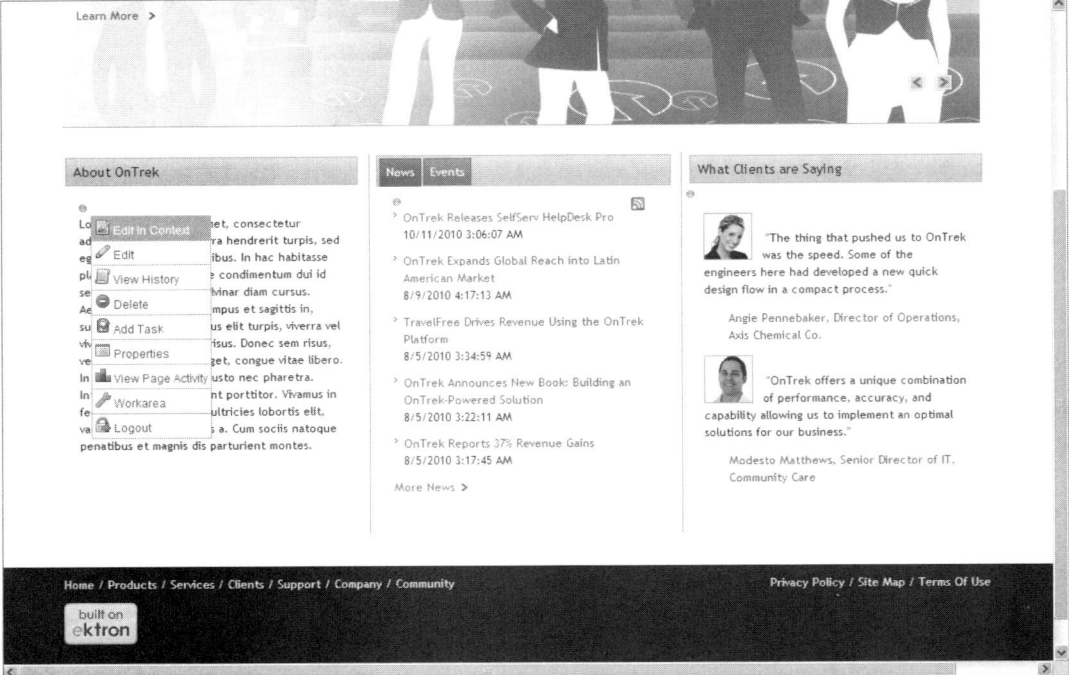

FIGURE 5-34

Content Entry and Display | 81

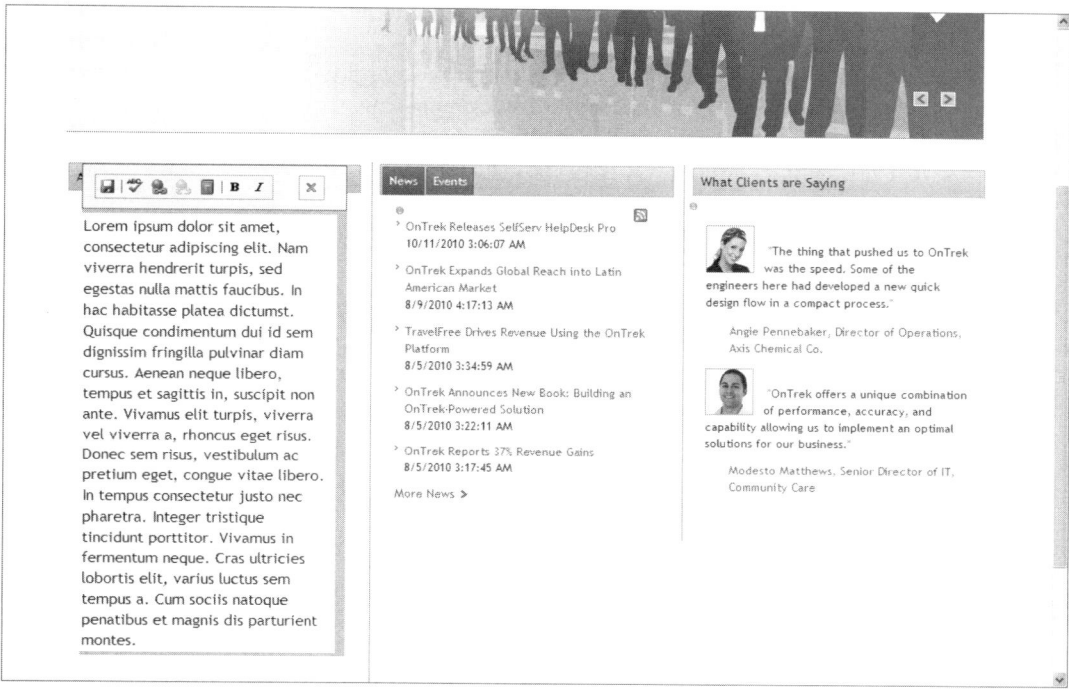

FIGURE 5-35

TABLE 5-5: Edit in Context Options

ICON	NAME	DESCRIPTION
	Save	Saves the content with the current changes. This will also check the content in, and submit it to the approval chain. In the in-context editor, these actions cannot be separated.
	Spell Check	This will spell check the content currently entered. Spell Check is not live as content is entered.
	Add/Remove Hyperlink	Manages hyperlinks in the content.
	Add Library Item	Allows for adding items from the library, and managing existing library items.
	Bold/Italic	Text styling.
	Cancel	Cancels the edits and returns the content to the original state.

In-context editing is not too useful for managing content layout or styling. Instead it is more useful for immediate textual changes.

Using the Content Block Server Control

The *Content Block Server Control* is probably the most commonly used server control in the Ektron Framework. Its function is simple: It reads content items from the database and displays them on the website. It can be hardcoded to a specific content item, it can be configured to read the content ID from the query string, or the ID of the content to display can be set programmatically at runtime.

For authors, the Content Block Server Control shows the Editors menu access point, which is a silver bullet rendered just above the content display on the Web page. The access point exposes options to manage the content item directly from the website, including editing in context, managing tasks, and viewing the history of the item. Most of these items launch the Workarea directly to the area of interest. A few of them, including items that moved the content through the workflow, just perform the selected action.

This section covers implementing the Content Block Server Control on a page. Follow these steps:

1. Open Visual Studio, and then open the website by selecting File ➪ Open ➪ Web Site.

2. On the Open Site dialog box that comes up, select File System and browse to C:\Inetpub\wwwroot\OnTrek. In the Solution Explorer, right-click the root of the site, and select Add New Item.

3. In the Add New Item dialog box, which is pictured in Figure 5-36, select Web Form with Visual C# as the language. Check the Place code in separate file checkbox, without choosing a master page. Enter in **content.aspx** for the filename.

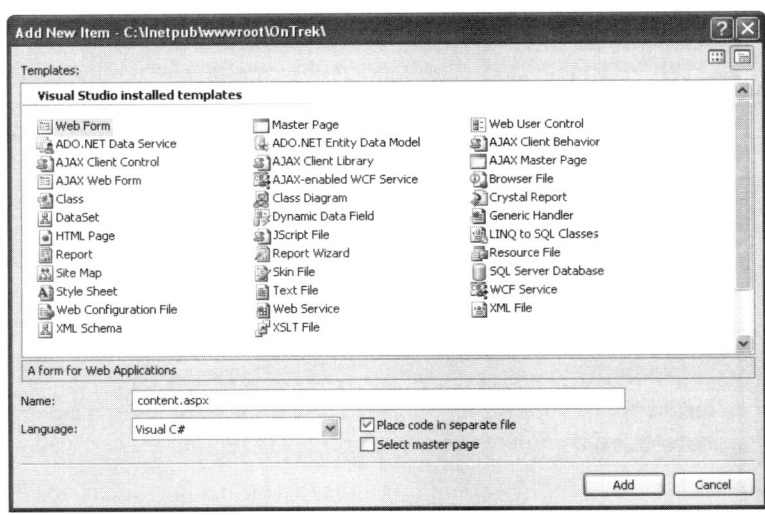

FIGURE 5-36

The dialog box creates the content.aspx file, as well as the content.aspx.cs codebehind file.

4. To add the Content Block Server Control, you don't need the codebehind, but the ASPX file itself is where you will declaratively add your control. Make sure the ASPX file is open now.

5. Once you are looking at the content.aspx file, switch to code view, and open the toolbox. As part of the Ektron installation, the Ektron Server Controls are registered with Visual Studio. This adds all the available controls into the toolbox, which allow you to simply drag the controls onto the page. At this point, the code on the page should look like the code in Listing 5-1.

LISTING 5-1: Content.aspx

```
<%@ Page Language="C#" AutoEventWireup="true" CodeFile="content.aspx.cs"
  Inherits="content" %>

<!DOCTYPE html PUBLIC "-//W3C//DTD XHTML 1.0 Transitional//EN"
   "http://www.w3.org/TR/xhtml1/DTD/xhtml1-transitional.dtd">

<html xmlns="http://www.w3.org/1999/xhtml">
<head runat="server">
    <title></title>
</head>
<body>
    <form id="form1" runat="server">
    <div>
    
    </div>
    </form>
</body>
</html>
```

6. Now select the Content Block Server Control from the Ektron Server Controls tab in the toolbox, and drag it between the `<div>` tags, as shown in Figure 5-37.

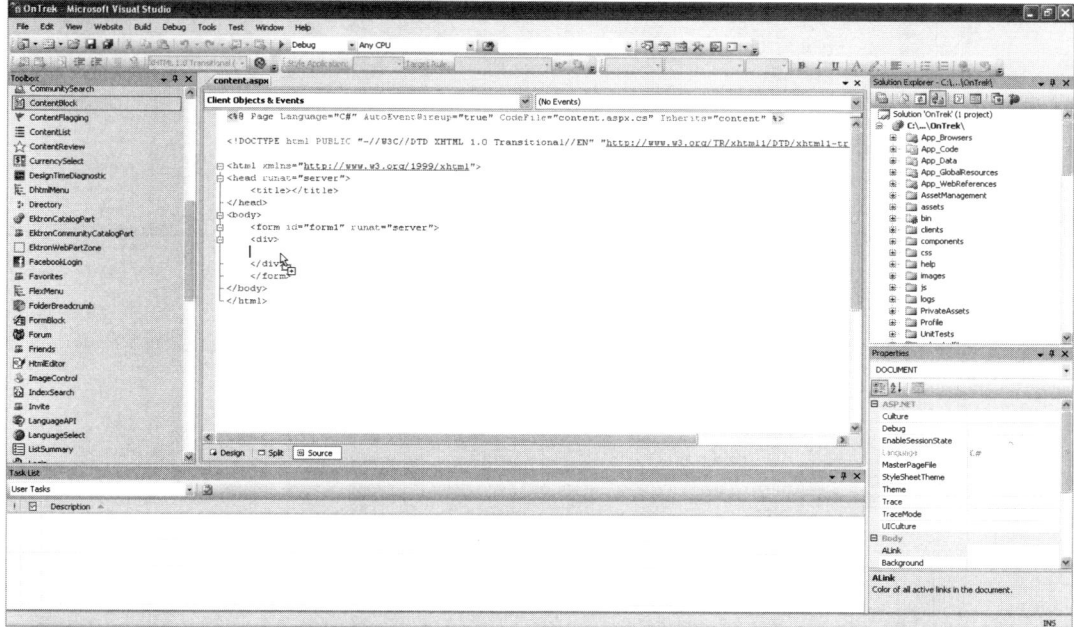

FIGURE 5-37

Dragging the Content Block Server Control onto the page modifies the code to look like it does in Figure 5-38.

7. Now open the Properties window, as shown on the right of Figure 5-38. When organizing the properties by category, the Ektron properties are grouped together. The most important property is highlighted in the screenshot — `DefaultContentID` specifies the ID of the content item to display by default. Additionally, the `DynamicParameter` property specifies which parameter from the query string to read in order to override the `DefaultContentID`.

8. The Content Block Server Control retrieves and displays the appropriate content item based on the permissions and language settings. To set the content item to display programmatically, set it on the server control using code like the following snippet, which will run in the Page_Load event.

```
public void Page_Load()
{
  ContentBlock1.DefaultContentID = 123;
  ContentBlock1.Fill();
}
```

Calling the `Fill` method forces the server control to read from the database or cache. The data can also be read from the content block programmatically after it has been loaded from the cache or database, by reading the `EkItem` property from the Content Block Server Control. The `EkItem` property returns an object of the type `Ektron.Cms.Common.ContentBase`, which in turn contains all the information about the content item itself. Content can also be retrieved programmatically without the use of the Content Block Server Control. This task is most frequently achieved through the use of the `Ektron.Cms.Core.Content.Content` object. This object exposes methods for adding content, updating content, deleting content, retrieving single pieces of content, and providing lists of content through the use of criteria objects.

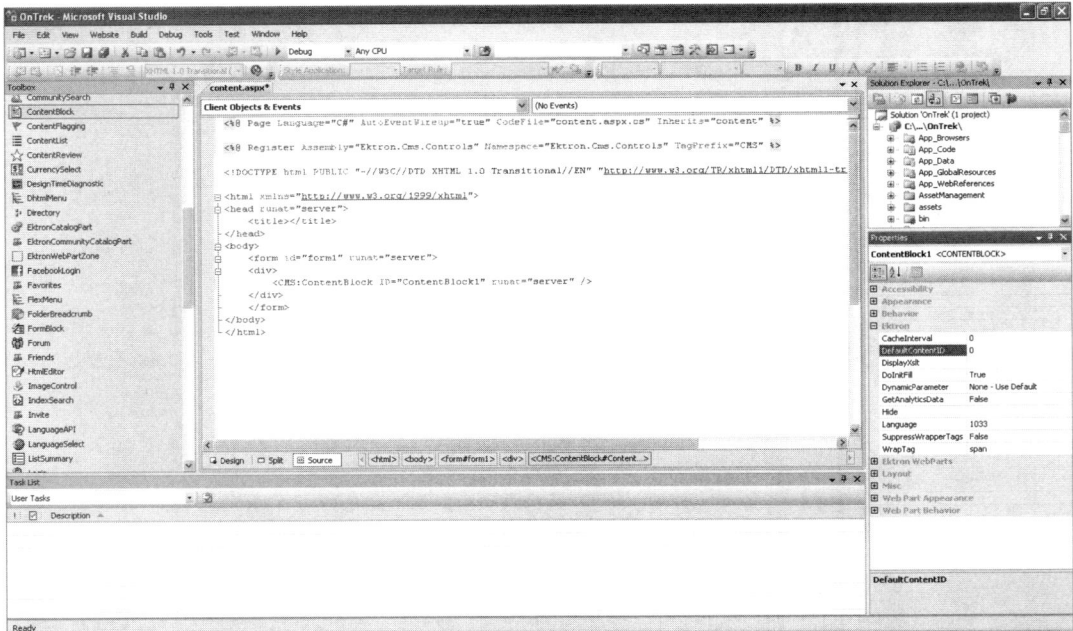

FIGURE 5-38

Content is the core of the Ektron Framework. Most items in the CMS are based on the concept of content, which allows these items to support related concepts such as metadata, permissions, and workflow. Content is mostly authored through the Workarea and displayed on the front end of the site. It can be retrieved and displayed through the use of the Content Block Server Control or through programmatic APIs.

FOLDERS AND THE LIBRARY

Folders are the categorizing tool of the Ektron Framework. They are the most basic way of categorizing content, and through the application of inheritance they also supply items contained in them with allowed properties such as metadata, assigned taxonomies, and permissions.

This section explores the process of creating folders, including the properties associated with them. It also covers the library and its uses.

In addition to containing content, folders are capable of storing other types of data. For instance, a standard content folder can store HTML content, Smart Form content, documents, and PageBuilder pages side-by-side. For consistency purposes, the Ektron Framework also has a concept of folder types. Items such as blogs, calendars, and forums are simply folders with a different subtype. All the APIs that allow a developer to interact with folders will also work with these other types of folders.

Folders have the concept of inheritance as well. By default, when a new folder is created, it inherits permissions, metadata definitions, taxonomy subscriptions, templates, and breadcrumbs from its parent folder. When content is created, it inherits from the containing folder any associated permissions and applicable properties.

You can create a folder programmatically, but the most common way to create folders is through the Workarea. The form to create a folder can be accessed by right-clicking the parent folder, in the folder tree on the Content tab and selecting the New Folder icon. You can access the same form by selecting the appropriate parent folder, and then selecting New on the menu in the right pane.

Folders can have many associated properties, ranging from permissions to approval chains, through metadata to taxonomy. Options such as associated templates and allowed types of content are covered in this section.

In addition to fundamental content types, folders can also store additional data such as images, multimedia files, and QuickLinks in what is called the library. The library is accessible through the Library tab in the top-right side of the Workarea.

Implementation: Adding a Folder and Managing Library Items

In this section you won't be following any particular part of the implementation guide, but instead you will spend time experimenting with some of the options in folder configuration. Since folders are one of the most fundamental parts of your site information architecture, it is important to understand the folder configuration options and what will be affected by those options. This section also explores the concept and management of the library.

The implementation tasks in this section are slightly more freeform than most. Specifically, this section covers:

- Navigating folders
- Creating a folder in the root of the site
- Modifying the properties for the folder

In later sections, you'll learn about the concepts of approval chains and permissions. This chapter will also cover:

- Navigating the library
- Adding items to the library
- More on the library

Navigating Folders

Open the Workarea and switch to the Content tab. The Content tab is where interaction with content and folders takes place. Looking at Figure 5-39, you can see the key elements of working with folders. On the left is the folder tree, starting at the root folder, marked Folders, and continuing down to list all the user-created folders. On the right is the folder menu, and below that the contents in the folder.

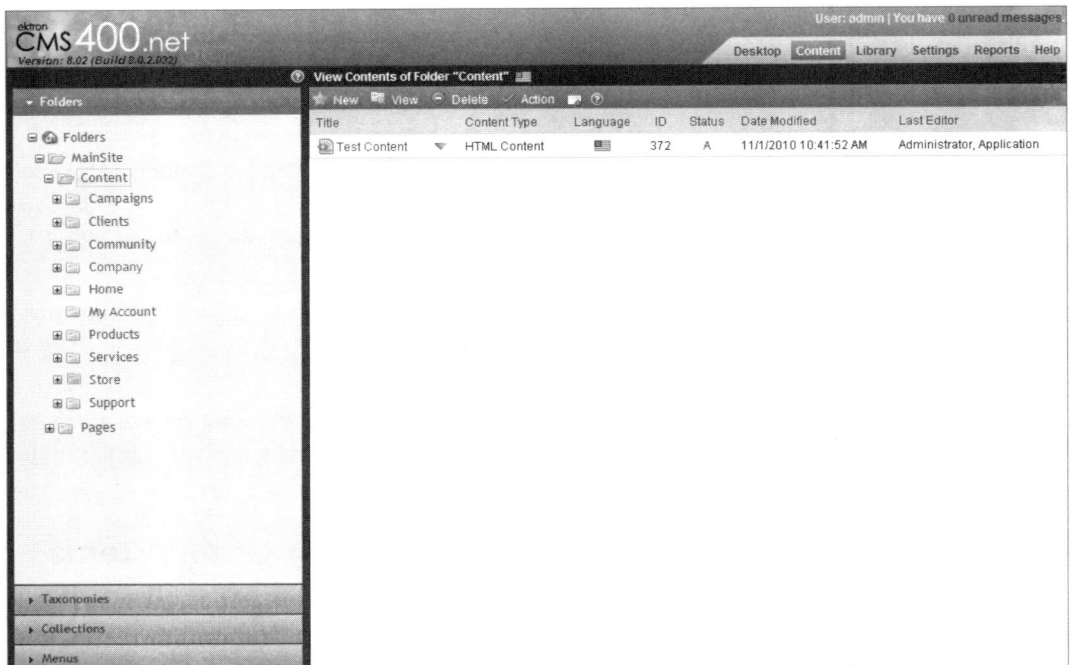

FIGURE 5-39

Starting with the tree, one of the first things you might notice is that some folders have different icons. As mentioned earlier, folders have a concept of type in which each icon corresponds to a different type of folder. Table 5-6 provides a description of each folder type.

TABLE 5-6: Folder Types

ICON	FOLDER TYPE	DESCRIPTION
	Root Folder	Contains all other folders in the installation. It is a normal folder in that it can contain any standard content items.
	Standard Folder	Contains any standard content item. Other folder types are based on this type.
	Multisite Folder	Serves as an artificial root in multisite configurations. Content within it will inherit from the multisite configuration for items such as QuickLinks.
	Community Folder	Where membership users can create content. It behaves differently during syncing operations in order to preserve the content when moving from a production server back to a staging server.
	Blog	Blogs contain regular content, but also have additional data such as links to external blogs and sites. This data is designed to be displayed in the Blog Server Control, which renders the content recognizably as a blog to users browsing the site.
	Discussion Board	Also known as a forum; allows membership users to interact on diverse topics. This folder type allows a structure to be created that mirrors the structure users see on the front end of the site.
	eCommerce Catalog	A special type of folder that allows for items to be added that can be interacted with as part of the eCommerce add-on.
	WebCalendar	This type of folder stores events for calendars.

Each of these folder types can be created either by selecting the folder you want to create it in, and then selecting New on the toolbar menu in the content pane or by right-clicking the parent folder and selecting the appropriate entry on the contextual menu. We will cover the majority of these folder types in later chapters.

On the right side of Figure 5-39 you can see the list of content contained in this folder. Above that are the menu items appropriate for this folder. Starting from the left are the following items:

➤ **New** allows a user to create new content and new subfolders where appropriate.
➤ **View** allows the user to filter the list of items by types, certain attributes, and language.
➤ **Delete** allows the user to delete content from the folder or the folder itself.
➤ **Action** allows the user to take additional actions such as copy and paste, or export content for translation to another language.

Creating a Folder in the Root Folder

To create a folder, right-click the Root folder and select Add Folder, as shown in Figure 5-40.

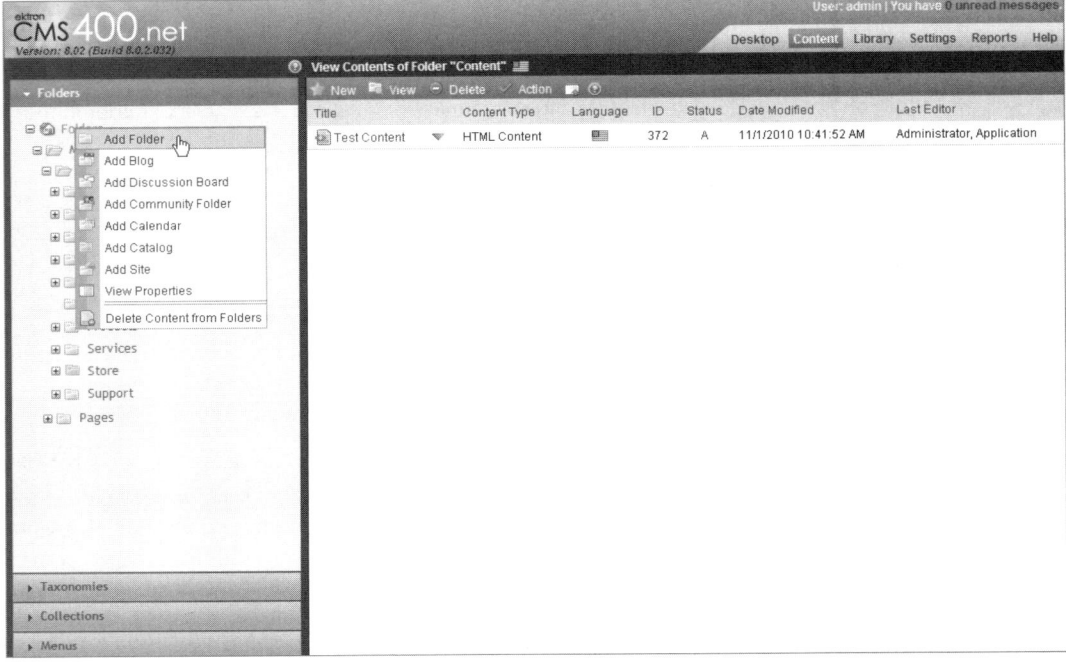

FIGURE 5-40

This brings up the Add Folder interface. This interface is the same when editing a folder, and allows for all properties of the folder to be modified. Consider the tabs from left to right, as displayed in Figure 5-41.

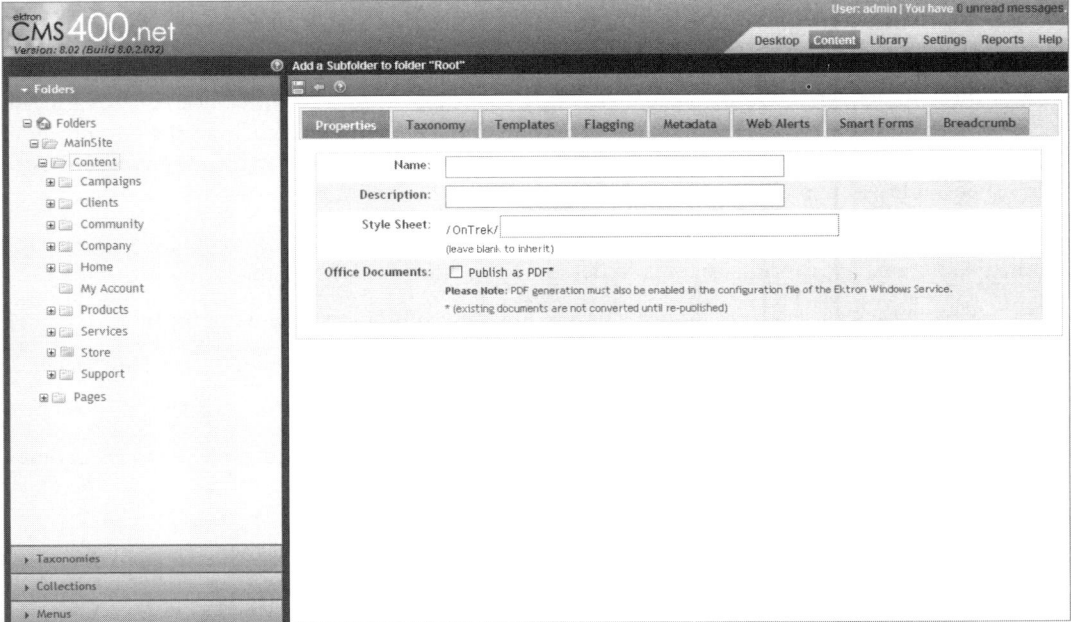

FIGURE 5-41

- **Properties:** This is where basic information is entered, such as the content name. The Properties tab has two options:
    - The stylesheet that's used in the editor so that editing matches the look and feel of the item when it is published.
    - The field Publish as PDF, which informs the system whether or not to automatically convert Office documents to PDF when published for greater accessibility by users browsing the site.
- **Taxonomy:** Controls which taxonomies are associated with this folder. Taxonomies can be marked either as assigned or as required. If required, content cannot be published until it is assigned to one or more categories. By default, the settings for taxonomy are inherited from the parent folder.
- **Templates:** Determine the form of QuickLinks for a given piece of content. Every time a piece of content is created, the system creates stored URLs to the content in the form of the assigned template, followed by a query parameter, which indicates which content item to load. When you assign templates to a folder, you are indicating which templates are allowed for users to base content on. Certain templates, called *Wireframes*, allow for PageBuilder content to be created in this folder. If a Wireframe is not associated with a folder, PageBuilder content cannot be created in that folder. Template configuration is inherited by default.
- **Flagging:** Allows you to select a set of flags that users can choose to flag content. These flags are frequently used for items as Helpful, or Inappropriate. Flagging is inherited from the parent folder by default.
- **Metadata:** As highlighted in Figure 5-42, this tab contains a list of all the metadata definitions in the system. The user is invited to mark some as assigned or required. These options are inherited by default from the parent folder.
- **Web Alerts:** Web Alerts are e-mail notifications sent to users who subscribe to them when new content is published on the site. The Web Alerts tab allows you to configure the form of the notifications. This tab inherits from the parent folder by default.
- **Smart Forms:** Smart Forms are most easily understood as a graphically designed DTD for XML. They are created within the CMS through eWebEditPro, which defines the HTML comprising the field elements, the format the XML is stored in, and the default XSLT data is rendered against for display on the site. Unlike standard HTML content, Smart Form content is not freeform. This allows for uniformity throughout the content.

    The Smart Form tab on the folder configuration allows the user to select which Smart Forms are supported in this folder. The user can opt to have no Smart Forms, or Smart Forms exclusively, or some combination thereof. The folder inherits these values from the parent folder by default.
- **Breadcrumbs:** These generate the site map for a site. They are also used to create the breadcrumb links that are frequently found at the top of a typical site design. These are inherited by default, but the inherited behavior is rarely desirable.

    When creating breadcrumbs, the items are displayed on the site in the same order they appear on the page in the folder properties, with a preview of what they look like appearing above the list. Reordering is achieved through the use of the green arrows, and the red minus sign deletes an item.

You use the fields that follow to create or edit a given item in the breadcrumb trail. These correspond with Figure 5-43.

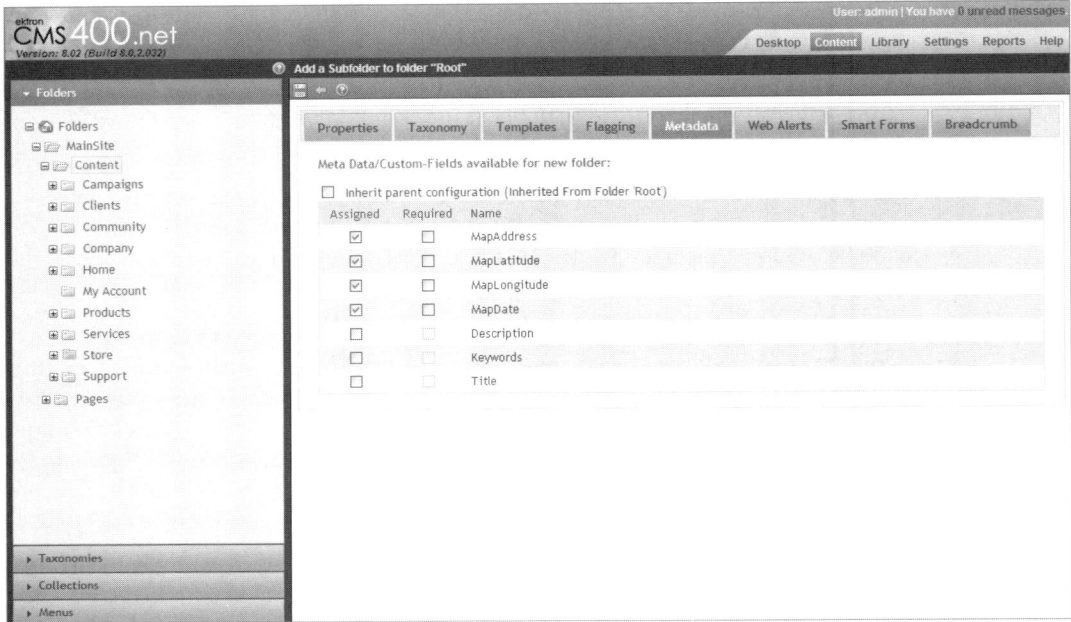

FIGURE 5-42

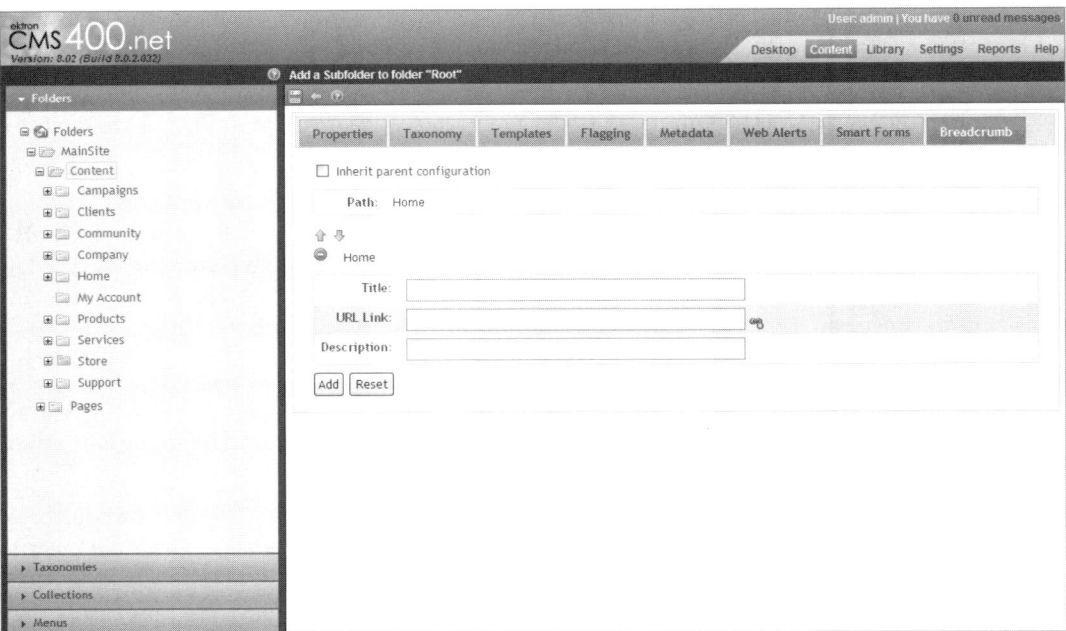

FIGURE 5-43

➤ **Title:** Sets what is displayed in the breadcrumb itself.

➤ **URL link:** Is the page or QuickLink the breadcrumb will route to.

➤ **Description:** Appears in the hover text for that item.

It is not necessary to configure most of the items on the tabs in the folder properties screen, except when overriding the default values. But for most users, the default values will achieve what is needed. To create the sample folder, simply enter the title Test Folder on the Properties tab, and click the Save icon.

Modify the Properties of the Folder

Modifying the properties for the created folder is done by simply right-clicking the folder in the tree and selecting Properties, or by selecting the folder in the tree and, on the right-side menu, selecting View ⇨ Properties. Once you're viewing the properties, select the Edit icon to edit them.

> *Remember that changing options on the folder will not un-publish content in that folder, even if it is in a broken state. For instance, removing a taxonomy from the folder will not unassign content in that folder from the taxonomy. Similarly, requiring an additional field of metadata in a folder does not automatically provide content in that folder with that additional metadata item until they are republished.*

Navigating the Library

The library, as displayed in Figure 5-44, is a parallel structure to the content tree. Every folder created in the Content tab has an equivalent folder in the library. The difference between the two is the type of stored content and the content's uses.

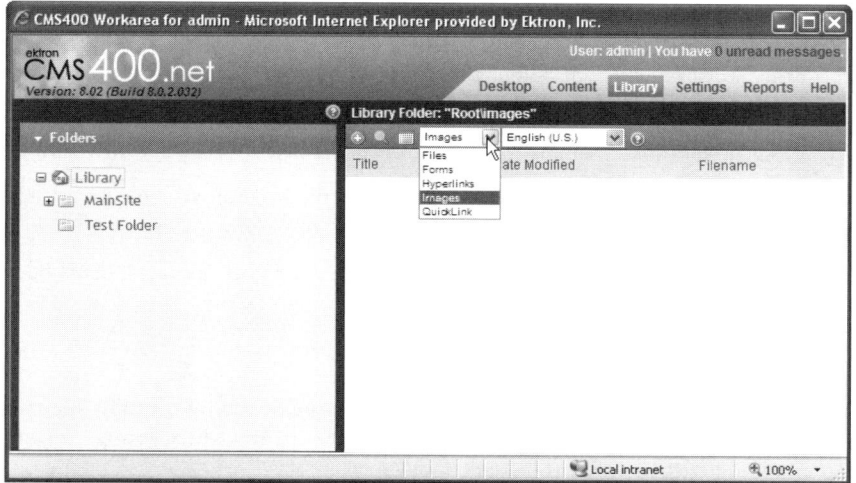

FIGURE 5-44

The library stores files, images, and three types of links. It also stores these objects on a per-language basis. Let's go through the five items on the list one-by-one.

- **Files:** The default allowed extensions for files uploaded to the library are PPt, PDF, XLS, and DOC. This is a legacy option, and is still supported, but uploading these files into the content tree, instead of the library, offers significant advantages, such as permissions, a history of modifications, approval chain support, and content scheduling. The library should be used for files only when you don't want the features provided by the content tree.

- **Forms:** This is a bit misleading, because the HTML forms themselves are stored in the content tab. What is stored here is the link that is used for the form, with an interface the same as that used for QuickLinks except that it uses `ekfrm` as the query string parameter rather than `id`.

- **Hyperlinks:** Hyperlinks are shortcuts to external sites. By storing them in the library, content authors can embed them into content throughout the site. By updating the URL in one location you can ensure that content authors are always using the most up-to-date version of the URL.

- **Images:** Images are the primary reason for everyday use of the library. By placing images into the library, it is easy for content authors to select the image and embed it in their content on the fly.

- **QuickLinks:** QuickLinks are the other main item in the library. QuickLinks store the URL that is used to reach a certain piece of content. They are automatically created when a piece of content is created, and follow the format `[template file name]?id=[id of content]`. These QuickLinks can be updated manually by selecting the Update QuickLink button.

Adding Items to the Library

Let's explore the functionality of the library by adding an image to the new folder. The image will then be available for embedding into content items to CMS users with view permissions. Follow these steps:

1. Start by selecting the Test Folder in the folder tree on the Library tab. From the dropdown of types on the toolbar, select Images.

2. Click the green plus Add icon. This opens the Add Library Item form pictured in Figure 5-45.

3. At the top of the form, you need to enter a title and select a file for upload. Select an image from your system and type in a title.

4. Below that you can enter a summary, metadata, and category for your image. This is because these items have inherited selected options on the parallel content folder.

5. Once this information is filled out, select the Save icon to return to the list view.

The list view, pictured in Figure 5-46, provides a preview and filename of the image. The file is served directly from that location by IIS when requested, with no pre- or post-processing. Selecting the item returns you to viewing the details for that item.

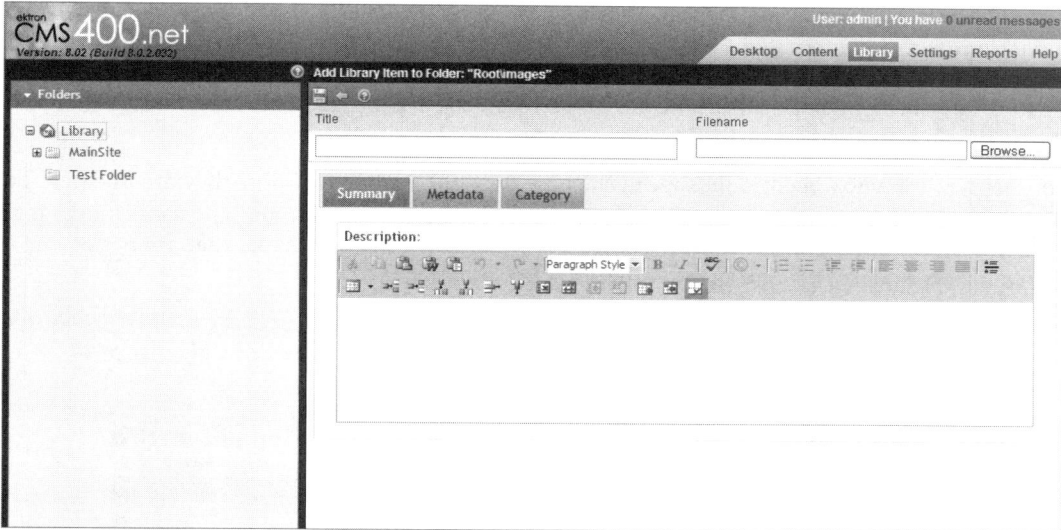

FIGURE 5-45

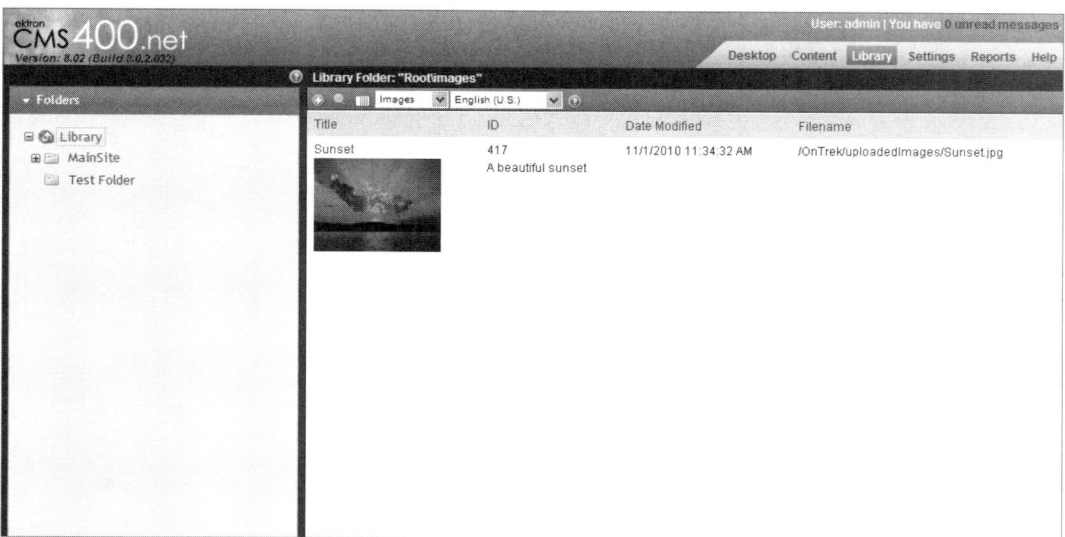

FIGURE 5-46

More on the Library

There are a couple of additional features in the library that haven't yet been covered. The first of these features is search, which exists for both the content folders and the library folders. Search is recursive, meaning you can search at the level of any ancestor folder of the content or library item you are trying to find. To search in the content, on the menu for your folder, select Action Í Search. To search in a library folder, select the icon from the toolbar in the folder.

There is another type of search also available in the library, called Link Search. Link Search allows you to find all the content items throughout the system that have the selected library item embedded. For example, this allows you to ensure that when you remove an item, all content items that rely on the item have been updated not to use the item. To use the Link Search feature, select an item in the library of any type, and select the Link Search icon.

Another feature worth mentioning about the library is the settings and how they are updated. For instance, we mentioned that files are only supported with a few extensions. The list is longer for images, but still holds true. However, you may want to add files to your site that are not on the supported file types list. This option and others can be updated.

As an administrator, select a folder in the library, and on the toolbar select the properties button. The screen that comes up has many possible customizations, displayed in Figure 5-47.

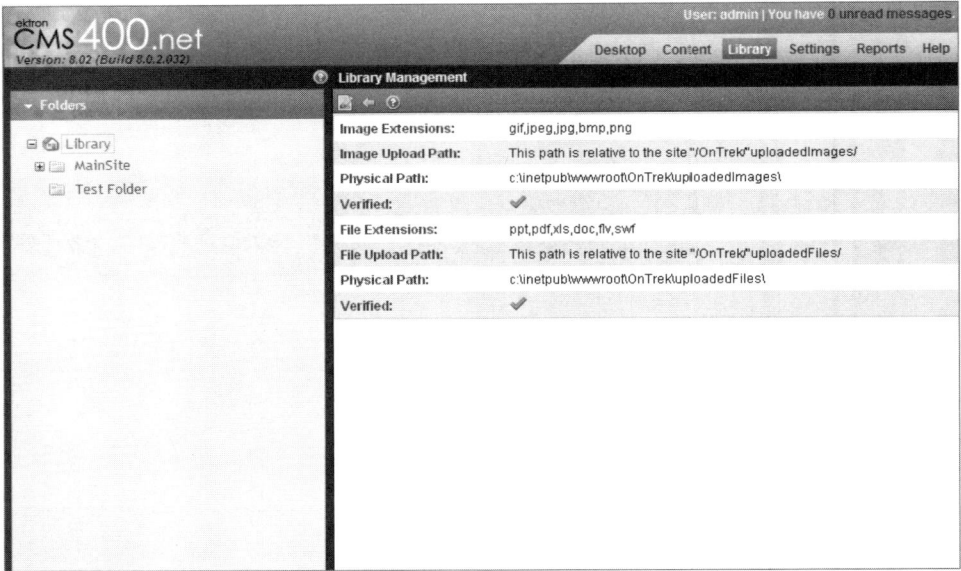

FIGURE 5-47

> - **Image Extensions:** A comma-delimited list of extensions allowed when uploading images.
> - **Image Upload Path:** The path that images uploaded to the library will be served from. It must be under the site path, since the files are served directly from the disk. It is used to build the appropriate URL to the library item.
> - **Physical Path:** This is the location on disk that the images are uploaded into. This is automatically generated based on the Image Upload Path.
> - **File Extensions:** The list of supported extensions for files added to the library.
> - **File Upload Path:** The path that files uploaded to the library will be served from. It follows the same pattern as the Image Upload Path.

➤ **Physical Path:** This is the location on disk that files are uploaded into. This is automatically generated based on the File Upload Path.

Under the Hood: Folders and Libraries

You won't always be accessing folders and their contents via the Workarea. From a developer perspective, you are very likely to approach the information from a programmatic standpoint. Ektron has a very large API for you to do so in addition to a lengthy series of server controls. For example, the ListSummary Server Control will create a list of the contents of a folder and display it on the Web page.

For API access, the `Ektron.Cms.Framework.Core.Folder.Folder` object contains all the operators for simple creation, retrieval, updating, and deletion (CRUD) operations. These operate with the `Ektron.Cms.FolderData` object.

The library is also accessible through the API, via the `Ektron.Cms.API.Library` object.

Folders and Library in Brief

Folders are one of the fundamental concepts in the Ektron Framework. They store many types of content, and associated data can be stored in the library. They support the concept of inheritance, and nearly all properties passed on to content come from the folder it is contained in. Folders determine how authors interact with and manage content, and support permissions and workflow on contained items.

PERMISSIONS, APPROVALS, AND ROLES

The Ektron Framework comes with a full permission model similar in nature to the permission model featured in Windows. This permission model is based around inheritance of properties, with the option to override at every level. It supports assigning permissions to individual users, as well as on a group level.

In addition to permissions, the framework also supports managing content access through the use of approval chain workflows, which allow content administrators to define a set of individuals or groups that must approve a piece of content before it goes live.

In this section you will explore the capabilities of the permission model for folders and content, the approval chain model for content, and the role model objects other than content. Although these systems perform their respective functions on different areas of the framework, they can be combined in order to operate together.

Understanding Permissions

Permissions comprise a structure that controls whether a given user has access to perform a given action on a given object. There are several methods of creating access control lists, but the method that Ektron follows is closest to the Windows access control. It has the concept of user groups, as well as single users for actors. Objects can be anything based on content. This group includes, but is not limited to, Smart Forms, documents, HTML content, events, and PageBuilder pages. The permission model in Ektron has a couple of points that must be understood.

One thing to be aware of is that the View action is slightly different from other actions in that it is checked only if a given piece of content is marked Private. If it is marked Private however, all permission entries are treated exactly the same.

Another point to keep in mind is the method by which a given permission request is checked. In the Ektron Framework, negative access control entries are not supported. The system will simply loop through the list of direct entries (naming the particular user directly), and the loop of inherited entries (naming groups the user is a member of), until it finds an entry that grants the user access. If it doesn't find an entry granting access to the request object and action, it blocks that action.

Understanding Approval Chain Workflows

Approval chains are similar to permissions in that they restrict publishing rights to a given piece of content. Approval chains in Ektron refer to a linear workflow, with each approval simply moving the content to the inbox of the next approver. If a piece of content resides in a folder that has an approval chain defined, any request to publish the content or delete the content forces the content to move through the entire approval chain before the requested action takes place. Each approver along the way has several options: He can modify the content, approve the content, or decline the requested modification. Depending on the configuration of the approval chain, modifying the content may force it back to the first approver, so that each approver is effectively approving the final version of the content, or the approval chain can simply move the content forward through the chain. Modifying the approval chain requires the Folder Admin role.

Understanding Roles

This leads the discussion into roles. *Roles* in Ektron are a secondary permission system that control access to all objects that are not directly inherited from content. For instance, there is a Taxonomy Administrator Role, as well as a Folder Admin Role. These roles respectively control whether a user can modify taxonomy structures or modify folder properties. Just like permissions, roles are a first positive system. If a user appears in the list of entries for the role directly, or is a member of a group in the list of entries for the role, that user is approved for that role. There are no negative entries.

Roles are not tied to individual items. For example, if a user has the Taxonomy Administrator role, she can modify all taxonomies. Additionally, the Ektron framework allows custom roles to be created and managed via the Workarea, and checked programmatically. This can be a useful way of managing access to custom functionality in your website.

Managing Permissions and Workflow

You won't be tying the implementation to any particular folder or set of functionality in this section; instead you will just try on some of the various types of tasks required to maintain your permission layout. The implementation section covers:

- Restricting permissions to a folder
- Setting up an approval chain
- Creating a custom role

Restricting Permissions to a Folder

To edit the permissions associated with a folder, follow these steps:

1. View the properties of that folder by either selecting View ➪ Properties on the toolbar in the content pane, or by selecting View Properties in the context menu in the content tree.

2. Once in the Properties pane, select the View Permissions icon from the toolbar. You should see the Permissions table for this folder, as pictured in Figure 5-48.

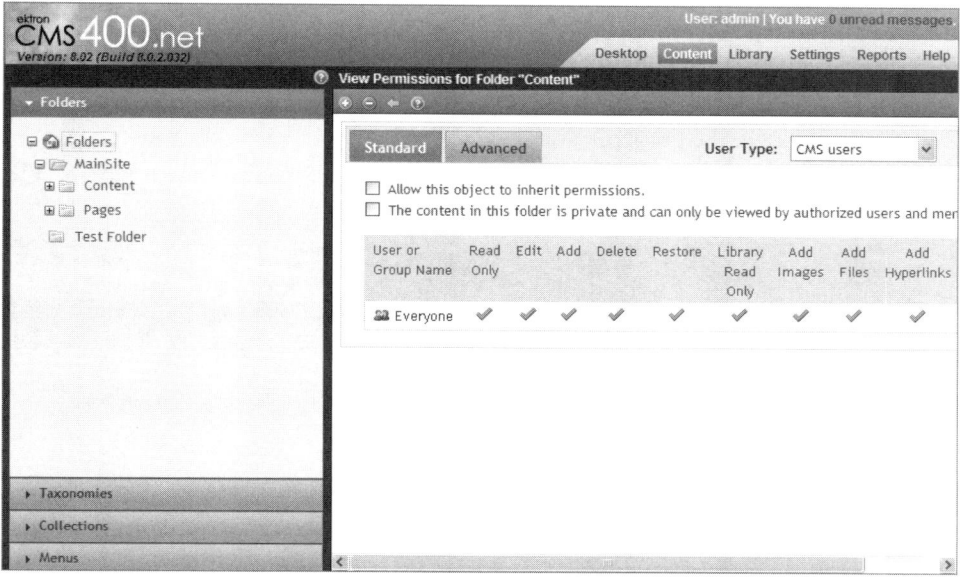

FIGURE 5-48

The first checkbox under the Standard tab is to enable or disable the inheritance of permissions. The second checkbox determines whether the folder is marked private. As previously noted, this only affects whether the read-only permission is followed as marked. If checked, it restricts users from viewing the content unless they are specifically approved. The reason this checkbox exists is that checking permissions can be costly, and because most content on a website is designed to be publically accessible, Ektron can improve performance by simply assuming everyone has read access unless specifically marked otherwise.

3. Uncheck the box for permission inheritance to modify the permissions associated with this folder. The Workarea asks for confirmation to break inheritance.

4. Approve the dialog box. When the Permission pane reloads, you see that the interface has not changed much:

   ➤ Note that two buttons have been added to the toolbar, a plus icon and a minus icon. The plus icon allows you to add actors to the list of entries. The minus icon allows you to remove them. The other change is less obvious, but you can now click the name of each actor in the list, Everyone for instance, to modify the permissions granted to that actor.

5. Add the user jedit to the list of users for the folder. Grant jedit all permissions and click Save to continue. You should now have jedit and Everyone as your list of actors for the folder, both with all permissions.

Setting Up an Approval Chain

Approval chains are also administered from the Folder Properties pane. Follow these steps:

1. Return to the Folder Properties pane by clicking View Properties in the context menu for a given folder in the Folders tree, or by viewing a folder and selecting View ➪ Properties in the toolbar.

2. Once you're in the Properties view, select View Approvals on the toolbar . The first pane that comes up is the summary of the current approval chain. It starts as an empty list shown in Figure 5-49.

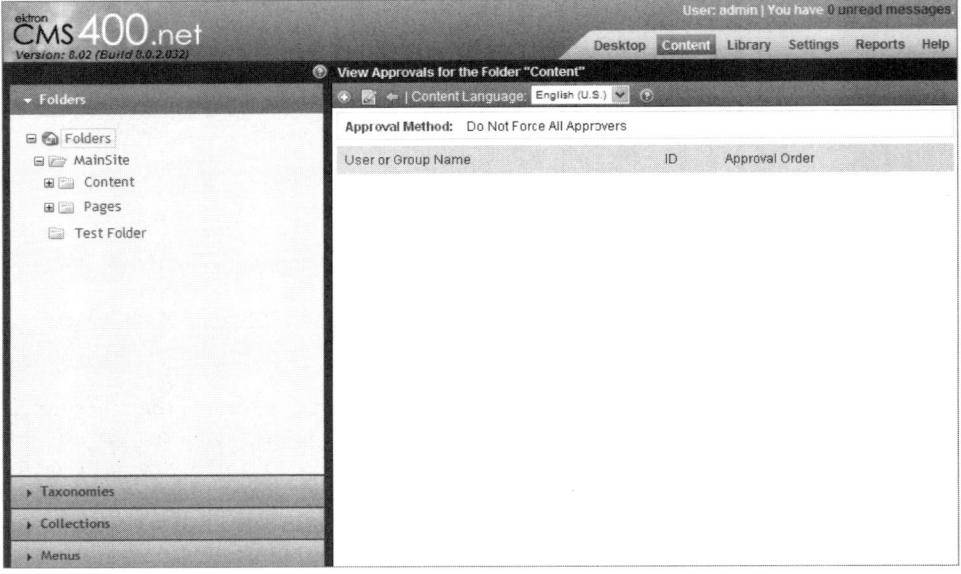

FIGURE 5-49

3. To modify the approval method, select the Edit icon on the toolbar. This presents you with two options: Force All Approvers and Do Not Force All Approvers. The difference between these two options refers to the behavior when an approver modifies the content during the approval process:

➤ If the chain is set to Force All Approvers, when the content is checked in after editing, the approval chain is restarted from the beginning. Every approver sees the content in its final form.

➤ If the chain is set to Do Not Force All Approvers, the content simply moves forward in the chain. Any approvers prior to the approver who edited the content do not see the final version.

4. Return to the main screen for the approvals. Click the plus icon to add an approver to the list. Figure 5-50 shows the User Selection Interface that appears.

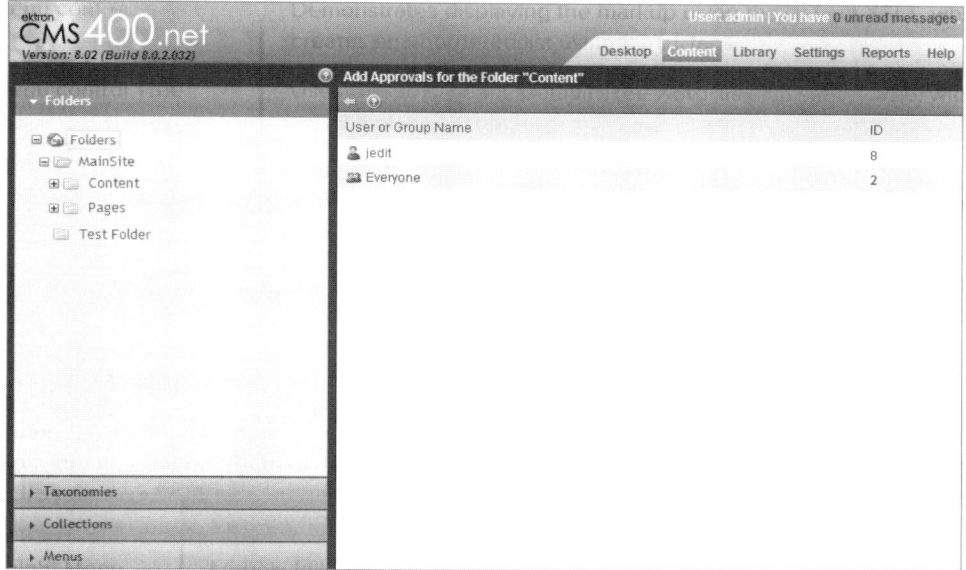

FIGURE 5-50

You'll notice the users and groups displayed for addition to the approval chain is not the complete list of all the users in the system. The list only displays those users explicitly granted permissions for the folder. This is why you added jedit to the list of users.

5. Select jedit from the list now. Doing so returns you to the approval chain with jedit in the list, as pictured in Figure 5-51.

Now that your approval chain has been configured with jedit, no piece of content in this folder will go live until jedit has approved it. Remember approval chains are always serial, meaning if you add a second user to the list, approval will first be required from jedit, and then from the second user. If you want any individual in a certain list of users to be able to approve the content, and not all of those users, you should add those users to a group, and require approval from the group instead.

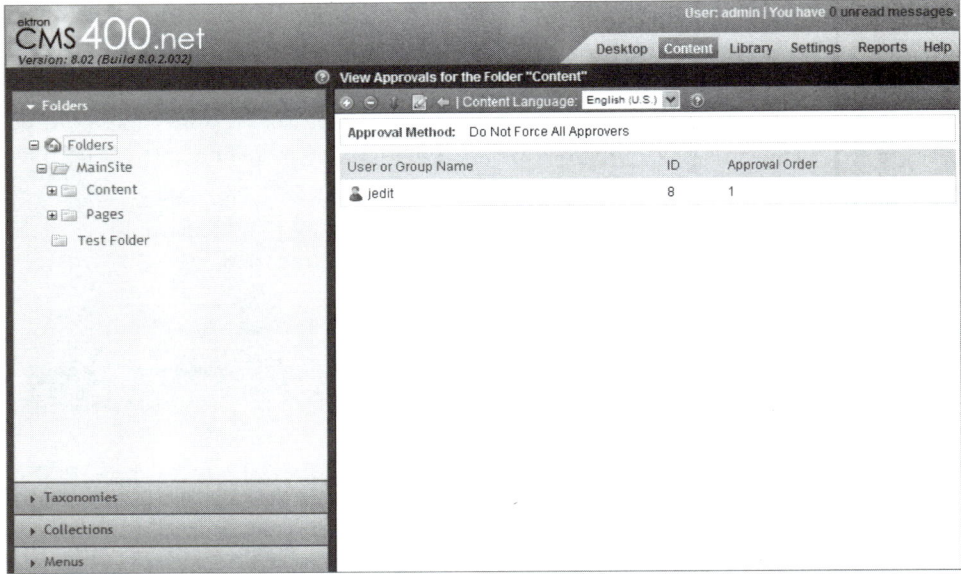

FIGURE 5-51

Creating a Custom Role

Custom roles allow you to create a list of users who have access to specific functionality on your site. They are configured in the Workarea and can be checked programmatically, allowing you to administer easily access lists for your feature. For instance, you might create a site moderator role, and add a Flag Server Control to pages throughout your site. You could then control the visibility of the Flag Server Control by checking if the user is a member of your moderators role. To get to where custom roles are defined in the Workarea, follow these steps:

1. Click the Settings tab, and navigate the tree to Settings ⇨ Roles ⇨ Custom Permissions. The display pane then shows a page called Manage Custom Roles, as shown in Figure 5-52.

2. When you click the plus icon to add a new role, you are presented with a page first asking for the name of this role.

3. Enter CustomRole and click the Save icon to continue. You now are returned to the previous screen, with your CustomRole showing up first on the list of roles.

4. Clicking the CustomRole now brings you to the Manage Members for Role screen, as shown in Figure 5-53.

   Just like in the permissions screen, clicking the plus icon lets you select the users and groups you want to add to this role. Clicking the minus icon removes them from the role.

5. To check programmatically whether a user is a member of the CustomRole, you simply call the following code.

```
Ektron.Cms.CommonApi _commonApi = new Ektron.Cms.CommonApi();
if (_commonApi.GetRolePermissionSystem("CustomRole", _commonApi.UserId))
{
```

```
        //is a member of role
}
else
{
        //is not a member of role
}
```

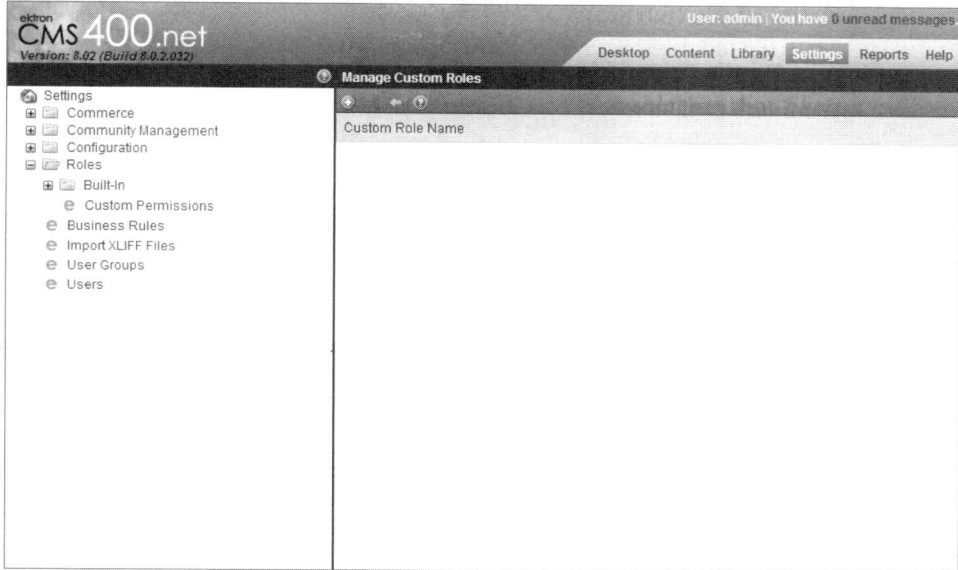

FIGURE 5-52

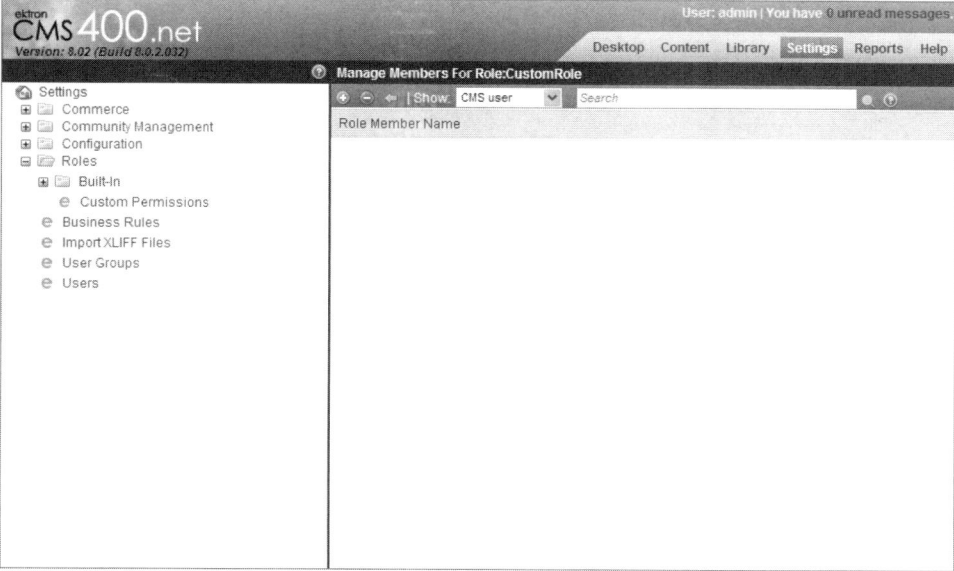

FIGURE 5-53

Under the Hood

There are a few things to remember when working with permissions, roles, and approval chain workflows. In this section we'll cover those notes and discuss some best practices when working with these subsystems.

Permission Types and Behaviors

There are over a dozen types of permissions that can be set in the Ektron Framework. Each type of permission applies to a specific object and action type pair. If a positive setting is set, that user has permission. The administrator account and all members of the administrator group are automatically granted all permissions. Likewise, for programmatic access, the InternalAdmin account (`Ektron.Cms.Common.EkConstants.InternalAdmin`) is automatically granted all permissions. To use the InternalAdmin account for your programmatic calls, when you create an API object, set the `RequestInformation` member variables `CallerID` and `UserID` to the InternalAdmin constant.

Table 5-7 lists the permissions and what they affect.

TABLE 5-7: Permission Types

PERMISSION NAME	DESCRIPTION
Read Only	View permissions. This is ignored unless the content is marked "Private."
Edit	Edit permissions.
Add	Add new item permissions.
Delete	Delete item permissions.
Restore	Restore a version of the content from the history.
Library Read Only	View and download items in the corresponding library folder.
Add Images	Permissions to add images to the corresponding library folder.
Add Files	Permissions to add files to the corresponding library folder.
Add Hyperlinks	Permissions to add hyperlinks to the corresponding library folder.
Overwrite Library	Permissions to overwrite existing items in the corresponding library folder.
Collections	The ability to add or remove items from collections associated with this folder.
Add Folders	Permissions to add subfolders to this folder. This includes typed folders, such as Calendars and Blogs.
Edit Folders	Permissions to modify the folder properties for the selected folder.
Delete Folders	Permissions to delete subfolders from this folder. This includes typed folders, such as Calendars and Blogs.

PERMISSION NAME	DESCRIPTION
Traverse Folders	Permissions to access folders under this folder. This overrides permissions on subfolders, in that users must have traverse permissions on all parent folders to perform any operation on a specific folder.
Modify Preapproval	This lists the users that a piece of content is assigned to when a task is created for it. It is then up to this user or group of users to assign it to an editor to perform the task.

Approval Chain Notes

Due to the way approval chains are implemented in the Ektron Framework, there are a couple of things to keep in mind when developing against them. First, a user can't be in the same approval chain twice. The system sees the first approval as satisfying the second condition, so the content moves immediately past the user.

Also note that approval chains are language specific. If the site you are developing supports multilingual content, remember to select the language from the View menu that you want to administer, and then modify the approval chain to set it for that language.

When content is assigned to a user for approval, the system can send out an e-mail. There are a couple steps involved in setting this up. Check the manual for details on how to enable the sending of system e-mails.

Role Types and Actions

Roles in the Ektron Workarea are split into *folder-specific roles*, and *system-wide* roles. There is no technical difference in the way these roles are applied, only that roles in the system-wide section affect actions not associated with folders. Note also that administrators automatically pass all role tests. Finally, remember it is Ektron Best Practice to create a group for roles, and make users a member of the group, rather than having many users directly as role members. Table 5-8 displays the list of built-in roles.

TABLE 5-8: List of Built-In Roles

ROLE NAME	DESCRIPTION
Alias-Admin	Alias Admin members have the ability to modify the aliasing rules, including adding new automatic aliases, changing existing aliases, and activating or deactivating aliasing altogether.
Alias-Edit	This role applies to the granular ability to add and modify manual and secondary aliases.
Analytics Viewer	This allows users to view analytics reports on content and PageBuilder pages.
Business Rule Editor	Covers creating and editing business rules.

continues

TABLE 5-8 *(continued)*

ROLE NAME	DESCRIPTION
Collection and Menu Admin	Allows users to create, modify, and delete collections and menus.
Collection Approver	Defines the group of users that can approve changes to collections. Only takes effect if collections require approvals.
Commerce Admin	Allows for access to all eCommerce screens.
Community	Allows for management of default community preferences, activity types, messages, and management of notifications.
Community Group Admin	Allows for management of existing community groups, and the ability to create new groups.
Community Group Create	Allows users to create groups and manage groups they created.
Master Layout Create	Allows users to create Master Layout PageBuilder templates.
Message Board Admin	Allows users to approve pending comments and delete existing comments on message boards for groups, users, and content.
Metadata Admin	Allows for creation, modification, and deletion of metadata types.
Search Admin	Allows for management of synonyms and suggested results in search.
Smart Forms Admin	Allows for management of Smart Form definitions.
Synchronization Admin	Allows users to manage sync settings, and perform sync operations.
Task Create	Creates tasks.
Task Delete	Deletes tasks.
Task Redirect	Assigns tasks to users.
Taxonomy Administrator	Allows users to create and edit taxonomies.
Template Configuration	Manages system templates.
User Admin	Manages users and groups.
XLIFF Admin	Allows users to export and import content to XLIFF format for translation to other languages.
Folder User Admin	Allows users to manage the properties for all folders they have at least Read Only and Traverse permissions to. For more details, see the user manual.
Move or Copy	Allows users to perform Copy and Move operations in the Workarea in folders they have the appropriate permissions to.

To programmatically check whether a user is a member of a specific role, use the `GetRolePermissionSystem` and `IsARoleMember` system calls in `Ektron.Cms.CommonApi`. The built-in roles are defined in the enumeration `Ektron.CMS.Common.EkEnumeration.CmsRoleId`.

TAKE HOME POINTS

This chapter explored some of the fundamentals of the Ektron Framework. You may have noticed that some of the structuring decisions that the Ektron team took in developing their framework differ, sometimes significantly, from other content systems out there:

The biggest differentiator from many systems out there is that in the Ektron Framework, almost everything is based on content in an object-oriented pattern. This is helpful for developers in that once you understand how features that interconnect with content — such as the categorization tools like taxonomy, collections, and folders — function, you can generalize that understanding to features other than core content. For content managers the same holds true, but more with respect to the content creation and the process by which content goes live.

To recap, here are some of the ideas covered:

- The primary location of interaction from a content management perspective in the Ektron Framework is the Workarea. You learned how to log in to the system, content authoring, and how content and other features hang together in the Ektron Framework. You explored how content is authored both from the Workarea, as well as managed from the site itself.

- Folders and library content, specifically how folders and content then recombine to create other types of features, like blogs and forums.

- How inheritance factors into the system, and how the combination then informs the approach you take in your information architecture.

- How folders work in the Ektron system.

- Permissions and roles, which is the way all actions are verified and controlled in the Ektron Framework. The use of permissions is necessary to ensure that authors do not accidentally overstep into areas they should not be managing. Roles, on the other hand, are a great way for administrators to enable authors to go above and beyond, and manage subsystems they would not ordinarily be able to.

Configuring Commonly Used Components

- How do you author structured content using Smart Forms?
- How do you organize content through taxonomy?
- How do you use aliasing to improve URL readability?
- How do you create language-specific editions of your site?

Once you have a few Web projects under your belt, you will notice that Web projects are unique in their own way. Technical requirements vary significantly from project to project, and for any Web project to be truly successful, it needs to respond to the unique business requirements for each site, incorporating the needs of stakeholders and customers. But focusing on these differences might lead one to assume there is little commonality between them. In reality, this is not true. This assumption focuses on differences of functionality, information architecture, and even business requirements. But it overlooks the fact that the vast majority of websites share common fundamental requirements and they are built upon common technological underpinnings, in spite of their implementation differences. This chapter builds on the content management fundamentals of Chapter 5 by describing commonly used components found in Ektron implementations. The frequency of their use stems from the fundamental requirements of websites, which are:

- **Content needs:** Requirements often drive the need to repurpose information in many ways on the site and across different platforms, to separate data from the presentation, and to define information in such a way that improves consistency and information discovery. Each of these needs can be largely addressed in one fell swoop when information is properly structured and available in a media-agile format like XML.

- **Organize and classify information:** The human brain is an amazing general-purpose information processor. There is no computer available that comes close to matching the human brain's ability to identify patterns and classify information. This process of identification and classification is how you make sense of the world. It naturally follows that you use a similar process for ordering the information on your websites. This identification makes sense of Web content for your site visitors by organizing it into content hierarchies and creating meaningful information architectures.

➤ **Meaningful navigation cues:** These help orient your site visitors to their place and position in the overall information architecture. In the real world, you use visual cues to orient yourself spatially; it is something you do naturally without much thought. In the virtual world, URLs are one of the most valuable communication signals you can use. They make your information architecture visible and intelligible to your site visitors and provide descriptions rich with meaning to help your site visitors have a sense of place and position on the site.

➤ **Exposing the site's content to the widest possible audience:** There are many things that can be discussed here, but this chapter focuses on localization. Even though the primary language of the Internet began as English, this changed as the Internet proliferated globally. From a marketing standpoint, offering multilingual content exposes your website to an entirely new audience at the cost of translating existing content. Relative to the cost of other marketing efforts, this may prove to be among the most cost effective.

After reading this chapter, you will understand how to use the Ektron Framework to define and author structured content, how to organize content following your website's information architecture, how to craft meaningful URLs for navigation and SEO purposes, and how to expose your website to a global audience. This chapter covers each of these four technologies in depth, focusing on best practices, recommended configurations, and step-by-step instructions on implementing each within the context of further developing the OnTrek website.

UNDERSTANDING THE TECHNOLOGY

Let's take a look at each of the four needs described previously and see how they map to Ektron technology. Each of the four technologies is summarized in the following paragraphs and will have its own coverage in their respective "technical sections" later this chapter.

Structured content modeling and authoring are done using Ektron's *Smart Forms*. From a developer's perspective, Smart Forms provide a mechanism for creating strongly typed content definitions used for content authoring. These definitions are called Smart Form Designs and are created using the WYSIWYG form builder called Smart Form Designer. The designs can then be used as the basis for different content types available to content authors in the Workarea. The designs consist of three primary pieces:

➤ **Structural definition:** Visually expressed using user interface components like textboxes and checkboxes. Internally, this form is represented as XML Schema and the content created using it is defined as XML. From a content author's perspective, these details are hidden. Authors are simply presented with a Web form containing familiar user interface elements.

➤ **Validation definition:** Consists of the rules governing the validation of data provided by the content author.

➤ **Template:** This governs the display of this information. This piece consists of an XSLT which is designed to convert the XML to XHTML for use in the display layer on the site.

Ektron's *taxonomy* feature provides a categorization system authors use to organize information into meaningful hierarchies. These category structures can then be used to create navigation structures, such as menus and directories, which guide users to the information they're looking for. Multiple taxonomies can be created to match the expectations by different audiences. For example, on the OnTrek website, the product marketing material is managed in the content folder tree in a folder called Products, as is all content authored by OnTrek's marketing group. When authoring content, the marketing group classifies the marketing material related to software products by assigning the content one or more categories defined in the product taxonomy. This allows site visitors to access the information by navigating through a product directory. Because some products might exist in multiple categories, associating products, such as those with multiple categories, means customers can find software in multiple pathways.

The *URL Aliasing* feature of the Ektron Framework provides a powerful engine that lets you turn undescriptive URLs into meaningful resource identifiers. Using descriptive, keyword-rich URLs has SEO benefits and improves your site's position on search engine results pages. The human friendly URLs also provide a navigation aid. This helps your site visitors to better understand the overall site structure and determine their current location in the sitemap. This feature allows you to define such URLs in a number of ways. Automatic URL Aliasing can create URLs using the category structure of the taxonomy hierarchy along with the content item's title. For example, a content item titled Barack Obama is categorized in U.S. > Executive Branch > Presidents, maps to the URL `http://localhost/US/Executive-Branch/Presidents/Barack-Obama/`. Similarly, automatic aliases can be created using the content folder tree and regular expressions. *Manual aliasing* comes in handy when you need to override automatically generated URLs, or simply need to define a unique alias for a content item.

You can expose your website's content to a global audience using *content localization features*. The *Language Export feature* exports content items as a single bundle, packaged using XLIFF, an established XML standard for language translation. These bundles are compressed and then delivered to a translation company where the information is translated and returned in the same bundle, which is then imported back into the system. This process makes offering professionally translated content on your website a very straight forward and painless process. In addition to the Language Export feature, Ektron's localization technology offers the ability to translate content using manual translation or machine translation. Manual translation is often used when an organization employs a translation specialist and has a small amount of content to translate. Machine translation uses computer generated translations when there is no budget for professional translation yet a requirement exists for multilingual content.

SMART FORMS

Another pattern you will notice when having a number of websites under your belt is that websites often contain the same types of information such as press releases, employee bios, and product descriptions. You will find these data types have the same discrete elements regardless of the type of site you're building. A press release has a title, an author, and a subtitle, whereas an employee has a name, title, contact information, and bio. Using a freeform WYSIWYG content editor to produce content having a highly consistent structure like this will predictably result in a few snags:

- **Content items are often inconsistently authored**: Sometimes press releases end up without subtitles, others without descriptions.
- **Content authors often make design decisions that cause the designers to cringe**: Authors inadvertently add spacing where it doesn't belong, or changing fonts and colors.
- **Information frequently ends up tied to a particular use**: This is because information may contain presentation markup for a specific purpose, making it impossible to reuse elsewhere.

Unstructured content certainly has its place, but it does present the types of problems described here. Namely, there's no way to force structure, no way to separate the content from the presentation, and no way to reuse the content in other contexts such as mobile and syndication feeds.

To start, let's look at how the term *structured content* is commonly defined. Wikipedia defines it in the following way:

> *Structured content refers to information or content that has been broken down and classified using metadata. Structured content often refers to information that has been classified using XML, but can also relate to information classified using other standard or proprietary forms of metadata.*

This definition touches on the key idea that the information has been broken into discrete chunks having been classified in some way. Web CMSs take different approaches as to how they support chunking content into discrete pieces. Some favor using relational database structures while others use metadata. At the core of the Ektron Framework, structured content is defined and stored as XML.

The Difference between Smart Forms and HTML Forms

Structured content is authored in Ektron using Smart Forms. These are not to be confused with HTML forms as they are two completely separate technologies serving different purposes. The primary difference being what is done with the data that is submitted through them. Data submitted through the HTML form is stored in the database as unchangeable name-value pairs. This data is almost exclusively used for report generation, and is submitted by site visitors. In contrast, Smart Forms store content entered by site authors as first class content items, which means they have every behavior of content — they obey content permissions, flow through approval processes and offer scheduled publishing. Everything content does, Smart Forms can do as well.

In spite of the fact that Smart Forms and HTML forms are entirely separate entities, they do share some similarities simply because they both deal with technology for displaying forms on Web pages. They both provide a wide variety of standard form input fields (such as textboxes, select lists), and ways to validate input data. They are also both designed in similar ways, using a WYSIWYG form designer. Chapter 9 has an entire section that discusses HTML forms. After reading about Smart Forms, see that section for more information about HTML forms.

Understanding Smart Form Design

Before you can author content using a Smart Form, you need to first define a Smart Form Design. If you're familiar with Relation Databases Management Systems (RDBMS), you can think of a Smart

Form Design as the database table schema, however under the covers, a Smart Form Design is represented as an XML Schema. A Smart Form Design is what you create to break down your information into discrete chunks, each chunk having its own data type and User Interface (UI) for gathering strongly typed values from the user. Because the Ektron Framework uses XML for storing these custom defined chunks of information, it follows that these form elements map directly to the core XML building blocks — XML Elements and XML Attributes — that are used to create content that conforms to a schema.

Structuring your content well may sometimes feel like a form of art, but there are good resources available to help with this. A recommended book is *Content Management Bible*, Bob Boiko, Wiley Publishing, 2001.

Creating Smart Form Designs

The process of creating a Smart Form Design begins by navigating to the Data Designer in the Workarea by following these steps:

Navigate to Settings ➪ Configuration ➪ Smart Form Configurations, and use the Smart Form Data Designer. Only members of the Administrators group or those given the Smart Form Admin Role have the ability to create these. This interface allows you to build a Smart Form Design visually using the user interface shown in Figure 6-1, called the Smart Form Data Designer.

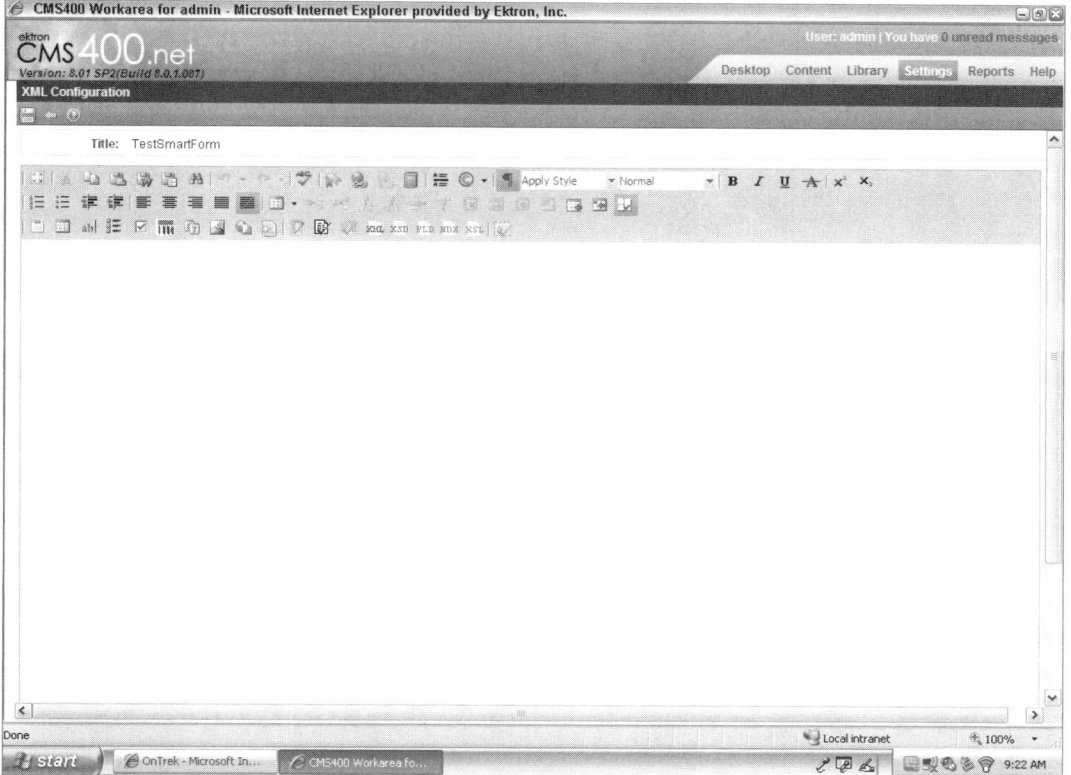

FIGURE 6-1

As you move through the Data Designer, you'll see dialog boxes that give you the ability to set the properties on the input elements defined in the design. The properties include the options to define the structure of the XML to be produced, so you can specify whether data is stored as an XML Element or XML Attribute or Text. Figure 6-2 shows a comparison of a simple Smart Form Design (top) and the XML source of the Smart Form Content (bottom) created from it.

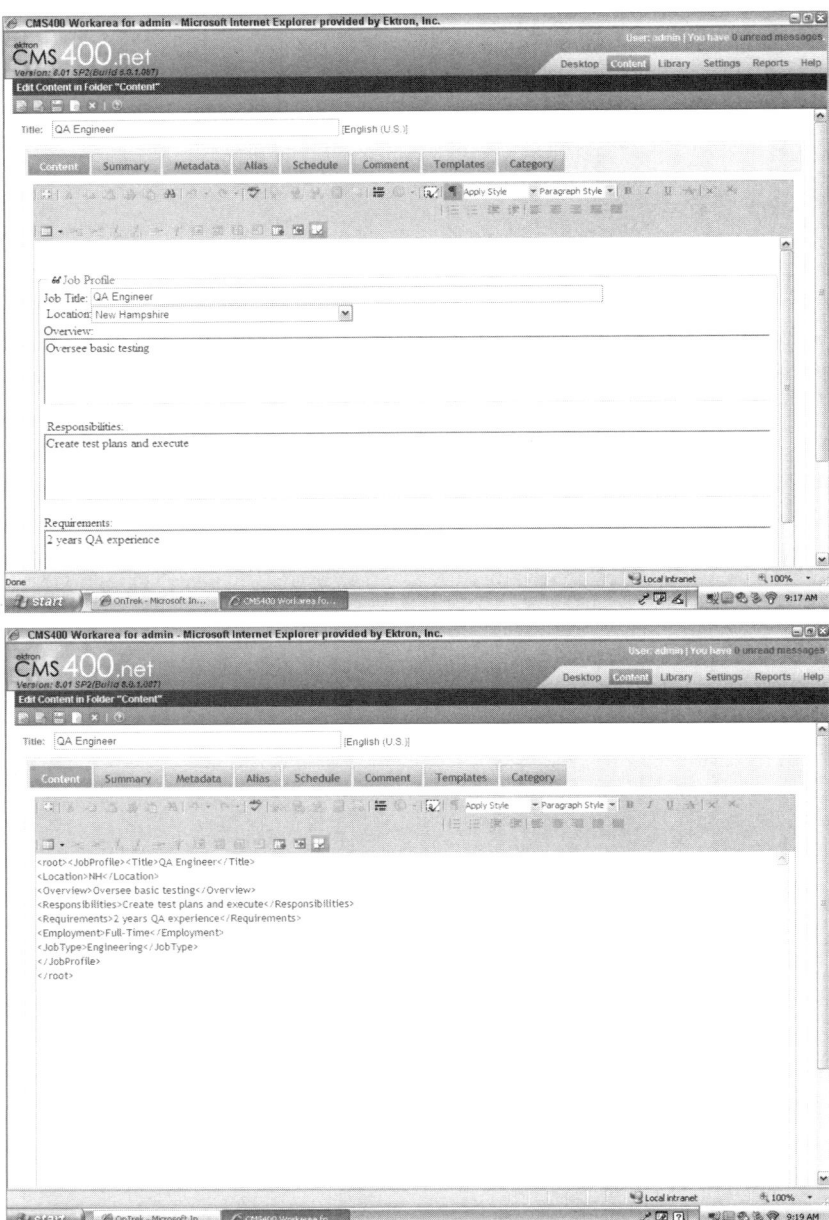

FIGURE 6-2

Once the Smart Form Design is defined, associate it to folders in your content folder tree. This has the effect of defining which Smart Form Designs are available to content authors for creating Smart Form Content. Figure 6-3 shows how this association affects the New Content Menu for content authors.

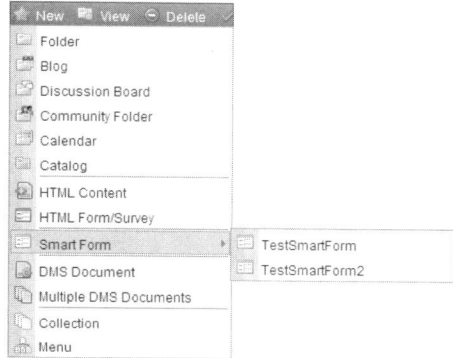

FIGURE 6-3

From a content authoring standpoint, the details of the XML Schema, elements, and attributes are entirely hidden. Content creators need only focus exclusively on authoring content and need not worry about the system implementation details or Smart Form Design process discussed so far. Filling out the form and submitting it is as simple as filling out any form-based interface, and once the form is submitted, structured XML content is created.

At this point, structured content has been authored and is stored using the schema you created when you defined your Smart Form Design. But what would happen if you tried to display this on a Web page; what would it look like? By default, each Smart Form Design has an associated default presentation style associated with it. This default presentation is automatically generated by the system when the definition is published and is defined using XSLT. This can be overridden by providing a custom XSLT file, as shown in Figure 6-4. You can specify up to three custom presentation styles on this screen. It is recommended that you use the default display XSLT file as a starting point for your own custom display XSLT file. You access the Default Display XSLT through the XSLT icon in the Smart Form Design. The Default Display XSLT is also discussed in the "Under the Hood" section, later.

Retrieving, Manipulating, and Rendering Structured Data

The Ektron Framework provides a number of ways to retrieve, manipulate, and render structured data, such as APIs, server controls, and widgets. The .NET XML Framework can be used as well. Let's look at each of these.

Using the Content Block Server Control

The Content Block Server Control (Chapter 5) allows you to retrieve and render content, including Smart Form content, by its content ID. Unless you specify a custom defined XSLT, the default display XSLT is used. Figure 6-5 shows how you override the default XSLT using the Content Block `DisplayXSLT` property. XSLT is the primary method for customizing the markup of the Content Block Server Control.

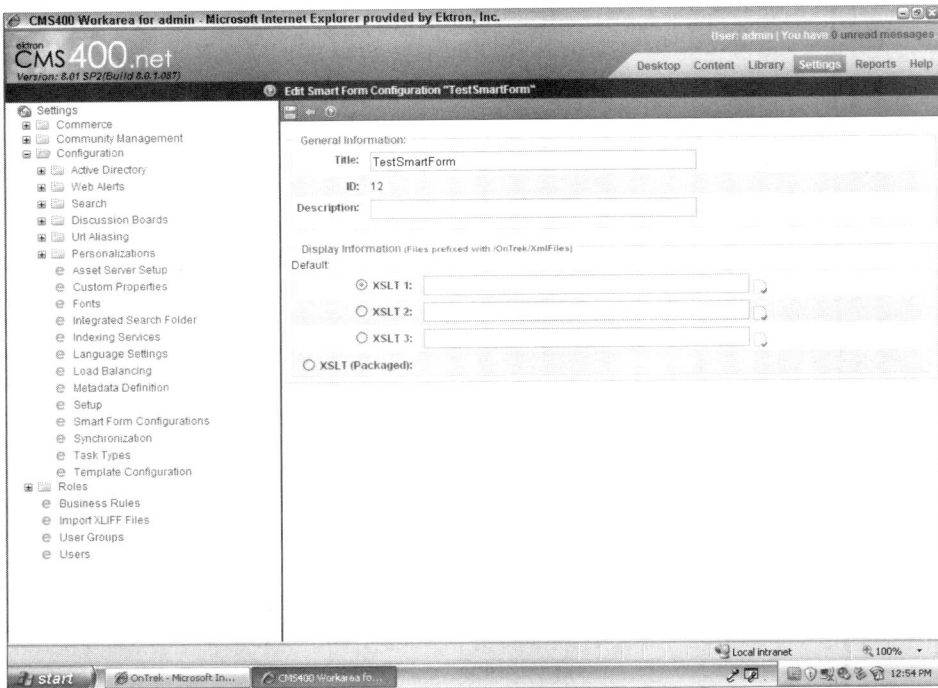

FIGURE 6-4

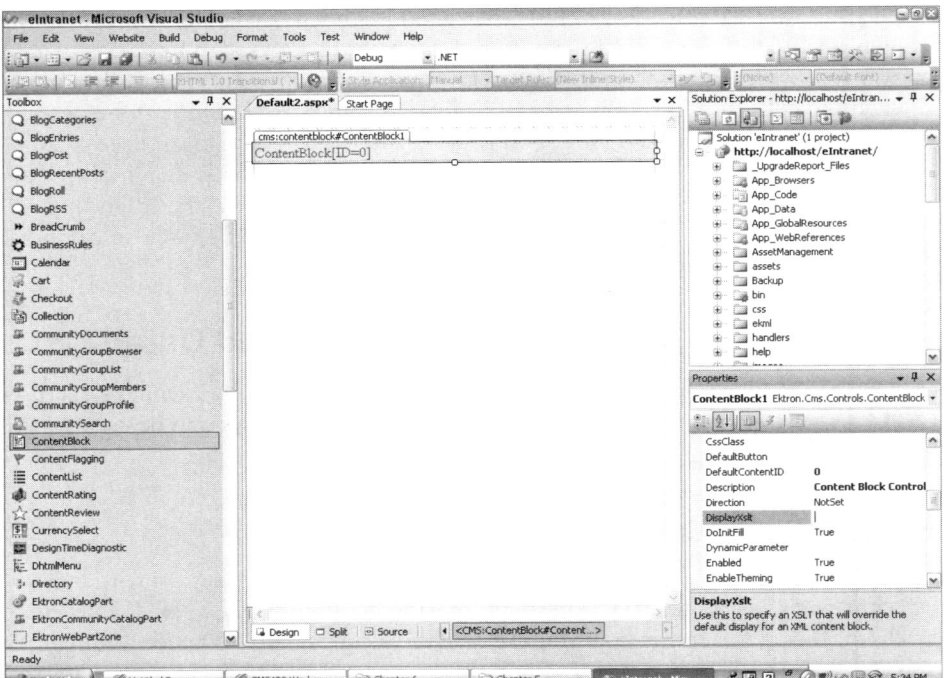

FIGURE 6-5

Although it is somewhat common to hear a .NET developer voice resistance to using XSLT for transforming XML into HTML, it's important to keep in mind that XSLT is a language specifically designed for this purpose and it is an extremely powerful tool to have in your toolkit. Good developers always strive to use the right tool for the job, and in many cases, XSLT is just that tool. The benefits of using XSLT are listed as follows:

- It is a declarative language and can be easily interspersed between HTML tags. This provides a much more visual understanding of the markup structure.
- You don't have to recompile every time you make a change to the presentation. Markup in an XSLT becomes a sort of presentation configuration file, separate from the website's application business logic.
- Complex transformations that take many lines of imperative code to express (procedural or object oriented) can be achieved with a few XSLT statements.

Resistance to XSLT typically comes into play when developers are not familiar with it. To help developers overcome common hurdles while learning XSLT, Ektron has written a number of Knowledge Base articles on the Dev Center such as those shown in the following list. These articles give solutions to common "gotchas." Most issues occur when developers fail to recognize that XSLT is a declarative language and try to write it using the imperative programming paradigm (writing XSLT as if it were a procedural or object oriented language like VB or C#).

Helpful KB articles related to XSLT include:

- **KB 0485:** Gallery of Templates: `http://dev.ektron.com/kb_article.aspx?id=485`
- **KB 9240:** XSLT Support Summary: `http://dev.ektron.com/kb_article.aspx?id=9240`

Using the .NET Framework

The .NET Framework provides a number of ways to transform and render XML data, ranging from the brute force approach of iterating over an XML data structure using XPath selectors and building up HTML markup using StringBuilder, to data binding. The approach that Ektron developers seem to be most comfortable with, however, is a hybrid of both approaches, which falls somewhere in the middle, and is a best practice recommended by Ektron. This hybrid approach is to create .NET code that maps the elements of your Smart Form Design to .NET data classes. Using this approach makes it possible for you to access the Smart Form content directly in .NET without having to think about XML, XSLT, or XPath in cases where it is not appropriate. With a native .NET data class in hand, representing Smart Form data, you have two options:

- Databind to .NET Server Controls and use Server Control Templating provided by controls, such as ListView or Repeater, to reference your field properties right in your declarative ASP.NET markup (See "Which Controls Support Templates?" on the MSDN `http://msdn.microsoft.com/en-us/library/h59db326.aspx`).
- Programmatically access your class properties and manipulate the data as you need.

The process for generating a .NET Class from a Smart Form Design is simple and straightforward, albeit somewhat manual. The general steps are listed as follows:

1. Export the Smart Form Design as XML Schema (*.XSD).

2. Transform the XSD into a C# class definition.
3. Retrieve Smart Form data and deserialize it into an instance of your class.

The more detailed steps are as follows:

1. Begin by retrieving your Smart Form Design as an XML Schema Definition file (*.XSD). This is done through a RESTful interface provided by the Ektron Framework. Plug the following URL into your browser: `http://localhost/workarea/webservices/rest.svc/xmlconfigs/{SMART-FORM-ID}.xsd`. Replace **SMART-FORM-ID** with the ID of your Smart Form Design.

You can also access the XML Schema Definition file (*.XSD) by clicking the XSD button in the Smart Form Design in the Workarea.

2. Use Microsoft's XML Schema Definition tool, a command-line tool xsd.exe, to convert XML Schema to a C# class. This tool is provided with Visual Studio and is also available as a free download from Microsoft (binaries, documentation, and configuration options are available through the MSDN, `http://msdn.microsoft.com/en-us/library/x6c1kb0s(VS.80).aspx`).

For example, if you have a Smart Form Design representing a book that contains elements such as ISBN, title, author, summary, and description, creating a C# class with the same structure would be done by issuing the following command on the command line:

`c:\>xsd.exe book.xsd /classes /language:CS /namespace:SmartForm.Book`

The XML Schema Definition tool then creates a file named book.cs containing C# code defining a class named Book in the namespace SmartForm, a portion of which is shown in Listing 6-1.

Available for download on Wrox.com

LISTING 6-1: A class generated using the Microsoft XML Schema Definition tool

```
//------------------------------------------------------------------------------
// <auto-generated>
//     This code was generated by a tool.
//     Runtime Version:2.0.50727.3603
//
//     Changes to this file may cause incorrect behavior and will be lost if
//     the code is regenerated.
// </auto-generated>
//------------------------------------------------------------------------------

//
// This source code was auto-generated by xsd, Version=2.0.50727.42.
//
namespace SmartForm.BookStore
{
    using System.Xml.Serialization;


    /// <remarks/>
    [System.CodeDom.Compiler.GeneratedCodeAttribute("xsd", "2.0.50727.42")]
    [System.SerializableAttribute()]
```

```
[System.Diagnostics.DebuggerStepThroughAttribute()]
[System.ComponentModel.DesignerCategoryAttribute("code")]
[System.Xml.Serialization.XmlTypeAttribute(AnonymousType=true)]
[System.Xml.Serialization.XmlRootAttribute(Namespace="", IsNullable=false)]
public partial class Book {

    private string TitleField;
    private string IsbnField;
    private string AuthorField;
    private string DescriptionField;
    private float PriceField;

    /// <remarks/>
    [System.Xml.Serialization.XmlElementAttribute("Title")]
    public string Title {
        get {
            return this.TitleField;
        }
        set {
            this.TitleField = value;
        }
    }
...
```

3. Retrieve Smart Form data. This can be done using the Content Block Server Control or the API. The following code sample shows a C# example that accesses this content using the Content Block Server Control's EkItem.Html property in codebehind. An alternative implementation might use the Content API methods as shown in Appendix B.

   ```
   string xml = ContentBlock1.EkItem.Html;
   SmartForm.Book book = Ektron.Cms.EkXml.Deserialize
   (,
   typeof(SmartForm.Book), xml) as SmartForm.Book;
   ```

4. The process of retrieving and deserializing Smart Form content can then be wrapped into a utility class to provide a nice way to request and retrieve a strongly typed data object in one line. The following snippet shows code that does just that:

   ```
   Book book1 = SmartFormHelper.GetBook(bookId);
   ```

An alternative approach is to load the XML into the .NET XmlDocument and use XPath to select elements. The situation where you may possibly use this approach is when you just want to access a few pieces of data from the XmlDocument. If you don't need to access all of the data available, you might want to consider using XmlDocument and XPath to select the data you need, instead of mapping each of the XML elements to a data class.

Implementation

This section focuses on creating a Smart Form Design that you'll use in Chapter 7 to build a JavaScript-based banner rotator for the OnTrek homepage. Don't worry about the technical implementation of that component at this point. Chapter 7 will cover those details. For now, suffice it to say that the component rotates through a series of images and their associated text. The image caption, text description, and other information driving the component are defined through the Smart Form Design that you will create here.

Figure 6-6 shows a screenshot of the component as it appears on the OnTrek homepage (top) and the form that content editors will use to place new images, or modify existing ones, on the component of the homepage (bottom).

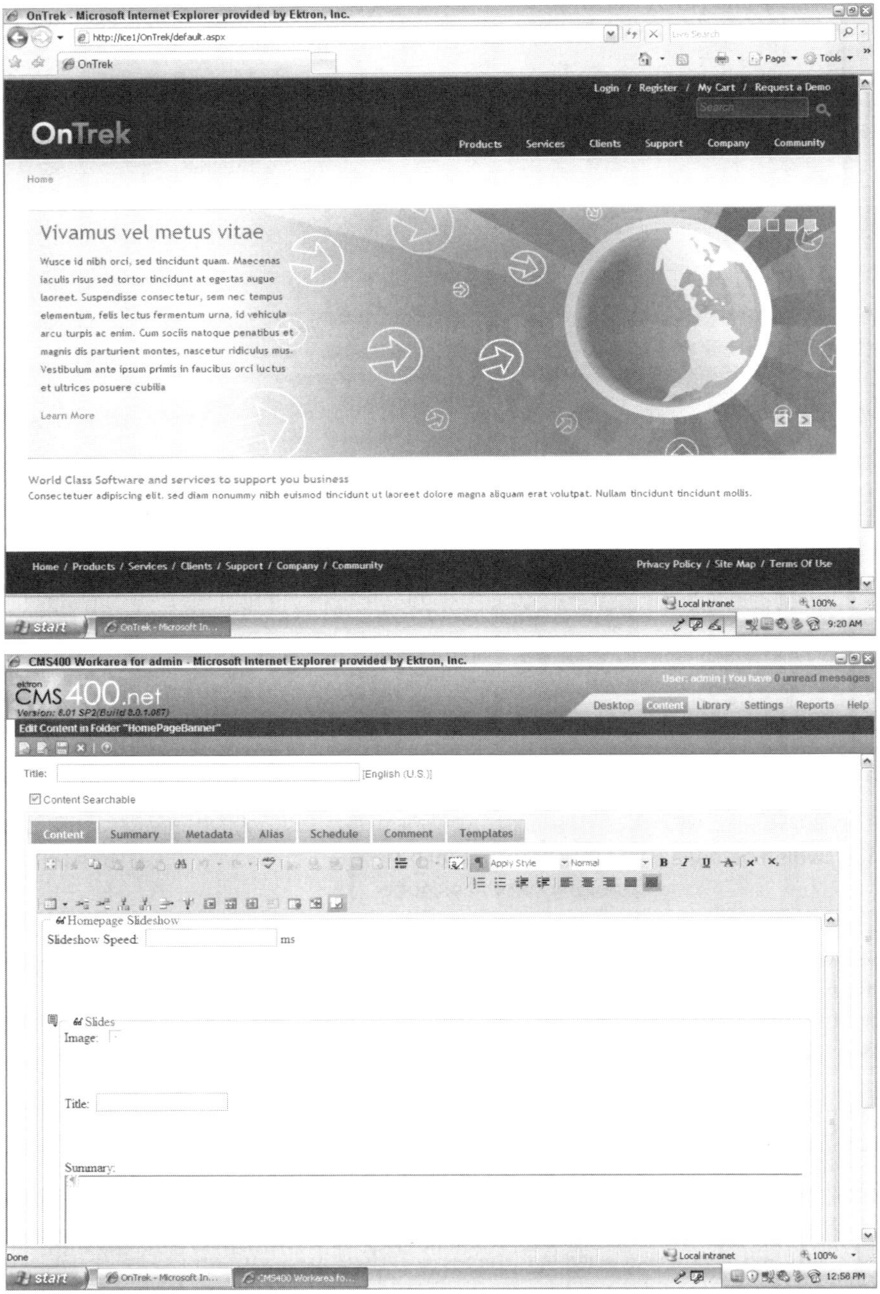

FIGURE 6-6

Creating a Smart Form Design

Although this form is relatively simple, the following steps walk through the process of building a new Smart Form Design. The form contains the four form input fields shown in Figure 6-7 (Heading, Text, URL, and Duration).

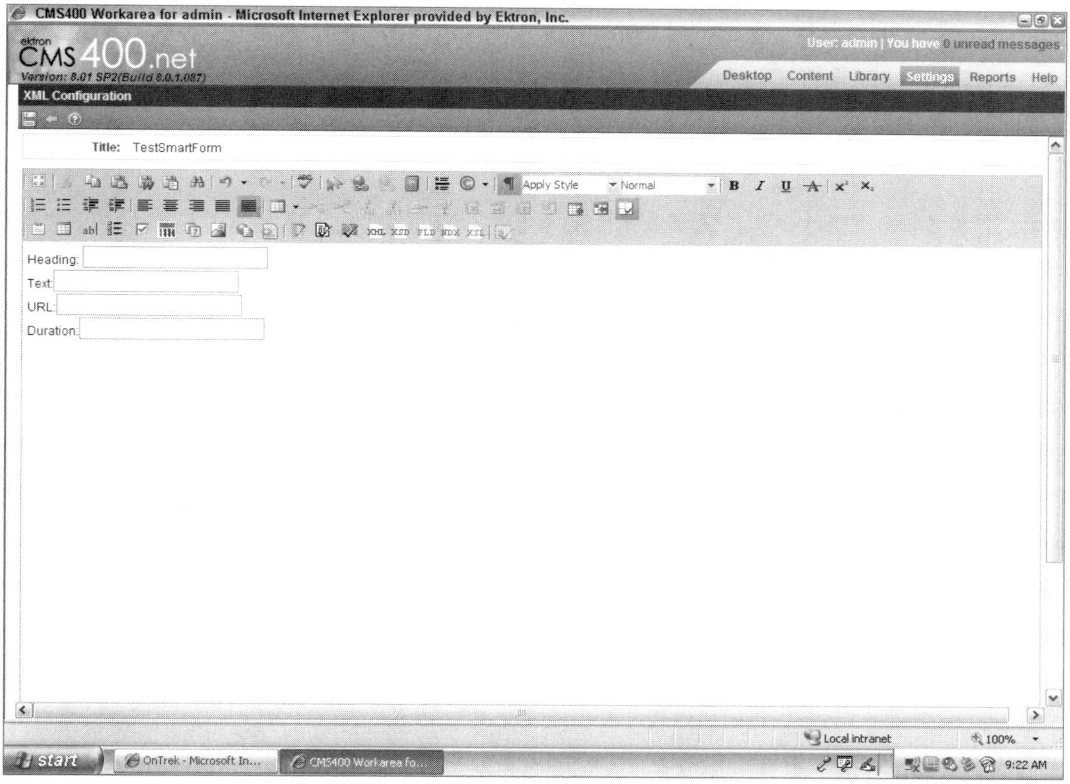

FIGURE 6-7

1. Open the Workarea and navigate to Settings ➪ Configuration ➪ Smart Form Configurations.

> *Once upon a time, Smart Forms were called* XML Configurations. *Although this terminology has been removed from Ektron's Workarea, documentation, and website, you might run across references to this terminology on the Ektron Dev Center in older forum posts. Anytime you see XML Configurations, you can mentally replace that phrase with Smart Forms.*

2. Click the Add Smart Form icon.
3. In the Title field, provide the name of the Smart Form Design. Name the form design Featured Image.

4. Click the Save icon.
5. In the WYSIWYG Smart Form Designer, click into the main canvas and type in the string **Heading:**
6. Leaving your cursor at the end of Heading, click on the Text Field button. The Text Field dialog box appears as shown in Figure 6-8.

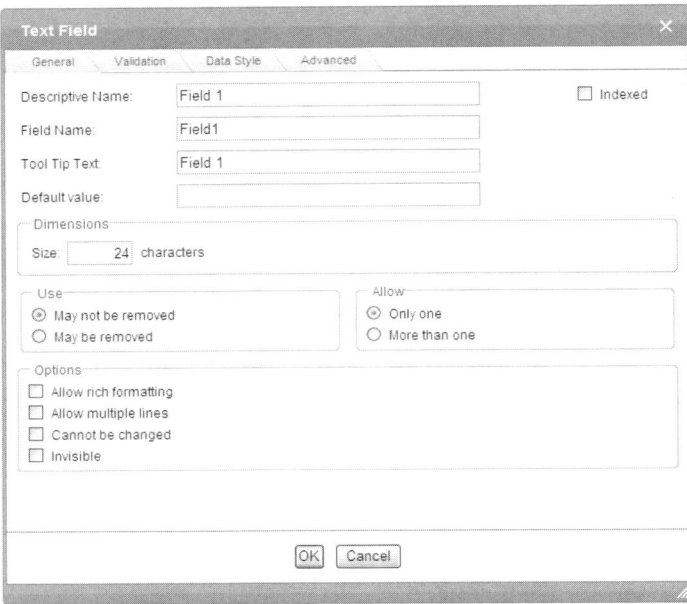

FIGURE 6-8

7. In Descriptive Name, provide the name **Featured Image Heading**; the other fields will auto-populate. Take this moment to explore each of the options you have available here. Leave all of the default values.
8. Repeat Steps 5-7 for the Text field.
9. Again, repeat the same process for the URL field; however, once the Text Field dialog box appears, click the Validation tab as shown in Figure 6-9.
10. From the Validation pull-down menu, select URL. This validates the input and ensures that a URL is provided.
11. Repeat the process for the Duration field; this time, select Decimal number or blank from the Validation menu.
12. Click the Update icon to save the Smart Form Design

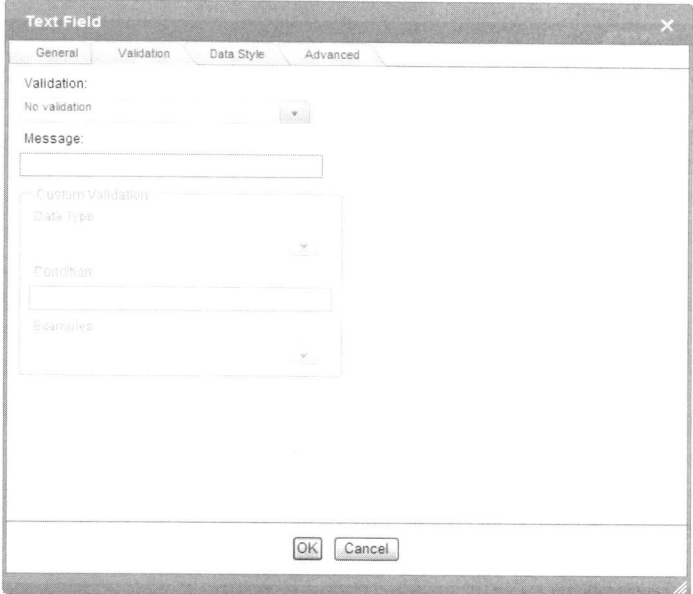

FIGURE 6-9

Associating the Smart Form Design to the Content Tree

Before a Smart Form Design can be used to author content, it must be associated to one or more folders in the content folder tree.

1. Open the Workarea and navigate to the content folder tree, MainSite/Content/Home/HomePageBanner.

2. From the View menu, select Properties as shown in Figure 6-10

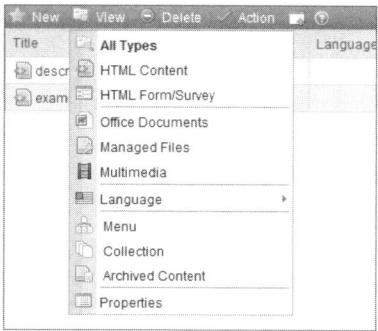

FIGURE 6-10

3. Click the Edit icon from the toolbar.
4. From the Edit screen, select Featured Image from the select menu on the Smart Forms tab as shown in Figure 6-11.

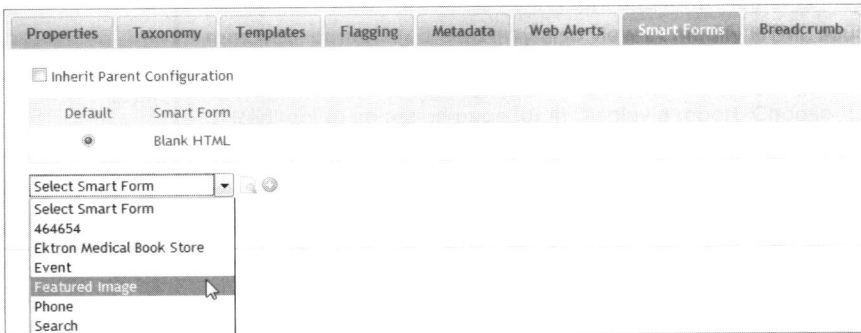

FIGURE 6-11

5. Click the Add icon.
6. Save the folder configuration by clicking the Save icon from the toolbar.

Creating Smart Form Data

Once the Smart Form Design is associated to the content folder tree, a content author can complete a Smart Form and author structured content.

1. Open the Workarea and navigate to the content folder tree, MainSite/Content/Home/HomePageBanner.
2. From the New menu, select Smart Form ⇨ Featured Image.
3. In the content Title field, provide the title of the featured image. In this case, name it **New Product Image**.
4. In the Smart Form's Heading field, type the heading of the image, **New Product Image**.
5. In the Smart Form's Text field, type the text that displays at the bottom of the image, **The Newest Addition to Our Product Line**.
6. In the Smart Form's URL field, type the URL path to the image, `http://localhost/OnTrek/images/img-banner1.png`.
7. Click the Submit icon.

Under the Hood

Earlier in this section, we made the statement that Smart Form data is stored as XML in the content table. This is true, but keep in mind that some select system attributes are defined as fields in the database. This should not be too surprising, since Smart Form data is content stored in the content table, and as discussed in Chapter 5, the content table contains a number of fields for core content properties, such as Title and Author. One of the core fields in the content table is a field titled Content HTML, which stores the raw content itself. The Content HTML field either contains structured

XML in cases when Smart Forms are being used or unstructured XHTML when content is authored using the free-form WYSIWYG editor. In all cases, this field must contain well formed XML.

Any content added through the Workarea or the site through server controls ensures that the content is well formed XML and does so by running the content through a *Tidy process*, which closes unclosed tags. However, be advised that there are content APIs outside of the Framework API namespace that intentionally circumvent the Tidy process. If you are adding XML content directly into the system using a content API outside of the Framework namespace, you must ensure that the XML content is well formed prior to the API call. Adding malformed XML to the content table will have undesired effects on many parts of the system, like content rendering and search.

The Smart Form Designs themselves are stored in the xml_collection_tbl table. Understanding the internal XML structure of the Smart Form Design might not improve your ability to work with the Smart Form data produced; however, it certainly helps you to understand how the system behaves. This might be helpful at some point when trying to debug your application. All the elements that comprise a Smart Form Design are encapsulated into an XML entity called the *Smart Form Design Package*, which consist of five parts, described in Table 6-1. You can query the xml_collection_tbl to see what the Smart Form Design Package looks like for a given Smart Form Design and copy the Package XML into an XML reading tool (such as Altova's XMLSpy) to see how your data maps to the elements in Table 6-1.

TABLE 6-1: Internal Elements of a Smart Form Design

#	PART	DESCRIPTION
1	Form Elements	The form elements that make up the user interface of the data entry aspect of the Smart Form Design. That is, the user interface that displays when a content editor is authoring Smart Form data. This content is composed of XHTML with custom tags and attributes that are needed for the editor and for the internal behaviors of the content processing engine.
2	XML Schema	Defines the structure of the XML as XML Schema. Earlier in this section, you exported the Smart Form Design as XML Schema — this data was extracted from the Smart Form Design Package.
3	Data Entry XSLT	This is run against the XML described earlier containing the XHTML UI elements. The results of this transformation define how the Smart Form Design renders in the browser. This XSLT is not something that should be customized or modified, and there are no Workarea screens or public APIs for changing it.
4	Default Display XSLT	Defines how the Smart Form Data renders by default in the Workarea and on the website. This XSLT can be overridden both in the Workarea as described earlier, and at runtime using something like the Content Block Server Control's Display XSLT property.
5	Default XML Document	This is used when new content is created. Think of this as an XML template that's used internally to stub out what values exist by default during the process of creating new Smart Form data.

TAXONOMY

The Ektron Framework gives administrators and those users who have been granted the taxonomy administrator role, the ability to categorize content using its taxonomy engine, providing content item level categorization using one-to-many relationships between content and categories.

Using a taxonomy for content organization lets you classify content in a way that reflects how people think, allowing you to build effective site navigation and pathways for accessing content through search, menus, and sitemaps. These navigation paths can and should differ from how the content is physically stored and managed in the content folder tree, since typically the set of people creating content is different from the set of people accessing content. As such, in practice, it is common to see companies store content in folders organized by department (engineering, marketing, sales) and use taxonomy categorization to control how that information is displayed on the website. This allows you to leverage the content folder tree for defining things such as permissions and approval processes (see Chapter 5, under the section "Permissions and Workflow" for more information). Through taxonomies, you gain the ability to adapt and expand the site navigation as the content repository grows and the site visitors' needs change.

Ektron's taxonomy is simple to use, but don't let its simplicity belie its power. The taxonomies you create will make themselves useful in many ways throughout the system.

From a data structure perspective, a taxonomy manifests itself as a boundless hierarchical structure consisting of many nodes representing categories and subcategories. The arrangement of the hierarchy is such that the top-level nodes correspond to the most general categories and the lower-level nodes to more specific ones. Because the taxonomy supports one-to-many relationships between content and categories, there may be multiple pathways to reaching a given content item. Technically, this means the *taxonomy tree* is not technically a tree because a cycle emerges once a single content item has been associated with multiple categories. Conceptually it is fine to think of the taxonomy as a tree because the category nodes themselves represent a tree structure and the documentation refers to them as such.

Once configured, each category node in a taxonomy tree can be assigned custom properties that can be populated by taxonomy administrators while creating and managing taxonomy categories. These properties are similar to folder metadata and their values are available to the items associated with the category node through the Taxonomy API covered in the section "Under the Hood" later in this chapter.

The taxonomy system is also language aware, which gives multi-language support. Once a language-specific version of a taxonomy is created, a taxonomy is also created for each enabled language. The Taxonomy ID for each of these is the same; therefore to uniquely identify a particular taxonomy, you need the compound key consisting of Language ID and Taxonomy ID. For example, if you create a taxonomy in English, and enable Spanish and Italian, you'll have three taxonomies, all with the same Taxonomy ID and each with their own Language ID.

Within Ektron Search (Chapter 7, "Search"), taxonomy plays a critical role in two significant use cases:

- ➤ It can be used to power a faceted search that allows you to narrow search results by attributes.
- ➤ Content categorization also provides an effective way to disambiguate search results.

For example, when a user searches for Saturn it may be unclear if they are looking for information on Saturn the car or Saturn the planet. By configuring the Search Server Control to display taxonomy categories, as shown in Figure 6-12, taxonomy can be used in such situations, to disambiguate search results and provide more accurate search results.

Browsing by category provides a powerful navigation paradigm, as it allows content authors to create multiple taxonomies for different audiences, and provide different Menu Navigation structures based on those taxonomies, giving navigation that matches the way your audience expects to find the content. There are a number of widgets and modules available through Ektron's Developer Exchange that create menu navigation from a taxonomy. You can view them at: `http://dev.ektron.com/exchange/searchcode.aspx?searchtext=taxonomy`.

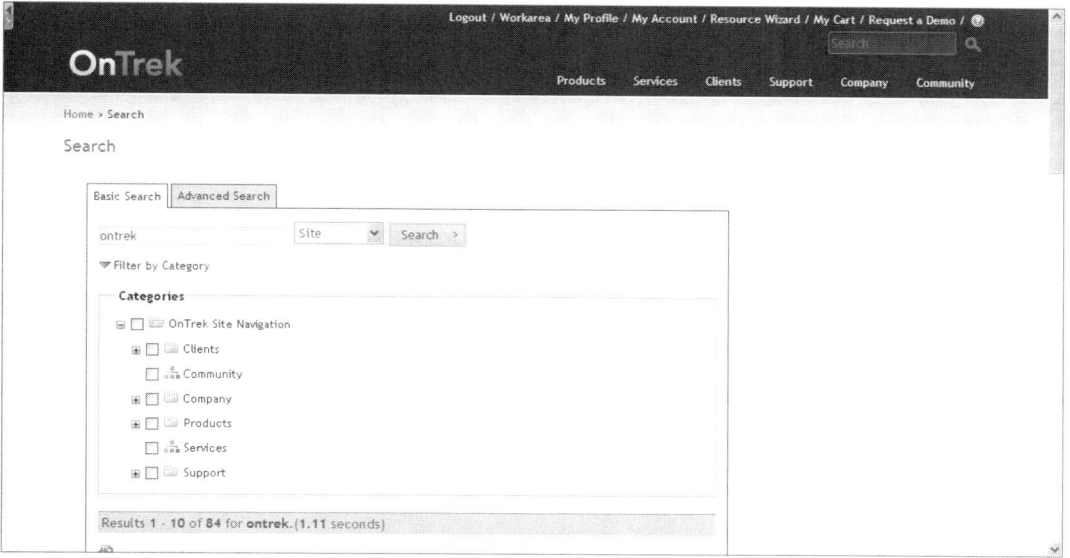

FIGURE 6-12

Taxonomy also plays an important role with URL aliasing, as described later in this chapter. Once this type of automatic aliasing is enabled and configured, URLs are automatically generated based on the hierarchical structure of the taxonomy.

Implementation

This section shows how to enable and configure the taxonomy used to define OnTrek's Information Architecture. There are three concepts covered here:

➤ How to create a taxonomy

➤ How to associate that taxonomy with the folder structure so content authors can use it to create content

➤ Two ways to categorize content

Creating a Taxonomy

Follow these steps to create your taxonomy:

1. From the Workarea, go to Content ➪ Taxonomies ➪ Taxonomies.
2. Choose a language for the taxonomy by using the View ➪ Language selector pull-down menu.
3. Click the Add Taxonomy button. Also note that you can hover your cursor over Taxonomies in the left panel, right-click the mouse, and click the Add Taxonomy menu item. The Add Taxonomy screen appears.
4. Use Table 6-2 to complete the screen shown in Figure 6-13.

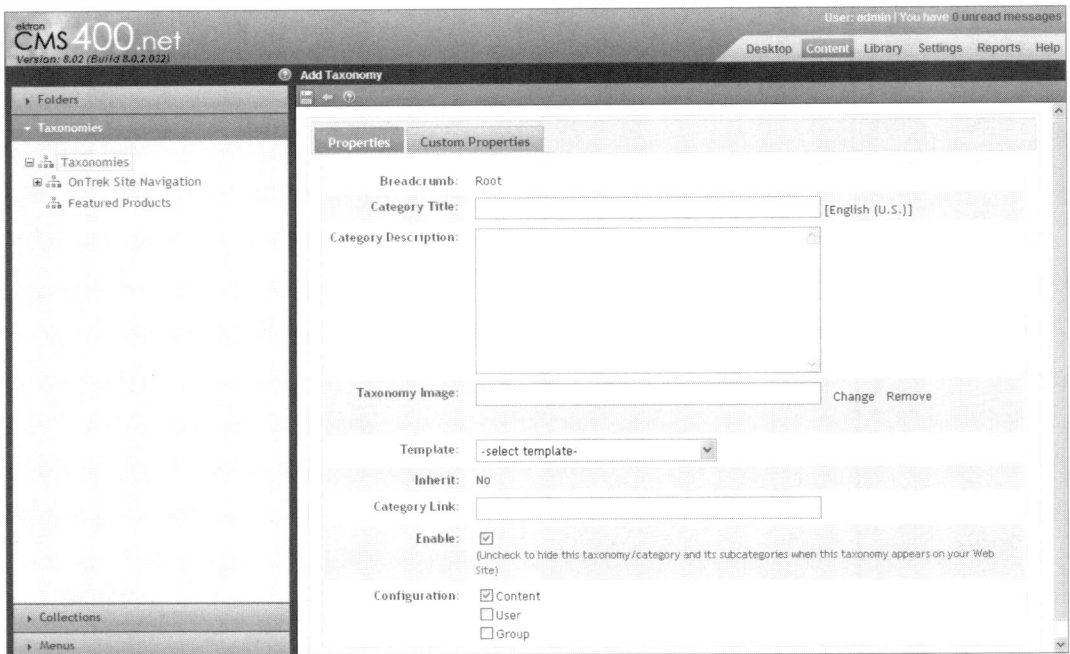

FIGURE 6-13

TABLE 6-2: Taxonomy Field Descriptions

FIELD	DESCRIPTION
Category Title	Give the taxonomy a title. OnTrek uses two taxonomies, **OnTrek Site Navigation** and **Featured Products.** You'll create the **OnTrek Site Navigation** taxonomy here, so type that title in this field.
Category Description	A description appears on the Edit Taxonomy screen and is also available when programmatically accessing taxonomies through the API. Populating this field is optional.

FIELD	DESCRIPTION
Taxonomy Image	Populating this field is optional for OnTrek. In general, however, you can assign an image to a taxonomy and access this data through the API to display a taxonomy image. See the section "Under the Hood" for a code sample.
Template	You'll not populate this field for OnTrek. If specified, the template provided here will be used by taxonomy-oriented controls such as the Directory Server Control for its links rather than the one normally associated with the content item. The value provided here is also made available through the taxonomy API. OnTrek uses the default links associated with the content item.
Inherit (only appears when creating a category underneath a taxonomy)	Select this checkbox. Doing so indicates that you want this category to inherit its template from the parent category or taxonomy. **Category Link:** When the taxonomy node is displayed in a directory control, this will render the node as a link to another page. If left blank, the directory will update to show the contents of the node on the same page.
Enable	Select this checkbox. Doing so indicates that you want this category and its subcategories to appear when this taxonomy appears on your website. In the future, you can use this field to block certain categories from appearing as part of this taxonomy.
Configuration	A taxonomy can be associated with content, users, or groups. The "OnTrek Site Navigation" taxonomy is a Content taxonomy, so select that item here.

5. At this point, you have a taxonomy with no categories defined. To add categories to this new taxonomy, click the Add Category button and populate the fields following the same process outlined in Table 6-2. You can model your categories after the hierarchy defined in the OnTrek website.

Assigning a Taxonomy Configuration to a Folder

To allow content authors to categorize content while it is being authored, you must first assign a taxonomy to a folder. To do this, follow these steps.

1. Navigate to the root OnTrek folder by clicking Content ⇨ Folders.
2. Choose View ⇨ Properties and click Edit.
3. On the Taxonomies tab, select the OnTrek Site Navigation taxonomy. This will make this particular taxonomy available to content authors creating content in all subfolders of this root folder.

Assigning Content to a Taxonomy/Category

The OnTrek website uses the OnTrek Site Navigation taxonomy to classify content as types of "Knowledge Base Articles" and "Job Postings." The Ektron Framework allows content authors to categorize content items like these by associating it with one or more taxonomy categories. There are two ways to assign content to a taxonomy.

The first way is by associating a content item to a taxonomy category by way of the content item. To make this association:

1. Navigate to a content block.
2. Click the Category tab.
3. Expand the taxonomy to locate the desired category.
4. Select the appropriate categories by clicking the checkbox next to the category name.

The second way is by associating content to a taxonomy category by way of a specific category. To do this, navigate to the Workarea ⇨ Content ⇨ Taxonomies and then:

1. Select the language of the taxonomy.
2. Select the category to which you want to associate content.
3. Click the "Assign Item(s) to the Taxonomy" icon in the toolbar, or alternatively, right-click the category and choose "Assign Item(s)" from the context menu.
4. Navigate to the content item to which you want to associate a category.
5. Select the checkbox next to all content items you want to associate.
6. Click the Update icon to finish.

Additionally, in situations where you have a number of content items to categorize, selecting Assign Folder(s) from the context menu allows you to categorize all content in a selected folder in one fell swoop. Note, however, that this does not assign a taxonomy configuration to the folder — it simply creates an association between all content in that folder to the selected taxonomy category.

Under the Hood

The Taxonomy data object is stored in the system as a hierarchical structure in the content_taxonomy_tbl. A Taxonomy ID can be considered a Category ID and the two are essentially the same. In some cases you work with a control that asks you to define a Taxonomy ID, and in other situations, a Category ID. You can use these IDs from the taxonomy_tbl interchangeably. The following snippet shows how to retrieve a taxonomy tree structure using the Content API and its TaxonomyRequest object.

```
Ektron.Cms.TaxonomyRequest taxonomyRequest =
   new Ektron.Cms.TaxonomyRequest();
taxonomyRequest.TaxonomyId = id;
taxonomyRequest.TaxonomyType =
   Ektron.Cms.Common.EkEnumeration.TaxonomyType.Content;
taxonomyRequest.IncludeItems = true;
taxonomyRequest.Depth = 2;
taxonomyRequest.TaxonomyLanguage = contentAPI.ContentLanguage;

Ektron.Cms.API.Content.Taxonomy taxonomyManager =
```

```
            new Ektron.Cms.API.Content.Taxonomy();
        TaxonomyData taxData = taxonomyManager.LoadTaxonomy(taxonomyRequest);
```

You can also use the API to retrieve and render additional information, such as the Taxonomy Image mentioned in Table 6-2, by referencing the `TaxonomyImage` property of the `TaxonomyData` object. The following snippet displays all images assigned to a taxonomy node by recursively calling the *ShowTaxonomyImages* method.

```
            protected void ShowTaxonomyImages(long id)
            {
                Ektron.Cms.ContentAPI contentAPI = new Ektron.Cms.ContentAPI();

                Ektron.Cms.TaxonomyRequest taxonomyRequest =
                   new Ektron.Cms.TaxonomyRequest();
                taxonomyRequest.TaxonomyId = id;
                taxonomyRequest.TaxonomyType =
                   Ektron.Cms.Common.EkEnumeration.TaxonomyType.Content;
                taxonomyRequest.IncludeItems = true;
                taxonomyRequest.Depth = 2
                taxonomyRequest.TaxonomyLanguage = contentAPI.ContentLanguage;

                Ektron.Cms.API.Content.Taxonomy taxonomyManager =
                    new Ektron.Cms.API.Content.Taxonomy();
                TaxonomyData taxData =
                   taxonomyManager.LoadTaxonomy(taxonomyRequest);

                if (null != taxData)
                {
                  // render each taxonomy nodes' image
                  if (!String.IsNullOrEmpty(taxData.TaxonomyImage))
                  {
                      string imagepath = contentAPI.SitePath + taxData.TaxonomyImage;
                      literal1.Text  = "<div>image: " + imagepath + "</div>";
                      literal1.Text += "<div> ID: " + taxData.TaxonomyId + "</div>";
literal1.Text += "<div> Title: " + taxData.TaxonomyName + "</div>";
                  }

                  // if child taxonomies exist, call recursively
                  if (null != taxData.Taxonomy)
                  {
                      for (long i = 0; i < taxData.Taxonomy.Length; i++)
                      {
                          ShowTaxonomyImages(taxData.Taxonomy[i].TaxonomyId);
                      }
                  }
                }
            }
```

Taxonomy is used in many ways throughout Ektron. For an additional look at how taxonomy is used see the Under the Hood section of "Users, Friends, Profiles" in Chapter 10, which covers how the Community Framework uses the taxonomy for managing social relationships between users, groups, and content.

ALIASING

URL aliasing, also referred to as URL mapping, URL redirection, or URL rewriting, is the process of modifying a URL's appearance to be more easily understood by both humans and computers (like search engines). Although a developer would recognize the URL `http://localhost/default.aspx?pageid=231&compid=832&userid=912&q=profile&cat=root` to be syntactically valid, even a skilled developer would need to closely examine each parameter and its value to guess the page's function. For someone other than a developer, it's practically meaningless. Contrast this with the following aliased URL, `http://localhost/users/gsmith`, which can be immediately identified as a profile page by developers and non-technical folks alike. The aliased URL uses meaningful terms to describe the resource, instead of exposing the applications raw query string parameters and values.

Unfriendly URLs, like the first one shown previously, present three fundamental problems:

➤ **The URLs introduce usability issues for humans:** Consider the frequency in which URLs are read, recited, and exchanged in print and electronic communications. Beyond being difficult to read, they often cause technical problems when they're copied into e-mail or text messages and can result in broken hyperlinks spanning multiple lines.

➤ **File extensions come and go:** You especially see this if you look over the past 10 years of Microsoft Web applications. In the early days, content was frequently served as static HTML and the .htm extension was commonplace, which gave way to dynamically generated ASP pages using an .asp extension, which faded as ASP.NET replaced it with its .aspx extension. Suffice it to say, application frameworks will come and go, and your URLs should be technology agnostic. They should not reflect the technology used to build it.

➤ **URL aliasing is fundamental to a sound SEO strategy.** This is the most important thing to remember! Creating human-readable keyword-rich URLs optimizes a search engine's ability to rank and categorize your website, which improves the ability for search engine users to find your content.

Ektron's URL aliasing makes is possible for content contributors to create and manage a site's URL structure. Back when websites were created and content was managed exclusively by IT folks, content editors and marketers had little direct control over the site's information architecture exposed through its URLs. The Ektron Framework makes it very straightforward for any contributor, when granted the proper roles, to create and manage human readable and SEO friendly URLs, either through an automatic or manual process.

Getting started with URL aliasing involves enabling and configuring the feature, and then creating and managing aliases. URL aliases can be generated in a number of ways, but in general, they fall into three categories:

➤ **Automatically created:** Uses the structure of a taxonomy or folder tree

➤ **Manually created:** Created and managed by content authors

➤ **Dynamically generated:** Uses regular expressions or the name of a user or community group

Taxonomy Based Aliasing

Taxonomy based URL aliasing uses the site's information architecture defined by a taxonomy to create URLs that follow the same structure. This is a nice feature, as aliases can be automatically created based on a taxonomy that is already in use. Taxonomy aliases use the nodes of the taxonomy tree plus the title of the content to create a URL. A URL alias for a content item titled "George Washington" categorized within the taxonomy of United States politicians might be:

    http://www.example.com/executive-branch/president/george-washington/

Since content can be associated with multiple categories, this means there might be more than one alias for your content. For example, the content item titled Ronald Reagan might be categorized as a president within a taxonomy of United States politicians, as well as an actor within a taxonomy of movie actors. Enabling taxonomy aliasing for multiple taxonomies may be useful for finding information, but might have unwanted implications from an SEO perspective, as search engines such as Google often reduce the rank of a page when the same content appears on multiple pages.

Folder Based Aliasing

Folder based URL aliasing is similar to taxonomy aliasing, with the difference that folder aliases use the folder structure of the content tree to derive their URL aliases. Folder aliasing is useful when you have a meaningful and logical structure to your content tree and want to expose content using this folder structure. One specific use for folder aliases is on an Intranet where content is organized into separate folders by company department, so folder aliasing would create meaningful URLs for corporate documents such as

    http://intranet/departments/engineering/products/v1/specs/

RegEx Based Aliasing

RegEx based URL aliasing is useful when your website contains URLs that follow a certain predictable pattern, such as the URLs for blog posts. Typically such URLs follow a pattern like

    http://www.example.com/my-blog/2001/12/31/my-blog-post/

When RegEx aliasing is enabled, the Ektron Framework will try to match requested URLs with those patterns defined in the RegEx alias settings.

Community Aliasing

Community aliasing lets you assign an alias for community groups or users (Chapter 11, "Community Groups") so that a site visitor can enter a simple URL to find them. For example, if John wants to make a URL for a community group called Marketing, he sets the Community alias so that a friendly URL such as

    http://www.example.com/Marketing/

can be used to find the group.

Manual Aliasing

Manual aliasing offers content editors tight control over URL aliases assigned to content items. Manual aliasing is useful when a URL falls outside of the patterns defined by the other types of aliasing, such as when you need to include optional tracking parameters for marketing campaigns. Manual aliases are defined in the content editing screen's Alias Tab depicted in Figure 6-14, or in the Manual Aliasing Settings in the URL Aliasing Settings screen in the Workarea.

Implementation

The OnTrek website uses both manual and automatic aliasing. This implementation section walks through the process of enabling, configuring, and defining aliases.

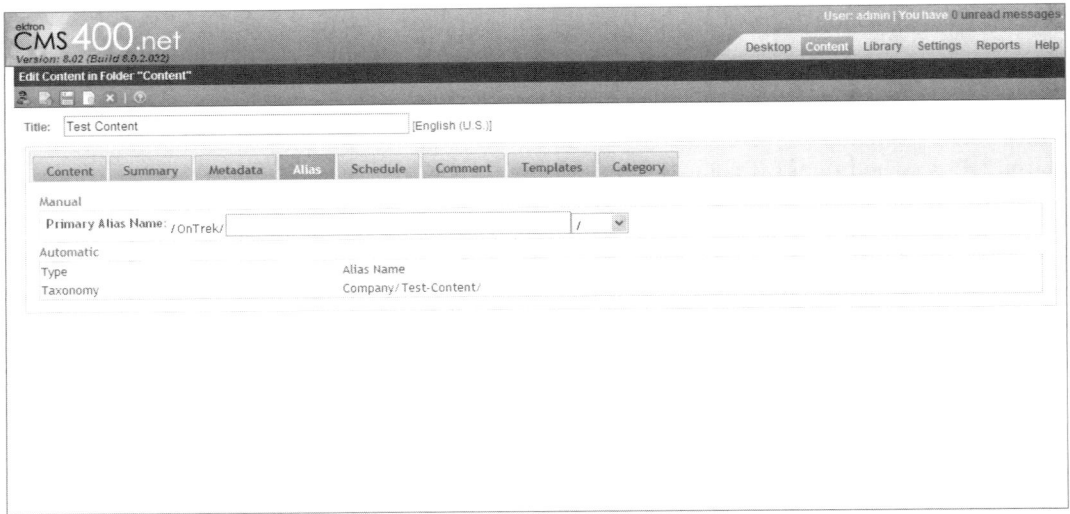

FIGURE 6-14

Enabling URL Aliasing

Only an administrator or a CMS user that has the role of URL Aliasing Administrator can enable and configure this feature. Once this role has been granted, you will have access to the URL Alias settings screen, shown in Figure 6-15, in the Workarea. To enable URL aliasing, first decide which of the types you want to use.

The OnTrek website uses all four types of aliasing (RegEx, Automatic, Manual, and Community). To enable all four of these, do the following.

1. Go to Workarea ⇨ Settings ⇨ Configuration ⇨ URL Aliasing ⇨ Settings.
2. Click the Edit icon.

3. Select the checkboxes in the Enabled column next to the Manual, Automatic, Community, and RegEx Labels.

4. Click the Save icon.

On this screen, as shown in Figure 6-15, you have the ability to enable and configure settings for each of the four types of aliases shown (Manual, Automatic, RegEx, and Community).

To configure any of these options, click the Edit icon. From this screen you can define what types of pages can be aliases by listing their extension types in the Extension field, with each extension separated by a comma. A default configuration will have both .aspx and the forward slash.

In cases where you've defined a URL alias, such as /default.aspx, that conflicts with the path of an ASPX template that exists on the file system (e.g. c:\inetpub\wwwroot\default.aspx), you can use the Override Template checkbox to define whether the URL alias will be used. Checking this checkbox tells the system to use the URL alias in place of the physical ASPX template.

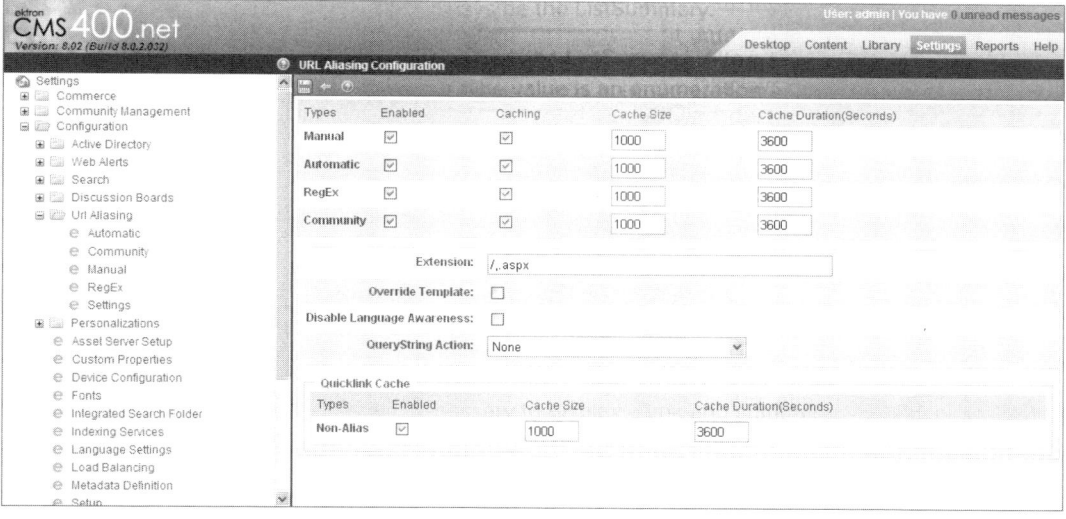

FIGURE 6-15

The Disable Language Awareness property defines what happens when a visitor browses to content using an alias and the site visitor changes the language of the site. In cases where this is checked (enabled), content in the newly selected language appears. Otherwise, when unchecked, the site visitor receives a 404 File Not Found message.

The Query String Action property defines a rule to handle query string parameters appended to an aliased URL. Be careful to note that these rules apply to the aliased URL, not the target of the alias. There are four possible rules each described in Table 6-3.

If a query string parameter is appended to an alias ...

TABLE 6-3: URL Aliasing Parameter Resolution Logic

AND THE SELECTED RULE IS...	THEN ...
None	The appended query string parameter is ignored.
Resolve Matched Parameters within Alias	The Ektron Framework checks if the appended parameter is already defined in the target URL. If so, the alias' query string parameter takes precedence. For example: **Target**: `http://www.OnTrek.com/contact.aspx?id=84&cat=user` **Alias**: `http://www.OnTrek.com/user/jsmith?id=100` **Result**: `http://www.OnTrek.com/contact.aspx?id=100&cat=user` Note the result here: The final URL has been updated with the new ID.
Replace All Parameters within Alias	The Ektron Framework checks if the appended parameter is already defined in the target URL. If so, the target URL's query string parameters are replaced with the alias' query string parameter values. For example: **Target**: `http://www.OnTrek.com/contact.aspx?id=84&cat=user` **Alias**: `http://www.OnTrek.com/user/jsmith?id=100` **Result**: `http://www.OnTrek.com/contact.aspx?id=100` Note the result here: The query string parameters on the target URL have been replaced by those appended to the aliased URL.
Append Parameters to Alias	The Ektron Framework will take all query string parameters added to the aliased URL and append them to the target URL. **Target**: `http://www.OnTrek.com/contact.aspx?id=84&cat=user` **Alias**: `http://www.OnTrek.com/user/jsmith?id=100` **Result**: `http://www.OnTrek.com/contact.aspx?id=84&cat=user&id=100` Note the result here: The query string parameters on the aliased URL are appended to those defined in the target URL.

Configuring Taxonomy-Based URL Aliasing

Follow these steps to configure automatic aliasing using a taxonomy:

1. Go to Workarea ⇨ Settings ⇨ Configuration ⇨ URL Aliasing ⇨ Automatic to bring up the page shown in Figure 6-16.
2. Click the Add a New Alias icon .

3. Select Source Type of Taxonomy from the pull-down menu.
4. To define the Alias Root, click the Select button and choose the root element of the OnTrek Site Navigation taxonomy.
5. For the Alias Format, choose ContentTitle.
6. For the Extension, choose the forward slash (/).
7. For the remaining values, select the default values provided.
8. Click the Save icon to save the configuration.

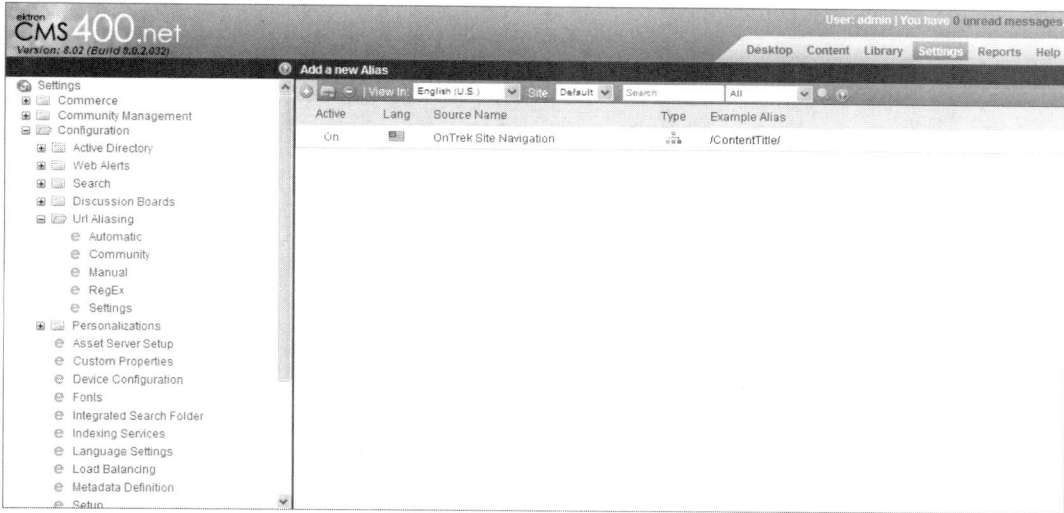

FIGURE 6-16

Under the Hood

Because aliasing provides a level of indirection between the friendly URL and the actual target URL, any performance-minded developer might be concerned with the perceived overhead of this additional lookup occurring with every page request. Ektron has designed its URL aliasing engine with these concerns in mind and has implemented an aliasing-caching engine that mitigates the potential performance hit. The caching engine stores static objects in a list container in application memory and holds those data objects for the duration of time, or Time To Live (TTL), specified on the Workarea ⇨ Settings ⇨ Configuration ⇨ URL Aliasing ⇨ Settings screen. When caching is enabled, the cache is checked for every request to the system. If there is a cache miss, the database is accessed to retrieve the appropriate target URL for the alias and is then stored in the cache. If there is a cache hit, the system returns with the cached URL. A cache hit with an expired TTL is considered a cache miss.

A powerful feature provided by Ektron's URL aliasing is its *RegEx aliasing engine*. As described earlier, this is a particularly useful feature when you need to define URLs that follow a certain predictable pattern, such as the URLs for blog posts. The system comes preconfigured with aliases to match common patterns. You can see the available expressions through the Expression Library, which is accessible through the Add a Regular Expression screen. To access this screen and define a RegEx alias pattern:

1. Go to the Workarea ➪ Settings ➪ URL Aliasing ➪ RegEx.
2. Click the Add a Regular Expression screen, as shown in Figure 6-17.
3. In the Expression Name text field, enter **Blog Post Aliases**.
4. Click Expression Library button to launch the Expression Library dialog box, shown in Figure 6-18.
5. Click the second item in the list.

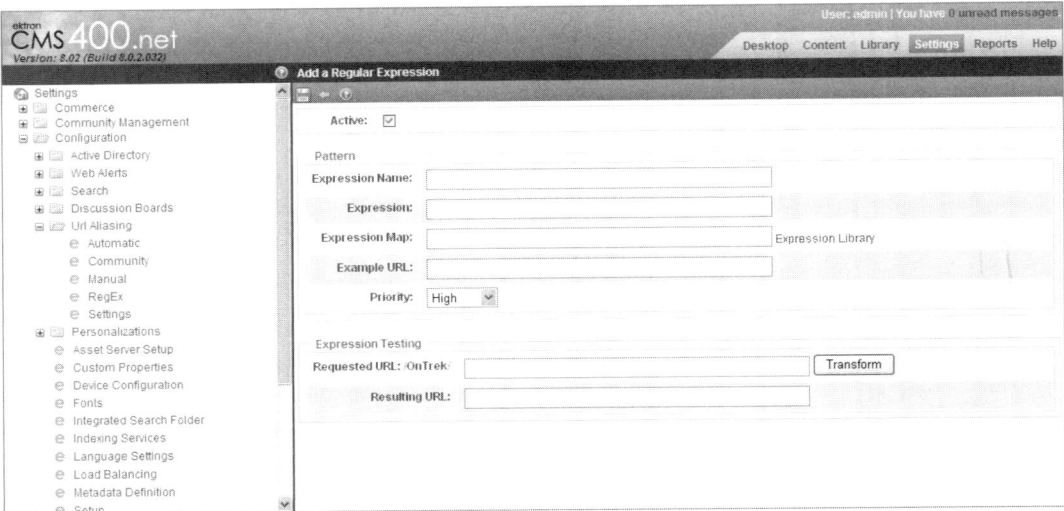

FIGURE 6-17

With this configured, now you have a URL that matches the pattern commonly found in URLs for blog posts, which includes a four digit number representing the year, followed by a two digit number representing the month, (e.g. /2011/01/default.aspx). This URL maps to /pagename.aspx, and passes along the year and month to it as query string parameters. These parameters can be used within your application to retrieve all posts that have been created during that particular month and year.

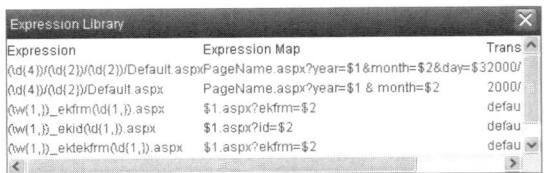

FIGURE 6-18

MULTILINGUAL SITES

The Ektron Framework makes it possible for Web developers to create fully localized versions of websites offering language specific editions to visitors based on their language preferences. It also provides content authors with the tools to manually author content in multiple languages, instantly translate text between many langua[...] export content to a professional translation company.

The requirements for the OnTrek w[...] on the website must be available in both Spanish and Engli[...] mation architecture, navigation, and page layout. This is amon[...] ite requirements. The architectural considerations and best pra[...] implementing this approach are described in this section.

Designing an Ektron Multilingual Website

Creating a successful multilingual website requires special consideration at each step of the website design process. Graphic designers need to consider how their websites will render and behave in foreign languages. A Web designer who speaks English, for example, might not consider what their design looks like when rendering German text, which contains words that are typically 30 percent longer than those in English. This increase in average word size can affect how things such as menus, text, and images are positioned in potentially unexpected ways. Ektron recommends that the targeted languages are defined as soon as possible in the discovery process, thereby allowing designers time to consider these languages in their designs.

When designing the information architecture of the site, it is essential to understand how Ektron has designed its multilingual capabilities, as it should influence the approach you take in organizing your content folder tree. You need to understand how Ektron manages the relationship between each content item and each *edition*, or translated version of the content item. As you have already learned, each content item has a number of properties, including a content ID and language ID. Each edition has its own language specific properties, such as title and history. The unique identifier for a specific edition of content is represented by a compound key { Content ID, Language ID }.

To understand this better, let's look at an example directly querying Ektron's primary content table, content_tbl. Figure 6-19 shows a query that selects content that has a Content ID of 84. The query returns two records because this content has two editions available, English and Spanish. Translating content will never change the content ID, but other properties, such as title, are unique for that specific edition of content and may change according to the language.

Also notice in Figure 6-19 that the folder_id is the same for both editions. This is because translated content is automatically placed into the same folder as the original source content. Although the folder ID for an edition *can* change, meaning a specific edition can exist in a folder separate from the original source content (for example, when a specific edition is moved from one folder to another through the Workarea interface), it is highly recommended that each edition remain in the same folder. Just as you typically create folders for related documents but don't create separate folders for document types (an Excel folder, Word folder), the folder tree structure should not map to language-specific editions of content.

Ektron's multisite feature creates a unique folder for managing the content for each site. Therefore, it is not a best practice to use multisite to create separate sites for each language. Instead, manage each subsequent language edition of a given site in the same folder as the original language for that edition.

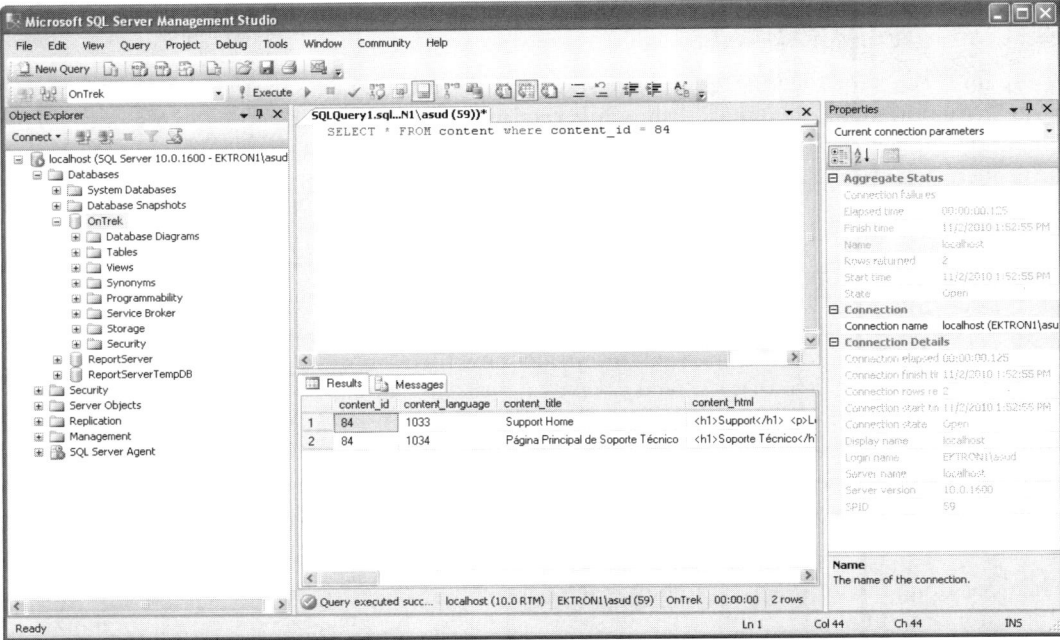

FIGURE 6-19

Although the OnTrek site does not use the content approval process, it is worth highlighting that you can use the content approval process to create language-specific approval processes. Individuals designated to approve content will most likely differ for each language and this feature allows for separate approval chains for each edition of a content item. Chapter 5 has more information on configuring approval chains.

When the information architecture of your site differs from the organization of the content in the folder tree, you can use taxonomies as described in the "Taxonomy" section of this chapter. Because taxonomies are language aware, you can use them to control the rendering of the site in a way that differs from its location in the content folder tree. This gives you the ability to create and organize different multilingual hierarchies and provide different categorization structures, navigation aids, and site maps for each language.

As a Web developer creating a multilingual website, you'll need to look at content a little bit differently, primarily because the content that appears on a Web page may actually originate from any one of a number of sources. Consider the various sources for content on a Web page: There is text that is embedded directly into ASPX templates, codebehind, and JavaScript. There is also managed content — that is, content stored and managed within the Ektron Framework. Lastly, there is content that originates from external data sources, such as syndication feeds and third-party Web services.

The Ektron Framework handles and simplifies the process of displaying localized editions of content. Its server controls, widgets, and APIs retrieve the proper edition of the content based on the current locale of the site, typically defined either by the site visitor or overridden by setting the language ID through the API or server control properties. Any text requiring localization on your website that falls outside of Ektron requires leveraging standard .NET localization strategies. This typically consists of two activities:

➤ Managing text that would otherwise be directly embedded in buttons or labels in localized XML files (files with a *.RESX extension).

➤ Using .NET localization APIs for retrieving and displaying the language appropriate text from these files in your application.

> *The process of localizing non-managed content is beyond the scope of this book. There are many resources available online on this topic. The Microsoft Developer Network (MSDN) has good documentation on .NET Localization APIs and the tools available for managing these *.RESX resource files. See* `http://msdn.microsoft.com/en-us/magazine/cc163609.aspx`.

Content authors use Ektron to create language-specific editions of content in one of the following three ways:

➤ **Manual translation:** This is great to use in situations where editors are translating a small amount of content, under a dozen content items or so. This is performed by CMS users and is performed through the content editing interface of the Workarea. Content authors can use the editor's multilingual spell checking capabilities to check for misspelled words in a number of languages. By default, the spell checker refers to the dictionary for the target language. For example, if the content is U.S. English, the U.S. English dictionary is referenced. If the spell checker does not have a dictionary that matches the target content language, it attempts to find related dictionaries. If unsuccessful, it defaults to U.S. English. The spell checker also supports custom language dictionaries and the Ektron reference manual covers the steps needed to define and register one.

> *As stated, manual translation is ideal for small amounts of content. In cases where more content must be translated, the best practice recommendation is to use the language export feature described later.*

➤ **Machine translation:** Refers to the process of using language translation algorithms to translate text. Websites such as Babelfish (`http://babelfish.yahoo.com/`) and Google Translate (`http://translate.google.com/`), as well as the slew of translation plug-ins for Web browsers such as Firefox, have made the use of machine translation fairly commonplace. As such, people have become aware of technology's inability to produce translations that compare to those crafted by professional translators. In spite of their reputation for producing less than perfect translations, machine translation technology is improving and might prove useful in the following scenarios.

➤ You have discussion board posts that are authored in one language but are relevant to a wider, global audience. These posts are informal by nature, written by the public, and are time-sensitive, yet are often too copious to warrant spending time and money to translate.

➤ You have no budget for professional quality translations and don't mind presenting a possibly imperfect translation (and potentially offending your readers).

➤ The translation is needed immediately and can't wait for professional translation.

In cases such as these, you can use Ektron's machine translation to translate content through its Workarea interface in Figure 6-20. The process for translating content using machine translation follows the same process for manually translating content, with the exception that you click the Translate Content icon rather than translate it manually.

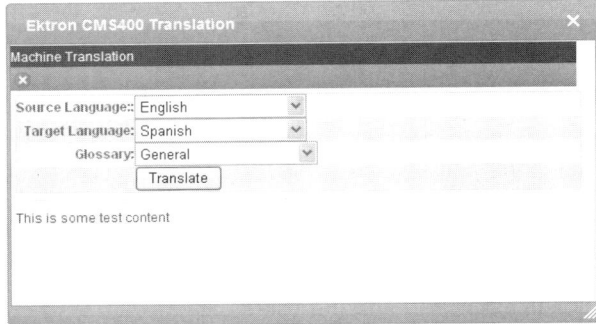

FIGURE 6-20

➤ **Language export:** This is Ektron's recommended process of translating content. Language export uses XLIFF, an XML format, to simplify and standardize data exchange between translation companies and content providers. Ektron has been an early adopter of the XLIFF standard and has received recognition for its localization capabilities. Through the Workarea interface, content editors mark items for translation, and then export these items in bulk to submit to a translation company. The export process copies the content marked for translation into XML documents following the XLIFF structure, and then compresses them into a ZIP file. The translation company takes the compressed file, translates the content, and then returns a translated version for importing into Ektron.

Even if you are not using a translation company, it will most likely benefit your organization to use the language export feature instead of the manual translation process. This can help you to avoid accidentally missed translating elements, especially non-visible elements such as ALT attributes. The text from attributes like the ALT marker on an IMG tag is included in XLIFF documents, automatically marking them as phrases requiring translation. Another benefit is that XLIFF-compatible translation tools often employ the use of translation memory, which remembers how phrases have been previously translated, saving time and creating a more efficient translation process.

Ektron recommends using the following tools for translating content using its language export feature.

➤ **SDL Trados** (http://www.trados.com/en/): The industry standard application most commonly used by professional translation companies.

➤ **Heartsome Translation Studio** (http://heartsome.net/EN/home.html): Costs much less than SDL Trados and still provides many time- and money-saving features like translation memory.

Managing the Displayed Content Language

The Ektron Framework provides a number of ways to control which content language to display to a site visitor. With the LanguageSelect Server Control placed on a page, site visitors see the dropdown menu shown in Figure 6-21. It contains the languages that are enabled on the site so visitors just manually select the language for the site.

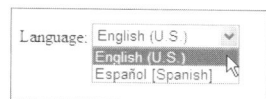

FIGURE 6-21

When you want to force users to view a site in a particular language, you can use the LanguageAPI Server Control or the language APIs directly to achieve this. Doing so is often useful in situations where you are using the following:

➤ **Top Level Domain (TLD):** This determines the country code and site language. For example, if your site is accessible through the TLD .it (Italy), you might want to set the default language to Italian.

➤ **IP address location services:** This provides another way to determine the location of the site visitor. There are many services available online that can translate a visitor's IP address into a physical location, including their country.

➤ **The browser's locale:** This is an effective way to determine the browsers preferred language as `string language = Request.ServerVariables("HTTP_ACCEPT_LANGUAGE");` this value can then be parsed and used to force the site to display the appropriate language.

➤ **A custom user interface for selecting languages:** An example of such an interface is one that displays a list of flags representing the languages spoken by those countries. Site visitors can click on a flag to select a language.

You can use the LanguageAPI Server Control in either of these situations. For example, the following code looks at the hostname used to access the website and sets the site language accordingly. Note the single line that sets the site language — you can find this on the last line of the *SetSiteLanguage* method. The remainder of the code extracts the Top Level Domain from the URL. With the LanguageAPI Server Control on the page, you can then do the following:

```
public void SetSiteLanguage(string url)
{
    string tld = ExtractTLD(url);
    int lang = 1033; // default english
    switch( tld )
    {
        case "it":
            lang = 1040; //Italian
            break;
        case "es":
```

```
            case "mx":
                lang = 1034; //Spanish
            default:
                lang = 1033; //default English
        }

        // Use the LanguageAPI Server Control to set the Language
        LanguageApi1.SiteLanguageID = lang;
}
    protected string ExtractTLD(string url)
    {
        string topLevelDomain = String.Empty;
        string host = ExtractHost(url);
        string[] tld = host.Split('.');
        if (tld.Length > 0)
        {
            topLevelDomain = tld[tld.Length-1];
        }

        return topLevelDomain;
    }

    protected string ExtractHost(string url)
    {
        string domain = String.Empty;
        Regex rg = new Regex(@"http://([a-z\.]+)",RegexOptions.IgnoreCase);

        if (rg.IsMatch(url))
        {
            domain = rg.Match(url).Result("${1}");
        }

        return domain;
    }
```

Implementation

As covered earlier in this chapter, there are many issues to consider when designing and creating a multilingual website. The implementation process should follow the steps outlined in the Ektron reference manual (see the section "Setting Up a Multilingual Web Site"), which are:

- Enabling support for multiple language content
- Setting the default language
- Enabling languages your site will support
- Adding the language selection function to templates
- Creating metadata definitions for each supported language *
- Setting up approval chains for multilingual content *
- Setting up multilingual menus, collections, and taxonomies*

> *The * steps are not covered in this book as the OnTrek website's configuration does not require them. However, if your site configuration does require them, see Chapter 14 of the Ektron reference manual.*

Enabling Support for Multiple Language Content

To enable support for multiple language content, follow these steps:

1. Open the web.config file in a text editor.
2. Locate the ek_EnableMultilingual key and set it to 1 to enable this feature. To disable this feature entirely throughout the site, set it to 0. Disabling the feature after multilingual content has been created does not delete any of this content from the repository, but it removes it from displaying on the website. For the OnTrek website, you'll need to set this to 1.
3. Save the web.config file (but keep it open if you need to set the default language in the following steps).

Setting the Default Language

By setting the default language, you are defining which edition of content will display when the site visitor has not specified a language, and when one has not been set programmatically through the API or server controls.

To set the default language for your multi-language website:

1. Open the web.config file in a text editor.
2. Set the value of ek_DefaultContentLanguage to the locale ID of the default language. For example, the locale ID for Spanish is 1034. For a list of locale IDs, go to the Workarea ⇨ Settings ⇨ Configuration ⇨ Language Settings screen. For the OnTrek website, let's set this to English, 1033.
3. Save the web.config file.

Enabling Languages Your Site Will Support

To determine or configure which languages are available for creating content, see the Workarea's Language Settings screens.

1. Go to Workarea ⇨ Settings ⇨ Configuration ⇨ Language Settings to display the Language Settings page shown in Figure 6-22.
2. Click the Edit button to edit the Language Settings.
3. Each language has two checkboxes. To enable a language in the Workarea, select the checkbox in the column with the yellow yield sign .

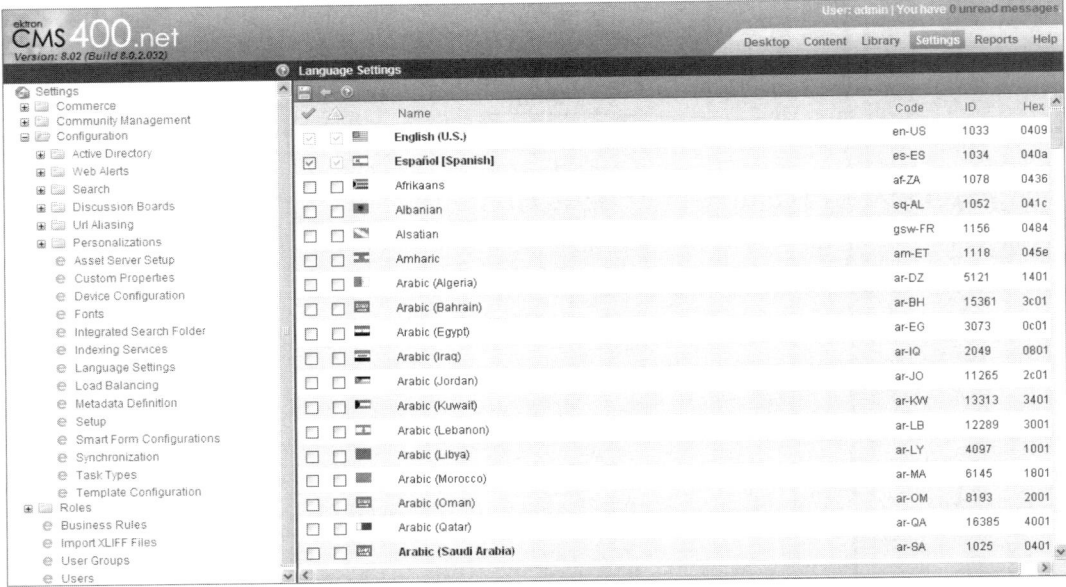

FIGURE 6-22

Checking this column populates the language dropdown menus in the Workarea so content editors can create content in this language.

4. Once the content has been translated and is ready to display on the website, select the checkbox under the column headed with a green checkmark .

For the OnTrek website, since you'll have English and Spanish available in the Workarea and the website, you should have both checkboxes enabled next to those languages.

Under the Hood

It's worth pointing out that the Local Identifier values used by Ektron are the same that are defined and used by Microsoft, available in this Technical Reference on the MSDN: `http://msdn.microsoft.com/en-us/goglobal/bb964664.aspx`. In this list you can see that Local Identifier 1033 is English, and 1034 is Spanish.

The Ektron reference manual contains a chapter dedicated to discussing working with multilingual content. As mentioned earlier, this book covers the most common configuration and the one used by the OnTrek website. The Ektron reference manual covers other configurations, such as a configuration where your site has only one language and that language is something other than U.S. English as the default.

TAKE HOME POINTS

This chapter built upon the content-management fundamentals outlined in Chapter 5 by discussing the components found commonly on Ektron powered websites. These components are used so frequently because they address the basic needs and requirements of most websites, namely, structured content authoring, content categorization, URL naming, and multilingual content rendering:

- **Ektron Smart Form technology:** Provides information architects and developers with the ability to create Smart Form Designs to define structured data types using a WYSIWYG form designer. The Smart Form Designs are used by content editors to create Smart Form data which is stored in the system as XML and is available to developers through APIs, server controls, and widgets. These offer a number of ways of retrieving, manipulating, and rendering this information, such as through using .NET data binding or XSLT transformations.

- **Taxonomy:** Helps your site visitors find content using a navigation structure that is familiar to them. Content authors create content and categorize it into the taxonomical structures defined by information architects, allowing developers to retrieve that information by category using the Directory Server Control and the Taxonomy APIs.

- **URL aliasing:** Allows for rewriting URLs to be more easily understood by humans and machines such as search engines. With the Ektron Framework, you can create URL aliases either manually or automatically by leveraging the structure of your folder structure and taxonomies or through patterns defined as regular expressions.

- **Localization capabilities:** It is often a requirement that an organization's website be available in multiple languages. With Ektron's localization capabilities, the process of translating and delivering content in multiple languages has been greatly simplified. Editors can translate content manually or use its language export feature to send the content to a translation house.

The Homepage

> ➤ How do you use JavaScript and Smart Forms to build rich interfaces?
> ➤ How do you navigate using menus?
> ➤ How do you use search to navigate?
> ➤ How do you increase discoverability using breadcrumbs and sitemaps?
> ➤ What do you do to allow users to register with your site?

With all the emphasis on campaign landing pages, micro sites, and search engine friendly interior content pages, it is reasonable to ask whether a website's homepage matters much anymore. Although the homepage is often the most visited page on a website, its importance has been overshadowed by the increased focus on lead generation by marketing groups. But lead generation is not the only purpose for a website. Other major objectives mentioned by marketing managers include supporting branding initiatives, creating a positive image for the company and its products, building awareness of the organization, and distributing product and company information to existing and potential customers. The homepage plays an extremely important part in satisfying these objectives — no other page on your site will have such a pivotal and multipurpose role.

This chapter discusses ways to implement a successful homepage by focusing on a number of the most important elements of a homepage. Because the homepage must satisfy the needs of many types of visitors, this chapter focuses on using navigation to guide site visitors in the right direction through the use of menus, sitemaps, breadcrumbs, and search and goes in depth on the technology available through Ektron Framework used to implement them. In addition to navigation, the chapter also focuses on a specific technique for delivering attention-grabbing content that appeals to a wide audience. The technique uses a jQuery plug-in for rotating through images and is a nice way to deliver multiple messages on the homepage without diluting the focus and attention. Lastly, the chapter concludes with a discussion of the registration methods available for membership users, showing the internal registration methods as well as how to integrate Facebook Connect onto your site.

USE CASE

This section introduces the use cases implemented for this chapter. Most of the remaining technical chapters contain such a section. These sections give a discussion a meaningful context in which to understand the technology. Each of these sections contain: a wireframe describing the organization and composition of the page; the actors involved defining the roles and requirements of the site visitor; the scenario, which includes bullet points that capture the expected actions performed by the site visitor; and the outcome, which specifies the success criteria for the scenario in quantifiable terms and is typically tied to Web metrics for measurability.

LAUNCHING THE ONTREK WEBSITE

The OnTrek marketing team is leading the effort to launch the OnTrek website, with careful attention being given to the look, feel, and function of the homepage. The marketing team's objectives for the homepage include: supporting the marketing department's branding initiatives, creating a positive image for the company and its products, and distributing information to existing and potential customers.

Wireframe

The Wireframe is a critical part of the Implementation Guide. In Chapter 2, you learned about the Discovery Phase and the process by which the Implementation Guide and Wireframes are created. Chapter 3 focused exclusively on the Implementation Guide and in this chapter, you learned what a best-practice Implementation Guide includes. For more detail on Wireframes and the Implementation Guide, see those chapters. The Wireframe for the OnTrek homepage is shown in Figure 7-1.

Actor

John is the Director of IT at Acme Inc. and is researching security-related software packages for his company's network. He is specifically looking for information on product functionality, supporting services, and licensing costs. In addition, John is looking for basic information about the company such as the number of years in business and the location of its headquarters.

Scenario

In this scenario, John:

1. Performs a Web search using an online search engine like Google or Bing to find companies that sell security related software packages.
2. Searches and clicks on a result in the results page that takes him to the OnTrek homepage.

3. Arrives on the site with the primary objective being to find product information.
4. Uses the site search and the menu navigation to locate the product info.

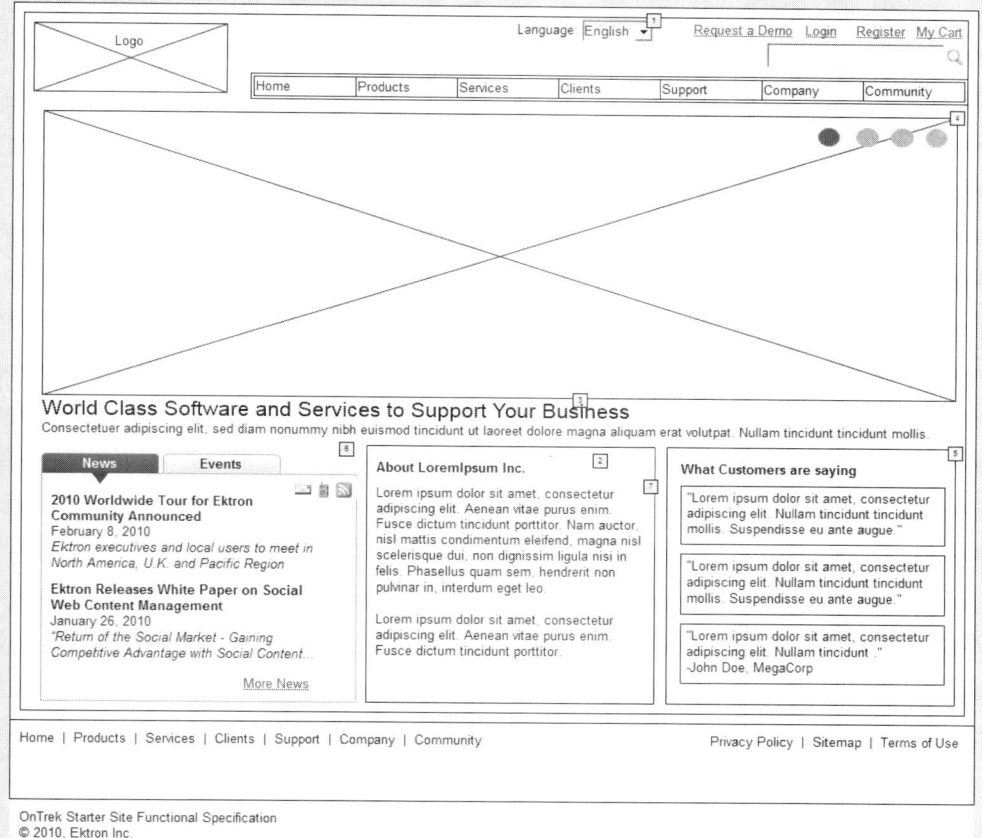

FIGURE 7-1

Outcome

A successful outcome in this use case is one where John visits the homepage and then travels to the product and company information pages. In general, by using Web Analytics (Chapter 9), you can track the abandon rate for the homepage, which is the number of homepage visits that result in no further page views. A high abandon rate implies that people visit the homepage and do not proceed any further. A general metric for success is a low abandon rate for the homepage.

TECHNOLOGY

It is difficult to predict why visitors will come to a homepage. Contrast this with a campaign-landing page, where you know exactly how someone arrived (through a search advertisement or e-mail marketing message) and you know what they're looking for (a particular product or service). In order to adequately address this visitor's needs, the homepage needs to do two apparently competing things:

- ➤ The homepage needs to be general enough so that it is applicable to different users with diverse goals, both in terms of the content presented and the navigation structures available.
- ➤ The homepage needs to deliver specific content and not dilute its message by being all things to all people.

If you add these requirements so that content is consistent with the marketing department's branding efforts, you'll begin to see how designing a persuasive homepage can be challenging.

Using Rotating Graphics

One popular way to present relevant and compelling information to a diverse set of users is through the use of a prominently featured set of *rotating graphics*. This technique also increases the attractiveness of your site and provides an opportunity to display rich and interactive content. In this chapter you'll use the jQuery to create an RIA component for rotating through images promoting OnTrek's products and services. This component will be built using ASP.NET to generate markup, jQuery to render it as a slider, and CSS to style the presentation. Although the implementation uses jQuery, the described approach can be applied to components designed using Silverlight and Flex as well.

Adding Navigation

Another important factor for a successful homepage is *navigation*. The importance of navigation stems from the general purpose nature of the homepage and the need to present site visitors with clear indicators of possible next moves. There are a number of navigation aids that can be used and this chapter focuses on the use of menus, website search, sitemaps, and breadcrumbs. You'll use Ektron Menus to manage the global navigation structure in the Workarea and you'll render these on the page using the Flex Menu Server Control. The implementation shows how you can override the default behavior of the server control to provide tight management over the markup and the presentation using XSLT, CSS, and jQuery.

Using Menu Links and Search

A good menu structure usually only provides links to a subset of the site's overall content. Considering that it's realistic for an average-sized website to have hundreds of pages of content, it makes sense for a navigation structure to provide site visitors with *links* to only the most important and relevant items and not overload them with links to all possible resources. *Search* is a good way to provide access to the remaining items and also give an alternative to menu navigation for those who prefer it. The implementation section discusses how to develop a successful search strategy using Ektron's search technology, including the use of Web Analytics for tracking search terms site visitors use and tweaking results based on that data. The section also covers a deep look into Ektron Search and provides architectural diagrams and code samples showing how to leverage the search architecture.

Adding Navigation Indicators

Providing site visitors with *navigation indicators* that help them understand their current position in the overall information architecture of the website is another critical factor for ensuring a happy visitor and increasing page views. This chapter will show how to implement navigation using Ektron's *Breadcrumb* and *Sitemap* features.

Keep in mind that not all visitors to the homepage are first-time visitors. The homepage is visited by new users and existing membership users alike. It's a good idea to offer membership users the ability to log in directly from the homepage. This chapter also discusses ways to use Ektron's registration functionality, including both its native registration methods as well as its ability to integrate with Facebook Connect.

RICH INTERACTION USING JQUERY, SMART FORMS, AND HANDLERS

Rich Internet Applications, or *RIAs*, have been an important part of Internet design ever since Flash became a commonly used Web element over a decade ago. Today the concept of RIAs has been greatly extended. RIAs have gone from being a replacement for traditional HTML-based development to including the concept of small pieces of rich functionality within a more typical page experience. The collection of technologies has grown from the basic functionality of Flash, to an ecosystem that includes Java, advanced Flash with server side data management, Silverlight, AJAX, and HTML 5. Whether or not you as a developer agree with the development of RIA interfaces as part of a Web experience, it is something that needs to be supported, and Ektron has made sure that there are ways of doing so.

In order to support as many developer use cases as possible, the Ektron approach has always been to supply a rich API in addition to the more typical server controls that are the usual first stop for developers. In addition to the API, there is also a built-in Web service package that is part of the Workarea. This collection of Web services was originally created as part of the Plugin and Extension architecture, but these Web services are also available to RIAs.

Types of Interaction

Solutions for rich client interaction can be logically divided into two areas:

➤ When you want more than just a statically displayed page, but you don't require additional data round trips from the server

➤ When you need to return to the server for more information based on user interaction

These are discussed in more detail in the following sections.

Adding More Than a Static Display

The first group pertains to the original designs of rich interfaces. A typical solution was to create a splash page, which might show a movie or some information before the users moved on to the site itself. This type of interstitial is widely regarded today as detrimental to the usability of the site, and is generally frowned upon.

The group of solutions that don't require additional data from the server today has grown to be more oriented towards producing a richer experience for the visitor. For instance, creating a client side sorted table through the use of JavaScript is a very typical interface requirement. Like many solutions requiring a richer sort of technology, this requirement can be solved through the use of a simple link that informs the server to render the page again with a different sort order. However, the modification to use JavaScript client side eliminates a round trip to the server. That round trip is a very expensive call, both in terms of wait time for the users, as well as in terms of server load, so eliminating the call is very desirable.

Returning to the Server for More Information

The second group of solutions — those that require returning to the server for more information in order to update the page for the users — first became common with the use of AJAX. Microsoft supplies a set of tools dubbed ASP.NET AJAX, which can simplify the development of these requirements through wrapping the calls back to the server in a standard framework that requires nothing of the developer except to wrap the portion of the page to be rendered again in an ASP.NET UpdatePanel Server Control. This solution provides a very simple way for developers to create a lighter feeling Web solution and in many cases is perfectly acceptable. However, using the standard Microsoft AJAX toolkit still requires a full-page lifecycle to occur on the server, even though only the updated portion of the page is returned to the user. This means that of the two downsides to using a standard anchor tag to update the page — the server render time and the client transfer time — only the transfer time is reduced; the server render time remains the same.

The use of Web services, or RESTful services, has increasingly become an accepted method for reducing both the bottlenecks at this point. While this solution is typically more complicated to develop, the decrease in server load can sometimes be a worthwhile reason for this approach. Any of the list of currently popular client side technologies allow for this mode of development. Additionally, ASP.NET makes it very easy to develop a simple Web handler that can respond in any format required.

Examples in This Chapter

This chapter covers two simplified examples to help you understand how best to approach these types of problems. The first example you will explore using the jQuery library to animate the slider on the homepage of the OnTrek website. The example starts by discussing the storage of content specific for the interface, allowing for benefits like localization and easy updating. You will then move onto generating appropriate output for the content to be displayed, and finally create some code to actually render the slider.

The second example is about the creation and consumption of RESTful generic handlers. For this example, you'll create a simple ASHX Web handler that responds to queries with JSON, and the authors will talk about consuming the results through the use of jQuery.

On the homepage of the OnTrek website, there is an image rotator at the top of the page. The images displayed, along with the accompanying text, all come from a settings content item stored in the CMS as Smart Form content based on the Rotating Ad Smart Form definition. You created that definition in the Smart Form section of Chapter 6. In this section, you will explore the following:

➤ Homepage image rotator using serialization

➤ Homepage image rotator using XSLT

➤ Web service creation and consumption

Homepage Image Rotator Using Serialization

In this section, you'll be building the same example, that of the image rotator from the homepage of the OnTrek starter site, in two different forms. The first form, which you'll produce now, uses the same method used in the site itself. You'll use Smart Forms to create the structured content types, and then use existing query methods to render that data. In the next section, you'll build the same example, but with more home-grown code. In most cases, you'll want to follow the approach used in the first case as demonstrated on the OnTrek website, particularly if you're already familiar with jQuery. However, there is almost always more than one way to accomplish a task; it can pay to evaluate each method for the lessons learned.

The OnTrek start site comes prebuilt with a Smart Form definition called *Home Page Banner.*" One of the common uses of Smart Forms is to use them to store settings for rich interface applications as they allow for simple management of XML based options. Since XML is such an open standard across languages and platforms, this allows developers to consume those settings from whatever platform they may be developing on. In addition, using content as the basis for the options means you have the ability to protect the configuration through permissions and have multilingual versions of the settings.

You read about how to use the Microsoft XML Schema Definition Tool in Chapter 6. In this approach, you'll build the class definition from the XSD for the Rotating Ad Smart Form, and then use that to deserialize the settings from the Smart Form settings content item. You will then databind the results into an ASP.NET Repeater Control to convert it to HTML. Once the results are in an HTML format, you will use a jQuery plug-in to render the results into a slider interface.

Follow these steps to create an Image Rotator using Smart Form Serialization, databinding, and jQuery.

1. Make sure your content item, based on the Home Page Banner Smart Form, has been created. Open the Workarea content tab and go to `MainSite/Content/Smart Forms/HomePageBanner`. There should be a content item called HomePageBanner there. If there isn't, create a new piece of content based on the Home Page Banner Smart Form now, and make note of the ID of the newly created piece of content.

2. Retrieve the XSD for the Smart Form and convert it using the Microsoft XML Schema Definition Tool into a serializable data class. Go to Settings ⇨ Configuration ⇨ Smart Form Configuration in the Workarea, and then find the row for the Home Page Banner Smart Form.

3. At this point, you can either retrieve the XSD for the Smart Form through the RESTful service as covered in Chapter 6, or you can enter the Data Designer for the Smart Form, and

find the icon of a document overlaid with XSD. Clicking that icon on the toolbar brings up a modal window that contains the XSD. In either case, put the results into a file called HomePageBanner.xsd in the path c:\. The HomePageBanner.xsd file is shown in Listing 7-1.

LISTING 7-1: HomePageBanner.xsd

```xml
<xs:schema elementFormDefault="qualified"
          attributeFormDefault="unqualified"
          xmlns:xs="http://www.w3.org/2001/XMLSchema">
  <xs:element name="GroupBox">
    <xs:complexType>
      <xs:sequence>
        <xs:element name="SlideSpeed">
          <xs:simpleType>
            <xs:restriction>
              <xs:simpleType>
                <xs:union memberTypes="xs:nonNegativeInteger">
                  <xs:simpleType>
                    <xs:restriction base="xs:string">
                      <xs:length value="0"/>
                    </xs:restriction>
                  </xs:simpleType>
                </xs:union>
              </xs:simpleType>
            </xs:restriction>
          </xs:simpleType>
        </xs:element>
        <xs:element name="Slides" maxOccurs="unbounded">
          <xs:complexType>
            <xs:sequence>
              <xs:element name="Image">
                <xs:complexType>
                  <xs:sequence>
                    <xs:element name="img" type="imgDesignType" minOccurs="0" />
                  </xs:sequence>
                </xs:complexType>
              </xs:element>
              <xs:element name="Title" type="xs:string" />
              <xs:element name="Summary" type="rich" />
              <xs:element name="Link">
                <xs:complexType>
                  <xs:sequence>
                    <xs:element name="a" type="aDesignType" minOccurs="0" />
                  </xs:sequence>
                </xs:complexType>
              </xs:element>
            </xs:sequence>
          </xs:complexType>
        </xs:element>
      </xs:sequence>
    </xs:complexType>
```

```xml
      </xs:element>
      <xs:attributeGroup name="coreattrs">
        <xs:attribute name="id" type="xs:ID" />
        <xs:attribute name="class" type="xs:NMTOKENS" />
        <xs:attribute name="style" type="xs:string" />
        <xs:attribute name="title" type="xs:string" />
      </xs:attributeGroup>
      <xs:attributeGroup name="i18n">
        <xs:attribute name="lang" type="xs:language" />
        <xs:attribute name="dir">
          <xs:simpleType>
            <xs:restriction base="xs:token">
              <xs:enumeration value="ltr" />
              <xs:enumeration value="rtl" />
            </xs:restriction>
          </xs:simpleType>
        </xs:attribute>
      </xs:attributeGroup>
      <xs:attributeGroup name="attrs">
        <xs:attributeGroup ref="coreattrs" />
        <xs:attributeGroup ref="i18n" />
      </xs:attributeGroup>
      <xs:simpleType name="FrameTarget">
        <xs:restriction base="xs:NMTOKEN">
          <xs:pattern value="_(blank|self|parent|top)|[A-Za-z]\c*" />
        </xs:restriction>
      </xs:simpleType>
      <xs:complexType name="aDesignType" mixed="true">
        <xs:sequence>
          <xs:any namespace="##any" processContents="skip" minOccurs="0"
maxOccurs="unbounded" />
        </xs:sequence>
        <xs:attributeGroup ref="attrs" />
        <xs:attribute name="href" type="xs:anyURI" />
        <xs:attribute name="target" type="FrameTarget" />
      </xs:complexType>
      <xs:simpleType name="ImgAlign">
        <xs:restriction base="xs:token">
          <xs:enumeration value="top" />
          <xs:enumeration value="middle" />
          <xs:enumeration value="bottom" />
          <xs:enumeration value="left" />
          <xs:enumeration value="right" />
        </xs:restriction>
      </xs:simpleType>
      <xs:simpleType name="Length">
        <xs:restriction base="xs:string">
          <xs:pattern value="[-+]?(\d+|\d+(\.\d+)?%)" />
        </xs:restriction>
      </xs:simpleType>
      <xs:complexType name="imgDesignType">
        <xs:attributeGroup ref="attrs" />
        <xs:attribute name="src" use="required" type="xs:anyURI" />
```

continues

LISTING 7-1 *(continued)*

```
      <xs:attribute name="alt" use="required" type="xs:string" />
      <xs:attribute name="height" type="Length" />
      <xs:attribute name="width" type="Length" />
      <xs:attribute name="align" type="ImgAlign" />
      <xs:attribute name="border" type="Length" />
      <xs:attribute name="hspace" type="xs:nonNegativeInteger" />
      <xs:attribute name="vspace" type="xs:nonNegativeInteger" />
    </xs:complexType>
    <xs:complexType name="rich" mixed="true">
      <xs:sequence>
        <xs:any namespace="##any" processContents="skip" minOccurs="0"
maxOccurs="unbounded" />
      </xs:sequence>
    </xs:complexType>
</xs:schema>
```

4. Use the Microsoft XML Schema Definition Tool to convert the XSD file into a C# class for use in serializing and deserializing data. Chapter 6 mentions where this tool could be found. It is run from the command line with the following syntax.

    ```
    c:\>xsd.exe HomePageBanner.xsd /classes /language:CS /namespace:SmartForm
    .HomePageBanner
    ```

5. Run that line now, after copying the HomePageBanner.xsd file to your C:\ drive. It generates a file called HomePageBanner.cs. A portion of this file is reproduced in Listing 7-2.

LISTING 7-2: AdRotator.cs

```
//------------------------------------------------------------------------------
// <auto-generated>
//     This code was generated by a tool.
//     Runtime Version:2.0.50727.3615
//
//     Changes to this file may cause incorrect behavior and will be lost if
//     the code is regenerated.
// </auto-generated>
//------------------------------------------------------------------------------

//
// This source code was auto-generated by xsd, Version=2.0.50727.3038.
//
namespace SmarForm.HomePageBanner {
    using System.Xml.Serialization;
    
    
    /// <remarks/>
    [System.CodeDom.Compiler.GeneratedCodeAttribute("xsd", "2.0.50727.3038")]
    [System.SerializableAttribute()]
    [System.Diagnostics.DebuggerStepThroughAttribute()]
    [System.ComponentModel.DesignerCategoryAttribute("code")]
    [System.Xml.Serialization.XmlTypeAttribute(AnonymousType=true)]
    [System.Xml.Serialization.XmlRootAttribute(Namespace="", IsNullable=false)]
```

```
public partial class GroupBox {

    private string slideSpeedField;

    private GroupBoxSlides[] slidesField;

    /// <remarks/>
    public string SlideSpeed {
        get {
            return this.slideSpeedField;
        }
        set {
            this.slideSpeedField = value;
        }
    }

    /// <remarks/>
    [System.Xml.Serialization.XmlElementAttribute("Slides")]
    public GroupBoxSlides[] Slides {
        get {
            return this.slidesField;
        }
        set {
            this.slidesField = value;
        }
    }
}

...
```

Now you have the basis for deserializing the homepage banner settings into an object that you can then databind to. The remaining steps are:

1. Create a repeater with the desired HTML structure.

2. Add some CSS.

3. Animate the results using jQuery.

The OnTrek site demonstrates this behavior in the default.aspx page, which then references a user control that lives at ~\UserControls\slider\slider.ascx. This user control contains all the code to build the slider interface, but for your efforts, you will create a new blank page that will recreate the functionality.

6. Create a new page now in the root of your site called HomePageBannerSerialization.aspx.

7. Open the new page and put an ASP.NET Repeater Server Control on it.

8. Build the format for the HTML output. You have specific needs for the format of this output, since you are using an existing jQuery plug-in to create the slider effect.

9. For this plug-in, you need to output each frame to be displayed as an li in a ul element. Within each li, you need to display the title, summary, link, and background image for that frame. With that in mind, update the Repeater to match the output you need. You also need to add a Content Block Server Control so that you can retrieve the contents of the Ad Rotator Smart Form content item in order to deserialize it. The code to achieve this is shown in Listing 7-3.

Available for download on Wrox.com

LISTING 7-3: HomePageBannerSerialization.aspx

```aspx
<%@ Page Language="C#" AutoEventWireup="true"
    CodeFile="HomePageBannerSerialization.aspx.cs"
    Inherits="HomePageBannerSerialization" %>
<%@ Register Assembly="Ektron.Cms.Controls"
    Namespace="Ektron.Cms.Controls" TagPrefix="CMS" %>
<!DOCTYPE html PUBLIC "-//W3C//DTD XHTML 1.0 Transitional//EN"
 "http://www.w3.org/TR/xhtml1/DTD/xhtml1-transitional.dtd">

<html xmlns="http://www.w3.org/1999/xhtml">
<head runat="server">
  <title></title>
</head>
<body>
  <form id="form1" runat="server">
  <div>
    <CMS:ContentBlock ID="uxBannerContentBlock"
      runat="server" Visible="false" />
    <ul class="site-slider">
      <asp:Repeater runat="server" ID="uxBannerRepeater">
        <ItemTemplate>
          <li>
            <div class="content"
                style="background: url('<%# DataBinder.Eval(
                                        Container.DataItem,
                                        "SlideImage")%>') no-repeat;">
              <div class="slideContent">
                <h1>
                  <%# DataBinder.Eval(Container.DataItem, "Title")%>
                </h1>
                <p>
                  <%# DataBinder.Eval(Container.DataItem, "Summary")%>
                </p>
                <p class="moreLink">
                  <a href="<%# DataBinder.Eval(Container.DataItem, "LinkUrl")%>">
                    <%# DataBinder.Eval(Container.DataItem, "LinkText")%>
                  </a>
                </p>
              </div>
            </div>
            <div class="clear">
            </div>
          </li>
        </ItemTemplate>
      </asp:Repeater>
    </ul>
  </div>
  </form>
</body>
</html>
```

10. Do the background data binding and ensure that the SmartForm.HomePageBanner classes are included properly. For this example, put the generated classes inline in the

HomePageBannerSerialization.aspx codebehind. You will also hook into the `Page_Load` event to retrieve and deserialize the settings and do the databinding to the Repeater. This code is shown in Listing 7-4.

Available for download on Wrox.com

LISTING 7-4: HomePageBannerSerialization.aspx.cs

```csharp
using System;
using System.Collections.Generic;
using System.Linq;
using System.Web;
using System.Web.UI;
using System.Web.UI.WebControls;

public partial class HomePageBannerSerialization : System.Web.UI.Page
{
  protected void Page_Load(object sender, EventArgs e)
  {
    //Fill CB with SmartFormData//
    uxBannerContentBlock.DefaultContentID = 31;
    uxBannerContentBlock.Fill();
    string xml = uxBannerContentBlock.EkItem.Html;
    SmarForm.HomePageBanner.GroupBox groupBox = (SmarForm.HomePageBanner.GroupBox)
        Ektron.Cms.EkXml.Deserialize(
          typeof(SmarForm.HomePageBanner.GroupBox), xml);

    List<BannerSlide> slides = GetBannerSlides(groupBox.Slides);
    //DataBind//
    uxBannerRepeater.DataSource = slides;
    uxBannerRepeater.DataBind();
  }

  protected List<BannerSlide>
      GetBannerSlides(SmarForm.HomePageBanner.GroupBoxSlides[] groupBoxSlides)
  {
    List<BannerSlide> bSlides = new List<BannerSlide>();
    foreach (SmarForm.HomePageBanner.GroupBoxSlides gbSlide in groupBoxSlides)
    {
      bSlides.Add(new BannerSlide(gbSlide.Image.img.src, gbSlide.Title,
          gbSlide.Summary.Any[0].InnerText,
          gbSlide.Link.a.Any[0].InnerText, gbSlide.Link.a.href));
    }
    return bSlides;
  }

  public class BannerSlide
  {
    //properties//
    public string SlideImage { get; set; }
    public string Title { get; set; }
    public string Summary { get; set; }
    public string LinkText { get; set; }
    public string LinkUrl { get; set; }
```

continues

LISTING 7-4 *(continued)*

```
        //constructor//
        public BannerSlide(string slideImage, string title, string summary,
                           string linkText, string linkUrl)
        {
            SlideImage = slideImage;
            Title = title;
            Summary = summary;
            LinkText = linkText;
            LinkUrl = linkUrl;
        }
    }
}

#region SmartForm.HomePageBanner autogenerated classes
```

For brevity's sake, this chapter has folded the autogenerated classes into the region marker at the end of the file. Aside from that, there are a number of moving parts in the codebehind. The first thing that happens is in the `Page_Load` *event; you set the Content Block Server Control on the declarative side to retrieve the* `HomePageBanner` *content item. Then use the* `EkXml` *object to deserialize the object into your generated class.*

This chapter uses the `EkXml` *object because it intelligently caches serializers. You could just as easily use the built-in serialization routines in* `System.Xml`, *but those are not logically cached in all situations, causing much longer page load times in certain circumstances. It also simplifies the calls into a single line versus the several lines necessary for a normal deserialization call using the* `System.Xml` *objects.*

11. The banner settings are then handed off to the `GetBannerSlides` method, which converts them into a list of `BannerSlide` objects. You do this intermediate step just to ease the databinding that takes place on the declarative side. Once that is done, simply set the list as the datasource for the repeater, and call databind. The repeater then converts the objects into your desired HTML.

12. Now that the hard part is done, include some CSS and fire off some jQuery to convert the results into an actual rotating display. Of these two parts, you will use the CSS built for the homepage banner. On the jQuery side, the homepage uses a third party library called bxSlider (available at `http://bxslider.com`) to perform the animations. So in all, you will add two calls to register JavaScript files in the codebehind, and one call to register CSS in the codebehind. These lines should be put in the `Page_Load` event of the page as the first methods called in the event.

```
Ektron.Cms.API.JS.RegisterJS(this,
    "js/plugins/bxSlider/ektron.bxslider2.0.1.js", "EktronBxSliderJS");
```

```
Ektron.Cms.API.JS.RegisterJS(this,
    "components/usercontrols/slider/ektron.site.slider.js", "EktronSiteSliderJS");
Ektron.Cms.API.Css.RegisterCss(this,
    "components/usercontrols/slider/ektron.site.slider.css", "EktronSiteSliderCSS");
```

The methods for registering client side scripts on a Web page are used for a couple of reasons. The register methods ensure that all registered files are only included once. They can additionally aggregate all registered files into a single JavaScript file and optionally minify the results.

The first register call includes the `bxSlider` library. The second call includes the JavaScript required to initialize the `bxSlider`. Finally, include the CSS to render the whole thing properly. Now when the browser points to `http://localhost/mainsite/homepagebannerserialization.aspx`, the banner is displayed properly. The rotating image banner is shown rendered on the homepage in Figure 7-2.

FIGURE 7-2

Homepage Image Rotator Using XSLT

The method covered in the previous section, using serialization and an ASP.NET Repeater Server Control to render the markup, is how the rotator built into the OnTrek starter site functions. In the interest of expanding your knowledge, you will now build the same example with a different approach. In this approach, you'll use an XSLT to transform the settings into HTML, and you won't use a pre-built jQuery plug-in. Instead, you'll write some custom jQuery to animate the results.

Creating the Custom XSLT

To create the custom XSLT, follow these steps:

1. Retrieve the XML for the settings content item. Log in to the Workarea, and in the content tree browse to /MainSite/Content/Smart Forms/HomePageBanner.

2. In the content list pane, select HomePageBanner and click the Edit icon.

3. When the data is published, it is saved as an XML document with a reference back to the Smart Form Design Package, which contains the automatically generated XSLT. Whenever the content is displayed through a Content Block Server Control, the XML is transformed against the built-in XSLT. Since that XSLT does not format the data as you want, you will write a custom XSLT for the content now. In order to do so, you need to look at the generated XML. At the bottom of the eWebEdit400 editor, there are two buttons.

   These buttons switch between the data designer view and the XML view. Click the second of these buttons now to view the automatically generated XML, and copy it to a text document for later reference. A portion of the generated XML is listed in the following code snippet.

```xml
<GroupBox>
  <SlideSpeed></SlideSpeed>
  <Slides>
    <Image>
      <img
        src="/OnTrek/uploadedImages/Content/Home/HomePageBanner/img-banner1.png"
        alt="Banner1" />
    </Image>
    <Title>Lorem Ipsum</Title>
    <Summary>Vusce id nibh orci, sed tincidunt quam. Maecenas
    iaculis risus sed tortor tincidunt at egestas augue laoreet.
    Suspendisse consectetur, sem nec tempus elementum, felis lectus
    fermentum urna, id vehicula arcu turpis ac enim. Cum sociis
    natoque penatibus et magnis dis parturient montes, nascetur
    ridiculus mus. Vestibulum ante ipsum primis in faucibus orci
    luctus et ultrices posuere cubilia</Summary>
    <Link>
      <a href="http://www.Ektron.com">Learn More</a>
    </Link>
  </Slides>
  <Slides>
```

```xml
      <Image>
        <img
        src="/OnTrek/uploadedImages/Content/Home/HomePageBanner/img-banner2.png"
        alt="Banner2" />
      </Image>
      <Title>Vivamus vel metus vitae</Title>
      <Summary>Wusce id nibh orci, sed tincidunt quam. Maecenas
      iaculis risus sed tortor tincidunt at egestas augue laoreet.
      Suspendisse consectetur, sem nec tempus elementum, felis lectus
      fermentum urna, id vehicula arcu turpis ac enim. Cum sociis
      natoque penatibus et magnis dis parturient montes, nascetur
      ridiculus mus. Vestibulum ante ipsum primis in faucibus orci
      luctus et ultrices posuere cubilia</Summary>
      <Link>
        <a href="http://www.ektron.com">Learn More</a>
      </Link>
    </Slides>
  </GroupBox>
```

4. Based on this XML, you need to output some simple HTML that can be read by indexing engines such as Google for SEO purposes. The HTML format you want to achieve is in the following code snippet.

```html
    <div class="rotator">
      <div class="panel"
        style="background-
        image:url(
        '/OnTrek/uploadedImages/Content/Home/HomePageBanner/img-banner1.png');">
        <h1>Lorem Ipsum</h1>
        <p>
          Vusce id nibh orci, sed tincidunt quam. Maecenas
          iaculis risus sed tortor tincidunt at egestas augue laoreet.
          Suspendisse consectetur, sem nec tempus elementum, felis lectus
          fermentum urna, id vehicula arcu turpis ac enim. Cum sociis
          natoque penatibus et magnis dis parturient montes, nascetur
          ridiculus mus. Vestibulum ante ipsum primis in faucibus orci
          luctus et ultrices posuere cubilia
        </p>
        <a href="http://www.Ektron.com">Learn More</a>
      </div>
      <div class="panel"
        style="display:none;background-
        image:url(
        '/OnTrek/uploadedImages/Content/Home/HomePageBanner/img-banner2.png');">
        <h1>Vivamus vel metus vitae</h1>
        <p>
          Wusce id nibh orci, sed tincidunt quam. Maecenas
          iaculis risus sed tortor tincidunt at egestas augue laoreet.
          Suspendisse consectetur, sem nec tempus elementum, felis lectus
          fermentum urna, id vehicula arcu turpis ac enim. Cum sociis
          natoque penatibus et magnis dis parturient montes, nascetur
```

```
            ridiculus mus. Vestibulum ante ipsum primis in faucibus orci
            luctus et ultrices posuere cubilia
        </p>
        <a href="http://www.ektron.com">Learn More</a>
    </div>
</div>
```

The elements in the HTML closely correspond to the elements in the XML. The items in the HTML should be self-evident.

5. Wrap the whole structure in a `div` with class rotator, and then that in turn contains panels. Each panel has a background image, and displays the heading, the text, and a link to more information. Then use jQuery to appropriately scroll through the items by hiding the current item and showing the next item.

6. Next, you need to develop an XSLT that transforms from the XML into the format just discussed.

7. Finally, you need to add some minimal styles and JavaScript to animate the final rotator. The XSLT is listed in the following code snippet.

```
<?xml version="1.0" encoding="utf-8"?>
<xsl:stylesheet version="1.0"
   xmlns:xsl="http://www.w3.org/1999/XSL/Transform">
  <xsl:template match="/">
    <div class="rotator">
      <xsl:for-each select="/GroupBox/Slides">
        <div class="panel">
          <xsl:choose>
            <xsl:when test="position() != 1">
              <xsl:attribute name="style">
                display:none;background-image:url('<xsl:value-of
                            select="Image/img/@src"/>');
              </xsl:attribute>
            </xsl:when>
            <xsl:otherwise>
              <xsl:attribute name="style">
                background-image:url('<xsl:value-of
                            select="Image/img/@src"/>');
              </xsl:attribute>
            </xsl:otherwise>
          </xsl:choose>
          <h1>
            <xsl:value-of select="Title"/>
          </h1>
          <p>
            <xsl:value-of select="Summary"/>
          </p>
          <xsl:copy-of select="Link/a"></xsl:copy-of>
        </div>
      </xsl:for-each>
```

```
        </div>
    </xsl:template>
</xsl:stylesheet>
```

This XSLT is as simple as it can be while achieving the goals set here. After the header information, there is a single template, which matches the root of the document. Inside that template, there is a containing `div` element, which is the root of the output. Then do a `for-each` on the panels contained in the root node. Each panel is contained in a panel `div`. The panel `div` contains several other elements, like an `h1`, a `p`, and an `anchor`. Each of these elements contains the corresponding data. The `choose` acts as a switch based on whether or not the current panel is the first panel. In the case that it is, you simply set the background-image CSS property on the element. If it is not the first panel, then set the background-image property, but also mark the panel as invisible. You will then use jQuery to animate between them.

XSLTs can be very complex; fortunately there are many resources for learning more about writing them effectively. One point to consider that may assist your development efforts is how to debug an XSLT in Visual Studio. While this is not foolproof, as the Ektron Framework's internal XSL Transform engine can switch between two types of engines, it can frequently help a developer figure out just what is wrong with the transform.

Debugging the XSLT in Visual Studio

To debug an XSLT in Visual Studio, you need to have a file for the input XML, and a file for the XSLT:

1. Take the XSLT shown in the previous section and save it into a file at `~\Xml\HomePageBannerRotator.xslt`.

2. Take the XML you copied from eWebEdit400, and save it to `~\Xml\HomePageBannerRotator.xml`.

3. Open both files in Visual Studio at the same time, and view the XSLT. In the Properties pane, one of the items listed is Input. This property informs Visual Studio where the XML file is against which it should perform the transform. This is shown in Figure 7-3.

4. Set the input to `C:\Xml\ria.xml`.

5. Test your transform by selecting XML ➪ Show XSLT Output.

Remember that .NET does not support XSLT 2. Ektron has worked around that by using the built in XSLT 1 engine by default for transforms, but using the bundled Saxon XSLT 2 processor for certain XSLT files that are marked appropriately. To signal to the Ektron Framework that your XSLT should be transformed via Saxon, you can either store the XSLT in a folder called "saxon," or you can include the line `<saxon></saxon>` inside your XSLT. Remember that XSLT 2 files cannot be tested in Visual Studio.

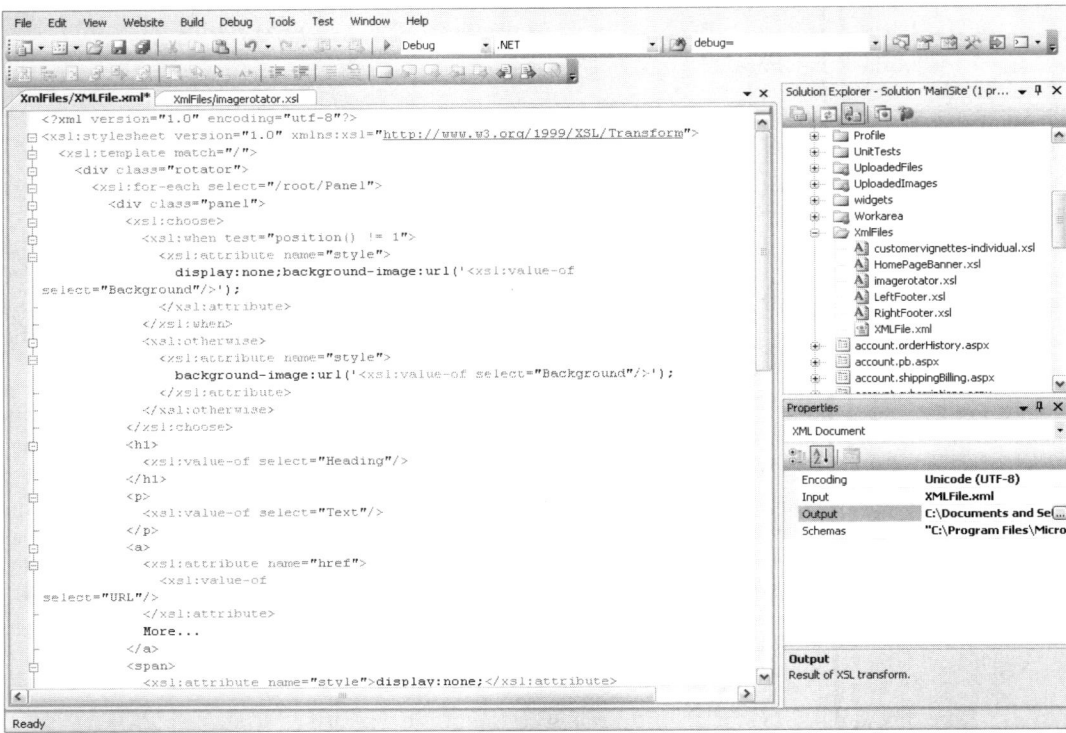

FIGURE 7-3

Setting Code to Use the XSLT

Now that you have the XSLT you wish to use, you need to set up your code to use it. You created the first example in the file HomePageBannerSerialization.aspx. Now, follow these steps:

1. Add a new Web Form to the root of your site, and call it **HomePageBannerXSLT.aspx**.

2. Make sure that the language is set to Visual C#, and that the Place Code in Separate File checkbox is selected.

3. Once the file is created, drag a Content Block Server Control into the form element.

4. Set the `DefaultContentID` to the ID of the RIA Settings content item. For now, don't set the `DisplayXSLT` property. The code for HomePageBannerXSLT.aspx is shown in the following code snippet.

```
<%@ Page Language="C#" AutoEventWireup="true"
    CodeFile="HomePageBannerXSLT.aspx.cs"
 Inherits="HomePageBannerXSLT" %>
<%@ Register Assembly="Ektron.Cms.Controls" Namespace="Ektron.Cms.Controls"
TagPrefix="CMS" %>

<!DOCTYPE html PUBLIC "-//W3C//DTD XHTML 1.0 Transitional//EN"
```

```
    "http://www.w3.org/TR/xhtml1/DTD/xhtml1-transitional.dtd">

<html xmlns="http://www.w3.org/1999/xhtml">
<head runat="server">
    <title></title>
</head>
<body>
    <form id="form1" runat="server">
    <div>
        <CMS:ContentBlock ID="SmartFormSettingsRetrieve" runat="server"
DefaultContentID="31" />
    </div>
    </form>
</body>
</html>
```

5. Save the file and then load it in the browser at `http://localhost/OnTrek/HomePageBannerXSLT.aspx`. The loaded page is shown in Figure 7-4.

> The ContentBlock Server Control will use the default XSLT from the Data Design Package, which displays the data similarly to how it looked in the editor.

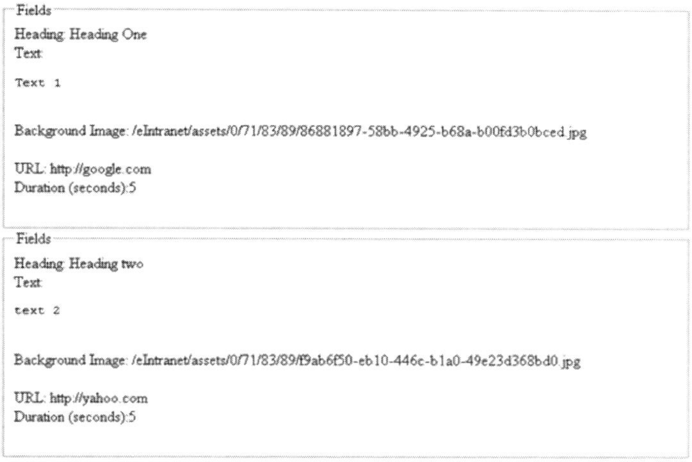

FIGURE 7-4

6. Set the Content Block Server Control to use the XSLT you developed. Set the property called `DisplayXSLT` to the path `~/xmlfiles/ HomePageBannerRotator.xslt`. This modification is shown here:

```
<CMS:ContentBlock ID="SmartFormSettingsRetrieve"
    runat="server" DefaultContentID="554"
DisplayXslt="~/xmlfiles/HomePageBannerRotator.xslt" />
```

7. Refresh the page in the browser to see the transformed HTML, as shown in Figure 7-5.

FIGURE 7-5

Clearly, you'll need some CSS to make this look right. The main thing you need to do is set the width and height of the panels to the size of the images you are displaying. On the homepage there are additional styles to set the font and display the text in appropriate places, but for this example you'll skip those complications.

8. Update the head of the HomePageBannerXSLT.aspx file to look like the following code snippet.

```
<head runat="server">
    <title></title>
    <style type="text/css">
        div.rotator {
            width:470px; height:296px; min-height:296px; }
        div.panel {
            background-position:center;
            background-repeat:no-repeat;
            width:470px; height:296px; }
    </style>
</head>
```

9. Finally, you need some JavaScript to do the actual rotation. The Ektron Framework internally uses jQuery for most of the client side heavy lifting, so you'll piggyback on that for your own code.

Remember that the Ektron copy of jQuery is renamed to $ektron rather than $ so it won't conflict with your code, but in all other respects it is effectively the same. The JavaScript to run the rotator is listed in the following code snippet.

```
<script type="text/javascript" language="javascript">
    //initialization of the rotator. We wrap it in the document ready so it
    //only runs after the entire DOM has been loaded.
    $ektron(document).ready(function() {
      if ("undefined" != typeof HomePageRotator) {
        //set up rotator
        HomePageRotator.setupRotator();
        //set up callback to switch to second item. from then on,
        //the movenextrotator function will set up the timers.
        window.setTimeout(
          HomePageRotator.moveNextRotator, HomePageRotator.TimeOut)
      }
    });

    //this will be our namespace for objects and
    //functions created for the rotator.
    if ("undefined" == typeof HomePageRotator) {
      var HomePageRotator = {
```

```
          Panels: {}, //this stores the set of panels to rotate through
          TimeOut: 3000, //this stores the length of time to show each panel
          CurrentItem: 0, //this is the panel currently being displayed
          setupRotator: function() {
            //set the panels property to the retrieved set of panels
            HomePageRotator.Panels = $ektron("div.panel");
          },
          moveNextRotator: function() {
            //current displayed panel
            var curItem = HomePageRotator.CurrentItem;
            //next panel to display
            var nextItem = curItem + 1;
            if (nextItem >= HomePageRotator.Panels.length) nextItem = 0;
            //Animate the fade out of the current panel. Once the
            //animation has completed, start fading in the next panel.
            //Wait until that animation has completed, then update the
            //current item pointer and set up the callback to perform
            //the action again once the timer has run out.
            HomePageRotator.Panels.eq(curItem).fadeOut(500, function() {
              HomePageRotator.Panels.eq(nextItem).fadeIn(500, function() {
                HomePageRotator.CurrentItem = nextItem;
                window.setTimeout(
                  HomePageRotator.moveNextRotator, HomePageRotator.TimeOut);
              });
            });
          }
        };
      }
    </script>
```

This JavaScript might be a little unfamiliar looking — you're using object oriented code for this. You can think of this in three chunks of code:

➤ The first serves as the initialize, which only runs after the document has been loaded. This ensures when you run queries to find the panels, they exist in the DOM.

➤ The second, as indicated in the comments, defines the namespace for your functions and variables. In it you store the panel set, the length of time to display each panel, and the current item that is displayed. You also have the setupRotator function, which sets the Panels object.

➤ The third is the moveNextRotator function, which animates the transitions between panels and sets up the callback to itself after the appropriate amount of time.

You've now created the image rotator for the homepage. This was a simple example of using JavaScript to create a richer interface than displaying static HTML would yield. A common need, however, is for the interface to dynamically update itself with fresh data based on user interaction.

Web Service Creation and Consumption

In this example, you will create an interface that lists the child nodes of a taxonomy, and uses an AJAX call to retrieve the content items associated with the selected node. This particular set of functionality would typically be implemented through the use of the Directory Server Control, which does this out-of-the-box, but the example illustrates how to approach an AJAX requirement in an extensible way. The same approach can be used to create any interface that requires fast responses on the client page. In this example, you will do the following:

- Create a page that renders the child nodes of a specified node.
- Create a simple handler that accepts a JSON argument specifying the selected child node and returns a JSON object containing the list of items to display.
- Modify the page to have a reusable template to display those items.
- Create the JavaScript using jQuery to retrieve and render the children.

Rendering the Children of a Specific Node

Start by creating a Web Form called `SimpleHandler.aspx`. Create this at the root of the site. The purpose of this file is to list the taxonomy nodes that are children of a given node. In this case, you will use the `Taxonomies/OnTrek Site Navigation` node, which has an ID of 189 in the default OnTrek database. The page you create will have three main elements on it:

- A repeater to list the taxonomy nodes
- A `div` that will be the container that you use to display the children of the selected node
- The JavaScript to tie it all together

The code listing for SimpleHandler.aspx follows. In its current state it will display the ID of the clicked taxonomy node in the results `div`, as displayed in the following code snippet.

```
<html xmlns="http://www.w3.org/1999/xhtml">
<head runat="server">
  <title></title>
</head>
<body>
  <form id="form1" runat="server">
    <asp:Repeater ID="repeaterItemList" runat="server">
      <ItemTemplate>
        <a href="#" class="taxonomyLink" onclick="return false;">
          <span style="display:none;" class="taxonomyId">
            <%#
              DataBinder.Eval(Container.DataItem, "TaxonomyId")
            %>
          </span>
          <%#
            DataBinder.Eval(Container.DataItem, "TaxonomyName")
          %>
        </a>
        <br />
      </ItemTemplate>
    </asp:Repeater>
    <div id="ItemResults">
    </div>
```

```
<script language="javascript" type="text/javascript">
  //initialization of the Taxonomy links.
  //We wrap it in the document ready so it only runs
  //after the entire DOM has been loaded.
  $ektron(document).ready(function() {
    if ("undefined" != typeof TaxonomyHandler) {
      //When the link is clicked, fire the
      //getTaxonomyItems handler.
      $ektron("a.taxonomyLink").click(
        TaxonomyHandler.getTaxonomyItems
      );
    }
  });

  //this will be our namespace for objects and functions
  //created for the handler example.
  if ("undefined" == typeof TaxonomyHandler) {
    var TaxonomyHandler = {
      getTaxonomyItems: function() {
        //this function will look inside the clicked link
        //to retrieve the id of the taxonomy item clicked.
        //It will then display the taxonomy id in the results div.
          var clickedAnchor = $ektron(this);
          var taxonomyId = clickedAnchor.find("span.taxonomyId").text();
          $ektron("div#ItemResults").html(taxonomyId);
        }
      };
    }
  </script>
  </form>
</body>
</html>
```

In the codebehind for the page, register the jQuery library to include it on the page, retrieve the children nodes using the API, and then databind the nodes to the repeater. This code is listed in the following snippet.

```
public partial class SimpleHandler : System.Web.UI.Page
{
  protected void Page_Load(object sender, EventArgs e)
  {
    //include jQuery library
    Ektron.Cms.API.JS.RegisterJS(
      this,
      Ektron.Cms.API.JS.ManagedScript.EktronJS
    );

    //set up objects we will use
    Ektron.Cms.API.Content.Taxonomy taxonomyAPI
      = new Ektron.Cms.API.Content.Taxonomy();
    Ektron.Cms.TaxonomyRequest taxonomyRequest
      = new Ektron.Cms.TaxonomyRequest();
    Ektron.Cms.TaxonomyData taxonomyData
      = null;
```

```
        //initialize the taxonomyrequest object
        //whether to include items or just sub nodes
        taxonomyRequest.IncludeItems
          = false;
        //the taxonomy id to retrieve the children of
        taxonomyRequest.TaxonomyId
          = 189;
        //the language of the items we should retrieve.
        //set it to the currently selected language
        taxonomyRequest.TaxonomyLanguage
          = taxonomyAPI.RequestInformationRef.ContentLanguage;
        //the taxonomy type
        taxonomyRequest.TaxonomyType
          = Ektron.Cms.Common.EkEnumeration.TaxonomyType.Content;

        //get the taxonomy item and children
        taxonomyData = taxonomyAPI.LoadTaxonomy(ref taxonomyRequest);

        //ensure the result is good, and databind it to the repeater
        if (taxonomyData != null && taxonomyData.TaxonomyHasChildren)
        {
          repeaterItemList.DataSource = taxonomyData.Taxonomy;
          repeaterItemList.DataBind();
        }
      }
    }
```

Creating a Simple Handler

Now that you have a page that lists the nodes, the next step is to create the handler to retrieve the children content of a selected node. You do this by following these steps:

1. Create a generic handler. You'll use a handler because it is significantly lighter than a full page in the .NET Framework. You then return results to the query through JSON.

2. In the root of your site in Visual Studio, add a new item. Select Generic Handler for the template, and Visual C# as the language, as shown in Figure 7-6. Name it **TaxonomyExampleService.ashx**.

   The code for this file uses the `DataContractJsonSerializer` class bundled with ASP.NET 3.5 to serialize the response and deserialize the request object. You also have the option at this point of using the `Serialization.JavaScriptSerializer` object to serialize the JSON, but using a `DataContract` has two large benefits:

   ➤ By marking the class as a `DataContract`, you can serialize to anything that there is a serializer for, including XML.

   ➤ The `DataContract` gives you additional flexibility because you can specify the property names to serialize to in the JSON object.

Rich Interaction Using jQuery, Smart Forms, and Handlers | 173

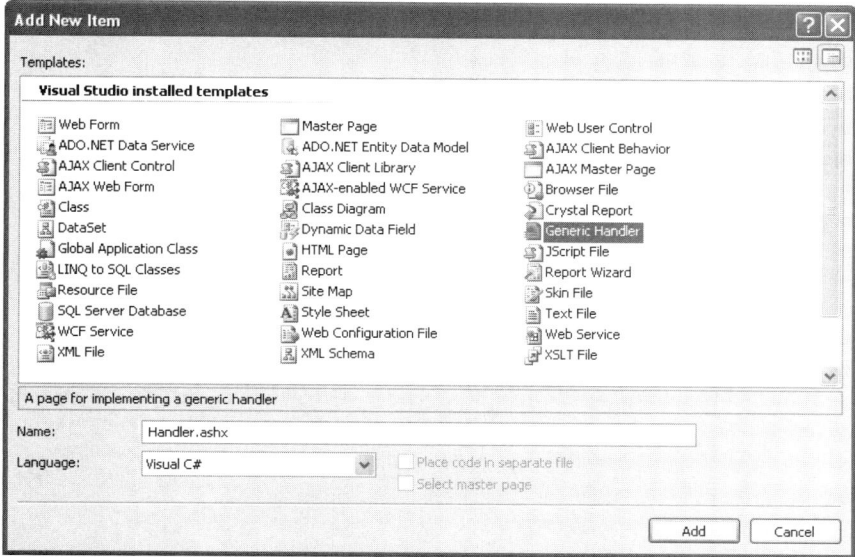

FIGURE 7-6

3. Using the standard serialization methods requires that you have a class definition for the objects being serialized. The first portion of the code is in the `RequestItem` class shown in the following code snippet.

```
//this class is marked with the DataContract attribute
//to specify that it is serializable.
[System.Runtime.Serialization.DataContract]
public class RequestItem
{
  //this attribute marks that this property should be serialized.
  //the attached property specifies the parent taxonomy node of
  //the requested children.
  [System.Runtime.Serialization.DataMember]
  public long TaxonomyID { get; set; }

  //this static method will take the serialized
  //requestitem object and deserialize it
  public static RequestItem Deserialize(string serializedItem)
  {
    System.IO.MemoryStream memoryStream = null;
    //declare a new requestitem so we don't return a null object
    RequestItem requestItem = new RequestItem();

    if (serializedItem != null) // ensure the argument string exists
    {
      //create a new serializer object
      System.Runtime.Serialization.
```

```csharp
              Json.DataContractJsonSerializer requestItemSerializer
                = new System.Runtime.Serialization.Json.DataContractJsonSerializer(
                  typeof(RequestItem));

            try
            {
              //get the bytestream for the serialized object
              memoryStream = new System.IO.MemoryStream(
                System.Text.Encoding.Unicode.GetBytes(serializedItem));
              //deserialize the object
              requestItem = requestItemSerializer.ReadObject(memoryStream)
                as RequestItem;
            }
            catch (Exception e)
            {
              throw new Exception("Could not deserialize request", e);
            }
            finally
            {
              //ensure the memorystream gets emptied
              memoryStream.Dispose();
            }
          }
          else
          {
            throw new Exception("Request is null");
          }
          return requestItem;
        }
    }
```

4. The other class you need to define is `TaxonomyItem`. The handler will return a generic list of these, each of which will store the content ID, title, and QuickLink for a content item. This class has a `SerializeList` method rather than a deserializer method, as you will serialize the list to return it to the requesting page. Otherwise it is very similar to the `RequestItem` class. The `TaxonomyItem` class' code is listed in the following code snippet.

```csharp
//this class is marked with the DataContract
//attribute to specify that it is serializable.
[System.Runtime.Serialization.DataContract]
public class TaxonomyItem
{
  //the properties listed below store the relevant
  //data for a given piece of content.
  //each is marked as a serializable property.
  [System.Runtime.Serialization.DataMember]
  public long ItemID { get; set; }
  [System.Runtime.Serialization.DataMember]
  public string ItemName { get; set; }
  [System.Runtime.Serialization.DataMember]
  public string ItemQuicklink { get; set; }

  //the constructor takes all three properties to initialize the object
  public TaxonomyItem(long ID, string Name, string Quicklink)
```

```
    {
      ItemID = ID;
      ItemName = Name;
      ItemQuicklink = Quicklink;
    }

    //this method takes a list of taxonomyitems and serializes it as one unit.
    public static string SerializeList(List<TaxonomyItem> itemlist){
      System.IO.MemoryStream memoryStream = null;
      string serializedList = ""; //the return value

      if (itemlist != null) //ensure the input is valid before continuing
      {
        //create the serialization object
        System.Runtime.Serialization.Json.
          DataContractJsonSerializer responseItemSerializer
          = new System.Runtime.Serialization.Json.DataContractJsonSerializer(
            typeof(List<TaxonomyItem>));

        try
        {
          memoryStream = new System.IO.MemoryStream();

          //serialize the object and then write it to the output string
          responseItemSerializer.WriteObject(memoryStream, itemlist);
          serializedList = System.Text.Encoding.
            Default.GetString(memoryStream.ToArray());
        }
        catch (Exception e)
        {
          throw new Exception("Could not serialize results", e);
        }
        finally
        {
          memoryStream.Dispose();
        }
      }

      return serializedList;
    }
  }
```

5. Now that you have your input and output classes, you need to fill in the `ProcessRequest` method, and also the code that actually retrieves the child content. You do this by:

➤ Writing the method to get the content. The method will be called `GetChildren`, and is mostly a modified version of the taxonomy code you wrote to list the categories in the first place. The first modification to the earlier code is that you specify in the `TaxonomyRequest` object to include content.

➤ Once you have the results, do not databind them to a repeater, but instead iterate over them building a `List<TaxonomyItem>` to return from the method.

The code is listed in the following code snippet.

```csharp
public List<TaxonomyItem> GetChildren(long taxonomyId)
{
  List<TaxonomyItem> contentItems = new List<TaxonomyItem>();

  //set up objects we will use
  Ektron.Cms.API.Content.Taxonomy taxonomyAPI
    = new Ektron.Cms.API.Content.Taxonomy();
  Ektron.Cms.TaxonomyRequest taxonomyRequest
    = new Ektron.Cms.TaxonomyRequest();
  Ektron.Cms.TaxonomyData taxonomyData
    = null;

  //initialize the taxonomyrequest object
  //whether to include items or just sub nodes
  taxonomyRequest.IncludeItems = true;
  //the taxonomy id to retrieve the children of
  taxonomyRequest.TaxonomyId = taxonomyId;
  //the language of the items we should retrieve.
  //set it to the currently selected language
  taxonomyRequest.TaxonomyLanguage
    = taxonomyAPI.RequestInformationRef.ContentLanguage;
  //the taxonomy type
  taxonomyRequest.TaxonomyType
    = Ektron.Cms.Common.EkEnumeration.TaxonomyType.Content;

  //get the taxonomy item and children
  taxonomyData = taxonomyAPI.LoadTaxonomy(ref taxonomyRequest);

  //ensure the result is good
  if (taxonomyData != null
    && taxonomyData.TaxonomyItems != null
    && taxonomyData.TaxonomyItems.Length > 0)
  {
    //iterate over the results, adding
    //converted items to the contentItems list
    foreach (TaxonomyItemData item in taxonomyData.TaxonomyItems)
    {
      contentItems.Add(
        new TaxonomyItem(
          item.TaxonomyItemId,
          item.TaxonomyItemTitle,
          item.TaxonomyItemQuickLink));
    }
  }

  return contentItems;
}
```

6. Add the `ProcessRequest` method. This method is very straightforward; it simply deserializes the request item passed to the handler, calls `GetChildren`, and responds to the request with the serialized results. The code is listed in the following snippet.

```csharp
public void ProcessRequest (HttpContext context) {
  //we will return an empty string if there is a problem retrieving the
  //children.
```

```
      string serializedResult = "";
      List<TaxonomyItem> results = null;

      //deserialize the request
      RequestItem request = RequestItem.Deserialize(context.Request["request"]);

      //get the child content items
      results = GetChildren(request.TaxonomyID);

      if (results != null)
      {
        //serialize the results
        serializedResult = TaxonomyItem.SerializeList(results);
      }

      context.Response.ContentType = "text/plain";
      //write the serialized results
      context.Response.Write(serializedResult);
    }
```

7. Now you have the complete code for your handler. Call this handler with an AJAX request from the Web page, specifying a single argument with the key request. That argument will be a serialized object containing the taxonomy ID. The complete code is reproduced in Listing 7-5.

Available for download on Wrox.com

LISTING 7-5: TaxonomyExampleService.ashx

```
<%@ WebHandler Language="C#" Class="TaxonomyExampleService" %>
using System;
using System.Web;
using Ektron.Cms;
using System.Collections.Generic;

public class TaxonomyExampleService : IHttpHandler {

  //this class is marked with the DataContract attribute
  //to specify that it is serializable.
  [System.Runtime.Serialization.DataContract]
  public class TaxonomyItem
  {
    //the properties listed below store the relevant
    //data for a given piece of content.
    //each is marked as a serializable property.
    [System.Runtime.Serialization.DataMember]
    public long ItemID { get; set; }
    [System.Runtime.Serialization.DataMember]
    public string ItemName { get; set; }
    [System.Runtime.Serialization.DataMember]
    public string ItemQuicklink { get; set; }

    //the constructor takes all three properties to initialize the object
    public TaxonomyItem(long ID, string Name, string Quicklink)
    {
```

continues

LISTING 7-5 *(continued)*

```
      ItemID = ID;
      ItemName = Name;
      ItemQuicklink = Quicklink;
    }

    //this method takes a list of taxonomyitems and serializes it as one unit.
    public static string SerializeList(List<TaxonomyItem> itemlist){
      System.IO.MemoryStream memoryStream = null;
      string serializedList = ""; //the return value

      if (itemlist != null) //ensure the input is valid before continuing
      {
        //create the serialization object
        System.Runtime.Serialization.Json.
         DataContractJsonSerializer responseItemSerializer
           = new System.Runtime.Serialization.Json.DataContractJsonSerializer(
               typeof(List<TaxonomyItem>));

        try
        {
          memoryStream = new System.IO.MemoryStream();

          //serialize the object and then write it to the output string
          responseItemSerializer.WriteObject(memoryStream, itemlist);
          serializedList = System.Text.Encoding.Default.GetString(
                              memoryStream.ToArray());
        }
        catch (Exception e)
        {
          throw new Exception("Could not serialize results", e);
        }
        finally
        {
          memoryStream.Dispose();
        }
      }

      return serializedList;
    }
}

//this class is marked with the DataContract
//attribute to specify that it is serializable.
[System.Runtime.Serialization.DataContract]
public class RequestItem
{
  //this attribute marks that this property should be serialized.
  //the attached property specifies the parent taxonomy node
  //of the requested children.
  [System.Runtime.Serialization.DataMember]
  public long TaxonomyID { get; set; }
```

```csharp
    //this static method will take the serialized requestitem
    //object and deserialize it
    public static RequestItem Deserialize(string serializedItem)
    {
      System.IO.MemoryStream memoryStream = null;
      //declare a new requestitem so we don't return a null object
      RequestItem requestItem = new RequestItem();

      if (serializedItem != null) // ensure the argument string exists
      {
        //create a new serializer object
        System.Runtime.Serialization.Json.
          DataContractJsonSerializer requestItemSerializer
          = new System.Runtime.Serialization.Json.DataContractJsonSerializer(
                                                    typeof(RequestItem));

        try
        {
          //get the bytestream for the serialized object
          memoryStream = new System.IO.MemoryStream(
                      System.Text.Encoding.Unicode.GetBytes(
                        serializedItem));
          //deserialize the object
          requestItem = requestItemSerializer.ReadObject(memoryStream)
                      as RequestItem;
        }
        catch (Exception e)
        {
          throw new Exception("Could not deserialize request", e);
        }
        finally
        {
          //ensure the memorystream gets emptied
          memoryStream.Dispose();
        }
      }
      else
      {
        throw new Exception("Request is null");
      }
      return requestItem;
    }
}

public void ProcessRequest (HttpContext context) {
  //we will return an empty string if there is a
  //problem retrieving the children.
  string serializedResult = "";
  List<TaxonomyItem> results = null;

  //deserialize the request
  RequestItem request = RequestItem.Deserialize(
                    context.Request["request"]);
```

continues

LISTING 7-5 *(continued)*

```csharp
  //get the child content items
  results = GetChildren(request.TaxonomyID);

  if (results != null)
  {
    //serialize the results
    serializedResult = TaxonomyItem.SerializeList(results);
  }

  context.Response.ContentType = "text/plain";
  //write the serialized results
  context.Response.Write(serializedResult);
}

public List<TaxonomyItem> GetChildren(long taxonomyId)
{
  List<TaxonomyItem> contentItems = new List<TaxonomyItem>();

  //set up objects we will use
  Ektron.Cms.API.Content.Taxonomy taxonomyAPI
    = new Ektron.Cms.API.Content.Taxonomy();
  Ektron.Cms.TaxonomyRequest taxonomyRequest
    = new Ektron.Cms.TaxonomyRequest();
  Ektron.Cms.TaxonomyData taxonomyData
    = null;

  //initialize the taxonomyrequest object
  //whether to include items or just sub nodes
  taxonomyRequest.IncludeItems = true;
  //the taxonomy id to retrieve the children of
  taxonomyRequest.TaxonomyId = taxonomyId;
  //the language of the items we should retrieve.
  //set it to the currently selected language
  taxonomyRequest.TaxonomyLanguage
    = taxonomyAPI.RequestInformationRef.ContentLanguage;
  //the taxonomy type
  taxonomyRequest.TaxonomyType
    = Ektron.Cms.Common.EkEnumeration.TaxonomyType.Content;

  //get the taxonomy item and children
  taxonomyData = taxonomyAPI.LoadTaxonomy(ref taxonomyRequest);

  //ensure the result is good
  if (taxonomyData != null
    && taxonomyData.TaxonomyItems != null
    && taxonomyData.TaxonomyItems.Length > 0)
  {
    //iterate over the results, adding converted
    //items to the contentItems list
    foreach (TaxonomyItemData item in taxonomyData.TaxonomyItems)
    {
```

```
      contentItems.Add(
        new TaxonomyItem(
          item.TaxonomyItemId,
          item.TaxonomyItemTitle,
          item.TaxonomyItemQuickLink));
    }
  }

  return contentItems;
}

public bool IsReusable {
  get {
    return false;
  }
  }
}
```

Using a Reusable Template to Display Items

Now you need to return to the `SimpleHandler.aspx` file to create the glue to retrieve and display these results. The first section you add to the `SimpleHandler.aspx` file is a `div` just below the repeater. This `div` is used by the JavaScript as a template for each item returned from the handler. There are other methods of handling this sort of templating, but we have found this method allows for the most flexibility to developers, and keeps the template as part of the HTML. The template then contains tokens that are replaced with the values from the handler. The HTML for the template is listed in the following code snippet.

```
<div id="ItemResults">
  <div id="ItemTemplate" style="display:none;">
    #ID#: <a href="#QUICKLINK#">#NAME#</a><br />
  </div>
  <div id="DisplayedItems"></div>
</div>
```

Compared to the earlier version of this file, you modified the contents of the existing `ItemResults div` to contain a template container, as well as a `div` with ID `DisplayedItems`. This second `div` is what displays the results, rather than the outer `div`. The template `div` is styled to `"display: none;"` as it will not be displayed to the user.

Creating JavaScript Using jQuery to Retrieve Children

Now you need to update the `getTaxonomyItems` method in the JavaScript to actually call the Web service, and update the displayed items `div`. The update JavaScript is listed in the following code snippet.

```
//initialization of the Taxonomy links.
//We wrap it in the document ready so it only runs
//after the entire DOM has been loaded.
$ektron(document).ready(function() {
  if ("undefined" != typeof TaxonomyWebService) {
    //When the link is clicked, fire the
    //getTaxonomyItems handler.
```

```
      $ektron("a.taxonomyLink").click(
        TaxonomyWebService.getTaxonomyItems
      );
    }
  });

//this will be our namespace for objects and functions
//created for the handler example.
if ("undefined" == typeof TaxonomyWebService) {
  var TaxonomyWebService = {
    getTaxonomyItems: function() {
      //this function will look inside the clicked link
      //to retrieve the id of the taxonomy item clicked.
      //It will then display the taxonomy id in the results div.
      var clickedAnchor = $ektron(this);
      //get the child span of the anchor-this contains the taxonomy id
      var taxonomyId = clickedAnchor.find("span.taxonomyId").text();
      //build the requestitem object
      var requestItem = { 'TaxonomyID': taxonomyId };
      //use the Ektron JSON library to serialize it
      //and build the complete object to send to the handler.
      var dataObject = { 'Request': Ektron.JSON.stringify(requestItem) };

      //use the jQuery ajax method to perform an ajax call to the handler.
      $ektron.ajax({
        url: 'taxonomyexampleservice.ashx',
        //this will cause jQuery to evaluate the return object as json
        dataType: 'json',
        type: 'POST', //the data should be sent as POST, not GET
        data: dataObject, //the ItemRequest object
        //the method to call when we get data back
        success: TaxonomyWebService.updateDisplay
      });
    },
    //the ajax method calls this when data is returned
    updateDisplay: function(data, textStatus, XMLHttpRequest) {
      //retrieve the template contents
      var template = $ektron("div#ItemResults div#ItemTemplate").html();
      //the string that will be built containing the html to display
      var results = "";
      for (var i in data) {
        //perform string replacements for each token with the content
        //of the results
        var tmp = template;
        tmp = tmp.replace(/#ID#/g, data[i].ItemID);
        tmp = tmp.replace(/#QUICKLINK#/g, data[i].ItemQuicklink);
        tmp = tmp.replace(/#NAME#/g, data[i].ItemName);
        results += tmp;
      }
      //update the displayed items div with the constructed html
      $ektron("div#ItemResults div#DisplayedItems").html(results);
    }
  };
}
```

Rich Interaction Using jQuery, Smart Forms, and Handlers | 183

The changes in the JavaScript start with the addition of the AJAX call. You are setting the `dataType` to JSON so the results are evaluated, rather than returned as a string. You are also passing the `dataObject` as the POST data. The `dataObject` is comprised of a simple object you created, which you used the Ektron JSON library to serialize. Remember that to use the Ektron JSON library, you need to include the JSON file. The following code when placed in codebehind for this page does this.

```
Ektron.Cms.API.JS.RegisterJS(
    this, Ektron.Cms.API.JS.ManagedScript.EktronJsonJS);
```

The AJAX method also has a parameter called *success* which accepts a method. This method is set to `updateDisplay`. The `updateDisplay` method handles the templating output. With these changes your example is complete.

The Completed Code and Page

The complete code for the `SimpleHandler.aspx` file is shown in Listing 7-6.

Available for download on Wrox.com

LISTING 7-6: SimpleHandler.aspx

```
<%@ Page Language="C#" AutoEventWireup="true"
    CodeFile="WebService.aspx.cs" Inherits="WebService" %>

<!DOCTYPE html PUBLIC "-//W3C//DTD XHTML 1.0 Transitional//EN"
"http://www.w3.org/TR/xhtml1/DTD/xhtml1-transitional.dtd">
<html xmlns="http://www.w3.org/1999/xhtml">
<head runat="server">
  <title></title>
</head>
<body>
  <form id="form1" runat="server">
    <asp:Repeater ID="repeaterItemList" runat="server">
      <ItemTemplate>
        <a href="#" class="taxonomyLink" onclick="return false;">
          <span style="display: none;" class="taxonomyId">
            <%#
              DataBinder.Eval(Container.DataItem, "TaxonomyId")
            %>
          </span>
          <%#
            DataBinder.Eval(Container.DataItem, "TaxonomyName")
          %>
        </a>
        <br />
      </ItemTemplate>
    </asp:Repeater>
    <div id="ItemResults">
      <div id="ItemTemplate" style="display:none;">
        #ID#: <a href="#QUICKLINK#">#NAME#</a><br />
      </div>
      <div id="DisplayedItems"></div>
    </div>
    <script language="javascript" type="text/javascript">
```

continues

LISTING 7-6 *(continued)*

```javascript
        //initialization of the Taxonomy links.
        //We wrap it in the document ready so it only runs
        //after the entire DOM has been loaded.
        $ektron(document).ready(function() {
          if ("undefined" != typeof TaxonomyWebService) {
            //When the link is clicked, fire the
            //getTaxonomyItems handler.
            $ektron("a.taxonomyLink").click(
              TaxonomyWebService.getTaxonomyItems
            );
          }
        });

        //this will be our namespace for objects and functions
        //created for the handler example.
        if ("undefined" == typeof TaxonomyWebService) {
          var TaxonomyWebService = {
            getTaxonomyItems: function() {
              //this function will look inside the clicked link
              //to retrieve the id of the taxonomy item clicked.
              //It will then display the taxonomy id in the results div.
              var clickedAnchor = $ektron(this);
              //get the child span of the anchor-this contains the taxonomy id
              var taxonomyId = clickedAnchor.find("span.taxonomyId").text();
              //build the requestitem object
              var requestItem = { 'TaxonomyID': taxonomyId };
              //use the Ektron JSON library to serialize it, and build the complete

              // object to send to the handler.
              var dataObject = { 'Request': Ektron.JSON.stringify(requestItem) };

              //use the jQuery ajax method to perform an ajax call to the handler.
              $ektron.ajax({ url: 'taxonomyexampleservice.ashx',
                dataType: 'json', //this will cause jQuery
                                  //to evaluate the return object
                type: 'POST', //the data should be sent as POST, not GET
                data: dataObject, //the ItemRequest object
                success: TaxonomyWebService.updateDisplay
                //the method to call when
                //we get data back
              });
            },
            //the ajax method calls this when data is returned
            updateDisplay: function(data, textStatus, XMLHttpRequest) {
              //retrieve the template contents
              var template = $ektron("div#ItemResults div#ItemTemplate").html();
              //the string that will be built containing the html to display
              var results = "";
              for (var i in data) {
                //perform string replacements for each token with the
                //content of the results
                var tmp = template;
```

```
                tmp = tmp.replace(/#ID#/g, data[i].ItemID);
                tmp = tmp.replace(/#QUICKLINK#/g, data[i].ItemQuicklink);
                tmp = tmp.replace(/#NAME#/g, data[i].ItemName);
                results += tmp;
            }
            //update the displayed items div with the constructed html
            $ektron("div#ItemResults div#DisplayedItems").html(results);
        }
      };
    }
    </script>
  </form>
</body>
</html>
```

Now visit `http://localhost/OnTrek/simplehandler.aspx` to see the completed page. As shown in Figure 7-7, the page first lists a set of links that correspond to the taxonomy nodes. When a user selects a link, the jQuery performs an AJAX call to the `TaxonomyExampleService.ashx`, where the request is deserialized and the child content is retrieved. The child content is then serialized and returned to the jQuery where it is evaluated and templated before being displayed as output.

Company-Wide
Marketing
Engineering
HumanResources
Sales
Training
516: Activity Stream
517: Calendar
518: Group Spaces
519: Home

FIGURE 7-7

USING MENUS FOR NAVIGATION

You may have heard the phrase "content is king." The idea behind this is that the importance of quality content on a website is second to none. The better the information, the more likely you will have happy site visitors and growing traffic. But if content is king, then navigation is queen, because without navigational aids such as menus to direct site visitors to the content they're looking for, the content might as well not exist. Navigational structures such as menus make content accessible, and are therefore just as important as the content itself. It's no exaggeration to say that one of the most fundamentally important tasks for a developer is creating effective website navigation. Failing to create a well designed navigation will result in an overall decrease in your website's visitors, sales, conversions, and other metrics that define your website's success.

In the Implementation section, you'll learn to create the main navigation for the OnTrek website. This section focuses exclusively on the Ektron Menus feature and discusses strategies and best practices for using Ektron Menus. After reading this section, you'll understand what it takes to create a well designed navigation structure. You'll go through the process of implementing a globally accessible menu on the OnTrek website using the Ektron Flex Menu Server Control.

Ektron Menu Basics

Let's start by covering the basics of Ektron menus. The term *menu* in this section refers specifically to the type of navigation structure that is created and managed using Ektron's Menu feature. Although you can use Ektron's other navigation aids, such as collections, to create single-level menu-like structures, this section covers only Ektron Menus.

At a high level, creating a menu in Ektron is a two-phase process:

➤ The menu hierarchy is created by content managers in the Workarea shown in Figure 7-8

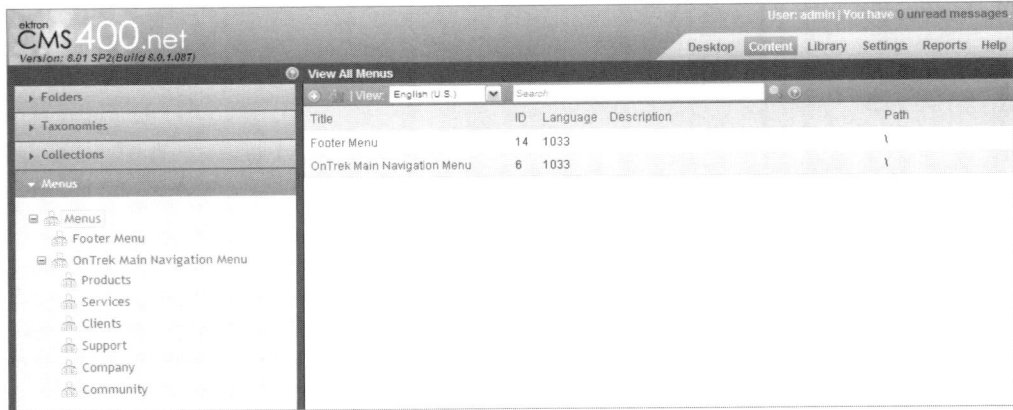

FIGURE 7-8

➤ It is then displayed on the site by developers using a menu server control.

Once the menu is available through the website, further management of the menu (adding, updating, and removing menu items) happens in one of two ways. Since the server controls provides authenticated users with the GUI needed to do this, as shown in Figure 7-9, management can be done through the website itself or through the Workarea.

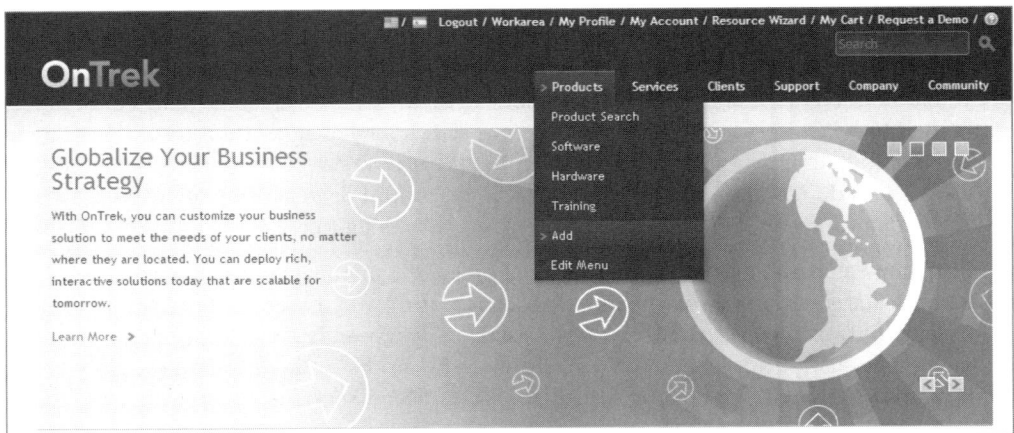

FIGURE 7-9

To manage and create menu structures, CMS users need to be part of either the Administrators group (a CMS user belonging to the Collection and Menu Admin role) or be granted permissions to the collections on the root folder.

Menus contain links to managed content items, library assets, external hyperlinks, or other menus to create nested submenus. Because menus are language aware, you can create a language specific edition of any menu in each supported language. The main menu object itself has a number of properties that are defined through the menu creation process, such as a title, description, and an image link that controls the icon that appears on the Web page next to, or in place of, the menu item text.

To display a menu on the Web page, developers use one of the two Ektron Menu Server Controls:

- The Flex Menu Server Control
- The CMS Menu Server Control

The Flex Menu is extremely feature rich, has more configuration options and server control properties, and is therefore a bit more complex than its counterpart. The CMS Menu, on the other hand, has a minimalist feature set by design, and is less complex to set up and configure. Each menu has its pros and cons and which you choose should be determined by your project's requirements. Here are some things to keep in mind when choosing between the Flex Menu and the CMS Menu.

Using the Flex Menu

The Flex Menu's most prominent feature is its ability to intelligently highlight submenu items, based on the page that is being visited, when the page is loaded. For example, if a site visitor navigates directly to a website's "product page," the Flex Menu can automatically expand and highlight the appropriate submenu item. This is an extremely valuable feature — consider the annoyance site visitors often experience while navigating through a website using a standard hierarchical left-hand menu, only to have it collapse with each click and page refresh. Without auto-expanding menus, the site visitors have less indication of where they are in relation to the rest of the site and may miss opportunities to discover related information.

All the configuration information that determines which menu item to select is defined in the Workarea and executed by the server control, and therefore requires no custom coding. The server control derives which item to select based on a set of conditions that take into account both the menu's configuration options defined during the menu creation process and the data available at the page runtime, such as the page being visited and the ID of the content item displayed. The "Working with Menus" chapter of the Ektron Reference Manual lists the complete set of these rules; there are nine in all. It's a good idea to read through the complete list available in the Reference Manual before working with the Flex Menu, but the first two in the list are included here to give an understanding of what the rules look like.

1. The Flex Menu looks in the query string for parameters that indicate if a user has clicked on a menu item. If it finds the item, it marks all ancestor menus as selected and processing stops.
2. The Flex Menu looks in the query string to see if a query string parameter defining a Content ID or Form ID is present, and if so, checks to see if it matches an item in the menu. If a match is found, the item is selected and processing stops.

This type of processing continues through all of the nine rules listed in the Reference Manual. If a particular rule doesn't find a match, the processing continues to the next rule, otherwise it stops processing. Once all rules are executed, if no matches are found, the menu renders collapsed with no menu items selected. The processing rules are fixed and cannot be changed. However, the item that's selected is determined by your specific menu's configuration. The Flex Menu Server Control has a debug mode that logs information to help developers understand why the Flex Menu made a particular selection. The following steps describe the process of enabling this logging feature.

1. Open the website's web.config in a text editor.
2. In the system.diagnostics section, locate the setting for the LogLevel, and set it to verbose by using the value `"4"`, that is, `<setting name="LogLevel" value="4"/>`.
3. The Flex Menu Server Control has a property called LogInfo that must also be set to True. This value is False by default. See Table 7-1 for an abbreviated list of Flex Menu Server Control properties. For a complete list, refer to the Flex Menu Server Control section of the Ektron Reference Manual.
4. Refresh the page and view the recent events in the system's event viewer.

TABLE 7-1: Flex Menu Server Control Properties

PROPERTY	VALUE	DATA TYPE
AutoCollapseBranches	When set to true, all open submenus close once a new submenu is expanded. When false, all open submenus remain open as new submenus are expanded.	Boolean
CacheInterval	Specifies the amount of time in seconds that the menu's data is cached by the server control.	Double
DefaultMenuID	The ID of the menu to display.	Long
DisplayXslt	The path to an XSLT file for rendering the menu.	String
EnableMouseOverPopup	When set to true, submenus expand once the cursor moves over them. When false, submenus appear only when clicked.	Boolean
EnableSmartOpen	When set to true, submenus will open automatically according to the menu configuration defined in the Workarea. When false, submenus do not automatically expand.	Boolean
IncludeJS	When set to true, the default JavaScript is loaded. When false, it is not. You may want to set this to false if you're using a custom XSLT.	Boolean
SuppressAddEdit	When set to False, additional Add and Edit menu items are displayed and can be used from the site to further manage the menu. When set to True, the Add and Edit menu items are suppressed..	Boolean

The last thing to cover on the Flex Menu is controlling its presentation. The recommended method for styling the Flex Menu is to use CSS. There are a number of samples available in the

CMS400Developer starter site (~/CMS400Developer/Developer/Menu/FlexMenu/) showing different menu styles achieved by changing exclusively the CSS, including rendering the Flex Menu horizontally (as used in a header navigation menu) and vertically (as used on a left-hand navigation menu).

Modifying the markup produced by the Flex Menu Server Control is achieved through modifying an XSLT file. Keep in mind that the default JavaScript produced by this control expects its HTML markup to conform to a particular schema. So if you decide to modify the markup through the XSLT, you'll also want to write your own JavaScript for manipulating it. This also requires an understanding of the XML structure produced by the Flex Menu Server Control, which contains attributes noting things such as a particular item being selected. This approach is demonstrated as you implement OnTrek's global navigation menus.

Using the CMS Menu

There is much less to say about the second of the two menu server controls since the CMS Menu Server Control does not try to solve the problem of auto-expanding menu items, and as such, is much more simplistic in its implementation. The CMS Menu renders the menu structure into the page and provides the markup, CSS, and JavaScript for default `click` event handling. If you don't need the menu to open itself, this is the menu to use. This control also allows you to modify its markup by modifying its default XSLT. However, in this case, the XML is simplified since it does not contain the same markup elements to denote when a menu item is selected. The benefit of using this control is that there is little overhead since it does not auto-expand menus. The obvious drawback of using this control is that your site visitors need to drill back into the menu each time the page loads, or you will need to write your own expansion logic.

There are three CMS Menu Server Control samples included in the CMS400Developer Menu section. Two of them include JavaScript for their demos: One is the local file called CSSMenu.js, and the other is the Workarea file ~/Workarea/java/cmsmenuapi.js. Both of these files are short and only a few JavaScript functions. The third sample (menu.aspx) does not include any JavaScript and does not open or close; it renders fully open.

You may have seen or used the DHTML Menu Server Control before. This is a legacy menu that is still supported for upgrades and backwards-compatibility, but it should otherwise not be used. If you're using the DHTML Menu Server Control and have the opportunity to revisit old code, it's best to upgrade to either the CMS Menu or the Flex Menu. The Smart Menu Server Control, which was available in earlier versions of Ektron, has also been deprecated. You should not use the DHTML Menu or the Smart Menu, and instead, use the CMS Menu or the Flex Menu.

Understanding Menu Configuration Options

Now that you understand the basics of how to create a menu and how to render the menu on the site using either one of two menu server controls, let's go into more depth on the menu configuration options that influence which menu item is automatically selected when using the Flex Menu Server

Control. Since the CMS Menu does not provide the auto-expanding capabilities of the Flex Menu Server Control, the Folder and Template Associations described next are ignored by the CMS Menu. You should know which type of menu you plan on using on your website prior to creating the structure in the Workarea, since one requires more configuration information than the other.

As discussed earlier, a menu can contain links to content items, library assets, external hyperlinks, or submenus. The Add Menu Screen in Figure 7-10 shows the fields available when choosing to add a new menu (or submenu).

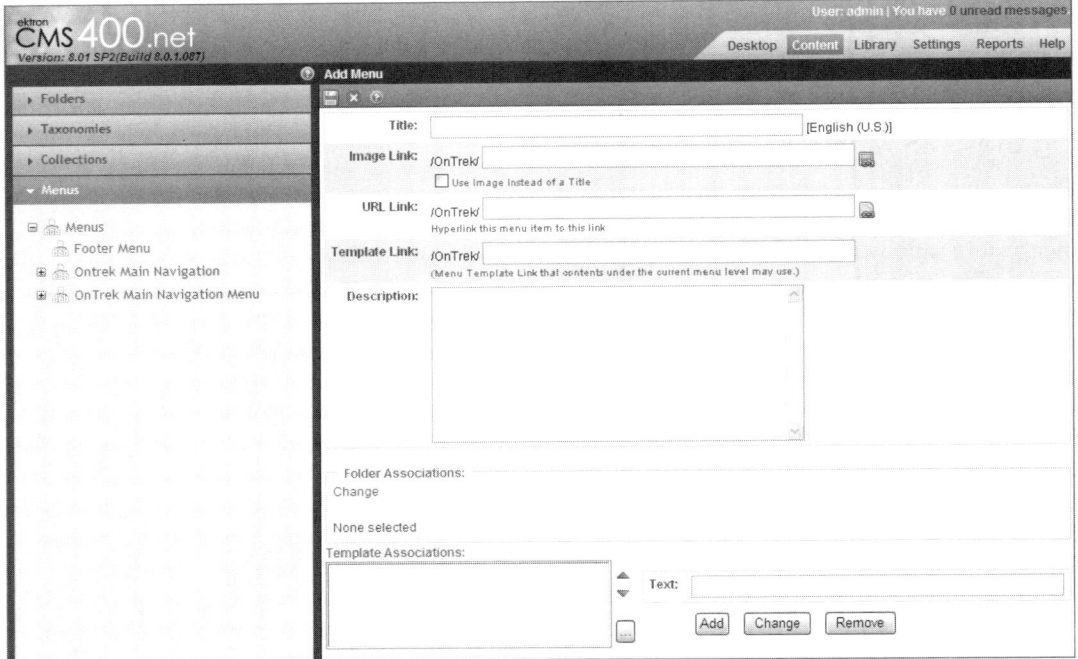

FIGURE 7-10

The field values are described in the Table 7-2. The final two fields, Folder Associations and Template Associations, are described outside of the table.

TABLE 7-2: Fields on the Add/Edit Menu Screen

FIELD	DESCRIPTION
Title	The label that displays in the menu on the Web page.
Image Link	The image that appears next to, or in place of, the title. This field is optional.
URL Link	The URL that defines the hyperlink for the Title and Image Link. This field is optional.
Template Link	This field applies to content only and defines the template used for all content on this menu. This field is optional. Not specifying a Template Link means the content's QuickLink is used.

FIELD	DESCRIPTION
Description	The description of the menu used mostly in the Workarea.
Folder Associations	See the following section.
Template Associations	See the following section.

The Folder Associations field and The Template Associations field are applicable only to the Flex Menu and provide it with the information needed by the Flex Menu to control which items are selected by default. Folder associations are used to instruct the menu to automatically expand when a user visits a page containing a content item that lives in the specified folders. For example, if you associate the menu to the `/MainSite/Pages/Products` folder, and a user navigates to any content item that resides in this folder, the Flex Menu automatically displays the items on the associated submenu. The template associations are used in a similar way. They allow you to instruct the menu to automatically expand when a user visits a page that uses the specified template. For example, suppose you have a template called ProductDetails.aspx that provides a detailed description for a given product, and you associate this template to the Products Menu. Any time a visitor travels to the Product Details template, the Flex Menu automatically displays the Products menu.

Designing your menu structure up front will help avoid a couple of painful pitfalls when working with the Flex Menu. These include creating nested associations that result in unexpected content from expanding, or creating impossible conditions that prevent any menus from expanding. If you run into such a situation, refer back to the steps described in earlier sections to enable its verbose logging.

Implementing the Global Navigation Menu

There are two ways to create the menu structure in the Workarea. The first is through the Workarea's Content ➪ Menu tab, and the second is through the New ➪ Menu option located in the content folder tree. Creating a menu through the content folder tree has the added benefit of being able to use folder level permissions to control who has access to manage the menus. If you do not need such granular control, use the Workarea's Content ➪ Menu tab UI, which places the menus in the root folder. This section shows the Content ➪ Menu option.

Creating a Subset of the Our Company Menu

The OnTrek website uses a persistent global navigation that displays in the header of each page on the site. The following steps walk through the process of creating a subset of the "Our Company" menu shown in Figure 7-11.

To create a new menu item via the Menus tab, follow these steps.

1. From the Workarea ➪ Menu tab, right-click the Menus item and then click Add Menu.

2. In the Add Menu screen, shown in Figure 7-10, provide the title: **OnTrek Main Navigation** and leave all other fields blank.

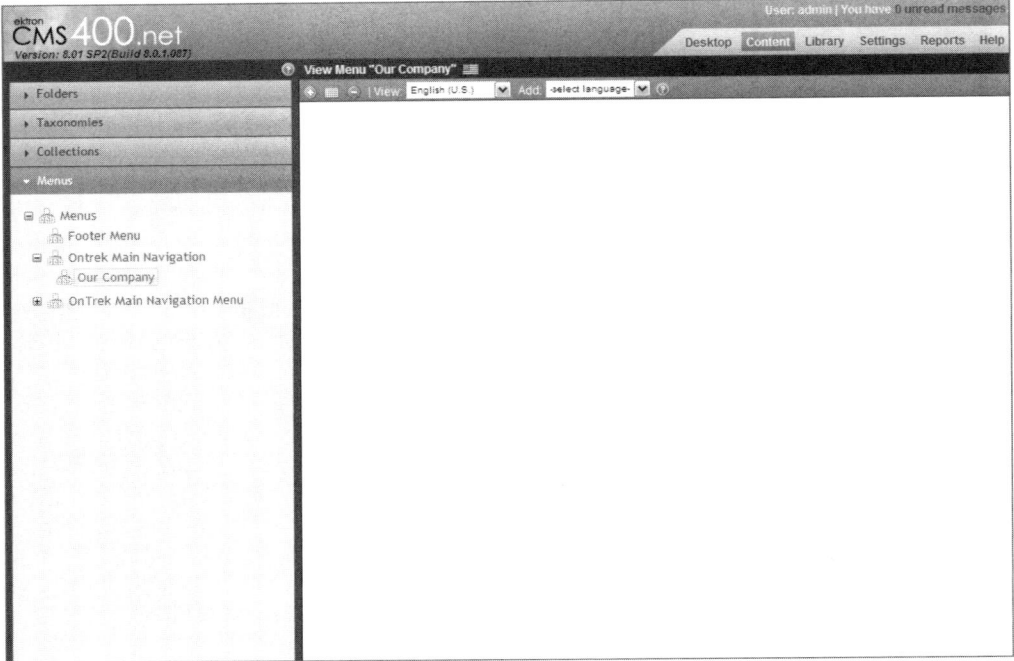

FIGURE 7-11

3. To add items to this menu, click the Add button [Add], or alternatively, hover the cursor over the menu in the left panel, right-click the mouse, and click Add Items. The Add New Item screen displays a list of items that you can add to the menu.
4. Click the radio button next to Submenu and click Next.
5. In the Add Menu Item screen, provide the title **Our Company** and leave the other fields blank.
6. To add items to the "Our Company" submenu, click the Add button.
7. Click the radio button next to Content Item and click Next.
8. From the Add New Item "Our Company" screen, select the Contact Information item, then click the Save button.

If you've installed the OnTrek Starter Site, the complete navigation structure will already exist in the database.

Placing a Flex Menu in the Master Page

The global navigation of the OnTrek website is located in the header section of each page on the site. You will now use a single Flex Menu rendered horizontally and placed in the website's master page. This implementation will use a custom XSLT to modify the markup, and also use the jQuery Superfish plug-in to provide its styling and subtle animations.

1. From Visual Studio, open `~/templates/masterpages/main.aspx`.

2. Place the Flex Menu Server Control onto the page by dragging and dropping from the Visual Studio Toolbox into the header region of the template, just after the opening BODY tag. Use the following Flex Menu parameter values to guide your implementation.

```
<CMS:FlexMenu
    ID="uxMenu"
    runat="server"
    DefaultMenuID="6"
    DisplayXslt="~/components/usercontrols/menu/lightweight.xsl"
    WrapTag="div"
    AutoCollapseBranches="True"
    StartCollapsed="True"
    EnableMouseOverPopUp="False"
    EnableSmartOpen="False"
    StartLevel="1"
    MenuDepth="0"
    EnableAjax="False"
    MasterControlId=""
    CacheInterval="600"
    IncludeJS="false" />
```

> *In this snippet, you can see that the* DefaultMenuID *is 6, which points to the ID of the root of the OnTrek menu created in the Workarea. Also note how the Flex Menu specifies its custom XSLT through the* DisplayXslt *property and then suppresses the output of the default JavaScript by setting the* IncludeJS *attribute to False. Custom JavaScript is needed anytime the Flex Menu's HTML is customized, as mentioned earlier, since the default JavaScript looks for HTML that conforms to a particular schema.*

Internally the Flex Menu Server Control receives the menu structure from the business tier in the following XML format. The custom XSLT is used by the Flex Menu to transform this XML into HTML, as shown in the following code snippet:

```
<MenuDataResult>
  <Info>
    <ControlMenuId>6</ControlMenuId>
    <CssFileName></CssFileName>
    <XslFileName>/OnTrek/components/usercontrols/menu/lightweight.xsl</XslFileName>
    <WrappingClassName></WrappingClassName>
    <ControlId>uxMenu</ControlId>
    <ControlIdHash>e6aab43b8</ControlIdHash>
    <MasterControlIdHash></MasterControlIdHash>
    <GroupId></GroupId>
    <AppPath>/OnTrek/WorkArea/</AppPath>
    <SitePath>/OnTrek/</SitePath>
    <ButtonNoScriptLink>http://ws10247/OnTrek/default.aspx</ButtonNoScriptLink>
    <AjaxEnabled>false</AjaxEnabled>
    <MenuFragment>false</MenuFragment>
```

```xml
        <AutoCollapseBranches>true</AutoCollapseBranches>
        <StartCollapsed>true</StartCollapsed>
        <EnableSmartOpen>false</EnableSmartOpen>
        <EnableMouseOverPopUp>false</EnableMouseOverPopUp>
        <IsSlaveControl>false</IsSlaveControl>
        <StartLevel>1</StartLevel>
        <MenuDepth>0</MenuDepth>
        <SelectLevel>-1</SelectLevel>
        <SelectMenuIdString></SelectMenuIdString>
        <SelectItemIdString></SelectItemIdString>
        <SlaveStartLevelIds></SlaveStartLevelIds>
        <DefaultMenuIdString></DefaultMenuIdString>
        <SWRevision>8.0.0.073</SWRevision>
        <CacheInterval>600</CacheInterval>
        <UseCssHardLink>true</UseCssHardLink>
        <UseJavascriptHardLink>false</UseJavascriptHardLink>
    </Info>
    <Item>
      <Item>
        <ItemId>7</ItemId>
        <ItemType>Submenu</ItemType>
        <ItemSubType>0</ItemSubType>
        <ItemTitle>Products</ItemTitle>
        <ItemDescription></ItemDescription>
        <ItemImage></ItemImage>
        <ItemImageOverride>false</ItemImageOverride>
        <ItemSelected>false</ItemSelected>
        <ItemLevel>1</ItemLevel>
        <ItemIdString>e6aab43b8_6_7_7</ItemIdString>
        <Menu>
          <MenuId>7</MenuId>
          <Title>Products</Title>
          <Template></Template>
          <Type>content</Type>
          <Link></Link>
          <ParentId>6</ParentId>
          <AncestorId>6</AncestorId>
          <FolderId>0</FolderId>
          <Description></Description>
          <Image></Image>
          <ImageOverride>false</ImageOverride>
          <MenuIdString>e6aab43b8_6_7</MenuIdString>
          <MenuSelected>false</MenuSelected>
          <MenuLevel>1</MenuLevel>
          <ChildMenuSelected>false</ChildMenuSelected>
          <ChildMenuSelRelDepth>0</ChildMenuSelRelDepth>
```

3. Copy the lightweight.xsl file from your samples directory into the `~/compontents/usercontrols/menu/` directory.

4. Open this XSLT and see how it uses various templates for matching and transforming the XML.

Under the Hood

In the CMS400Developer starter site, there are several fully functioning code samples showing various ways to use the Flex Menu and the CMS Menu (`~/CMS400Developer/Developer/Menu/`). These samples are shown in Tables 7-3 and 7-4.

TABLE 7-3: Example Customizations of the CMS Menu

SAMPLE	DESCRIPTION
Cms:Menu control	Demonstrates displaying the markup using the default XSLT, which creates an unordered list using UL/LI tags.
Cms:Menu control Tree	Uses CSS to style the default Tree-XSLT as a navigable tree, without the use of JavaScript.
Cms:Menu control Tree 2	Displays the markup using the internal Unordered-List-XSLT together with styling from CSSMenu.css and client-side control from CSSMenu.js.
Cms:Menu control as XML	This demonstrates how to display the control's XML, using the internal Unordered-List-XSLT (default) and a literal control; the codebehind sets the menu to invisible and copies the controls XML to the literal control for viewing.

TABLE 7-4: Example Customizations of the Flex Menu

SAMPLE	DESCRIPTION
Lightweight Menu	Largely follows the implementation steps of this chapter, though it may be useful as a starting point for future projects, as it uses a minimal yet functional JavaScript and XSLT files.
Expanding	Demonstrates how to use CSS exclusively to render the Flex Menu as a vertically oriented accordion menu.
Horizontal	Shows how to configure the Flex Menu to render horizontally for use in a header navigation.
508 Compliance	This sample shows how to render the Flex Menu in such a way that it is Section 508 compliant to ensure visually impaired site visitors can access and navigate the menu structure.

In addition to these samples, there is another called the Master Slave Menu sample that demonstrates a specific configuration of the Flex Menu commonly implemented. The Master Slave Flex

Menu is a two-part menu system that uses two Flex Menus together on a single page. Before getting into the code sample, let's clarify its purpose and outline its approach.

The first of the two menus is the Master located in the page header, rendered just like the horizontally oriented navigation menu you created for the OnTrek website. The second of the two menus is located in the left-hand navigation area of the page, and renders vertically like an accordion menu, as shown in the CMS400Developer starter site in Figure 7-12.

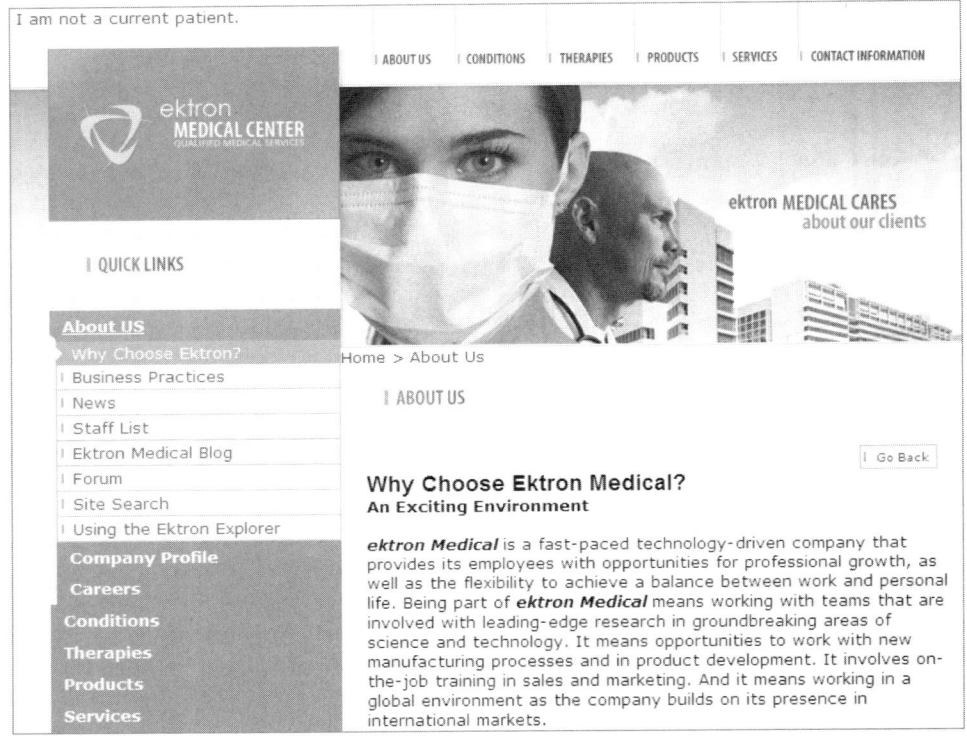

FIGURE 7-12

The Master menu renders the entire first level of the menu horizontally while the Slave menu renders the first level and its children vertically. The Slave is called such because it follows the lead of the Master and automatically expands based on the item selected from the Master menu. So for example, if you click Departments ➪ Engineering ➪ Infrastructure from the horizontal navigation menu, the left-hand navigation menu automatically expands out to highlight this location in the menu structure. This is an extremely powerful way to give site visitors a solid sense of their current location on the site. Historically, achieving this type of functionality with the Flex Menu was somewhat complex. But with the Version 8 release, this process has been simplified noticeably by leveraging an approach using ASP.NET Master Pages and a new Flex Menu Server Control property called the `StartMenuId`.

The ASP.NET Master Page is basic and it is simply used to render the Master Flex Menu horizontally. Use the following code snippet.

```
<cms:FlexMenu
    ID="TopMenu"
    runat="server"
    DefaultMenuID="89"
    EnableMouseOverPopUp="True"
    EnableSmartOpen="False"
    Stylesheet="top_horizontal.css"
    DisplayXslt="Demo.xsl"
    CacheInterval="0"
/>
```

There are two tricks to getting the Slave Flex Menu to expand automatically.

- **The brute force approach:** This uses a separate ASP.NET template for each second level node in the navigation menu and manually sets the `StartMenuId` parameter to the ID of the sub-menu item to expand. Note that this `StartMenuId` parameter does not need to be the root of the menu. Then, you configure your menu in the Workarea to expand (using the Template Associations described earlier) using a URL that references each of these ASP.NET templates. Use the following code snippet.

```
<cms:FlexMenu
    ID="SideMenu"
    runat="server"
    DefaultMenuID="89"
    StartMenuId="91"
    EnableSmartOpen="True"
    Stylesheet="side_expand.css"
    DisplayXslt="Demo.xsl"
    CacheInterval="0"
/>
```

- **Some codebehind required:** This uses a single ASP.NET template and dynamically sets the `StartMenuId` in programmatically based on rules that you have to define and manage in your codebehind.

The CMS400Developer sample has a complete working sample for you to analyze and use as a starting point for your own Master Slave Flex Menu implementation.

USING SEARCH FOR NAVIGATION

Search is an important part of your website's navigation and fills a specific void not handled by the other navigation aids previously discussed. The importance of search appears to be well understood, given that almost all companies report search as one of the primary means of navigation on their sites. Unfortunately, as the study "Enriching Search: Efficiency Without Spending," by Jupiter Research found out, almost 70 percent of all visitors using site search report that their searches yielded useless information.

Deploying a successful site search requires more than simply making the Search textbox available on a Web page. This is where search-strategy planning comes in. Developing a search strategy requires you to consider the information needs of your site visitors and the information architecture of the website, and to understand what information is not readily available through the website's navigation structures. A successful search strategy takes these factors into account, uses search analytics to monitor its effectiveness, and tweaks the results in response regularly. The Ektron Framework provides technology to complement this process. This section discusses how a site search strategy can be used to ensure that your site search is effectively providing site visitors with the information they want.

Starting with Ektron version 8.5, Ektron's search technology leverages the Microsoft search stack. The 8.5 release featured a major architectural overhaul of search, replacing its previous search implementation which relied on Microsoft Index Server and redesigned it to leverage Microsoft's state of the art search technology.

Defining Your SiteSearch Strategy

Making sure that all information is accessible through a search interface is the most obvious and critical part of any search strategy. Ektron's core search engine satisfies this requirement by providing full text search for content such as HTML, Microsoft Office Documents, Smart Forms, and Shockwave Flash files. When content is published into the system, it is indexed and becomes available to site visitors through widgets, server controls, and any other code using Ektron's search APIs. All types of managed content, including those previously listed and community generated content, such as blog posts and discussion board topics, are indexed by default, as are searchable metadata values if any have been defined (see the metadata section in Chapter 5). If there are cases where you want to exclude particular content items from the search result, you have the ability to remove them by selecting the Content Searchable checkbox shown in Figure 7-13.

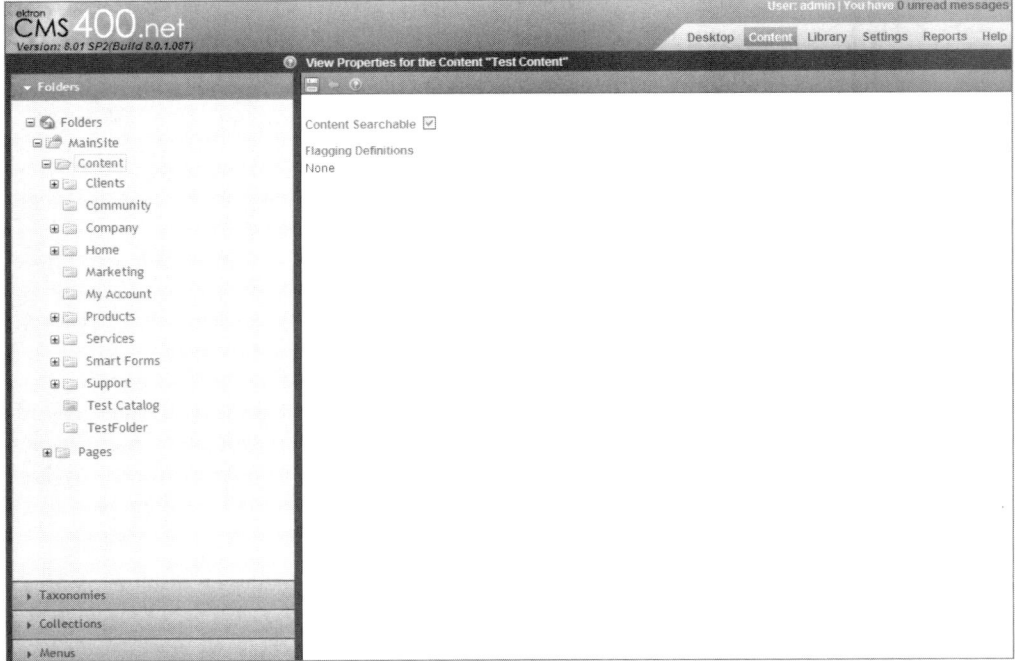

FIGURE 7-13

In addition to full text searches, Ektron also offers the ability to perform structured searches through the XML fields stored in Smart Form Designs (see the Smart Forms section in Chapter 6), taxonomy categories, as well as through searchable metadata definitions associated to content. Structured search is useful when you want to retrieve and filter data by a specific field, such as ContentType or ContentID. Combining both structured and full-text search is extremely powerful and lets you formulate queries equivalent to "get only PDF documents that contain the text OnTrek."

Including Folders in a Search Index Using Integrated Search

Continuing with the thread of making all information accessible through search is using Ektron's Integrated Search to include content from an external repository. Integrated Search is a natural fit when you have directories filled with files such as unmanaged HTML or Word documents in the server's file system (or accessible through a virtual path) and want them included in the search index.

To include a folder in the search index, follow these steps:

1. Click Workarea's Settings ➪ Configuration ➪ Integrated Search.
2. Click the Add Icon. This begins the process and allows you to specify the directories and file types to include or exclude from the search results.

Searching with Social Networking

Ektron's social networking functionality demonstrates how Ektron Search can be used to search for people, colleagues, and community groups. The CommunitySearch Server Control allows you to find users by name and customize user properties, such as what department you work in, or your favorite type of food. There are also APIs available for retrieving this type of information about users and groups; these are discussed in more detail in Chapter 10 along with the rest of the community framework.

Tracking Searches with Ektron's Search Phrase Report

Knowing what people are searching for and understanding whether their searches are successful are essential parts of establishing an effective search strategy. The first part of this is straightforward. Start by looking at what search phrases people are using to find information. Ektron's Search Phrase Report displays a unique list of all the terms entered by site visitors, along with a count representing the number of times a term was used in a search, sorted in descending order with the most popular search terms at the top of the list.

To find this report, do the following:

1. This report is found in the Workarea by going to Reports ➪ Contents.
2. Click Search Phrase Report. You can see the form used to generate the report in Figure 7-14.
3. To make the most of the data, you need to filter the results. You can do this by specifying a date range, a particular language, the minimum number of occurrences of the term, and whether or not you want to include terms from the Workarea or the website, or both.

Determining whether a particular search was successful using the Search Phrase Report is not always easy. The crux of the issue is that it's close to impossible to determine whether a search is successful simply by identifying the search term and determining whether the searcher clicked on the result. This is because the search term alone does not give an accurate picture of a searcher's intent. Even still, there are a number of warning flags to look out for in this report that can indicate potential problems. These are discussed in detail in the following sections.

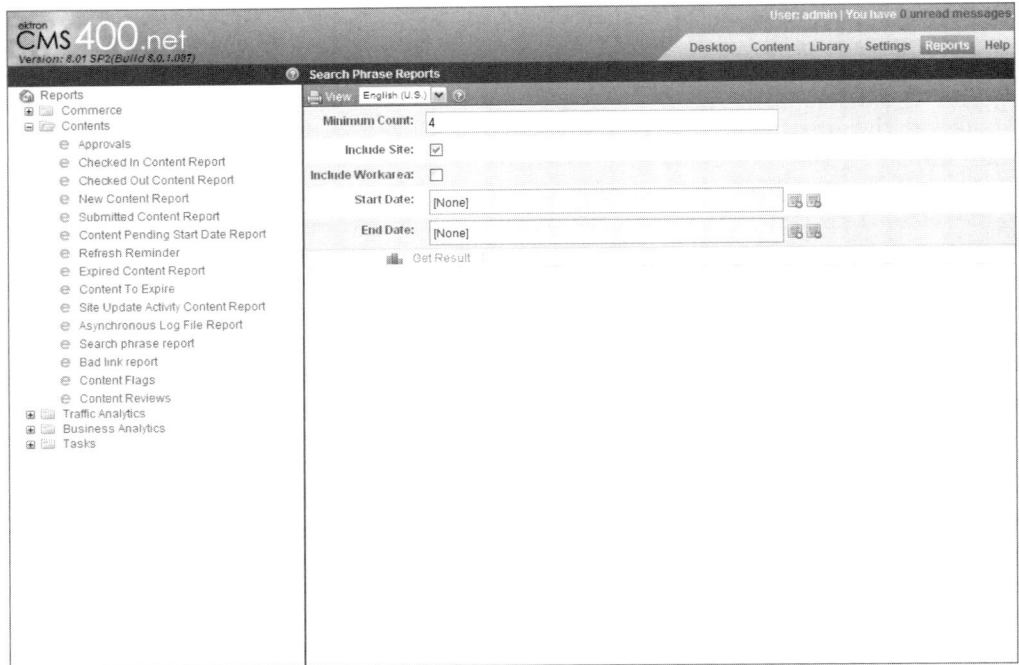

FIGURE 7-14

A Search Phrase Report That Lacks Sufficient Search Terms

This could indicate an obscured or improperly positioning Search textbox. Do people recognize that search is available? You will most certainly have unhappy visitors if they don't recognize that search is a part of your navigation strategy. Offer search as part of your global navigation. Either put a Search box or a link to one on the global navigation header on every page of your site.

Ambiguous Queries

These are searches resulting in two sets of results, each with completely different meanings. For example, a search for the term "Saturn" might indicate a search for information on the planet, but might also be a term used by someone researching a car. The WebSearch Server Control has a property called ShowCategories that, when set to True, displays a navigable category tree when a search term is entered that exists in a taxonomy. To return to the Saturn example, assuming your content was categorized appropriately in a taxonomy and the ShowCategories property was set to True, the "Filter by Category" link would appear and display choices allowing the visitor to filter by Automobiles or Planets. If no content in the search results are assigned categories, the "Filter by Category" link would not appear. This feature provides a nice way to disambiguate queries as well as help site visitors filter search results when a site search returns too many results.

Searches That Yield No Search Results

When this situation does occur, you have the opportunity to do a few things:

➤ **Adding a collection:** Because a page with no results is typically a dead end, it's a good idea to give the site visitor some further search instruction or a list of potentially useful links. You might use a collection here to provide editorial control over which links are available.

➤ **Logging the event:** You might want to consider logging this event in some way. The Search Phrase Report currently does not provide a report detailing search terms that yield no results, but this is forthcoming. In the meantime, this is a situation that is easily detected and logged. On the search results page, evaluate the number of search results available. If no results are returned, you can use standard .NET logging to capture the search term. Evaluate this information to determine why no results are returned. Is content missing? Are phrases commonly misspelled?

Misspellings

One common way to deal with common misspellings is to use Ektron's *synonym search* feature. When you create a set of synonyms, Ektron searches for all terms in the set when a site visitor searches for any of the terms. You can create a synonym set to contain each of the misspellings of the name, product or object, so that users who searched for those misspellings receive results containing the correct spelling. For example, assume that OnTrek has a common misspelling of OnTerk (notice the transposed 'e' and 'r'), which yields no results. Creating a synonym set containing the set {OnTerk, OnTrek} yields the same results, even when someone searched using an incorrect spelling. In addition to handling common misspellings, synonym search is also often used to:

➤ **Expand acronyms:** For example, a synonym set could contain the terms {Web CMS, Web Content Management, WCMS}.

➤ **Create common word stems:** Unless wildcards are used explicitly, search does not perform stemming or pluralize nouns. For example, if you think a site visitor might enter {run, running, runs} enter that set as a synonym set.

The following steps walk through the process of creating a synonym set for the misspellings, OnTech and OnTeck.

> You must be a member of the Administrators Group or assigned the Search Admin role to create, edit, and delete Synonym Sets.

1. In the Workarea, go to Settings, Configuration ➪ Search ➪ Synonym Sets.
2. Click the Add Icon.
3. Give the synonym set a meaningful name. This is only used for identifying the search set in the Workarea.
4. Add the terms OnTech Plus and OnTeck Plus.

5. Click the Check for Duplicates button. This compares terms in this set against the other synonym sets in this language.

6. Click Save .

An additional way to deal with misspellings is to use the *Did You Mean Search* Widget available through the Ektron Developer Exchange site. According to the developer of the widget, this component "provides a list of terms similar to the terms a visitor performs a search on. Additionally, CMS Administrators can promote items to *Suggested Results* or set a content item as *unsearchable* from within the display of items returned. The Did-You-Mean terms are generated from your website content, ensuring only relevant terms are returned. Each term in this result set has a corresponding number (displayed in parentheses), which represents the number of items associated with that term." This widget is available for free on the Ektron Exchange at `http://dev.ektron.com/exchange/codeDownload.aspx?id=30638`.

Overly General Search Terms

When site visitors use overly general search terms, they do not produce meaningful search results. Ektron's Suggested Results feature can be used here to force certain results to the top of the search results for specific queries.

You add a suggested result through the Workarea. Once a suggested result has been created, it is available immediately through all search APIs and server controls.

You must be a member of the Administrators Group or assigned the Search-Admin role to create, edit, and delete Suggested Results.

1. From the Ektron CMS400.NET Workarea, go to Settings ➪ Configuration ➪ Search ➪ Suggested Results.
2. From the language dropdown, select a language for the suggested results.
3. Click the Add button .
4. Provide a title, link, and text, or browse to select an existing content item.
5. Click Save .

Popular Search Terms

You need to look for the presence of popular search terms that exist prominently in your primary navigation. This is because a high correlation between the Phrase Report and your primary navigation may indicate a possible flaw in the navigation's organization and design. Use this information as a call to action to perform another round of quick informal task-based usability testing on your menu navigation. Search should not be used as a crutch for poorly designed information architecture.

Adding Search to the Global Navigation

The OnTrek website follows the best practice recommendation of making search globally accessible by placing a search textbox in the header on each page of the website. The implementation has two parts:

- The search textbox placed on the website's master page
- The page that handles the form submit, performs the search, and displays the results

The SiteSearch Server Controls are used to display the search results and the following steps show how to configure SiteSearch Server Controls to handle submitting queries to another page. To see how this is implemented on the OnTrek website, start by looking at the global header code:

1. Open ~\components\userControls\header\header.ascx.
2. Navigate to the bottom of the file, you'll find the following snippet:

Available for download on Wrox.com

```
            <asp:TextBox ID="inputText" runat="server"></asp:TextBox>
  Insert IconMargin    [FILENAME]
            <asp:LinkButton ID="search" runat="server" Text="Search"
  onclick="search_Click" />
```

code snippet header.ascx

In this snippet you can see the code that defines the look and feel of the Search textbox, which is very basic but which you can customize in any way you need. To force the search results to display on a separate page, the `onclick` property is used to reference the `search_Click` event handler, whose implementation can be seen in the following snippet:

```
protected void search_Click(object sender, EventArgs e)
{
    Response.Redirect("~/SearchResults.aspx?q=" +
      Server.UrlPathEncode(inputText.Text));
}
```

The SearchResults.aspx page then has the sole job of rendering search results for the search query that is passed to in the query string. The complete source code for the SearchResults.aspx.cs code-behind file is shown in code Listing 7-7.

Available for download on Wrox.com

LISTING 7-7: ~/SearchResults.aspx.cs

```
using System;
using System.Collections.Generic;
using System.Linq;
using System.Web;
using System.Web.UI;
using System.Web.UI.WebControls;
using Ektron.Cms.Controls;

public partial class SearchResults : System.Web.UI.Page
```

continues

LISTING 7-7 *(continued)*

```csharp
{
    protected void Page_PreRender(object sender, EventArgs e)
    {
        string searchText = Request.QueryString["q"];
        TextBox inputText = searchInput.FindControl("inputText") as TextBox;
        inputText.Text = searchText;

        searchDataSource.QueryText = searchText;
        searchResults.DataBind();
    }

    protected void search_Click(object sender, EventArgs e)
    {
        LinkButton searchButton = sender as LinkButton;
        TextBox inputText =
            searchButton.NamingContainer.FindControl("inputText") as TextBox;
        searchInput.BasicQuery(true, inputText.Text);
    }
}
```

Reviewing the code in Listing 7-7 reveals that the SearchResults.aspx has two server controls on it, one defining a datasource, and the other displaying the results. The relevant aspects of the SearchResults.aspx template are shown in the following snippet, showing how these server controls are used.

```
<CMS:SiteSearchInput
    ID="searchInput"
    DataSourceID="searchDataSource"
    runat="server">
    <ItemTemplate>

        <asp:TextBox
            ID="inputText"
            runat="server">
        </asp:TextBox>
        <asp:LinkButton
            ID="search"
            runat="server"
            OnClick="search_Click"
            Text="Search"
        ></asp:LinkButton>

    </ItemTemplate>
</CMS:SiteSearchInput>
<CMS:SiteSearchDataSource
    ID="searchDataSource"
    runat="server"></CMS:SiteSearchDataSource>
<CMS:SiteSearchResults
    ID="searchResults"
    DataSourceID="searchDataSource"
    runat="server"></CMS:SiteSearchResults>
```

code snippet SearchResults.aspx

The SiteSearchInput Server Control defines how the search input displays on the page. Because it supports nesting an ItemTemplate, you have full control over how the markup renders. Additionally you'll notice two more server control:

- **SiteSearchDataSource:** Allows you to define the query data source and source text.
- **SiteSearchResults:** Allows you to customize the markup and display of the search results.

These decoupled controls give you ultimate control over how the search results display on the page.

Under the Hood

This section starts by discussing Ektron's new search architecture and the deep integration Ektron provides with Microsoft's advanced search technology. The three search technologies that Ektron supports are:

- Microsoft Search Server Express 2008 and 2010
- Microsoft Search Server 2008 and 2010
- Microsoft FAST Enterprise Search

A standard installation of Ektron includes Microsoft Search Server Express by default. But don't let the *Express* lead you to believe that it is feature disabled — in fact, Microsoft Search Server Express is functionally equivalent to Microsoft Search Server in every way with only one important exception: That is, Search Server Express lacks the ability to run in a distributed search environment. This means if you need to create a load balance search cluster, Microsoft Search Server must be used. Otherwise, Microsoft Search Server Express will suit your needs. Additionally, integration with Microsoft FAST Enterprise Search Server is also available as an upgrade option, which gives you additional unique capabilities.

The version of Microsoft Search Server Express that is installed depends on the version of your Windows Server operating system. If you installed Windows Server 2008 64 bit, Ektron will install Search Server 2010 because it depends on this version to operate. Otherwise, Search Server 2008 will be installed.

On top of this Search Server, Ektron has built its deeply integrated Search Framework, which includes all the plumbing that handles crawling content, catalog management, as well as developer facing features like the Search Framework API, Search Widgets, SiteSearch Server Controls, Faceted Search, Federated Search, and Site Search Analytics, to name a few. All these features depend on the Ektron's Search Framework, so this section covers how Ektron integrates with Microsoft Search Server at the core, to give you an understanding of how content is crawled, indexed, and queried.

Crawling, Indexing, and Querying

In Figure 7-15, you can see the Ektron Search Framework's overall architecture and process for crawling and indexing content.

The process begins on the left hand side of the diagram with the Ektron user authoring content either through the Workarea or directly on the website. This content item can be any type of managed content, such as a content block, structured Smart Form data, or document through a content

API, server control, or widget. Through a CMS Extension (see Appendix A), the publish pipeline is modified to notify the Ektron Windows Service that new content has been pushed. The Ektron Windows Service then invokes a request for either a full or incremental crawl.

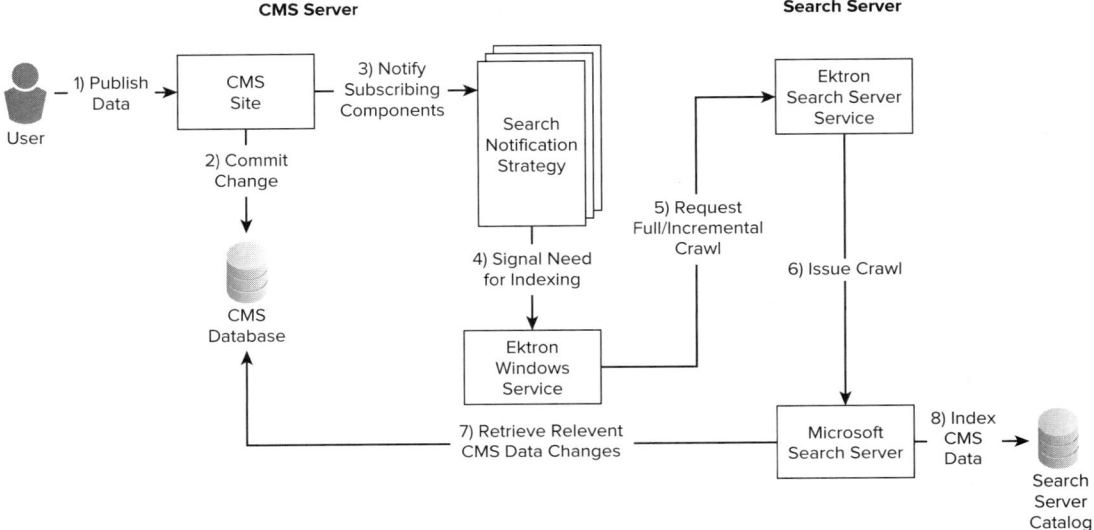

FIGURE 7-15

➤ **Incremental crawl:** Crawls only what has changed without needing to rebuild the content index. Most data changes result in an incremental crawl, including the creation of new content, deleting content, adding a user, and such. So as not to over-burden the Search Server and the service, incremental crawl requests are issued on a user-configurable interval. The request to crawl is flagged and is issued when the interval expires. If no requests for an incremental crawl have been issued when the interval expires, no crawl occurs.

➤ **Full crawl:** Crawls everything. The one type of action that requires you to initiate a full crawl is one in which metadata (or any other object that results in the creation of new searchable properties within Search Server, such as a taxonomy) is added. Full crawl requests, unlike the incremental ones, are issued immediately. If a crawl (incremental or full) is already in progress, it will be interrupted and restarted. Upon completion of a full crawl, new searchable properties in the system are mapped so that they can utilized in queries.

During the crawl, Search Server retrieves content by querying the database through the use of stored procedures — it does not spider the website in the way that public internet search engines do — and it is important to understand why. Crawling the database means that the search architecture has access to rich metadata, taxonomy, and other forms of structured information. This is an advantage that site search has over public search engines like Google, who are limited in this knowledge since all content is visible only through loosely structured HTML documents. It is because of this type of indexing that Ektron can provide faceted search on custom user properties.

The process of content indexing is performed using *IFilters*, which are components that understand how to handle a specific file format, such as Microsoft Word. The Ektron Framework is distributed with IFilters to handle all common file formats such as Office documents, text documents, Shockwave Flash files, and PDF documents. It's worth pointing out that IFilters can also index custom attributes on files. These attributes include the file level metadata you see when you right-click a file and choose Properties ➪ Advanced Option (or choose Details on Windows 7), as well hidden ones not available through the Windows interface. All of this data is stored in the content index.

In Figure 7-16, you can see the overall architecture and process for querying and retrieving information.

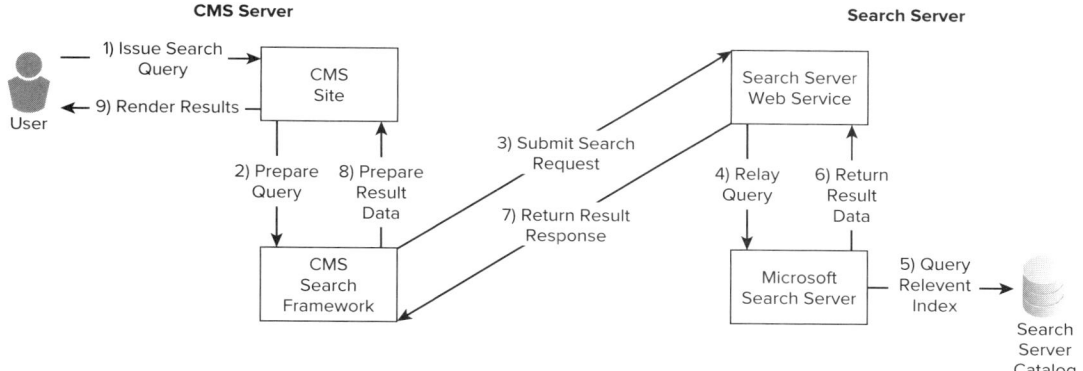

FIGURE 7-16

The process is as follows:

➤ The site visitor initiating a query through a website search interface built using any of the site search server controls or APIs.

➤ The query is processed and formatted into XML in preparation for querying the Search Server. The XML document can be thought of as a search request configuration file, and includes the search phrase and configuration parameters value, such as whether or not duplicates should be trimmed, stemming is enabled, spellcheck should be used, and so forth.

> *The Microsoft Developer Network has an article describing the Schema for this XML document available here* `http://msdn.microsoft.com/en-us/library/ms563775.aspx`.

➤ Once the XML search request has been created, it is passed to the Search Server Web Service which manages all communication between Ektron and Microsoft Search Server.

➤ Once the request has been received, the Search Server Query Engine is then responsible for performing the lookup against the relevant catalog indices and returning the results back.

Using the Search Framework APIs

The Search Framework APIs follow the overall pattern established in the Framework API, which was introduced briefly in Chapter 1 and is covered more thoroughly as a whole in Appendix B. This section builds on this by presenting code samples that implement various search-driven use cases. The Ektron Dev Center also features a screencast highlighting the design goals of the Framework API, why it was introduced, and how to work with it here: http://dev.ektron.com/FrameworkAPI/. Although it isn't required, it is recommended that you look through Appendix B and watch the screencast before reading through these samples.

In this section, you look at a use case and see the constructs used to implement it. The following snippet implements a search that defines two filters:

- One that specifies that the content title must contain the phrase "ektron"
- The other that specifies that the title must contain the phrase "corporation"

These two filtering criteria are grouped together using the SearchCriteriaFilterGroup. Because the LocalOperation is set to AND, both of these filters must be true for a search result to be included in the set. So content with the title "the ektron corporation" would be included, but "ektron, inc." would not.

```
public void SearchTitleWithTwoFilters()
{
    SearchServerContentCriteria contentCriteria =
        new SearchServerContentCriteria();
    ISearchCriteriaFilter filter1 =
    New SearchCriteriaFilter<string>(
            SearchCriteriaContentFields.Title,
            SearchCriteriaFilterOperator.Contains,
            "ektron");
    ISearchCriteriaFilter filter2 = new SearchCriteriaFilter<string>(
        SearchCriteriaContentFields.Title,
        SearchCriteriaFilterOperator.Contains,
        "corporation");

    SearchCriteriaFilterGroup groupFilter =
        new SearchCriteriaFilterGroup();
    groupFilter.AddFilter(filter1);
    groupFilter.AddFilter(filter2);
    groupFilter.Condition = LogicalOperation.And;

    contentCriteria.AddFilter(groupFilter);
    contentCriteria.PagingInfo = new PagingInfo(10, 1);

    ContentSearchResponse response = SearchManager.Search(contentCriteria);
    string query = response.ExecutedQuery;

    OutPutResult(response.RelevantResults);

    Console.WriteLine("Query '{0}'...", query);
    Console.WriteLine("Showing results {0} - {1} out of {2}\n",
        contentCriteria.PagingInfo.StartRow,
        contentCriteria.PagingInfo.EndRow,
        response.AvailableResultCount.ToString());
}
```

You can also nest filter groups, which gives you the full ability to create complex, nested filter expressions. The `PagingInfo` object defines how many results are returned and the current page in the resultset. In cases where you are using search as an Application Search, you might only need to return three results. Setting the paging info object to 3 ensures that you're never returned more results than needed.

The Search Framework APIs are also permission aware. This means that the results returned are properly trimmed according to the content permissions granted to the site visitor. Developers have the ability to force an administrator level access mode in cases where you're looking to use the Search Framework APIs as a general purpose API for content information retrieval. The following show the enumeration values that can be passed to the Search Manager constructor to force the Search Framework API into administrator level access mode.

- `ApiAccessMode.Admin`
- `ApiAccessMode.LoggedInUser`

This approach is often used when search is used for dynamic page generation using search. This approach is also sometimes referred to as "application search" which is a term used to describe applications built using search's highly denormalized search catalogs as a delivery system, instead of the highly normalized SQL database.

SITEMAP AND BREADCRUMBS

A major requirement of a website is to provide simple user and machine resources for discoverability. In addition to menus, breadcrumbs and sitemaps allow for simple discovery in different ways:

- **Sitemaps:** Useful for indexing content by third-party search engines. The spiders that these search engines use are designed to follow links to find other pages. A sitemap makes it easy for the spider to find all the other pages on your site. The spider is a way of ensuring that all of your pages are cross-linked.
- **Breadcrumbs:** These serve a slightly different purpose by allowing a site visitor to easily discover the information architecture of your site. This, in combination with a well thought out aliasing scheme, allows users to infer the location of interesting content based on where they have already been in your site.

In the Ektron Framework, breadcrumbs can function in two different ways:

- **The BreadCrumb Server Control acts as a positional indicator.** It reads information from the folder the content belongs to, and displays a list of parent links. For example, if you are browsing a job listing, you may wish to display a breadcrumb like the following.

    Jobs ⇨ Engineering ⇨ Nashua, NH
- **The breadcrumbs can alternatively display a click trail for the current user.** This shows users the pages they landed on leading them to the current page. This type of breadcrumb trail is less common, and less accepted due to usability concerns, but the option is there.

One point to remember is that the breadcrumb for a given piece of content is actually associated with the folder that content belongs to. The breadcrumbs are also not generated recursively from each folder, but are instead stored in their entirety in the folder the content appears in. These breadcrumbs can also be inherited down the folder chain.

This section includes three implementation tutorials:

➤ Setting up breadcrumbs on the /Content/Products folder

➤ Implementing breadcrumbs on the products.aspx page

➤ Creating a sitemap.aspx page

On the dynamix.aspx page, from where most free content is loaded, part of the Wireframe indicates that between the menu and the Content Block Server Control there is a breadcrumb acting as a positional indicator.

Creating Breadcrumbs for the Products Folder

As covered in the Folder section of Chapter 5, breadcrumb settings are managed through the folder properties screen in the Workarea. Enter the Workarea now, and navigate in the Content tab to /Content/Products. Select View ➪ Properties, and then select Edit from the toolbar in the Display pane.

As shown in Figure 7-17, the last tab in the folder properties is for breadcrumb settings. The top checkbox is marked Inherit from parent folder. Breadcrumbs can be inherited from the parent folder. This can simplify creating a basic structure for breadcrumbs, but it is also frequently a point of confusion for content managers trying to set up breadcrumbs.

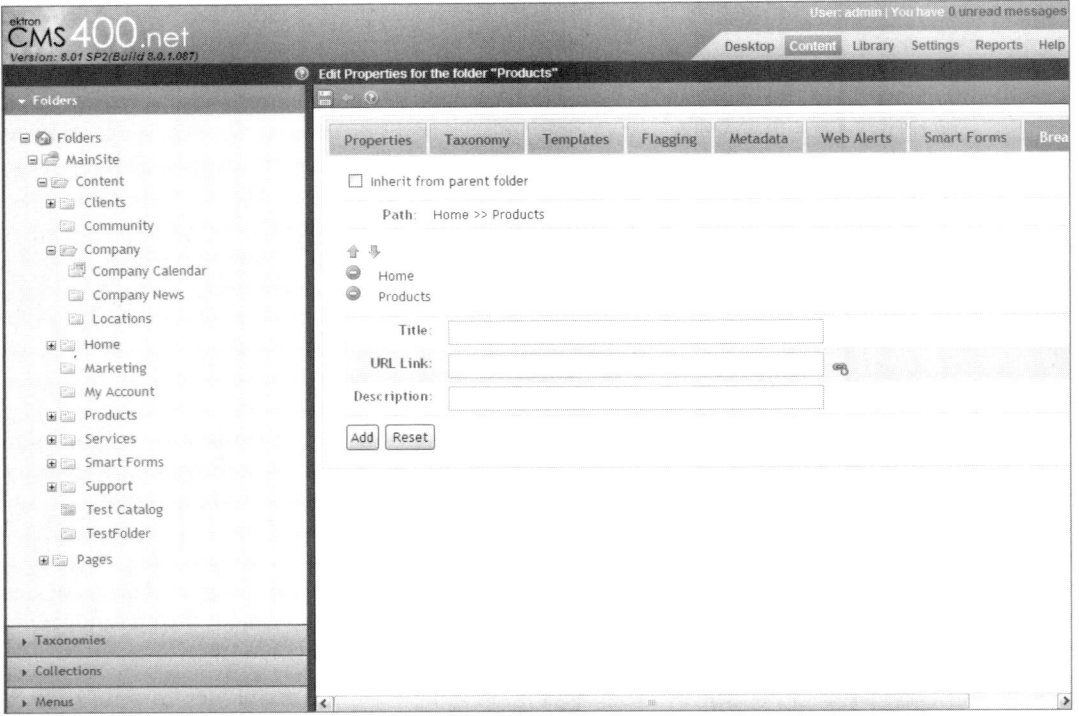

FIGURE 7-17

One might expect the breadcrumb structure to automatically recurse through parent folders to retrieve the appropriate list of links to display. Unfortunately, this is not how the system actually works. Instead, from a given Content ID, the folder is retrieved. The system then checks if the folder is marked to inherit breadcrumbs. If so, the system climbs through the parent folders until it finds a folder that is not set to inherit. Once found, the list of links is listed from that folder, and no other folders. What this means is that to construct the breadcrumbs you want to display, you create the root-most folders breadcrumb settings first and then move deeper into the tree breaking inheritance as you go. Each time you break inheritance, the parent breadcrumb structure is copied to the current folder, so you only are adding one level at a time.

Let's create the breadcrumb trail for a folder now.

1. Make sure the inheritance checkbox is deselected, and you have the rest of the options to work with. Because you are creating the root products folder, you want products directly within this folder to have a breadcrumb like the following:

    Home ⇨ Products

2. To create the breadcrumb, fill out the title, URL link, and description fields shown in Figure 7-17 with the following settings listed in Table 7-5.

TABLE 7-5: Settings for Home Breadcrumb

FIELD	VALUE
Title	Home
URL Link	default.aspx
Description	Home Page

3. Once you enter the settings, click the Add button, and the item will be added to the list displayed above the form.

4. Repeat the process for the Products breadcrumb fields in Figure 7-18 with the settings listed in Table 7-6.

TABLE 7-6: Settings for Products Breadcrumb

FIELD	VALUE
Title	Products
URL Link	products.aspx
Description	Products Home

The list of items can now be reordered, and a preview is displayed in the Path box.

5. Confirm that what is displayed is what you intended, and then click Save on the toolbar. Remember that this process must be repeated for each folder containing content that should have a different breadcrumb trail.

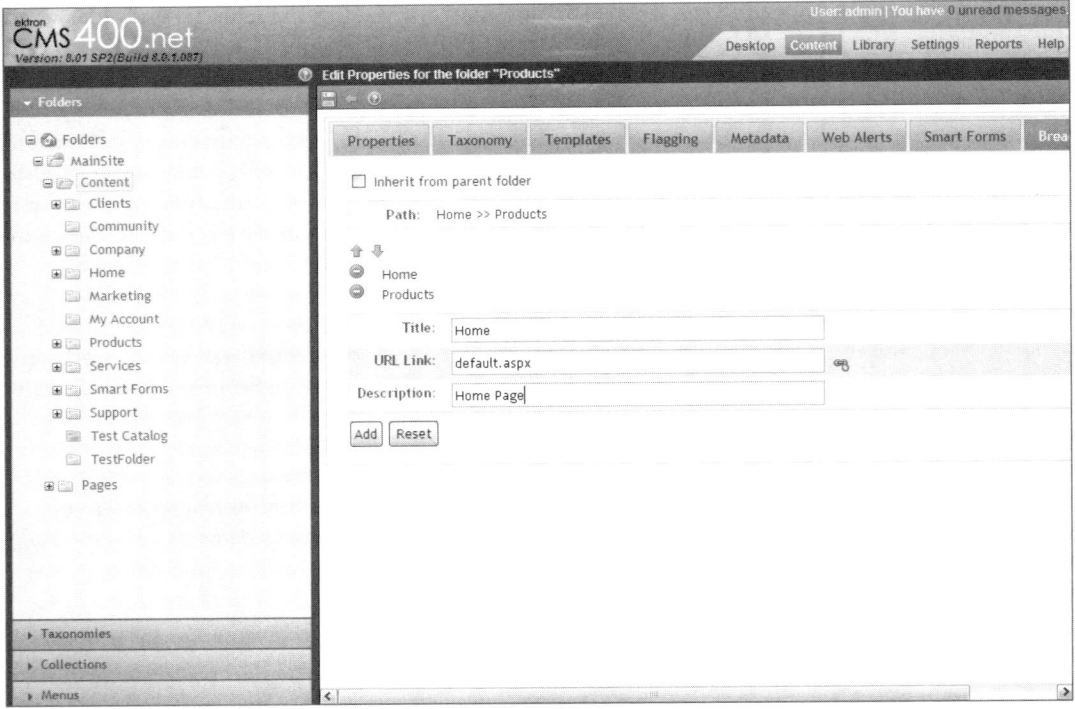

FIGURE 7-18

Implementing the BreadCrumb Server Control

Now that the folder is configured, you need to implement the server control to display the breadcrumb on the page. Follow these steps:

1. Fire up Visual Studio, and open the Products.aspx file.

2. Just above the Content Block Server Control, place the following line.

    ```
    <CMS:FolderBreadCrumb ID="Breadcrumb" runat="server" />
    ```

3. There is also a BreadCrumb Server Control, instantiated with the following line. The difference between the two is that the FolderBreadCrumb Server Control reads the breadcrumb you set in the folder properties, and the BreadCrumb Server Control uses the user history, where each page on the site that the user visits is appended to the breadcrumb trail.

    ```
    <CMS:BreadCrumb ID="Breadcrumb" runat="server" />
    ```

The FolderBreadcrumb Server Control reads the ID parameter from the query string. The control then loads the appropriate breadcrumb for that piece of content. There are several other parameters that are useful in configuring the breadcrumb controls. These are listed in Table 7-7.

TABLE 7-7: BreadCrumb Server Control Properties

PROPERTY NAME	DESCRIPTION
DefaultContentID	If there is not a valid value in the query string, this is the value used for the Content ID.
DynamicParameter	Defaults to ID, which is what is used for normal content in QuickLinks. Depending on the use case, you may want to manage breadcrumbs based on a PageBuilder page rather than a content item displayed in a ContentBlock control, in which case you may want to set this to "pageid."
Language	The LanguageID to use for display.
Mode	Can be set to Normal or DisplayOnly — DisplayOnly will not render any links; it will only display text.
Separator	This is the character to separate entries with. It defaults to ">."

Creating a Sitemap Page

Now that you covered how to create the breadcrumb settings, you can move onto the SiteMap Server Control. You use the SiteMap Server Control to create a list of all the contents, recursively, from a given folder. Each item is listed with its corresponding breadcrumb from the parent folder.

The following steps show you how to create a new Web form in Visual Studio, in the root of your site.

1. Name it **Sitemap.aspx**, and set it to use a separate codebehind file.
2. Drag the SiteMap Server Control from the toolbox to the inside of the Form element on the page, as shown in the following code snippet.

```
<%@ Page Language="C#" AutoEventWireup="true" CodeFile="sitemap.aspx.cs"
Inherits="sitemap" %>
<%@ Register Assembly="Ektron.Cms.Controls" Namespace="Ektron.Cms.Controls"
TagPrefix="CMS" %>

<!DOCTYPE html PUBLIC "-//W3C//DTD XHTML 1.0 Transitional//EN" "http://
www.w3.org/TR/xhtml1/DTD/xhtml1-transitional.dtd">

<html xmlns="http://www.w3.org/1999/xhtml">
<head runat="server">
    <title></title>
</head>
<body>
    <form id="form1" runat="server">
    <div>
      <CMS:Sitemap ID="Sitemap1" runat="server" />
    </div>
    </form>
</body>
</html>
```

The SiteMap Server Control works without any additional properties. When you load the page in the browser, you get the output shown in Figure 7-19.

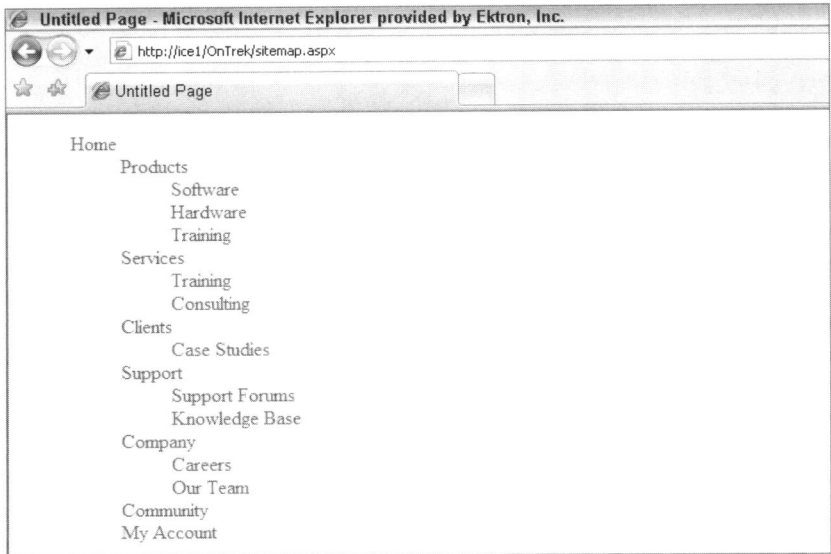

FIGURE 7-19

3. You can optionally fine-tune the display to match your needs. These parameters are listed in the Table 7-8.

TABLE 7-8: SiteMap Server Control Properties

PROPERTY	DESCRIPTION
ClassName	The CSS class to wrap the sitemap display.
FolderID	The folder ID to display the sitemap below. Defaults to zero, which specifies the root folder.
MaxLevel	Specifies the depth to go below the FolderID. Zero means unlimited.
StartingLevel	Sets the number of levels to skip in the SiteMap. For instance, you may want to only show the third tier folders, but show all of them. In this case, FolderID would be zero, but StartingLevel would be three.

Like most Ektron controls, the SiteMap Server Control also outputs XML and allows for custom transforms using XSLT. The SiteMap Server Control exposes a property called XmlDoc, which exposes the XML used for rendering; by setting the DisplayXSLT property you can specify a custom XSLT to transform that XML.

REGISTRATION

It is increasingly common for Web presences to invite interaction from visitors which can range from posting on forums to authoring wiki entries or just rating content. Most sites with these interactions have users to register on the site rather than just posting anonymously. The Ektron Framework provides for this necessity by supporting user membership.

Membership users in the Ektron Framework are a close relative to CMS users. The main distinction is that CMS users have access to the Workarea where membership users do not. With a typical Ektron license, the number of CMS users allowed is limited, whereas the number of membership users is usually unlimited.

Because membership users are a subset of CMS users, the management techniques and capabilities of the two groups are very similar. Membership users can be granted read permissions on private content, they can be members of groups, and they can even edit content from the website if allowed.

There are several server controls that make it easy to implement membership management on your site. This section covers these server controls.

When setting up membership capabilities on your site, there are a couple of main capabilities that you need to implement. These are:

- Allowing users to register on the site
- Allowing users to modify their properties
- Implementing a password reset feature
- Implementing Facebook registration

The last item on the list refers to Ektron's feature that lets a user log in to your site with their Facebook credentials. Ektron will then retrieve the user details from Facebook and create a user in the system for them.

The Membership Server Control handles three out of the four situations previously listed. By determining whether the user is logged in, and by setting attributes on the server control, you can have it handle most of the details of administering users. All of these examples are handled in the OnTrek starter site, but the following sections have you using a simple page to demo these examples.

Allowing a User to Register on the Site

Registration is handled through the Membership Server Control, along with many other functions. The Membership Server Control enforces custom attributes, and allows users to set up every aspect of their membership on the site through a single interface. You start this example by following these steps:

1. Create a new page called **Membership.aspx**. In Visual Studio, right-click the site root in the Solution Explorer and select Add New Item. Select Web Form, and name it **Membership.aspx**.

2. Make sure you are in Source view, and drag the Membership Server Control from the toolbox to within the form element. Listing 7-8 shows what the code will look like after you have done this.

Available for download on Wrox.com

LISTING 7-8: Membership.aspx

```
<%@ Page Language="C#" AutoEventWireup="true" CodeFile="Membership.aspx.cs"
Inherits="Membership" %>
<%@ Register Assembly="Ektron.Cms.Controls" Namespace="Ektron.Cms.Controls"
TagPrefix="CMS" %>

<!DOCTYPE html PUBLIC "-//W3C//DTD XHTML 1.0 Transitional//EN" "http://www.w3.org/
TR/xhtml1/DTD/xhtml1-transitional.dtd">

<html xmlns="http://www.w3.org/1999/xhtml">
<head runat="server">
    <title></title>
</head>
<body>
    <form id="form1" runat="server">
    <div>
      <CMS:Membership ID="Membership1" runat="server" />
    </div>
    </form>
</body>
</html>
```

The Membership control, when no options are specified, serves two functions. If the user on the site is not logged in, the Membership Server Control displays the registration interface, shown in Figure 7-20. The tabs for this interface are as follows:

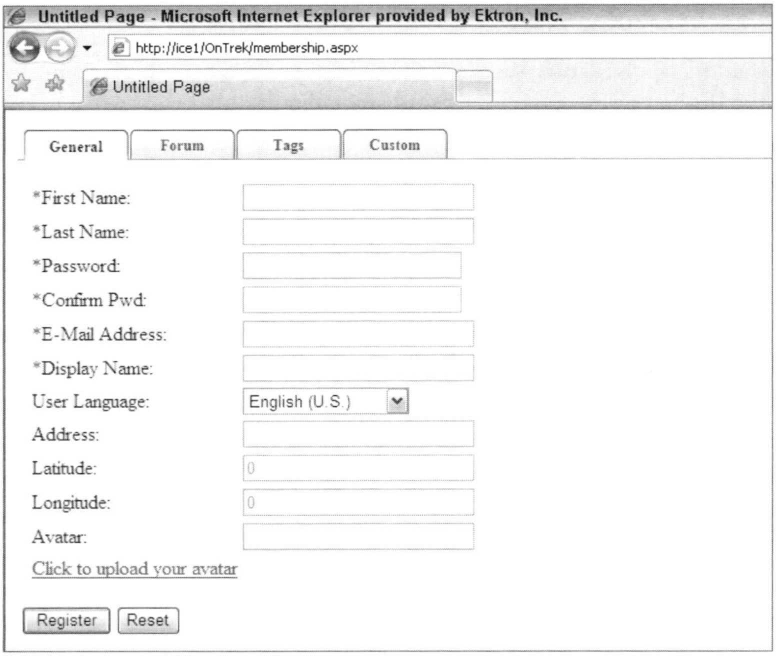

FIGURE 7-20

➤ **General:** This has s for each category, starting with the key fields such as username and password. The option that might be non-obvious is the Address field. This field exists so that GeoMapping Server Control can search for users. By specifying the address, the Ektron Framework can convert it to an appropriate latitude and longitude behind the scenes.

➤ **Forum:** Allows the users to specify options specifically for Forums on the site, such as which editor to use, and what the forum signature should be.

➤ **Tags:** Allow the users to specify things such as interests or locations, which are then searchable by other users.

➤ **Custom:** Contains a group of options that don't fit into the other categories. This tab is shown in Figure 7-21.

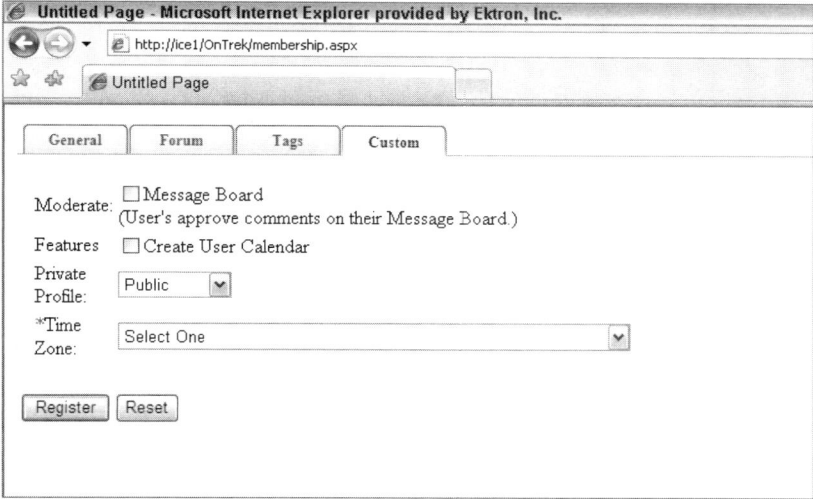

FIGURE 7-21

For the most part, these options are configured in the Workarea on the Settings tab as Custom User Attributes. More attributes can be added there, and some of the existing options can be modified or deleted. There are, however, a few options on this tab that cannot be modified:

➤ **Features:** This checkbox creates a user calendar for the users. A user calendar allows users to add and share their schedules on the site through the WebCalendar interface. For more information on user calendars, see Chapter 8.

➤ **Time Zone:** Also has to do with the WebCalendar. The WebCalendar internally stores events in GMT, and converts them to the logged-in user's time zone. This time zone list is the same list used in Windows, so it allows for an appropriate amount of granularity in location.

This interface may not be exactly what you as a developer want to display to the user at registration time. As usual, the Ektron Framework provides for developing custom interfaces through the use of the API. See the following code snippet for programmatically creating users.

```
Ektron.Cms.UserData memDetails = new Ektron.Cms.UserData();
memDetails.Username = "Username";
memDetails.FirstName = "First";
memDetails.LastName = "Last";
memDetails.Password = "Password";
memDetails.DisplayName = "Displayname";
try
{
  Ektron.Cms.Framework.Users.User user = new Ektron.Cms.Framework.Users.User();
  user.Add(memDetails);
}
catch (Exception ex)
{
  throw ex;
}
```

Allowing Users to Modify Their Properties

In addition to allowing a user to register for the site, the Membership Server Control supports many other features. As you saw in the previous section, the server control generates an interface for users to enter the initial details of their accounts. The default interface also works when users are already logged in. Log in to your OnTrek site and refresh the Membership.aspx page. The interface now displays with your information populating the fields, as is shown in Figure 7-22.

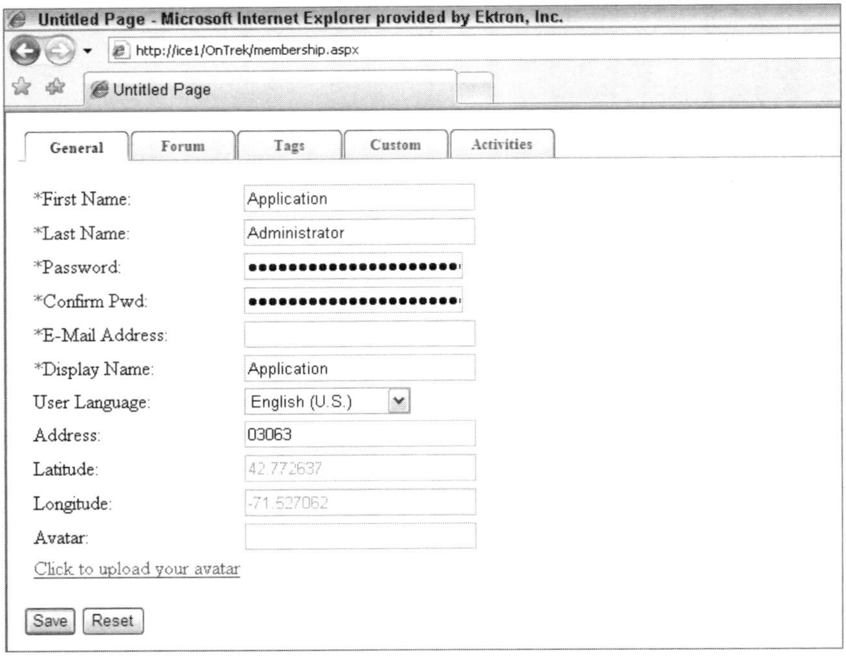

FIGURE 7-22

The membership control handles CMS user accounts, including the admin account, not just membership users. As before, if you do not like the interface as shown, all of the actions can be performed through the API. The Framework User API class has methods for `Update` and `Delete` in addition to the `Add` method.

Implementing a Password Reset Feature

As mentioned earlier, the Membership Server Control handles more than just registering and managing users. By modifying the `DisplayMode` property on the Membership Server Control, you can have it manage other functions. The following figures show what these options mean.

➤ `DisplayMode="AccountActivate"` is shown in Figure 7-23.

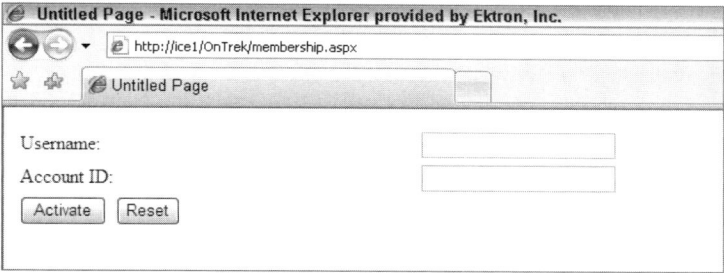

FIGURE 7-23

This screen is needed only if the option Enable Verify E-mail in the Configuration ➪ Setup screen of the Settings tab in the Workarea is checked. If that option is turned on, then when a user registers on the site, an e-mail is sent with a link to Workarea/ActivateUser.aspx. You can specify your own page with the Membership Server Control by modifying the Verification e-mail in the Workarea. System e-mail messages are managed in the Settings tab under Community Management ➪ Messages.

➤ `DisplayMode="ResetPassword"` is shown in Figure 7-24.

FIGURE 7-24

This mode allows users to reset their passwords. It will send an e-mail to the registered account. The e-mail sent will include a new randomly generated password. Remember that the System E-mail address must be specified in the Settings tab in the Workarea, under Configuration ➪ Setup.

➤ `DisplayMode="UnsubscribeSecured"` is shown in Figure 7-25.

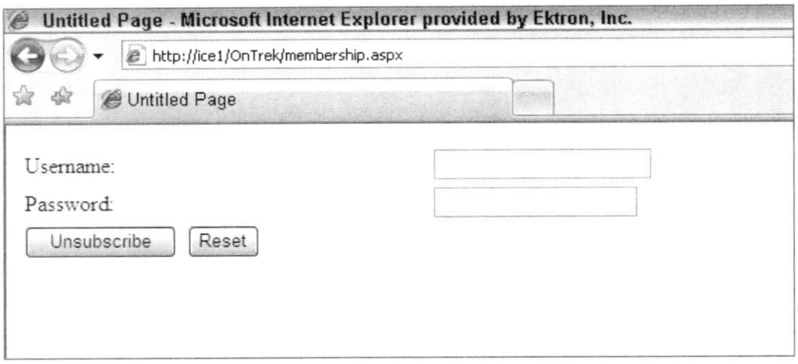

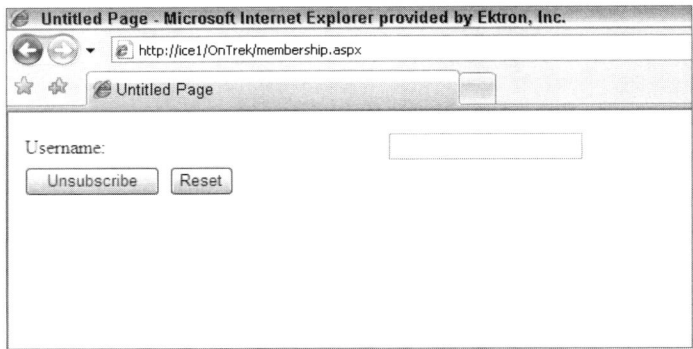

FIGURE 7-25

It allows users to unsubscribe. Requires the username and password.

➤ `DisplayMode="UnsubscribeUnsecured"` is shown in Figure 7-26.

FIGURE 7-26

It allows users to unsubscribe. It does not require the users to be logged in or enter a password.

➤ `DisplayMode="UserRegistration"` was shown previously in Figure 7-20.

This mode is the default and was covered in the previous examples. It allows users to create and manage their accounts by inputting all the details necessary to deal with the Ektron Framework.

Implementing Facebook Registration

A relatively new feature in the Ektron Framework is support of Facebook authentication. Using the FacebookLogin Server Control allows users to authenticate against the Facebook servers. The process opens a window on the Facebook site — prompting the users to log in to their Facebook accounts and authorize the site to connect to their profiles — and then passes a token to your site. The token allows the Ektron Framework to connect to Facebook and retrieve details about the users.

The FacebookLogin Server Control allows users to simply log in to the site using their Facebook accounts. If the user is already logged in, the control allows connection between the two accounts. If details are updated on the Facebook side, the modifications are replicated to the other site.

The following steps walk through the user experience of the Facebook Connect feature.

1. The user clicks the Connect with Facebook button, shown in Figure 7-27.

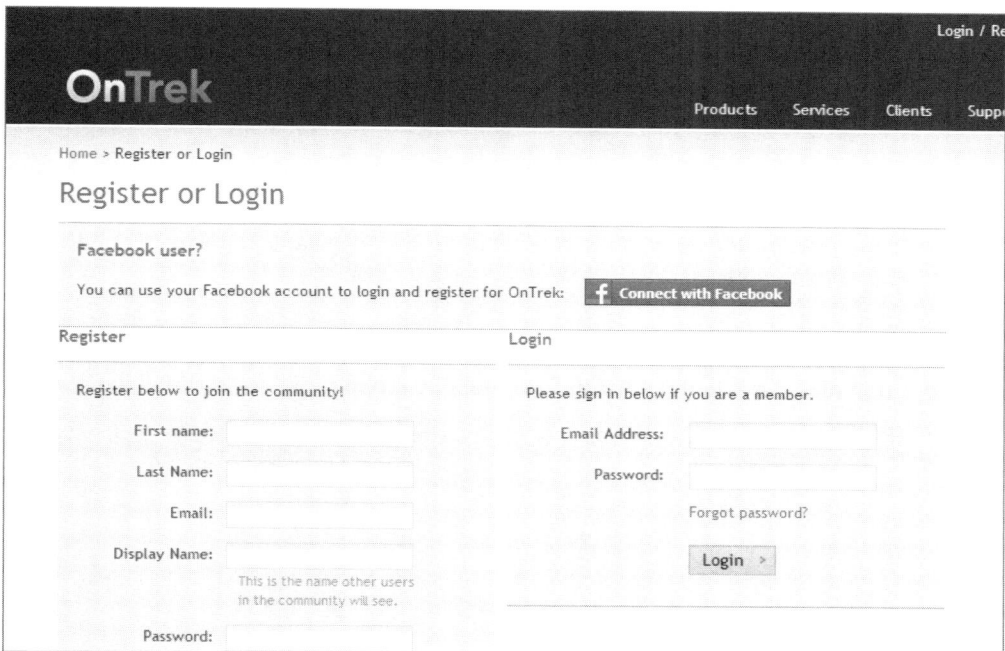

FIGURE 7-27

2. When the user clicks the button, a new window pops up inviting the user to log in to Facebook and authorize the site to connect to their Facebook profile, as depicted in Figure 7-28.

FIGURE 7-28

3. Once the users have authenticated with Facebook, they are returned to your site, where they are invited to log in if they have an account, or register if they do not have an account. This step allows the system to collect any additional details that are required, such as the users' time zones.

Allowing for this process requires a few steps from developers. They must first create a Facebook application for their website, and then they must log the details for that application in the web.config. Then the user interface must be defined for logging in.

The following steps walk you through creating a Facebook application.

1. First, if you don't have a Facebook account, register on `www.facebook.com`.
2. Go to the Facebook Developer site at `www.facebook.com/developer` and log in.
3. Click the link Set up New Application.
4. Fill in the name for your application. This name is displayed to the users allowing access to their profiles. It cannot contain any variation recognizable to the user as Facebook. The best bet is to go with your site's name or a variation of it.

   A screen will come up displaying your Application ID, as shown in Figure 7-29, API key, and Secret key. Ektron Framework uses these keys to authenticate itself with Facebook, allowing it to connect to authenticated user profiles.

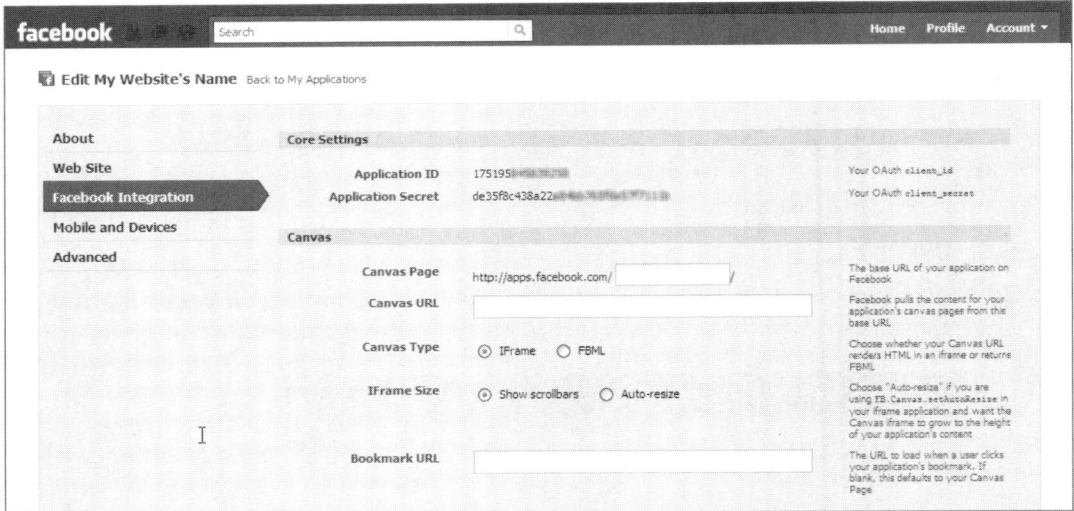

FIGURE 7-29

5. Open your web.config file in the root of your website, and copy the values you just received from Facebook into the corresponding keys — these keys are listed next. The default keys provided in your site are for use with localhost:

   ```
   <add key="ek_FacebookApiKey" value="fed65adedd83eec7e1e56f32f03d7303" />
   <add key="ek_FacebookSecret" value="92b7e5245d455fd9213c0b9af14f5805" />
   ```

6. Save your modifications to the web.config, and return to the Facebook developer site. Select the Connect tab, and enter your website's URL, as shown in Figure 7-30. You can change this URL to the final address at any time.
7. Save your settings on Facebook.

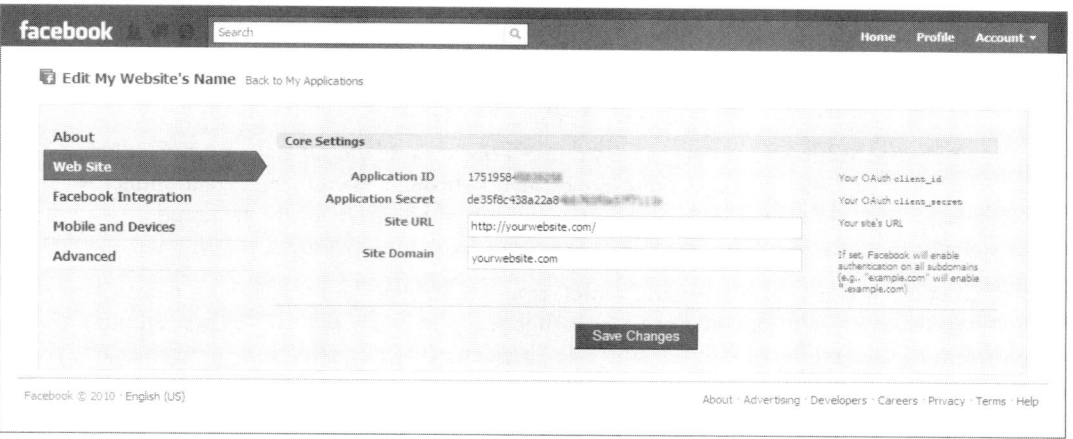

FIGURE 7-30

Once this configuration has been complete, you can simply place the FacebookLogin Server Control on your page, and it will walk the users through the previous steps. For more information about modifying the Facebook login process, see section 3-19 in the CMS400 Manual, which is installed alongside the Ektron Framework in the Documentation folder (e.g. C:\Program Files\Ektron\CMS400v80\Documentation\CMS400Manual.pdf).

TAKE HOME POINTS

This chapter focused on the main elements of a successful homepage:

- **RIA:** This section discussed using Smart Forms to store information usable in a rich format. Smart Forms are a powerful way of storing settings for rich interfaces and applications. Since the backend of a Smart Form is designed to store the content as straight XML, it is even possible to design a Smart Form to be directly serializable and deserializable from a class, while remaining editable in the eWebEdit400 editor. This flexibility means that content authors can update settings directly, rather than relying on developers to do so for them.

- **RESTful services:** You use these to retrieve information from the Ektron Framework with light call backs. The chapter didn't cover platforms, such as Silverlight or Flash in these examples. However, you can certainly extend these examples in that direction. For example, a developer can use the same handler developed for the taxonomy example, and modify the JSON serializer to be an XML, YAML, or even some other type of serializer depending on the requirements of the consuming platform.

- **Menus:** This covered creating the global navigation for the OnTrek website using Ektron's native menu feature and for displaying the menu on the website using a customized Flex Menu Server Control. You saw alternative ways to use the Flex Menu, including the Master Slave implementation, which uses two menus in tandem. A Master displays the global horizontal navigation menu. A Slave displays the left-hand vertical navigation menu, which alters its currently selected item based on the item selected from the Master menu.

- **Search:** You learned the best practice strategies for creating a successful website search implementation, including implementation strategies and how to flag potential problems that your site visitors are having issues with finding relevant content. You saw how to create a globally accessible search box and did a deep dive into the search architecture.

- **The breadcrumb and sitemap:** This showed basic navigational elements. The Ektron Framework easily manages these site elements through the information architecture and content. It also allows you to separate the conceptual hierarchy of the frontend of your site from the backend content management perspective by manually setting the sitemap entries.

- **BreadCrumb and FolderBreadCrumb Server Controls:** The BreadCrumb Control creates easy-to-implement position indicators that you place site-wide so visitors can infer and deduce the architecture of the site. The SiteMap Server Control allows for the same thing for software discovery agents. When you team up both, you can expose the underpinnings of your site to the world, ensuring that your content is easy to find.

- **Registration:** Showed the process of registering users for your site, keeping user details up to date, and allowing users to register through Facebook Connect. Membership management is a crucial part of any website that allows for user interaction, and these tools should be used as part of your site build out.

- **The Membership Server Control:** A versatile tool that can handle a large portion of that user management. It allows for user registration, updating user profiles, and managing items like password reset functionality and unsubscribing users.

- **The Facebook Login Server Control:** Users can connect their profiles to your website. This is desirable to users because they can maintain their profiles at a single location. It's desirable for website administrators because it can serve as a traffic driver. For instance, a user commenting on a story on your site can opt to cross-post her comment and a link to your story to her wall on Facebook. This can alert the entire network to the story on your site, driving what may be a substantial amount of traffic to your site.

Reaching Prospects

> - What is the ListSummary Server Control and how do you use it?
> - How do you make use of calendars and events in the Ektron Framework?
> - How do you manage video on your website?

Reaching prospects and maintaining connections with existing customers are two of the most important functions of your website. One of the ways this is done is through the use of corporate event calendars. Calendars allow your users to see what public events your company is holding, find out about webinars, better understand the lifecycle of your technology, or simply better connect with your service or sales representatives.

Video can also be a great connector of the Web, whether to disseminate technical information and provide how-to's, or to tap into your current customer base as an advertising technique to sell your company's wares. More and more frequently, if people have the option to find information through reading marketing copy or watching a five-minute video, they are turning to the video.

In this chapter, you'll learn how to implement these fundamental tools, allowing you to utilize them to increase your conversion rate. You'll be looking at things from the perspective of a testimonial page, but with slightly more generic examples that allow you to use these features throughout your site, wherever they make sense.

USE CASE

This section gives you a continuation of the use cases that started in Chapter 7. It connects the exercises you will perform in this chapter with the plan laid out in the implementation guide, and puts a story to the features we will cover in this chapter, specifically the ListSummary Server Control, calendars, and the DMS.

CONNECTING TO CLIENTS

Having developed the homepage in the last chapter, the OnTrek marketing team is now looking to disseminate information to potential prospects. Their objectives are to create a section of the site where they can list Customer Testimonials. This section is a go-to location for the sales team for reaching potential clients, by helping them understand how the OnTrek system can help their businesses. Additionally, they need to implement calendars to keep clients up-to-date on trainings, open houses, Webinars, and other corporate events. The combination of these two efforts allow them to more clearly connect to potential and existing clients by maintaining that connection in a more solid way, so clients are never in a position of not having enough information about OnTrek's product line and service offerings.

Wireframe

The example Wireframe for this chapter, shown in Figure 8-1, is the Video Testimonials page. The goal of this page is to showcase existing customers, helping drive interest in the OnTrek suite of products.

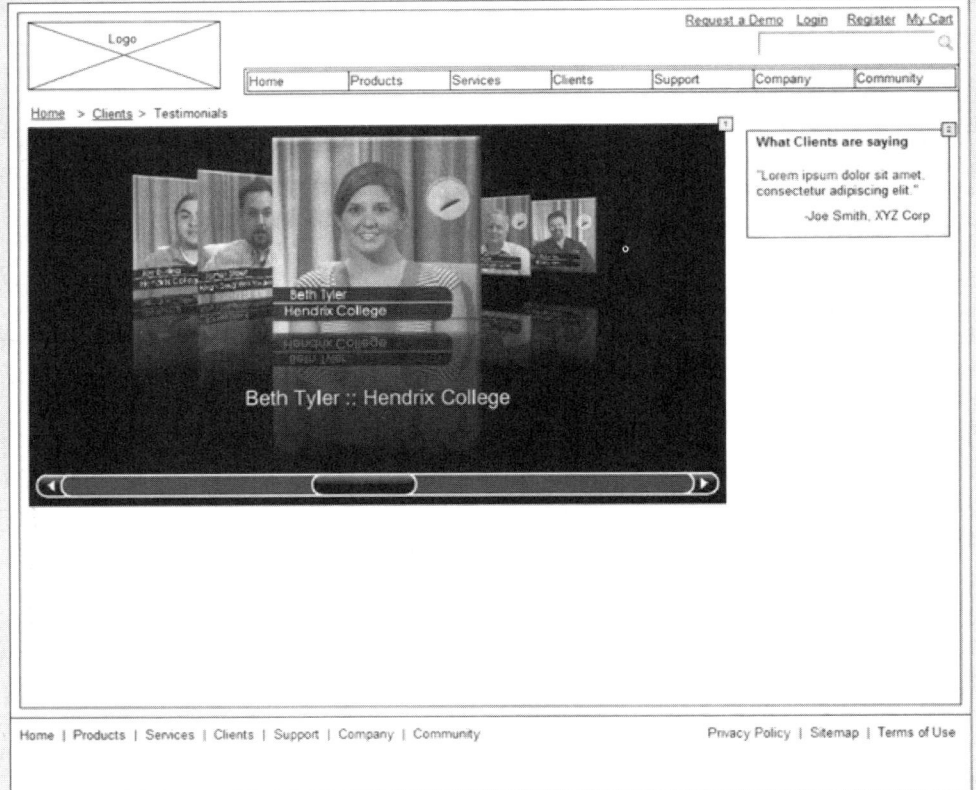

FIGURE 8-1

Actor

Jack is the Director of IT at Acme Inc. and is researching security related software packages for his company's network. He is looking to understand how OnTrek's solution set has helped other companies in need of security related services and products. Additionally, he wants to know how in-depth OnTrek's support for its existing customer base is, which means knowing the schedules for trainings and technical Webinars.

Scenario

In this scenario, Jack:

Analyzes OnTrek and is interested in the product line, but needs to know how the relationship will grow over time between Acme and OnTrek.

Needs to find out about existing partnerships with current clients of OnTrek.

Looks at the menu of the site, and finds a section for Customer Testimonials.

Follows the link and arrives at the page with the primary objective being to find information about satisfied customers.

Uses the videos on the page to learn that information.

Outcome

A successful outcome in this use case is one where Jack can easily find useful information about current OnTrek customers. Using the videos, he should be able to determine the satisfaction level of the existing customer base, as well as learn about potential uses of the technology. Additionally, he should feel satisfied that there is enough existing customer outreach through the use of the calendar to feel comfortable in closing a deal to purchase. The success rate of this group of technologies can be measured through the use of *analytics*, and through customer reports sent directly to the sales people.

TECHNOLOGY

It's become a standard practice for companies to request references and testimonials when shopping for expensive packages. When a company has a very good relationship with its existing customer base, it's a point of pride, and marketing is always interested in showing them off in the hopes of higher conversion rates in their sales cycles. To answer these needs, it has become more and more common to include videos of customer testimonials on company websites.

There are other reasons why videos are becoming a more popular way to disseminate information. As mentioned earlier, people are increasingly interested in collecting information through a well-crafted video than they are through trudging through pages of marketing copy. Additionally, some forms of information are more easily delivered through video than through the written word. As Webinars and other video tools become more popular, there is an increasing desire to house that information in a viewable location. The Ektron Framework has solidly integrated such tools into its feature set over time.

This chapter covers the use of calendars and ListSummaries. ListSummaries tend to be one of the cornerstones of Web designs, by producing simple navigational elements that are always automatically up-to-date. Through their rich customizability, they can produce simple lists of links or can be the fundamental driver behind interfaces such as photo galleries. By allowing for customization through XSLT, data binding, and EKML, ListSummaries and calendars have become one of the chief problem-solving tools when building towards high-gloss projects.

Calendars, much like video, have become a de facto must-have on both client facing websites and internal websites. As part of the rebuild of the feature in version 8.0 of the Ektron Framework, calendars received the ability to behave more like content, by storing event definitions in an XML back end. Being based on content allows them to utilize other features inherent in the content model including permissions, workflow, categorization, and so on. This update also introduced a much richer front-end interface modeled on Outlook, and a complete overhaul of the recurring event capabilities.

The new calendar feature has a feature set commensurate with any other calendar on the market — whether it's exporting entire iCal feeds of calendars, sorting by category, or mashing up multiple event feeds, the calendar feature can take your requirements and make them reality.

Taking this collection of three features, this chapter will run through the fundamentals of each and discuss how they work under the covers. You will then practice implementing these features into various scenarios.

LISTSUMMARY

ListSummaries are used to display a list of the content in a folder, and optionally, recursively down the child folders. This is a typical feature on a website, and one of the oldest features in the Ektron Framework. The usefulness of this server control fundamentally depends on how closely the Information Architecture of your site matches the front end organization of your site, but in most cases the two nearly mirror each other.

Due to this mirroring, you can use ListSummaries to show content related to what's currently being viewed, or a list of recently updated content, among other types of output. You can also use ListSummaries with custom XSLTs. They can include the full HTML of the content they refer to, allowing developers to provide features such as aggregated updates.

This section discusses the various ways you use a ListSummary on your site, and how to approach the different uses from a development perspective. The specific examples you will work through are based on the most common needs, which usually involve displaying a basic list of links, while still matching the format and style of the page that the ListSummary occurs on. This section shows how to:

➤ Implement a basic ListSummary.

➤ Change the markup using XSLT.

➤ Change the markup using EKML.

Implementing a Basic ListSummary

The ListSummary is a versatile control in the Ektron Framework tool belt. It serves a very basic function, but through the use of a wide variety of properties, it can be stretched to provide a list of links in almost every way imaginable. Table 8-1 contains these properties.

TABLE 8-1: ListSummary Server Control Properties

PROPERTY	DESCRIPTION
CacheInterval	Defines, in seconds, how long to cache the results. A value of zero specifies not to cache the results.
ContentParameter	Specifies the query string parameter for content IDs. If the query string contains a match for this, the ListSummary is replaced with a content block displaying the specified content item. If left unspecified, the display will always be the ListSummary.
ContentType	If this is specified, the ListSummary filters to display only matching items of that type. The value is an enumeration.
DisplayXslt	Specifies the path to the XSLT to render the results against.
FolderID	The ListSummary retrieves the contents of the folder specified by this property.
GetAnalyticsData	Returns Content View Count, Content Rating, and Content Rating Average in the XML document. This information can then be used in a custom XSLT.
GetHtml	Specifies whether to retrieve the HTML of the content items, or just the details necessary to display a link and summary. This is typically set to true only when you're using a custom markup file that shows the HTML.
IncludeIcons	Sets whether to display icons next to the displayed links. This property has an effect only when one of the default XSLT values is used.
LinkTarget	Sets the target on anchor tags in the default output. Can be set to _blank, _self, _parent, or _top. Leave blank for normal link behavior.
MarkupLanguage	Specifies the path to an EKML file. If this is set, it will override any value in DisplayXslt. EKML is a simplified token replacement display layer that can be easier to understand than XSLT.
MaxResults	The number of results to retrieve.
OrderBy	The key to sort items. Can be set to Title, DateModified, DateCreated, LastEditorFname, LastEditorLname, StartDate (the go live date of the content), Rated (the content rating of the item), or ContentViewCount (the number of times the item has been viewed).

continues

TABLE 8-1 *(continued)*

PROPERTY	DESCRIPTION
OrderByDirection	Ascending or descending order.
Recursive	Specifies whether to retrieve items in subfolders.
SelTaxonomyID	Specifies the default category to add content to if added through the access point displayed to logged-in authors just above the ListSummary.

As is clear from Table 8-1, the methods for modifying the ListSummary Server Control are quite varied. Let's explore how some of those properties react when you use the ListSummary on a page:

1. Start by creating a new Web form on your site called ListSummary.aspx. On the declarative ASPX file, drag the ListSummary Server Control from the toolbox on the left into the page between the form tags. This is shown in the following snippet.

    ```
    <CMS:ListSummary
       ID="uxListSummary"
       runat="server" />
    ```

2. The snippet, as is, defaults to show only content items from the root folder in the Workarea. The first thing you might try is specifying a different folder to display, and turning recursive display on.

    ```
    <CMS:ListSummary
       ID="uxListSummary"
       FolderID="72"
       Recursive="true"
       runat="server" />
    ```

    With the updated code in place, you now see all the content below the Pages folder in the Workarea. It's displaying a pretty long list of content now, as displayed in Figure 8-2, so you should probably set a maximum on the number of items displayed.

3. The following snippet configures the ListSummary Server Control to display a maximum of five results per page, with paging set to on. It's also set to display the results in alphabetical order by title.

    ```
    <CMS:ListSummary
       ID="uxListSummary"
       FolderID="72"
       Recursive="true"
       MaxResults="5"
       EnablePaging="true"
       OrderBy="Title"
       OrderByDirection="Ascending"
       runat="server" />
    ```

This combination of settings provides a much more useful layout, as seen in Figure 8-3. The paging is done via AJAX, which allows for fast and seamless user interaction.

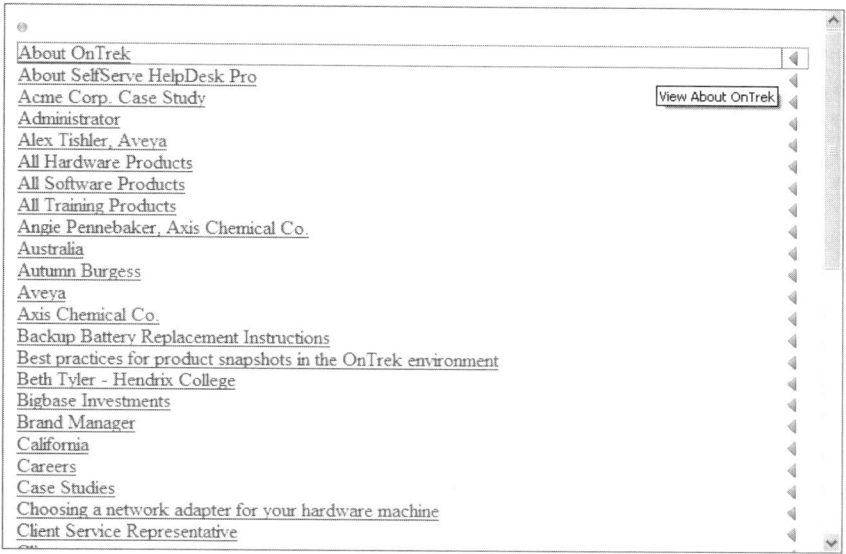

FIGURE 8-2

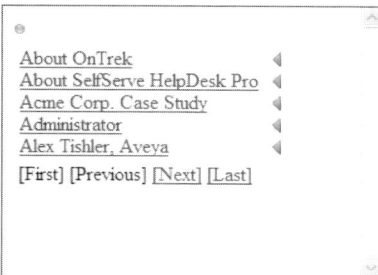

FIGURE 8-3

There are also a few ways to change the way the ListSummary Server Control looks. By default, if you don't set the DisplayXslt property, the server control will use the ecmNavigation template. There are, however, three other predefined options for display. You can set the DisplayXslt property to None–Databind, which does not display anything, but populates the EkItems property so the results can be worked with programmatically.

You can also set the DisplayXslt property to ecmTeaser or to ecmUnorderedList. These are prebuilt documents that cannot be modified, but can help you avoid having to author new XSLT's by covering common use cases. Figure 8-4 shows what the display looks like when set to ecmTeaser.

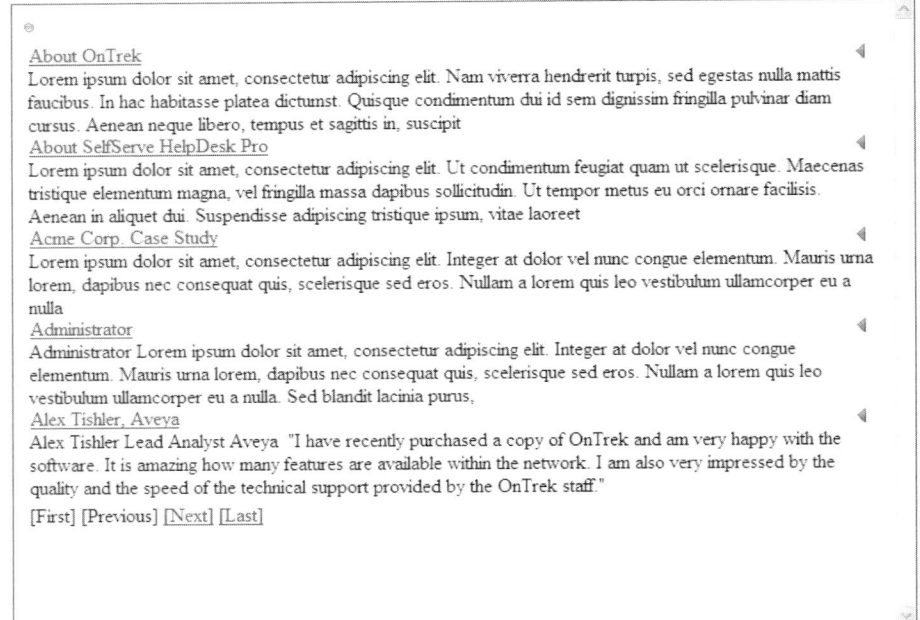

FIGURE 8-4

Changing the HTML Markup Using XSLT

If you want to change the display layer to something that the standard options won't allow for, you can use a custom XSLT in those situations. To do so , follow these steps:

1. Retrieve the XML you will be transforming. You can do this by reading from the `XmlDoc` property on the ListSummary Server Control at runtime, which involves adding a textbox to the declarative ListSummary.aspx file.

2. In the codebehind, set the Text property of the textbox to the `XmlDoc` property, as in the following snippet.

    ```
    Textbox1.Text = uxListSummary.XmlDoc.OuterXml;
    ```

    When you view the page in the browser, the textbox appears with the generated XML inside it. A sample of the XML produced by the ListSummary is reproduced in Listing 8-1.

LISTING 8-1: ListSummary Server Control XML output

Available for download on Wrox.com

```
<Collection>
  <Content>
    <ID>58</ID>
    <Type>Content</Type>
    <Title>All Hardware Products</Title>
    <QuickLink>
    http://thunder2/OnTrek/Products/Hardware/All-Hardware-Products/</QuickLink>
```

```xml
      <Teaser></Teaser>
      <Html></Html>
      <StartDate>1/1/0001 12:00:00 AM</StartDate>
      <DateModified>7/15/2010 5:50:29 AM</DateModified>
      <DateCreated>7/15/2010 5:47:18 AM</DateCreated>
      <EndDate>12/31/9999 11:59:59 PM</EndDate>
      <LastEditorFname>Application</LastEditorFname>
      <LastEditorLname>Administrator</LastEditorLname>
      <Hyperlink>
        <a href="http://thunder2/OnTrek/Products/Hardware/All-Hardware-Products/">
        All Hardware Products</a>
      </Hyperlink>
      <DisplayStartDate></DisplayStartDate>
      <FolderID>84</FolderID>
      <ContentStatus>A</ContentStatus>
      <Language>1033</Language>
      <AssetInfo>
        <Id></Id>
        <Icon></Icon>
        <FileName></FileName>
        <FileExtension></FileExtension>
        <ImageUrl></ImageUrl>
        <Language>0</Language>
        <MimeName></MimeName>
        <MimeType></MimeType>
        <PluginType></PluginType>
        <PublishPdfActive>False</PublishPdfActive>
        <Status></Status>
        <Type>0</Type>
        <Version></Version>
      </AssetInfo>
      <DisplayDateModified>7/15/2010 5:50:29 AM</DisplayDateModified>
      <DisplayDateCreated>7/15/2010 5:47:18 AM</DisplayDateCreated>
      <DisplayEndDate></DisplayEndDate>
      <EndDateAction>Archive_Expire</EndDateAction>
      <Comment></Comment>
      <Image>/OnTrek/WorkArea/images/application/spacer.gif</Image>
      <ImageThumbnail>
      /OnTrek/WorkArea/images/application/thumb_spacer.png</ImageThumbnail>
      <FilePath>
      http://thunder2/OnTrek/Products/Hardware/All-Hardware-Products/</FilePath>
    </Content>
    <Content>
      <ID>57</ID>
      <Type>Content</Type>
      <Title>All Software Products</Title>
      <QuickLink>
      http://thunder2/OnTrek/Products/Software/All-Software-Products/</QuickLink>
      <Teaser></Teaser>
      <Html></Html>
      <StartDate>1/1/0001 12:00:00 AM</StartDate>
      <DateModified>7/15/2010 5:51:07 AM</DateModified>
      <DateCreated>7/15/2010 5:44:58 AM</DateCreated>
      <EndDate>12/31/9999 11:59:59 PM</EndDate>
```

continues

LISTING 8-1 *(continued)*

```xml
    <LastEditorFname>Application</LastEditorFname>
    <LastEditorLname>Administrator</LastEditorLname>
    <Hyperlink>
      <a href="http://thunder2/OnTrek/Products/Software/All-Software-Products/">
      All Software Products</a>
    </Hyperlink>
    <DisplayStartDate></DisplayStartDate>
    <FolderID>84</FolderID>
    <ContentStatus>A</ContentStatus>
    <Language>1033</Language>
    <AssetInfo>
      <Id></Id>
      <Icon></Icon>
      <FileName></FileName>
      <FileExtension></FileExtension>
      <ImageUrl></ImageUrl>
      <Language>0</Language>
      <MimeName></MimeName>
      <MimeType></MimeType>
      <PluginType></PluginType>
      <PublishPdfActive>False</PublishPdfActive>
      <Status></Status>
      <Type>0</Type>
      <Version></Version>
    </AssetInfo>
    <DisplayDateModified>7/15/2010 5:51:07 AM</DisplayDateModified>
    <DisplayDateCreated>7/15/2010 5:44:58 AM</DisplayDateCreated>
    <DisplayEndDate></DisplayEndDate>
    <EndDateAction>Archive_Expire</EndDateAction>
    <Comment></Comment>
    <Image>/OnTrek/WorkArea/images/application/spacer.gif</Image>
    <ImageThumbnail>
    /OnTrek/WorkArea/images/application/thumb_spacer.png</ImageThumbnail>
    <FilePath>
    http://thunder2/OnTrek/Products/Software/All-Software-Products/</FilePath>
  </Content>
</Collection>
```

This XML document contains all the information you need to generate anything you want to display. You may notice that the `Html` tag is empty for each content item; the property `GetHtml` on the ListSummary determines whether or not to retrieve the HTML. There is a slight performance hit to retrieve the HTML, which is why it defaults to off, but if required, the HTML can be retrieved as well.

3. For the output, you're going to generate some very simple HTML that will output an unordered list of links. The output is very similar to the `ecmUnorderedList` output, but it should serve as a reasonable basis for future development you may need to do. The output looks like the following code snippet.

```
        <ul>
          <li>
            <a href="target.aspx?id=1">title of content</a>
          </li>
          <li>
            <a href="target.aspx?id=2">title of content 2</a>
          </li>
          <li>
            <a href="target.aspx?id=3">title of content 3</a>
          </li>
        </ul>
```

To achieve this output, the XSLT shown in Listing 8-2 will match the Collection/Content section and then retrieve the inner tag for the hyperlink, and simply render it into a list.

LISTING 8-2: UnorderedListSummary.xslt

Available for download on Wrox.com

```xml
<?xml version="1.0" encoding="utf-8"?>
<xsl:stylesheet version="1.0" xmlns:xsl="http://www.w3.org/1999/XSL/Transform"
    xmlns:msxsl="urn:schemas-microsoft-com:xslt" exclude-result-prefixes="msxsl">
    <xsl:output method="xml" indent="yes"/>
  <xsl:template match="Collection">
    <ul>
      <xsl:for-each select="Content">
        <li>
          <xsl:copy-of select="Hyperlink/a"/>
        </li>
      </xsl:for-each>
    </ul>
  </xsl:template>
</xsl:stylesheet>
```

4. This listing should be saved as a new file called ~\XmlFiles\UnorderedListSummary.xslt. To set your ListSummary Server Control to use it, set the `DisplayXslt` property to the new location, as shown in the following snippet.

```
<CMS:ListSummary
  ID="ListSummary1"
  FolderID="72"
  Recursive="true"
  MaxResults="5"
  EnablePaging="true"
  OrderBy="Title"
  OrderByDirection="Ascending"
  DisplayXslt="~\XmlFiles\UnorderedListSummary.xslt"
  runat="server" />
```

This updates the display on the Web page to what is shown in Figure 8-5.

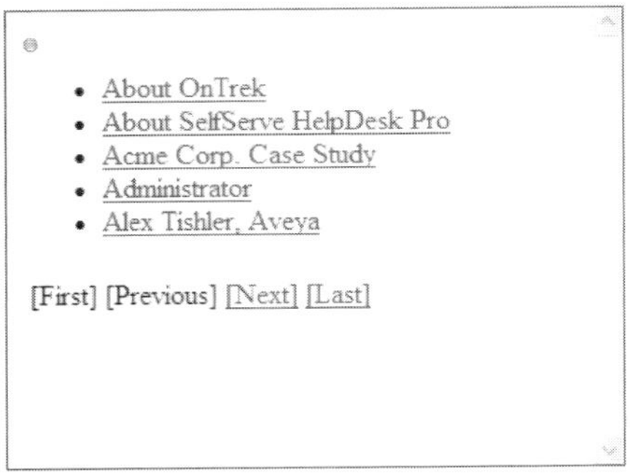

- About OnTrek
- About SelfServe HelpDesk Pro
- Acme Corp. Case Study
- Administrator
- Alex Tishler, Aveya

[First] [Previous] [Next] [Last]

FIGURE 8-5

As you can see in Figure 8-5, paging is still functional, and the ListSummary respects the sorting options you have specified. This makes it simple to update the display because you don't have to reinvent the wheel by adding custom paging or internal sorting. It also means that under-the-hood performance will be as fast as possible, since the transform is taking place on as small a portion of the data as possible. The XML supplied for the transform only contains the information that is currently being displayed to the end user, rather than the full result set.

Changing the Markup Using EKML

While XSL transforms are a powerful way of translating the display layer, Ektron is aware that not all developers are completely comfortable with writing XSL transforms. To solve this issue, Ektron has introduced EKML, short for Ektron Markup Language, which can handle basic transformations through simple looping and string replacement of tokens. This language was introduced by Ektron to allow developers to avoid complex XSLT's in simple use cases.

The way EKML hooks into the ListSummary Server Control is very similar to the procedure for XSLT documents. You create an EKML document, and set the `MarkupLanguage` property to the location of the file. The ListSummary then caches the file and transforms the output according to the structure defined in the markup document. The structure of the file is mostly HTML, with some tags that define where special processing needs to be done, such as loops. Table 8-2 contains the list of special tags used in EKML.

TABLE 8-2: EKML Tags

TAG	DESCRIPTION
ekmarkup	The root element for EKML documents.
ekoutput	The output from the server control goes between these tags.
ekrepeat	Anything between these tags will be repeated for each item in the list.
ekbubbleinfo	Defines the contents of a popup bubble. The bubble is invoked when a link, which is inserted with the token [$ShowBubble], is clicked on by the user. This tag is a sibling to the ekoutput tag.

The EKML tags define the basic structure of the EKML document. In addition to the tags there are a whole series of tokens that are replaced with the appropriate values for the objects being displayed. These tokens are outlined in Table 8-3.

TABLE 8-3: EKML Tokens Usable in ListSummaries

TOKEN	DESCRIPTION
[$Comment]	The item's comment information.
[$ContentId]	The ID of the content item.
[$DateCreated]	The date the content item was created.
[$DateModified]	The date the content item was last modified.
[$EditorFirstName]	First name of the most recent editor.
[$EditorLastName]	Last name of the most recent editor.
[$FolderDescription]	Description of the folder.
[$FolderId]	ID of the folder.
[$FolderName]	Name of the folder.
[$Html]	The actual HTML of the content item.
[$HyperLink]	Hyperlink to the item.
[$Image]	Replaced with the path to the image defined in the item's metadata.
[$ImageIcon]	Replaced with an image tag corresponding to the content type of the current item.
[$ImageThumbnail]	Replaced with the path to the thumbnail generated for the image defined in the item's metadata.
[$ItemCount]	The number of items returned.
[$Language]	The language currently being displayed.
[$QuickLink]	The QuickLink of the content from the Library.
[$SERVER_NAME]	The domain for the current page.
[$ShowBubble]	Creates a link to display a bubble containing the template defined in the ekbubbleinfo tag. Optionally, you can specify the width and height in pixels in parentheses after the variable. For example: [$ShowBubble(300,400)].
[$Status]	Displays the status of the content item.

continues

TABLE 8-3 *(continued)*

TOKEN	DESCRIPTION
[$Teaser]	Displays the teaser for the item.
[$Title]	Displays the title for the item.
[$UrlEncode('string')]	Runs a URL encoding function against the passed in string. The passed in string can be the output of another token.
[$UrlParam('parameter')]	Outputs the value from the specified query string parameter. For example, on the url test.aspx?id=233, the token [$UrlParam('id')] will output 233.

Now that you know the allowed tokens, you can create an EKML document that outputs the same HTML as the XSLT you created earlier. Take the code from Listing 8-3 and save it in ~\XmlFiles\ as UnorderedListSummary.ekml.

LISTING 8-3: UnorderedListSummary.ekml

Available for download on Wrox.com

```
<ekmarkup>
  <ekoutput>
    <ul>
      <ekrepeat>
        <li>
          [$HyperLink]
        </li>
      </ekrepeat>
    </ul>
  </ekoutput>
</ekmarkup>
```

Now you simply need to point the ListSummary Server Control at the new file by setting the `MarkupLanguage` to point to the new file. This is outlined in the following snippet.

```
<CMS:ListSummary
    ID="uxListSummary"
    FolderID="72"
    Recursive="true"
    MaxResults="5"
    EnablePaging="true"
    OrderBy="Title"
    OrderByDirection="Ascending"
    MarkupLanguage="XmlFiles\UnorderedListSummary.ekml"
    runat="server" />
```

The output of this update is shown in Figure 8-6. As is visible in the output, the HyperLink token is actually replaced by a DMS menu style link. There is a bit more intelligence in the token then there is following the same process with an XSLT. Using EKML can be a great way to simplify your development efforts while creating rich and complex displays.

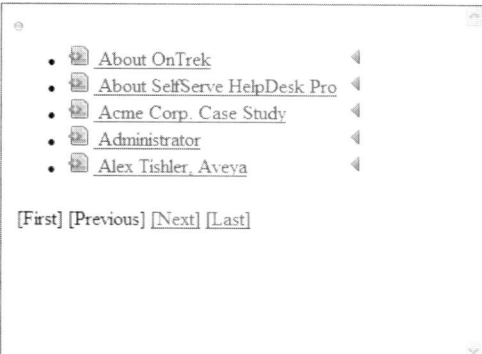

FIGURE 8-6

CALENDARS

Calendars have been a long-time feature of the Ektron Framework, but with version 8.0 they received a major overhaul. Where the old version had calendars stored outside of content, the new version makes calendars more like folders of events. Events themselves are stored as a subtype of content, which allows events to take advantage of the feature set built around content. This includes the capability of being categorized via taxonomy and the storage of associated metadata.

The interface also received a big facelift, and rather than using a simple table for output, they now use a rich, complex interface. The interface comes by way of Telerik's Scheduler component, and is similar in look and feel to Outlook. Because the items themselves are now content, they can also be displayed in the Content Block Server Control, the ListSummary Server Control, and almost any other control designed to work with content.

In this section, you learn how to administer calendars in the Ektron Framework, and then you move on to the many modes of displaying the events to users on your site. Finally, you learn how the events are stored in the system.

Most calendar administration takes place in the Workarea. There are three types of calendars in the Ektron Framework: system calendars, user calendars, and group calendars. The process of creating each type is slightly different. The first thing you do in this section is create one of each and learn the differences.

Next, you work through some of the different methods of displaying these calendars on your site. There are two modes of displaying calendar information: either as content or as a calendar. When displaying an Ektron calendar using the calendar interface, you use the WebCalendar Server Control. When displaying it as content, you can use a ListSummary, or any other content control. This chapter covers using the WebCalendar, ListSummary, and Content Block Server Controls to display events. Finally, it discusses how to use the API to retrieve a list of upcoming events from the system, and how to modify the way some of the server controls render the information. In this section, you:

➤ Create a system calendar, a group calendar, and a user calendar.

➤ Display events using a WebCalendar Server Control with customizations.

➤ Display events using a ListSummary Server Control.

➤ Display events using a Content Block Server Control.

➤ Display a list of upcoming events.

➤ Output iCal feeds.

Creating a System Calendar, User Calendar, and Group Calendar

Creating a system calendar follows the same process as creating a standard folder in the Workarea. The difference is what is displayed in the Content pane after creating it. To create a system calendar:

1. Open the Workarea after logging in as Admin, and go to the Content pane.

2. Right-click a folder in the folder tree and select Add Calendar. This brings up the Add Calendar form, as seen in Figure 8-7.

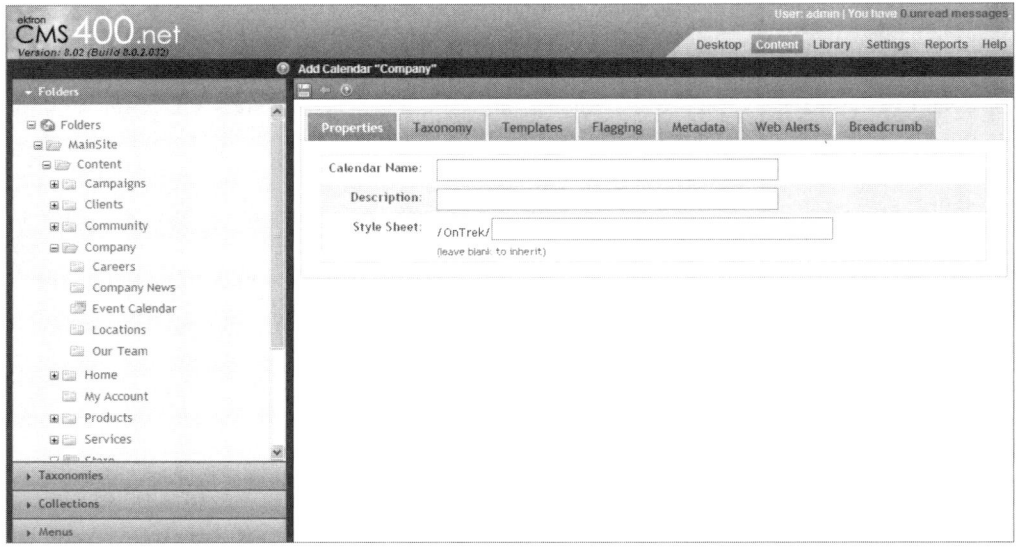

FIGURE 8-7

This form is almost exactly the same as the Add Folder form, covered in Chapter 5.

3. Enter in a Calendar Name, select a taxonomy node, and then click Save. When the page returns, it shows you an interface that is similar to the Folder View page, but with the exception that a calendar view is also visible. This is shown in Figure 8-8.

Interacting with the calendar in this view is the same as from the front end WebCalendar Server Control, which is covered in more depth later in this section. The key point to note about this view is that it supports dealing with events in two ways:

➤ **Via the calendar itself**: You use this to create new events, update event details, and reschedule events.

➤ **Via the interface you are used to using for content:** The classic content interface is useful in updating metadata, templates, and other related content details.

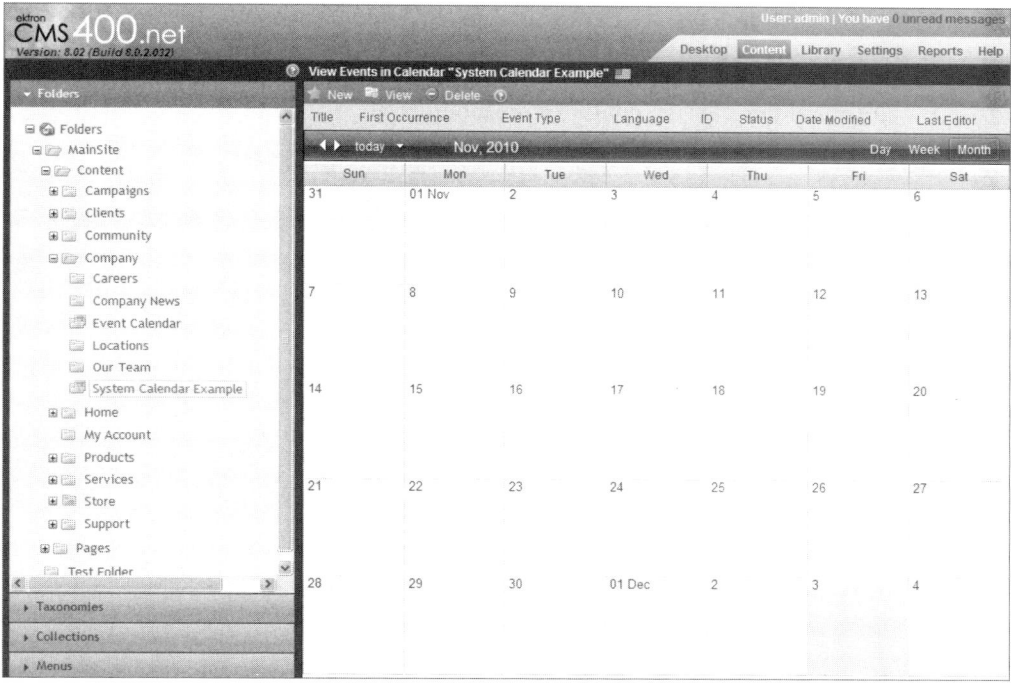

FIGURE 8-8

4. Try out the content interface now by first creating an event. Double-click the calendar on a day of your choice. This brings up the Edit Appointment form, shown in Figure 8-9.

5. The Title, Location, and Description fields are self-explanatory. The start date for the event is shown underneath those three primary fields. By deselecting the All Day checkbox, three additional fields will be shown. These fields allow you to specify the start time, as well as the end date and time. Using these options allows you to specify the exact period that your event will run. It is possible to create events that run for multiple days, but generally the preferred practice is to use recurrence to define the additional days, as each recurrence can then be managed separately with its own details.

6. On the Recurrence tab, a single checkbox is shown, unchecked by default. By checking the Recurrence checkbox, a group of additional fields is shown. These fields allow you to specify the type of recurrence, as well as how long the event should run — definable as forever, after a certain number of occurrences, or up until a specific date and time. The supported recurrence modes are:

   ➤ Daily
   ➤ Weekly

➤ Monthly by Date

➤ Monthly by Day

➤ Yearly

The difference between by Date and by Day is that the by Date option allows you to specify a specific day number, where the by Day option is used for settings such as the first day of the month, or the last Sunday of the month.

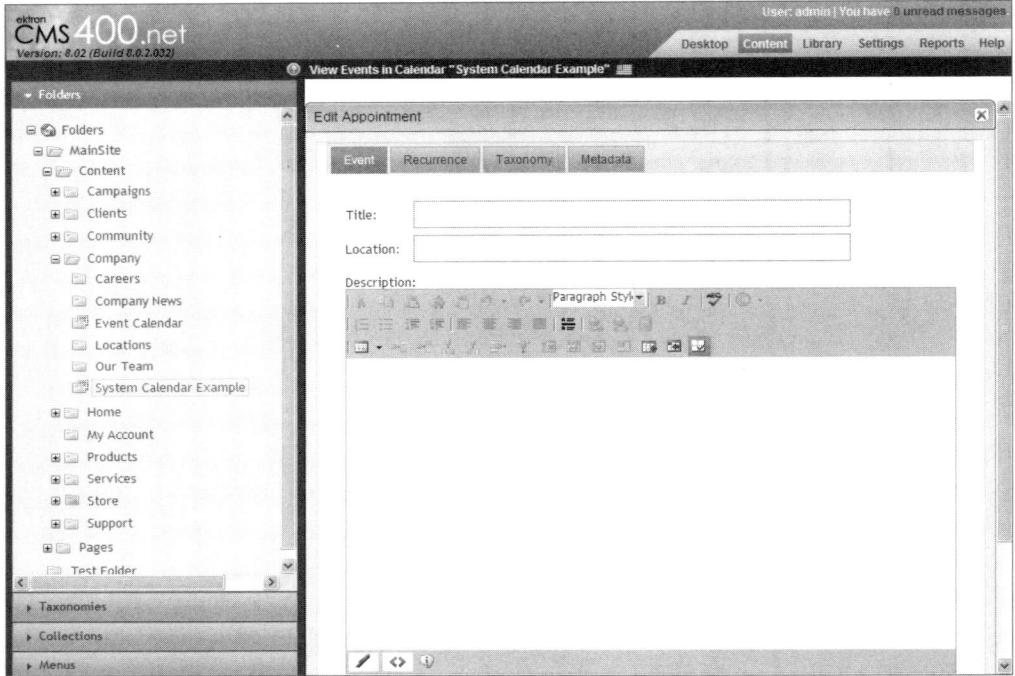

FIGURE 8-9

7. There are two additional tabs on this form; these allow for setting taxonomy associations and metadata settings. Because this calendar was associated with a taxonomy when you created it, clicking that tab allows you to categorize this event into one or more taxonomy nodes. Taxonomy categorization can be an integral part of how events are displayed, as each created interface allows them to be filtered by taxonomy.

8. Enter **My Event** as the title for your event now, and and click Save, which returns you to the calendar view, with the event listed above the calendar as well as shown on the calendar itself, as shown in Figure 8-10.

As you can see, the new event has been added to the event list, along with the details of when the event occurs and what type the event is. This event has the type Original, which means that it is the base definition of the event. The other types are "Variance - Extra Occurrence" and "Variance - Cancelled Occurrence." Extra Occurrence means that it is a member of a recurring series whose details have been changed for that day. A cancellation means that the event that should have occurred on that day, due to a recurrence rule, has been cancelled.

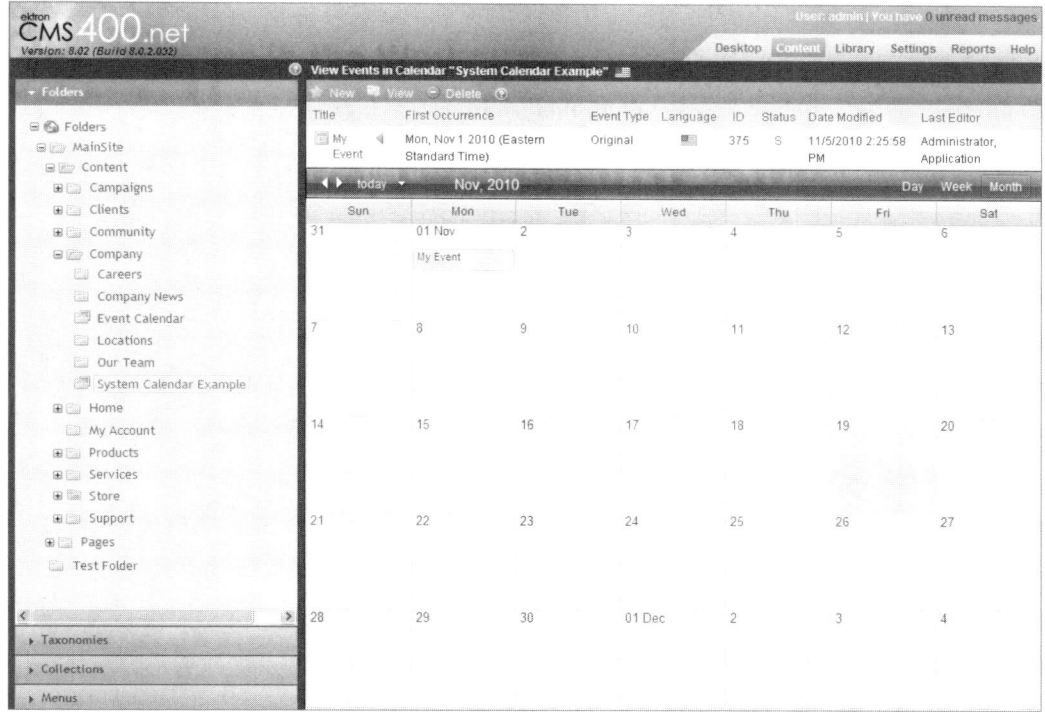

FIGURE 8-10

The event is also shown with a DMS Menu instance, which allows content authors to perform immediate actions on the content such as deleting it or moving it through an approval chain. Click the title of the event on the list now to be taken to the detail view of the event. The detail view is also shown in Figure 8-11.

The event detail view does not allow you to edit the event itself, but does allow you to manage the summary, metadata, alias, content scheduling, templates, and taxonomy associations.

User and Group Calendars

User and group calendars are similar to system calendars in that they store events in the same way. The difference is the location that these events are stored internally. When a user or community group is created in the Ektron Framework, the system automatically adds a hidden folder for that user or group. One of the properties available during the creation process is whether to create a calendar for the new object — if checked, then a calendar folder is added underneath the private folder.

The upside to group and user calendars is that they maintain proper permissions automatically for groups and users. The downside is that there is no content interface for the events or calendars in the Workarea the way there is for System Calendars.

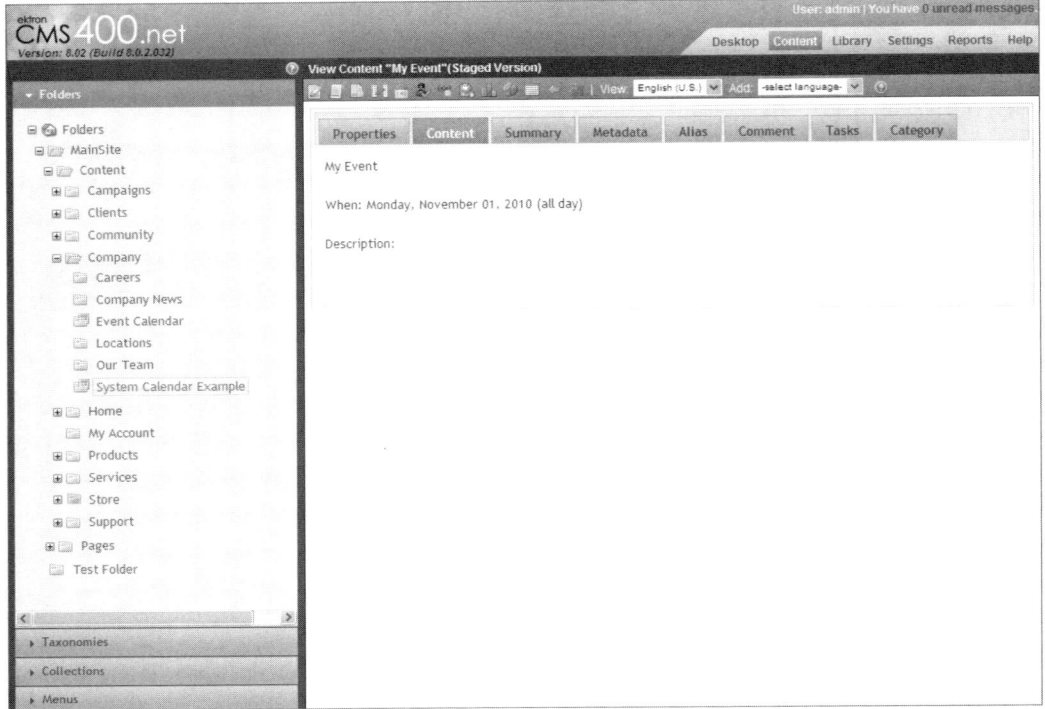

FIGURE 8-11

Let's create a user calendar now.

1. Start by going to Settings ⇨ Users in the Workarea, and select Admin.
2. Clicking the edit button brings up the edit user properties interface, with a tab labeled Custom, shown in Figure 8-12.

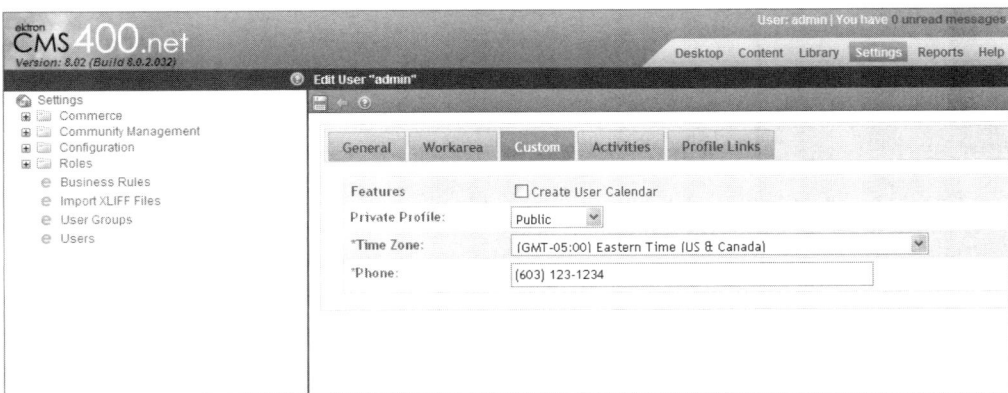

FIGURE 8-12

3. On the Custom tab, there are two settings that are related to the calendar:

   ➤ **Create User Calendar**: Checking this box and saving creates the user calendar and makes it available for use as a data source. It is not possible to roll back the creation of a user calendar or a group calendar, as this can lead to loss of data. It is an option on the user profile for performance reasons — if your users do not create calendars, this can make the system more responsive by reducing the number of folders in the system.

   ➤ **Time Zone property**: This list is generated from the Windows time zone list. When a user selects a time zone, all calendar events from that time forward are calculated from the version stored (based on GMT) to the user's time zone. This allows users across the globe to all see the event in their appropriate time zones. It is a required field, but if it has not been entered, for example for a user who was created programmatically, the system displays the events in the server time zone.

4. Community groups have a similar method of creating user calendars, but the interface is slightly different. Go to Settings ➪ Community Management ➪ Community Groups. Clicking the Add Icon or selecting an existing group brings up the community group form. This form has two checkboxes under the Features group, one of which is for Group Calendars, as shown in Figure 8-13. The same caveats apply to this calendar as to user calendars.

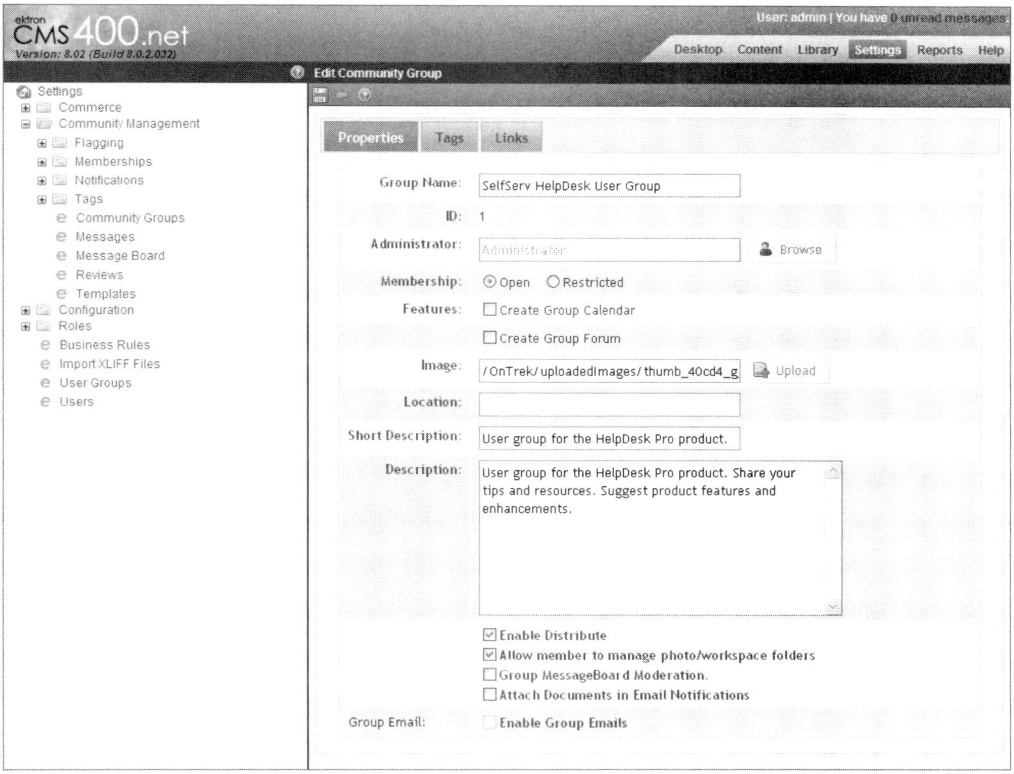

FIGURE 8-13

Displaying Events Using a WebCalendar Server Control

The WebCalendar Server Control is the primary interface for Ektron calendars. The control uses the Telerik Scheduler component internally for rendering, but supports a variety of overrides. Using the server control with its default settings is straightforward. You'll create these examples on a new Web form. Create the Web form in the root of your site and call it Calendars.aspx, shown in Listing 8-4, and drag the WebCalendar Server Control from the toolbox into the form of the new page.

LISTING 8-4: Calendars.aspx

Available for download on Wrox.com

```
<%@ Page Language="C#" AutoEventWireup="true"
    CodeFile="calendars.aspx.cs" Inherits="calendars" %>
<%@ Register Assembly="Ektron.Cms.Controls"
    Namespace="Ektron.Cms.Controls" TagPrefix="CMS" %>

<!DOCTYPE html PUBLIC "-//W3C//DTD XHTML 1.0 Transitional//EN"
    "http://www.w3.org/TR/xhtml1/DTD/xhtml1-transitional.dtd">

<html xmlns="http://www.w3.org/1999/xhtml">
<head runat="server">
    <title>Calendars</title>
</head>
<body>
    <form id="form1" runat="server">
        <CMS:WebCalendar ID="uxWebCalendar" runat="server">
        </CMS:WebCalendar>
    </form>
</body>
</html>
```

The WebCalendar Server Control has a few key properties that are used as attributes on the control, but data sources are encoded as inner XML. Table 8-4 shows the properties.

TABLE 8-4: WebCalendar Server Control Properties

PROPERTY	DESCRIPTION
AllowEventEditing	Setting this to `false` disallows editing (creating, updating, and deleting) of events on the page. When `true`, events are editable only if the logged-in user has the appropriate permissions.
DefaultDisplayType	The display mode the calendar is set to by default. Can be set to Month, Week, or Day. Defaults to Month.
DisplayTemplatePath	The path to the user control that will render the event on the calendar. Defines bubble behavior as well as what text displays. Defaults to ~\Workarea\WebCalendar\DefaultTemplate\Display.ascx.

PROPERTY	DESCRIPTION
IncludeJqueryTheme	If set to `false`, this prevents the WebCalendar from loading a jQuery theme, which is used to style the form for creating and editing events. If set to `true` the WebCalendar includes the Remond jQuery theme to style the Edit Event form.
IncludeScriptManager	The WebCalendar attempts to detect if there is already a ScriptManager instance on the page. If there isn't, it adds one internally. Occasionally, depending on where the external ScriptManager is in the control tree, it falsely detects no ScriptManager. Set this to `true` if you run into this issue.
UseUpdatePanel	The WebCalendar uses an UpdatePanel internally to allow for Async Postbacks. If you don't want this behavior, set UseUpdatePanel to `false`.
CssFile	Defaults to ~/Workarea/WebCalendar/View/WebCalendar.css. This can be pointed elsewhere to modify the base styles.

In addition to the properties listed in Table 8-4, there are internally encoded properties to define the data sources for the calendar. The following code snippet shows a few examples of how this can be achieved.

```
<CMS:WebCalendar ID="uxWebCalendar" runat="server">
  <DataSource>
    <CMS:CalendarDataSource
      backColor="AutoSelect"
      defaultId="111"
      queryParam="calendarId"
      sourceType="SystemCalendar" />
    <CMS:CalendarDataSource
      backColor="Blue"
      defaultId="222"
      queryParam="groupCalendarId"
      sourceType="GroupCalendar" />
    <CMS:CalendarDataSource
      backColor="DarkRed"
      defaultId="333"
      queryParam="userCalendarId"
      sourceType="UserCalendar" />
  </DataSource>
</CMS:WebCalendar>
```

The WebCalendar in the previous snippet has three sources defined. Each source then has several properties. Table 8-5 outlines the properties for CalendarDataSource.

TABLE 8-5: CalendarDataSource Properties

PROPERTY	DESCRIPTION
defaultId	The default ID to use. If the source is a system calendar, this is the folder ID. If the source is a user or group calendar, this should be set to the user or group ID.
queryParam	The query string parameter to use. If this is specified and the query string contains a parameter by the same name, the value overrides the `defaultID` property.
sourceType	The type of the calendar. Can be `GroupCalendar`, `UserCalendar`, or `SystemCalendar`. This switches the `defaultID` to key off the appropriate type.
backColor	The color to display the event in. This is an enumeration.

In addition to these baseline data source properties, the `CalendarDataSource` tag also supports an inner encoded list of taxonomy IDs to use as a filter against the particular source. For instance, a developer can specify that the calendar should only show events from category ID 23 or 24 that are in system calendar 432 using the following code snippet.

```
<CMS:WebCalendar ID="uxWebCalendar" runat="server">
  <DataSource>
    <CMS:CalendarDataSource
        backColor="AutoSelect"
        defaultId="432"
        sourceType="SystemCalendar">
      <CMS:CategoryID categoryId="23" />
      <CMS:CategoryID categoryId="24" />
    </CMS:CalendarDataSource>
  </DataSource>
</CMS:WebCalendar>
```

When specifying multiple category IDs for a single data source, all events from each category are included — it is an OR operation rather than an AND operation.

All of these settings can be configured through codebehind, allowing for items like a taxonomy tree filter to be applied to the WebCalendar. The properties are stored as generic *lists*, making it straightforward to manage the sources. The following example achieves the same effect as the previous snippet.

```
Ektron.Cms.Controls.CalendarDataSource Source;
Source = new Ektron.Cms.Controls.CalendarDataSource();
Source.backColor = Ektron.Cms.Controls.EventColor.AutoSelect;
Source.defaultId = 432;
Source.sourceType = Ektron.Cms.Controls.SourceType.SystemCalendar;

Source.CategoryIDs.Add(new Ektron.Cms.Controls.CategoryID(23));
Source.CategoryIDs.Add(new Ektron.Cms.Controls.CategoryID(24));

uxWebCalendar.DataSource.Add(new Ektron.Cms.Controls.CalendarDataSource());
uxWebCalendar.Fill();
```

These steps allow you to display calendars on your site with a minimum of fuss, while achieving a rich interface for your users and administrators. Deeper customizations can also be performed on the WebCalendar — three main areas that people frequently want to customize on the WebCalendar are the event rendering, the event editing form, and the styling on the calendar.

When referring to the event rendering of the WebCalendar, we are talking about the information displayed for each event in the day, week, or month view. An example of the bubble is shown in Figure 8-14. This bubble is created through the instantiation of a user control that is normally in the Workarea at ~/Workarea/WebCalendar/DefaultTemplate/Display.ascx. To override this display, copy the user control from the Workarea to another location on your site, and update the property `DisplayTemplatePath` on the WebCalendar to reflect the new location. The user control can then be modified to display anything you want.

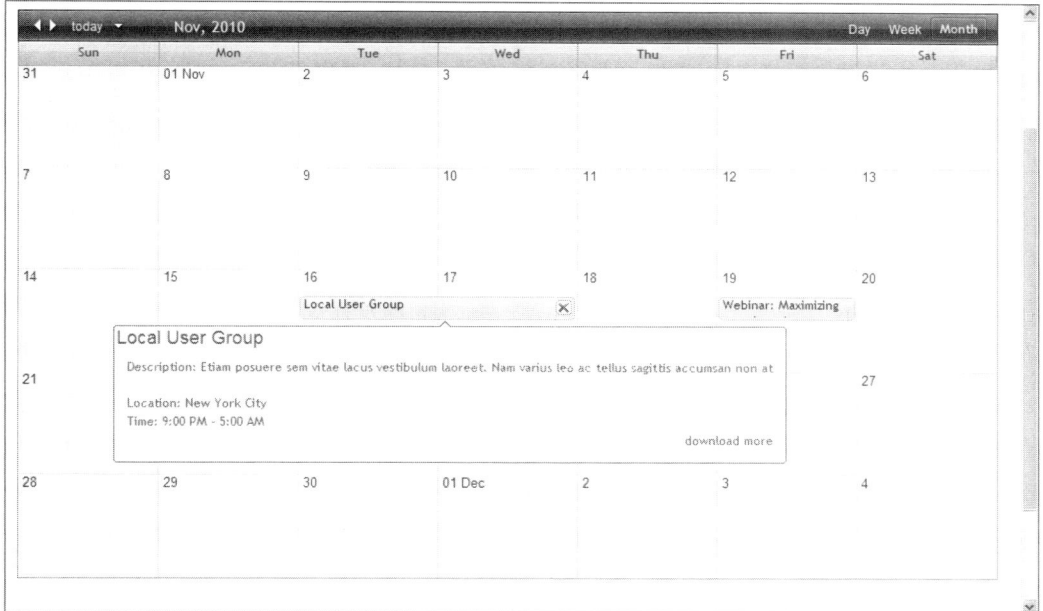

FIGURE 8-14

As mentioned earlier, another common need is to modify the event editing form. This is also a user control in the Workarea that is instantiated on demand. In this case, the user control is stored at ~/Workarea/WebCalendar/DefaultTemplate/AdvancedForm.ascx. There is no property that allows this to be overridden to another location, but as the control is exposed, modifications can be made directly to the control to support alternate functionality.

> *A caveat to modifying Workarea files is to remember that when you upgrade your installation of the Ektron Framework, your modifications will be overwritten by the new versions of these files from Ektron.*

A final common set of modifications made to the WebCalendar is to customize the CSS included by the control. The property `CssFile` allows you to point the WebCalendar somewhere other than the default location for the CSS. The unmodified file is stored in ~/Workarea/WebCalendar/View/WebCalendar.css. To modify it, copy it somewhere else in the site, and update the `CssFile` property to point at the new location. Inside the file, the style rules are broken into three main sections. The file starts with the styles defined for the advanced form, followed by the base layout styles for the WebCalendar view. That is then followed by a theme section, which defines the look and feel including colors and images.

Displaying Events Using a ListSummary Server Control

Events stored in Ektron calendars are stored as a subtype of content. What this means is that all the features that standard HTML content supports are also supported by WebCalendar events, including taxonomy, metadata, search, permissions, and workflow.

Additionally, since the events are stored in what is effectively a folder, they can be displayed by most controls as standard content. For example, it is possible to use a ListSummary Server Control to display a list of events from a calendar. As an example, the following code snippet will output the result shown in Figure 8-15.

```
<form id="form1" runat="server">
  <CMS:ListSummary runat="server" ID="uxListSummary" FolderID="124" />
</form>
```

The tradeoff with this approach comes from how the events are stored under-the-hood. As mentioned earlier, the events are stored similarly to the iCalendar standard. What this means is that the rules for recurrence are stored as part of a master event, and that additional occurrences or cancellations of recurrences are stored as variances in secondary content. The outcome of this type of storage is that if you have an event that recurs every week, it only shows up once as a single piece of content. If you then cancel a single occurrence of the event, the cancellation shows up as

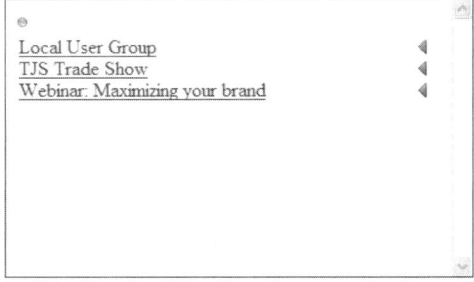

FIGURE 8-15

a second piece of content. If you were then to modify a different occurrence and save it, you end up with four total pieces of content. One of the additional items is the cancellation for that day, and the other is the additional variance for that day.

For some uses this is fine, as you can write a custom XSLT against the XML to display what you need from the event details, but in other cases you will be actually looking for a list of upcoming events, which is covered later in this section.

Displaying Events Using a Content Block Server Control

In the same way the ListSummary Server Control can display a list of events from a calendar, you can use the Content Block Server Control to display a detail view of an individual event. The Ektron Framework internally uses an XSLT to transform the stored data for the event into a standardized display layer. You can then combine this display layer with other standard Ektron controls, such as the MessageBoard Server Control, to create a rich interface for people to interact with these events. This section covers how to display the event on a Content Block Server Control, as well as how to modify the display of the event by changing the XSLT.

In the Smart Form section of Chapter 6, you read how Smart Form designs are stored in packages. A package contains five major elements, from the schema to the input form. The key part of the package that is used to display the data in a content block, however, is the default XSLT.

Events in the Ektron Framework are based at their core on a Smart Form, which means the behavior is almost exactly the same as any other Smart Form.

This includes the way the data is rendered through the Content Block Server Control. The hidden Smart Form package contains a default XSLT that has the smarts to render the event definition in an appropriate manner, depending on the language and time zone of the user. When an event ID is specified for a Content Block Server Control, it automatically renders the event using that predefined XSLT. In this section, you render the event you created earlier using a content block. Once you've investigated how the system behaves by default, you'll learn how to create a custom XSLT for rendering the data, while maintaining the intelligence supplied in the original.

To render an event into a Content Block Server Control, you need to know the event's ID:

1. In the Workarea, navigate to the calendar built into the OnTrek site, at /MainSite/Content/Company/Event Calendar.

2. Once there, look at the list of events that's rendered just above the calendar in the Content pane — the starter site ships with three events. We'll display the Local User Group event, which is ID 252, as shown in Figure 8-16.

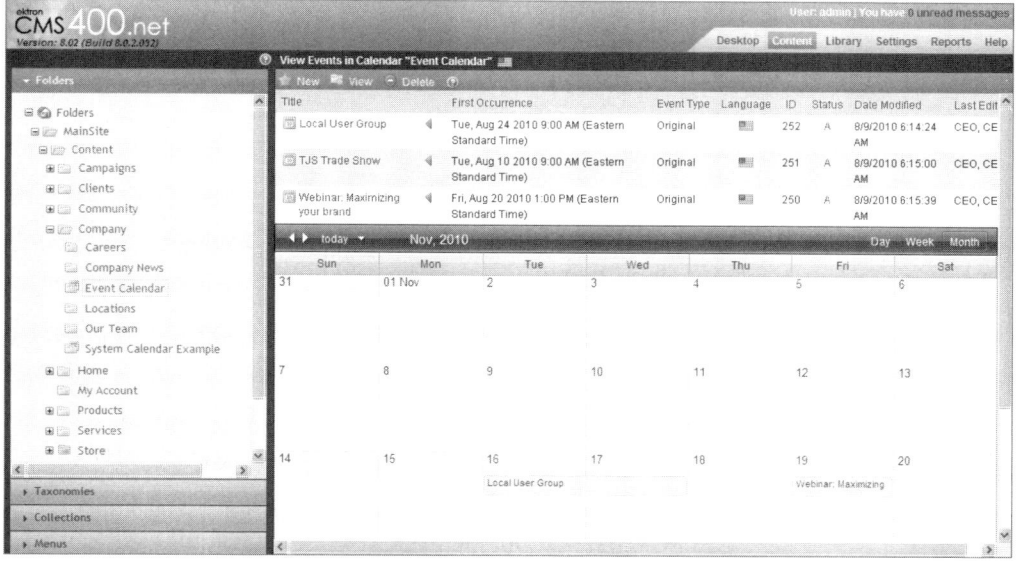

FIGURE 8-16

You will use that value as the `DefaultContentID` value in the Content Block Server Control.

3. Return to the Calendar.aspx file in Visual Studio, and replace the ListSummary Server Control with a Content Block Server Control, as shown in the following snippet.

```
<form id="form1" runat="server">
  <CMS:ContentBlock
    runat="server"
    ID="uxContentBlock"
    DefaultContentID="252" />
</form>
```

When you reload the page in your browser, you should see something that resembles the output shown in Figure 8-17. In this example, the event has a complex recurrence rule, which is correctly interpreted by the XSLT and rendered into a verbal description of that rule, displayed with the event.

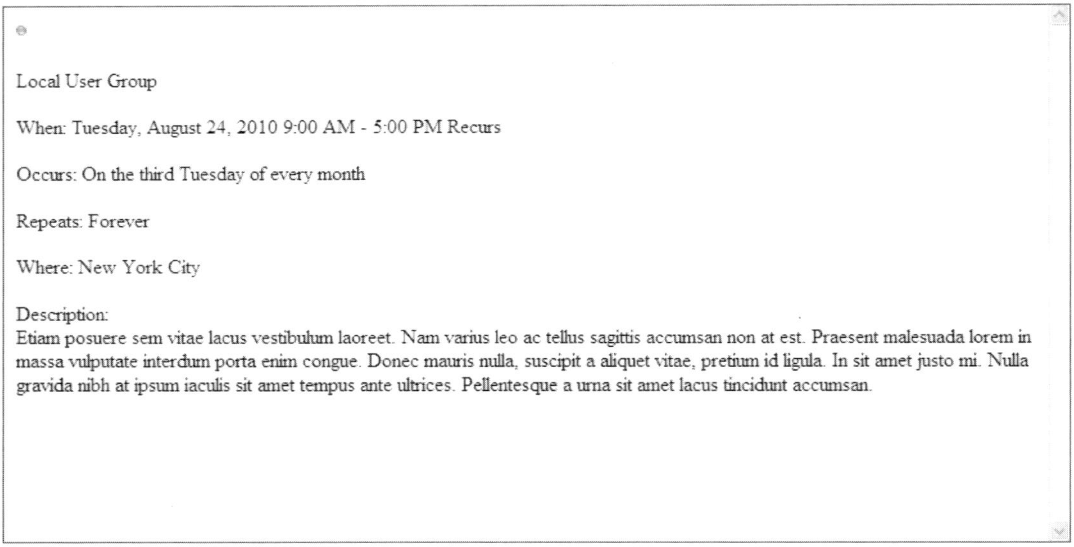

```
Local User Group

When: Tuesday, August 24, 2010 9:00 AM - 5:00 PM Recurs

Occurs: On the third Tuesday of every month

Repeats: Forever

Where: New York City

Description:
Etiam posuere sem vitae lacus vestibulum laoreet. Nam varius leo ac tellus sagittis accumsan non at est. Praesent malesuada lorem in
massa vulputate interdum porta enim congue. Donec mauris nulla, suscipit a aliquet vitae, pretium id ligula. In sit amet justo mi. Nulla
gravida nibh at ipsum iaculis sit amet tempus ante ultrices. Pellentesque a urna sit amet lacus tincidunt accumsan.
```

FIGURE 8-17

While, the output is a bit bland, the markup is clean enough, so the display layer can be formatted using CSS to match the site it is being displayed on. But if you want to use different words for some of the output, or change the order, or even skip some elements, a copy of the XSLT used in the package is also provided in ~/Workarea/WebCalendar/XSL/default.xslt. This file can be copied elsewhere into your site, modified at will, and then used to override the default package XSLT for Web events.

To point your content block at the custom XSLT, use the `DisplayXSLT` property on the Content Block Server Control. For example, on your site you copied the default XSLT to the XMLfiles directory, so you could update your content block code to look like the following snippet. Once you have rewired it to use your custom XSLT, you can modify the webevent.xslt file until you are satisfied with the format or language.

```
<form id="form1" runat="server">
  <CMS:ContentBlock
    runat="server"
    DisplayXslt="~/XmlFiles/webevent.xslt"
    ID="uxContentBlock"
    DefaultContentID="252" />
</form>
```

The XSLT file itself is fairly complex, and this section doesn't go into it in depth, but there are a few decisions that were made in the development of the WebCalendar system that may not be apparent immediately. The main item to note is the custom extension functions that are used in the XSLT — specifically `ekext:convertUTCtoLocal` and `ekext:formatDateTime`. By using the Saxon processor packaged with the Ektron Framework to perform an XSLT2 conversion rather than an XSLT1 conversion, Ektron could have avoided the need for these custom extensions, as date logic is included with the XSLT2 specification. However, the decision to use custom extensions was made for two reasons: The localization included with the Saxon processor does not include data for all regions, meaning that in some cases the localization of dates would fail. Additionally, by moving the functions into the core Ektron stack, the XSLT became substantially simpler.

Display a List of Upcoming Events

The WebCalendar infrastructure also has a rich API for retrieving and modifying events. The majority of this API can be accessed through the `Ektron.Cms.Framework.Calendar.WebEvent` class, but there are a few additional functions available only through the `Ektron.Cms.Content.Calendar.WebEventManager` class. Many of these functions are self-explanatory. For example there are functions to `Add`, `Delete`, `Update`, and `CancelOccurence`. But the key function covered right now is the `GetEventOccurenceList` function.

Whereas the ListSummary Server Control was useful in showing a list of events from the perspective of content — one item per event definition, regardless of recurrences — the `GetEventOccurenceList` is used to expand the recurrence rules into a full set of event occurrences, and then correlate them with cancellations and additional occurrences. What this means is that when you call `GetEventOccurenceList` you get output that matches exactly what you see on the WebCalendar display for a given time period.

The output of this function is not added into a mode of display on the WebCalendar Server Control because it is very straightforward to use one of the standard ASP.NET controls to display the output. A common method of displaying the event list is to use the ASP.NET Repeater Server Control.

Let's walk through an example now of setting up the retrieval and display.

1. Return to the Calendar.aspx file in Visual Studio and open the codebehind for the file.
2. Retrieve the list of events. In this example, you'll start with the current time and get the list of events covered over the next month. You can optionally provide a Category ID to filter by, but let's skip that in this example.
3. Add the following code snippet to your file.

```
protected void Page_Load(object sender, EventArgs e)
{
  List<Ektron.Cms.Common.Calendar.WebEventData> eventList;

  Ektron.Cms.Content.Calendar.WebEventManager webEventApi;
  webEventApi = new Ektron.Cms.Content.Calendar.WebEventManager();
  eventList = webEventApi.GetEventOccurrenceList(
    88, DateTime.Now, DateTime.Now.AddMonths(1));
}
```

This code retrieves the list of `WebEventData` instances, each of which contains a single occurrence of an event.

4. At this point, you can create an ASP.NET Repeater Server Control on the declarative side and create that output formatting. Flip over to the Calendar.aspx file, and put the following snippet in between the Form tags.

```
<asp:Repeater ID="uxRepeater" runat="server">
  <ItemTemplate>
    Event Name: <%# Container.DataItem as
              Ektron.Cms.Common.Calendar.WebEventData).DisplayTitle%><br />
    Event Start: <%# Container.DataItem as
              Ektron.Cms.Common.Calendar.WebEventData).EventStart
.toString()%>
    <br />
    Event Location: <%# Container.DataItem as
                Ektron.Cms.Common.Calendar.WebEventData).Location%>
    <br /><br />
  </ItemTemplate>
</asp:Repeater>
```

5. Now all that remains is to databind the Repeater Server Control to the list of occurrences you retrieved through the API. The following amendment to the codebehind does this.

```
uxRepeater.DataSource = eventList;
uxRepeater.DataBind();
```

Now when you visit Calendar.aspx in your browser, you should get output like that shown in Figure 8-18.

```
Event Name: Webinar: Maximizing your brand
Event Start: 11/19/2010 1:00:00 AM
Event Location: Online

Event Name: Local User Group
Event Start: 11/16/2010 9:00:00 PM
Event Location: New York City
```

FIGURE 8-18

For posterity's sake, Listing 8-5 lists the complete code (both declarative and codebehind) for the
Calendar.aspx and Calendar.aspx.cs files.

LISTING 8-5: Calendar.aspx and Calendar.aspx.cs

CALENDAR.ASPX

```
<%@ Page Language="C#" AutoEventWireup="true"
  CodeFile="calendars.aspx.cs" Inherits="calendars" %>
<%@ Register Assembly="Ektron.Cms.Controls"
  Namespace="Ektron.Cms.Controls" TagPrefix="CMS" %>

<!DOCTYPE html PUBLIC "-//W3C//DTD XHTML 1.0 Transitional//EN"
  "http://www.w3.org/TR/xhtml1/DTD/xhtml1-transitional.dtd">

<html xmlns="http://www.w3.org/1999/xhtml">
<head runat="server">
    <title>Calendars</title>
</head>
<body>
<form id="form1" runat="server">
  <asp:Repeater ID="uxRepeater" runat="server">
    <ItemTemplate>
      Event Name: <%# (Container.DataItem as
        Ektron.Cms.Common.Calendar.WebEventData).DisplayTitle%>
      <br />
      Event Start: <%# (Container.DataItem as
        Ektron.Cms.Common.Calendar.WebEventData).EventStart.toString()%>
      <br />
      Event Location: <%# Container.DataItem as
        Ektron.Cms.Common.Calendar.WebEventData).Location")%>
      <br /><br />
    </ItemTemplate>
  </asp:Repeater>
</form>
</body>
</html>
```

CALENDAR.ASPX.CS

```
using System;
using System.Collections.Generic;
using System.Linq;
using System.Web;
using System.Web.UI;
using System.Web.UI.WebControls;

public partial class calendars : System.Web.UI.Page
{
    protected void Page_Load(object sender, EventArgs e)
    {
      List<Ektron.Cms.Common.Calendar.WebEventData> eventList;

      Ektron.Cms.Content.Calendar.WebEventManager webEventApi;
```

continues

LISTING 8-5 *(continued)*

```
        webEventApi = new Ektron.Cms.Content.Calendar.WebEventManager();
        eventList = webEventApi.GetEventOccurrenceList(
          88, DateTime.Now, DateTime.Now.AddMonths(1));

        uxRepeater.DataSource = eventList;
        uxRepeater.DataBind();
    }
}
```

Outputting iCal Feeds

One final frequently asked question about the feature set that WebCalendars provides is how to export events from the Ektron Framework and import them into another application such as Outlook, and vice versa. The Ektron Framework does not support importing iCal or vCal files from other sources, but it generates them in order to move events from the framework to another software platform.

In fact, the default interface for the WebCalendar Server Control includes a link to download the .ICS file for each event. By hovering over the event link, the event bubble appears on the calendar, including a download link, as seen in Figure 8-19.

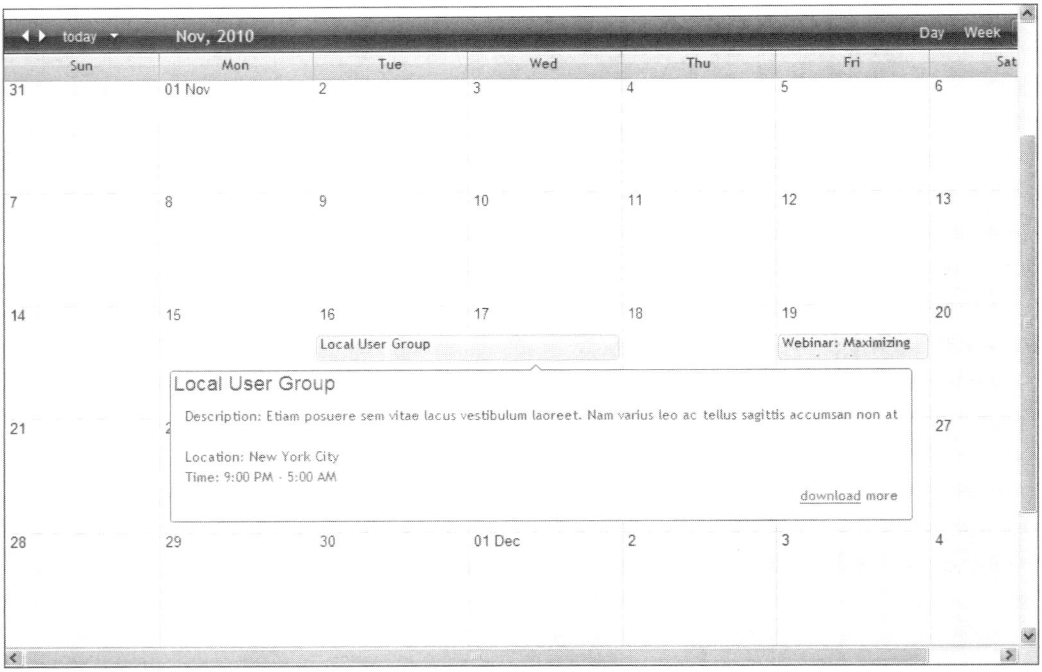

FIGURE 8-19

The download link in the bubble points to the file ~/Workarea/WebCalendar/View/IcalGenerator.ashx and includes the query string parameter `eventid`. This file generates feeds for entire calendars as well, by specifying the `calid` query string parameter instead. This ability allows for programs to have live feeds of calendars if they support it.

The feed generated supports version 2 of the iCal standard, which allows it to also specify the originating time zone information for the event. This means that whenever users worldwide add the event to their calendars, the event appears in their local time zones, and respects the translation effects of moving across potentially two daylight savings boundaries in the case of a recurring event.

VIDEO/CUSTOMER TESTIMONIALS

This section covers how to work with video files and Flash in the CMS. The Ektron Framework is designed to make this as straightforward as possible, while allowing developers to treat the videos as content so that attributes can be set on the files and concepts such as metadata can still be applied to them.

There are also options other than managing your videos within the Ektron Framework. For example, the Ektron Framework ships with a BrightCove PageBuilder Widget, which allows you to use the BrightCove video management service and distributed content network to embed corporate videos into your site and easily track statistics. We'll cover these in more depth after we discuss how to serve your files from the Ektron Framework.

This section corresponds to the Testimonials section of OnTrek. The testimonials page is comprised of a single Flash object that retrieves the testimonial information from a Smart Form configuration, and then displays it inside the container. In this scenario, you will simplify the example by working with a single Flash object. This section covers how to add the object to the system, manage options on it, and display it. It also discusses some of the alternatives to managing the video within the Ektron Framework. The specific items in this section will be:

- Adding an object to the DMS
- Modifying settings on the managed object
- Displaying the managed object
- Alternatives to using the Ektron Framework to manage your assets

Adding an Object to the DMS

Adding assets to the framework is an action performed in the Workarea.

1. Open the Workarea and log in as Admin.
2. Once in the Workarea, navigate to the Content tab, and drill down in the tree to Mainsite/Content/Clients/Client Testimonials.
3. Once in the folder, there is an icon on the toolbar that shows a window with a green arrow. This is the main method of adding assets to the DMS. Clicking the icon brings up the File Upload interface, which has two tabs:

➤ **File Upload:** Shown in Figure 8-20 this tab uses a standard file upload button normal in most browsers. Simply navigate to the file and click upload to add the media to your site as a managed item.

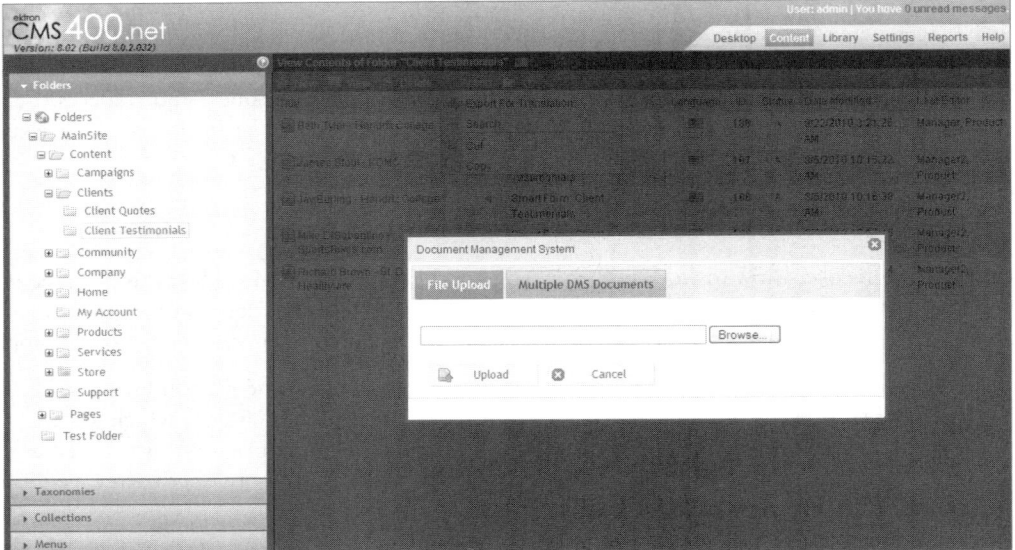

FIGURE 8-20

➤ **Multiple DMS Documents:** Shown in Figure 8-21 this tab provides an interface that displays a file selector inline on the page, and can be used to upload multiple files at the same time. It uses DAV as the backend service, which can be very user friendly, but the downside is that it can be temperamental about its configuration. This is why both options are presented, so that even if DAV has a hiccough, you can still add files to the DMS.

4. Go to the Multiple DMS Documents tab.

5. Navigate using the presented folder tree in the Web page to C:\Inetpub\wwwroot\OnTrek\uploadedfiles\MainSite\Client_Testimonials, and check the box next to Beth tyler.flv. Then click Upload. When the file finishes uploading, the Content pane in the Workarea will refresh to the list view of the content in the folder. The list now includes the Testimonial .swf file.

The alternative to uploading through the upload interface is to select New ⇨ DMS Document. This interface is more similar to authoring HTML content, in that you can enter the summary, categories, and metadata at the same time as you upload the file through the standard file browser interface. This is shown in Figure 8-22. Either method of adding files is fine, as you can get to the same interface now on your drag-and-drop uploaded file by simply clicking it in the list of content in the folder.

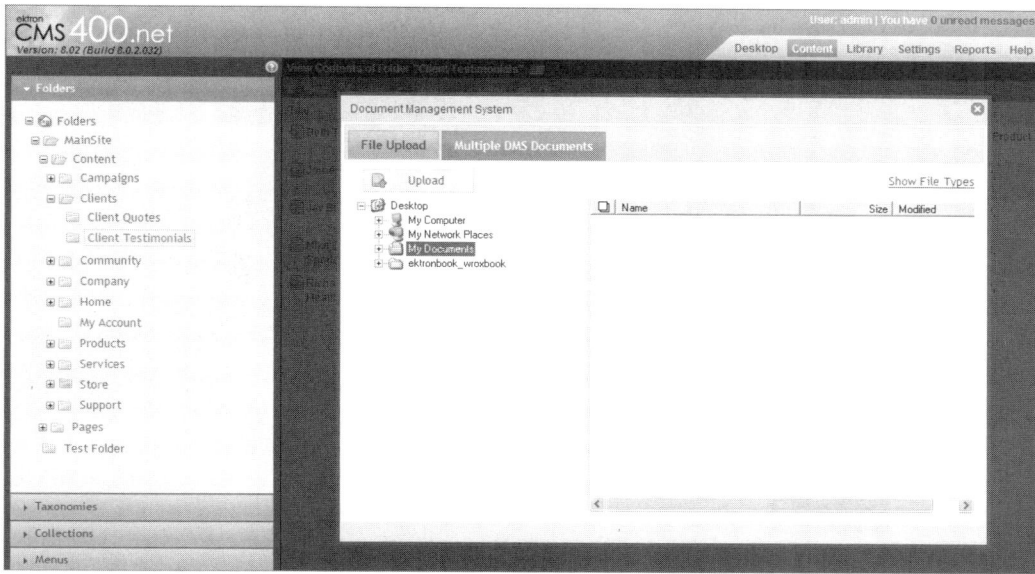

FIGURE 8-21

FIGURE 8-22

Click the file now to bring up the properties. In this interface, you can see that working with your assets is exactly the same as working with normal HTML content, with all the same capabilities.

Modifying Settings on Managed Objects

Editing the settings on the uploaded Flash video also works the same way as normal content. Simply click the edit icon on the toolbar, and you will be shown all the options available for the current type of content. The edit screen is shown in Figure 8-23.

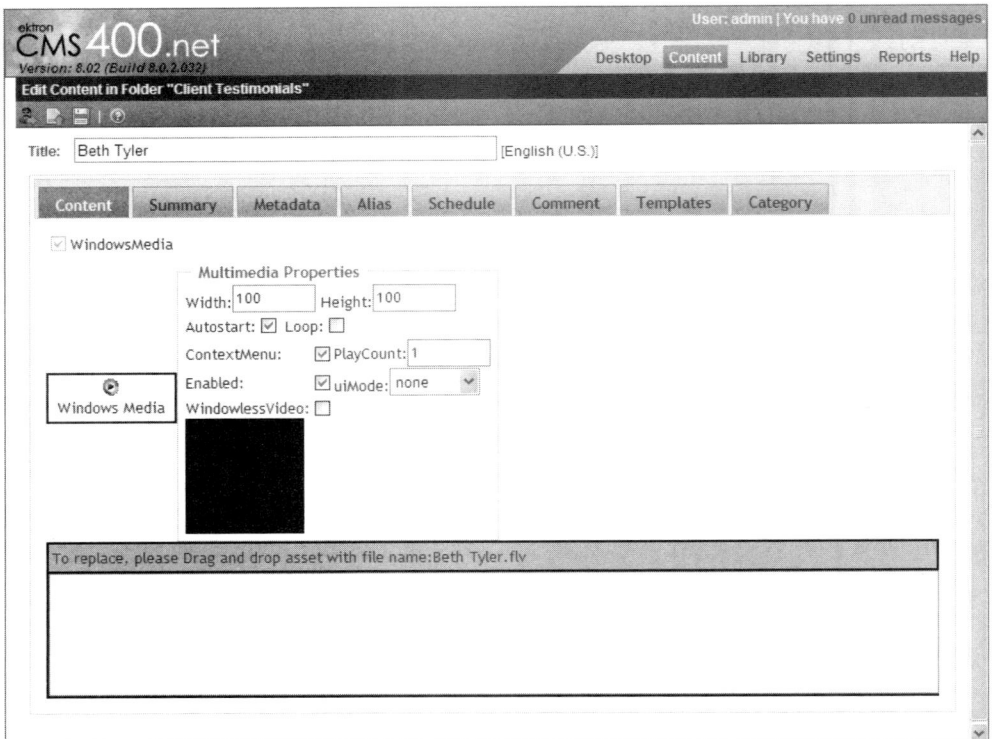

FIGURE 8-23

The main difference from normal content is that the Content tab shows a series of options that affect how the Flash object is shown on the site. The options differ based on whether the object is a SWF or other type of media. These options are outlined in Table 8-6.

TABLE 8-6: Flash Settings in the Workarea

SETTING	DESCRIPTION
Width	Width of the object in pixels. The DMS attempts to automatically retrieve this value when the file is uploaded.
Height	Height of the object in pixels. The DMS attempts to automatically retrieve this value when the file is uploaded.
AutoStart	A Boolean to determine whether the video should start playing immediately, or whether it should be clicked on to initiate playing on the page.
Loop	Sets whether to infinitely loop the video. Use PlayCount if you want to loop a specific number of times.

SETTING	DESCRIPTION
Menu	Determines whether to show the menu.
ContextMenu	Enables the right click context menu on videos.
BGColor	Sets the default background color of the object tag when rendered in a content block.
Align	Determines where to align the object in its containing element. Can be set to Left, Right, Top, or Bottom.
SAlign	More specific align options for browsers that support it. Can be set to Left Edge, Top Edge, Right Edge, Bottom Edge, Top Left, Top Right, Bottom Left, and Bottom Right.
Quality	The default quality level to use for the Flash player.
Scale	Determines how to scale the object. Can be set to Default (Show all), No border, or Exact Fit.
WMode	Sets Flash to the corresponding window mode: can be set to Window, Transparent, or Opaque. This is frequently the issue in shine-through problems, where the Flash object covers up elements like menu navigation when it shouldn't. If you are having an issue with shine-through, try setting this to Transparent.
uiMode	Determines whether to show a full ui, or a minimized ui for video playback.
WindowlessVideo	Microsoft alternative to WMode.

In addition to the options on this screen, there is a preview of the object, as well as an upload interface. Remember that to update the object with a new version, it must have the same name; otherwise it is uploaded as a different object in the DMS.

These settings are applied whenever the item is displayed through a Content Block Server Control, and are implemented through setting the correct parameters on the object tag that is written to the page. Flash objects can override certain of these settings, but in general they can help you to achieve the exact look and feel you desire for your site.

Displaying the Managed Object

Working with objects in the DMS is very straightforward. All the logic to print the correct HTML to the page is contained in the Content Block Server Control, which means all you need to display them is that same control. Let's test it out by creating a new page in the root of the site called Video.aspx. Drag a Content Block Server Control onto the page so it looks like the code in Listing 8-6.

LISTING 8-6: Video.aspx

Available for download on Wrox.com

```
<%@ Page Language="C#" AutoEventWireup="true"
    CodeFile="Video.aspx.cs" Inherits="Video" %>

<%@ Register Assembly="Ektron.Cms.Controls"
    Namespace="Ektron.Cms.Controls" TagPrefix="CMS" %>

<!DOCTYPE html PUBLIC "-//W3C//DTD XHTML 1.0 Transitional//EN"
    "http://www.w3.org/TR/xhtml1/DTD/xhtml1-transitional.dtd">

<html xmlns="http://www.w3.org/1999/xhtml">
<head runat="server">
    <title></title>
</head>
<body>
    <form id="form1" runat="server">
    <div>
      <CMS:ContentBlock
        ID="ContentBlock1"
        runat="server"
        DefaultContentID="86" />
    </div>
    </form>
</body>
</html>
```

Return to the Workarea and make sure your file has been published and then view the properties to find out the content ID of the video. Replace the number 86 with the appropriate value for your object. When you save the file and view it in the browser, you will see your video playing with your options.

Alternatives to Using the Ektron Framework

The Ektron Framework works very well for certain situations, such as rich applications, or raw SWF files containing video. However, it isn't the end-all be-all when it comes to video. For instance, FLV videos, which require a Flash video player to be displayed, will not work with just a Content Block Server Control to display them. There is, however a Flash Widget that can be used with PageBuilder to display FLVs.

Ability to display is not the only consideration when making a choice about how to deliver your content. Also keep in mind that video is one of the most bandwidth-intensive functions you can perform with a site. Additionally, because of the way ASP.NET is structured, it is not very good at keeping connections open for long periods of time, which is something that downloading large files, like video, requires. There is also the question of the ability to stream files — ASP.NET can be configured to do stream files, but it does require some hacking around in the system to get streaming working.

Ektron is aware of these considerations. One solution supplied by Ektron is the BrightCove Widget, which integrates with the third-party vendor to allow you to create a collection of videos that can be displayed on your site with solid analytics and a clean player.

Another common solution is to use a free service like YouTube to manage your videos, and then embed the player onto your page. All of these options allow you to easily share videos with potential clients and site visitors.

TAKE HOME POINTS

In this chapter, you learned the following:

- **ListSummary Server Control:** You added one more fundamental feature to your tool belt in the ListSummary Server Control, which allows you to easily generate lists of content based on the folder they are contained in. It also allows for straightforward modification of the output layer through a rich selection of properties as well as the ability to modify the output entirely through the use of XSLT and EKML.
- **EKML:** This is the first time the book has covered EKML. While it can be simplistic, it can also be a powerful way of easing development time through the elimination of one of the more complicated aspects of developing for the Ektron Framework: the XSLT.
- **XSL Transforms:** These are an extremely powerful tool for translating from a raw data feed to user interface ready HTML. In them, you have a Turing complete language that can do nearly anything asked of it.
- **Creating and Managing Calendars:** These were completely rewritten for version 8.0 of the Ektron Framework. Specifically, the chapter covered the concept of the three different calendar types: user calendars, group calendars, and system calendars. These three types are not very different in their underpinnings. But when displaying them, the system can simplify things greatly for you by not requiring you to find out a particular user's hidden calendar ID, as an example.
- **Displaying Calendars and Events:** This chapter also covered myriad ways of displaying the data from them, as well as how to customize those display layers in depth. The ability to significantly change how an event is rendered in a Content Block Server Control and how to modify the way event bubbles appear on the WebCalendar Server Control are both capabilities that you will likely need to tap into at some point in your development exercises, and now you have the tools to do so.
- **Videos:** You explored how videos are stored in the Ektron Framework. This increasingly useful feature has been explored on many of the sites Ektron has been used for, and is one of the primary identified needs of many companies' Web projects. The chapter discussed some of the tradeoffs of using an external video management service, and also discussed the strong capabilities and integration provided through object management in the DMS.

Through the judicious use of these features, you can deliver strong marketing campaigns to your company, as well as help customers find out about your organization and why they should become a customer.

Generating Leads through Campaign Optimization

- ➤ How do you create reusable PageBuilder Wireframes?
- ➤ How do you encapsulate functionality into PageBuilder Widgets?
- ➤ How do you optimize performance with Multivariate Testing and Web Analytics?
- ➤ What are collections and HTML Forms?

One of the primary purposes of websites is to support an organization's online marketing initiatives with SEO, branding, advertising, and lead generation. In many organizations, website modifications need to occur rapidly to respond to sales and marketing efforts. Unfortunately, these requests often overwhelm IT and development teams and create a backlog of work, interrupting development schedules and affecting production deadlines. To add insult to injury, there is often little understanding of how these online efforts are performing until there's a noticeable decline in leads (number of demo requests, downloads, search referrals, and so on). Improving the performance of such campaigns only adds more high-priority crisis-mode work to the IT and development backlogs.

The Ektron Framework provides developers with a set of tools that can improve an organization's overall efficiency by streamlining processes and removing the bottlenecks that commonly exist between marketers and Web developers. The Ektron PageBuilder helps you create reusable templates called *PageBuilder Wireframes*; with PageBuilder Widgets marketers can quickly assemble and launch campaign landing pages, micro-sites, or marketing forms without the involvement of IT or development; Ektron's Multivariate Testing and Web Analytics helps marketers determine page performance and optimize them as necessary; collections and HTML forms, two technologies that are commonly used on landing pages, are also discussed.

By the end of this chapter, you will understand how these tools help you launch and optimize new campaign or marketing initiatives. The Ektron Framework gives people the tools they need to do their jobs efficiently. Web developers focus on building Web technology, while marketers focus on assembling marketing pages, testing their performance, and optimizing their results.

USE CASE

This section gives you a continuation of the use cases that started in Chapter 8. It connects the exercises you will perform in this chapter with the plan laid out in the implementation guide, and puts a story to the features we will cover in this chapter, specifically the PageBuilder Feature, Multivariate testing, Analytics, Collections, and HTML Forms. The Use Case outlined here introduces the primary actor — Derek, a site visitor who is performing Internet research, describes the expected scenario, and defines the desired outcome.

> **THE ONTREK CAMPAIGN LANDING PAGE**
>
> OnTrek's Director of Marketing needs to launch a landing page to serve as a starting point for visitors arriving from a new online advertising campaign. This campaign is designed to attract technical people researching software products. The information offered by the landing page will accommodate a technical audience and highlights a particular product offering from OnTrek. The landing page includes a brief video clip featuring a product demonstration, links to product white papers, and other product related resources. Figure 9-1 shows the Wireframe taken from the OnTrek Implementation Guide discussed in Chapter 3.
>
> **Description**
>
> The OnTrek Software Evaluation Campaign Landing Page will provide technical people researching for Doodads with the technical information they need to choose OnTrek's Doodads. The landing page will highlight the OnTrek Doodads API, documentation, and training videos through a two-minute video. The goal of the landing page is to convince the site visitors to provide their contact information to receive a one-on-one demo from an OnTrek Sales Engineer.
>
> **Actor**
>
> Derek is an employee at Acme Inc. and is researching options for his company's new Doodad. Since Derek is a technical employee, he cares about the Doodad's ability to integrate with existing systems, so he is looking for something with an API and documentation. Derek is primarily performing his research online by reading reviews, discussion forums, and other information found through Web searches.

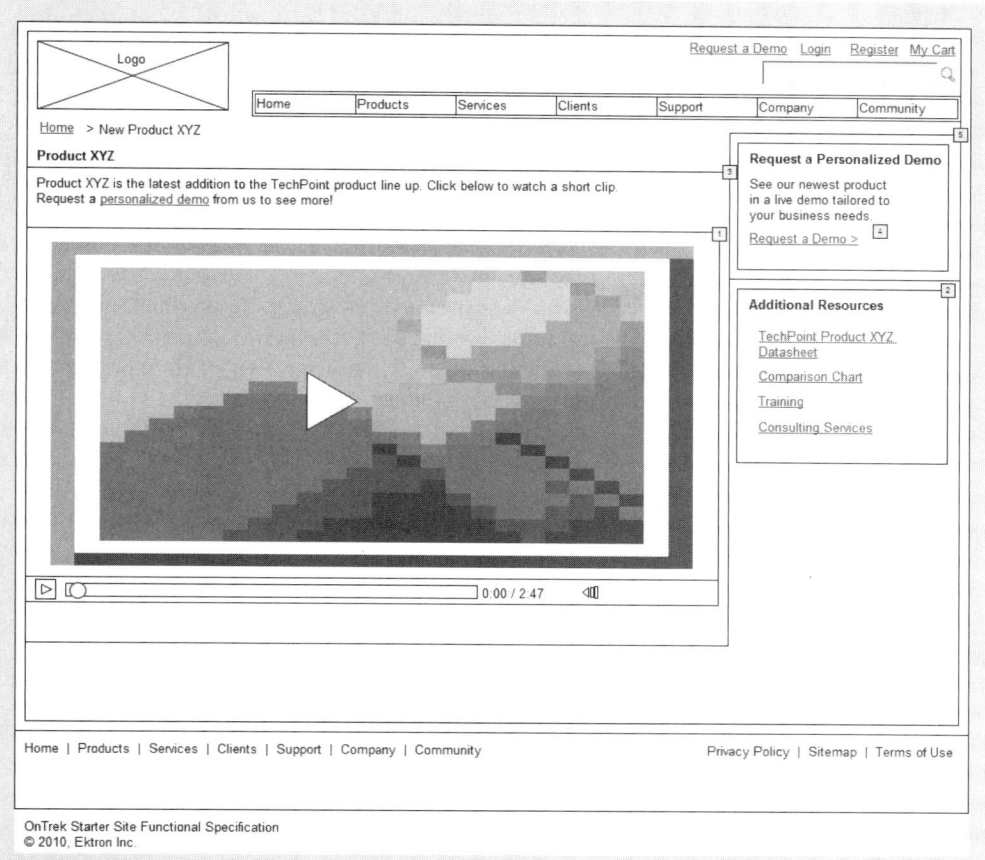

FIGURE 9-1

Scenario

In this scenario, Derek:

1. Performs a Web search using a search engine such as Google or Bing to find and compare products. He searches using the phrase "Doodad" and notices a highlighted search result at the top of the list. This is a paid search listing purchased by the OnTrek marketing group.
2. Clicks the paid search listing and is taken to the OnTrek campaign landing page.
3. Watches the two-minute video, which provides a technical overview of the OnTrek Doodad API.
4. Clicks the links listed beneath the video to read through the supporting documentation, which includes white papers and technical documentation.

continues

(continued)

> **5.** Clicks the call-to-action button to request a one-on-one technical demo with an OnTrek Sales Engineer and is taken to the Request a Demo form.
>
> **6.** Completes and submits the HTML form.
>
> **Outcome**
>
> We will track the number of visits to the landing page, the number of visits to the HTML form, and the number of form completions. A successful outcome is a request for a demo. A successful campaign is one where at least 2 percent of all visitors to the landing page Request a Demo by submitting a form with valid contact information.

UNDERSTANDING THE TECHNOLOGY

The cornerstone technology in this chapter is *Ektron PageBuilder*. From a developer's perspective, Ektron PageBuilder provides the framework on which the Ektron Widgets and Wireframes are created. Widgets are ultimately .NET User Controls (.ASCX files) that encapsulate site functionality and the user interface in a reusable way. Wireframes are reusable .NET templates (.ASPX files) that define *DropZones*, regions of the page that can be populated with widgets.

From a developer's perspective, you leverage everything you know about .NET ASCX User Controls and .NET ASPX Templates when creating Ektron PageBuilder Widgets and Wireframes. One advantage of using a widget over a standard UserControl is that they allow someone like a Marketer to manipulate the widget's properties through the browser that a developer chooses to expose.

From a marketer's perspective, PageBuilder allows non-technical people to quickly assemble Web pages visually, in the Web browser, without needing physical access to the Web server or assistance from a Web developer. The marketer selects a Wireframe, populates it with widgets, and publishes it using a friendly URL (see Figure 9-2).

A developer has complete control and flexibility over the Wireframes and widgets that are created and exposed to the marketer through PageBuilder. The process of creating an Ektron Widget is identical to the process of creating a .NET User Control; an Ektron Widget is ultimately an extension of a User Control since it derives from the System.Web.UserControl. Similarly, Wireframes are simply ASPX templates that use special Ektron Server Controls for denoting DropZones. From a developer's perspective, working with PageBuilder feels very much like building a componentized, User Control-based ASP.NET website.

In this chapter, you'll create a number of widgets componentized for the functionality required for the Request a Demo landing page. One of these widgets encapsulates the Ektron Collections Server Control. You can think of the *Ektron Collections* as a static list of managed content items, similar in concept to a playlist in a music player such as Apple iTunes, in that the list is manually defined. The added benefit is that any modifications to the collection can require the approval of an administrator, so you have a single authority or group responsible for the collection content. Collections are also language-aware, which means different versions of the content can display depending on the visitor's language selection for the site. The "Collections" technical section will walk you through the process of creating a Collections Widget and go into more depth on its capabilities.

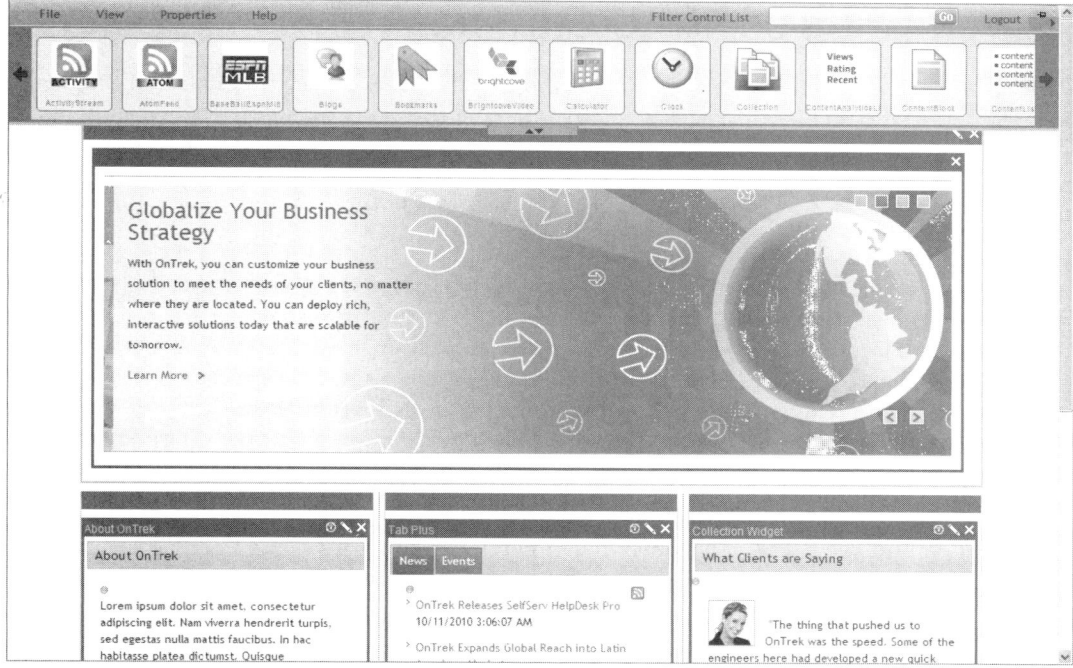

FIGURE 9-2

You'll create another widget containing an HTML form that will be used to build the Request a Demo form page. Ektron provides robust *HTML form* capabilities that allow you to build traditional HTML forms containing various input elements, such as textboxes, option lists, with the added ability to define client-side form validation rules, enable spell checking, and more, all using the WYSIWYG authoring environment.

The purpose for the campaign landing page is to gather information from prospects. To determine whether or not the marketing campaign's key success metrics are met, Web Analytics and Multivariate Testing will be used. Web Analytics allow us to measure the number of impressions and conversions, while Multivariate Testing will help us to optimize the overall performance of our campaign by testing the effectiveness of content and modifying it according to the results of the test.

In summary, this section covers:

- PageBuilder
- Widgets
- Collections

- HTML forms
- Multivariate Testing
- Web Analytics

IMPLEMENTATION USING COLLECTIONS

Collections have been referred to as the *butter knife* of the CMS — they're simple and can be used in a number of situations. As such, they're often the first tool a developer turns to when tight control over a list of items is needed. In practice, you see projects use collections for promoting job postings, announcing press releases, listing knowledge base articles, and providing the underpinnings of a banner ad rotator. Given their inherent simplicity, ease of use, and overall flexibility, you'll find collections to be a very valuable addition to your Ektron Web developer toolbelt.

In its simplest form, a *collection* is a hand-crafted list of content items. Content authors create these editorial-driven lists to serve as a navigation aid to help site visitors discover content objects such as documents, multimedia, PageBuilder pages, or any type of managed asset. A collection is similar in some ways to a ListSummary (see Chapter 8) because you can use a collection to display a list of content items and developers can customize it to render those items in any conceivable way, such as a bulleted list, Cover Flow, accordion, and so on. However, a collection is the only content list control that gives editors exclusive control over which items are included in the set and also control the order of the items.

Marketing will use the Collection Widget that you implement in this section to place specifically chosen content items (a white paper, technical documentation, and a customer testimonial) on the campaign landing page.

Creating a collection starts in the Workarea, either from the Collections menu (Figure 9-3) or from the content folder tree. Creating a collection follows the same two-step process regardless of which location you create it in — provide a name for the collection and then browse the content folder structure and select the items you want included. You can include any item available through the content folder tree such as content blocks, blog posts, calendar events, and documents.

Collections are *language-aware*, which means that a website publishing content in multiple languages can choose to create a language-specific edition of a collection. When a site visitor browses to a language-specific version of the site, any collections present display in the currently selected language.

The two options available for displaying a collection on a Web page are as follows; each has its own benefit:

- **The Collection Widget:** Available to use on PageBuilder-driven sites. This is useful in situations where a business user, such as a member of the marketing department, needs the ability to add or remove items from the collection.
- **The Collection Server Control:** Useful in cases where a developer needs to maintain control over its display and position and wants to effectively "lock down" a list of items to prevent modifications.

Implementation Using Collections | 271

 The implementation section focuses on the Collection Widget because the goal in this chapter is to allow a marketer to assemble the list of content items that displays on the landing page.

The Request a Demo campaign landing page uses a collection to display the list of links. In this section, you start the process of fleshing out the landing page using the Collection Widget to implement it. This section covers the following steps:

➤ Creating the collection
➤ Putting the Collection Widget on your site using PageBuilder
➤ Customizing the presentation of the collection

Creating a Collection

The process of creating a collection begins in the Workarea through either the Collections menu or the Content menu. To create a collection through the Collections menu, follow these steps:

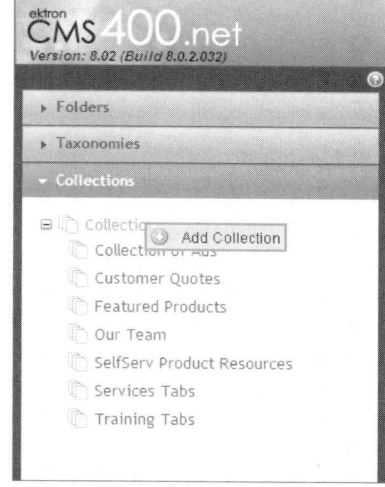

FIGURE 9-3

1. Click the Workarea's Content tab. From this screen you can either right-click the Collection list and select Add Collection or click the Add icon, as shown in Figure 9-3.

    The Add Collection Form appears in the display pane and allows you to define your collection options, as shown in Figure 9-4.

2. Enter **Request a Demo Promotion** as a name for your collection in the Title field. This must be a unique name and can contain letters, numbers, and other characters. The Title is available through the website if you choose to display it. In practice it is typically used only within the Workarea to identify your collection.

3. Enter the path to a .NET Template in the Template field. If you specify a template, all links in the list of content items will use this path. If you leave this field empty, each content item will use its QuickLink.

4. Enter a short description for your collection. Like the Title, this information is available to the website, but in practice it is used within the Workarea.

5. Select the Include Subfolders checkbox. This permits users to populate the collection with content items located in child folders; otherwise they're limited to choosing content items that exist in the selected folder exclusively.

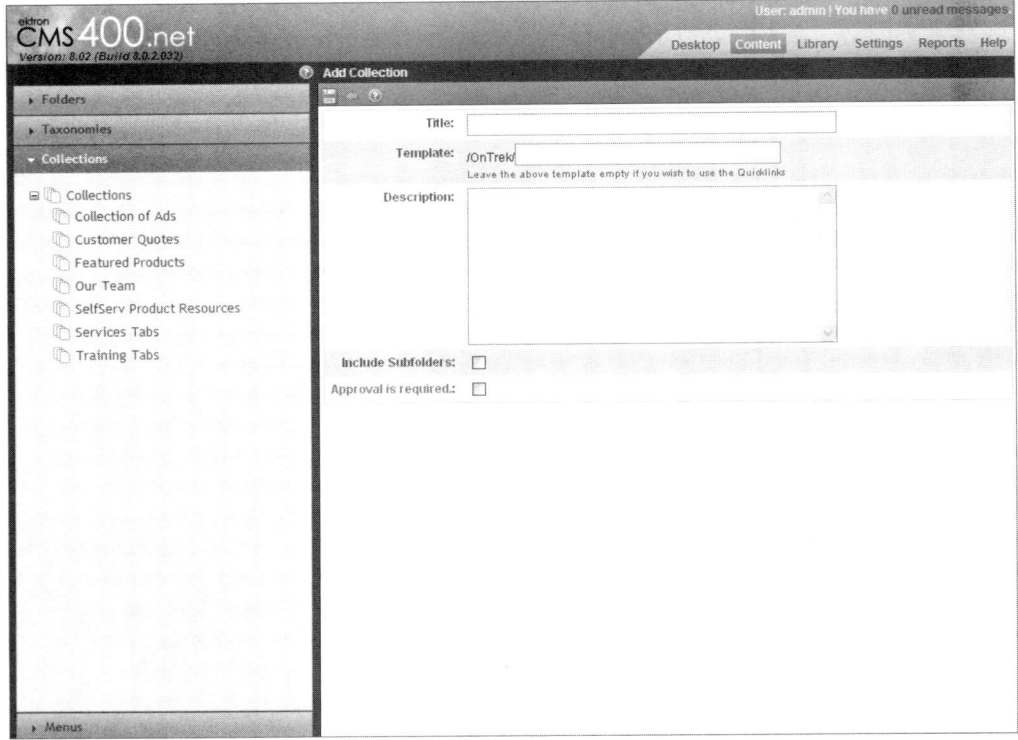

FIGURE 9-4

6. Deselect the Approval is a required checkbox. If this box is checked, changes to the content need to be approved by an authority before being published.

7. Click Save to save your collection. You are returned to the list of collections. You will see your newly created collection in the list, as shown in Figure 9-5.

Adding to the Collection

Now that you've created the collection, you need to add to it. For the sake of this example, add the following content items, located in the /MainSite/Content/Campaigns/SelfServe HelpDesk Pro Release folder of the OnTrek starter site:

➤ About SelfServe HelpDesk Pro

➤ SelfServe HelpDesk Pro Datasheet

To add these items:

1. Navigate to the collection to which you want to add items.

2. Click the Add icon.

3. Use the Path field to navigate through the content tree and select the content items to include in the collection, as shown in Figure 9-6. The Path value represents the location where the collection was created in the content tree. For collections created via the Collections Accordion item, the folder path is automatically set to the root.

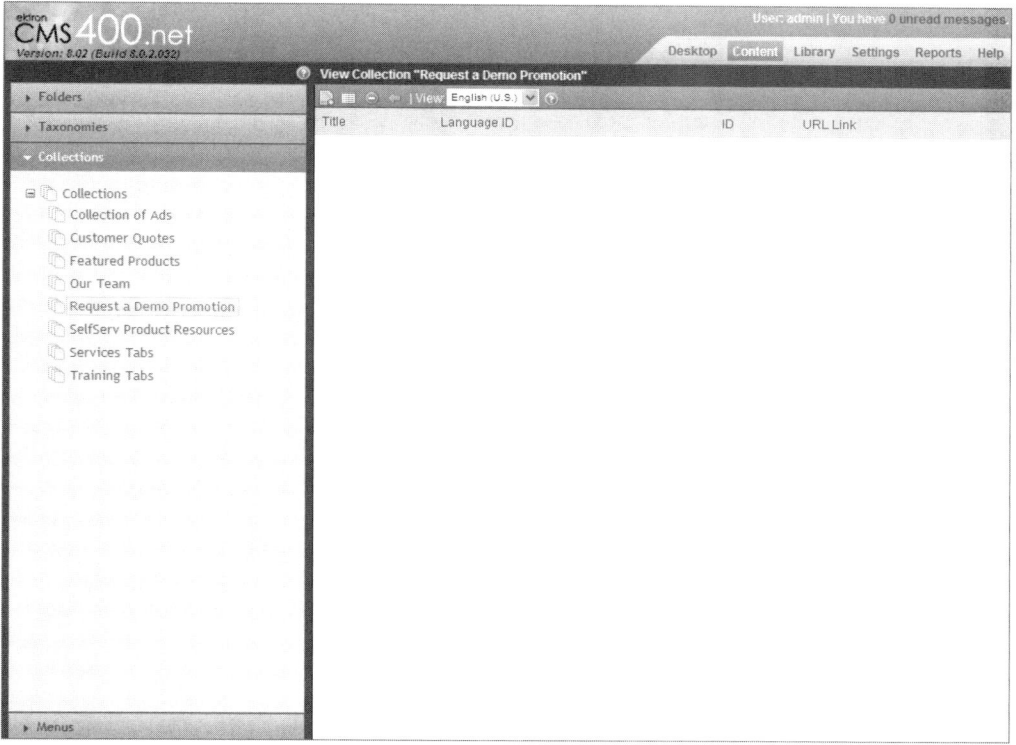

FIGURE 9-5

4. If you are adding a specific type of content to the collection, you can use the All Types filter to limit the content items displayed.

As previously noted, it is possible to have language-specific versions of each collection. From a developer's perspective this has little impact, since the CMS handles selection of the appropriate version of the collection based on the site's language.

Putting the Collection on the Landing Page

From a developer's standpoint, you can leverage the Collection Widget that comes with the CMS with very little modification, as it satisfies the requirements outlined in the Implementation Guide. The Collection Widget is provided with every installation of the CMS; you can find it in the Widgets directory under your site root.

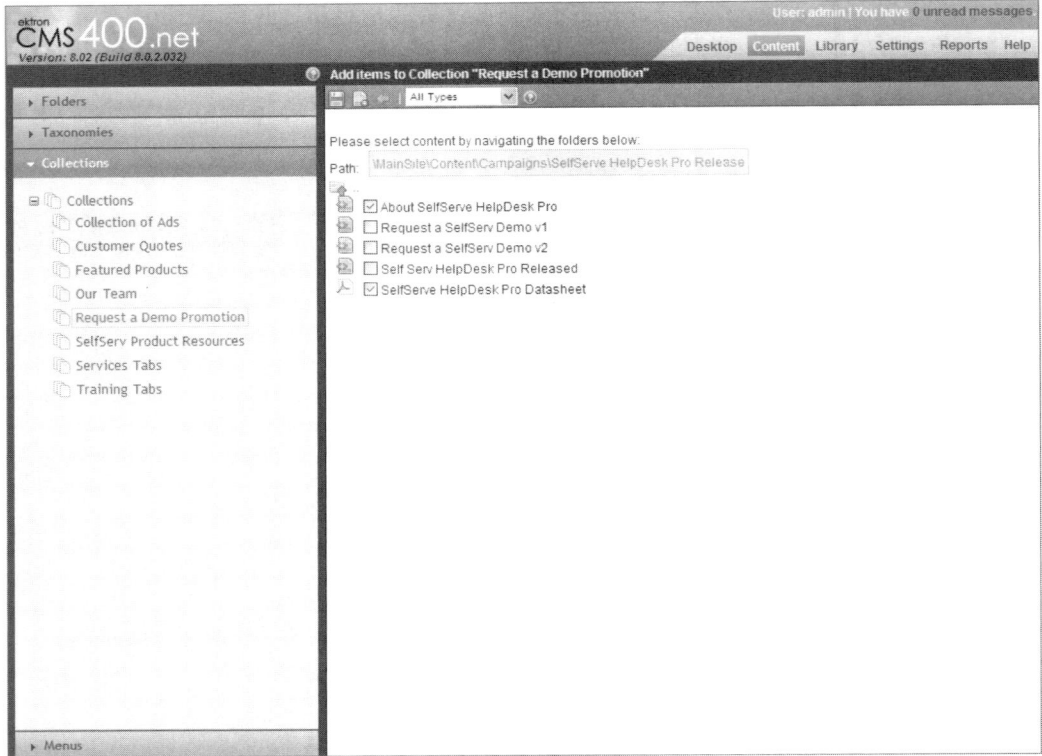

FIGURE 9-6

To put the Collection Widget on your page:

1. Edit the SelfServ HelpDesk Campaign landing page located at /MainSite/Pages/Experiments and expand the Widget Control Set (the process of Editing a PageBuilder page is discussed later in this chapter).

2. Filter the list of controls visible by typing **collection** into the Filter Control List textbox, as shown in Figure 9-7.

3. Drag and drop the Collection Widget into the location of the Wireframe defined in the Implementation Guide.

4. Click the Edit icon in the top-right corner of the Collection Widget (see Figure 9-8). You will now see the Editing Widget dialog box; the Collection Widget is in Edit mode, as shown in Figure 9-9.

5. Select the collection you just created from the dropdown list of available collections. The number preceding the name is its Collection ID.

6. Enter a page size. The Page Size field indicates the number of items displayed in the list before it starts to page. Although you only have three items to display, the Implementation Guide specifies that five links may be displayed here, so let's limit the number of items displayed.

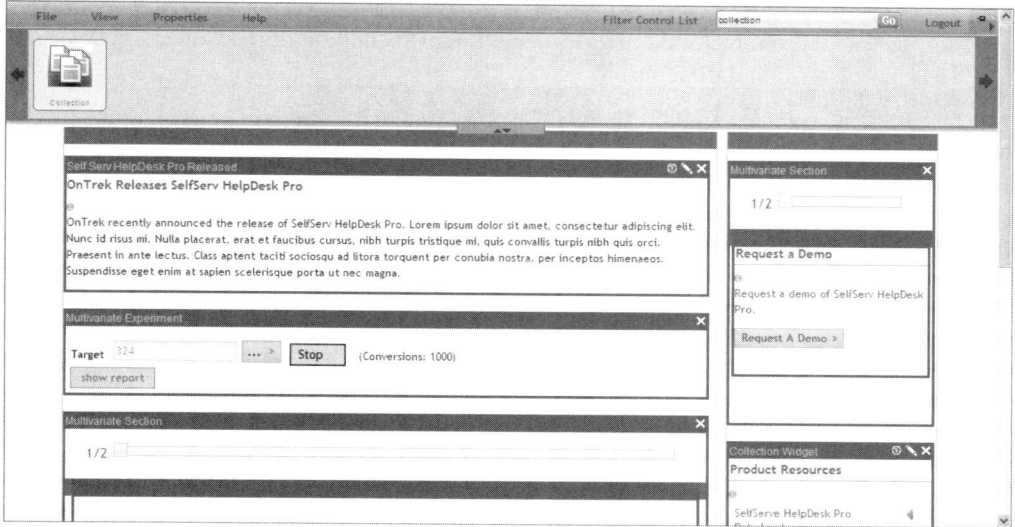

FIGURE 9-7

FIGURE 9-8

7. Deselect the Teaser checkbox. When selected, the Collection Widget displays the content item's link followed by its teaser.

8. Because the Implementation Guide limits the number of items to five without paging, deselect the EnablePaging checkbox.

9. The Implementation Guide calls for a list of links, with no icons displayed, so uncheck the IncludeIcons checkbox.

10. Because the links should follow the URL defined in the QuickLink, deselect the DisplaySelectedContent checkbox. When this is checked, links post back to the current page, passing the content ID of the item clicked. The Collection Widget then displays that content item inline.

Customizing the Presentation of the Collection Widget

From a developer's standpoint, it is important to note that the Collection Widget is implemented using the Collection Server Control. Just as with the Collection Widget, the Collection Server Control is used to display a collection on a Web page. The widget simply acts as a wrapper for the functionality.

The two are similar in that they both provide the ability to control which collection is displayed, how many items appear, whether paging is enabled, and so on, but the server control provides options not exposed through the widget. As a developer, you can take advantage of the Collection Server Control's additional capabilities by modifying the default implementation of the Collection Widget.

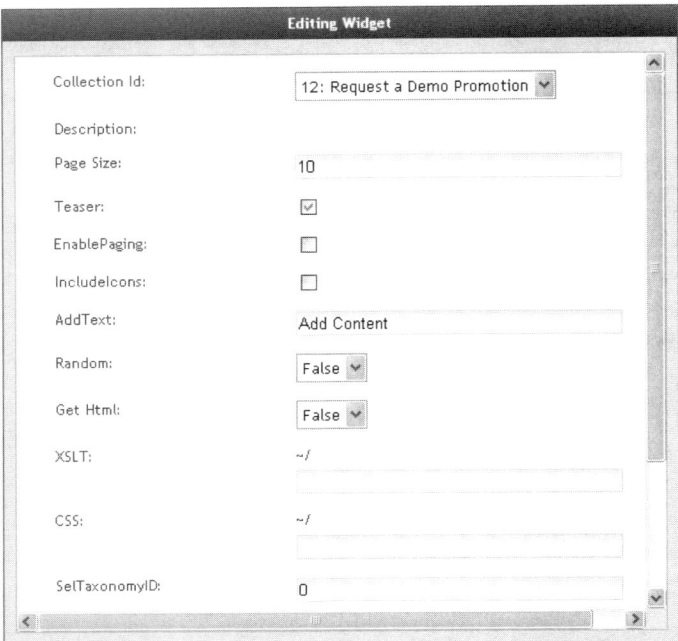

FIGURE 9-9

The Implementation Guide specifies that the collection should display as a simple bulleted list of links. If you look at the HTML source code produced by the widget, you will find that its markup uses an HTML `<table>`. We can modify its implementation and instruct the Collection Server Control to display the items as a bulleted list using unordered list HTML elements (`<UL>` and `<LI>`) instead of `<table>`, taking advantage that Ektron Server Controls expose their data as XML and provide a mechanism for defining an XSLT to control the markup rendered to the browser.

The file that implements the Collection Widget is Collection.ascx and its source code is located in the Widgets directory (~/Widgets/Collection.ascx). Opening the file shows a standard widget implementation using a MultiView Server Control with two view panels: View and Edit. Listing 9-1 shows the source code for the View panel containing only an ASP: Label Server Control. The Collection Server Control is instantiated in the Collection Widget's codebehind file, so we'll explore that next.

LISTING 9-1: ~/Widgets/Collection.ascx

```
<%@ Control Language="C#" AutoEventWireup="true"
    CodeFile="Collection.ascx.cs" Inherits="widgets_Collection" %>
<%@ Register Assembly="Ektron.Cms.Controls" Namespace="Ektron.Cms.Controls"
    TagPrefix="CMS" %>
<asp:MultiView ID="ViewSet" runat="server">
```

```
    <asp:View ID="View" runat="server">
      <asp:Label ID="Text" runat="server" Visible="false">Select a Collection</
asp:Label>
    </asp:View>
    <asp:View ID="Edit" runat="server">
      <div id="<%=ClientID%>_edit" class="LSWidget">
        <table style="width: 95%;" class="ekColEditView">
          <tr>
            <td>Collection Id:</td>
            <td>
              <asp:DropDownList ID="collectionlist" runat="server"></asp:DropDownList>
            </td>
          </tr>
          <tr style="font-size: 80%; color: #888;">
            <td>Description:</td>
            <td>
              <span class="ekcoldescription" id="description" runat="server"></span>
            </td>
          </tr>
          <tr>
            <td>Page Size:</td>
            <td>
              <asp:TextBox ID="pagesize" runat="server" Style="width: 95%;"></
asp:TextBox>
            </td>
          </tr>
          <tr>
            <td>Teaser:</td>
            <td>
              <asp:CheckBox ID="TeaserCheckBox" runat="server" Checked="true" />
            </td>
          </tr>
          <tr>
            <td>EnablePaging:</td>
            <td>
              <asp:CheckBox ID="EnablePagingCheckBox" runat="server" Checked="false"
/>
            </td>
          </tr>
          <tr>
            <td>IncludeIcons:</td>
            <td>
              <asp:CheckBox ID="IncludeIconsCheckBox" runat="server" Checked="false"
/>
            </td>
          </tr>
          <tr>
            <td>AddText:</td>
            <td>
              <asp:TextBox ID="AddTextTextBox" runat="server"></asp:TextBox>
            </td>
          </tr>
          <tr>
            <td>SelTaxonomyID:</td>
```

continues

LISTING 9-1 *(continued)*

```
              <td>
                <asp:TextBox ID="SelTaxonomyIDTextBox" runat="server"></asp:TextBox>
              </td>
            </tr>
            <tr>
              <td>DisplaySelectedContent:</td>
              <td>
                <asp:CheckBox ID="DisplaySelectedContentCheckBox" runat="server" />
              </td>
            </tr>
            <tr>
              <td></td>
              <td>
                <asp:Button ID="CancelButton" CssClass="LSCancel" runat="server"
    Text="Cancel" OnClick="CancelButton_Click" />
                <asp:Button ID="Button1" runat="server" OnClick="SaveButton_Click"
    Text="Save" />
              </td>
            </tr>
          </table>
        </div>
      </asp:View>
    </asp:MultiView>
```

To customize the markup created by the Collection Widget:

1. Open the Collection Widget codebehind, ~/Widgets/Collection.ascx.cs. The relevant section of code is the SetOutput() method and begins on line 62. The source code for this method is shown in Listing 9-2.

LISTING 9-2: SetOutput() Method from ~/Widgets/Collection.ascx.cs

```
protected void SetOutput()
{
    if (CollectionId > 0)
    {
        Ektron.Cms.Controls.Collection Collection1 = new Ektron.Cms.Controls.Collection();
        Collection1.Page = Page;
        Collection1.DefaultCollectionID = CollectionId;
        Collection1.DisplayXslt = (Teaser) ? "ecmTeaser" : "ecmNavigation";
        Collection1.IncludeIcons = IncludeIcons;
        Collection1.MaxResults = PageSize;
        Collection1.EnablePaging = EnablePaging;
        Collection1.AddText = AddText;
        Collection1.SelTaxonomyID = SelTaxonomyID;
        Collection1.ContentParameter = DisplaySelectedContent ? "id" : "no_id";
        if (DisplaySelectedContent && Request.QueryString["id"] != null)
        {
            long.TryParse(Request.QueryString["id"], out DynamicId);
```

```
        Collection1.DefaultCollectionID = DynamicId;
      }
      Collection1.CacheInterval =
        ((Page as PageBuilder) != null) ? (Page as PageBuilder).CacheInterval : 0;
      Collection1.Visible = true;
      View.Controls.Add(Collection1);
      Text.Visible = false;
    } else {
      Text.Visible = true;
    }
  }
}
```

  2. Find and Modify the `Collection1.DisplayXSLT` property to the following:

```
Collection1.DisplayXSLT = (Teaser) ? "ecmTeaser" : "UnorderedList.XSLT";
```

> *UnorderedList.XSLT is a file located in the Widgets directory alongside the Collection Widget; it defines an XSLT tranformation that customizes the markup for the control.*

  3. Save the modifications to the Collection.ascx.cs file.

The Collection Server Control has other properties that provide you with the ablity to customize many aspects of its behavior. Table 9-1 outlines the most common ones.

TABLE 9-1: Collection Server Control Properties

FIELD	DESCRIPTION
AddText	The text specified overrides the content for the Add Content menu item. For example, if you have a news website, you can change "Add Content" to "Add News Item."
CacheInterval	The amount of time in seconds the server control will cache the collection data. The default is zero (not cached).
ContentParameter	The name of a `QueryString` parameter. When the parameter is found in the `QueryString`, the collection is replaced with a content block.
DefaultCollectionID	The ID of a collection that appears if no other Collection ID is identified or is not available. If you don't know the ID of the collection, browse for it using the CMS Explorer in Visual Studio by clicking the […] button within the field.
DisplayXSLT	Defines an XSLT that can override the default presentation of the server control.
DynamicParameter	Defines whether the collection is dynamic.

continues

TABLE 9-1 *(continued)*

FIELD	DESCRIPTION
EnablePaging	This property, in conjunction with the `MaxResults` property, lets site visitors view an unlimited number of collection items while controlling the amount of screen space. To accomplish this, the collection display is limited to the number set in the `MaxResults` property. If you set this property to true, and the number of collection items exceeds the `MaxResults` number, navigation aids appear below the last item. The site visitor uses the aids to view additional items.
GetHTML	Set to true if you want to retrieve and display content (HTML body) for all content blocks in the collection, for example, to display content inside a Web Server Control such as a GridView.
IncludeIcons	In cases where you're using the control's default presentation, you can specify whether you want the icons next to the collection list's links using this field.
LinkTarget	Specifies the target for the links in the list. Valid choices are _blank, _self, _parent, and _top.
MemberMenuActive	Set this property to true to hide the dropdown menu next to a content item when a membership user is logged in. If the value is true, the menu will be hidden from Membership Users. If it is false, the menu will be displayed.
SelTaxonomyID	Defines the ID of a category node that is associated with the new content added to the collection from the server control.

Under the Hood: Collection Data Model

As a developer, you can use almost every feature of the framework without having to know what's going on under the hood; but sometimes the best way to learn something is to take it apart. In this section, you look at the collection data model to understand what's happening behind the scenes when a collection is added.

The recommended way of reading, writing, updating, and deleting data is through the APIs. ServerControls and widgets are also recommended as they utilize APIs underneath as well. This section, however, shows how to read information directly from the database using SQL statements for debugging purposes only. Ektron strongly recommends that developers do not access the database directly using SQL statements for any reason beyond debugging purposes.

The data model for collections is implemented much as you might expect. The table named `nav_tbl` stores information for each collection, such as the collection ID, name, description, and so on. Each row in this table corresponds to a collection added to the system, so if you went through the process of creating a collection in "Creating a Collection," you'll see that information stored here by issuing the following SQL query:

```
select * from nav_tbl
```

Table 9-2 shows a subset of the fields available.

TABLE 9-2: Available Fields

FIELD NAME	FIELD DESCRIPTION
nav_name	Name of the collection.
nav_template	The name and path of the ASPX template to use for links in the collection. If none is displayed, the content item's QuickLink is used.
nav_description	The description of the collection.
folder_id	The folder from which the collection's content items can be drawn.
recursive	When this field is true, it indicates that content items can be selected from subfolders of the folder specified by `folder_id`.
user_id	The user who created the collection.
status	The current status of the collection, such as A approved, O checked out, and so on.
published	Indicates whether the collection has ever been published.

By looking at the schema, you will notice there is no place to store content information. This is because it's found in a separate table, `nav_to_content_tbl`, which is a many-to-many relationship table that provides a place to map a collection to the content items assigned to it. To see this list of collections and their assigned content items, issue the following SQL query:

```
SELECT     nav_tbl.id, content.id
FROM       content, nav_tbl
WHERE
content.id = nav_to_content_tbl.content_id AND
nav_tbl.id = nav_to_content_tbl.nav_id
```

Because you have the ability to put collections through an approval process, you have a final table `nav_to_content_stage_tbl` that has the same structure and function as `nav_to_content_tbl` but is used for collections that are not yet published. If you're viewing a published collection on your website, content items are coming from the `nav_to_content_tbl` table. Otherwise, they're coming from the `nav_to_content_stage_tbl`.

PAGEBUILDER

PageBuilder addresses a typical issue in the lifecycle of sites: How does one keep the design of a site fluid and able to react quickly to marketplace needs, without involving a developer in every decision? By shifting layout design into the hands of content managers through a WYSIWYG editing interface, the need to have a developer making endless modifications to endless templates is eliminated. The number of templates is typically also reduced, frequently to just two Wireframes. The encapsulation of functionality into widgets promotes code reuse and ease of maintenance.

PageBuilder is a relatively recent feature in the CMS. Its goal is to simplify the process of creating pages, reduce dependencies on developer time, and allow for more varied designs. PageBuilder does this by separating a page into two components:

- **Wireframe:** This is the HTML shell of the page with any constant functionality.
- **Widgets:** These contain encapsulated functionality and content.

The two elements combine into a single item called a *layout*, which is then stored and managed similarly to content.

The process of working with PageBuilder begins by creating a Wireframe. A *Wireframe* is a normal CMS template, with a few exceptions: First, it contains two extra user controls — the PageHost and a number of DropZones. It also inherits from `Ektron.Cms.PageBuilder.PageBuilder`. The combination of these elements gives the Wireframe the supporting code it needs to render a given layout.

- **PageHost User Controls:** Manages the state of a given page, and displays the PageBuilder menu as well as the widget list, which contains the icons to instantiate any widget onto the layout.
- **DropZone User Control:** Usually exists in multiple locations on a given Wireframe, this control is where those widgets will wind up. These internally render horizontal lists of columns. Vertical lists of widgets are rendered within those columns.

Internal to the widgets are the Widget Settings, which effectively store any data the developer has determined should be stored. The Widget Settings are serialized into an XML string, which is stored as a component in the overall layout which is the term used to describe the serialized PageData stored in a content item. The other components in the layout XML are the definitions for the number and widths of the columns appearing in each DropZone. When the layout is serialized, it can in turn be stored into a content item in the database.

Since the PageBuilder architecture is built on top of the basic content stack, this allows it to take advantage of other CMS features, like aliasing, taxonomy, collections, and so on.

Once the Wireframe has been created, a layout is created based on that Wireframe by selecting "New Page Layout" within a folder. This brings up a Wizard which accepts the title of the new page, aliasing information, and metadata for the page. On completion of the Wizard, the user can then start adding widgets to the page.

Looking at the Implementation Guide, you can see that your requirement in this section is to create a landing page for capturing leads. This page will have a form, as well as a collection control, allowing potential leads to download information.

As covered in the technical overview, creating the landing page for the lead center will have a number of steps. You won't actually be constructing the widgets you use in this chapter, but in the next technical section we'll walk through constructing a widget for use on PageBuilder pages.

This section covers the following steps:

- Creating the Wireframe
- Associating the Wireframe to a folder
- Creating a layout based on the Wireframe
- Modifying the layout

Creating the Wireframe

Creating a Wireframe starts by creating the file in the website root. Once you've created the Web form, you add it to the Workarea so that the CMS is aware of the form.

1. Open Visual Studio and add a Web form to the root of your site and select the master template TwoColumnChannelRight.Master from ~\components\templates. Call the Web form **Promotions.pb.aspx**.

2. Open the newly created file and add three register statements. These statements inform the .NET runtime of the controls and assembly that will be referenced in the page.

3. Add the PageHost User Control, followed by a DropZone User Control. Note that you can add the user controls and two of the register statements by switching to design view and dragging them from ~\Workarea\PageBuilder\PageControls, or you can simply type the code in.

```
<%@ Page Language="C#"
  MasterPageFile="~/components/templates/2ColumnChannelRight.master"
  AutoEventWireup="true" CodeFile="promotions.pb.aspx.cs"
  Inherits="Ektron.Site.Promotions" Title="Promotions" %>

<%@ Register Assembly="Ektron.Cms.Widget"
  Namespace="Ektron.Cms.PageBuilder" TagPrefix="PB" %>
<%@ Register Src="Workarea/PageBuilder/PageControls/PageHost.ascx"
  TagName="PageHost" TagPrefix="Ektron" %>
<%@ Register Src="Workarea/PageBuilder/PageControls/DropZone.ascx"
  TagName="DropZone" TagPrefix="Ektron" %>

<asp:Content ID="contentBody"
  ContentPlaceHolderID="uxContentBody" runat="Server">
  <Ektron:PageHost ID="pageHost" runat="server" />
  <Ektron:DropZone ID="dropZoneContentBody" runat="server"
AllowColumnResize="false" AllowAddColumn="false">
    <ColumnDefinitions>
      <PB:ColumnData columnID="0" unit="percent" width="100" />
    </ColumnDefinitions>
  </Ektron:DropZone>

</asp:Content>

<asp:Content ID="channelRight" ContentPlaceHolderID="uxChannel"
Runat="Server">
```

```
        <Ektron:DropZone ID="dropZoneChannelRight" runat="server"
AllowColumnResize="false" AllowAddColumn="false">
          <ColumnDefinitions>
            <PB:ColumnData columnID="0" unit="percent" width="100" />
          </ColumnDefinitions>
        </Ektron:DropZone>
    </asp:Content>
```

4. Now open the code of the page. You'll have this page inherit from the PageBuilder class, which in turn requires you to override the `Error` and `Notify` functions.

```
using System;
using System.Collections.Generic;
using System.Web;
using System.Web.UI;
using System.Web.UI.WebControls;
public partial class PSResources : Ektron.Cms.PageBuilder.
PageBuilder
{
    protected void Page_Load(object sender, EventArgs e)
    {

    }

    public override void Error(string message)
    {
        throw new NotImplementedException();
    }

    public override void Notify(string message)
    {
        throw new NotImplementedException();
    }
}
```

The Wireframe is now completed. When you view it in the browser when you log in, you should see a page with the master page elements and the PageHost menu, but with all menu items disabled, as shown in Figure 9-10.

FIGURE 9-10

The remaining step is to inform the CMS of your new Wireframe. This is done in the Workarea.

1. Log in as an administrator.
2. In the Workarea, go to Settings/Configuration/Template Configuration, and click the Add Template button . See Figure 9-11.

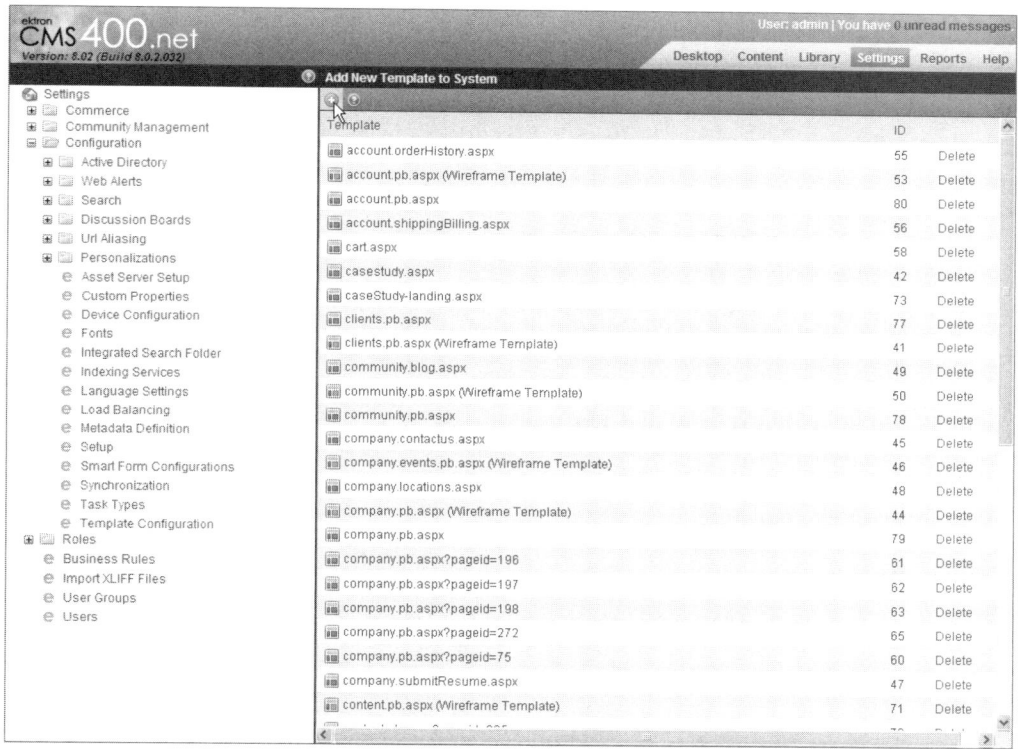

FIGURE 9-11

3. Click Add Template to bring up a new window that allows you to specify the location of your template.
4. Click the "..." button and browse to the new Wireframe. Select the PageBuilder Wireframe checkbox.
5. You can now choose which widgets will be allowed on layouts created for this Wireframe.
6. Select ContentBlock and Collection, and then click Save. See Figure 9-12.

At this point, the CMS creates a thumbnail of the Wireframe so layout editors can see where the DropZones are and what the page looks like in the Wizard when the editor creates a new page.

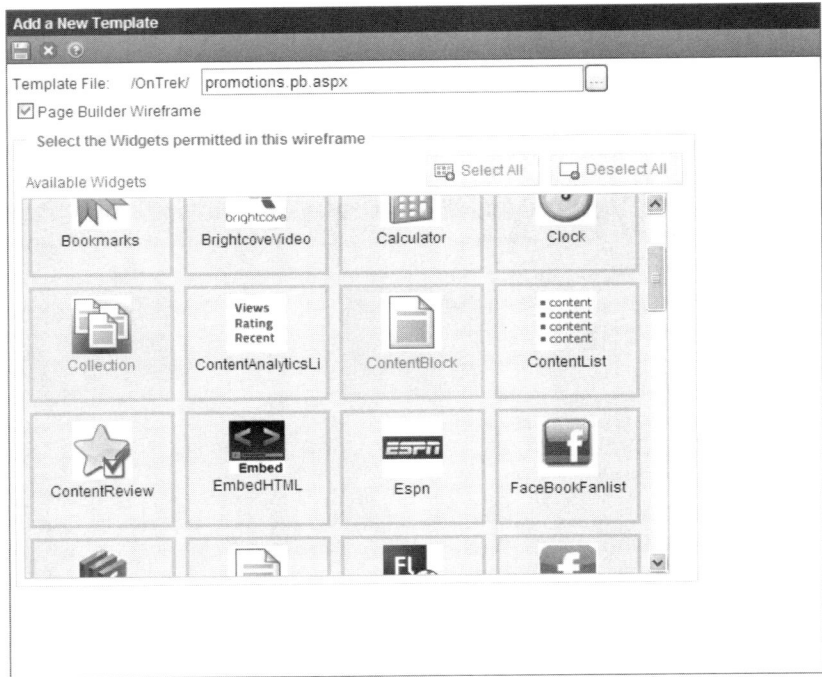

FIGURE 9-12

Associating the Wireframe to a Folder

The next step is to associate the Wireframe to a folder in the CMS so it can be used to create layouts.

1. In the Workarea, switch to the Content tab, and select /MainSite/Pages/Experiments.

2. In the campaign folder, select View ⇨ Properties. See Figure 9-13.

3. Click Edit in the Properties screen (see Figure 9-14), and then select the Templates tab. Make sure Inherit parent configuration is unselected. Select Promotions.pb.aspx in the dropdown list of templates. Finally, click the plus sign icon ⊕ to add the Wireframe to the list of allowed templates, as shown in Figure 9-14.

4. Click Save 💾 on the toolbar to save the properties. Now any user with permission can add a layout to this folder based on the new Wireframe.

Creating a Layout Based on the Wireframe

Now that the Wireframe is configured and ready to go, you need to add a layout based on the Wireframe. This layout displays the collection and form to the user browsing the site.

1. In the folder tree, browse to /Pages/Promotions.

2. When you hover over the New menu, you'll notice you have the option to add a Page Layout or a Master Layout.

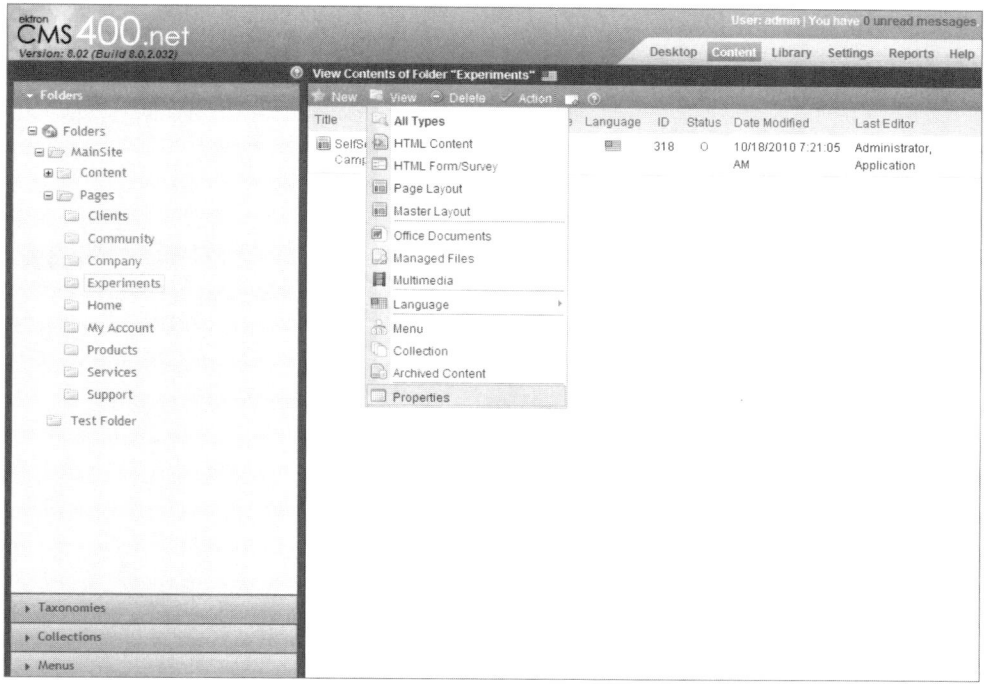

FIGURE 9-13

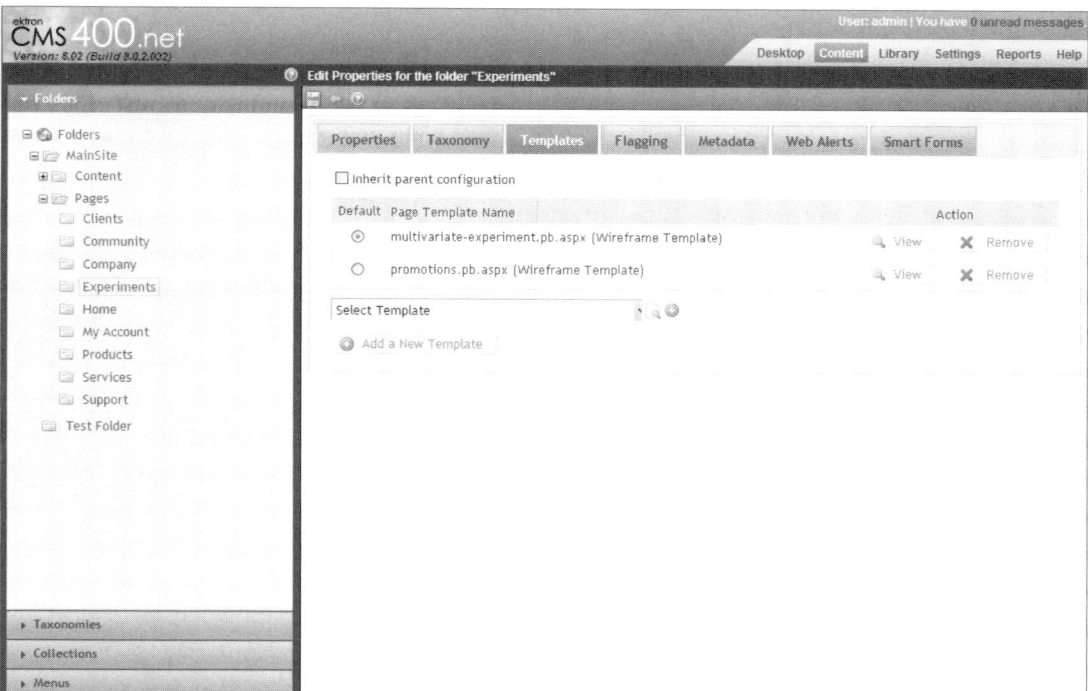

FIGURE 9-14

3. Click Page Layout, and the Add New Page Wizard appears. See Figure 9-15.

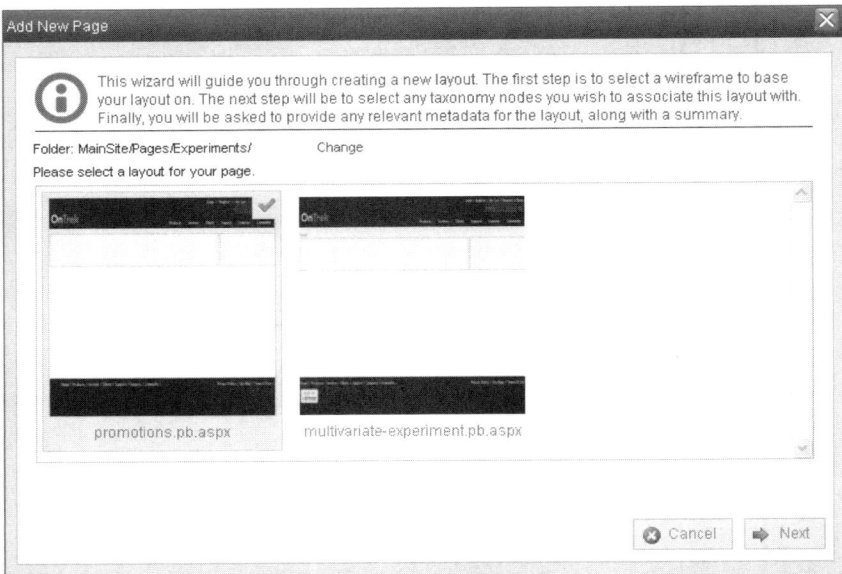

FIGURE 9-15

4. On the first page of the Wizard there are several available options:
   - One that allows you to change folders.
   - A list of all the Wireframes permitted in this folder along with thumbnails of the Wireframes. The thumbnails can be replaced by overwriting the corresponding file in ~/uploadedimages/Wireframesthumbnails. Editing the template options also automatically generates a new thumbnail.

5. Select Promotions.pb.aspx as shown in Figure 9-15, and click Next.

   The second page in the Wizard, shown in Figure 9-15, allows you to associate the layout with one or more taxonomy nodes, assign a title to the layout, and configure any enabled aliasing options. It displays the automatic aliases for selected taxonomy nodes in real time, as well as any automatic folder aliasing. It also allows you to optionally specify a manual alias for the page.

6. Enter **Request a Demo** in the Page Title field (as shown in Figure 9-16) and use the automatically generated Manual Alias, and then click Next.

   You are presented with two tabs to specify the summary for this page, as well as any metadata associated with the folder, as shown in figure 9-17.

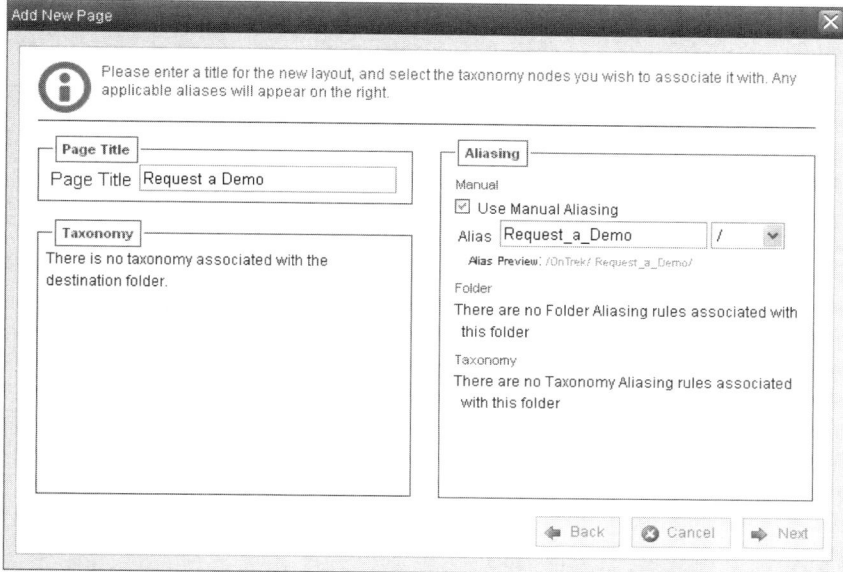

FIGURE 9-16

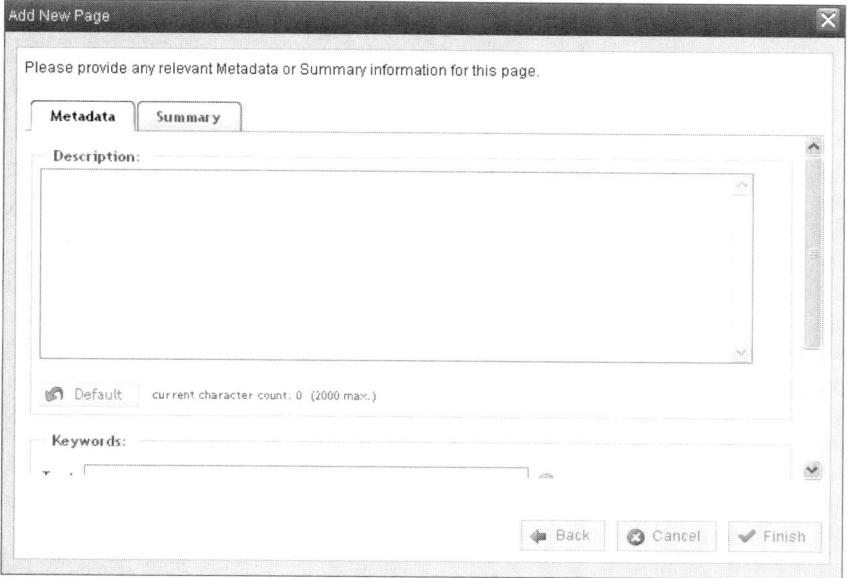

FIGURE 9-17

7. Click Finish. A dialog box will ask if you want to edit the new page. Select OK to be brought to the new page for editing. The editing interface for PageBuilder is shown in Figure 9-18.

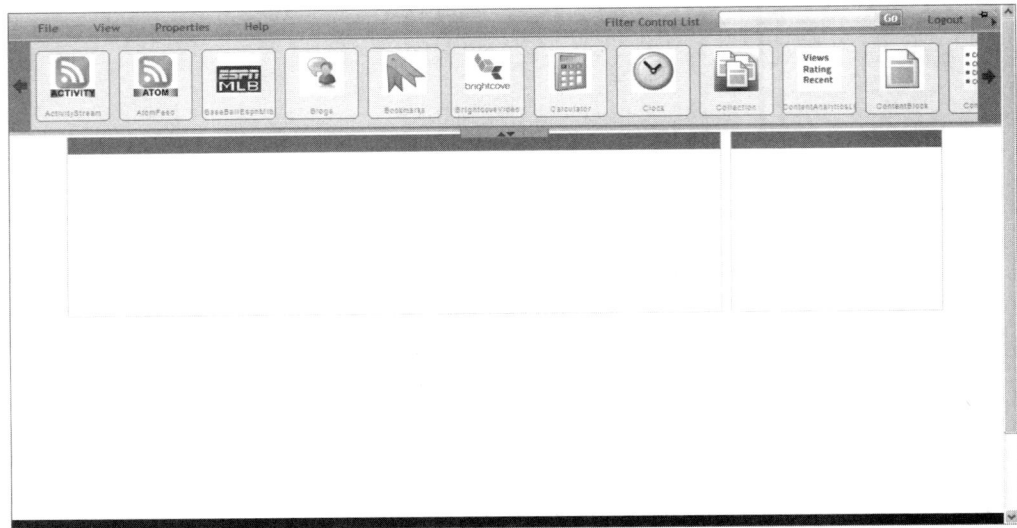

FIGURE 9-18

8. Clicking the up/down toggle brings down a list of widgets which you can drag and drop into the DropZone. You also see a box with a blue title bar is the first column in the DropZone. Note the following:

   ➤ In this example, we set the AllowAddColumn property to false on the DropZones. If we hadn't, the blue title bar would also contain an add icon, which is a button to add a new column to the DropZone.

   ➤ Likewise, we opted to disallow column resizing by setting AllowColumnResize to false. If we hadn't, a pencil icon would be shown that allows the layout editor to set the width of the column.

   ➤ We also set the width of the default column to 100%. We optionally could have left it unspecified, which would let the column grow dynamically with the width of the widgets contained in the column.

9. Place a content block in the column. Drag the Content Block icon from the widget tray into the column. This is shown in Figure 9-19.

10. Once you have the Content Block Widget on the page, click the pencil icon to bring up the Editing Widget dialog (shown in Figure 9-20) so you can edit the Content Block Widget's options.

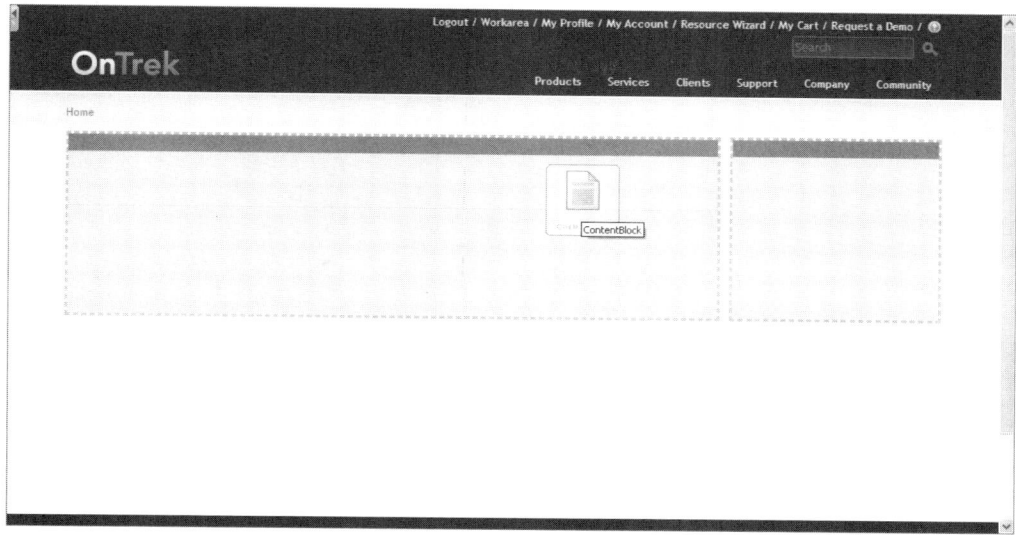

FIGURE 9-19

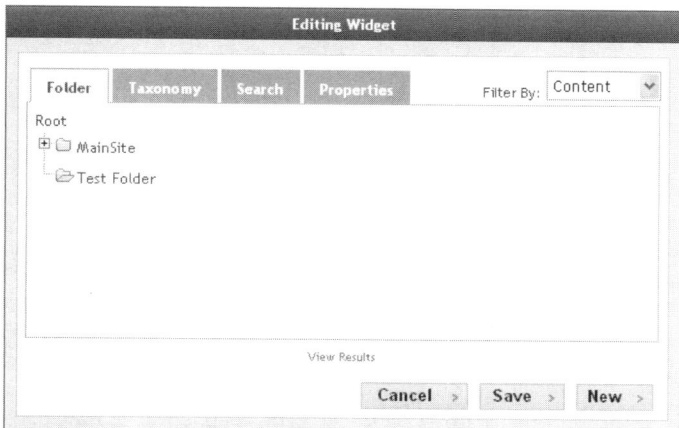

FIGURE 9-20

11. Since it's the lead capture page, put a form on here. Change the Filter By on the upper-right corner from Content to Forms, as shown in Figure 9-21, and then navigate to MainSite/Content/Company. In the results that appear below the folder list, select Contact Us and click Save.

12. Now go to File ➪ Publish.

The page is now live and users can interact with the form.

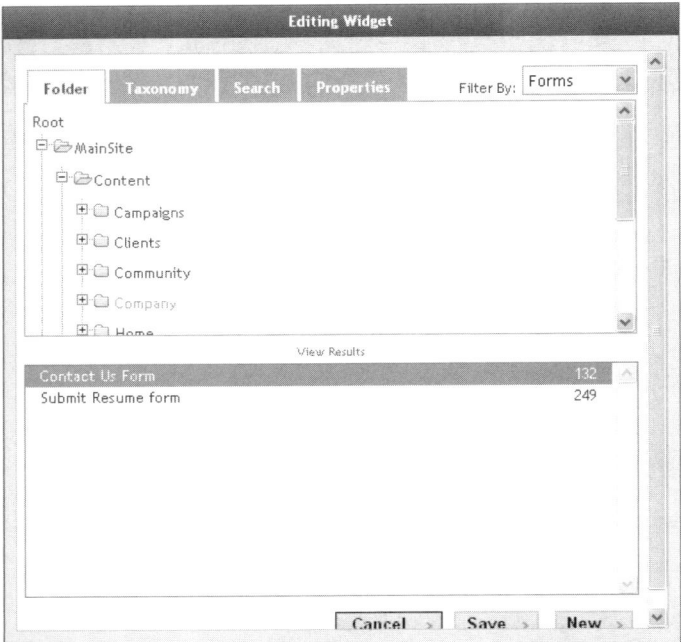

FIGURE 9-21

Under the Hood

The way that PageBuilder works versus earlier versions of the Ektron Framework (or other content management systems) may require a change in development approach. This is due to the large amount of encapsulation of functionality and UI. Whereas the old approach was to create conceptual Wireframes for pages and then build out the functionality of each template, or ASPX file to match that Wireframe, PageBuilder turns *conceptual* Wireframes into *actual* Wireframes. The new approach is to develop an ASPX Wireframe that has DropZones where the interchangeable functionality blocks go. Instead of developing 15 pages that are variations on the same theme, the developer now only needs to develop one Wireframe, and then allow the content author to drop predeveloped discrete pieces of functionality (called widgets) into those spaces to create each individual page. When paired with aliasing, this system provides a seamless experience for the end user, while drastically simplifying development, maintenance, and content management.

Understanding the PageBuilder Structure

One of the key benefits to using the PageBuilder feature is its relationship with normal content. Within the schema, PageBuilder layouts are stored as a subtype of standard content. All the normal content interactions such as workflow, permissions, and state transitions are present in PageBuilder layouts. They support multilingual representations, they can be displayed as part of a ListSummary or collection, and they interact with taxonomy structures. They are also compatible with metadata, aliasing, and social tools. The reliance on existing structures on the schema is also extended to the Wireframes, which are the empty ASPX pages defined as the basis for layouts. The Wireframe information is stored as a subtype of a standard template.

Conceptually, PageBuilder shares its roots with Smart Forms when it comes to storage of actual layout data. Page layouts are serialized to XML, along with all the instance data for the widgets on the page. Widgets have the ability to store any data desired through XML serialization. This serialization can be data intensive, but it has the benefit of being platform agnostic. Typically the data for the layout is divorced from the content displayed — for example, a layout may contain a ListSummary Widget and a Content Block Widget. The Content Block Widget would only store the ID of the content to display, and the ListSummary Widget would only contain the ID of the folder to generate the list, along with any instance display options such as which XSLT. The design pattern has several benefits. As the underlying content is updated, the page always displays the most recent version of the content. The design pattern has the implication that a CMS administrator can choose to have one person or team in charge of layouts, with a separate person or team in charge of the content itself. We'll come back to how the data actually looks, but let's first discuss the structure of a PageBuilder page.

PageBuilder uses several classes for behind-the-scenes data management, and several user controls for display and interaction. We'll go through all these in steps.

Understanding the Difference between a Layout and a Wireframe

The first concept to understand is the difference between a layout and a Wireframe. As discussed earlier, a *layout* is the data stored in the database that dictates the size of display areas, as well as the contents of those areas in the form of widget data. A *Wireframe* is the physical file used to render the page. These Wireframes are simply ASPX pages registered in the CMS with a few modifications:

➤ The Wireframe must inherit from `Ektron.Cms.PageBuilder.PageBuilder`.

➤ The `PageBuilder` base class inherits from `System.Web.UI.Page` in turn.

This means you can do anything on a Wireframe that you can do on a standard page, but the intermediate class can hook into events on that page early in the page lifecycle. The `PageBuilder` class automatically handles the state of the page, the loading of PageData, and so forth. You'll notice when implementing the `PageBuilder` class you must also add two overrides to the Wireframe. The two overrides are the Error and Notify functions, and are used to pass messages to the end user. These functions are left abstract so the developer can handle the messages in a manner that fits the page.

There are also a few user controls in the Workarea that must be referenced by your PageBuilder Wireframe.

The three registrations in the snippet that follows register the PageHost User Control, the DropZone User Control, and the PageBuilder namespace, which contains the `ColumnData` definition.

```
<%@ Register Src="~/Workarea/PageBuilder/PageControls/PageHost.ascx"
    TagPrefix="PB" TagName="PageHost" %>
<%@ Register Src="~/Workarea/PageBuilder/PageControls/DropZone.ascx"
    TagPrefix="PB" TagName="DropZone" %>
<%@ Register Assembly="Ektron.Cms.Widget" Namespace="Ektron.Cms.PageBuilder"
    TagPrefix="PB" %>
```

The PageHost and the DropZone perform nearly all the operations for editing and display of layouts. The PageHost Control renders the menu bar that appears at the top of every layout to logged-in CMS authors, as shown in Figure 9-22. The control allows for users to switch modes on the page and place widgets on the page, and provides shortcuts to some Workarea functions. The PageHost control should be placed on the page before all DropZones. CSS will force the PageHost control to the top of the page, but the PageHost control should be placed as close to the beginning of the page as possible within the `<Body>` tag.

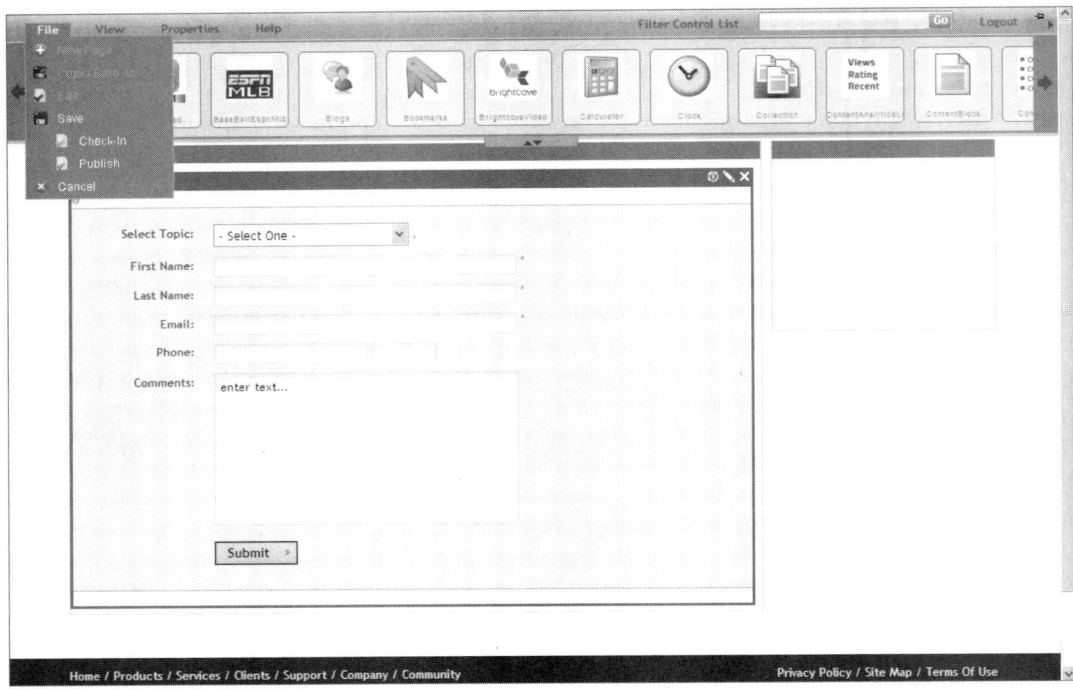

FIGURE 9-22

Table 9-3 is a subset of the properties available on the PageHost User Control.

TABLE 9-3: Properties on the PageHost User Control

PROPERTY	DESCRIPTION
CacheInterval	Controls the length of time, in seconds, that the page layout data should be cached upon reading from the database. Some widgets inherit from this setting; for example, the Content Block Widget will cache for the same length of time as its host Wireframe is set.
FolderID	The folder that holds new layouts by default.
SelTaxonomyID	The taxonomy node to associate new layouts with by default.

PROPERTY	DESCRIPTION
DefaultPageID	The layout to load into this Wireframe if no layout is specified via an alias or query string.
ThemeName	The theme to load for the DropZones and PageHost User Controls. This defaults to TrueBlue. Theme packs are stored in ~/Workarea/PageBuilder/PageControls/Themes.

The DropZone User Control renders the area into which widgets are placed. They internally render out a list of columns, each of which can have a width applied, either in absolutes or percentages. Within the columns, a vertical list of widgets is rendered. The widgets themselves are rendered within another user control called the WidgetHost, which is dynamically created by the DropZone as required for each widget. All these user controls are contained in ~/workarea/PageBuilder/PageControls.

The DropZone User Control also has adjustable properties, and also allows you to optionally preset column definitions as inner-encoded XML.

Table 9-4 is a subset of the properties available on the DropZone User Control.

TABLE 9-4: Properties on the DropZone User Control

PROPERTY	DESCRIPTION
AllowAddColumn	Controls whether the layout editor is allowed to add columns to the DropZone.
AllowColumnResize	Controls whether the layout editor is allowed to modify column widths within the DropZone.
ColumnDefinitions	Presets the columns that will appear to the layout editor on a new layout. This is encoded as an inner element.

Understanding Storage

Now that you understand the concepts of Wireframes and layouts, let's return to the question of storage.

The layout information — all the data required to recreate the layout and inject it into a Wireframe — is stored as an XML document in the database. The class that is serialized to produce the XML is called the `PageData` class, and it has two main properties: `Widgets` and `Zones`.

The `Widgets` property is a `List<WidgetData>` object, and the `Zones` property is a `List<DropZoneData>` object. These contain all the elements necessary to reconstruct the page layout. `WidgetData` is a simple class. It contains a `Settings` string, the `ColumnID` the widget appears in, an `Order` indicating where the `WidgetData` appears in the column, and a Boolean called `Minimized`, which controls whether the widget is visible. The `DropZoneData` class is equally simple; it contains a string called `DropZoneID`. When this string matches the control ID on a given

`DropZone`, the data stored in the `DropZoneData` instance is used to instantiate a list of columns and widgets inside that `DropZone`. The `DropZoneData` class contains a property called `Columns`, which is a `List<ColumnData>`. The `ColumnData` class stores the information necessary to relate back to the widgets, such as the `ColumnID`, in addition to display options, such as `width` and `unit`. In the code Listing 9-3, you can see the serialized data.

LISTING 9-3: Serialized PageData Object

```xml
<PageData>
    <pageID>909</pageID>
    <languageID>1033</languageID>
    <title>EktronTechPlus</title>
    <Widgets>
      <WidgetData>
        <ID>7</ID>
        <ControlURL>ContentBlock.ascx</ControlURL>
        <ColumnID>0</ColumnID>
        <Order>0</Order>
        <Minimized>false</Minimized>
        <Settings>
            <ArrayOfDataStore>
              <dataStore>
                <Property>ContentBlockId</Property>
                <Value xsi:type="xsd:long">951</Value>
                <TypeName>System.Int64</TypeName>
                <AssemblyAndType>System.Int64, mscorlib, Version=2.0.0.0, Culture=neutral, PublicKeyToken=b77a5c561934e089</AssemblyAndType>
              </dataStore>
            </ArrayOfDataStore>
        </Settings>
        <DropID>Middle</DropID>
        <ColumnGuid>00000000-0000-0000-0000-000000000000</ColumnGuid>
        <ChildColumns />
      </WidgetData>
    </Widgets>
    <Zones>
      <DropZoneData>
        <DropZoneID>Middle</DropZoneID>
        <Columns>
            <ColumnData>
              <Guid>00000000-0000-0000-0000-000000000000</Guid>
              <Display>true</Display>
              <columnID>0</columnID>
              <width>100</width>
              <unit>percent</unit>
            </ColumnData>
        </Columns>
      </DropZoneData>
    </Zones>
</PageData>
```

You can see there is some basic information about the page, and then a list of widgets followed by a list of DropZones. The DropZone corresponds to the DropZone with an ID value of "Middle" on the Wireframe and contains a single column of 100 percent width. In the widgets list is a single widget, which is, in this case, the Content Block Widget, and it is set to appear in DropZone Middle, column 0, at the top. The Content Block Widget has a single property to be set, and that is the `ContentBlockId` property, type `Int64` with a value of 951.

The next question we'll look at is, "How does storing layouts affect the information architecture of a site?"

A typical information architecture (IA) in a PageBuilder site has two main folders, one for content, and one for layouts, as you can see in Figure 9-23. This allows a separation of permissions, workflow, and taxonomy based on the type of content. It also allows searches to be specified only on pages, or only content, depending on which is preferable. However, layouts and content can exist side-by-side in the same folder.

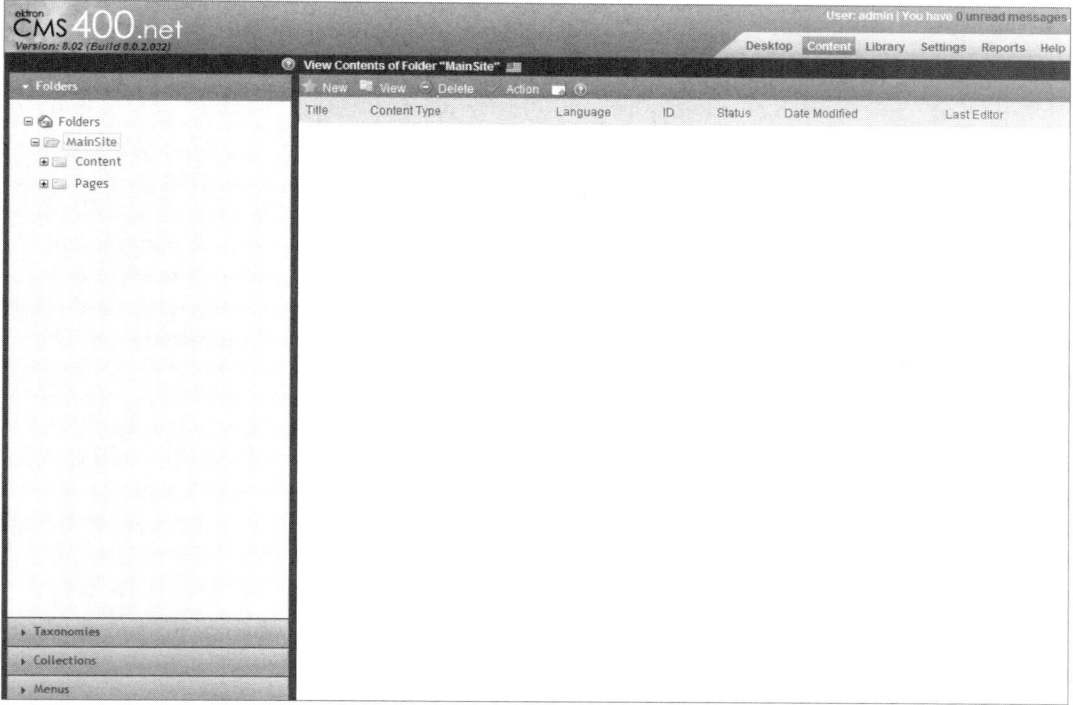

FIGURE 9-23

WIDGETS

Widgets are a simple and straightforward way to encapsulate parts of your site for easy re-use. They are designed for use with PageBuilder and Personalization, and are composed of a user control that implements the interface `Ektron.Cms.Widget.IWidget`.

Using widgets as part of your site implementation allows you to grant greater leeway to content managers in the system. By allowing them to work with PageBuilder to create entire layouts, they can utilize the exact functionality required while maintaining the specified look and feel across the site.

Widgets are composed of a user control that's instantiated at runtime according to the needs of the page layout being displayed or the personalization dashboard being interacted with. Widgets manage their own data stores, include any relevant CSS and JavaScript, and have built-in code to handle any user interaction occurring within the particular widget. If you have built a user control before, working with widgets will be straightforward, with only a few modifications to the typical build process required.

Widgets usually have a built-in editing screen for authors to set any required properties from the Web interface. Since widgets are instantiated at runtime, the ways that CSS and JavaScript are implemented slightly different. As a developer, you should also be aware that widgets are rendered within a standard .NET UpdatePanel, meaning that most interactions with them will be by way of Asynchronous PostBacks, rather than a standard full PostBack.

Development of a widget starts by creating a user control. The user control must live in the Widgets directory under the site root. The primary modification required is that user control should implement `IWidget`. `IWidget` doesn't require any function overrides, but the `IWidget` decorator allows for the underlying framework to determine via reflection whether the user control is an Ektron Widget. This allows you to create supporting user controls in the same directory or in subdirectories without having the system identify them as additional widgets. For instance, you can create a tabbed interface user control without the IWidget interface, put it in ~/widgets/usercontrols, and reference it from several widgets. Because it cannot implement `IWidget`, it cannot display in the list of available widgets within a PageBuilder page.

Once the widget has been created, the widget can be registered against the framework and associated with one or more Wireframes or master layouts. This association step allows an administrator to determine which sections of the site the widget should be allowed to be instantiated in.

At this point, the widget can be utilized on any layouts based on the associated Wireframe. To liven up the widget, you can hook in several events programmatically. These events allow for switching to an editing interface. There are also methods available on the container host that allow for data access.

Reviewing the implementation guide, you can see that the out-of-the-box widgets for collections and HTML forms serve their purpose. However, you may run into a situation that demands the creation of a new widget. In this section, you'll work through creating a simpler version of a Collection Widget.

In order to implement your new Collection Widget and set up the widget for use by content managers, you will follow a full development process — you'll create the user control, set up the event hooks, and finish by associating the Collection Widget to a Wireframe for use.

This section covers the following steps:

- ➤ Creating the widget
- ➤ Hooking to events
- ➤ Creating an edit interface
- ➤ Handling instance data storage

➤ Handling Edit, Cancel, and Save clicks

➤ Rendering the output

➤ Associating to the Wireframe

Creating the Widget

The public-facing widgets all live in ~/Widgets. If you want to build a widget for use in the Workarea dashboard, those live in ~/workarea/Widgets. Because you are building a front-end widget, create it in ~/Widgets.

1. In Visual Studio, right-click the Widgets directory in your site, and select Add New Item.
2. Select Web User Control and name the control MyTestControl.ascx.
3. Select Visual C# as the language and make sure that Place Code in Separate File is checked.
4. After you click OK, you should have a nearly blank source file. Go to the code on your new widget, where you can make modifications to ensure the CMS recognizes it as a widget.

In Listing 9-4, you can see the required changes (highlighted in bold) that allow the CMS to recognize this as a widget. Specifically, when the widget is first loaded, the system attempts to cast it into an `IWidget` object. If that fails, further operations halt with the object.

LISTING 9-4: ~/Widgets/MyTestControl.ascx.cs

Available for download on Wrox.com

```csharp
using System;
using System.Collections.Generic;
using System.Web;
using System.Web.UI;
using System.Web.UI.WebControls;
using Ektron.Cms.Widget;

public partial class Widgets_MyTestControl : System.Web.UI.UserControl, IWidget
{
    protected void Page_Load(object sender, EventArgs e)
    {

    }
}
```

Hooking to Events

Now add some detail to have the WidgetHost display information about the widget. In Listing 9-5, you perform two main actions. First, you retrieve the widget instance's WidgetHost and store the host locally. The WidgetHost fires several events you can subscribe to, and several properties you can populate.

LISTING 9-5: ~/Widgets/MyTestControl.ascx.cs

Available for download on Wrox.com

```csharp
public partial class Widgets_MyTestControl :
   System.Web.UI.UserControl, IWidget
   {
     private IWidgetHost _host;

     protected void Page_Load(object sender, EventArgs e)
     {
       _host = Ektron.Cms.Widget.WidgetHost.GetHost(this);
       _host.Title = "My Collection Widget";
       _host.Maximize +=
         new MaximizeDelegate(delegate() {
           this.Visible = true; });
       _host.Minimize +=
           new MinimizeDelegate(delegate() {
           this.Visible = false; });
       _host.HelpFile =
 "http://localhost/ontrek/workarea/help/Widget%20Chapter/Using%20Widgets.htm";
     }
```

First set the `Title` property. The contents of the `Title` property are displayed in the bar that is visible above the widget when in edit mode. `Minimize` and `Maximize` are events that fire when the corresponding buttons are pressed on the host, and are only fired when the widget is used on a personalization dashboard. Usually these control whether the widget is collapsed or visible. `HelpFile` populates the URL the Help button links to.

If there is no subscribed function for any of the events on the WidgetHost, the icons will not show up. For instance, if you do not set the *HelpFile* location, no Help File button will appear on the host.

Creating an Edit Interface

You also need to hook up the edit event, and set up some properties for storing instance data. But before you do that, you must set up the front end. A typical approach to this is to use an ASP.NET MultiView Control, which allows you to programmatically switch between two completely different display interfaces, but other approaches, such as creating a UserControl for each view and setting the `Visible` property on them can also be used. In this example we will be using a MultiView, so start by adding the ASP.NET MultiView from the toolbox. One side of the control will contain the edit, and one side will contain the view. Then add a simple form for capturing the configuration for the instance, and add the collection control for viewing the data.

As you can see in code Listing 9-6, you've created a very basic form for entering the instance data required to display the user-selected collection. You've also created the display interface, which is just a collection object. By putting both panes into a MultiView, you can easily switch between them in code based on user interaction.

LISTING 9-6: ~/Widgets/MyTestControl.ascx

Available for download on Wrox.com

```
<%@ Control Language="C#" AutoEventWireup="true"
  CodeFile="MyTestControl.ascx.cs" Inherits="Widgets_MyTestControl" %>
<%@ Register Assembly="Ektron.Cms.Controls" Namespace="Ektron.Cms.Controls"
```

```
    TagPrefix="CMS" %>

<asp:MultiView ID="rootMultiView" runat="server">
  <asp:View ID="editView" runat="server">
    <div class="myTestControlEditView">
      <fieldset>
        <legend>Editing My Collection Widget</legend>
        <table>
          <tr>
            <td>XSLT</td>
            <td>
              <asp:DropDownList
                ID="ddlDisplayXSLT"
                runat="server">
                <asp:ListItem>ecmNavigation</asp:ListItem>
                <asp:ListItem>ecmTeaser</asp:ListItem>
              </asp:DropDownList>
            </td>
          </tr>
          <tr>
            <td>MaxResults</td>
            <td>
              <asp:TextBox
                ID="txtMaxResults"
                runat="server">
              </asp:TextBox>
            </td>
          </tr>
          <tr>
            <td>DefaultCollectionID</td>
            <td>
              <asp:TextBox
                ID="txtDefaultCollectionID"
                runat="server"></asp:TextBox>
            </td>
          </tr>
        </table>
      </fieldset>
      <asp:Button ID="btnSave" runat="server" />
      <asp:Button ID="btnCancel" runat="server" />
    </div>
  </asp:View>
  <asp:View ID="displayView" runat="server">
    <CMS:Collection runat="server" ID="collectionControl" />
  </asp:View>
</asp:MultiView>
```

Handling Instance Data Storage

Now that you have a front-end interface defined, you can return to the codebehind and add some properties. As is visible in Listing 9-7, you have opted in this widget to include only three properties — the XSLT used for display, the number of results to display, and the Collection ID. A more useful widget would probably have an interface that retrieves the collections currently defined in the system and displays them in a dropdown. In fact, the Collection Widget that ships with the

CMS has exactly that ability. Now go ahead and create the storage properties for the options, as shown in Listing 9-7.

LISTING 9-7: ~/Widgets/MyTestControl.ascx.cs

```
public partial class Widgets_MyTestControl : System.Web.UI.UserControl, IWidget
{
  private IWidgetHost _host;
  private string _displayXSLT;
  private int _maxresults;
  private long _defaultcollectionid;

  [WidgetDataMember("ecmNavigation")]
  public string DisplayXSLT
  {
    get { return _displayXSLT; }
    set { _displayXSLT = value; }
  }

  [WidgetDataMember(10)]
  public int MaxResults
  {
    get { return _maxresults; }
    set { _maxresults = value; }
  }

  [WidgetDataMember(-1)]
  public long DefaultCollectionID
  {
    get { return _defaultcollectionid; }
    set { _defaultcollectionid = value; }
  }
```

Listing 9-8 inserts some backing members as well as property assessors. The properties have been tagged with the `WidgetDataMember` attribute, specifying they should be filled and managed as part of the PageData. You may have noticed the argument for each of the attributes. For instance, on the DisplayXSLT you have specified `ecmNavigation`. This argument specifies the default value the property should be filled with if there is no value already stored for this instance of the widget.

You may feel something is missing from this implementation, namely how you will save and populate these properties at runtime. The framework handles this in large part for you. When the widget is instantiated, the WidgetHost automatically fills these properties with the stored values from the PageHost object. The WidgetHost handles all serialization and deserialization for you automatically, as long as the properties are tagged with the `WidgetDataMember` attribute. Saving is only slightly more complicated in that you have to call the `SaveWidgetDataMembers()` method on the WidgetHost.

Handling Edit, Cancel, and Save Clicks

Now that you have the scaffolding of the widget completed, you need to hook it up to the remainder of the events that can be fired. Editing is triggered by clicking the Edit button on the WidgetHost, which in turn fires the `WidgetHost.Edit` event.

As is visible in Listing 9-8, you have create a method called `EditButtonClicked` to handle initializing the edit screen, switching the view, and attaching it to the Edit event on the WidgetHost at the end of the Load section.

LISTING 9-8: ~/Widgets/MyTestControl.ascx.cs

```csharp
protected void Page_Load(object sender, EventArgs e)
  {
    _host = Ektron.Cms.Widget.WidgetHost.GetHost(this);
    _host.Title = "My Collection Widget";
    _host.Maximize += new MaximizeDelegate(delegate() {
this.Visible = true; });
    _host.Minimize += new MinimizeDelegate(delegate() {
this.Visible = false; });
    _host.HelpFile = "http://www.wrox.com/Ektron/
collectionhelp.HTML";

    _host.Edit += new EditDelegate(EditButtonClicked);
  }

  protected void EditButtonClicked(string settings)
  {
    ddlDisplayXSLT.SelectedValue = DisplayXSLT;
    txtMaxResults.Text = MaxResults.ToString();
    txtDefaultCollectionID.Text =
DefaultCollectionID.ToString();
    rootMultiView.SetActiveView(editView);
  }
```

Next you can wire up the Edit Pane buttons.

Listing 9-9 creates a Cancel method and a Save method. Not pictured here is the code that declaratively associates these methods to the corresponding buttons.

LISTING 9-9: ~/Widgets/MyTestControl.ascx.cs

```csharp
    protected void btnCancel_Click(object sender, EventArgs e)
    {
      rootMultiView.SetActiveView(displayView);
    }

    protected void btnSave_Click(object sender, EventArgs e)
    {
      DisplayXSLT = ddlDisplayXSLT.SelectedValue;
      if (!int.TryParse(txtMaxResults.Text, out _maxresults))
MaxResults = 0;
      if (!long.TryParse(txtDefaultCollectionID.Text,
out _defaultcollectionid)) DefaultCollectionID = 0;
      _host.SaveWidgetDataMembers();
      rootMultiView.SetActiveView(displayView);
    }
```

The Cancel method is comparatively simple, because all that must be done is to disregard the data on the form and then switch back to the display view. There is a bit more going on in the Save method. As mentioned earlier, by marking the properties as `WidgetDataMember`'s, you have informed the WidgetHost that these are properties you want to have managed for you. What this means is that in the Save method all you need to do is read the values selected by the author, store them in the properties, and then call `_host.SaveWidgetDataMembers()`. The WidgetHost takes care of the details from there, reading all the values and serializing them to XML for you. In the context of PageBuilder, the values aren't written to the database until the user decides to Save, Check In, or Publish the page. In the context of a dashboard, they can be written immediately to the user or group's personalization information.

The final act of the Save method is to set the view back to the display pane, since the user finished editing the widget.

Rendering the Output

The last bit of coding required for your widget is to add a function to set the properties on the Collection Server Control from the properties on the widget. You'll call that function from page load, as well as Save and Cancel, to make sure that each time the active view changes to display view, the collection has been updated with the most recent properties.

Listing 9-10 shows how the properties are updated in the `Page_Load` method. As you read in the "Implementing Using Collections" section of this chapter, you can set the properties that display the results on the Collection Server Control programmatically, which we are doing here. Remember to call Fill when modifying properties, to ensure the control is rendered with the appropriate options.

LISTING 9-10: ~/Widgets/MyTestControl.ascx.cs

Available for download on Wrox.com

```
protected void Page_Load(object sender, EventArgs e)
{
    _host = Ektron.Cms.Widget.WidgetHost.GetHost(this);
    _host.Title = "My Collection Widget";
    _host.Maximize += new MaximizeDelegate(delegate() {
this.Visible = true; });
    _host.Minimize += new MinimizeDelegate(delegate() {
this.Visible = false; });
    _host.HelpFile = "http://www.wrox.com/
Ektron/collectionhelp.HTML";

    _host.Edit += new EditDelegate(EditButtonClicked);
    SetOutput();
}

protected void btnCancel_Click(object sender, EventArgs e)
{
    SetOutput();
    rootMultiView.SetActiveView(displayView);
}

protected void btnSave_Click(object sender, EventArgs e)
{
```

```
        DisplayXSLT = ddlDisplayXSLT.SelectedValue;
        if (!int.TryParse(txtMaxResults.Text, out _maxresults))
    MaxResults = 0;
        if (!long.TryParse(txtDefaultCollectionID.Text, out _defaultcollectionid))
          DefaultCollectionID = 0;
        _host.SaveWidgetDataMembers();
```

Associating to the Wireframe

Now that the widget is code complete, you are almost done. All that's left is to register the widget with the CMS and associate the widget with a template. Start by opening the Workarea.

1. Go to Settings ➪ Configuration ➪ Personalizations ➪ Widgets. This page is shown in Figure 9-24.

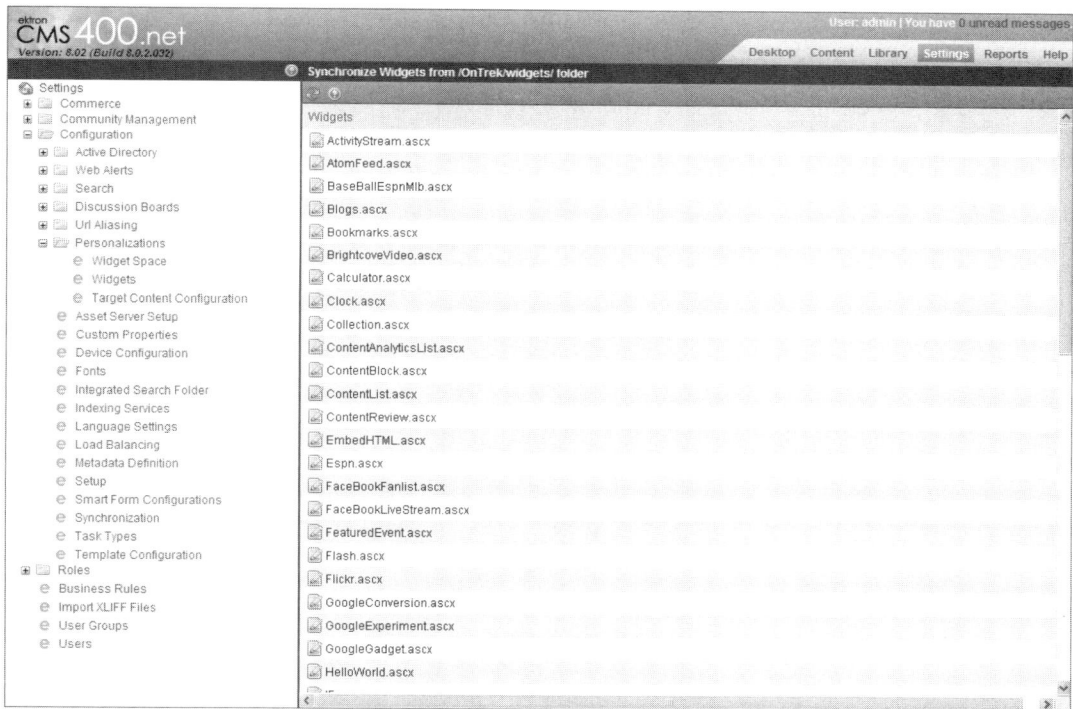

FIGURE 9-24

2. Click the Widget Sync button on this page.

> *The Widget Sync button does not refer to eSync, but rather to synchronizing the list of widgets in the database with what is in the file system. Clicking this button synchronizes* `~/Widgets` *and* `~/workarea/Widgets`. *You should perform synching only when you are adding or removing widgets from the system; if you are modifying an existing widget, there is no need to resync.*

3. Now that you have synchronized your widgets, you can see the new widget has been registered by the system. By clicking the image to the left of the name of the file, you open up the editor for the global properties of the widget.

4. Click the edit icon next to MyTestControl.ascx. You can see in Figure 9-25 that you can modify the Title and Label for the widget on this screen.

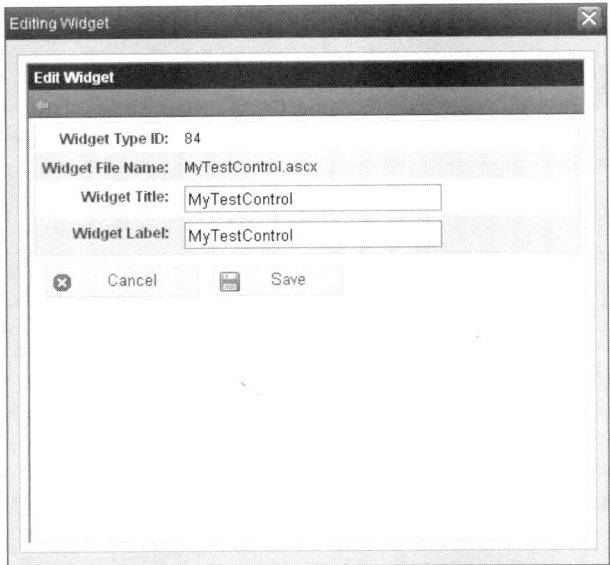

FIGURE 9-25

5. Change the Title and the Label to **CustomCollection**.

 If you mark one of the properties as `GlobalWidgetData`, *it shows up with a simple editing interface. More detail on* `GlobalWidgetData` *can be found in the "Under the Hood" section.*

6. Click Save.

7. There is one final step before you can use this widget on a page. You must associate the widget with a template by clicking Settings ➪ Configuration ➪ Template Configuration and selecting Promotions.pb.aspx. This brings up the template configuration screen, shown in figure 9-26.

8. Ensure that PageBuilder Wireframe is checked. Once it is checked, you are provided with a list of all the widgets defined in the system. Scroll down until you find CustomCollection at the end of the list. Select the CustomCollection and it should turn green. Content editors can now use that widget on any layout based on this template.

9. Click Save.

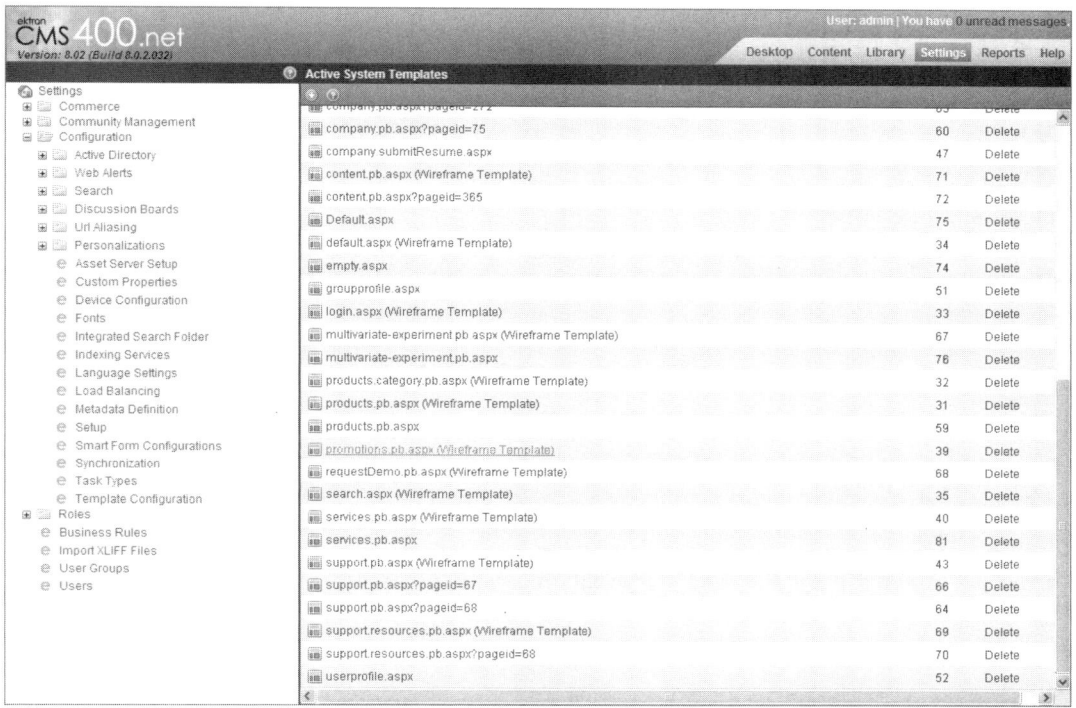

FIGURE 9-26

You'll notice on the template-management page there is no icon showing the CustomCollection Widget. Once you decide which icon to use, simply name it **MyTestControl.ascx.jpg** and put it in the Widgets directory with the widget itself.

Under the Hood: Widgets

Going through the exercise of building a widget exposed most of the functionality of the framework with regards to widgets, but we deliberately simplified some of the aspects. It can be helpful to understand the underlying structure of the platform being used, so we'll cover those details here, and examine some limitations and common issues developers run into when developing with PageBuilder and Personalization.

The widget itself is instantiated through LoadControl into another user control, called the WidgetHost. The WidgetHost contains the events we mentioned earlier, as well as the properties. The WidgetHost also handles data storage and retrieval for the properties on the widget itself. Let's discuss the lifecycle of the widget first.

On `page_init`, the WidgetHost reads the data stored for the widget being instantiated and the type of the widget. The WidgetHost then instantiates the widget, and after instantiating, sets the properties marked with `WidgetDataMember` and `GlobalWidgetData` with the appropriate values. It also adds the widget to the internal controls collection. At this point, the widget catches up to the page's lifecycle status, meaning the widget runs through its `pre_init` and its `init`. Page progression continues as normal. At the time the constructor in the widget runs, the properties have not been set, but you can read their values at any point in the page lifecycle.

The events exposed by the WidgetHost are `Edit`, `Maximize`, `Minimize`, `Create`, and `Close`. These events are fired upon certain conditions, outlined in Table 9-5.

TABLE 9-5: Properties on the Events

EVENT	OCCURS
`Edit`	When the user clicks the Edit button on WidgetHost
`Maximize`	When the user clicks the Restore button on WidgetHost (only in Personalization)
`Minimize`	When the user clicks the Minimize button on WidgetHost (only in Personalization)
`Create`	When the user first drags the widget onto the page
`Close`	When the user removes the widget from the page

The widget should subscribe to whatever events you want it to handle. If the widget does not subscribe to the Edit event, for example, the Edit button will not appear on the WidgetHost.

There are also some properties on the WidgetHost you should be aware of, as described in Table 9-6.

TABLE 9-6: Properties on the WidgetHost

PROPERTY	DESCRIPTION
`HelpFile`	The URL used for the Help link on the WidgetHost. If left empty, the Help button will not show up.
`IsEditable`	A read-only Boolean that informs the widget whether it is editable. For instance, on a PageBuilder page, the widget is only editable when the page is actually in Edit mode.
`Title`	Use this property to set the string to be displayed on the WidgetHost above the widget. This is always visible in Personalization, but is only visible while editing in PageBuilder.
`WidgetInfo`	The internal data construct used by PageBuilder to restore the widget. It can be used to determine areas such as location on the page and to read the widget settings manually.
`ExpandOptions`	This enumeration controls the modal operation of the widget. If set to `Expandable.DontExpand`, the widget will always render inline on the page. If set to `Expandable.ExpandOnEdit`, when the user clicks on Edit, the widget's settings screen will automatically appear within a modal dialog box. The last option, `Expandable.ExpandOnExpand`, creates another icon that takes the current display of the widget and puts it into a modal. In PageBuilder, the Expand button is only available while editing a page.

The `WidgetHost` assists with storage and retrieval of instance data. As covered in the "PageBuilder" section, each PageBuilder page is stored in the database as XML. Within the page, each widget also has storage available in the form of a string. In a given widget, the developer can decorate any public properties on the widget with the attributes `WidgetDataMember` or `GlobalWidgetData`. Such attributes take an argument for the default value of the property, but the real achievement is to inform the system that the properties should be maintained as part of the PageData, or should be filled by the system from the global data store. All properties decorated with the `WidgetDataMember` attribute will be saved to the current `PageData` object when the method `SaveWidgetDataMembers()` is called on the `WidgetHost` object. The data is loaded into those properties just after the constructor.

`GlobalWidgetData` is useful in situations where you have one property across the entire site that needs to be maintained for all instances of a widget. An example might be if you have a SalesForce Widget with a developer log-in and password. By marking those properties as `GlobalWidgetData`, you make it easy to update later across the entire site. That editing occurs in the widget settings page in the Workarea.

`GlobalWidgetData`, unlike `WidgetDataMember`, only supports a subset of data types for the property. Where `WidgetDataMembers` can serialize any object whose class has been marked Serializable, global properties have an automatically generated editing interface that respects data types. For instance, if the property is marked as an Int, the editing interface for that widget only allows numerics to be entered into the field. Conversely, for DateTime types, the editing interface automatically creates a datepicker instance for ease of data entry, and for enumerations, the editing interface automatically creates a dropdown list. Here are the supported data types:

- DateTime
- Int
- Long
- Double
- Bool
- String
- Enumeration

Common Pitfalls

One of the most common areas of confusion for developers working with widgets is that inline CSS and JavaScript do not appear to function. This is due to widgets having one or more ASP.NET UpdatePanels in their ancestor trees. The standard ASP.NET method of dealing with UpdatePanels is to use the ScriptManager to register scripts with the page. When using CMS400.NET however, the recommended standard is to use the `Ektron.Cms.Api.JS.RegisterJSInclude()` function to register the JavaScript, and the `Ektron.Cms.Api.Css.RegisterCss()` function to register CSS.

The first benefit of using these methods is that JavaScript is always run when the page finishes loading, which is equivalent to `Ektron.ready()`. More importantly, it causes your scripts to work in any location. `RegisterJSInclude` detects the situation for the current request — whether it is a full postback or an asyncpostback — and include the script on the page in the appropriate way. For CSS, the primary benefit is that all the files for a given request/response cycle are aggregated, cutting back on overhead. The client does not download many small files, but rather a few slightly larger files.

The biggest reason for aggregating CSS is that Internet Explorer places a limit of 32 CSS files at the root level. By using RegisterCSS rather than appending a style tag to each widget, CSS files are aggregated automatically, circumventing the limit, and style tags stay in the head, better conforming to standards.

Debugging widgets can also trip up developers from time to time. The two places where code errors can occur are compilation errors and runtime errors. The first step in debugging is to determine the type of error. You can do this easily by creating an empty ASPX page and directly referencing the widget within the page as you would any other user control. Fix any thrown error until you have no more compilation errors. If the widget is still functioning incorrectly, try attaching to the ASP .NET worker process or w3wp process. Within Visual Studio, press Ctrl+Alt+E. This brings up an exceptions screen. Make sure that Common Language Runtime Exceptions are checked and then try interacting with the widget. Execution should break at the point where the widget fails.

HTML FORMS

You'll use HTML forms when you need to collect information from site visitors. Ektron's HTML forms give authors the tools they need to create custom-tailored forms in a WYSIWYG editor and deploy them on a page using PageBuilder.

In addition to capturing data, the set of tools provides those without HTML knowledge the ability to create forms with advanced capabilities, such as validating against business rules and assigning tasks for follow-up. The data that's captured is available through Web-based reports for export to Microsoft Excel, or to developers through APIs, server controls, and widgets.

The form rendered in the browser is no different from forms you may have handcrafted using HTML. The difference is in how the form is created and deployed onto the website. Let's explore both in order to begin to understand HTML forms.

Creating a Form

HTML forms are entities that exist within the content structure of the Workarea. HTML forms are actually extensions of the content data type and, therefore, inherit many types of capabilities, namely language support, permissions, and scheduling (allowing authors to specify the time and date a form should "go live" on the website).

Creating an HTML form with eWebEdit400 is done visually through dragging and dropping form elements from the toolbar to the editor's canvas. eWebEdit400 has further simplified the process of creating an HTML form by offering an HTML Form Wizard, which allows you to create a number of popular types of forms (such as Polls, Contact Forms, and so on) quickly.

Displaying a Form

As is true with almost every object in the CMS, you retrieve and render HTML forms using a widget, a server control, or the HTML form API.

- **Widget:** Every installation includes a Content Block Control Widget that allows a CMS user with proper permissions to build a page that includes an HTML form. In the implementation section, you'll use this widget to place the "Request a Demo" form (as we'll create shortly) on a page.
- **Server Control:** Although an HTML form is ultimately content, you must use the FormBlock Server Control and not the Content Block Server Control to render the form on a page. The fields available for the FormBlock Server Control are listed in Table 9-7.

TABLE 9-7: Properties of the FormBlock Server Control

PROPERTY	DESCRIPTION
ID	The ID of the form that appears where you inserted the server control. If you don't know the ID of the form block, you can find the ID in the Workarea or use the CMS explorer to browse for it.
DynamicParameter	The value specified here will be used by the control when it looks in the query string for a parameter by this name.
CacheInterval	Sets the amount of time the server control's data is cached. The default is 0 (zero).
AddValidation	Set this parameter to true if you want to add validation to your HTML Form.

- **HTML Form API:** The data classes, methods, and properties available through the `Ektron.CMS.API.Content` namespace provide you with everything you need for creating, deleting, editing, and retrieving data from the system. The following shows a snippet of C# code for retrieving an HTML form by its ID from the system.

Using the `Ektron.CMS.API.Content` namespace, you can do the following:

```
Ektron.Cms.API.Content.Form formApi = new Ektron.Cms.API.Content.Form();
Ektron.Cms.FormData form = formApi.GetForm(23);
```

Implementation: The "Request a Demo" Form

In this section, you'll look at the implementation guide to review the requirements for the "Request a Demo" form and work through the process of implementing the form. The purpose of the form is to gather the contact information from the site visitors so that a sales engineer can follow up with a technical one-on-one demo. Another requirement is that a sales engineer must be notified by e-mail when a form is submitted and a task must be assigned to the sales engineer to follow up with the lead.

Implementation Tasks

In this section, you'll complete the process of building the "Request a Demo" form using the basic form you created earlier as a starting point. The requirements you have are:

- The HTML form must capture the site visitors' contact information.

- The HTML form must notify the sales engineer that a "Request a Demo" form has been submitted.
- The HTML form uses the task functionality to assign a task to a sales engineer upon form submission.

This section covers the following procedures:

- Reviewing the basic "Request a Demo" form created earlier
- Displaying the form on the Web page using the Content Block Widget and PageBuilder

Creating the Basic Contact Information Form

When you choose to create a new HTML form using the New menu in the Workarea, you're presented with a Wizard that guides you through the process, beginning with a list of sample forms installed by default, as shown in Figure 9-27. Because the implementation guide specifies that you need to capture an individual's basic contact information, you can choose the "Contact Information" form from this Wizard or use the form created earlier.

1. Access the content folder by expanding the Folder accordion item in the Workarea.
2. Select the Folder that will contain the form. Because content permissions apply to forms, it should also be noted that only administrators or content authors with sufficient folder privileges have the ability to create HTML forms. Put this form in /Content/Promotions/Forms.
3. In the Workarea File menu, hover over New to open the New menu.
4. From the New menu, select HTML Form/Survey.
5. As shown in figure 9-27, there are a number of HTML forms already set up for you to choose from. You can pick the one that most closely matches your form or start with a blank form. For now, choose Contact Information and click Next.
6. Enter the form's Title and Description and click Next.
7. Select the individuals you want to assign a task to every time form data is submitted. For now, leave this empty and click Next. This selection can be changed later by modifying the form properties.
8. Specify the action you want the Form Block Server Control to take when the form is submitted.
9. Customize the response message that displays when the form is submitted. The Merge Field button appears on the toolbar, which lets you select from available fields to display in the message. Click Next, and then click Done.

As you can see in Figure 9-28, you now have a basic "Contact Information" form that is ready to publish and capture information. All of the information provided in the Wizard is accessible through the form properties and can be modified at any point if needed. Table 9-8 describes the purpose of the two HTML Form specific tabs. The other tabs are covered when discussing content in Chapter 5 (see Chapter 5: Content Management Fundamentals).

HTML Forms | **313**

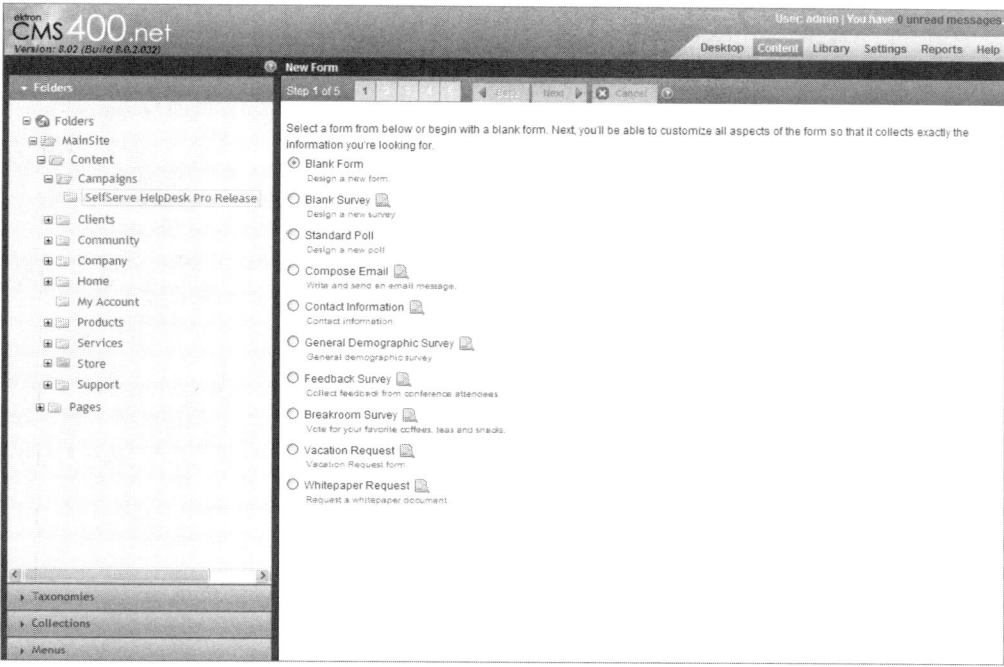

FIGURE 9-27

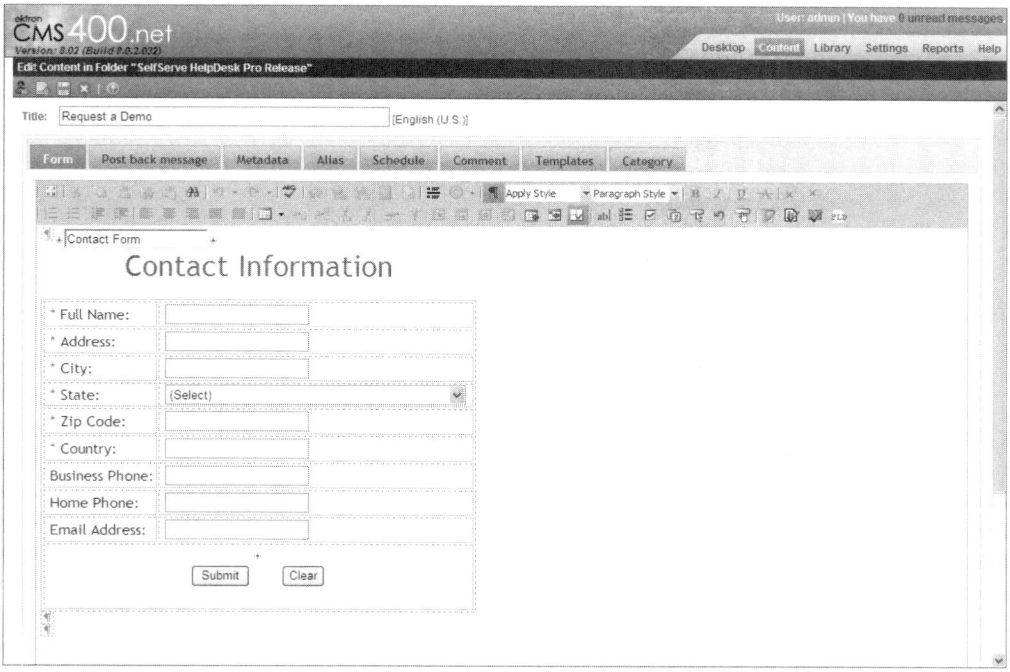

FIGURE 9-28

TABLE 9-8: Properties of Tabs

TAB NAME	PURPOSE
Form	A WYSIWYG display of the form. If the form is being edited, it will appear within the eWebEdit400 authoring tool and form elements may be added, removed, or modified. You may also view or modify HTML source directly.
Post back message	You can choose to 1) Display a message, 2) Redirect to a file or page, 3) Redirect to an action page, or 4) Display a report. Choose "Display a Message" and customize the response message that is displayed when the form is submitted.

This form uses an HTML table to display the labels and form elements in separate columns. The Text Field form element is used for every field except for State, which uses the Choices Field. The red asterisks indicate the form field has some type of validation associated with it. Table 9-9 lists the validation properties for an input field.

1. Right-click the form field.
2. Select Field Properties from the context menu.
3. Click the Validation tab and notice that the validation is set to **Cannot be blank,** as shown in Figure 9-29.

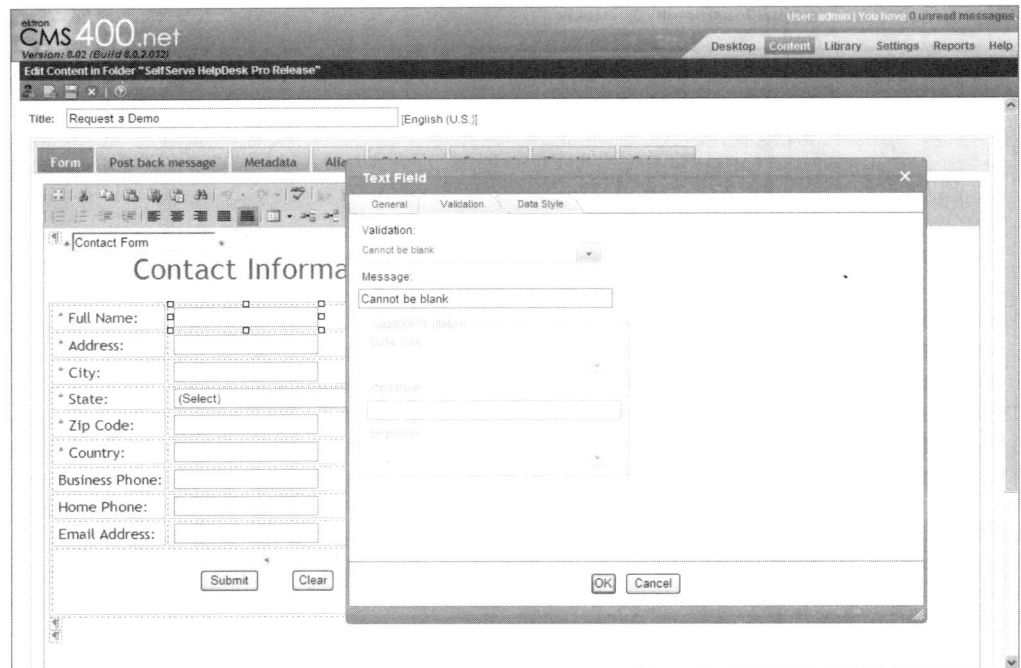

FIGURE 9-29

TABLE 9-9: Properties on Field Inputs

FIELD TYPE	DESCRIPTION
Text Field	Use a text field when you want the user to enter a free text response, or to display text on the screen.
Choices Field	Use when you want a site visitor to select from a predetermined list. You can allow a site visitor to select only one choice or more than one choice. You can also determine the list's items and appearance.
Checkbox Field	A Checkbox Field is one character wide and accepts one of two possible values: checked or unchecked.
Calendar Field	Use to insert a field that lets a site visitor select a date.

Placing the "Request a Demo" Form on the Page

You should be fairly comfortable with the concept of dragging and dropping PageBuilder Widgets from the Widget Tray into a PageBuilder Wireframe. Because HTML forms are ultimately content items, the widget to use for placing an HTML form on a page is the Content Block Control Widget. To select an HTML form using the Content Block Control Widget:

1. Drag and drop the Content Block Control Widget onto your page from the Ektron Widget Tray.

2. Set the Filter By option to Forms. This is an important step because HTML forms are not included in the result set by default.

3. Navigate the folder tree to find the "Request a Demo" form, or click the Search tab and search for your form by its name.

4. Hover your mouse over an item in the result set to see more information about that item in the Content Preview Bubble, as you can see in Figure 9-30.

5. With your choice selected, click the Save button.

Under the Hood: HTML Form Data Model

Now that you understand the basics of working with HTML forms, you can dive into some detail and look at the HTML form data model to see how the information is represented and stored in the database. This knowledge isn't required to use the feature or create HTML forms. Spending the time familiarizing yourself with the inner workings gives you a solid understanding of how the system is operating and inevitably saves you development time.

The core terminology to understand is:

- **Form Fields:** Text field, text area, hidden text, choices, checkbox, select list, and so on
- **Form Design:** The HTML markup that composes the HTML form
- **Form Properties:** Attributes of the form, such as Title, ID, and so on

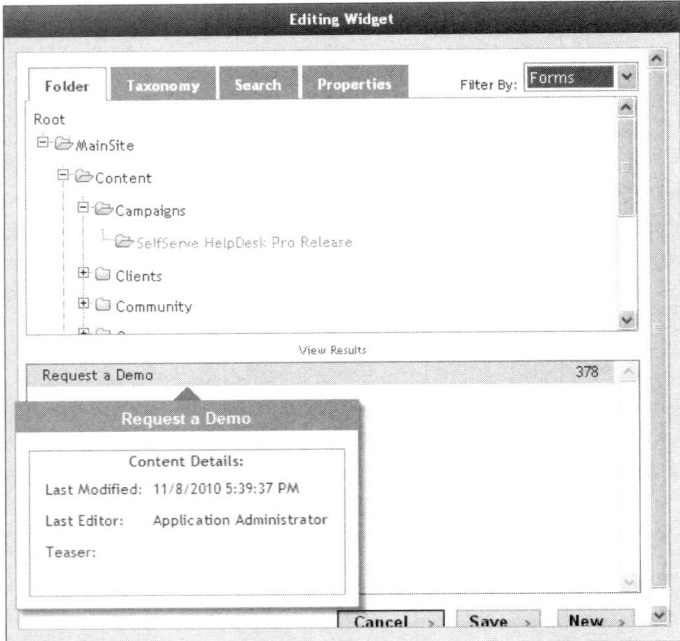

FIGURE 9-30

Form designs and core form properties are stored in the primary content table, `content_tbl`. Take a look at the form design for the HTML form you created earlier and focus on three fields: `type`, `content_HTML`, and `summary`. To find this information in the database, do the following:

1. Open SQL Server Studio.
2. Issue this SQL command: `SELECT id, content_HTML, summary FROM content_tbl WHERE type=2 AND title='My Test Form'`. You'll need to change the title to the one you created, or leave the title clause out to see all of the forms available.

The `type` field stores an integer that describes the type of content contained within the record. As you can see in the SQL query, the type for HTML forms is 2. The `content_HTML` field contains the HTML for the form. A close look at the markup reveals standard HTML form elements along with elements referencing custom tags and attributes. The custom elements are prefixed by `ekt_design_ns` and are used by the system for internal validation functions. All custom attributes are removed prior to page rendering, except for those attributes used for form field validation, so you see those fields in your markup if you're using the system's HTML form validation functionality.

Because HTML forms are stored in `content_HTML`, they are ultimately a type of content. The forms inherit the same features that content has including the ability to have different versions of the same form available for different languages and the ability to schedule forms to "go live" at a specific time.

If you continue to explore the `content_HTML` table, you find the properties that an HTML form derives from content, such as Title, Summary, and ID. Properties that are unique to HTML forms are found in the `form_properties_tbl` table.

HTML Forms | 317

The last table you should familiarize yourself with is the one that stores the form submissions, called `form_data_tbl`. If you noted the ID of the form you created previously, you can find the data submitted against it by executing this query, replacing the ID with the ID of your form: `SELECT * FROM form_data_tbl WHERE ID=23`. The data is stored as name-value pairs (and *not* as content), with the name representing the ID given to the form field and the value representing the information provided by the site visitor in that form element.

 See Chapter 7 for coverage on Smart Forms and the differences between Smart Forms and HTML Forms.

Multivariate Testing

Multivariate testing is process designed to increase the conversion rate of a given page. As a Web design concept, this is typically achieved through varying the layout, graphics, and content of a page through a series of possible configurations, and determining which collection of settings has the highest level of conversions.

The strength of multivariate testing comes from its ability to test a number of variables at the same time. The system creates a list of all possible combinations of layouts and content (called a *full factorial*) and allows a marketer to run an experiment that shows each combination to site visitors a roughly equal number of times. The success rate of each variation is then calculated by determining what percentage of users follow a call to action to the determined target page. This allows marketers to easily determine an optimum configuration for a given page through automated trial and error. Multivariate testing relies on PageBuilder for its foundation. There are three widgets that come into play, the first is called the Multivariate Experiment Widget, the second is the Multivariate Section Widget, and the third is the Multivariate Target Widget.

- ➤ Multivariate Experiment Widget
- ➤ Multivariate Section Widget

Multivariate Section Widget

The Multivariate Section Widget allows a marketer to create an internal set of columns, each containing further widgets. In display mode, the section widget randomly shows one of the internal columns, displaying the list of widgets defined for that column in its place. By adding a series of columns in a given section widget, it is possible to create a series of different configurations, called *variants*, which will be shown to end users browsing the site. If you use a single section widget on a given layout, you are approximating A/B testing, which varies a single item on a given page in order to determine which variation works best.

However, by using the flexibility of PageBuilder to turn this section functionality into a widget, Ektron built the functionality in such a way that multiple section widgets can be placed on the same page, delivering full multivariate capabilities. Each section widget can have multiple columns, each containing a set of widgets. The experiment widget, covered in the next portion of this section, then uses factorial logic to determine all the possible combinations of the the columns in the section widgets. The final page delivered to each user will contain one of these variations.

The columns created internally in the section widget are stored in the widget settings for the section widget, and the columns are instantiated by the widget at render time. This means that only the widgets currently being displayed are actually instantiated.

Multivariate Experiment Widget

The *Experiment Widget* is used to manage the settings for the overall experiment being run. Behind the scenes, it determines which combinations of content are displayed to users visiting the site, and it stores statistics on what was shown to users. Combining the data that the experiment widget collects with the data the target widget collects allows the experiment widget to display reports on the overall efficacy of each combination. This widget is the key that allows marketers to actually run experiments.

When a marketer interacts with the experiment widget, they are shown two key interface elements. The first portion of the widget allows them to select a target page, which is where conversions will actually be recorded. It also allows them to stop and start the experiment. Below the experiment settings, a list of the available combinations is shown, along with details on the current conversion rates, if an experiment is currently running.

When a site visitor views the page, the experiment widget remains invisible to them, but it performs several key functions during their visit. The first of these things is that it randomly selects a combination, also known as a variant or variation, from the list of available combinations. It then records which variation it selected by storing it as an incomplete conversion in the database, and also in a cookie on the user's system, allowing it to reshow the exact same layout if the user returns to the page. Finally, it informs the section widgets which column they should display in order to match the selected variant.

Once an experiment is underway, the experiment widget will continue to follow the process outlined above until the target number of test cases have been displayed, at which point the variant with the highest percentage of successful conversions is promoted to always being displayed, and the experiment ends. Typically, the number of test cases is set to a figure around 1,000, which is high enough that statistical anomalies can be averaged out, but not so high that the experiment runs inordinately long. A good way to determine what number to set this figure to is to take the number of combinations available, determined by multiplying the number of columns in each section together, and multiplying it by a number between 100 and 250. This means that each combination will be shown to over 100 users, which is usually considered a band large enough to glean accurate information from.

Multivariate Target Widget

The target widget is the third piece of the puzzle. This widget is designed to capture statistics on successful conversions, and is placed on the target page. For instance, if a marketer is trying to drive traffic to a membership signup page, they may try several different combinations of graphics and text on a campaign landing page. The target page would be the page that actually contains the form to create an account. As each variation is shown to a user on the site on the campaign landing page, the act of showing the particular combination is logged. When the user follows the link to the signup page, the target widget then analyzes the cookie on the visitors system, and determines that they participated in the experiment on the campaign page. It then reads which combination they were shown, and logs it as a successful conversion.

Multivariate Use Example

Putting this flow together into an example, imagine a scenario in which you have two section widgets and an experiment widget. In the first section widget you might choose to have two variations, resulting in two hidden columns. In the first variation, you may use a Content Block Widget and a YouTube Widget to show a video. In the second variation, you might opt to put in a different Content Block Widget and a Collection Widget to display associated documents. The items in these variations can be extended, modified, or more variations or columns can be added at any time. Variation settings are stored in the WidgetData object for the section widget, which also means the settings are part of the underlying data structure for the layout itself.

In addition to the center content defined by the first section widget, in the right column you choose to have your second section widget with another two variations, this time selecting two different images for your call-to-action graphic, one in each variant. The variations are then defined by a combination of a column selected from the first section widget and a column selected from the second section widget. For example, the first section could display column A and the second section column C, or the first section could display column B and the second column D. Combinations consisting of column B and C, or A and D are also valid. This totals four variations for the page. The experiment widget calculates all the possible vaiations and shows each of these combinations roughly equally, so at the end of the experiment you have a clear understanding of which combination of settings is most optimal to funnel conversions.

Looking at the implementation guide, you can see that an experiment is required in the campaign landing page. This page deals with accepting incoming page views from e-mail and Web campaigns, and funneling them through to a conversion page that contains a form. The form collects information from users requesting a demo about the company's software solutions.

Continuing the examples from this chapter, you now have one page completed which contains a Collection Widget with documentation about OnTrek's solutions and awards, and an HTML form to accept information from visitors requesting further information and demos. Extend the example in this section by splitting the contents of the single layout you have into two separate pages, one with the collection and one with the form. Then modify the collection page to be the experiment page and add HTML content from the site. Add the form page as well and set it as the target page.

The remaining sections cover the following steps:

➤ Creating an experiment.

➤ Modifying the contents of the section widget.

➤ Viewing the results and modifying the parameters of the experiment.

Creating an Experiment

To create an experiment, you need to have the experiment page and the target page ready to go:

1. Create a new page in /MainSite/Pages/Experiments called "Request a Demo Form Page" using the Promotions.pb.aspx template.

2. On this target page, place a Content Block Widget in the center column, and set the source to /MainSite/Content/Campaigns/SelfServe HelpDesk Pro Release/Request a Demo.

3. Also place a Multivariate Target Widget on this page. This will record successful conversions.
4. Publish the page.
5. Create the landing page, at /MainSite/Pages/Experiments/ Request a Demo Promotion, using the Promotions.pb.aspx template and edit the layout.
6. Now that the groundwork is complete, start by adding a Multivariate Experiment Widget to the center column. Click the "..." button on the widget to bring up the target page browser as shown in Figure 9-31, and navigate to the Target page in /MainSite/Pages/Experiments/Request a Demo Form Page. Before you click Start, you need to add a Multivariate Section Widget.

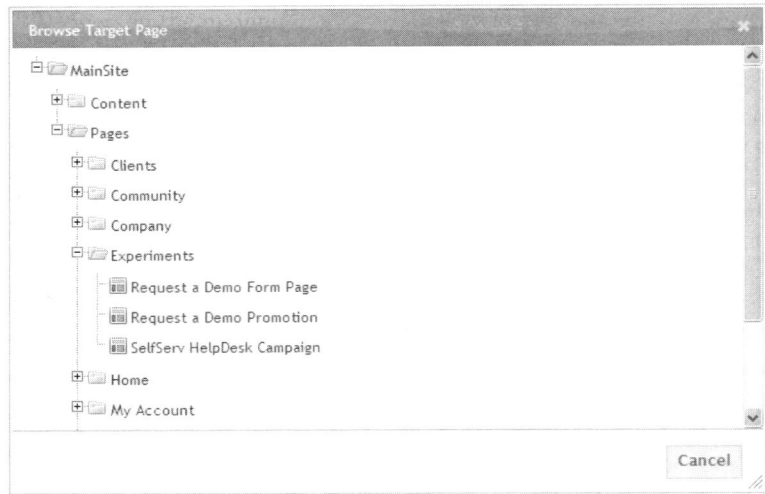

FIGURE 9-31

7. Go back to the toolbar and drag a Multivariate Section Widget into the center column. The Multivariate Section Widget is shown in Figure 9-32.

The Multivariate Section Widget has some key UI elements. The 1/1 indicator tells you which variant of the section you're looking at. Next to the indicator is a slider which can be dragged to select a different variation. Finally, there is a + button, which allows you to add a variation to the section. You can add as many of these section widgets to a page as you want.

Modifying the Contents of the Section Widget

Below the navigation tools in the widget is a blue header. The header indicates you can interact with the contents just as you can with any column in a DropZone. Follow these steps:

1. Add a Content Block Widget inside the Multivariate Section Widget, as shown in Figure 9-33.

    You can see there is now a Content Block Widget defined for Variation One with the same user icons you are accustomed to seeing — Edit, Delete, and Help. No customization needs to be done to a widget to allow it to be used in multivariate, as it is automatically supported.

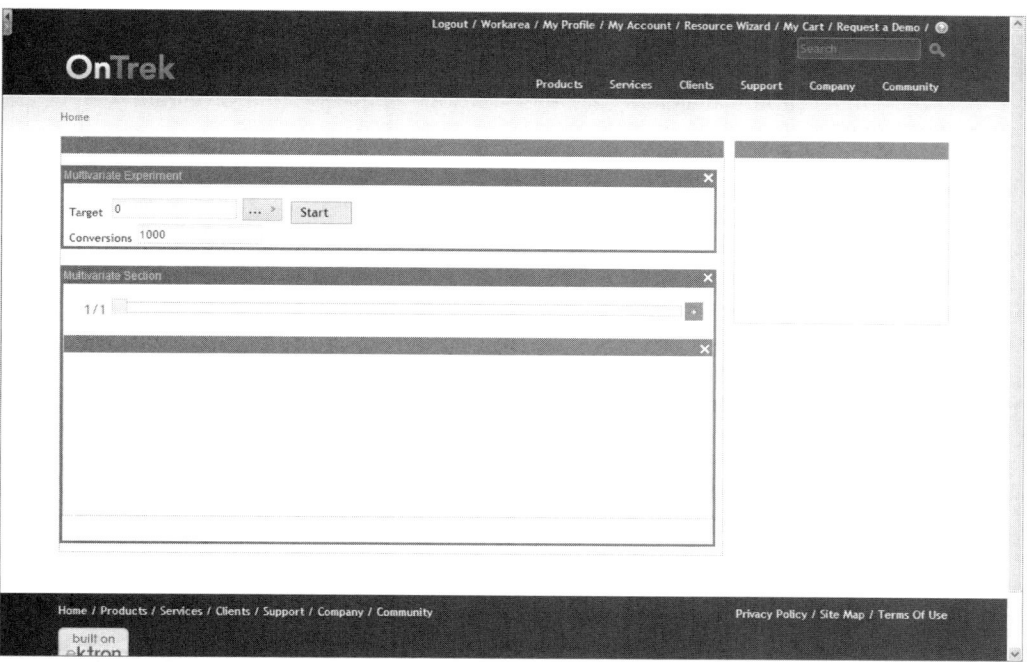

FIGURE 9-32

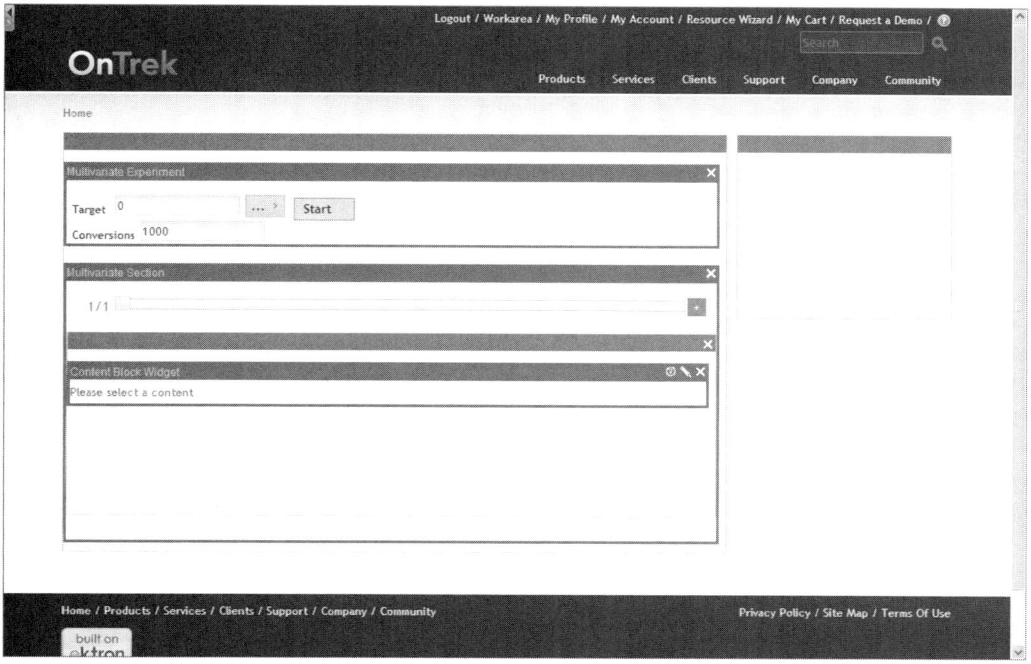

FIGURE 9-33

2. Set the Content Block Widget to use at /MainSite/Content/Campaigns/SelfServe HelpDesk Pro Release/ Request a SelfServ Demo v1.

3. Return to the section widget and click the + button to add a second variation.

4. Drag another Content Block Widget into the second variation, and set its source to /MainSite/Content/Campaigns/SelfServe HelpDesk Pro Release/ Pages/Promotions/Request a SelfServ Demo v2.

   You now have two variations of content on the page. Once you start the experiment, both versions will be shown roughly equally to site visitors until the conclusion of the experiment.

5. Start the experiment to see how the reporting works.

Viewing the Results and Modifying the Parameters of the Experiment

Once the experiment has been started in the Multivariate Experiment Widget, the report becomes available for viewing. You can see in Figure 9-34 that you have two variations available. If you have a second section, also with two variations, there can be four combinations. If you have a third section, this time with three variations, the number of combinations can be 2x2x3, or 8. Each combination represents one variant from each section.

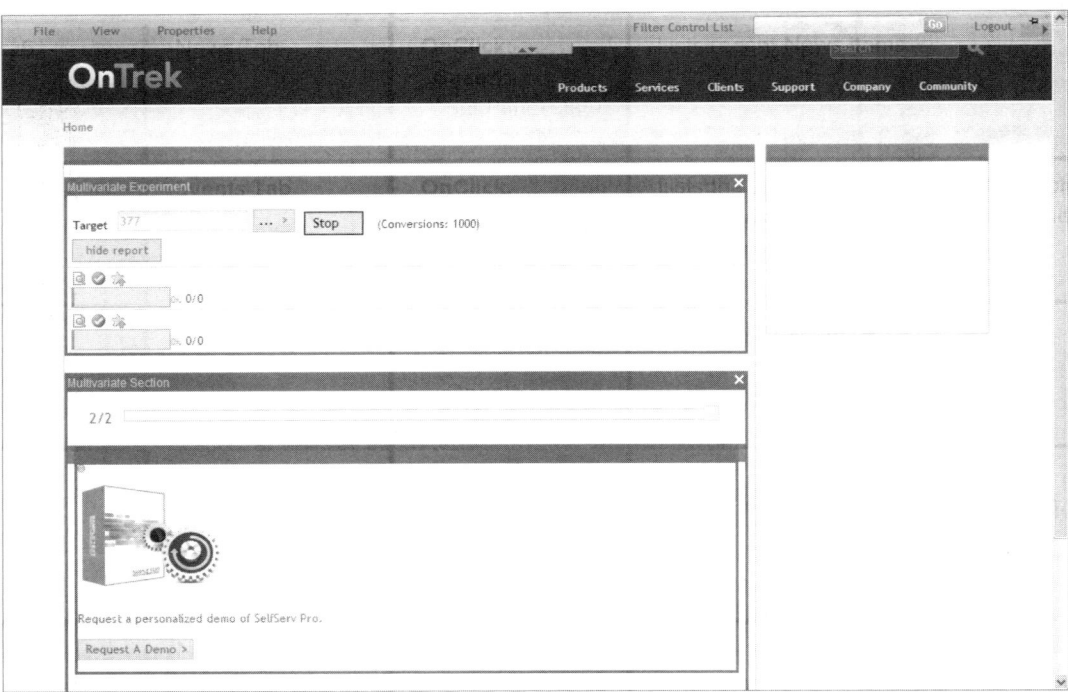

FIGURE 9-34

There are three options available above each combination:

- **Preview:** Allows a preview of the combination by adjusting each section to display the selected variant.
- **Disable:** Allows you to disable a specific combination. For instance, you may be measuring the effectiveness of having a call-to-action in the center column versus right column. You want to disable the combination that has the call to action in both columns.
- **Promote:** Clicking this button ends the experiment, and removes the section widgets while moving the contents in the corresponding variation to the page itself. This happens automatically when the target number of conversions happens.

You can start, stop, or modify the experiment at any time. The only limitation is that only administrators and users with the Multivariate-Tester role can manage the experiment. Any user with editing privileges can modify the contents of an experiment.

Under the Hood: Multivariate

The data model for Multivariate is broken into two tables. The first table, `multivariate_experiment`, stores the experiment details such as the target page, maximum conversions, and the experiment page ID. Listing 9-11 shows a select statement retrieving this information.

LISTING 9-11: SQL Query to Retrieve Experiment Details

```
SELECT TOP 1000 [id]
    ,[experiment_page_id]
    ,[target_page_id]
    ,[max_conversions]
FROM [multivariate_experiment]
```

The main table for results of the experiments however, is the `multivariate_report` table. As seen in Listing 9-12, this table stores the unique GUID for the combination viewed, the total number of hits, and the total number of conversions.

LISTING 9-12: SQL Query to Retrieve Experiment Conversions

```
SELECT TOP 1000 [id]
    ,[page_id]
    ,[hits]
    ,[conversions]
    ,[combination_guid]
    ,[disabled]
FROM [multivariate_report]
```

When a new variation is added by clicking the + icon on the Multivariate Section Widget, the variant is stored in the `PageData` object for the layout in the columns list. These column variations are not given a numerical column ID, but are instead given a random GUID for an ID. Combinations of variations also have GUIDs for IDs. The combination GUIDs are created by XORing the variation IDs together. This gives a reasonable assurance that each combination will have a unique identifier.

To speed up the page-load process and minimize hits to the database, the current hits are counted in the application cache until the threshold of 100 new results is reached. Hits are then bulk written to the database. The safest way of getting the results of an experiment is to use the cached model as is done in Listing 9-13

LISTING 9-13: Creating a Cached Multivariate Report Model

```
IMultivariateReportModel _reportModel =
    CachedMultivariateReportModel.FromModel(new
SqlMultivariateReportModel());
```

The cached model always returns the most up-to-date results.

Multivariate Brief

Multivariate testing is a powerful method of determining the effectiveness of varying versions of a page. It leverages PageBuilder to allow for ease of running experiments, and can help an organization to increase conversion rates with a minimum of fuss. There are many solutions to running A/B tests or Multivariate tests on your website, but by using the Ektron Framework, you ensure that these transformations take place server side, meaning better search engine optimization with less JavaScript. Using the Ektron Framework also means no development effort when integrating with a test suite.

WEB ANALYTICS

The key hallmark of a good objective is its ability to be measured. Web Analytics plays a fundamental role in validating the success of a website by recording and reporting on the metrics that will help determine whether or not your site's business objectives are being met. The Web metrics used to determine this are called *Key Performance Indicators (KPIs)*.

In this final technical section, you learn how to use Ektron's Traffic Analytics to measure the effectiveness of the Request a Form campaign by looking at the number of impressions, the click through rate, and the conversions rate.

Traffic Analytics versus Business Analytics

Ektron makes an important distinction between two different types of metrics collected on websites and categorizes them separately as *Traffic Analytics* and *Business Analytics*.

- **Traffic Analytics:** Encompasses capturing and reporting of metrics related to all aspects of Web traffic, including where site visitors come from, what they click, what pages they visit, how they respond to the content presented, covering all activities down to the page level.
- **Business Analytics:** Collects and provides similar data from a different perspective. For instance, it can look at activities related to a particular content block or business event.

The combination of Traffic Analytics and Business Analytics makes the Ektron Framework's Web Analytics Framework extremely powerful. Leveraging both can help you to make more informed decisions to determine quantitatively whether your website's objectives are being met.

The Traffic Analytics engine is designed to support a number of different Analytics providers such as Google Analytics and Omniture through its use of the *Provider Model Design Pattern*. This approach means that your website inherits all the tracking and reporting features provided by those systems, allowing Ektron to take full advantage of the tools and reports of the top analytics providers. It also means that Ektron can combine this information with its own data to provide even more insightful reports, such as the effect that changing content has on the page traffic or the effectiveness of different versions of the same content item.

Ektron simplifies the process of using these providers, eliminating the need to manually tag pages with snippets of tracking code, and offering the ability to track Web traffic on the entire website or limit data gathering to specific pages. The Ektron Framework automatically adds the tracking beacon to any PageBuilder page or ASPX template that contains an Ektron Server Control. It is strongly recommended that you enable site-wide tracking and filter data through the reports as needed. Once Web traffic analytics is enabled at the site level, the process of data collection starts and information is stored by the provider on their servers.

Analytics Reports

Although traffic analytics data is stored remotely, the reporting is integrated closely with your website and its content. A full suite of reports can be viewed through any Ektron-managed Web page or through the report section of the Workarea. You can also view the reports from any interface offered by your provider. For example, if you use Google Analytics, you can continue to use its Web interface http://www.google.com/analytics/ as you normally would. Widgets are also available for displaying Web traffic analytics data. With the Analytics Report Widget, you can display a traffic report for the past seven days, customize it as needed, and integrate it into a PageBuilder page or the Dashboard.

In cases where you need to provide metrics on custom events or the activities related to a particular content item or user, you'll want to look at Ektron's Business Analytics engine. In contrast to the Traffic Analytics engine, the Business Analytics engine uses an Ektron Server Control for tagging individual pages and logging statistical information related to custom defined events, the page URL, content ID, user ID, and more. The server control writes this information to the database and can be configured to store information in memory to minimize the number of transactions to the database. You'll see how to configure this later in the "Under the Hood: Analytics" section.

In the Report section of the Workarea, you can view Business Analytics reports covering the entire site, individual templates, and individual content items. To view analytics data you must be a member of the administrator group or assigned the Analytics Viewer role. A screenshot of the Business Analytics report section is shown in Figure 9-35.

This section walks through the process of implementing a solution that uses Web Traffic Analytics to determine the effectiveness of the campaign landing page by measuring the number of impressions (the number of times the page was viewed by a site visitor), the click through rate (the percentage of visitors that click the "Request a Demo" button), and the conversion rate (the percentage of visitors that complete the "Request a Demo" form).

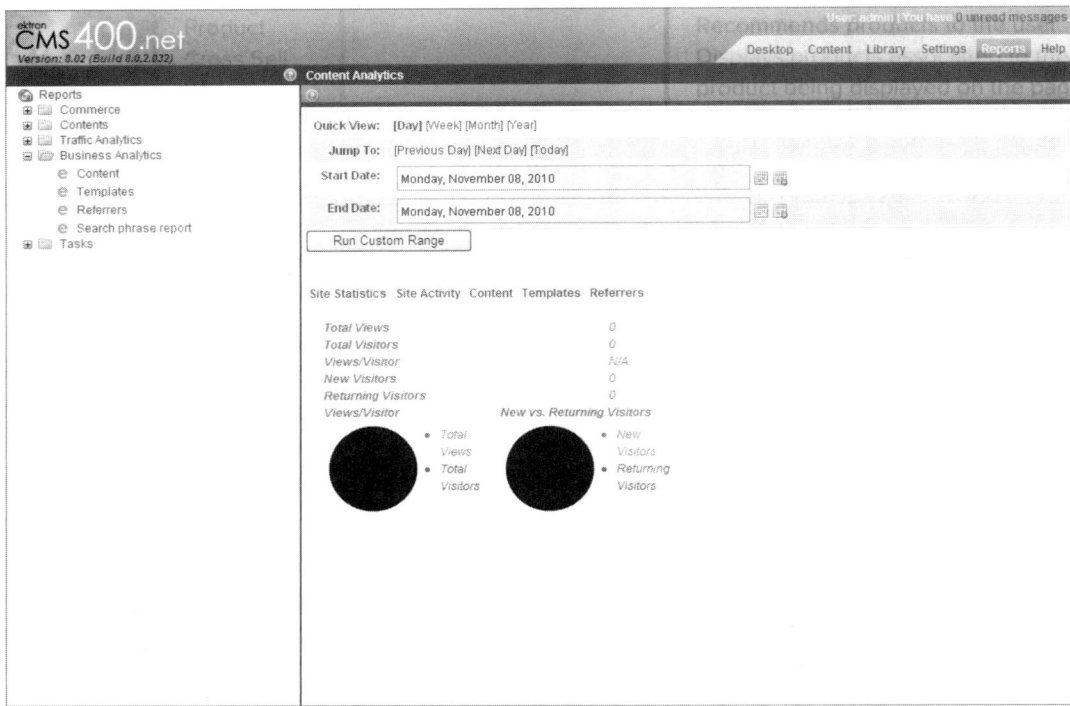

FIGURE 9-35

Setting Up Site Wide Traffic Analytics

These steps assume you are using Google Analytics as your Web Analytics provider. For steps on configuring the Omniture Provider, see the Web Analytics section of the Ektron Reference Manual.

1. If you don't have one already, create a Gmail account (http://www.google.com) and sign up for Google Web Analytics. When you set up a Google Web Analytics profile for your site, you are assigned a Profile ID and a User Account. Take note of these as you will need them to enable Traffic Analytics on your site.

2. On the server that hosts Ektron CMS400.NET, go to c:\program files\ektron\ cms400v80\"Utilities\EncryptEmailPassword.exe.

3. Use that utility to encrypt the Gmail username and password that you obtained.

4. Open your website's web.config file, located in the root of your site.

5. Find the AnalyticsdataProvider tag, which is shown in the following code snippet.

```
<AnalyticsDataProvider defaultProvider="Google">
<providers>
<add name="www.techpoint.com-Google" type="Ektron.Cms.Analytics.Providers.
GoogleAnalyticsProvider,
```

```
Ektron.Cms.BusinessObjects" Username="" Password="" ProfileId="" SiteURL=""
UserAccount=""
GoogleAnalyticsTrackingCodePath="Analytics\template\googletrackingcode.ascx"
/>
    </providers>
</AnalyticsDataProvider>
```

6. Use the element in Table 9-10 to populate the values of the AnalyticsDataProvider.

TABLE 9-10: Elements of the AnalyticsDataProvider Tag

ELEMENT	PURPOSE
Name	The text name of the site being tracked. Ektron recommends using the site name followed by the provider name. For example, `www.techpoint.com-Google`.
Username	The Gmail username you encrypted.
Password	The Gmail password you encrypted.
Profile ID	The Google Analytics Profile ID you obtained during your account creation.
Site URL	The URL of your site. For example, you could set up one `<providers>` tag for the dev.ektron.com site, and another for the www.ektron.com site. Do not include a protocol, such as `http://`. The Site URL needs to match the development site URL when you test in your development environment. For example, if the site path is `http://localhost/default.aspx`, the site URL attribute needs to be localhost. If there is no match, the Google beacon is not inserted onto your page.
User Account	The Google Analytics Site URL you defined during your account creation.

7. You also have the ability to define whether or not you want to include the traffic from CMS or membership users in your reports. Many site administrators want to exclude the activity from these users, and the `SuppressBeacon` setting found in the web.config code snippet below allows you to control this. Table 9-11 that follows lists the possible settings for this element.

```
<analyticsSettings>
    <!-- Valid options: None, Members, Authors, All -->
    <add key="suppressBeacon" value="None"/>
</analyticsSettings>
```

TABLE 9-11: SuppressBeacon Element Settings

VALUE	DESCRIPTION
None	Track all users, including authenticated membership and CMS users.
Members	Track unauthenticated and log-in CMS users only. Do not track membership users.
Authors	Track authenticated and logged-in membership users only. Do not track CMS users.
All	Track unauthenticated users only. Do not track membership and CMS users.

Once the steps to enable Traffic Analytics have been successfully completed, you will see client side tracking code, shown in the snippet that follows, automatically added to each PageBuilder page, as well as any ASP.NET template that contains at least one Ektron Server Control. You can verify site wide Traffic Analytics is configured properly by loading such a Web page, viewing its source, and finding the Google Web beacon.

```
<!-- Start Google Code -->
<script type="text/javascript">
var gaJsHost = (("https:" == document.location.protocol) ? "https://ssl." :
"http://www.");
document.write(unescape("%3Cscript src='" + gaJsHost + "google-analytics.com/ga.js'
type='text/javascript'%3E%3C/script%3E"));
</script>
<script type="text/javascript">
try {
var pageTracker = _gat._getTracker("[USER ACCOUNT STRING]");
pageTracker._trackPageview();
} catch(err) {}</script>
<!-- End Google Code -->
```

Measuring Effectiveness of the Campaign Using Traffic Analytics

To determine the number of times the landing page was viewed by a site visitor:

1. Log in to your website and navigate to the campaign landing page.
2. Hover your cursor over the website Content Menu.
3. Click View Page Activity from the website Content Menu as shown in Figure 9-36 below.
4. The SEO page's Traffic Tab appears with traffic information for this page.

Use the same process to determine the number of impressions to the Request a Demo form, and the number of times the Request a Demo form has been submitted. The click through rate (CTR) can be computed by dividing the number of request a demo form impressions by the page impressions. The conversion rate can be determined by dividing the number of form submissions by the page. Use the formulas shown in Table 9-12 for reference.

TABLE 9-12: Determining the Success of the Request a Demo Campaign

METRIC	DESCRIPTION
Impressions	Visits to the campaign landing page
Click Through Rate	Form impressions ÷ page impressions × 100
Conversions	Form submissions ÷ page impressions × 100

These reports can also be found through the Report section of the Workarea and through the Google Web Analytics Dashboard http://www.google.com/analytics/.

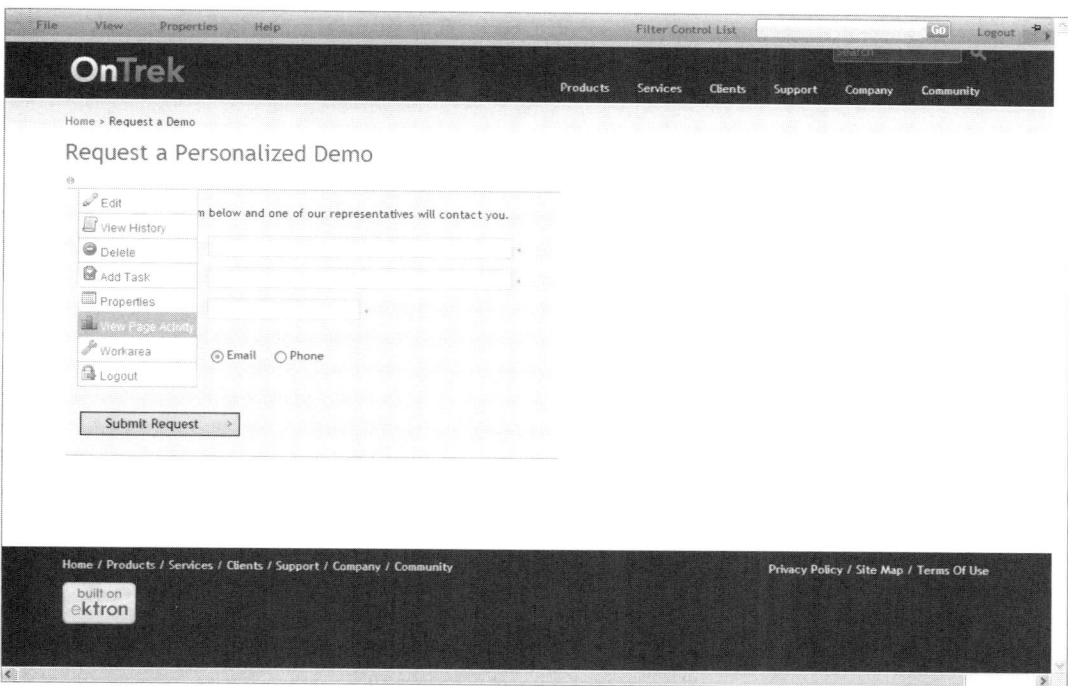

FIGURE 9-36

Under the Hood: Analytics

There may be times when you want to retrieve Traffic Analytics data programmatically from the system to use within the context of a custom report or application. Retrieving data from the Ektron Framework is straightforward and its API simplifies the process of access data from the Traffic Analytics providers, keeping the API classes and methods consistent regardless of which provider is being used. Listing 9-14 provides an example of how to retrieve a report using the Analytics API `GetAllTrafficSources`.

LISTING 9-14: Reports.ascx

Available for download on Wrox.com

```
using Ektron.Cms;
using Ektron.Cms.Analytics;
using Ektron.Cms.Analytics.Reporting;
using Ektron.Cms.Interfaces.Analytics.Provider;
using Ektron.Cms.Analytics.Providers;

class Example()
{
  public void DisplayReport()
```

continues

LISTING 9-14 *(continued)*

```
    {
        // Define the report objects and criteria
        IAnalytics _dataManager = ObjectFactory.GetAnalytics();
        string provider = "techpoint.com-google";
        DateTime startDate = DateTime.Today.AddDays(-1).AddDays(-30);
        DateTime endDate = DateTime.Today.AddDays(-1);
        AnalyticsCriteria criteria = new AnalyticsCriteria();

        // Get traffic sources report
        AnalyticsReportData report =
        _dataManager.GetAllTrafficSources(
    provider, startDate, endDate, criteria);

        // Display report by databing to DataGrid
        DataBind(report);

        // for a complete sample including DataBind(), see
        // c:\Inetpub\CMS400Developer\Workarea\Analytics\reporting\Report.ascx
    }
}
```

If you're planning on using the Business Analytics feature to capture custom defined or CMS events, it is important to know that the logging of these events occurs with each request to a Web page. This means that the application is potentially writing to the database with each Web request. To mitigate the stress that activity could put on the database, the Ektron Framework buffers this data in the website's application memory and keeps it until a predetermined amount of information is collected, at which point the information is written to the database in one transaction. To configure these parameters, open the website's `web.config` file and set the values of the parameters outlined in Table 9-13. Note that decreasing the default values causes an increase in database writes, and increasing the values decreases the frequency in which the database is written to.

TABLE 9-13: Controlling Business Analytics Caching

NAME	DESCRIPTION
recordsBeforeWrite	The number of unique template visits
timeBeforeWrite	The number of seconds since the last time a database write occurred

TAKE HOME POINTS

Now that you've gone through the process of creating a complete landing page that satisfies the business case outlined by OnTrek's marketing department, take a step back to appreciate all that you accomplished and learned.

You placed the right tools in the hands of the right people to generate leads, optimized the process by which these types of campaigns are launched, and provided a clear window into how these campaigns perform. By any measure, you are set up to be a rock star with your marketing department.

To recap, here are the highlights of the technology sections we've covered:

- **Collections:** These provide a way to manage and display a static list of content items. You used collections to provide tight control over the list of documents a site visitor is shown while visiting the campaign landing page. Collections are also language-aware and can require approval before modifications are visible on the website.
- **PageBuilder:** The biggest overall benefit of this is ease of maintenance. Making it a strict requirement that functionality be broken out into widgets forces developers into good habits about encapsulating functionality. It also offloads interface design from developers, meaning there is less housekeeping to do in the long run.
- **Widgets:** These are a powerful method of encompassing functionality in such a way that a developer is no longer required to instantiate them in a given instance. Widgets support a string platform that minimizes the amount of code required, but the tradeoff is they do require a bit more code than simply placing a server control on a given template.
- **HTML forms:** These improve upon standard HTML form technology by providing advanced form input elements like Rich Text Editing and checkbox form validation, and also put form creation in the hands of non-technical authoring and publishing through the WYSIWYG editor.
- **Multivariate Testing:** This involves increasing the conversion rate of a given page and is achieved through varying the layout, graphics, and content of a page through a series of possible configurations and identifying which has the highest conversion rate.
- **Web Analytics:** These are divided into two frameworks. *Traffic Analytics* integrates leading Web analytics providers like Google Analytics and Omniture into the Ektron Framework. *Business Analytics* provides content and user-specific reports, as well as the ability to track and report on custom business events.

ADDITIONAL PRACTICE STEPS

The following exercises aim to broaden your knowledge of PageBuilder and HTML forms. As you've seen, PageBuilder is a nice framework for building and deploying Web pages. The PageBuilder exercises have you trying to create a custom widget, using the Global Widget Data storage, and using PageBuilder master layouts. The practice step related to HTML forms references a KB article to create an HTML form that includes a dynamically populated select list.

- **For an advanced exercise in widget development, try creating a widget.** It should use the Twitter API to retrieve recent tweets from @Ektron and should allow the content author to specify a list of other authors.

➤ **For extra credit, rather than hardcoding @Ektron, make the default user that the widget will follow be configurable in the Global Widget Data for your new widget.** To get started, take a look at the Ektron Twitter Widget, supplied in your installation. It is also available at http://dev.ektron.com/exchange/codedownload.aspx?id=2147483754.

➤ **To extend your knowledge and understanding of PageBuilder, create a new master layout.** Master layouts allow for a layout to serve as the basis for another layout, allowing many pages to share elements in an inherited manner. Create a master layout that has navigation elements in the right column, but leave the center column open for use in layouts using it. For more information on master layouts, check pages 6–27 in the CMS400 Manual, installed with the CMS.

➤ **Consider reusing lists.** When creating an HTML form, you will inevitably repeat the same list of items in many forms, such as a list of products, office locations, and so on. There are Knowledge Base articles that explain how to define and manage a list of items in such a way that you can centrally manage that list making it easy to reuse them across multiple forms. The most popular approach is outlined in KB7244 (Static XML-Driven Datalist). To understand this approach, create a list using the method described in this article (Dynamic Data Driven Datalists: http://dev.ektron.com/kb_article.aspx?id=7244).

10

Supporting Customers

- ➤ How do you support an existing customer base with Forums?
- ➤ How do you use blogs to connect to a community?
- ➤ How can you use a wiki to create community content?
- ➤ Can you use the SocialBar to share pages and media?
- ➤ What's the easiest way to get feedback on content?

So far you have worked on managing the content and information architecture of your site. You made sure the navigational elements help clients find the content they are looking for quickly and accurately, and you had begun to explore community outreach in the form of calendars and surveys. The next step is to foster a deeper community, a natural meeting ground for the people who work with your product on a day-to-day basis. Getting your customers interacting on your site is one of the key pieces to building a community around your product.

One of the fundamentals of creating that type of interplay is allowing users to author content on your site, and manage it through the overall lifecycle. To that end, in this chapter you will review some of the basic building blocks to help your site garner more user interaction.

This chapter also covers some of the control mechanisms available to manage all this user-generated content. The ContentReview Server Control and ContentFlagging Server Control allow you to farm out moderation duties to your user base, and easily run reports to ensure that all the content you are exposing to the world is in good shape.

Of course, none of these features will bind your users into a community if you have no users. So, this chapter also covers the SocialBar Server Control, which allows your visitors to post, tweet, update Facebook statuses, and invite others to view the page without ever leaving it. This can help you to grow your user base organically by tapping into the social network of all your users.

UNDERSTANDING THE TECHNOLOGY

In this chapter you will cover a disparate group of technologies. They are all tools to drive customer interaction. Some of the classic tools discussion in this section have been around since the early days of the Internet, and some are more targeted at the particulars of the Ektron environment. All share the common ability to get users more involved and to generate a sense of collaboration.

Forums

Forums are one of the best ways to support an existing customer base. An evolutionary descendant of dial-up bulletin board systems and gaining in popularity in the 90s, forums have a long history of being a natural way of managing non-real-time conversations. Because they've been around so long, most Internet users are very comfortable at this point understanding how to interact with them.

As an example, Ektron uses forums extensively in the DevCenter to foster a community of developers. Even though the forum is on an Ektron property, questions are frequently answered by other users because of the depth and successful nature of this community.

Much like some other features covered in this section, forums also have the benefit of assisting not only a single customer, but every customer who comes to the site later with the same question.

Because of this reusability, many companies have decided to make forums their front-line support mechanism, backed up by a knowledge base, or wiki. This pairing of features allows for your company to disseminate answers to common and difficult questions, as well as to support the day-to-day needs of your existing and potential customer base.

The Ektron Framework's forum feature is a deep and well-developed piece of functionality. It's constructed from a basis of folders and content, with many boards being contained in a single forum folder. Each board then contains many topics, with each topic being an individual piece of content. The topics then contain responses, which are stored as associated data in a separate table.

The forum has several server controls specifically designed to display forum data, but because the data is comprised of fundamental content types, the rest of the server controls designed to interact with or rely on content, such as the ListSummary and ContentBlock, also work with topics. This makes the forum, like many other framework features, a very capable and extensible system. In addition to the server controls, there is a strong API available to retrieve and work with forum data.

Like so many other Ektron features, a wide variety of control mechanisms can be used without any complication with the particular data type. For instance, attaching a ContentReview Server Control to a post is easy.

Blogs

This feature can increase user involvement and communication. As a Web landmark, blogs have been around since 1994, and have exploded in popularity over the past 10 years. Many companies have successfully used blogs to keep customers and clients in the loop on key issues while posting very high hit numbers. For instance, the Google Blog at `googleblog.blogspot.com` posted as the 18th most popular blog on the Internet in the week of August 27, 2010. It only lost out to professional blogs like the Huffington Post, Gizmodo, and Engadget. Blogs can be a very key tool for your organization to drive user interaction.

The next piece of technology you will explore is the blog feature. Blogs in the Ektron Framework, like forums, are basically standard content. The major differentiators between blogs and standard content are the additional abilities (such as a calendar displaying dates of blog entries) that the server controls designed for blogs provide. The main Blog Server Control is actually composed of several smaller server controls, each of which provides for a particular desired function. This makes it very easy to mix and match the functionality for the specific requirements at hand. You'll explore the creation, moderation, and development of blogs in this section.

Wiki

This is a slightly more recent, but certainly no less popular, feature that the Ektron platform provides as part of its framework. Because one of the most trafficked websites on the Internet is Wikipedia, it's unlikely that any Web-savvy person has possibly avoided this type of tool. It's become a prized way of building an interacting customer base, due to the fact that any visitor can produce content. Ektron has made it a little easier to create this type of feature as a wiki in the Ektron Framework because:

- The ContentBlock Server Control allows you to display the content.
- The ListSummary Server Control provides simple navigation.
- The same rich text editor you use in the Workarea is used for the wiki on the front end.
- Community folders are the only basic folder type that allows membership users to create and manage content within them.

What this means is that your customers don't have to learn anything new to contribute to your wiki, including avoiding custom markup. The wikis simply operate in a Word-like environment. In-context editing is supported.

In this chapter you will build the wiki onto a PageBuilder page. You will then build a widget to explore the two final feature sets — the SocialBar Server Control and content flagging and review — which you will place onto the wiki PageBuilder page, easily and quickly extending its capabilities to allow for customer outreach as well as moderation and reporting on content usefulness. You will explore how to implement these features as well as how to use them going forward with respect to content-management needs.

In summary, the rest of this chapter covers the following in more detail:

- Forums
- Blogs
- Wikis
- The SocialBar Widget
- Content flagging and content review

USE CASE

This section gives you a continuation of the use cases that started in Chapter 7. It connects the exercises you will perform in this chapter with the plan laid out in the implementation guide, and puts a story to the features we will cover in this chapter, specifically the set of community building tools consisting of Forums, Wikis, Blogs, community authoring, and feedback tools.

> **ADDING A FORUM, A BLOG, AND A WIKI TO THE SITE**
>
> With the successful build-out of functionality of OnTrek's base site, the Director of Marketing would like to capture some excitement and involvement from the customer base the company has been cultivating over the past several years. To that end, marketing wants to add a forum for structured conversations, and a blog to help customers track OnTrek's business and technical directions. Marketing also wants a wiki for documentation and as a repository for less structured content. Finally, there's been a push to allow customers to easily tap into their social networks as a word-of-mouth mechanism. In addition to these basics, marketing wants to make sure that there are safeties in place, since much of the content for these new features may come from untrustworthy sources.
>
> This Use Case introduces the primary actor Derek, (a site visitor who has specific technical questions about the product), describes the expected scenario, and defines the desired outcome.
>
> ## Wireframe
>
> The example Wireframe for this chapter, shown in Figure 10-1, is the Support Forum page. This page contains the Forum Server Control. We will be covering features from additional sections of the Implementation Guide in this chapter as well.
>
> ## Description
>
> This three-piece implementation will addresses five separate needs. The third part of the implementation covers the last three needs.
>
> - A forum as a first line defense for support issues, which resides on its own page.
> - A CEO blog, which helps customers to understand the direction of OnTrek and managements goals. This also resides on its own page.
> - A PageBuilder-based wiki that serves as a documentation repository and promotes customer involvement. The wiki will also provide for the needs of word-of-mouth promotions, as well as flagging and reviewing of content.

Use Case | **337**

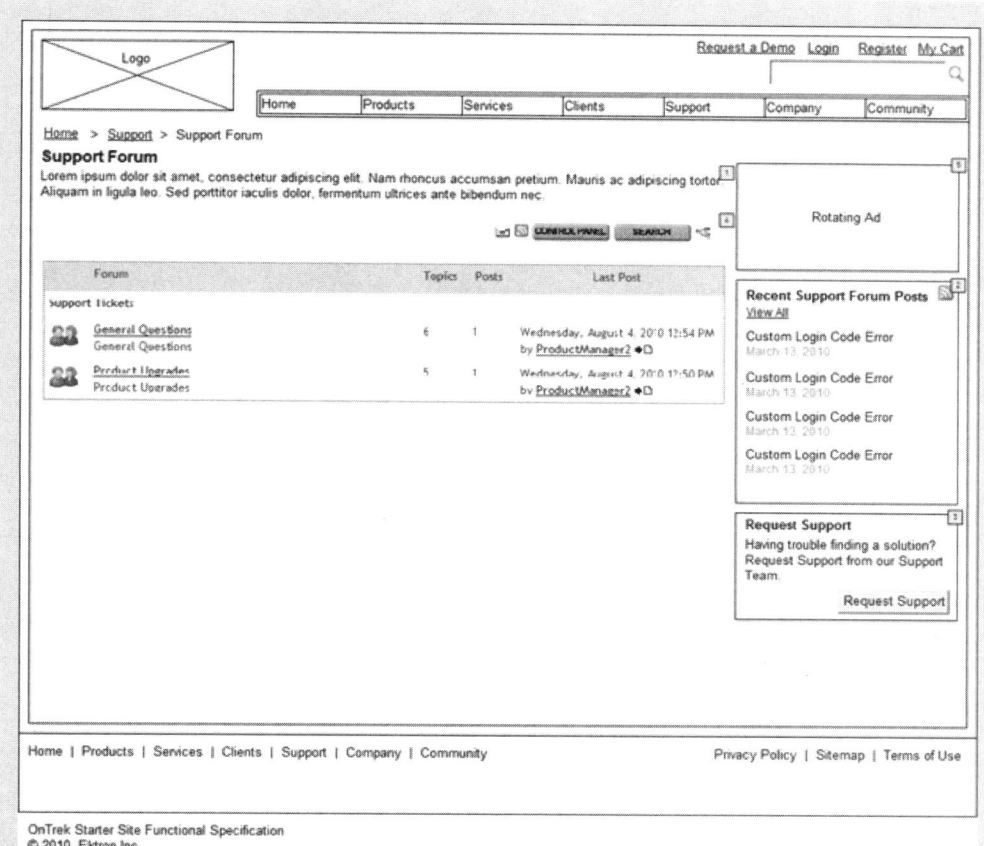

FIGURE 10-1

Actor

Derek is an employee at Acme Inc. Having selected OnTrek's venerable Doodad solution, he is now implementing it and has run into a road block. He is now attempting to use OnTrek's website to find a good solution to his technical issue. He wants to use the website as a primary resource rather than calling support immediately.

Scenario

In this scenario, Derek:

➤ Connects to the OnTrek site looking for a way to connect with other developers and potentially OnTrek support.

➤ Locates the forums and performs a search for similar issues, without finding any results.

continues

(continued)

> ➤ Posts the inquiry about his particular problem.
>
> ➤ Scans the documentation wiki for a solution to his issue.
>
> ➤ Flags a piece of content on the wiki as "needs updating" because it appears to refer to an older version of the product.
>
> ➤ Locating a page that discusses his issue, he notices a tip that solves his problem. Because the tip is something that should be made more visible, he adds a link through the editing functionality of the wiki.
>
> ➤ Solves his problem and continues on to the CEO blog, interested in what kinds of features are being analyzed for the next version of the OnTrek Suite. It already slices and dices; Derek is hoping that the next version will also julienne fries. Finding out that it does, he cross posts the blog to his Twitter account.
>
> **Outcome**
>
> The OnTrek team benefits from Derek's exercise because he made their documentation more concise, notified them about outdated content, and extended OnTrek's outreach through his social network.

BUILDING FORUMS

Ektron has provided forum capabilities since version 6 of CMS400.Net. The feature relies on the support infrastructure that is provided by the core content concepts in the Ektron Framework. Unlike many forum solutions on the market, the level of integration between forums and the rest of the framework is very strong, while still providing a full set of unique features such as RSS feeds of posts and sub-categorization of topics.

By relying on folders to create the information architecture of your forum, your site administrators can leverage their existing knowledge to manage the structure of the forums without having to learn a different system. This integration means better response time between changing support needs and implementation, which ultimately leads to a better overall customer experience.

This section discusses how the forums store data, and how they integrate with the rest of the Ektron Framework. You will create a forum, and then implement the forum control on an example page. You will then learn how to interact with the Forum Server Control from the front end of the site. Finally, this section discusses how to customize the forum, and some of the other controls and APIs that allow you to retrieve related data. The specific tasks in this section you will complete are the following:

➤ Creating forums in the Workarea

➤ Implementing the Forum Server Control

➤ Interacting with the Forum Server Control

➤ Using additional server controls, APIs, and customizations

Creating Forums in the Workarea

The forum feature in the Ektron Framework is built on the same foundation as Folders and Content. The structure of the forum mechanism, as you will see, is based around the concepts of boards, which contain forums, which contain topics. A *board* is a type of folder that can only contain other folders of the forum type. Forums, in turn, can contain topics, which are actually a single piece of content. Topic responses are stored in the Task table associated with the topic.

This construction means that a list of topics can be generated through something as simple as the ListSummary Server Control. It also means that topics can support taxonomy and content ratings. Content ratings are commonly used by enabling the `EnableThreadRating` property on the Forum Server Control, because other people's opinions on the usefulness of the content can aid users in scanning the topic list. Taxonomy is also gaining acceptance in allowing for additional, deeper categorization of posts. When combined with the Search function, this allows users to easily find topics that relate to their areas of interest.

The OnTrek site comes with a Discussion Board created at the path MainSite/Content/Support/Support Forums. Rather than recreating the forums that already exist in the site, you will create a new section for discussing Local User Groups. This section allows customers to connect at a local level, and discuss what they learned through the company outreach program. Customers can discuss their expectations and issues, and provide feedback to the OnTrek marketing team. You start with two local user groups: one in New York and one in San Francisco. Because the forums are based so closely on folders, the marketing team can utilize their existing knowledge and understanding of the Ektron Framework to create more forums as required.

Understanding the Forum Creation Flow

To create a forum in the Workarea, follow these steps:

1. Log into your site as admin and navigate to the Workarea.

2. Switch to the Content tab, and navigate the content tree to MainSite/Content/Community.

3. Create the board and define the topics for the board. Within the topic, create your forums (more about this in the next sections).

    Topics will then be created by users on the site, and responses will be added to those topics. This flow is shown in Figure 10-2.

4. Once in the Community folder, hover over the New menu. As shown in Figure 10-3, one of the options available is Discussion Board, the topic of our next section.

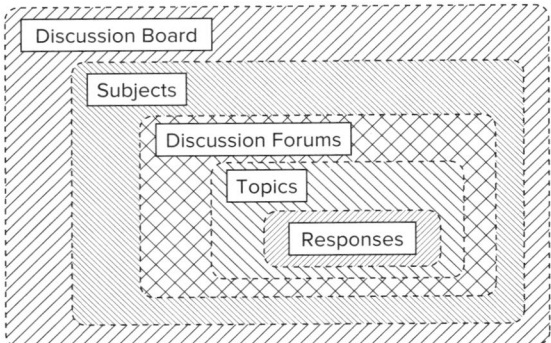

FIGURE 10-2

Creating a Discussion Board

You can create boards anywhere in the folder tree, and they inherit options from parent folders just as other folders do. A board, however, is limited in its contents — it can only support forums within it, and only topics can be created in forums.

Clicking New ➪ Discussion Board (see Figure 10-3) brings up the Add Discussion Board interface. This interface accepts all the key elements required to create the new board. It is comprised of three tabs outlined here: Properties, Template, and Subjects.

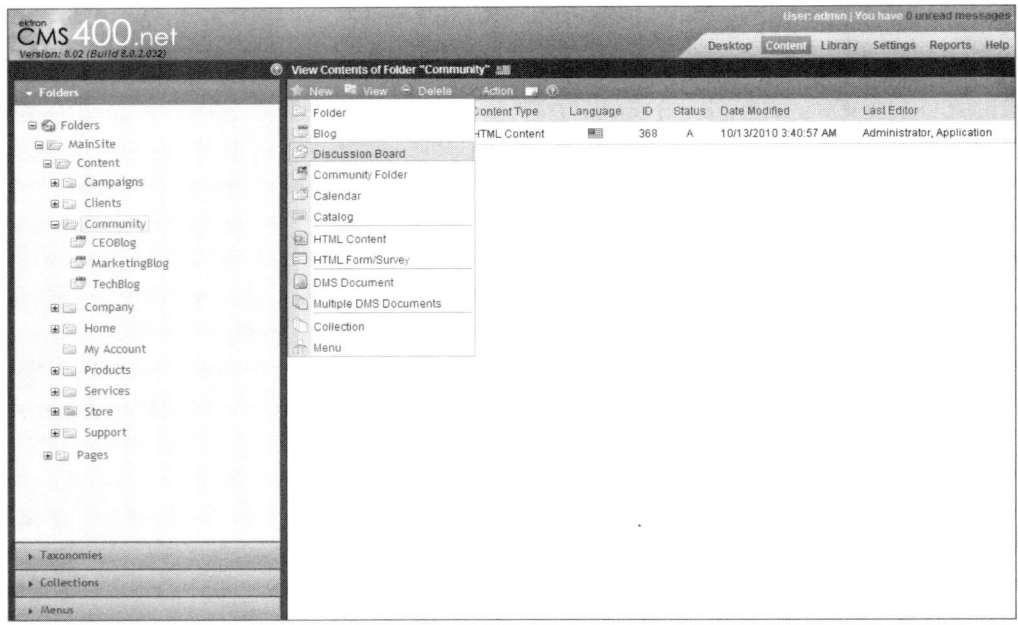

FIGURE 10-3

To create your new board, following these steps:

1. Click New ➪ Discussion Board (as shown in Figure 10-3).

2. Click the Properties tab (shown in Figure 10-4). This is where the basic information about the board is entered. The options include:

   ➤ **Name:** This is the Board name and it displays in the content tree in the Workarea.

   ➤ **Title:** This is displayed at the top of the Forum Server Control on the Web page.

   ➤ **Require Authentication option:** Determines whether users are required to log in to the site in order to post.

   ➤ **CSS Theme:** This controls the overall look and feel of the forum control when rendered. There are many options, each of which constitutes a different visual theme, allowing you to match the forum control to the feel of the rest of your site.

   ➤ **Style Sheet:** Allows you to specify an additional CSS file to control the visual representation of the text of posts within the forum and editor.

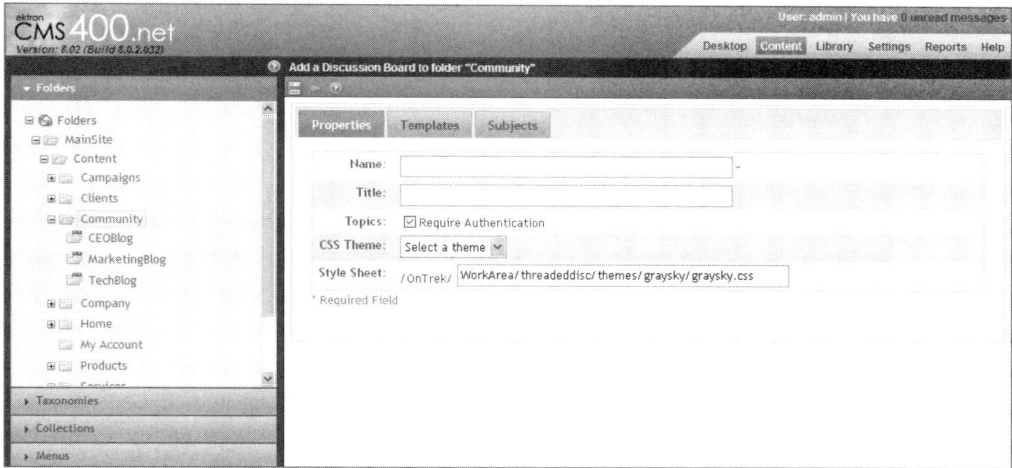

FIGURE 10-4

3. For the name and title, enter **Community Forums**.
4. Make sure Require Authentication is unchecked.
5. For the CSS Theme, select **Modern**.
6. Leave the stylesheet at its default value.
7. Click the Templates tab (shown in Figure 10-5). This tab allows you to select which template to use to render the posts in the forum. This is used primarily to control the creation of the QuickLinks for the forum posts.
8. For the template, select Login.aspx. You need to change this later when you have created the template that this board will be displayed on.
9. Click the Subjects tab (shown in Figure 10-6). This tab allows you to categorize the forums available into groups. This means that the subjects are not actual subfolders, but they still

group content together in the Workarea and the Forum Server Control. You'll be creating subject — **Local User Groups**. Your forums will be created within this subject since they all belong to that group.

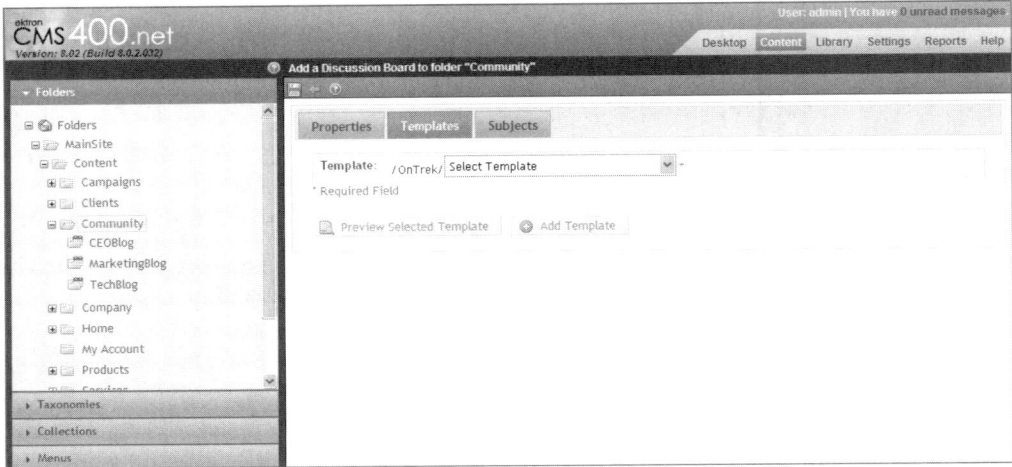

FIGURE 10-5

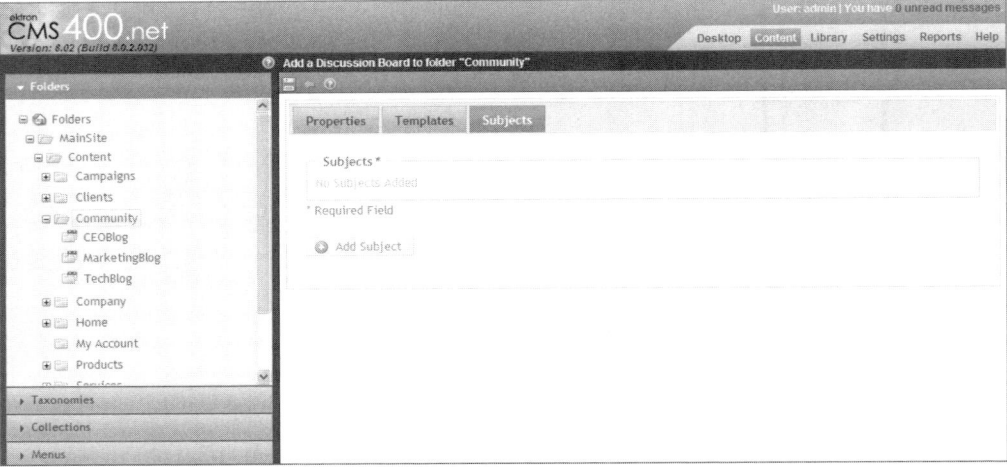

FIGURE 10-6

10. Click Save. This returns you to the content list view for the Community folder.

11. Select the newly created forum from the content tree to switch to the forum list view in the Content pane, as shown in Figure 10-7.

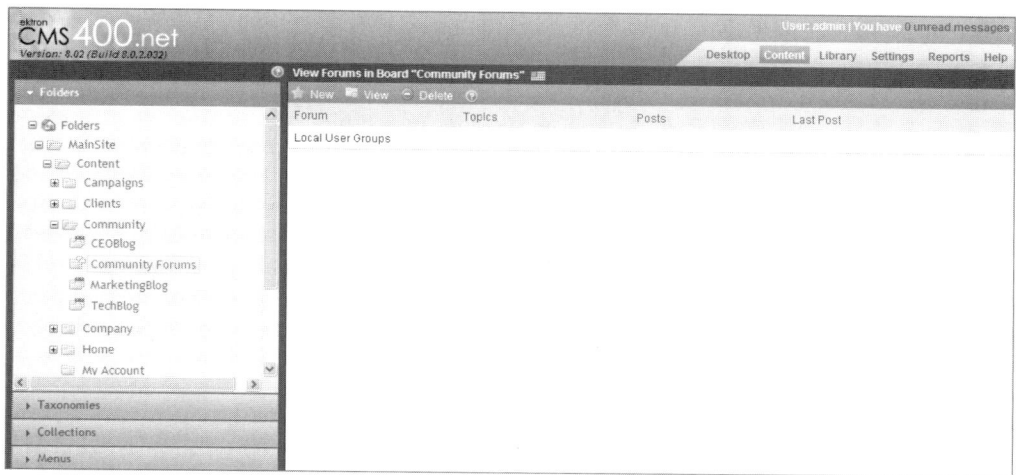

FIGURE 10-7

Understanding Discussion Forum Properties

Before you continue to create the discussion forums, go to the board's properties by clicking View ⇨ Properties. Normally in the Ektron Framework for folders, the properties are very similar to the interface shown when creating a new folder. However, in this case, you have a long list of newly available fields. Let's run through the new ones quickly in the following list.

➤ **Properties:** Shown in Figure 10-8, this has many more fields available when editing an existing board:

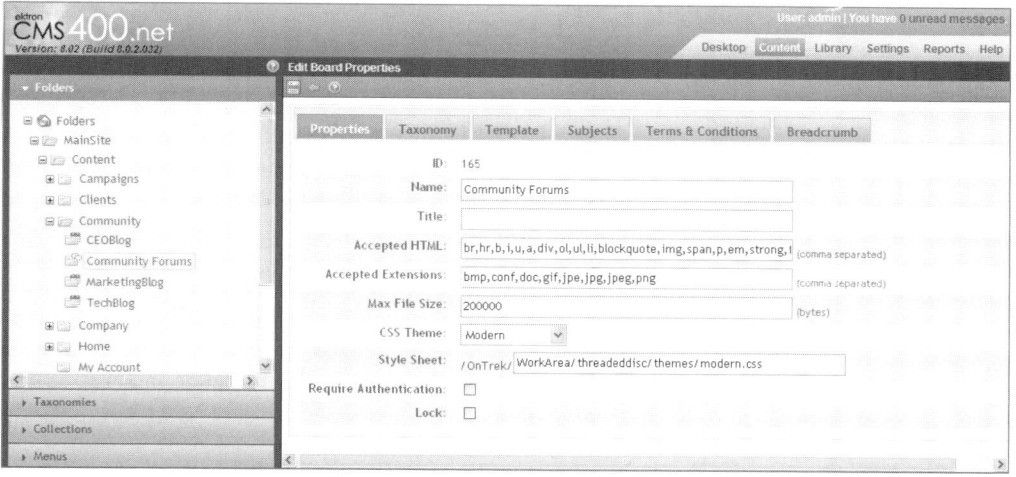

FIGURE 10-8

➤ **Accepted HTML field:** Allows you to specify a comma-delimited list of the HTML tags that are allowed in posts and comments. By default, the embed tag is not allowed, but depending on your site, you may want to add it to the list.

➤ **Accepted Extensions list:** Specifies which files may be uploaded as attachments. The notable exceptions you may want to override in this field are extensions relating to videos.

➤ **Lock:** This field to specify whether the board is locked. If a board is locked, no one can post topics or responses to it.

➤ **Taxonomy:** Shown in Figure 10-9, this allows you to specify whether topics must be categorized, as well as determine which taxonomy to attach to the board. These options allow users to specify which category nodes to search within.

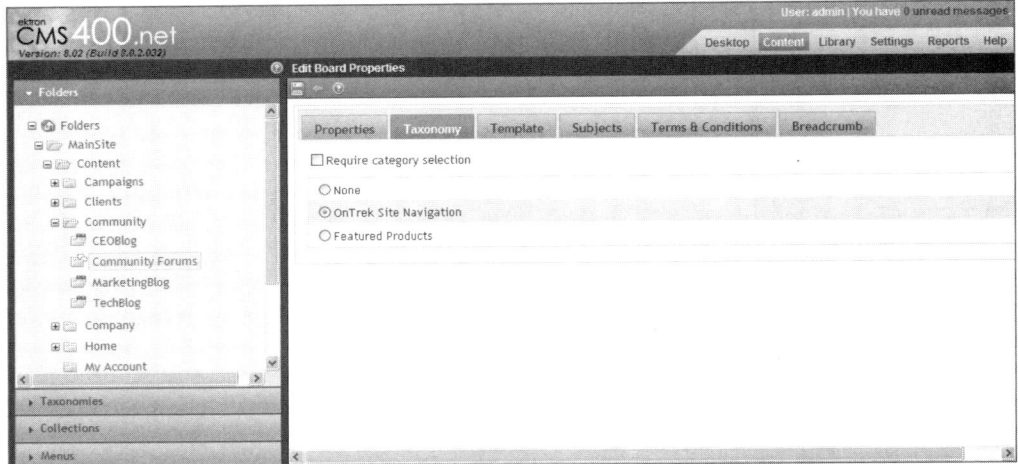

FIGURE 10-9

➤ **Template:** This tab is unchanged from the add board interface.

➤ **Subjects:** This tab is also unchanged from the add board interface.

➤ **Terms & Conditions:** Shown in Figure 10-10, this allows you to specify verbiage that users must accept before they are allowed to post a new topic or a response to a topic. Users are required to accept the terms only once, after which they are free to interact with the board.

➤ **Breadcrumb:** Shown in Figure 10-11, this tab allows you to define the breadcrumb for the board and forums underneath it.

Building Forums | **345**

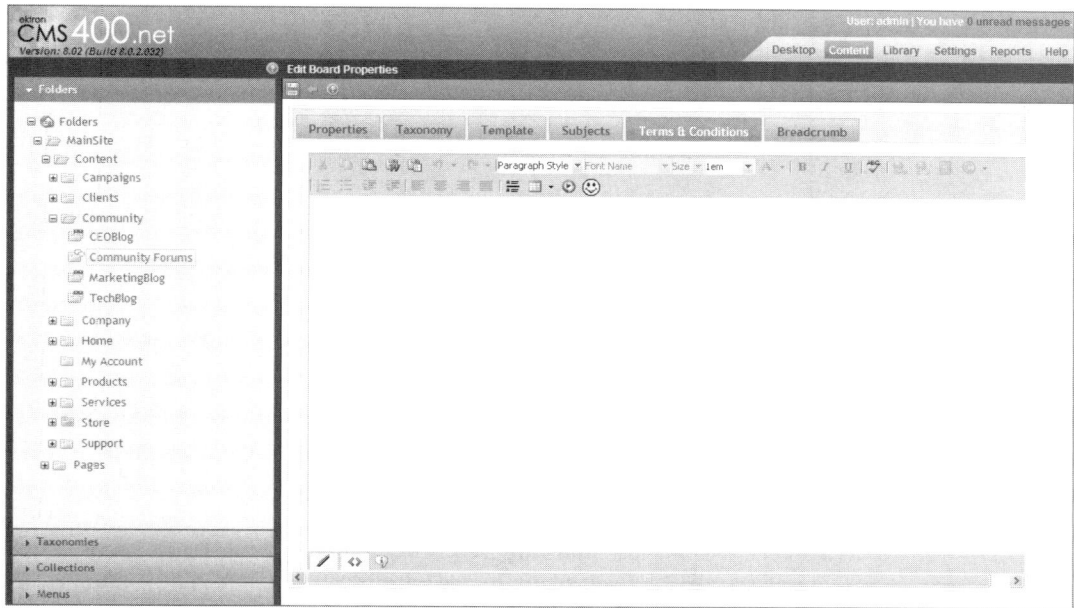

FIGURE 10-10

FIGURE 10-11

Creating Forums

At this point, you need to create two forums, one for New York, and one for San Francisco. To do so, follow these steps:

1. Hovering over the New menu, you see that there are many options that you haven't seen on other folders:

   ➤ **The Discussion Forum:** Allows you to create the individual forums that comprise the board.

   ➤ **Subject:** The internal group used to categorize posts.

   ➤ **Restricted IP:** Allows you to create a blacklist preventing problem users from posting to the board.

   ➤ **Replace Word:** Allows you to create word filters — a common use case is to create a bad word filter that automatically removes inappropriate words from user posts.

   ➤ **User Rank:** Allows you to create a ladder system so that users browsing the site can see at a glance which other users are frequently interacting with the system. It allows you to name the ranks, associate an image with each rank, and set the number of posts required to attain the rank. This information is then displayed with the user details whenever they post to the board.

2. Click New ➪ Discussion Forum now to create the new forums. The interface to create the forum is shown in Figure 10-12.

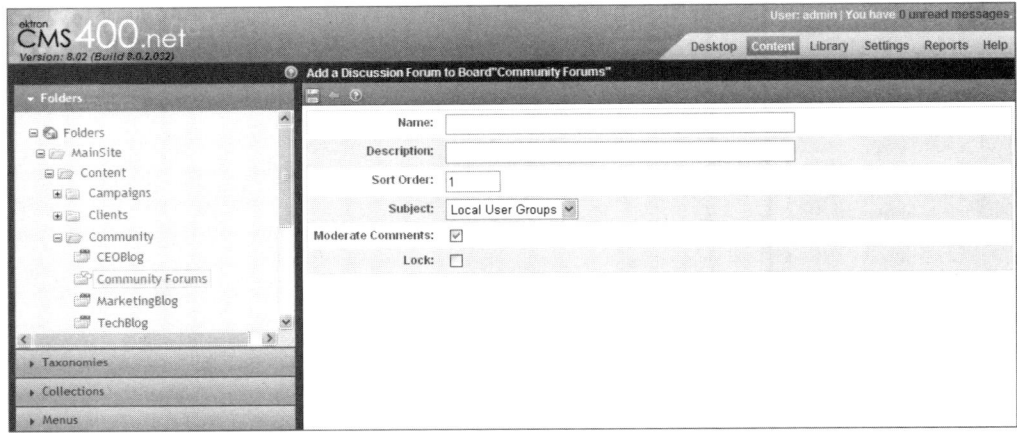

FIGURE 10-12

The fields shown on the Add Discussion Forum pane are explained in Table 10-1.

TABLE 10-1: Fields on the Add Discussion Forum Form

FIELD	DESCRIPTION
Name	Name of the forum. This is displayed in the list of forums on the Forum Server Control and in the Workarea.
Description	This is displayed just under the name and helps users to navigate to the appropriate location for their topic.
Sort Order	Allows you to specify what order to display the forums in within each topic. When the sort order is equivalent, alphabetical order is used. If you were to create both forums with a sort order value of 1, as in this example, the forums would be sorted ascending alphabetically.
Subject	Specifies which group this forum will be displayed in.
Moderate Comments	Sets whether the comments should go live immediately or whether they should not be displayed until a moderator specifies that they are acceptable.
Lock	If a forum is locked, no user can post new topics or responses to that forum.

3. Enter the details for your two forums now. Set the name of the first forum to **New York**, and the Description to **A place to discuss your user group expectations and experiences**. Leave the sort order as 1, and make sure that Moderate Comments is unchecked.

4. Click Save.

5. Repeat steps 2-4 with the same settings for the San Francisco forum. When finished, the Community Forums forum list will show your two new forums. These are, of course, empty at this point.

You'll now jump to Visual Studio to create the template for your forums.

Implementing the Forum Server Control

Like the previous examples, you can create a blank template to explore the options for the Forum Server Controls without the distraction of an intricate page surrounding it. To do so, follow these steps:

1. Open your site in Visual Studio and create a new Web Form in the root of the site.

2. Call it **UserGroupForum.aspx**, and set the language to Visual C# with the code in a separate file.

3. Once it has completed, drag the Forum Server Control from the Ektron section of the toolbox onto the document between the `Form` tags. Your code should now look like the following Listing 10-1.

LISTING 10-1: UserGroupForum.aspx

Available for download on Wrox.com

```
<%@ Page Language="C#" AutoEventWireup="true"
  CodeFile="UserGroupForum.aspx.cs" Inherits="UserGroupForum" %>
<%@ Register Assembly="Ektron.Cms.Controls"
  Namespace="Ektron.Cms.Controls" TagPrefix="CMS" %>

<!DOCTYPE html PUBLIC "-//W3C//DTD XHTML 1.0 Transitional//EN"
  "http://www.w3.org/TR/xhtml1/DTD/xhtml1-transitional.dtd">

<html xmlns="http://www.w3.org/1999/xhtml">
<head runat="server">
  <title></title>
</head>
<body>
  <form id="form1" runat="server">
  <div>
    <CMS:Forum ID="Forum1" runat="server" />
  </div>
  </form>
</body>
</html>
```

The Forum control has a long list of properties that can be set to change the behavior. These properties and their explanations are listed in Table 10-2.

TABLE 10-2: Forum Server Control Properties

PROPERTY	DESCRIPTION
AllowAnonymousPost	If set to true, the control adds a checkbox to the posting interface, allowing users to specify that the post should be created anonymously.
BoardID	Specifies the ID of the discussion board to display.
DefaultObjectID	Specifies a community group ID. If one exists, the Forum Server Control then displays that group's Community Forum.
DynamicForumParameter	Sets the query string parameter that contains the forum ID. Defaults to "f."
DynamicGroupParameter	Sets the query string parameter that contains the community group ID. Defaults to "g."
DynamicParameter	Sets the query string parameter that contains the board ID. If set to None - Use Default, only uses the value specified in `BoardID`.
DynamicThreadParameter	Sets the query string parameter that contains the thread ID. Defaults to "t."

PROPERTY	DESCRIPTION
EditorCSS	Overrides the stylesheet to use inside the JavaScript editor presented to the users when posting.
EditorToolbar	Overrides the default toolbars available inside the editor when posting topics or comments. Set as a comma-separated list, the default value is "StyleMenu,FontMenu,ParagraphMenu,TextFormatMenu,LinkMenu,ClipBoardMenu,SymbolsMenu,EmoticonSelect,WMV,Table."
EnableForumQuickSelect	If set to true, a dropdown with a list of all the forums is rendered under the topic list, allowing users to quickly jump to a different forum.
EnableThreadRating	If set to true, a five star rating control is rendered whenever a topic is displayed, allowing users to rate the thread. Additionally, the average ratings for each topic will be displayed inline in the topic display view.
JavaScriptEditorHeight	The height of the editor in pixels. Defaults to 400, with a minimum of 300.
JavaScriptEditorWidth	The width of the editor in pixels. Defaults to 625, with a minimum of 500.
ObjectType	Can be set to `CommunityGroup` or `DiscussionBoard`, and sets the type of object to retrieve.
ProfileLink	Formats the link to use when a user clicks on another user's link or avatar. The default is `?g=profile&u={0}`. There are two tokens that can be used in the url: `{0}` is replaced by the user's ID, and `{1}` is replaced by the user's display name.
ShowCategories	If set to true, the server control displays a filter by category option which allows them to navigate within a forum by taxonomy.
Theme	Overrides the theme set for the board in the Workarea. Prepend the path with a "/" to make it relative to the site root; otherwise it is relative to the current path.

4. Returning to the code, update the `BoardID` property to reflect the board you just created. Make sure to update the ID to reflect what it is in your installation. There is one other modification you must make to the page, which is to set `ValidateRequest` to false. This is because the forum control posts HTML back to the server, which, by default, causes ASP .NET to throw an error. The following code snippet shows the updated code.

```
<%@ Page Language="C#" AutoEventWireup="true"
  CodeFile="UserGroupForum.aspx.cs" Inherits="UserGroupForum"
  ValidateRequest="false" %>
```

```
<%@ Register Assembly="Ektron.Cms.Controls"
  Namespace="Ektron.Cms.Controls" TagPrefix="CMS" %>

<!DOCTYPE html PUBLIC "-//W3C//DTD XHTML 1.0 Transitional//EN"
  "http://www.w3.org/TR/xhtml1/DTD/xhtml1-transitional.dtd">

<html xmlns="http://www.w3.org/1999/xhtml">
<head runat="server">
  <title></title>
</head>
<body>
  <form id="form1" runat="server">
  <div>
    <CMS:Forum ID="Forum1" runat="server" BoardID="165" />
  </div>
  </form>
</body>
</html>
```

Now when you load the page in the browser, you are presented with the fully rendered Forum Server Control, displaying your one subject containing two forums. This is shown in Figure 10-13.

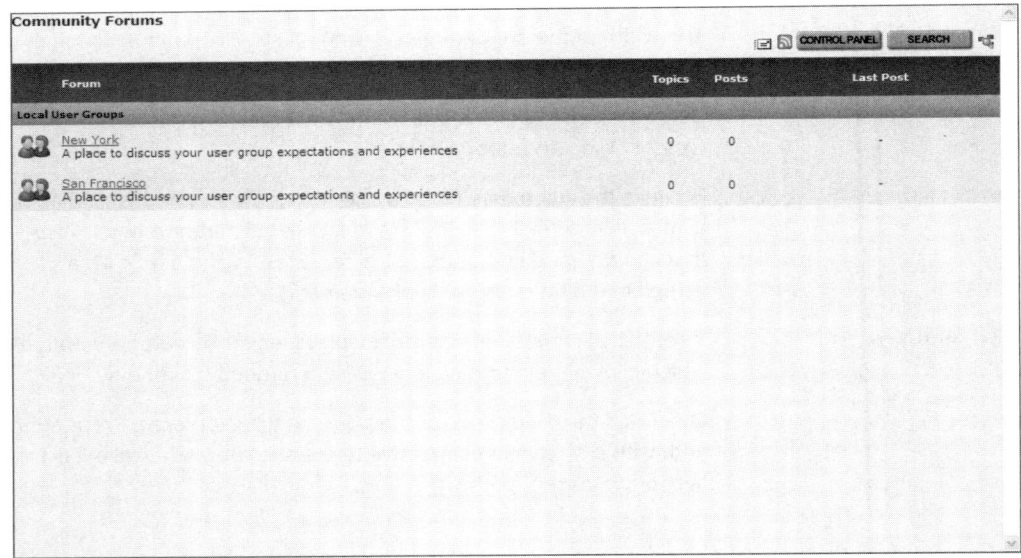

FIGURE 10-13

Interacting with the Forum Server Control

The front end of the Forum Server Control is going to be familiar to most Internet users. The initial display lists the available forums.

Follow these simple steps to view the forum:

1. Click any forum name to reveal a display listing its topics.

2. Click New Topic at the top of the display of the control. This displays the interface for adding posts to the forum, which is shown in Figure 10-14.

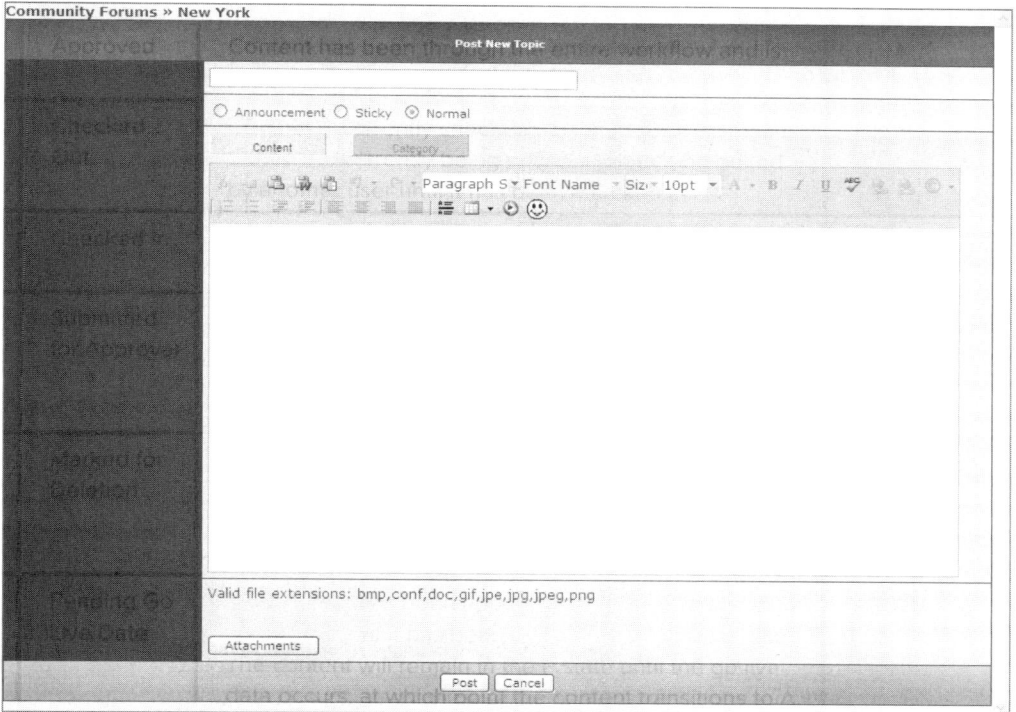

FIGURE 10-14

The interface for adding a post allows the users to specify the title, declare what type of post it is, enter the post itself, add attachments, and categorize the post. Once they're done, users must click Post to return to the list of topics.

Returning to the forum view as shown in Figure 10-15, there are a couple items at the top alongside the new topic button that may not be immediately obvious.

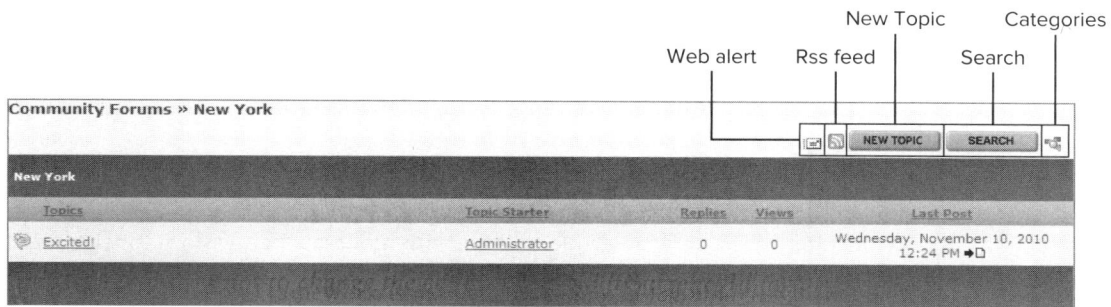

FIGURE 10-15

From left to right, the icons are as follows:

- **Web alert:** In a system with Web alerts set up, this allows users to subscribe to the forum to receive e-mail alerts when new topics are posted, or when responses are posted to existing topics.
- **RSS feed:** This summarizes the recent posts into a feed to be viewed in any RSS 2.0 capable viewer.
- **New Topic:** Allows the user to add a new topic or thread to the board where other users can respond.
- **Search:** The search interface allows users to perform a plain text search within a particular forum or across the entire board.
- **Categories:** This button displays a directory control relating back to the taxonomy defined for the board. This can be a simple way of allowing users to find topics relating to a particular issue with more granularity than just the list of forums within the board.

The final area available to forum users is the Control Panel. By returning to the board display rather than the forum display, the list of icons at the top right of the interface is updated, and the Control Panel button replaces the Add Topic button. Clicking the Add Topic button brings users to the Control Panel interface shown in Figure 10-16. The sections in the forum display are as follows:

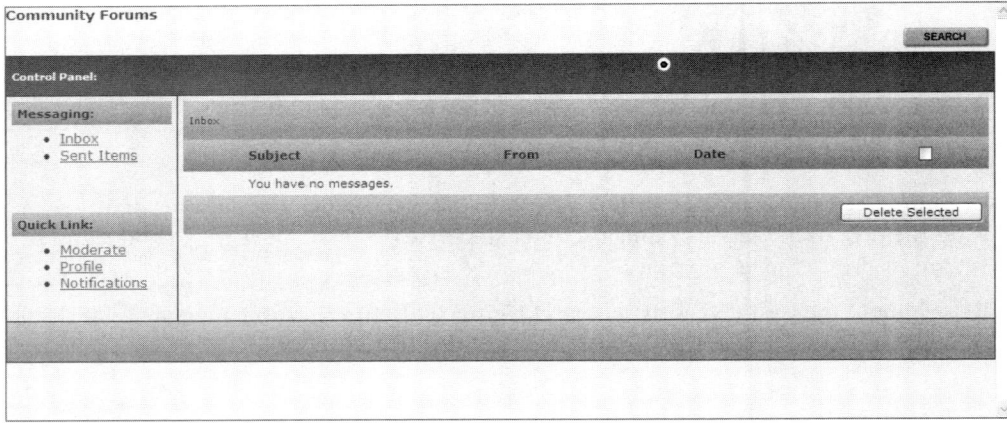

FIGURE 10-16

- **Messaging:** This is based around messaging, which allows users of the system to send notes to each other.
- **Quick Link:** These are links to a couple of other key areas:
  - **Moderate:** This is only available to users with moderate permissions for the board or forum. It allows the users to see posts that have not yet been moderated and to either approve or reject them.

> **Profile:** Clicking this displays recent posts by the user, as well as statistics about the user. It also includes a button to message the selected user.
> **Notifications:** Allows users to manage their subscriptions throughout the board.

Additional Server Controls and APIs

Now that you've learned about the fundamentals of the forum feature in the Ektron Framework, there are some peripheral areas that you should be aware of. In addition to the Forum Server Control, there are two other controls that return information about boards in the system.

> **ActiveTopics Server Control:** This returns the specified number of most recent topics in the board. This is similar to the way the ListSummary Server Control responds when it is pointed at a particular board. However, in this case the ListSummary only looks at the modified date of the original topic post, and ignores the responses when calculating the age of the topic. The ActiveTopics Server Control, by comparison, looks at the age of the most recent response to determine which links to display. When instantiating the server control, specify the board ID to examine, or optionally you can specify the query string parameters to evaluate instead. The ActiveTopics Server Control is instantiated using the following code snippet.
>
> ```
> <CMS:ActiveTopics ID="ActiveTopics1" runat="server" BoardID="125" />
> ```
>
> **PostHistory Server Control:** This is another server control that can help you with alternate displays. It displays a list of recently posted topics or responses submitted by a particular user. Because it is limited to a single user, both the board ID and the user ID need to be specified on this control. This control is instantiated through the following code.
>
> ```
> <CMS:PostHistory ID="PostHistory1" runat="server" BoardID="125" UserID="1" />
> ```
>
> **APIs:** In addition to the server controls to retrieve and display this information, there are a couple of key APIs that allow you to retrieve or update information relating to discussion boards". The `Ektron.Cms.API.Content` namespace contains a class called `ThreadedDiscussion`. The `ThreadedDiscussion` object, when instantiated, exposes several methods that are useful for programmatically controlling your boards. For instance, there are methods for `AddForum`, `DeleteForum`, and `GetForum`. There are also methods for managing forum subscriptions as well as getting the forums in a board and getting the active topics within a forum.

BLOGS

Like discussion forums, blogs have been on the Internet since the beginning of time. Like forums, blogs are stored in the system as a special type of folder, with special content within that folder. They are rendered by the Blog Server Control, which is actually a composite of several other controls. Because they are comprised of normal content, they have the same features as regular content, including metadata, taxonomy, and searchability.

Blogs serve as a great way to connect to the community around your company. Many tech companies use blogs to allow key personnel — including the CEO, CTO, product leads, or even developers — to connect with their clients and keep them informed about product updates and decision-making processes in real time. Internally blogs are also frequently used to provide daily or weekly summaries from individuals to managers, and in the reverse to disseminate information to the worker bees.

In this section you learn how to create a blog in the Workarea, and how to develop against it using server controls. You set up an executive blog for the CEO of OnTrek, which serves as a marketing tool to drive better customer relationships. Because this will be a point of public contact, you must configure the blog to have an approval chain so that the marketing department can have final review of content before it becomes publically visible on the Internet. In this section, you will:

- Create a blog in the Workarea with an approval chain.
- Create a blank template with a blog control on it.

Create a Blog in the Workarea

Creating a blog is very similar to creating any other folder in the Workarea. Like forums, blogs have a special interface when browsing their content through the Workarea, but much of the UI will be very familiar at this point. To create a blog:

1. Open the Workarea after logging in as admin, and go to the Content pane.
2. In the Content tree, browse to MainSite/Content/Company and right-click the Company Folder.
3. Select Add Blog to open the Add Blog interface, which is shown in Figure 10-17.

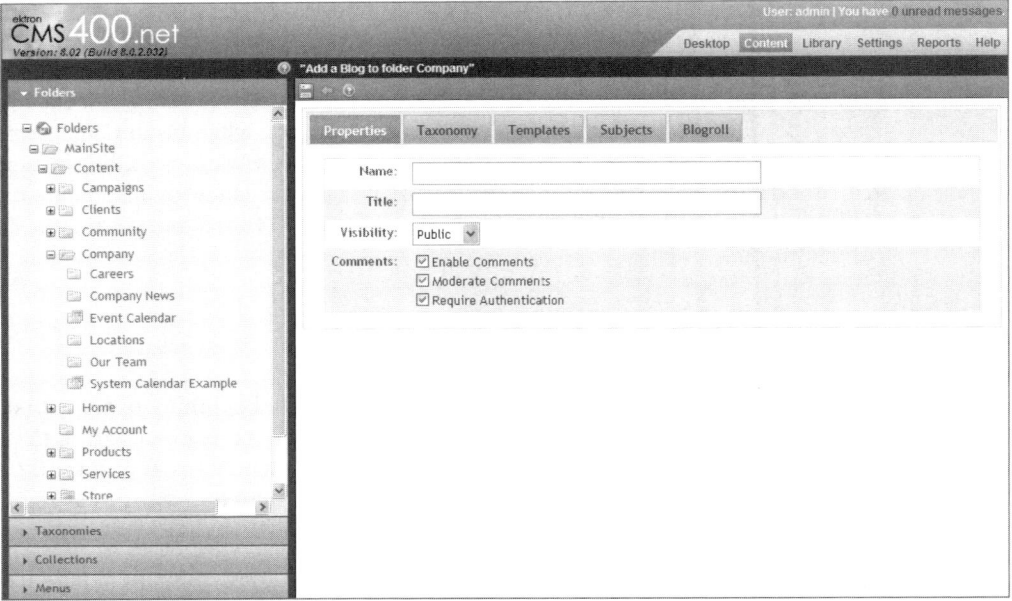

FIGURE 10-17

The form that comes up to add a blog is similar to the add folder form, with a subset of the functionality available. From left to right, the tabs accept basic properties of the blog, the taxonomies to assign content to, the default template to display the entries about subjects that the blog entries will belong to, and the list of links to display in the blogroll. These tabs are outlined in greater detail in Table 10-3.

TABLE 10-3: Tabs and Properties on the Add Blog Form

TAB	FIELD	DESCRIPTION
Properties	Name	Name of the blog.
	Title	Title of the blog.
	Visibility	Can be set to public or private; corresponds to the private setting for normal content. When set to public, permissions are not checked on the blog, and any site visitor can view the blog. If private, a user must be logged in and must have read privileges.
	Enable Comments	Enable or disable comments left on the blog by other users.
	Moderate Comments	Add comments posted by users to a queue that users with the correct permissions can then approve before they appear on the site.
	Require Authentication	Require users to be logged in before allowing them to comment on a post.
Subjects	Subjects	Creates and manages subjects for the blog. The list of subjects is then rendered as part of the Blog Server Control. When a user selects a particular subject, all posts tagged with that subject are displayed.
Blogroll	Blogroll	Creates a list of links to be rendered as part of the Blog Server Control output, and specify the foreign site's relationship to your blog.

4. Create your CEO's blog now. Enter **CEO Blog** as the title and name of the blog, and set the visibility to Public. Leave comments enabled with moderation on.

5. In the Subjects tab, add three subjects by clicking the Add Subject button. For the first subject, add **Technical Notes,** for the second add **Customer Stories,** and for the third add **Market Movements.**

6. Click Save. This returns you to the parent folder.

7. In the folder tree, click the new blog, which takes you to the CEO Blog, shown in Figure 10-18.

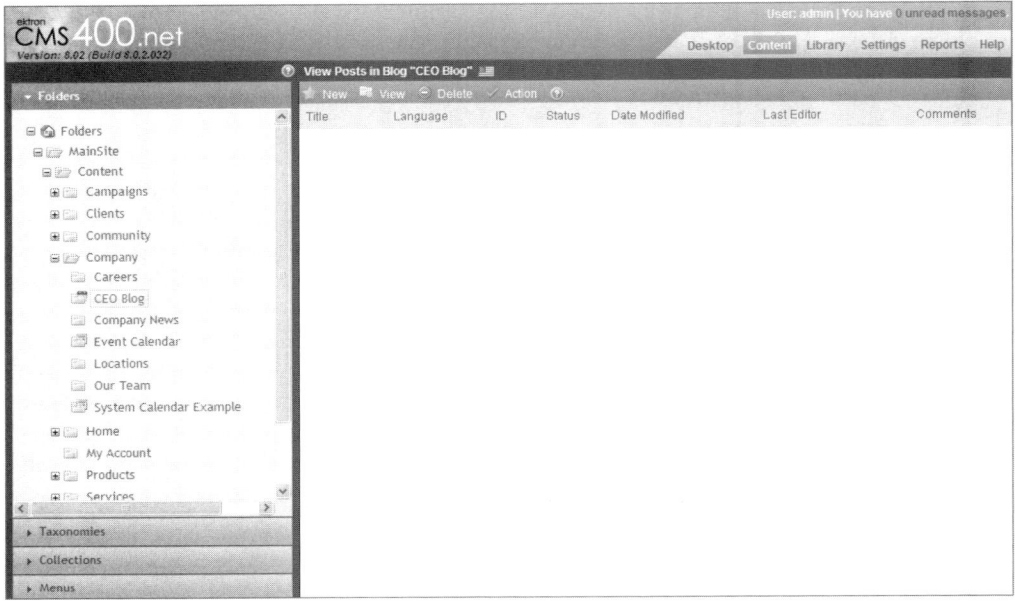

FIGURE 10-18

8. Let's add a new post now, by hovering over the New menu and selecting HTML Post. This brings up the Add Content screen.

 The Add Content screen was covered in Chapter 5. The only change from a basic content form is on the Summary tab. For normal content, all that is shown in this tab is a rich text field for the summary of the content. Because this is a blog, however, you have the opportunity to select the subject of the post from the list of subjects you entered for the blog.

9. You can specify a trackback URL for the post. These fields are shown in Figure 10-19. Again, since a blog post is just a special type of content, you can specify options applicable to content such as an alias and content scheduling.

WHAT IS A TRACKBACK URL?

A *trackback URL* is the URL to a service corresponding to a blog post on a foreign site. If trackbacks are enabled on a blog post you are reading, you will see a link or a trackback URL on the post. If you put that URL into the trackback field here, the Ektron Framework will notify the foreign blog that you have posted a followup post to the foreign post, and frequently this will create a link in the comments section of their post linking to your post. It is a way for users reading content on the foreign blog to be directed to your site, and thus can be useful in organically growing traffic.

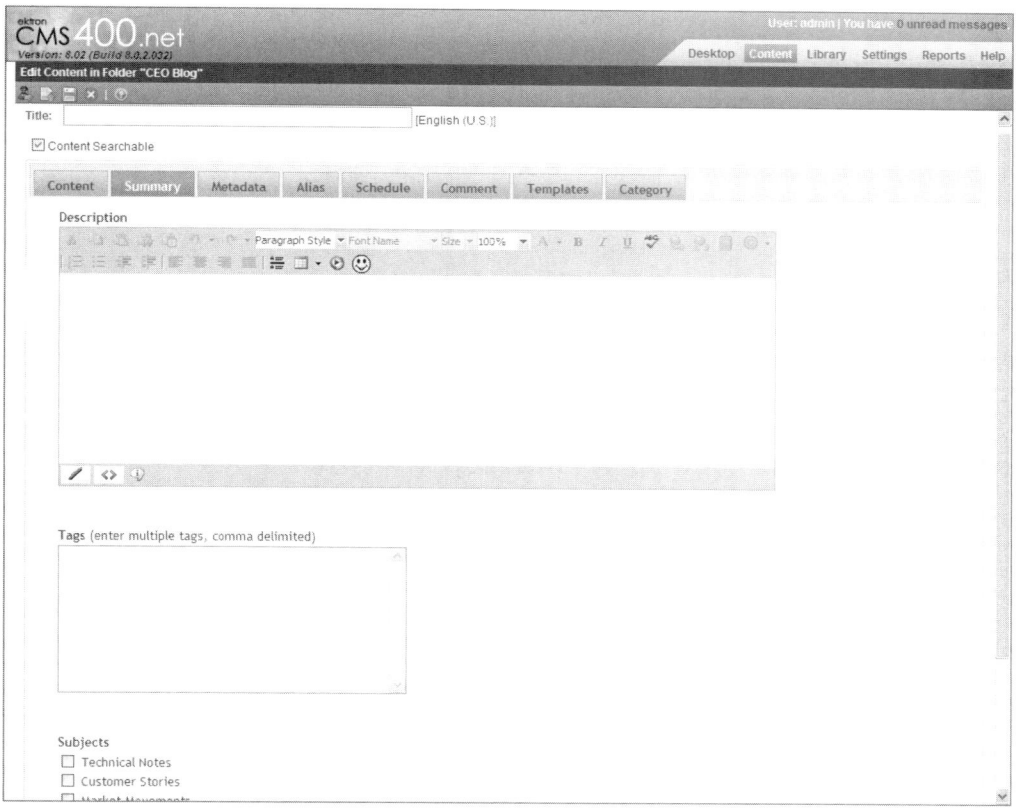

FIGURE 10-19

10. Enter some test content now for the post: Set the Title to be **OnTrek Launch Party**, and enter some content for the post. Under summary, select Market Movements as the subject.

11. Click Publish. Once you have published the content, the View Content pane displays.

12. You'll notice that under the HTML in the Content tab, there is a button to View Comments for the post. Clicking this button takes you to a list of the comments for the post, but of course there aren't any just yet. You'll add some when you set up the template for the blog.

13. Set up the approval chain for this blog. You do this by returning to the blog view and right-clicking CEO Blog in the Content tree. Then select View Properties.

14. Click View Permissions in the toolbar, which brings you to the Permissions pane you have seen a number of times before now.

15. Uncheck Allow This Object to Inherit Permissions, and then click Add Permissions. Select Marketing from the user list, and click Save. This brings up the Permission List pane.

16. Click Enable All in this interface, and click Save again.

Now that you have added Marketing as a specific user in the permission list, you have the ability to add this user as an approver in the approval chain.

17. Click the back icon to go back to the Properties view of the CEO Blog, and then click View Approvals.

18. Click the plus icon, and select Marketing from the user list.

You now have an approval chain on the CEO Blog.

Create a Template with a Blog Server Control

You've created the blogs in the Workarea, but currently there is no way for users to read or interact with the posts you author on the site. In this section, you'll create a template for the blog, and also explore how users can interact with the blog when browsing the site.

Creating the Page that Displays the Blog

Now you need to create the page that will display your blog. This involves knowing the ID of the blog you want to display, and setting the options you wish to enable on the Blog Server Control. The steps below outline this process.

1. Return to the folder properties for the CEO Blog folder, and make note of the ID of the folder. In the sample case the folder ID is 168, but in your case it may be different.

2. Open the OnTrek website in Visual Studio, and add a new Web form to the root of the site called CEOBlog.aspx.

3. Once the CEOBlog.aspx page comes up, drag the Blog Server Control from the Ektron section of the toolbox into the `form` element of the page. Your code will then look like Listing 10-2.

Available for download on Wrox.com

LISTING 10-2: CEOBlog.aspx

```
<%@ Page Language="C#" AutoEventWireup="true"
    CodeFile="CEOBlog.aspx.cs" Inherits="CEOBlog" %>
<%@ Register Assembly="Ektron.Cms.Controls"
    Namespace="Ektron.Cms.Controls" TagPrefix="CMS" %>

<!DOCTYPE html PUBLIC "-//W3C//DTD XHTML 1.0 Transitional//EN"
    "http://www.w3.org/TR/xhtml1/DTD/xhtml1-transitional.dtd">

<html xmlns="http://www.w3.org/1999/xhtml">
<head runat="server">
  <title></title>
</head>
<body>
  <form id="form1" runat="server">
    <CMS:Blog ID="Blog1" runat="server" BlogID="128" />
  </form>
</body>
</html>
```

When you load this page in the browser, the output will look like Figure 10-20.

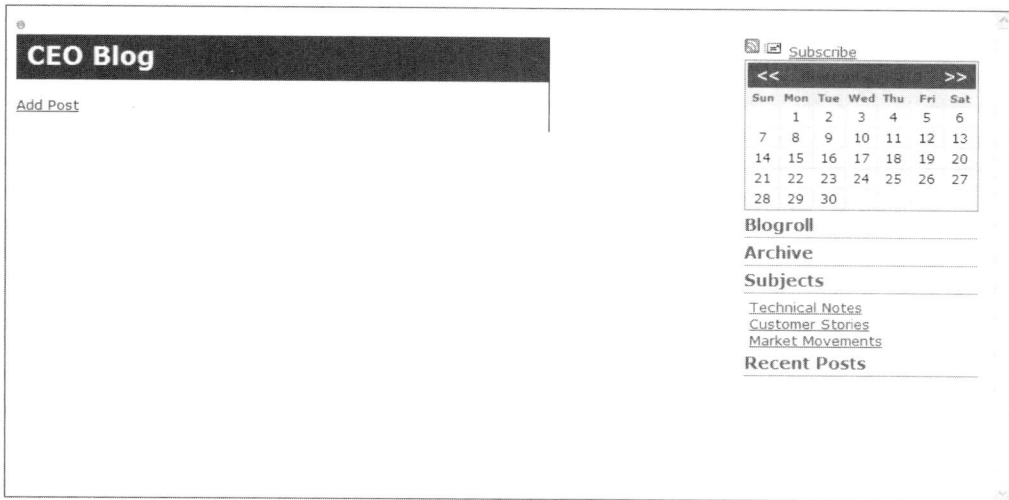

FIGURE 10-20

The Blog Server Control does have a series of properties that you can use to customize its behavior and user interface. Table 10-4 lists a subset of these properties.

TABLE 10-4: Blog Server Control Properties

PROPERTY	DESCRIPTION
ArchiveMode	Can be set to `year` or `month`. This property determines the grouping of the archive links. If set to month, which is the default, there is a link for each month which has an entry. If set to year, a list of years is displayed.
BlogID	Sets the ID of the blog to display.
BlogStartDateRange	Specifies the date to start displaying results from. Can be set to none, which displays all entries, monthly for entries in the past month, quarterly for three months, biyearly for six months, or yearly for all entries in the past year.
DateToStart	Similar to `BlogStartDateRange`, this allows you to select a specific date rather than a rolling time range for blog entries to appear.
DefaultUserID	The Blog Server Control is also used to display user blogs created as an option during registration. Setting `DefaultUserID` to the ID of the user retrieves that user's blog.
DynamicParameter	Set this to the query string parameter containing the Blog ID if you want to dynamically set the value.

continues

TABLE 10-4 *(continued)*

PROPERTY	DESCRIPTION
DynamicUserParameter	Similar to DynamicParameter but used to set the query string parameter containing the User ID.
MaxResults	The number of results to show. If set to zero, the Blog Server Control displays all the results matching the parameters selected.
ShowHeader	Selects whether to show the tagline for the blog.
ShowRSS	Determines whether to show the RSS feed link at the top of the blog.

In addition to managing the UI of the Blog Server Control through the properties, you can also manage the display layer in more depth by using the constituent server control of the Blog Server Control. There are eight of these sub-controls that comprise the full Blog Server Control as shown in Table 10-5.

TABLE 10-5: The Blog Server Sub-controls

SERVER SUB-CONTROL	DESCRIPTION	VISUAL REPRESENTATION
BlogEntries	Displays a list of blog entries.	
BlogPost	Displays a single blog post on a page.	

SERVER SUB-CONTROL	DESCRIPTION	VISUAL REPRESENTATION
BlogCalendar	Displays a calendar with the dates that have corresponding entries highlighted.	<< September 2010 >> Sun Mon Tue Wed Thu Fri Sat 1 2 3 4 5 6 7 8 9 10 11 12 13 14 15 16 17 18 19 20 21 22 23 24 25 26 27 28 29 30
BlogRoll	Displays the list of links for that blog.	• Ektron Bloghub • MSDN Blogs
BlogCategories	Displays the category links for the blog.	• Technical Notes • Customer Stories • Market Movements
BlogRecentPosts	Displays the most recent posts for a given blog. The number of posts to display is set through the NumberofPosts property.	• Record Quarter • Looking forward to Local User Groups
BlogRSS	Displays the RSS link for the selected blog.	

Through these individual controls, you can build any interface for your blog.

Working with the Commenting System

Now that you have a page for your blog, you can experiment with the commenting system. Allowing comments on your blog is a good way to build up a rapport with repeat visitors, and allows users to expound on content you have posted. It is another way of adding user generated content to your site, which increases the value of the site to future visitors. Follow these steps:

1. Go back to the Workarea and set your template properly. Go to Settings ⇨ Configuration ⇨ Template Configuration, and add a new template called CEOBlog.aspx.
2. Switch to the Content tab and browse to MainSite/Content/Company and right-click CEO Blog.
3. Select View Properties, and in the Properties pane select Edit Properties.
4. Switch to the Templates tab where you will deselect the Inherit Parent Configuration checkbox, and add CEOBlog.aspx to the list of templates from the template dropdown. Set it as the default for the folder, and click Save.

5. Return to the CEOBlog.aspx page in the browser, and you will see one entry for the OnTrek Launch Party. Click the comments link at the bottom of the entry, and the page will be updated with the interface shown in Figure 10-21.

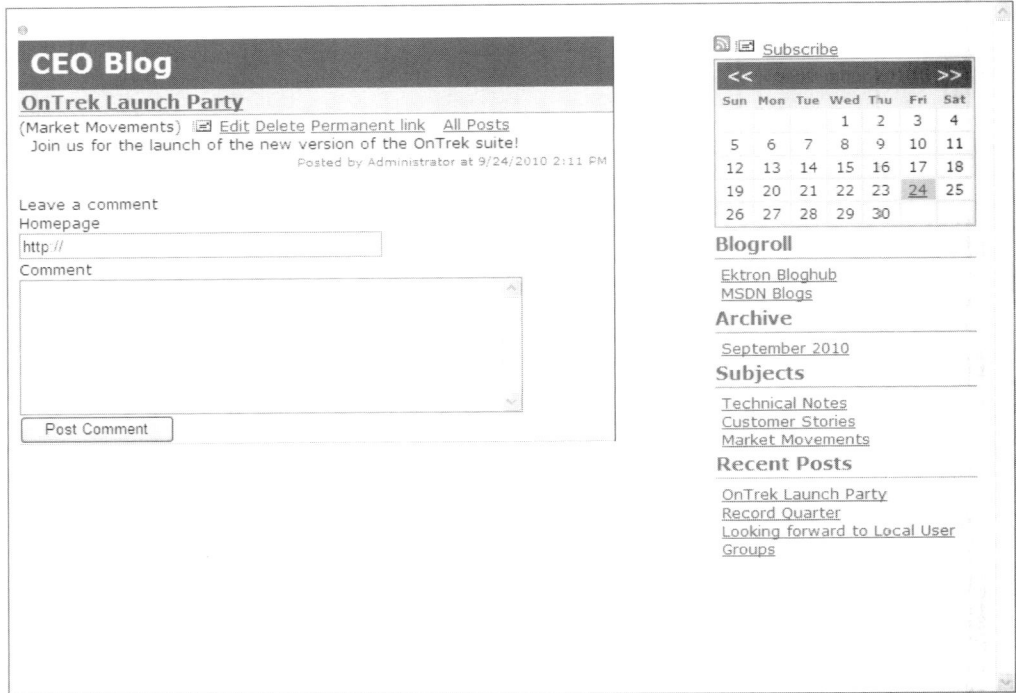

FIGURE 10-21

6. Enter a comment and click Post Comment. The page updates to thank you for posting a comment, but no new comments appear because Comment Moderation is turned on.

7. Return to the Workarea now, and in the CEO Blog folder, select OnTrek Launch Party. On the Content tab, select View Comments Now to show the comment you just posted, as in the example in Figure 10-22.

From here you have three options: approve, edit, and delete.

8. Click Approve Now.
9. Switch back to the front-end CEOBlog.aspx file, and refresh the page.

The new comment now appears in the blog.

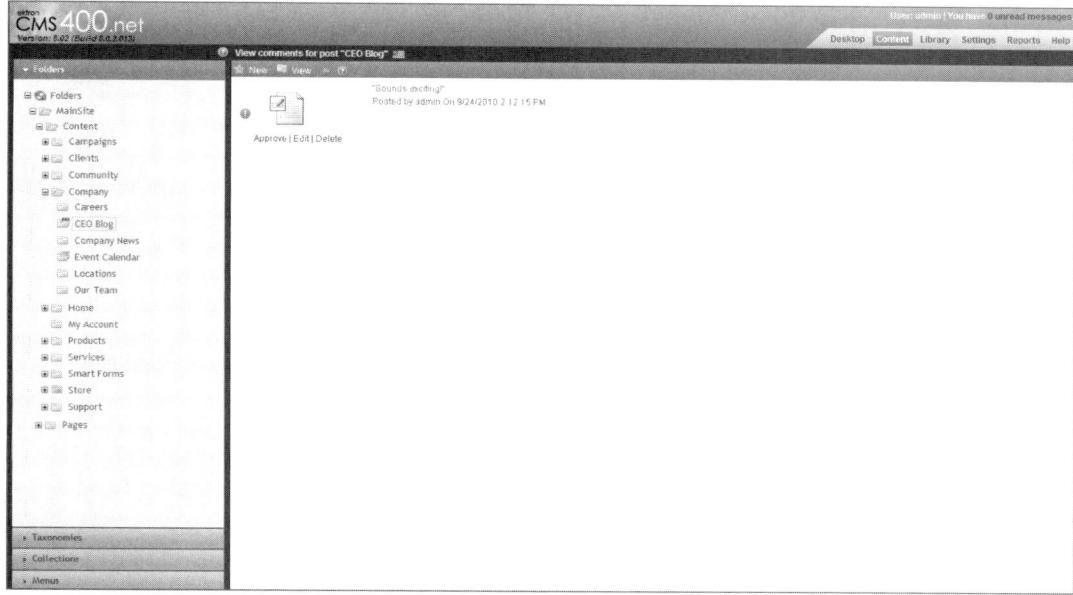

FIGURE 10-22

WIKIS

Wikis are designed to allow a combination of CMS authors and membership users to quickly develop a communal space of documents and content, which is useful in a number of scenarios. One example is as a documentation repository, or knowledge base, where technical representatives can post content that can later be expanded upon by anyone. Wikis are usually organized through taxonomy. The main difference between a wiki and any other folder is that you can add a wiki links to content that does not yet exist. When this occurs, the Ektron Framework creates the piece of content you link to so that you can edit and manage it in the future.

You've already learned about the primary folder type — regular content folders — which contain content mainly generated by CMS Authors. Wikis require you to utilize an alternative folder type called *community folders*. In community folders, content can be generated by either CMS authors or by membership users. The reason this different type of folder is needed for membership-generated content has to do with the way content is synchronized between staging servers and production servers.

In this section, you learn how to create and manage a wiki by performing the following tasks:

➤ Creating a wiki in the Workarea
➤ Using the wiki feature in the site

Creating a Wiki in the Workarea

Community folders allow membership users to add content to and edit content in that folder. The interface that allows membership users to add content is different from the normal interface because membership users don't have access to items like template management or workflow. The membership interface does, however, retain taxonomy management. Also keep in mind that community folders can only contain standard HTML content, and cannot include Smart Forms, HTML forms, or other types of special content.

To create a wiki, follow these steps:

1. Open the Workarea and click the Content tab.
2. In the Content tree, browse to MainSite/Content/Community, righting-clicking the Community folder, and selecting Add Community Folder.

The Add Community folder interface is exactly the same as the Add Folder interface covered in Chapter 5.

3. Name the new folder **Documentation Wiki**, and leave all other options as they are.
4. Click Save and you are returned to the community folder. Now you need to update the permissions to allow membership users to author content in the new folder.
5. Select the Documentation Wiki folder from the Content tree, and then select View ⇨ Properties.
6. Once the Properties pane is displayed, select the lock icon to enter into the Permissions pane, shown in Figure 10-23.
7. At the top-right of the Permissions pane, you'll notice a dropdown for User Type. Initially this displays CMS users, but you can change it to show the permissions for membership users as well. Uncheck Allow This Object to Inherit Permissions, and then switch the dropdown to Membership users.
8. Click the Add icon, and you are presented with a list of the membership users and groups currently defined in the system. Select the group All_Members checkbox, and then click Save.
9. On the next page, select the Read, Edit, Add, Add Images, and Add Files checkboxes. This ensures that your community can easily manage everything about the wiki.
10. Click Save and you return to the Permissions list with the new group added.

Using the Wiki Feature in the Site

The wiki feature front-end is based around the ContentBlock Server Control, and the ListSummary Server Control. The approach in the Ektron Framework is to enable WYSIWYG editing for users, and avoid the confusing normal wiki markup, while allowing users to create links to content that does not exist yet. Therefore, the interface for managing and interacting with content is very similar to the existing interface for CMS authors but it avoids contact with the Workarea itself. This implementation section focuses on a couple of areas:

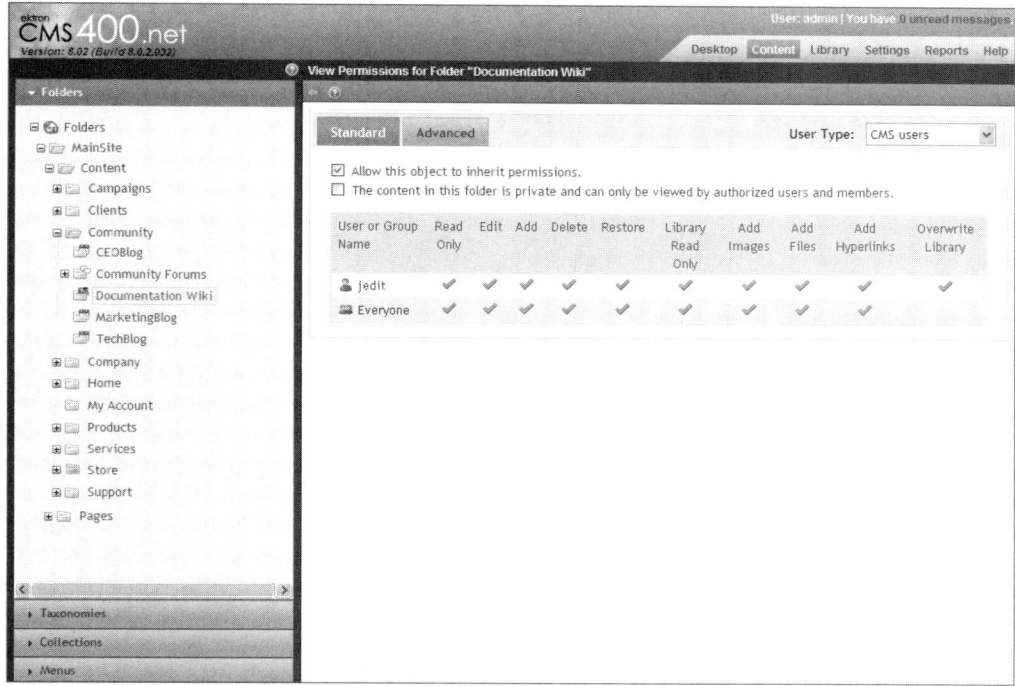

FIGURE 10-23

> ➤ Creating a new PageBuilder page with a ListSummary Widget and a ContentBlock Widget that you'll use to display the wiki.

> ➤ Learning the process of creating content as a membership user.

> ➤ Learning to edit existing content. You'll also create cross-links to existing content as well as content that has not yet been created, and explore how the wiki can grow organically over time.

Creating a New PageBuilder Page

In this example, you will build your Wiki out of a simple combination of a ListSummary Widget and a ContentBlock Widget on a PageBuilder page. This will allow us to easily add features from the community feature toolbox. You could also develop this on a non-PageBuilder page. To get started:

1. Open the Workarea, and switch to the Content tab.

2. In the Content tree, browse to MainSite/Pages/Community.

3. When the folder pane comes up for the community folder, hover over New, and select Page Layout. This brings up the Add New Page Wizard, shown in Figure 10-24.

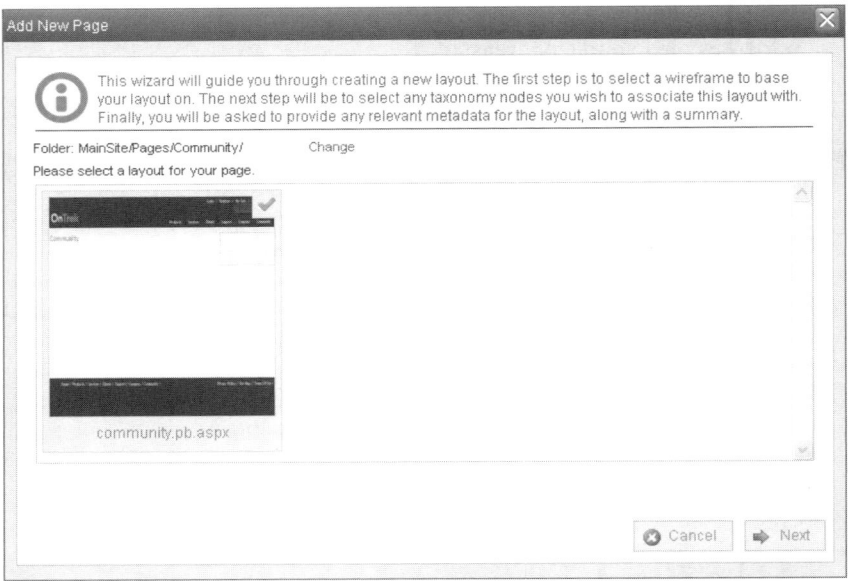

FIGURE 10-24

4. Make sure the community.pb.aspx template is selected, and click Next.

5. The next screen of the Wizard asks for the page title; call this page **wiki**. If manual aliasing has been enabled, this creates an alias called /wiki/, which is where you access this page.

6. In the taxonomy list, open the OnTrek Site Navigation node, and select the Community node under it. This creates an automatic taxonomy alias at /OnTrek Site Navigation/Community/Wiki/.

7. To proceed to the final screen, click Next.

8. The third screen of the Wizard has two tabs, the first for metadata, and the second for the summary. You can leave both of these blank for now, so click Finish. The server will work for a moment, and then ask if you want to begin editing the page now.

9. Click OK, and the new page opens in a new window. The page will be empty, as shown in Figure 10-25.

10. Open the widget tray and first drag a ListSummary Widget onto the right DropZone.

11. Reopen the widget tray and add a ContentBlock Widget to the left DropZone. Now that the two widgets are on the page, you need to hook them up to the community folder you created.

12. Click the Edit button on the ListSummary.

13. Switch to the Folder tab, and drill down in the tree to MainSite/Content/Community/Documentation Wiki.

14. Once you have selected the folder, switch back to the Property tab, and enable paging.

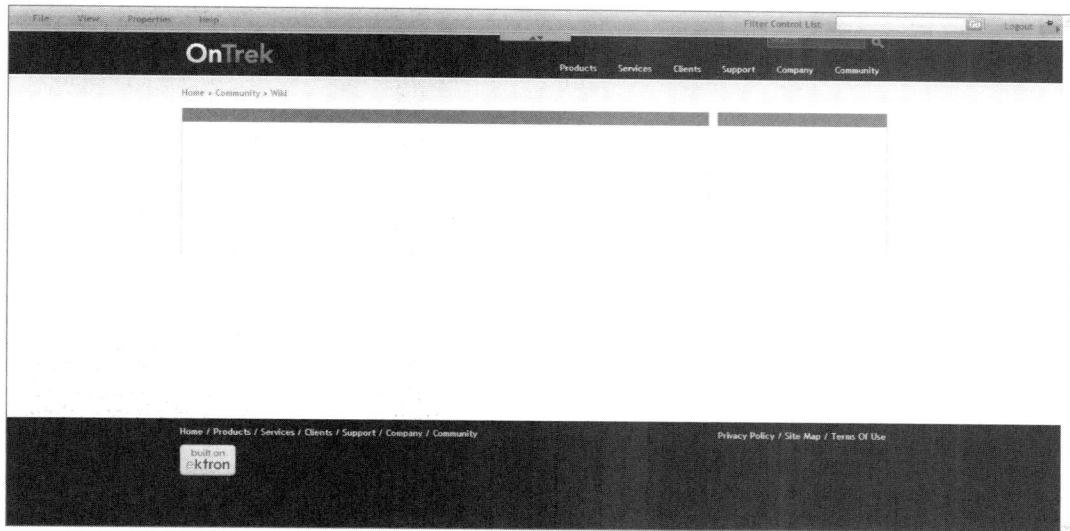

FIGURE 10-25

15. Click Save.

16. Publish the page now by selecting File ➪ Publish.

Using the Wiki and Creating Links

The barebones Wiki is now ready to use. You'll start by creating some content in the Wiki as a membership user, and learn about creating new content from existing content. The steps below will walk you through the process:

1. Log out of the system and log back in as jmember/jmember. This user is an automatically created membership user. Once you are logged in as jmember, and you return to the wiki page, you will see what is shown in Figure 10-26. The page consists of almost nothing, except for a silver access point where the ListSummary is rendered.

2. Hover over the access point, and you'll see two options: Add Content and Logout.

3. Click Add Content now, and a new window opens containing a two-tab interface. The first tab allows you to name and enter the content for the page, and the second tab allows you to categorize the content.

4. Enter the title **Welcome**. For content, enter **The OnTrek Documentation Wiki will help to keep you updated on recent products.**

5. Creating a wiki link from your page to a page that hasn't yet been created is straightforward from this point. Select the word products from the just entered text, and click the Add Wiki Link button on the toolbar. This brings up the Add/Edit Wiki Link form, shown in Figure 10-27, which has two tabs:

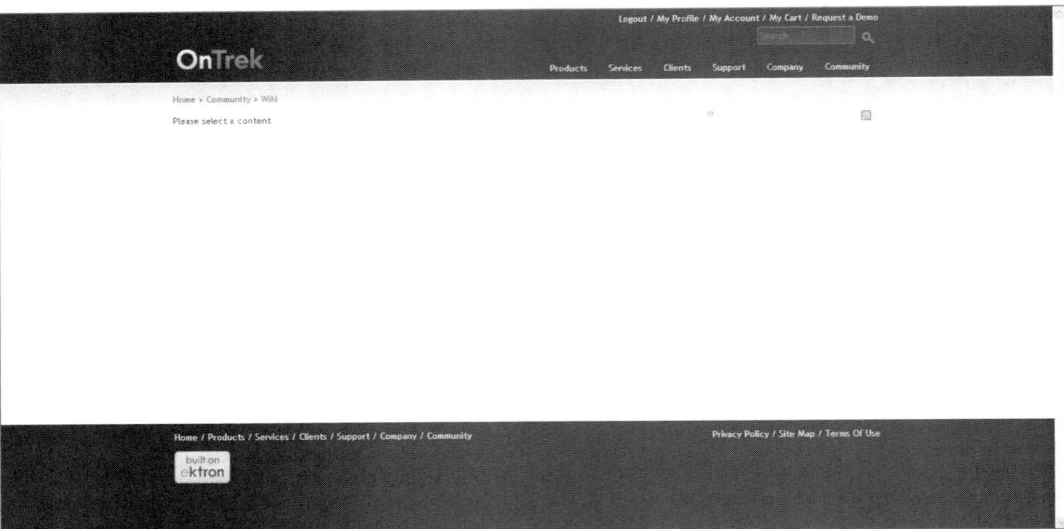

FIGURE 10-26

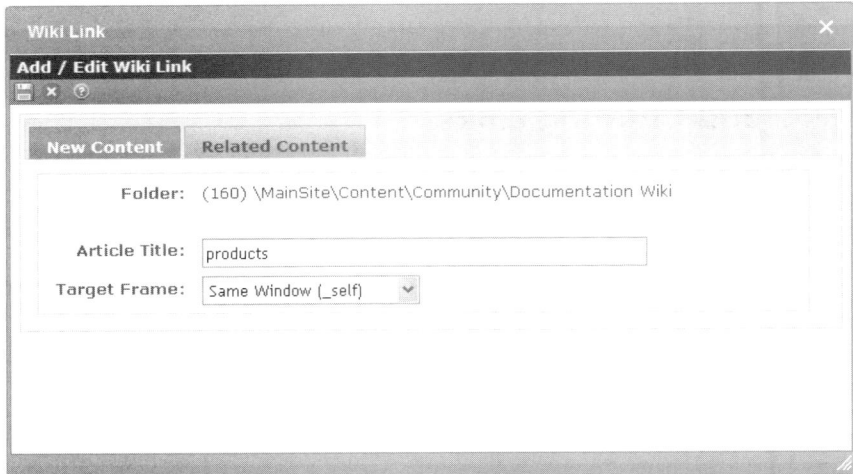

FIGURE 10-27

➤ **New Content:** This tab allows you to add wiki links and creates destination content item in the same folder as the current content. It also allows you to name the new content.

➤ **Related Content:** This tab allows you to search for already existing content related to the currently highlighted term.

6. For now, enter **products** for the Article Title field in the New Content tab and click Save. The form will go away, and your new link will be highlighted in blue. Click Publish Now, and the form closes. Your wiki page also refreshes, and you'll notice in Figure 10-28 that the ListSummary now has two items, one for the Welcome page, and one for the Products page.

FIGURE 10-28

Editing Existing Content

To edit the content you just created, click the Welcome link on the ListSummary. This updates the page showing the Welcome content you created in the ContentBlock Widget. Above the content itself, there is another access point. This time the menu items on the access point are:

➤ **Edit in Context:** This works the same way as it does for a CMS author.

➤ **Edit:** This brings up the same form you used to enter the content in the first place.

➤ **View History:** This will allow you to roll back in time and see what changes occurred to the content from it's original creation.

➤ **Logout:** Logs out the currently logged-in user from the site.

The content created in Community folders also supports all the same items as normal content. You can easily use taxonomy navigation in addition to the ListSummary, and use the MessageBoard Server Control, for instance, to create a more dynamic and easy-to-use page. This ability to easily construct a robust feature set can help you to develop against requirements quickly and flexibly.

THE SOCIALBAR SERVER CONTROL

The SocialBar Server Control is one of the simpler controls in the Ektron Framework toolkit. It allows users to easily share pages with social media sites such as Twitter, Facebook, and Digg, and integrates with Ektron Framework Favorites and Invites. It can be a great way to drive traffic to your site, by tapping into the network of your users to branch out further. A screenshot of the SocialBar Server Control is shown in Figure 10-29.

FIGURE 10-29

This section explores how to implement the SocialBar Server Control, and also investigates integrating it with the Invite Server Control and the Favorites Server Control. You will implement a widget using the SocialBar Server Control, and place it on the wiki page you created in the previous section.

Implementing the SocialBar Widget

Implementing a widget, as covered in Chapter 9, begins with creating a user control in the ~/widgets directory of your site. Follow these steps:

1. Open your site in Visual Studio, and in the solution explorer, browse to the Widgets directory.
2. Right-click the directory and select Add New Item.
3. In the pop-up menu, select Web User Control and name the widget **SocialBar.ascx**.
4. When the declarative file comes up, right-click it and select View Code.
5. Update the class definition to specify that the widget inherits from the UserControl class to also implement the `Ektron.Cms.Widget.IWidget` interface. This allows the system to determine that this user control is actually a widget and should be used as such. The widget codebehind should now look like the following snippet.

    ```
    public partial class widgets_socialbar : System.Web.UI.UserControl,
      Ektron.Cms.Widget.IWidget
    {
      protected void Page_Load(object sender, EventArgs e)
      {

      }
    }
    ```

6. Switch back to the declarative socialbar.ascx file and drag the SocialBar Server Control from the toolbox into the file. You will be building this widget without any edit screen, so the options are always the default. Table 10-6 outlines the properties available on the SocialBar Server Control.

TABLE 10-6: SocialBar Server Control Properties

PROPERTY	DESCRIPTION
DefaultObjectID	This value is used if the DynamicObjectParameter is blank, or there is no corresponding item in the query string. If this item is not specified and the DynamicObjectParameter is also left blank, the SocialBar Server Control operates with the URL of the current page instead.

The SocialBar Server Control | 371

PROPERTY	DESCRIPTION
DisplayXSLT	Allows you to override the stylesheet used to display the items on the page.
DoInitFill	If set to false, the server control postpones the fill event until the Page Render event rather than filling on Page Init. This is useful if properties will be changed in codebehind later in the lifecycle of the page.
DynamicObjectParameter	Sets the query string parameter used to retrieve the object ID to render the SocialBar against.
IncludeIcons	Sets whether icons are displayed for each link on the SocialBar.
InviteURL	Sets the URL for the invite page. Can contain two tokens that are replaced at render time with the appropriate values: {0} is used for the object ID and {1} is used for the object type. An example URL is invite.aspx?id={0}&type={1}.
Items	The Items property is the key to the SocialBar Server Control. It accepts a comma-separated list of names of services to display. The list is shown in Table 10-7.
MarkupLanguage	Specifies the path to the EKML file to use to display the items.
MessagingUrl	If PrivateMessageUser or PrivateMessageAdmin is in the Items list property, they render a link based on the URL specified in this property.
ObjectType	The type of the object the Social Bar is displaying links for. Can be set to Content, User, or Group. Group specifies a community group, not a user group.
Stylesheet	Path to the CSS file that styles the control.

The Items property determines the list of services to display links for. It accepts a comma-separated list. The supported options are listed in Table 10-7.

TABLE 10-7: Valid Options for the Items Property of the SocialBar Server Control

ITEM NAME	DESCRIPTION
Addto	The output of this option depends on the ObjectType specified. If the ObjectType is set to User, the SocialBar displays a link to Add a Colleague, Cancel Colleague request, or Remove From Colleagues depending on the current status of the relationship between the logged-in user and the user the SocialBar is associated with. If the ObjectType is a Group, the options are Join Group, Leave Group, or Cancel Request to Join. For Content, the options are Add to Favorites and Remove Favorites.

continues

TABLE 10-7 *(continued)*

ITEM NAME	DESCRIPTION
Invite	Displays the link specified in the InviteURL property. Allows a user to send an e-mail inviting another user to look at the content.
GroupInvite	Allows the logged-in user to invite colleagues or unregistered users to join the group. Displayed only if the ObjectType is Group.
Email	Displays a mailto: link that launches the users e-mail client to send a link to their friends.
Digg	Allows the user to submit to `Digg.com`.
Delicious	Allows the user to submit to del.icio.us.
Facebook	Allows the user to post the link to Facebook.
Google	Allows the user to post the link to Google's bookmarking service.
Furl	Allows the user to submit to Furl.
Technorati	Allows the user to submit to Technorati.
Twitter	Allows the user to post the link to Twitter.
Yahoo	Allows the user to submit to Yahoo's bookmarking service.
Print	Prints the page.
PrivateMessageUser	Links to a messaging page to allow the user to send a private message within the site to another user. Functions only when ObjectType is set to User.
PrivateMessageAdmin	Links to a messaging page to allow the user to send a private message within the site to the community group's administrator. Functions only when `ObjectType` is set to Group.

With these options in mind, set up the properties for the SocialBar Server Control inside the SocialBar Widget using these basic steps:

1. Set up the SocialBar to use an `ObjectType` of content and a `DynamicObjectParameter` of ID or PageID, but in this case it makes more sense to leave both properties blank and let the SocialBar work with the current URL instead.

2. You will also use a custom list of items, including the invite option, which means you'll need to specify the InviteURL. The declarative side of the widget then looks like Listing 10-3.

LISTING 10-3: SocialBar.ascx

Available for download on Wrox.com

```
<%@ Control Language="C#" AutoEventWireup="true"
    CodeFile="socialbar.ascx.cs" Inherits="widgets_socialbar" %>
<%@ Register Assembly="Ektron.Cms.Controls"
```

```
  Namespace="Ektron.Cms.Controls" TagPrefix="CMS" %>
<cms:socialbar
  runat="server"
  InviteURL="Invite.aspx"
  Items="Invite, Addto, Email, Digg, Delicious, Print, Twitter, FaceBook">
</cms:socialbar>
```

3. Also remember to create an icon for your widget. For now, simply make a copy of the content block icon at ~/widgets/contentblock.ascx.jpg and name the new copy **~/widgets/socialbar.ascx.jpg**.

4. Add the widget you just created to the Framework, associate it with the Wireframe you're currently using, and add it to the page.

5. You'll also need to configure the Invite Server Control on the invite.aspx page, and then you can test the whole thing.

6. To add the widget to the Framework, open the Workarea, and go to the Settings tab.

7. In the Settings tree, navigate to Configuration ➪ Personalizations ➪ Widgets.

8. In the toolbar of the Widgets pane, there is a button to resync the widgets. Click it now and OK the prompt, and the SocialBar Widget should be appended to the list.

9. Now you need to associate it to the template. In the settings tree, navigate to Configuration ➪ Template Configuration. In the list of templates that appears, select the file Community.pb.aspx (Wireframe Template). The Update Template screen will appear, as shown in Figure 10-30.

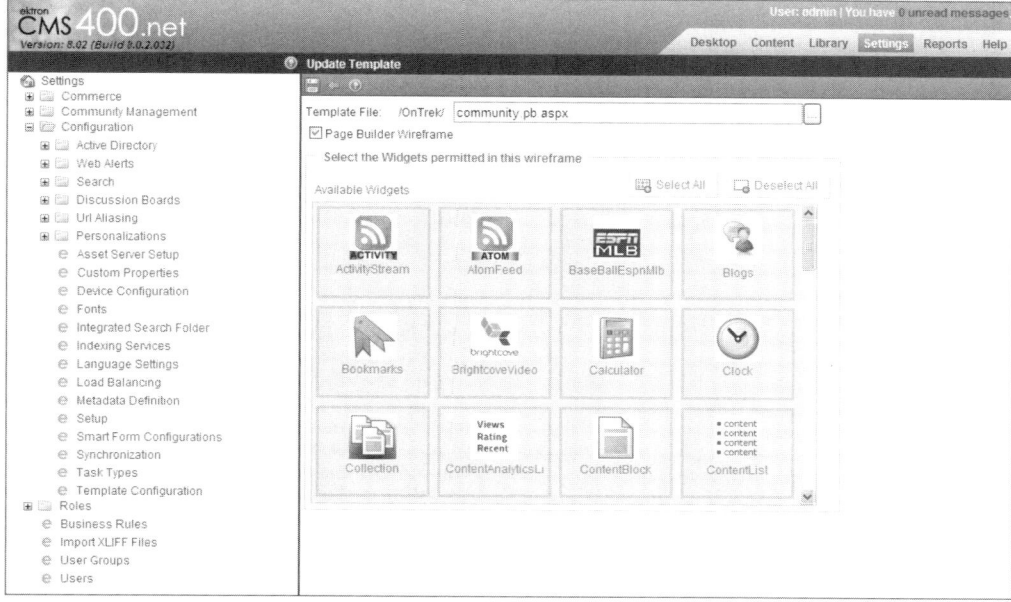

FIGURE 10-30

10. In the list of available widgets, find the SocialBar Widget. Select it so it turns green and click Update Template.

11. Return to the page you created for your wiki at /wiki.aspx, and enter editing mode by selecting File ⇨ Edit on the Pagehost menu.
12. Once in edit mode, type **socialbar** into the filter box at the right side of the pagehost toolbar, and drag the SocialBar to beneath the ContentBlock Widget, as shown in Figure 10-31.
13. Publish the page.

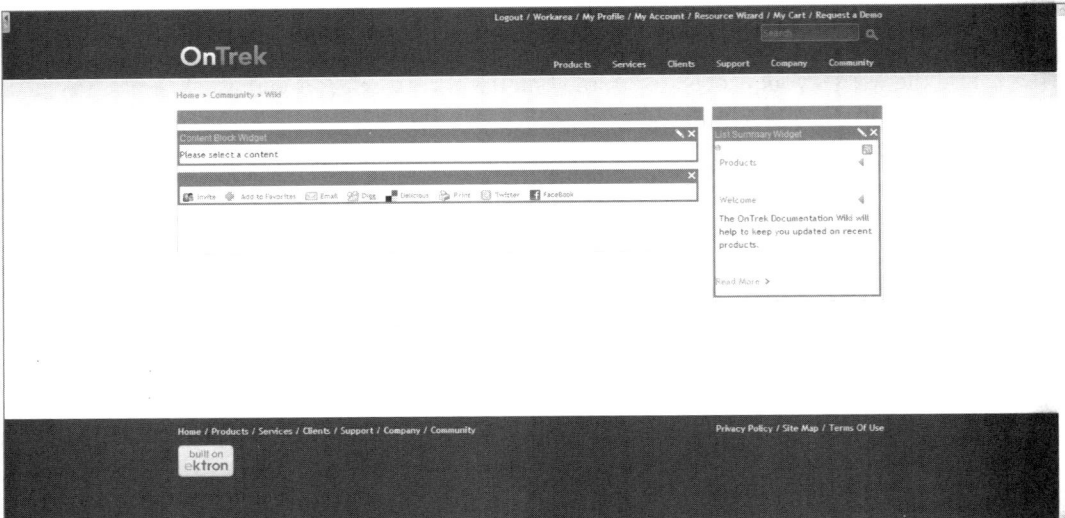

FIGURE 10-31

As you can see in Figure 10-31, the page now has a list of links to popular services, as well as an Invite link and a link to add the page to your favorites, which is a list of bookmarks kept on the site.

14. Now you need to create the Invite.aspx page so the invite link works. In Visual Studio, right-click the root of your site in the Solution Explorer and select Add New Item.
15. In the pop-up menu, make sure Web Form is selected, and name it **invite.aspx**. Also select the master page ~/components/templates/Full.master. This master page contains two placeholders, one for the breadcrumb and one for the content body.
16. When the declarative file appears, drag the Invite Server Control from the toolbox into the `uxContent` content section.

> *The Invite Server Control is part of the community framework. It allows users to send an e-mail inviting other users to come visit and register on your site. When the control is rendered, the user sees a two-part form, with one field allowing the user to add a list of e-mail addresses and a second field filled initially with a default message specified in the OptionalMessageText property. You'll define your text for this invite in the Workarea, but first...*

17. Run through the properties available to the Invite Server Control. These properties are listed in Table 10-8.

TABLE 10-8: Invite Server Control Properties

PROPERTY	DESCRIPTION
`DisplayXslt`	The path to a custom XSLT to render against.
`DoInitFill`	By default set to true; set to false to fill the control at the page render event. Use this if programmatically modifying the control properties later in the lifecycle.
`FriendMessageId`	The ID of the message to send for a `FriendInvitation` type e-mail.
`InviteMessageId`	The ID of the message to send for a `GroupInvitation` type e-mail.
`OptionalMessageText`	This text is displayed by default in the Invite form, and is folded into the form e-mail specified in the Workarea.
`Stylesheet`	Use this to override the default stylesheet. Accepts a path to a different stylesheet.

18. Go back to the Workarea to define the e-mail message to be sent. In the Workarea, switch to the Settings tab, and in the Settings tree, drill down to Community Management ➪ Messages. This brings up a list of all the messages currently defined in the system, as shown in Figure 10-32.

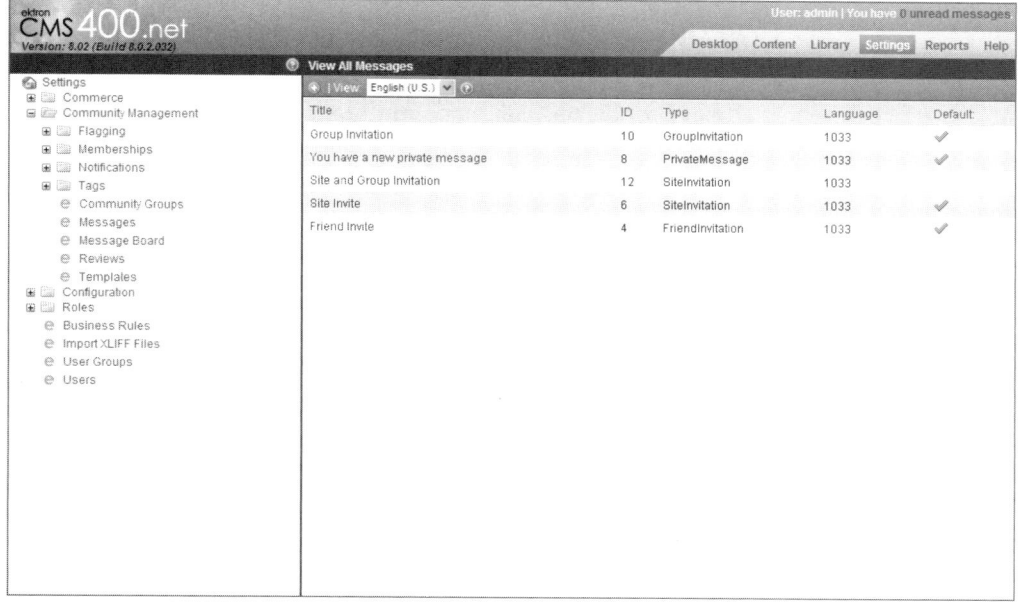

FIGURE 10-32

19. Click the plus icon to add a new message. The form that comes up has four fields. In the title field, enter **Join me at OnTrek**. In the type dropdown, select FriendInvitation. Leave the Default checkbox unselected. The text of e-mail messages uses a token-based string replacement system to allow you to easily create form e-mails. Table 10-9 shows a list of the tokens available.

TABLE 10-9: Community E-Mail Message Tokens

TOKEN	DESCRIPTION
`@appOptionalText@`	This is replaced with the text the user types into the Optional Message field on the Invite Server Control.
`@appSenderName@`	The name of the sender of the invitation.
`@appFriendDisplayName@`	The name of the recipient of the invitation.
`@appInvitedEmail@`	The e-mail address of the recipient of the invitation.
`@appInviteId@`	Replaced with the invite ID. This is typically used to track the invite through to registration so that the action the user was invited to do can be completed when the new user registers.
`@appGroupName@`	The group a person is being invited to join.

20. Enter the e-mail body as shown here:

```
@appSenderName@ has invited you to be part of the community at OnTrek.
@appOptionalText@
```

21. Click Add Email Message and you will be returned to the list of messages, with the new message in the list.

22. Make a note of the ID of the message, and return to the invite.aspx page in Visual Studio.

23. Update your options on the control so the declarative looks like Listing 10-4. Make sure to swap out the `InviteMessageId` value with the appropriate value for the message you just created.

LISTING 10-4: invite.aspx

Available for download on Wrox.com

```
<%@ Page Title="" Language="C#"
    MasterPageFile="~/components/templates/Full.master"
    AutoEventWireup="true"
    CodeFile="invite.aspx.cs"
    Inherits="invite" %>

<%@ Register Assembly="Ektron.Cms.Controls"
    Namespace="Ektron.Cms.Controls"
    TagPrefix="CMS" %>

<asp:Content ID="Content1" ContentPlaceHolderID="uxContentBody" Runat="Server">
    <cms:invite runat="server"
        InviteMessageId="91"
```

```
      OptionalMessageText="Hey, this site is pretty awesome. Come check it out!">
    </cms:invite>
</asp:Content>
```

24. Save the file and open /invite.aspx in your browser. It should look like Figure 10-33.

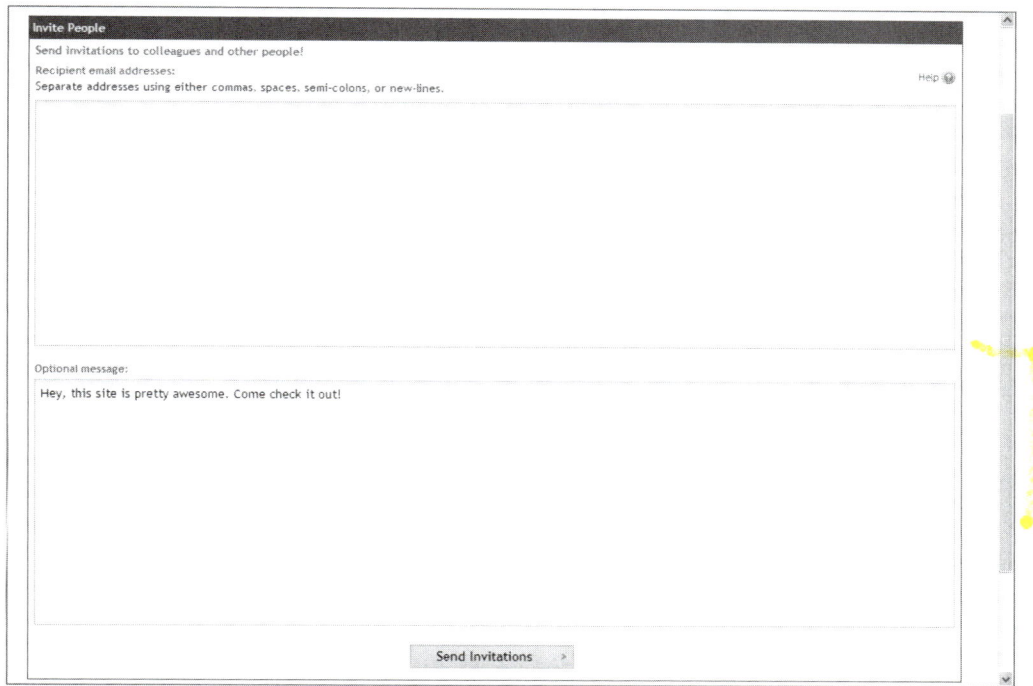

FIGURE 10-33

25. There is one step left to have the Invite Server Control completely functional, and that is to configure the e-mail server and outgoing e-mail address. The outgoing e-mail address defaults to `invitations@example.com`, but it can be updated by setting a key in the web.config file. Open the web.config file now, and find the line containing the key ek_InvitationFromEmail. Set the value to something appropriate for your organization.

> *The process of setting up your e-mail server depends on a few additional pieces. The Microsoft Messaging Queue must be installed, and the Asynchronous Processor Service must be configured. These steps are outlined in detail in the Ektron CMS400 manual, installed with the Framework. The manual is accessible by going through the Start menu, to All Programs ➪ Ektron ➪ CMS400v80 ➪ Documentation ➪ CMS400 Manual. The details on configuring the e-mail server are covered in Chapter 1 of the manual.*

Now that all your pieces are put together, users who visit the wiki page can easily notify their friends about the content they have found through the use of the SocialBar.

CONTENT FLAGGING AND CONTENT REVIEW

With the social nature of the wiki, content administrators of your site give up some basis of their control over the site. This is the nature of all social tools, but carries the risk of inappropriate content being added, as well as the possibility of subpar content remaining on the site due to lack of visibility and feedback. An easy way to combat these issues without sacrificing the positive feedback of user-generated content is to use the Content Flagging and Review features of the Ektron Framework.

These two pieces are also part of the social networking feature set of the framework, and support similar but different functionality. The ContentFlagging Control allows users to flag a piece of content with one of a set of predefined options. For example, you might use a list of options that allows users to identify inappropriate content, such as Sexually Explicit, Mature Content, Graphic Violence, or Hate Speech. This allows you to spread your moderation effort easily into the community, easing the workload of content administrators. The tags that users apply to content on the site are not visible on the site itself, but are instead used to generate reports in the Workarea.

The ContentReview Server Control, on the other hand, is used to collect information about a given piece of content and share it with other visitors. This is very common in eCommerce, but is also very useful in wiki settings as it can help your regular contributors understand the needs of the viewing audience. The server control can be used in a five-star manner, aggregating the ratings of many people into a visual indicator that can be taken in at a glance, or it can be used for textual reviews and comments.

In this section, you first explore how to set up flag definitions in the Workarea, then you implement both server controls into the widget you previously completed, and finally you explore how to run reports against them in the Workarea.

Setting Up Flagging Definitions

Flagging definitions are applied to content on a folder-by-folder basis, much like metadata definitions. This means that you can have a set of different flagging definitions for each folder if you want. All the flagging definitions are managed through the Workarea. You'll create a definition for your wiki, and assign it to that folder now. To do so, follow these steps:

1. Open the Workarea and log in as admin.
2. The flagging definitions are managed through the Settings tab, so switch to that tab.
3. In the Settings tree drill down to Community Management ⇨ Flagging ⇨ Flagging Definitions. This displays the list of current flagging definitions in the system.
4. Click the plus icon to add a new definition. The Add Flagging Definition pane should be up now, as shown in Figure 10-34.
5. The form has two fields and an interface to add the actual definitions. For the name field, enter **Wiki Flags**. Then add four options to the definition, Inappropriate Content, Inaccurate Content, Irrelevant Content, and Needs Updating. These are the four flags that users can apply to content in the wiki. Click Save.

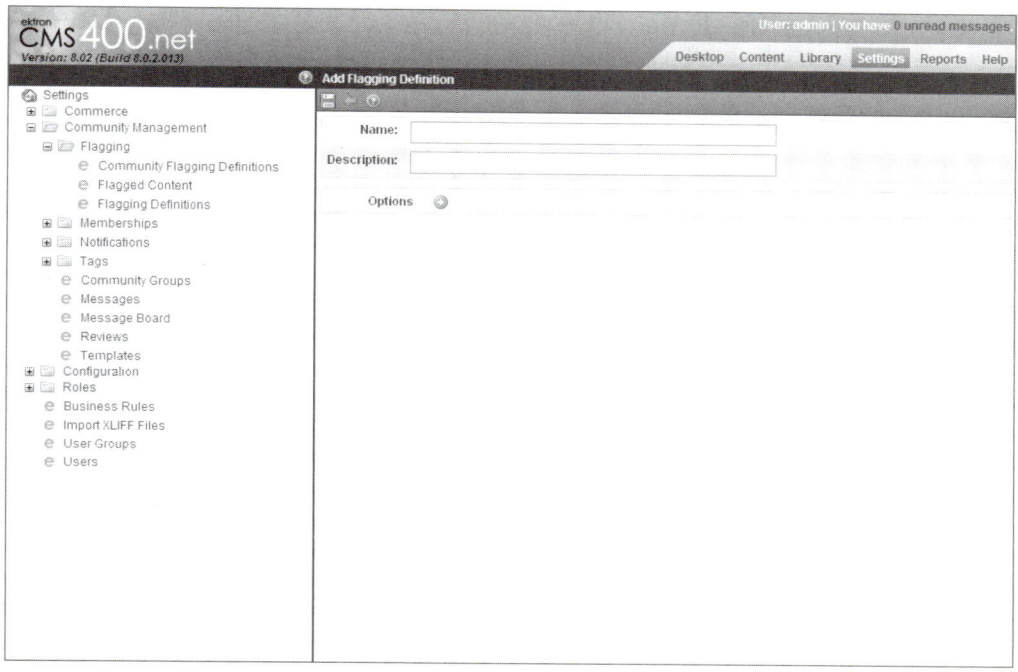

FIGURE 10-34

6. Apply the flags to the wiki folder. In the Content tab, go to the Content tree and drill down to MainSite ⇨ Content ⇨ Community ⇨ Documentation Wiki. On the Folder pane, select View ⇨ Properties from the toolbar. Once the properties come up, select Edit Properties on the toolbar, and switch to the Flagging tab. Deselect the Inherit Parent Configuration checkbox, which enables the dropdown underneath it. Select Wiki Flags and click Save. As is clear from the fact that the flag selector is a dropdown, only one flag definition can be applied per folder.

7. Move onto modifying the SocialBar Widget to display the ContentFlagging Server Control and ContentReview Server Control in addition to the SocialBar Server Control. This is covered in the next section.

Implementing the ContentFlagging and ContentReview Server Controls

In this section, you implement the additional server controls on the widget you previously created. You can easily create a new widget for each of the server controls, allowing for a bit more granularity in the decision of which controls to display, but in this scenario you know you want all three controls to appear on every wiki page, so it makes it a bit easier to just put them into the same widget. To do so, follow these steps:

1. Open Visual Studio, and open the previously created ~/widgets/socialbar.ascx file.

2. Beneath the SocialBar Server Control, drag a ContentFlagging Server Control onto the page from the toolbox. The properties for the ContentFlagging Server Control are listed in Table 10-10.

TABLE 10-10: ContentFlagging Server Control Properties

PROPERTY	DESCRIPTION
DefaultContentID	Sets the Content ID to review if DynamicParameter is not set or if there is no matching query string parameter.
DisplayXSLT	Path to a custom XSLT.
DoInitFill	If set to false, this prevents the control from filling the internal collection at Page Init, and instead waits until after any postbacks to do its fill. Use this if you are programmatically setting properties on the server control.
DynamicParameter	The query string parameter that will specify the content ID to flag.
FlagImage	Sets a path to an image to display rather than the text on the page.
FlagText	Sets the text to render for the link to flag the content. An example would be "Click here to flag this content." If FlagImage is set, this will be ignored.
StyleSheet	Set this to specify a custom stylesheet rather than the standard stylesheet.

3. With these properties in mind, you need to update the ContentFlagging Server Control to read the ID parameter from the query string. You also need to set the FlagText to be something a little less conspicuous. Update the socialbar.ascx file to match Listing 10-5.

LISTING 10-5: socialbar.ascx

```
<%@ Control Language="C#" AutoEventWireup="true"
   CodeFile="socialbar.ascx.cs" Inherits="widgets_socialbar" %>
<%@ Register Assembly="Ektron.Cms.Controls"
   Namespace="Ektron.Cms.Controls" TagPrefix="CMS" %>
<cms:socialbar
   runat="server"
   InviteURL="Invite.aspx"
   Items="Invite, Addto, Email, Digg, Delicious, Print, Twitter, FaceBook">
</cms:socialbar>
<CMS:ContentFlagging
   ID="ContentFlagging1"
   runat="server"
   DynamicParameter="id"
   FlagText="Problem with this content?" />
```

4. Add the ContentReview Server Control. This server control does not require you to add any definitions to the system, because it is much more free-form. You'll use the five-star plus

comment mode, so that users can provide textual feedback as well as a simple numerical rating. You'll also want to display the ratings on the page, rather than hiding them. Start by dragging the ContentReview Server Control onto the socialbar.ascx file, underneath the ContentFlagging Server Control. The properties for the ContentReview Server Control are listed in Table 10-11.

TABLE 10-11: ContentReview Server Control Properties

PROPERTY	DESCRIPTION
`DefaultContentID`	Sets the ID to use by default if the `DynamicParameter` is not set or no matching query string parameter was found in the URL.
`DoInitFill`	If set to false, this prevents fetching data until after the postback event. You use this if you plan to programmatically set properties on the server control later in the lifecycle to prevent fetching data twice.
`DisplayXslt`	This property accepts a path to a custom XSLT, or can be set to one of a list of pre-built XSLTs. The available options are: ➤ **Ajax 5 Stars:** Simple five-star rating that updates in place. ➤ **Ajax 5 Stars Comment:** Same as Ajax 5 Stars, but also shows a comment box for text entry. ➤ **Ajax 5 Stars with Increments:** Same as Ajax 5 stars, but allows for half-star increments. ➤ **5 Stars:** Non-Ajax version of Five Stars Comment. ➤ **5 Stars with Increments:** Allows for half-star ratings, as well as text reviews. ➤ **Review List:** Displays the list of reviews for a given piece of content or user.
`DynamicParameter`	Specifies the query string parameter used to set the current content ID. The server control then loads the reviews belonging to that content item.
`DynamicUserParameter`	The ContentReview Server Control can also display a single user's reviews from across the site. You can set this property to specify the query string parameter containing the User ID in that situation.
`GetReviews`	Specifies whether to retrieve reviews. You can set this to `None` so that reviews are not retrieved; `Content` so reviews for the appropriate content ID are retrieved; or `User` so reviews from the given user are returned.
`MaxReviews`	The maximum number of reviews to retrieve. When set to zero, all reviews are retrieved.

continues

TABLE 10-11 *(continued)*

PROPERTY	DESCRIPTION
`Moderate`	Setting this to true prevents reviews from being displayed until they are moderated.
`RatingsMinimum`	The minimum number of reviews a content item must receive before the average rating is displayed. When set to zero, the average is displayed after the first review.
`UserID`	Acts as a filter for reviews, so that you can display a user's review for a particular piece of content. If left blank, all user reviews for that content are displayed. `GetReviews` must be set to User for this property to have an effect.

5. As you may have noticed in the `DisplayXslt` property, you have several options for collecting data, but only one for displaying previously collected data. So for this example, you must actually have two ContentReview Server Controls on your widget, one to collect new ratings, and one to display the reviews. You set the first to not get reviews. You also turn moderation on. The code with these updates should look like Listing 10-6.

LISTING 10-6: socialbar.ascx

Available for download on Wrox.com

```
<%@ Control Language="C#" AutoEventWireup="true"
   CodeFile="socialbar.ascx.cs" Inherits="widgets_socialbar" %>
<%@ Register Assembly="Ektron.Cms.Controls"
   Namespace="Ektron.Cms.Controls" TagPrefix="CMS" %>
<cms:socialbar
   runat="server"
   InviteURL="Invite.aspx"
   Items="Invite, Addto, Email, Digg, Delicious, Print, Twitter, FaceBook">
</cms:socialbar>
<CMS:ContentFlagging
   ID="ContentFlagging1"
   runat="server"
   DynamicParameter="id"
   FlagText="Problem with this content?" /><br />
<CMS:ContentReview
   ID="ContentReview1"
   runat="server"
   DisplayXslt="5 Stars"
   DynamicParameter="id"
   Moderate="True" />
<CMS:ContentReview
   ID="ContentReview2"
   runat="server"
   DisplayXslt="Review List"
   DynamicParameter="id"
   GetReviews="content"
   MaxReviews="10" />
```

Now when you load the page in the browser, you see the three new elements:

➤ **The link that says "Problem with this content?"** When you click this link, you get the interface shown in Figure 10-35. This interface allows you to select one of the flags defined in the Workarea, as well as add a comment explaining the problem.

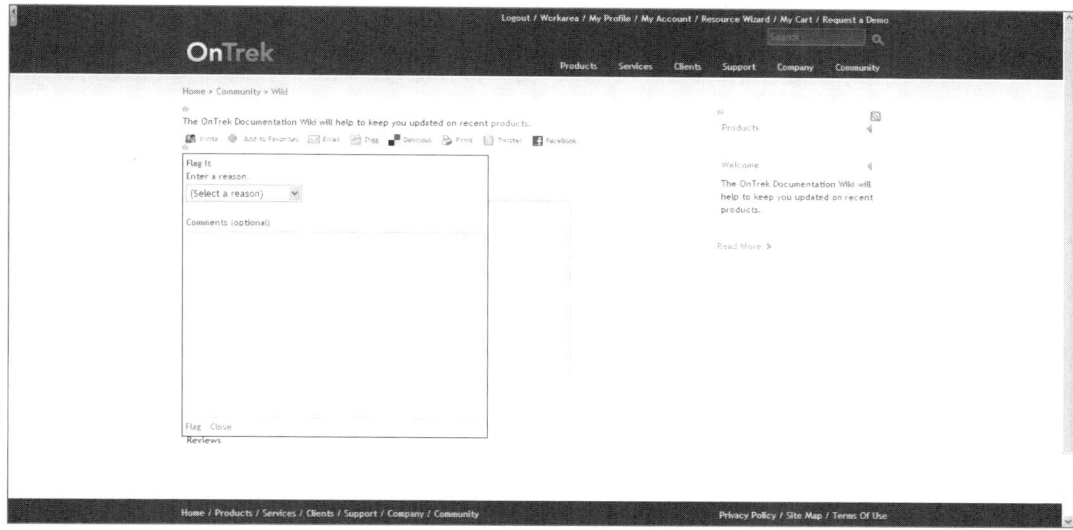

FIGURE 10-35

➤ **The five-star review interface:** Below the flagging interface, you'll see this interface. Here, you select the number of stars you want to give the content, as well as type a comment.

➤ **The list of reviews previously given for this content:** This is located below the five-star review area.

Flag and rate the content now. The next section explores how to report against the content flags and reviews.

Running Flagging and Review Reports, and Moderating Reviews

Now that you have entered some data into the flagging and review systems, you can jump into the Workarea to see how to report and deal with the information as it comes in. First you'll look at the flagging report to see which items have recently been flagged.

To work with the flagging and review data, follow these steps:

1. Open the Workarea logged in as admin. Most content reporting is handled through the Reports tab, so switch to that.

2. In the Reports tree, drill down to Contents ➪ Content Flags. The Content Reports pane displays in the right, showing the flagged content, as shown in Figure 10-36.

   As is shown, the list contains your wiki document, flagged as Needs Updating.

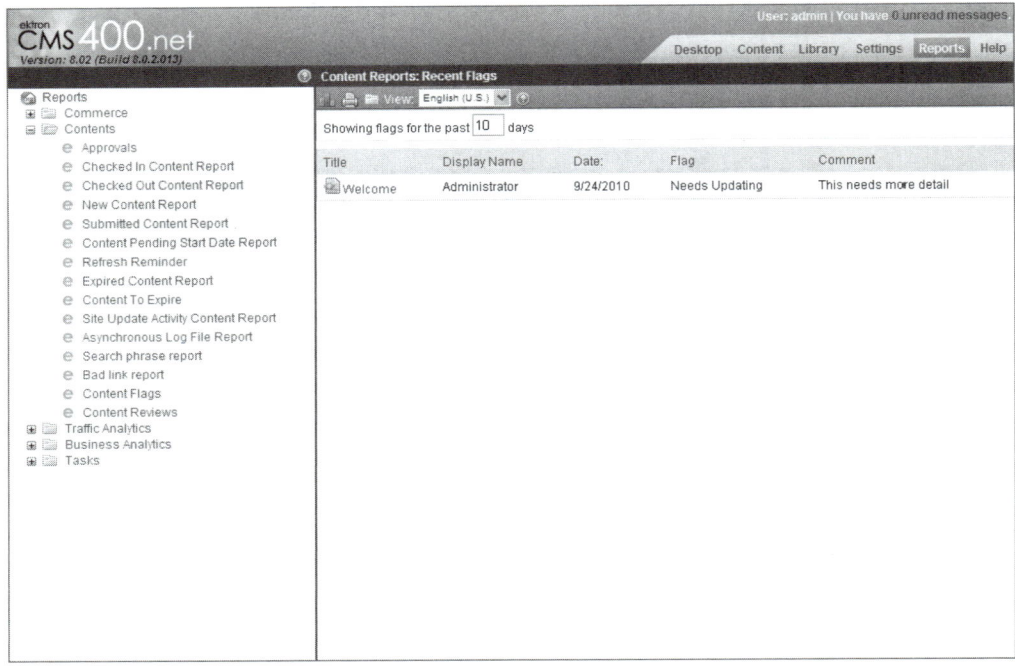

FIGURE 10-36

3. Click the link for the Needs Updating flag to update the display. This will show the flag details, and allow you to edit or delete the flag. You can see the details by browsing to the content item directly from the content as well.

4. You can also moderate reviews from the Reports tab. In the Reports tree, navigate to Contents ➪ Content Reviews. This shows a list of all the pending content reviews, as shown in Figure 10-37. By clicking one, you can see the specific details of that review and edit it as well.

> You can also quickly moderate many reviews by simply running down the left two columns of the report and selecting the Approve or Decline option for each one, and then clicking the Save icon. Once you have moderated a review, it will no longer appear in the report.

5. As mentioned earlier, these reports can be run against an individual piece of content as well. In the Content pane in the Workarea, navigate to MainSite ➪ Content ➪ Community ➪ Documentation Wiki in the Content tree.

6. Select the content you previously rated from the list in the Content pane, and the Workarea shows you that piece of content. On the toolbar in the Content pane, select the Content Report icon (). This brings up the Reporting pane, which displays the ratings as well as the flags for the particular piece of content. The initial display, shown in Figure 10-38, shows the ratings for the content.

Content Flagging and Content Review | **385**

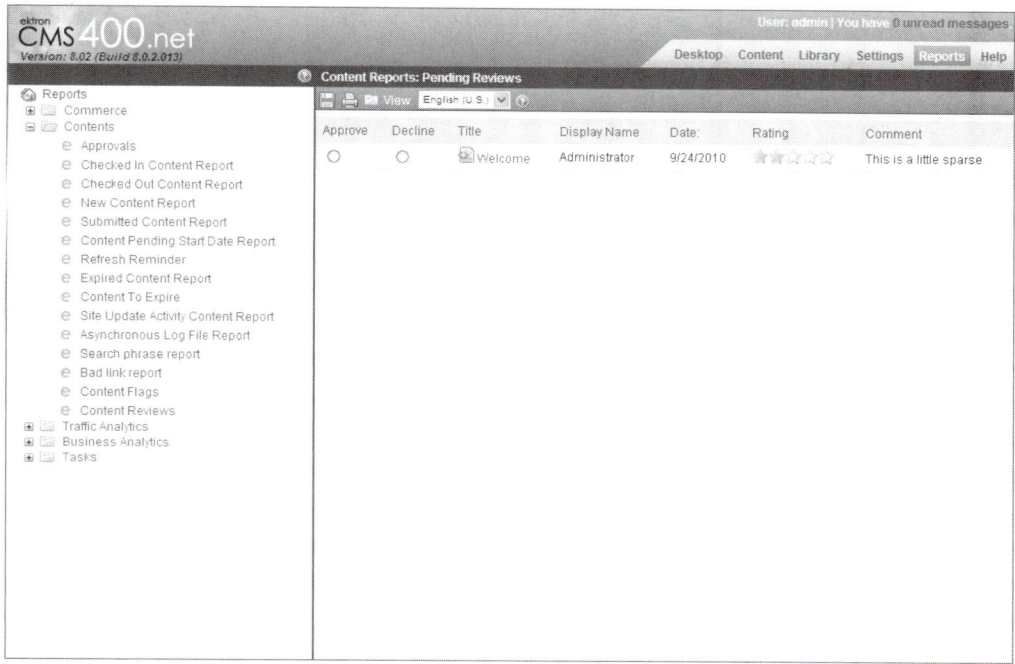

FIGURE 10-37

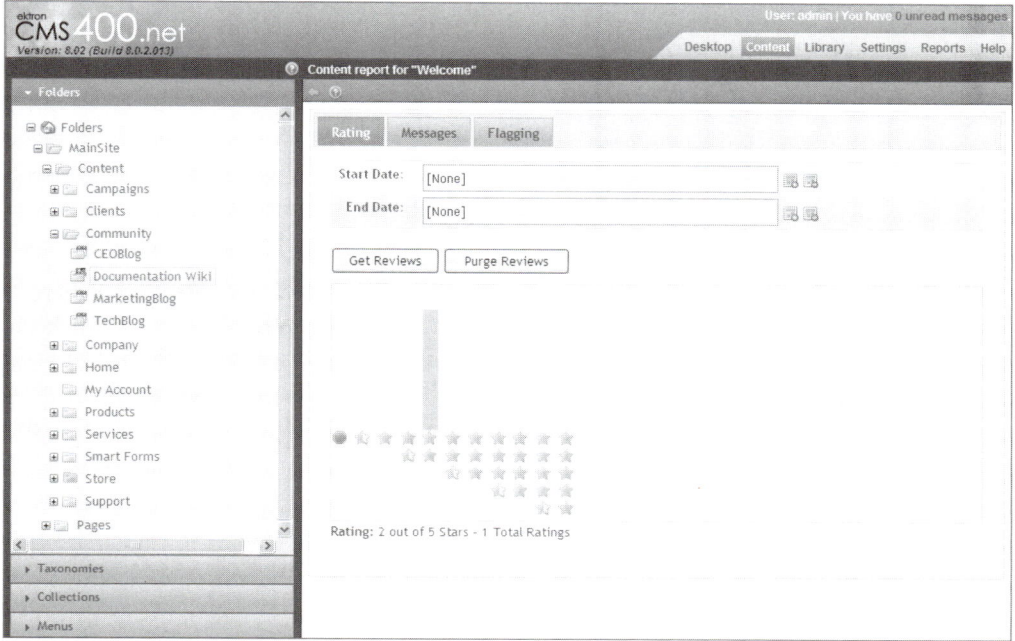

FIGURE 10-38

The Rating tab immediately summarizes the star ratings the content has received.

7. Click the Get Reviews button. You'll see a list of all the reviews for that comment, along with links to edit and delete them. You can also export to Excel from this interface.

8. The Flagging tab is very similar to the Rating tab — it allows you to specify a date range to retrieve the flags from. It does not allow you to edit the flags on the content, but it does allow you to purge them once they have been addressed. The Flagging tab is shown in Figure 10-39.

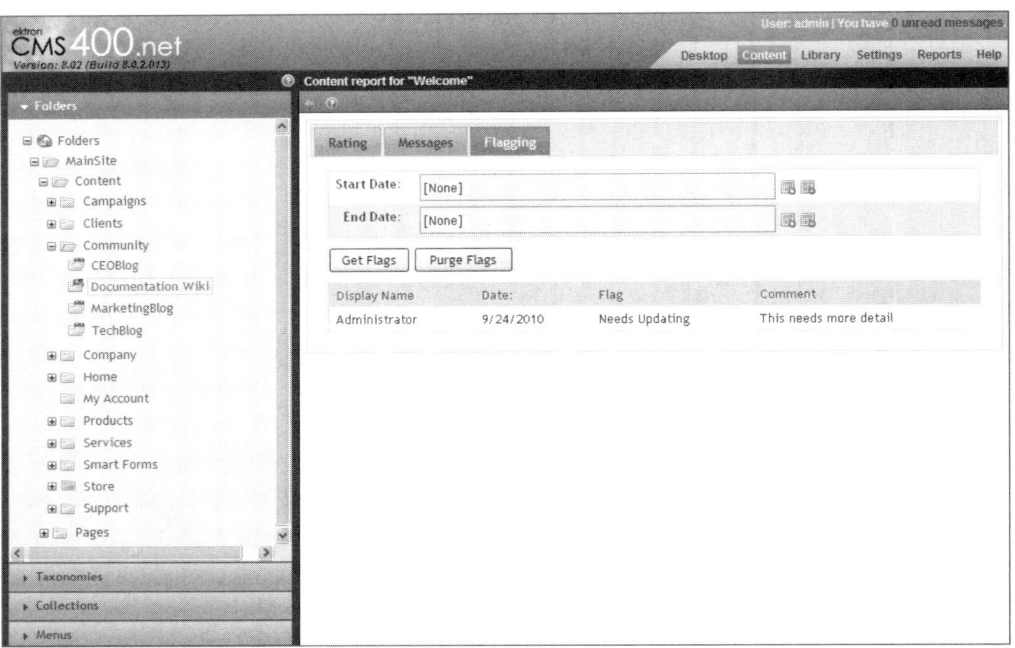

FIGURE 10-39

9. You can add widgets to your Smart Desktop in the Workarea to see the flags and reviews when you launch the Workarea. In the Desktop tab in the Workarea, click the wide down arrow on the right of the desktop title bar. This displays the list of widgets. Drag the ContentReviews and ContentFlags Widgets onto the desktop, as shown in Figure 10-40. These widgets allows you to quickly see if there is anything that needs to be dealt with.

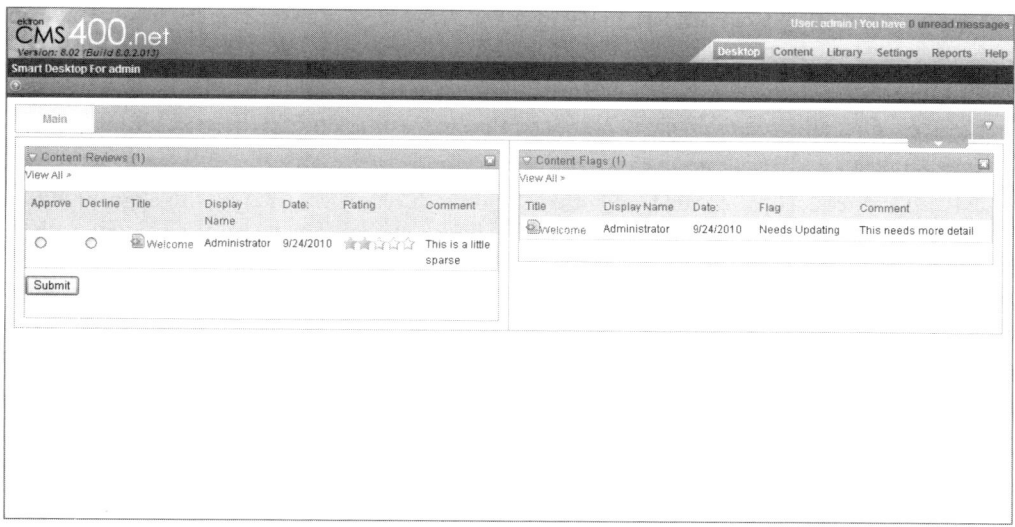

FIGURE 10-40

TAKE HOME POINTS

This chapter covered a diverse set of features, all targeted at a particular need — to involve the customer base in an active social life based around your company's product. The chapter covered the following:

➤   Fundamental tools: forums, blogs, and wikis.

➤   Some approaches to reach out through the current customer base into their social networks to provide for word-of-mouth advertising.

➤   How to manage the user-generated content going forward, by spreading some of the reviewing and moderation out to the existing customer base.

➤   How to create forums and manage them. You explored the server control set that supports forums, and learned about how to customize the user experience.

➤   How to create a blog in the Workarea, and how to manage and moderate comments on the blog. You also learned about the constituent pieces of the Blog Server Control, as well as how to recombine them to get specific functionality.

➤   All about wikis. You learned about community folders — the benefits and downsides. You learned how the existing server control library can utilize the community folder to invite users to participate with the site in a deeper way. You also constructed the wiki page using the PageBuilder feature, which provided a review of how to work with PageBuilder.

➤ Extending the wiki page you created by building a new widget to display the SocialBar Server Control. This allowed users to reach out to their networks on other sites.

➤ Extending the SocialBar Widget you created with the ContentReview and ContentFlagging Server Controls. These controls operate in slightly different ways, and with slightly different goals, but the final outcome of using them is similar in that they allow the content authors and managers to gain insight about the usefulness of the content on their sites.

➤ You also learned about the Invite Server Control, which allows users to send e-mails through the system to their colleagues, inviting them to become involved on the site.

By utilizing the community features in the Ektron Framework, the OnTrek team needs to give up a certain amount of control over what appears on the site, but is able to foster a vibrant community around the OnTrek suite. This community will help them secure more business in the future, through word of mouth advertising which occurs through cross-posting OnTrek's content to other social bookmarking and networking sites, and by demonstrating to potential customers that there is a wide array of current users. The net result is that OnTrek is able to spread its reputation in an easy and organic way.

11

Implementing the OnTrek Social Network

- ➤ How do you establish a social network including users, friends, and profiles?
- ➤ How do you connect members with community groups?
- ➤ Can you use dashboards as personalized portals of information?
- ➤ How do you stay up-to-date on members' activity streams?
- ➤ What is the purpose of micro-messaging?

It is no exaggeration to say that social media has fundamentally changed the way businesses operate and engage with customers. Changes are happening to the way corporations are doing business as a result. Information is being shared regularly through many different online venues. Organizations that listen and participate in such conversations gain an advantage over their customers by increasing sales, extending marketing opportunities, and increasing customer loyalty through improved support and public relations.

Prior to the age of social media, businesses were used to communicating directly both with customers and employees in one outward direction. This is no longer the case. Customers talk about the brands with which they interact in open forums on the Internet; employees blog about their company on personal websites and ask questions around the virtual water cooler. Businesses can no longer ignore the comments that people have. Communication is at the core of social media and if you are not engaging in the conversation on your own website, the conversation will happen elsewhere.

Social media is not just for external communities; it is also relevant for employees, which corporations are trying to leverage to improve their corporate culture and productivity. As new employees join the workforce, they expect or even demand that these social tools are a part of their everyday activities.

The OnTrek website uses social functionality to foster the community's involvement in many aspects of the website's functions. In Chapter 10, you learned how to use Web 2.0 type communication tools to provide support to existing clients through the use of blogs, wikis, and discussion boards. This chapter continues the conversation by showing how to use the social networking functionality for site visitors to discover relevant information, to discuss topics with like-minded individuals, and to discover community members in need of (or able to provide) help.

THE IMPORTANCE OF SOCIAL NETWORKING

To ensure that your site's social functionality can provide these services and meet the expectations of community members, this chapter looks at the components that form the core of social networking sites and shows how they are implemented in the OnTrek website using the Ektron Community Framework. Keep in mind that this framework encompasses both Web 2.0 and the social networking type functionality. Often times these two concepts are used interchangeably; however, Ektron does not do so. Ektron uses the phrase Web 2.0 to refer to the broad set of technologies that facilitates a two-way conversation between site visitors and site owners (through blogs, wikis, discussion boards, and so on; see Chapter 10). Ektron uses social software to refer specifically to the technology that allows users to form connections among one another and share information through those connections. This section and chapter focuses exclusively on the social networking aspects of the Ektron Community Framework.

The most important aspects of social networks are as follows:

➤ **The individual members:** Each member typically has his or her own profile that serves as their virtual presence on the website. Profiles often show contact information, various documents such as photos, videos, and blog posts, and list the member's *friends*, which signifies users who have been granted some elevated level of trust.

➤ **The community group:** This group allows members to unite around a common purpose and share information on a specific subject. A group also has a group profile, which serves as its homepage on the site and is usually the epicenter of the group activity. Group administrators can set permissions on groups so they are public and open to anyone or private, which means members must get approval to join. Group members can share information, discover others with similar interests, and work collaboratively to create documents.

➤ **Activity streams:** On both user profiles and group profiles it is common to find activity streams that list activities related to the group or member. The member profile includes the activities related to that individual, such as friending (for example, "John is now friends with Susan") and content creation (for example, "John uploaded a new video entitled Summer Vacation"). Similarly, on the group profile, the activity stream includes activities that occur within the group itself, such as membership activities (for example, "John is now a member of the Sales Group") and collaboration activities (for example, "John published a new document entitled Engineering Product Specification"). In addition to reading the activity stream online, members can often request updates to be delivered via instant messaging, SMS, or through e-mail.

➤ **Micro-messaging or micro-blogging:** This is a way of communicating that allows members to publish very short messages, share status updates (for example, "what are you doing now?"), and post relevant URLs and other interesting bits of information. Micro-messages can either be publicly visible to all members of the social network or only to friends. Twitter, which popularized micro-messaging, is often used in a number of ways — to crowd source for answers to questions in real-time, to keep aware of trending news topics, and to promote an event or other marketing event. Most micro-messages are text but some services allow for video and other multimedia formats.

TECHNOLOGY

When Ektron launched the first version of its Community Framework in 2006, there were no other Web content management vendors with this type of deeply integrated framework. Ektron recognized that a paradigm shift was underway that would fundamentally change what people would come to expect from websites, both public-facing websites and internal corporate intranets.

The Community Framework is composed of dozens of server controls and widgets, as well as a dozen more APIs, ranging from Web 2.0 type controls such as blogs and discussion boards, to the social networking components discussed here. This chapter focuses on the following aspects of the Ektron Community Framework:

➤ Community members, colleagues, and user profiles

➤ Community groups and group profiles

➤ Activity streams and notifications

➤ Micro-messaging

➤ Personalization dashboards

Any time a membership user is created, the user is automatically given the plumbing needed for participation in a social network, such as the ability to establish connections with other users called colleagues, and storage for personal information. From a developer's point of view, no work is needed to configure or enable this underlying structural aspect of a social network; it is an inherent part of the system. Once a user has been created, the User Profile Server Control and APIs can be used to display the profile for that user on the website. It is from the user profile that users manage their colleagues, personal information, privacy settings, and so forth.

User profiles are also a place for community members to establish personal "dashboards" of information. Similar in concept to iGoogle (www.google.com/ig), a member's personal dashboard becomes a place where information can be aggregated from across the Internet or the organization. The information kept on the dashboard can serve two purposes:

➤ Community members use it to organize information into one centralized location.

➤ Members use it to share information with others visiting the profile.

Ektron's Community Groups are created by community members as a place to discuss particular topics and share information with its list of members. Community members either join community groups out of interest or because they're invited to join by the group's administrator. Community profiles are displayed using the Community Group Profile Server Control and APIs and contain information similar to that found in the user's profile.

Keeping community members up-to-date on all of the activities occurring within their social network of colleagues and the community groups is of critical importance. As such, the Ektron Community Framework includes a general-purpose notification engine to alert members when certain activities of interest take place. These notifications can be delivered in a number of ways, including through e-mail and through the website's activity stream timeline, using the ActivityStream Server Control and APIs.

Later in this chapter, you'll see how to incorporate micro-messaging into the user profile, allowing members to publish micro-messages to the system and keep their colleagues and community groups apprised of their activity. Micro-messages are a type of activity, which means that members can choose to be notified of micro-message posts through a number of different channels, including SMS or the activity stream. Also, later in this chapter, you'll see how to work with micro-messaging through the Community Framework's MicroMessage Server Control, and you'll walk through its integration onto the user profile, as implemented on the OnTrek website.

USERS, FRIENDS, AND PROFILES

Community members, friends, and user profiles form three of the most basic elements of a social network.

As far as the Ektron database is concerned, the members of a website's community are one or the other of the following:

- **CMS users:** Created by a CMS admin.
- **Membership users:** Created either by a CMS admin through the Workarea, or by the site visitor through the website during the membership registration process (see the section "Allowing a User to Register on the Site" in Chapter 7).

Any time either type of user is created, they are automatically given the plumbing needed for participation in a social network, such as the ability to establish connections with other users (called *colleagues*) and storage for personal information. From a developer's point-of-view, no work is needed to configure or enable this underlying structural aspect of a social network; it is an inherent part of the system.

Understanding the Friending Process

Once a user is in the system, she can begin establishing connections with other members. This process is typically called *friending* and two users who have *friended* each other are called colleagues. It is worthwhile noting that the system uses a symmetric friending paradigm like Facebook, which means that both users need to establish the friendship connection before they're considered colleagues. It does not use the asymmetric follow approach used on sites such as Twitter, where one user can follow another without the approval of the person being followed.

The CommunitySearch Server Control is one of the primary methods for community members to discover other potential connections by searching by name, interests, tags, or even location. The search results display members of the social network and include a link that members can use to issue a friend request. Figure 11-1 shows the search results, including the friend request link as displayed by the CommunitySearch Server Control. In addition to the CommunitySearch Server Control, there are APIs available that can be used to issue friend requests. You'll read about these APIs later in the User Profile "Under the Hood" section.

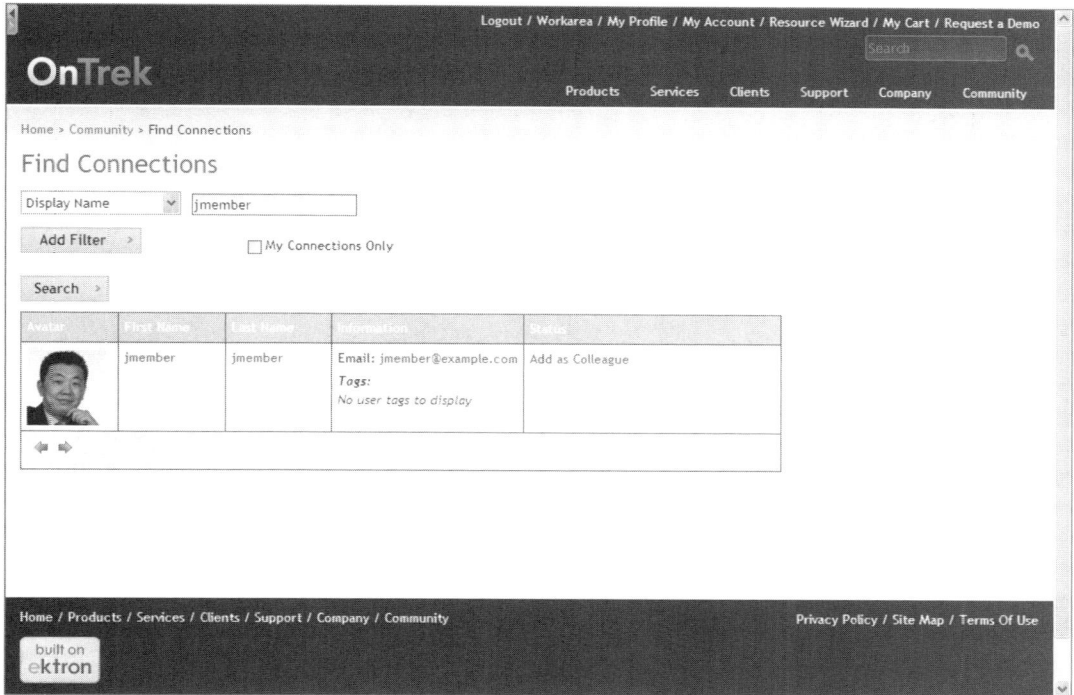

FIGURE 11-1

Understanding User Profile Functionality

A user profile is a Web page that contains personal information for a community member. This information often includes a photograph, avatar, contact information, and other personal details that define the member's digital identity. On a corporate social network, such as an intranet, a profile contains work-related information, such as an individual's role and their supervisor's name. A profile can also store and share data. Users of sites such as MySpace and Facebook often upload videos and publish blog posts through their profiles.

Profiles often provide community-generated content attribution, with the avatar and display name serving as the hyperlink pointing to the user's profile. In this way, profile links become a key aspect of social networking functionality, serving as a way to discover new users and learn more information about the person authoring the information. Figure 11-2 shows a posted message using the MessageBoard Server Control and shows how the post is attributed to a particular user through the use of an avatar and hyperlink to that user's profile.

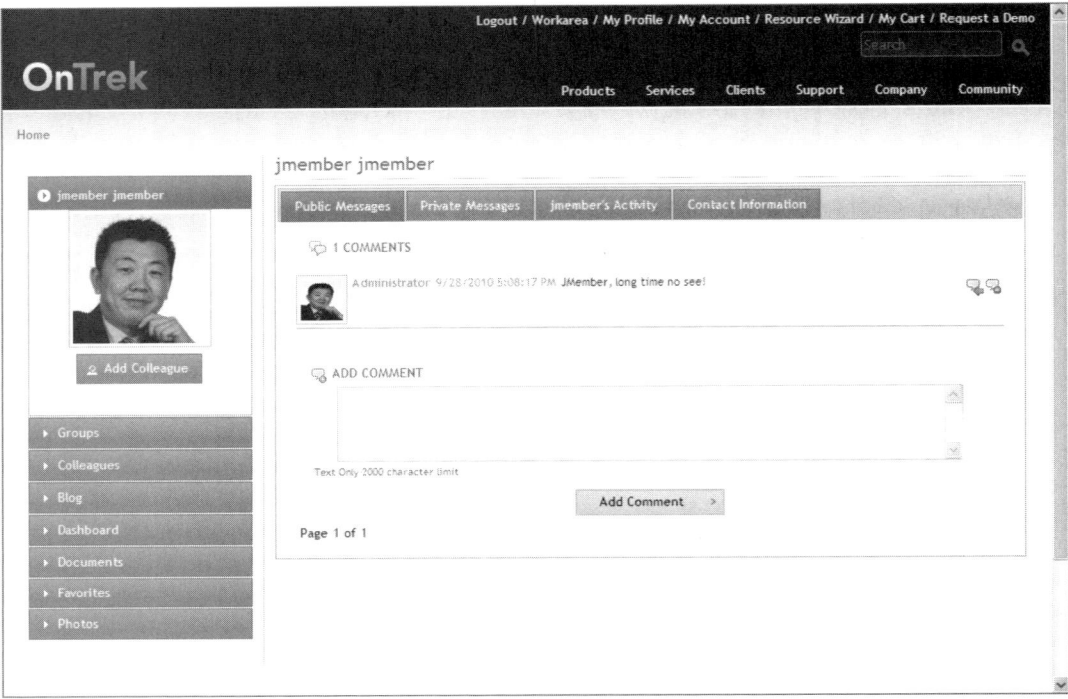

FIGURE 11-2

The UserProfile Server Control can be used to display a user profile for any CMS or membership user. The user profile displayed by the server control is very basic, and an example of its default display is shown in Figure 11-3. Users who are logged on have the ability to edit their profiles by clicking the Edit Profile link that appears in the top-right corner.

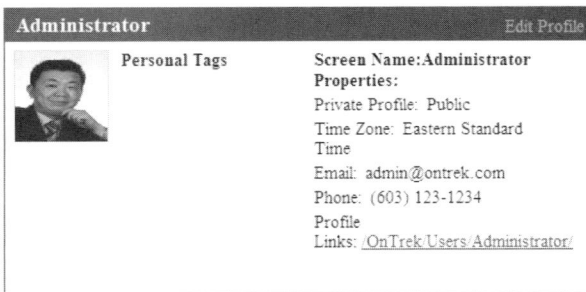

FIGURE 11-3

The default presentation can be customized by defining a custom XSLT and registering it using the server control's DisplayXSLT property. However, often the requirements for a website's user profile are more complex than the UserProfile Server Control can achieve, and so the stock server control may not be an option. Instead, the Ektron Community Framework APIs are frequently used to build a user profile. The OnTrek website is no exception — the user profile section of OnTrek is essentially an application unto itself.

You can create friendly URLs for your members' profiles. For example, rather than referring to a specific member's profile as /user/profile.aspx?id=239, you can use /users/john-smith, by enabling the Community Aliasing for Users feature. See the "Aliasing" section in Chapter 6 or more information.

In addition to this basic information, user profiles often also include links to other items:

➤ **Community Documents:** Every user in the system (both CMS and membership users) has a personal content repository associated with his account. This repository can be accessed and managed using the CommunityDocuments Server Control. This control allows users to create and share personal content on the website. Figure 11-4 shows the output of the CommunityDocuments Server Control prior to the user uploading any content.

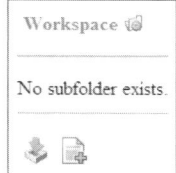

FIGURE 11-4

➤ **Private Messaging:** The Messaging Server Control allows community members to send and receive private messages. This is an important feature, as it offers a way for community members to communicate information that should not or cannot be shared publically on the website.

➤ **Colleagues:** The Friends Server Control displays a list of users who are colleagues of a particular community member. This control is typically located on a user profile and is set to display the list of the member's current colleagues, pending colleagues, and invited colleagues.

➤ **Community Groups:** The CommunityGroupList Server Control displays a list of community groups and can be used to present:

  ➤ Community groups a user has joined
  ➤ Community groups the user has been invited to join
  ➤ Community groups the user has requested to join

➤ **Message Boards:** The MessageBoard Server Control allows community members to author comments about a user, community group, or content item. The MessageBoard Server Control may be associated with a user, a community group, or with content. Moderation is also available, and requires that messages are approved prior to displaying on the website.

OnTrek's user profiles contain heavy client-side requirements, including the ability for users to:

➤ Create folders by right-clicking elements and invoking a context menu.
➤ Hide and show profile elements using sliding accordions.
➤ Organize colleagues by dragging and dropping their avatars into folders.

With such highly interactive and specialized behavior requirements, using the UserProfile Server Control is not possible. Instead, the user profile section of the OnTrek website uses the Ektron Community Framework APIs extensively, and it serves as a good example of how to use those APIs to power a rich, interactive user experience.

OnTrek's user profile is logically divided into three tiers:

- **Presentation tier:** Uses jQuery to create the interactive client-side experience.
- **Middle tier:** Uses ASHX handlers to encapsulate business logic.
- **Ektron's APIs:** For all data and CMS needs.

Overall, the OnTrek user profile presents a nice architectural model and clean pattern to follow when this type of rich functionality is required. It's a good example of what can be done with jQuery, .NET, and Ektron.

In this implementation section, you will focus your attention on the Ektron specific pieces of its implementation, namely the setup and configuration steps and the areas of the user profile application that use the Community Framework Server Controls and APIs. Later, in the User Profile "Under the Hood" section, you will continue to probe deeper into the implementation by looking into the source of the ASHX handlers and discovering a number of Community Framework API gems contained there.

If you're interested in learning more about jQuery and its possible uses with Ektron, you can find additional information in the RIA section of Chapter 6, which uses jQuery and Ektron Smart Forms to provide an interactive image rotation component.

Configuring Community Member Templates

For any community implementation, you'll need to define the location to the user profiles, community groups, and other community pages. This is done by specifying the URL to these pages in the Community Templates screen in the Workarea. These paths are used by the system when links to these pages are generated. For example, the search results displayed by the CommunitySearch Server Control include a hyperlink to the profile of the community member (as shown earlier in Figure 11-1). The hyperlink displayed by the control uses the information specified in this screen.

To specify these paths, do the following.

1. Go to Workarea ➪ Settings ➪ Community Management ➪ Templates. You will see the screen shown in Figure 11-5. This screen contains two sets of templates: user related and group related.

2. In the User Templates section, enter the values in Table 11-1 as defined in the OnTrek implementation guide:

Users, Friends, and Profiles | **397**

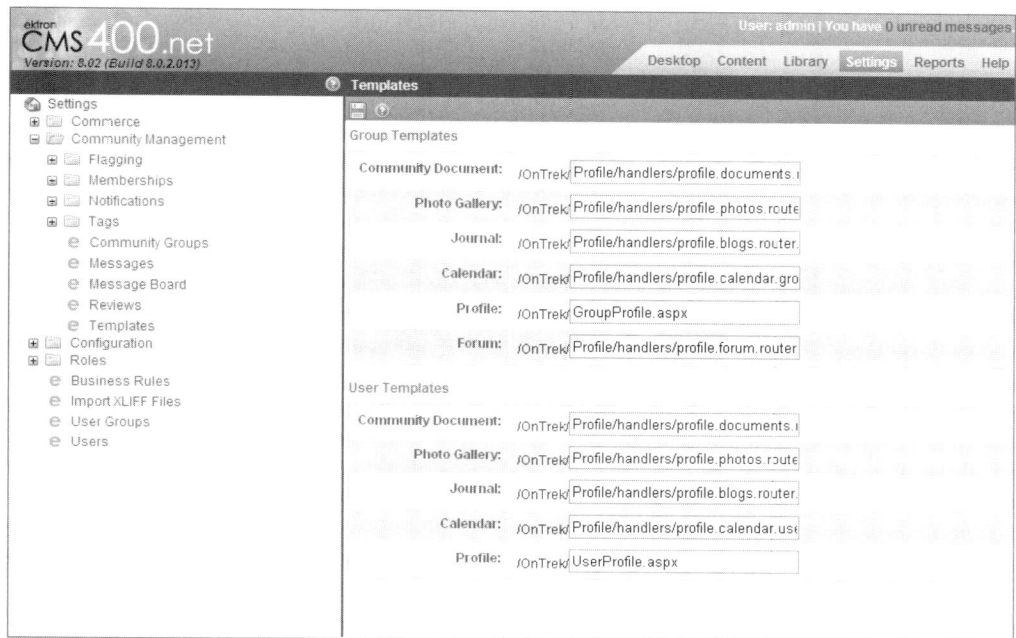

FIGURE 11-5

TABLE 11-1: User Templates values

DOCUMENT	VALUE TO ENTER	EXPLANATION
Community Document	exchange/codedownload.aspx	URL for the page hosting the CommunityDocuments Server Control (or similar functionality using the APIs)
Photo Gallery	/profile.aspx	URL for the page hosting the PhotoGallery Server Control
Calendar	/workarea/communitycalendar.aspx	The Calendar for the individual user
Profile	/user/profile.aspx	the URL for the user profile
Journal	/user/blog.aspx	URL for the page hosting a blog control or similar

OnTrek's User Profile User Control

When logged in as Admin, opening OnTrek's Admin user profile in your Web browser will show something similar to the screen shown in Figure 11-6. You'll notice that there are two major regions defined for the user profile.

- ➤ The first region occupies the left-side navigation and contains accordion items stacked vertically. At the top of the stack is the user's avatar, and then beneath it follows the Groups, Colleagues, Blog, Dashboard, Documents, Favorites, and Photos.
- ➤ The second region occupies the majority of the real estate of the profile's center. This contains information that is contextual to the selected accordion item. For example, when the accordion item containing the user's avatar is selected, the main region displays the five tabs shown in Figure 11-6.

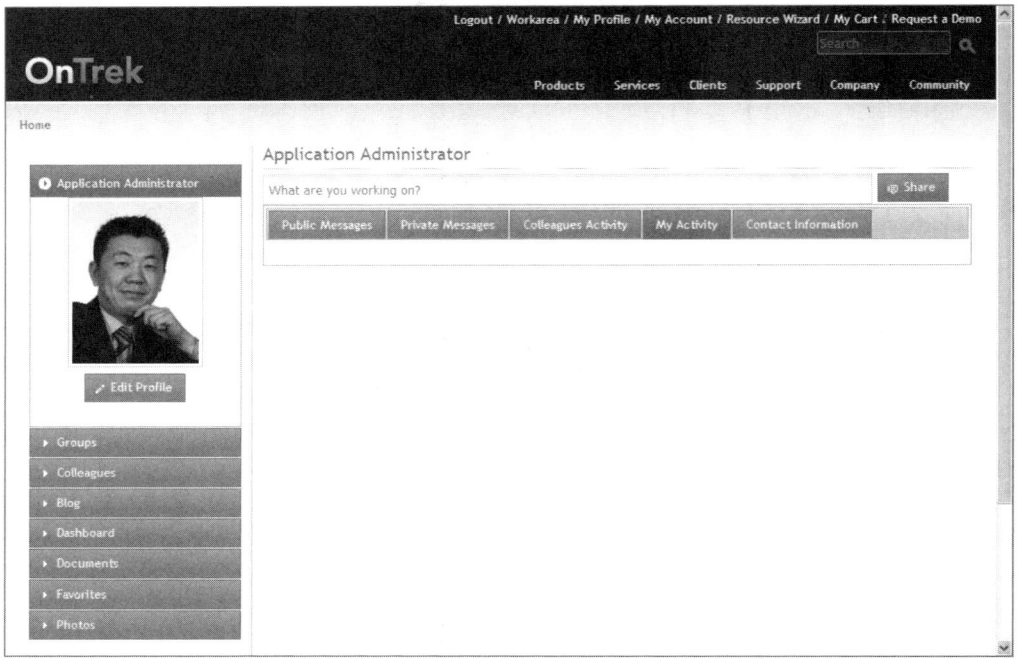

FIGURE 11-6

The implementation of the user profile is encapsulated into a single user control called ~/Profile/UserProfile.ascx; see Listing 11-1 (which is shorted for brevity). The two regions described previously (the accordion and the body) map to physical regions of this user control:

- ➤ The accordion items are wrapped with `<div class="accordion">` and define the content and behavior for each of the individual accordion items (shown in Listing 11-1).
- ➤ The main region, or body, is wrapped with `<div class="body">` and uses an ASP.NET MultiView Server Control to load the appropriate view based on the selected accordion item.

LISTING 11-1: ~/Profile/UserProfile.ascx

Available for download on Wrox.com

```
<%@ Control Language="C#" AutoEventWireup="true" CodeFile="UserProfile.ascx.cs"
Inherits="Ektron.Profile.UserProfile" %>

<%@ Register TagPrefix="CMS" Assembly="Ektron.Cms.Controls"
```

```
            Namespace="Ektron.Cms.Controls" %>
<%@ Register TagName="Blog" Src="./Accordion/Blog.ascx"
    TagPrefix="Ektron" %>
<%@ Register TagName="Calendar" Src="./Accordion/Calendar.ascx"
   TagPrefix="Ektron" %>
<%@ Register TagName="Colleagues" Src="./Accordion/Friends.ascx"
   TagPrefix="Ektron" %>
<%@ Register TagName="Dashboard" Src="./Accordion/Dashboard.User.ascx"
   TagPrefix="Ektron" %>
<%@ Register TagName="Documents" Src="./Accordion/Documents.ascx"
   TagPrefix="Ektron" %>
<%@ Register TagName="Favorites" Src="./Accordion/Favorites.ascx"
   TagPrefix="Ektron" %>
<%@ Register TagName="Groups" Src="./Accordion/Groups.ascx"
   TagPrefix="Ektron" %>
<%@ Register TagName="Photos" Src="./Accordion/Photos.ascx"
   TagPrefix="Ektron" %>
<%@ Register TagName="User" Src="./Accordion/User.ascx"
   TagPrefix="Ektron" %>
<%@ Register TagName="TreeView" Src="./Accordion/TreeView/treeview.ascx"
   TagPrefix="Ektron" %>
<%@ Register TagName="TreeviewContextMenu"
   Src="./Accordion/TreeView/treeview.contextmenu.ascx"
   TagPrefix="Ektron" %>

<asp:ScriptManager ID="uxScriptManager" runat="server" ScriptMode="Release" />
<Ektron:TreeviewContextMenu ID="treeviewContextMenu" runat="server" />
<div class="profileOverlay"></div>
<div class="userProfile profile">
    <input id="profile-focusHelper" type="hidden" name="profile" value="" />
    <div class="profile">

    <!-- REGION 1 - "accordion" -->
    <asp:UpdatePanel ID="upProfile"
                     runat="server"
                     ChildrenAsTriggers="false"
                     UpdateMode="Conditional">
      <ContentTemplate>
        <div class="width-6">
          <div class="rail">
            <CMS:UserProfile ID="cmsUserProfile"
                runat="server"
                Visible="true" />
            <div class="accordion">
            <h3>
            <asp:LinkButton ID="uxAccordionLinkUser"
                runat="server" CssClass="user" OnCommand="uxAccordion_Click"
                CommandArgument="user"></asp:LinkButton>
             <input id="uxAccordionDataUser" runat="server"
                type="hidden" name="accordionData"
                class="accordionData" />
            </h3>
           <div>
```

continues

LISTING 11-1 *(continued)*

```
            <div class="user">
              <asp:Literal runat="server" ID="uxAvatar" />
              <asp:MultiView ID="mvUserAccordion"
                  runat="server">
                <asp:View
                    ID="uxUserAccordionEditProfile"
                    runat="server">
                <a id="uxUserAccordionEditProfileLink"
                    runat="server"
                    class="ek_thickbox ui-button ui-widget
                          ui-state-default ui-corner-all
                          ui-button-text-icon">
                <span class="ui-button-icon-primary
                            ui-icon ui-icon-pencil"></span>
                <span class="ui-button-text">Edit Profile</span>
                </a>
                </asp:View>
              <!--
-- remaining Views removed for brevity, see
              -- source code for complete listing
              -->
              </asp:MultiView>
          </div>
        </div>
      </div>
    </div>
  </div>

  <!-- REGION 2 - "body" -->
  <asp:UpdatePanel ID="upBody" runat="server" UpdateMode="Always">
    <ContentTemplate>
    <div class="body">
      <input type="hidden" class="profileData"
            id="uxProfileData" runat="server" name="profile" />
      <input type="hidden" class="hostData"
            id="uxHostData" runat="server" name="profile" />
      <h3>
        <asp:Literal ID="uxHeaderUser" runat="server" />
        <span class="status">
          <asp:Literal ID="uxHeaderStatus" runat="server" />
        </span>
      </h3>
      <asp:MultiView ID="mvProfileBody" runat="server">
        <asp:View ID="vwUser" runat="server">
          <Ektron:User ID="ucUser" runat="server"
                Mode="User" />
        </asp:View>
        <!--
          -- remaining Views removed for brevity, see
          -- source code for complete listing
          -->
                        </asp:MultiView>
```

```
                    </div>
                </</ContentTemplate>
            </asp:UpdatePanel>
        </div>
    </ContentTemplate>
</asp:UpdatePanel>
</div>
</div>
```

In the associated codebehind file, ~/Profile/UserProfile.ascx.cs, the click event handler is responsible for handling the click events and loading the appropriate view:

```
protected void uxAccordion_Click(object sender, CommandEventArgs e)
{
    this.activeTabId = (string)e.CommandArgument;
    this.activeTabIndex = this.GetControlIndex(this.activeTabId);
    OnSelectedUserControl();
    SetBody();
}
```

The User Profile code so far has been more .NET code than Ektron Framework API; but it's important code to highlight for a few reasons. First, it demonstrates a practical real-world implementation of a user profile that incorporates most every standard element found in social networking profiles built using the Ektron Community Framework. Second, it will serve as a reference point for most every one of the remaining technical sections in this chapter.

The Friends User Control

At the very top of the UserProfile.ascx source code shown in Listing 11-1, you'll notice a number of Register statements that reference additional user controls. You'll now take a look at one of these specific user controls, the Friends.ascx control in order to better understand how this component of the User Profile is implemented and show how it uses the CommunityFramework API to display a list of the member's colleagues, as shown in code Listing 11-2.

LISTING 11-2 ~/Profile/Accordion/Friends.ascx

Available for download on Wrox.com

```
<%@ Control Language="C#" AutoEventWireup="true" CodeFile="Friends.ascx.cs"
    Inherits="Ektron.Profile.Friends" %>
<%@ Register Assembly="Ektron.Cms.Controls" Namespace="Ektron.Cms.Controls"
    TagPrefix="CMS" %>

<div class="colleagues members">
    <asp:PlaceHolder ID="uxFindColleague" runat="server">
        <div class="findColleagues clearfix">
            <label for="colleagues">Find a colleague...</label>
            <input type="text" id="colleagues" name="colleagues"
                maxlength="50" class="findFriend" value="" />
            <a href="#FindColleague"
                class="ui-button ui-widget ui-state-default
                ui-corner-all ui-button-text-icon"
                title="Find a colleague'
```

continues

LISTING 11-2 *(continued)*

```
                    onclick="Ektron.Profile.Colleagues.find(this);return false;">
                    <span class="ui-button-icon-primary ui-icon ui-icon-person"></span>
                     <span class="ui-button-text">Find</span>
                </a>
            </div>
        </asp:PlaceHolder>
        <asp:MultiView ID="uxColleagues" runat="server">
            <asp:View ID="uxColleaguesUser" runat="server">
                <div class="types">
                    <ul>
                        <li>
                            <a href="#colleagues-1">
                            <asp:Literal ID="uxFriendsLabel"
                                        runat="server" /></a>
                        </li>
                        <li id="uxColleaguesAwaitingTab" runat="server">
                            <a href="#<%= uxColleaguesInvitedPanel.ClientID %>">
                            <asp:Literal ID="uxOutgoingRequests"
                                        runat="server" /></a>
                        </li>
                        <li id="uxColleaguesNewInvitesTab" runat="server">
                            <a href="#<%= uxColleaguesPendingPanel.ClientID %>">
                            <asp:Literal ID="uxIncomingRequests"
                                        runat="server" />
                          <asp:Label id="uxNewInvites" runat="server">
                          <img id="uxColleaguesNewInvites"
                              runat="server" visible="false"
                              enableviewstate="false" /></asp:Label></a>
                        </li>
                    </ul>
                    <div id="colleagues-1">
                        <asp:Literal ID="uxColleaguesCurrent" runat="server" />
                    </div>
                    <div id="uxColleaguesInvitedPanel" runat="server">
                        <asp:Literal ID="uxColleaguesInvited" runat="server" />
                    </div>
                    <div id="uxColleaguesPendingPanel" runat="server">
                        <asp:Literal ID="uxColleaguesPending" runat="server" />
                    </div>
                </div>
            </asp:View>
            <asp:View ID="uxColleaguesNone" runat="server">
                <p class="noColleagues">
                    <asp:Image ID="uxNoColleagues" runat="server" />
                </p>
            </asp:View>
        </asp:MultiView>
        <CMS:Friends ID="cmsFriends" runat="server"
            Visible="false" MaxResults="200"  />
        <CMS:CommunityGroupMembers ID="cmsMembers"
            runat="server" Visible="false" />
</div>
```

The lines of particular interest are at the bottom, where you can see two references to two of the Ektron Framework's Server Controls, namely, the Friends Server Control (CMS:Friends) and the CommunityGroupMembers Server Control (CMS:CommunityGroupMembers). These two controls are placed side by side since this code file is shared across the implementation of the user and group profiles. On the user profile, the Friends Server Control is used to list a member's colleagues. On the group profile, the CommunityGroupMembers Server Control is used to display the group's members. Both of these controls have their visibility set to False, which means the display is being controlled through code. If you were to open its corresponding codebehind (Friends.ascx.cs), you would find the following code snippet:

```
private void GetUserProfile()
{
    bool hasColleagues = false;
    string colleagues;
    XsltArgumentList xsltArgs;
    xsltArgs = new System.Xml.Xsl.XsltArgumentList();

    //Get Colleagues
    cmsFriends.DefaultUserID = this.ProfileId;
    cmsFriends.DisplayMode =
       Ektron.Cms.Controls.Friends.eDisplayMode.Directory;
    cmsFriends.DefaultFolderID = this.UserCookieData.CookieData.Colleagues.Context[this.UserCookieData.CookieData.Colleagues.Context.Count - 1];
    cmsFriends.Hide = true;
    cmsFriends.Fill();
    xsltArgs.AddParam("mode", "", "colleagues");
    xsltArgs.AddParam("sitePath", "", this.contentApi.SitePath);
    xsltArgs.AddParam("permission", "", Enum.GetName(typeof(UserPermission), this.UserProfileData.Permission).ToLower());
    xsltArgs.AddParam("profileMode", "", Enum.GetName(typeof(ProfileType), this.Mode).ToLower());
    colleagues = EkXml.XSLTransform(cmsFriends.XmlDoc.InnerXml, this.xsltPathCmsFriends, true, false, xsltArgs, false, null, Constants.CacheProfileInterval);
    uxColleaguesCurrent.Text = colleagues;
```

In the underlying user control, the developer sets additional parameters to the Friends Server Control, namely, DefaultUserID, DisplayMode, and DefaultFolderID — the three most important parameters of the Friends Server Control.

The purpose of the DefaultUserID parameter is straightforward, with the specified value representing the default user ID that will be used by the control.

Since this server control has the ability to display four types of colleagues (current colleagues grouped by category, current colleagues listed in alphabetical order, pending colleagues, and invited colleagues), it is necessary to indicate which type you want returned. This is specified through the DisplayMode property, which is set to retrieve data in Directory mode (current colleagues grouped by category). The DefaultFolderID property correspondingly indicates which category colleagues should be selected from.

You may be wondering, though, why this code was manipulated in codebehind. Looking at this code further, it becomes apparent why the developer decided to set the control's visibility to False and to manipulate its display through codebehind: It presents a solution to a problem that many have run across previously. The problem is, when using the DisplayXSLT property of a server control, how can you pass along custom parameters to the transformation? The solution is one that can only be implemented in codebehind. You create an XsltArgumentList object, define your parameter values, and use the EkXml's transformation routine, which accepts an XSLTArgs object as a parameter. The result is the same had you used the DisplayXSLT property, with the exception and benefit that this transformation allows you to pass arguments.

Take a look through the other user controls that are registered at the top of the page, namely:

- *./Accordion/Blog.ascx*
- *./Accordion/Calendar.ascx*
- *./Accordion/Dashboard.User.ascx*
- *./Accordion/Documents.ascx*
- *./Accordion/Favorites.ascx*
- *./Accordion/Groups.ascx*
- *./Accordion/Photos.ascx*
- *./Accordion/User.ascx*

Each is worth exploring further as they contain useful lines of code that can save you time when building your own user profile.

Under the Hood

Given the heavy client-side requirements of the OnTrek profile, the application uses jQuery to achieve much of the rich client behavior. To facilitate client and server communication, the user profile application exposes Community Framework APIs over HTTP through the use of .NET ASHX handlers, and returns data formatted using JSON. ASHX handlers are a good choice when implementing this type of service because they avoid much of the overhead involved in rendering a full ASPX page. For example, ASHX handlers entirely skip the normal page lifecycle, reducing the computational overhead of a given request.

In the ~/Profile/Handlers/ folders, you'll find all of the following files:

- profile.blogs.router.ashx
- profile.calendar.group.router.ashx
- profile.calendar.user.router.ashx
- profile.colleagues.ashx
- profile.documents.ashx

- profile.documents.router.ashx
- profile.favorites.ashx
- profile.forum.router.ashx
- profile.groups.ashx
- profile.members.ashx
- profile.photos.ashx

Each handler uses the Framework API in some way, exposing features that are not available through the Workarea or server controls. This section cherry picks through a few of the hidden pearls of these handlers, but there are many others not covered here, so it is highly advised that you spend some time browsing through these files at some point since they provide examples for things that haven't been exposed before.

The ProcessRequest Entry Point in Services

Let's start by looking at how the ProcessRequest method defined in ~/Profile/Handlers/profile.colleagues.ashx handles various requests. It uses a `switch` statement to dispatch processing based on the type of action that is requested. The following snippet shows the relevant section of that ASHX handler:

```
public void ProcessRequest(HttpContext context)
{
    //set header info
    context.Response.ContentType = "application/json";
    context.Response.Cache.SetNoStore();
    context.Response.Cache.SetRevalidation(
        HttpCacheRevalidation.AllCaches);

    GetTaxonomyTreeData();
    TaxonomyRequest taxonomyRequest;

    switch (this.Action)
    {
        case RequestAction.AddColleague:
            this.friendsApi.AddPendingFriend(this.ColleagueId);
            this.response = @"{""Status"":""OK""}";
            break;
        case RequestAction.ApproveColleague:
            this.friendsApi.AcceptPendingFriendForUser(this.ColleagueId,
                                                       this.UserId);
            this.response = @"{""Status"":""OK""}";
            break;
```

Understanding the RequestAction.AddFolder Implementation

Reviewing the implementation details of some of the RequestAction handlers might not be necessary in some cases, as the source code spans only a few lines. However, there are others operations which are more complex, like the implementation for the `RequestAction.AddFolder` shown in the following code snippet, that need explaining:

```csharp
                    case RequestAction.AddFolder:
                    try
                    {
                     //add new node
                     taxonomyData = new TaxonomyData();
                     taxonomyData.TaxonomyDescription = String.Empty;
                     taxonomyData.TaxonomyName = Convert.ToString(this.CategoryName);
                     // community items have no language;
                     taxonomyData.TaxonomyLanguage = 0;
                     taxonomyData.TaxonomyType = (this.Mode == ProfileType.User) ?
                         EkEnumeration.TaxonomyType.User : EkEnumeration.TaxonomyType.
        Group;
                     taxonomyData.TaxonomyParentId =
                         long.Parse(this.RequestTaxonomyData.Id);
                     long newCategoryId =
                         contentApi.EkContentRef.CreateTaxonomy(taxonomyData);

                     //get new node
                     taxonomyRequest = new TaxonomyRequest();
                     taxonomyRequest.TaxonomyId = newCategoryId;
                     taxonomyRequest.TaxonomyType = EkEnumeration.TaxonomyType.User;

                     // limit the taxonomy to just the level required
                     taxonomyRequest.IncludeItems = false;
                     taxonomyRequest.ReadCount = false;
                     taxonomyRequest.Depth = 1;

                     taxonomyData = this.contentApi.LoadTaxonomy(ref taxonomyRequest);

                     //translate to treeview
                     TranslateTaxonomyData(taxonomyData);

                     //set response
                     this.response = this.jsonSerializer.Serialize(this.TreeView);
                    }
```

To understand the previous code snippet, you should first understand the use case for the code. In this instance, the use case is: "As a developer, I can create new folders for organizing colleagues." Allowing for this type of organization means that the user can place colleagues into logical groups based on their relationship to the colleague. For example, as a community member, you might choose to place all of marketing colleagues into a newly created folder called Marketing.

How Taxonomy Structures Relate to the Community Platform

Looking at the implementation, you might be surprised to find references to Taxonomy APIs and Taxonomy data classes in code for creating a new folder. This is because taxonomy is actually an extremely central part of the Community Framework and it serves a number of important purposes. By default, every user in the system has a user taxonomy associated to it. Although there is only one user taxonomy per user (a one-to-one mapping between a user and user taxonomy), there are predefined user taxonomy categories created to manage the relationships between the user and other community-related items, such as community groups, colleagues, and content. These predefined categories are child categories of the root folder.

The two significant differences between user taxonomies and content taxonomies are that user taxonomies are not language-aware, and also, there is no UI for managing them in the Workarea.

Given this new information, it now becomes clearer why the RequestAction.AddFolder handler references the Taxonomy API to create a new "folder" for organizing colleagues. You're actually creating new categories for this information behind the scenes and through the process of categorizing colleagues, documents, and community groups. You're establishing an organized relationship between a user and these objects.

Exploring the ~/Profile/Handlers/profile.colleauges.ashx further, you will see a number of references to the Ektron.Cms.Community.FriendsAPI namespace. This provides an interface for performing many of the actions you'd expect to have, including the ability to issue friend requests and approve friend requests. The following code snippet from that file shows how to do each of these respectively.

```
case RequestAction.AddColleague:
    this.friendsApi.AddPendingFriend(this.ColleagueId);
    this.response = @"{""Status"":""OK""}";
    break;
case RequestAction.ApproveColleague:
    this.friendsApi.AcceptPendingFriendForUser(this.ColleagueId,
                                                this.UserId);
    this.response = @"{""Status"":""OK""}";
    break;
```

Retrieving a List of Friends Using the API

Another important point to know and highlight is how to retrieve a list of friends using the API. The following code snippet shows the procedures needed to get a list of colleagues for a given user. This code uses the same GetList/Criteria pattern that the Ektron's Framework APIs use (See Appendix B for more information about the Framework API, including cookbook style code snippets). The nice thing about the Framework API is its consistent use of GetList() for retrieving a list of items. Once you've used it, you know how to use it for other datatypes.

```
Ektron.Cms.API.Community.CommunityGroup groupApi =
  new Ektron.Cms.API.Community.CommunityGroup();

Criteria<Ektron.Cms.CommunityGroupProperty> criteria =
  new Criteria<Ektron.Cms.CommunityGroupProperty>();
criteria.AddFilter(Ektron.Cms.CommunityGroupProperty.GroupName,
                CriteriaFilterOperator.StartsWith,
                "H");
List<Ektron.Cms.CommunityGroupData> groupList = groupApi.GetList(criteria);

gvCommunitGroups.DataSource = groupList;
gvCommunitGroups.DataBind();
```

The next code snippet shows how to retrieve a list of favorites using the same GetList/Criteria pattern. Notice the similarity between the two, despite the fact that they're querying for and returning entirely different datatypes.

```
Ektron.Cms.API.Community.CommunityGroup groupApi =
  new Ektron.Cms.API.Community.CommunityGroup();

Criteria<Ektron.Cms.CommunityGroupProperty> criteria =
```

```
             new Criteria<Ektron.Cms.CommunityGroupProperty>();
       criteria.AddFilter(Ektron.Cms.CommunityGroupProperty.GroupName,
                    CriteriaFilterOperator.StartsWith,
                    "H");
       List<Ektron.Cms.CommunityGroupData> groupList = groupApi.GetList(criteria);

       gvCommunitGroups.DataSource = groupList;
       gvCommunitGroups.DataBind();
```

In both cases you'll also notice that the lists are data-bound to data-bindable server controls like the .NET ListView Server Control and the GridView Server Control. This pattern can be replicated for many of the community datatypes, making the process of data retrieval intuitive and straightforward.

For a developer screencast covering the Framework API, including code samples and documentation, see `http://dev.ektron.com/FrameworkAPI/`.

COMMUNITY GROUPS

One way to draw people to join a social network is to show that it is possible to connect with other members of the community who have similar interests. *Community groups* often serve this purpose and offer members the ability to discuss topics and discover new members in the process. Community groups often have profiles much like community users, which contain the same types of capabilities. They have their own message boards, or walls, threaded discussion boards, and displays of members belonging to the group.

Community groups also serve a purpose on internal intranets. In this context, community groups function as a collaborative workspace where members can work cooperatively to author content, manage project calendars, blog about project status, and use the activity stream timeline to see what has recently happened in the group.

Active community groups are often major hubs of activity on social networking sites, and it is important to make sure that community members are aware of them. These groups help members connect and give them a strong connection to the site, increasing the likelihood that they'll remain an active part of your community. The Ektron Community Framework supports the creation of community groups and also the technology to keep people informed of new community groups, activity community groups, and others.

The CommunityGroupProfile Server Control displays the basic information about a community group, including attributes such as group name, description, number of members, and the group administrator. The CommunityGroupProfile Server Control shares much of the purpose and function of the UserProfile Server Control covered in the previous section, and there are many parallels between the two server controls and the set of APIs used to manage and display them.

How Users Discover Community Groups

There are a number of ways for community members to discover new community groups, including the following:

➤ **Community group search:** This facilitates the discovery of new members by exploring group names, descriptions, tags, and other custom defined attributes. The CommunitySearch Server Control and related APIs were covered in a previous section in this chapter (see "Users, Friends, and Profiles").

➤ **List of most popular and most active community groups:** The CommunityGroupList Server Control displays a list of community groups and can be configured to display them by name, how recently they were created, or how popular they are. When associated with a user, this control can also be used to show community groups with which a user is associated, a list of community groups the user has been invited to join, or any restricted community groups the user has asked to join, where his acceptance is pending.

➤ **The community's activity streams:** In real life, what compels someone to join a group, purchase a car, or eat particular foods, is often influenced by what other people are doing. If you see a number of people lined up to purchase the latest gadget, your instincts might compel you to check it out and maybe even purchase it. The activity stream provides a window into what people are doing, and when community members see others flocking to particular groups, they'll stop to explore and see if it is something that interests them. Activity streams are covered in the upcoming section in this chapter called "Activity Streams".

Creating a Community Group

Community groups can be created through the Workarea and through the website. In many cases, the website is the primary place where community groups are created since membership users do not have access to the Workarea. If you're interested in exposing this functionality to your site visitors, consider using the CommunityGroupBrowser Server Control, which, in addition to allowing visitors to browse existing groups, also has the ability to create a new group. Offering visitors the ability to create community groups "on demand" is an extremely important piece in the social technology puzzle. Site administrators will never be able to predict which groups should be created and who should administer them. Putting this power in the hands of the community is the right way to approach this.

The Difference between a Member User Group and a Community Group

It is important to keep in mind that membership user groups and community groups are two completely different concepts and are used in entirely different use cases. There has been some confusion in the past about this, mostly because some use the terms "membership users" and "community members" interchangeably. To clarify this, CMS Administrators use membership user groups to grant content permissions to groups of membership users, whereas community groups are created by the community to facilitate information exchange around a topic or idea, as discussed here.

If you read through the previous section in this chapter titled "Users, Friends, and Profiles," recall that the OnTrek user profile had heavy client-side requirements and needed to use the Community Framework APIs for its implementation. If you haven't read that section yet, take a few minutes to do so. Much of what was described there, in terms of requirements and implementation approach, holds true for the group profile. In fact, OnTrek's group profile code is organized into the same three logical tiers discussed earlier (a presentation tier using jQuery, a middle tier encapsulating business logic using ASHX handlers, and a data tier using Ektron Framework APIs for CMS and data needs). In addition, it was implemented in such a way that a fair amount of the source code is shared across both the group and user profiles.

Creating a New Community Group

Community groups are used on the OnTrek website to facilitate conversations around the OnTrek product line. Since having this community group was a planned part of the initial site requirements and design, the group was created by a CMS admin. The following is a walkthrough of creating a new community group in the Workarea.

1. Open Workarea ➪ Settings ➪ Community Management ➪ Community Groups. This command shows the list of existing community groups, as shown in Figure 11-7.

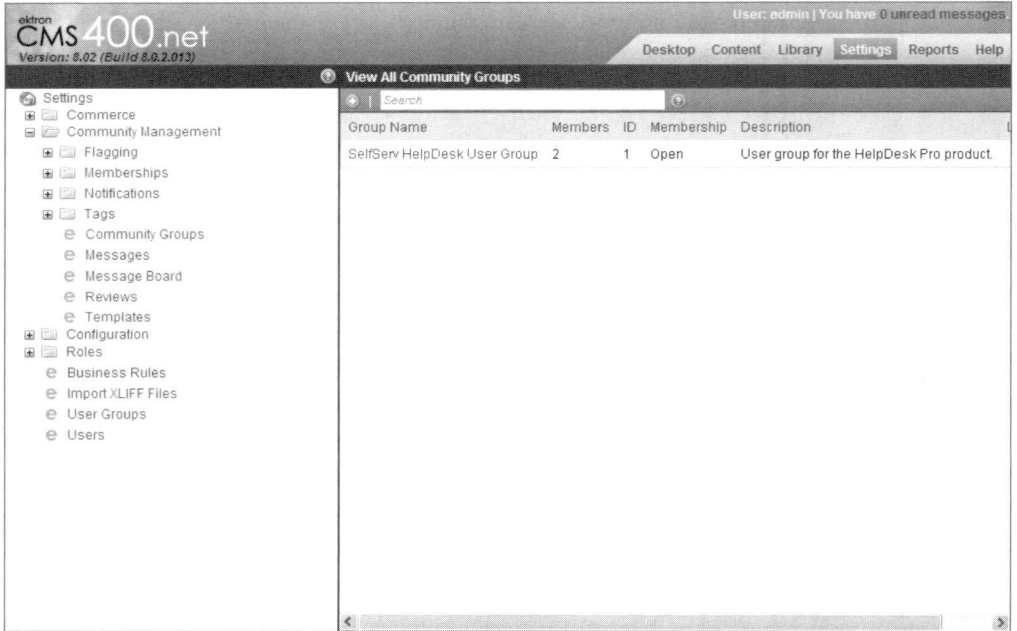

FIGURE 11-7

2. Click the Add New Community Group icon .

3. On the Add New Community Group screen, you have a number of form fields available to describe the community group. These fields are grouped into three categories, organized and separated by tabs.

> **Properties tab:** Here you are required to provide a group name, assign an administrator, and specify whether the group is open or restricted. The following list describes select fields for data entry.
>> **Administrator:** Administrator here refers to the group administrator, which is an individual who has the privilege to delete a group or edit its properties. By default, the person who created the group is the group administrator. You can delegate administrative responsibilities to a user by clicking the Browse button and selecting a different user.
>> **Membership:** Membership can either be extended to everyone (public) or restricted to those users who have been granted access to join (private).
>> **Enable Distribute:** If you want to offer the administrator the ability to move content from the Community Group to the content folder tree, check this box.
> **Tags tab:** Use this to associate short, one word descriptions to the community group. For example, tags for an "New England Patriots Fans" community group might be "football," "sports," or "fans."
> **Categories tab:** Note that this tab might not be displayed on your installation. It will not show up if you have not defined at least one taxonomy for community groups. To enable the tab, simply create a new taxonomy (see Chapter 6) and make sure to select the group checkbox to indicate you want to categorize community groups using the taxonomy.

4. Click Save.

Configuring Community Group Templates

Just as you previously defined the location to various community member pages, you'll follow the same process for community group templates. To review, you must specify the URL paths used by the system when links to group pages are used. For example, the community group search results displayed by the CommunityGroupList Server Control include a hyperlink to the profile of the community group. This hyperlink uses the URL specified in this screen.

To specify these paths, do the following.

1. Go to Workarea ⇨ Settings ⇨ Community Management ⇨ Templates. You will see the screen shown in Figure 11-8. This screen contains two sets of templates — user related ones and group related ones.
2. In the Group Templates section, enter the values shown in Table 11-2, as defined in the OnTrek implementation guide.

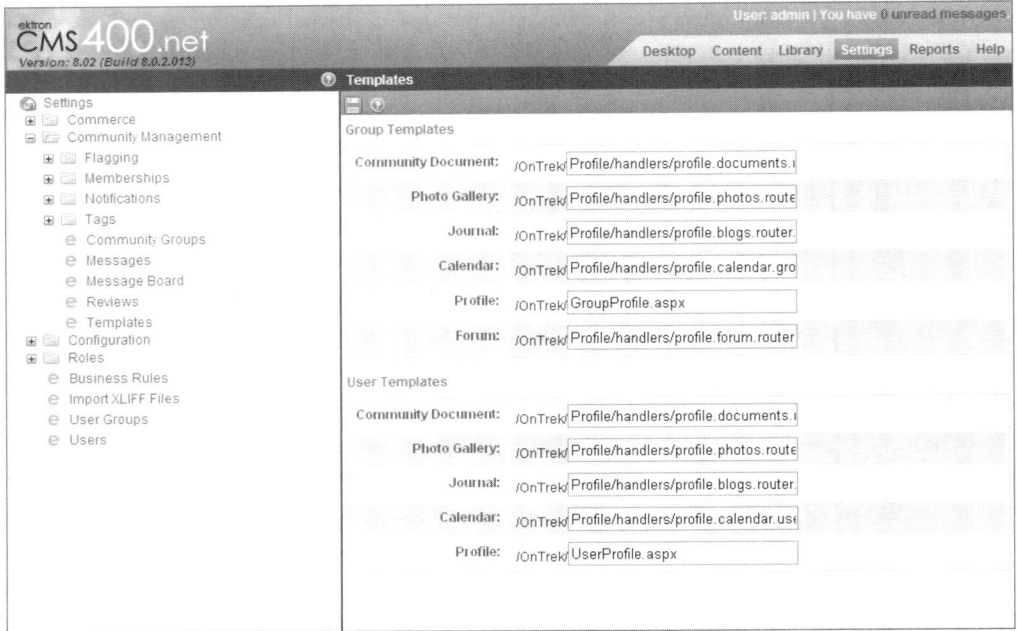

FIGURE 11-8

TABLE 11-2 Community Group Templates in OnTrek

TEMPLATE NAME	TEMPLATE PATH	DESCRIPTION
Community Document	/Profile/Documents.aspx	The URL for the page hosting the CommunityDocuments Server Control
Photo Gallery	/Profile/GroupPhotos.aspx	The URL for the page hosting the PhotoGallery Server Control
Profile	/ GroupProfile.aspx	The URL for the group profile
Journal	/ GroupProfile.aspx	The URL for the page hosting the group blog
Forum	/Workarea/CommunityForum.aspx	The URL for the page hosting a threaded discussion control

OnTrek's Group Profile User Control

The primary use of a community group is to facilitate communication and interaction between community members, and OnTrek's Group Profile User Control includes many features to achieve this. The screen in Figure 11-9 shows its primary view, which contains a list of the activities that have recently taken place in the group, notes that have been posted to the group message board, and group information.

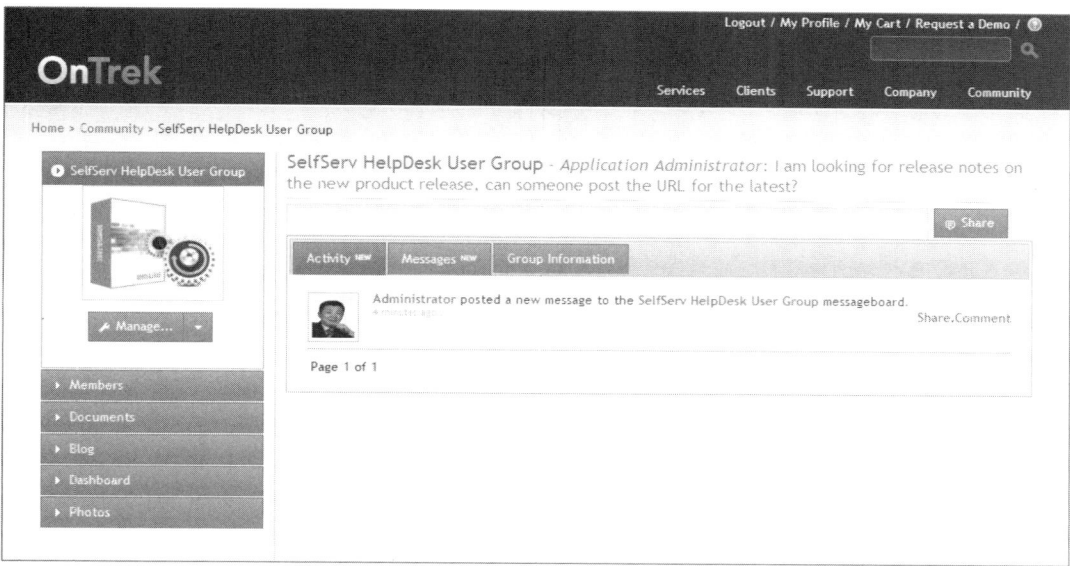

FIGURE 11-9

If you've read the previous section of this chapter (called "Users, Friends, and Profiles"), this interface should look very familiar. The implementation of the Group Profile User Control for the OnTrek website breaks the functionality into two groups (just as was done in the User Profile User Control) and those two groups are: the functionality contained within the accordion and the functionality contained within the main body. The items in the main body are contextual to the selected accordion item, and change accordingly when a new accordion item is selected.

Main Body Functionality

The source code for the Group Profile User Control can be found in ~/Profile/GroupProfile.ascx. As this was covered in the previous technical section, this section focuses on a few of the real workhorses of the profile, which are the user controls that are registered at the top of the document. These are:

- ./Accordion/Blog.ascx
- ./Accordion/Calendar.ascx
- ./Accordion/Dashboard.Group.ascx
- ./Accordion/Documents.ascx
- ./Accordion/Forum.ascx
- ./Accordion/Friends.ascx
- ./Accordion/Group.ascx
- ./Accordion/Photos.ascx

Each is used to define the behavior of the main body of the profile. Which control is loaded is determined through the use of a .NET MultiView Server Control in the following way:

```
<asp:MultiView ID="mvProfileBody" runat="server">
  <asp:View ID="vwGroup" runat="server">
    <Ektron:Group ID="ucGroup" runat="server" Mode="Group" />
  </asp:View>
  <asp:View ID="vwMembers" runat="server">
    <Ektron:Members ID="ucMembers" runat="server" Mode="Group" />
  </asp:View>
  <asp:View ID="vwDocuments" runat="server">
    <Ektron:Documents ID="ucDocuments" runat="server"
      Mode="Group" />
  </asp:View>
  <asp:View ID="vwBlog" runat="server">
    <Ektron:Blog ID="ucBlog" runat="server" Mode="Group" />
  </asp:View>
  <asp:View ID="vwCalendar" runat="server">
    <Ektron:Calendar ID="ucCalendar" runat="server"
      Mode="Group" />
  </asp:View>
  <asp:View ID="vwForum" runat="server">
    <Ektron:Forum ID="ucForum" runat="server" Mode="Group" />
  </asp:View>
  <asp:View ID="vwDashboard" runat="server">
    <Ektron:Dashboard ID="ucDashboard" runat="server"
      Mode="Group" />
  </asp:View>
  <asp:View ID="vwPhotos" runat="server">
    <Ektron:Photos ID="ucPhotos" runat="server" Mode="Group" />
  </asp:View>
</asp:MultiView>
```

Accordion Functionality

When a user clicks the accordion item labeled "Members," the Members User Control is loaded. Looking up at the register statements on the top of the page, you can see that the Member control is defined in Friends.ascx. You might recall that you looked into this file in Listing 11-2 in the previous section, since the user and group profiles share this code file. In this section, you'll examine this file again, except this time you'll see how it is used to display a list of the group members. At the bottom of Listing 11-2, you'll find the following snippet:

```
<CMS:CommunityGroupMembers ID="cmsMembers" runat="server" Visible="false" />
```

The visibility for this control is set to false, which previously has meant that it is being used in codebehind. Opening ~/Profile/Accordion/Friends.ascx.cs, you see the following snippet defined for retrieving member information in the GetGroupProfile method. You can see it follows a very similar pattern to the User Profile implementation seen earlier. Specifically, it references the CommunityGroupMembers Server Control by its ID cmsMembers to populate the DefaultCommunityGroupID and DisplayMode properties.

```
private void GetGroupProfile()
{
    this.communityGroupApi = new CommunityGroupAPI();
```

```
this.communityGroupData =
  communityGroupApi.GetCommunityGroupByID(this.ProfileId);

this.xsltPathCmsFriends = this.contentApi.SitePath +
  "profile/xslt/cmsGroupMembers.xsl";
bool hasColleagues = false;
string colleagues;
XsltArgumentList xsltArgs;
xsltArgs = new System.Xml.Xsl.XsltArgumentList();

//Get Members
cmsMembers.DefaultCommunityGroupID = this.ProfileId;
cmsMembers.DisplayMode = CommunityGroupMembers.eDisplayMode.Members;
cmsMembers.Hide = true;
cmsMembers.Fill();

xsltArgs.AddParam("mode", "", "members");
xsltArgs.AddParam("sitePath", "", this.contentApi.SitePath);
xsltArgs.AddParam("permission", "",
        Enum.GetName(
            typeof(GroupPermission),
            this.GroupProfileData.Permission).ToLower());
xsltArgs.AddParam("isGroupAdmin", "",
        this.GroupProfileData.IsGroupAdmin.ToString().ToLower());
xsltArgs.AddParam("myId", "", this.UserId);
xsltArgs.AddParam("groupAdminId", "",
        this.communityGroupData.GroupAdmin.Id.ToString());
colleagues = EkXml.XSLTransform(cmsMembers.XmlDoc.InnerXml,
        this.xsltPathCmsFriends, true, false, xsltArgs, false,
        null, Constants.CacheProfileInterval);
uxColleaguesCurrent.Text = colleagues;
```

Table 11-3 shows a list of the commonly used properties of the CommunityGroupMembers Server Control, and a description of what the impact of each property is.

TABLE 11-3: Select Properties of the CommunityGroupMembers Server Control

PROPERTY	DESCRIPTION
CacheInterval	Sets the amount of time, in seconds, that the server control's data is cached. The default value is 0.
DefaultCommunityGroupId	The community group ID that is used by default.
DisplayMode	Defines which type of members are displayed, Members or PendingMembers.
DisplayXSLT	Defines the XSLT that is used to customize the markup presented by the control.
DynamicParameter	Gets or sets the QueryString parameter to read a community group ID dynamically. To use the default community group ID, leave this blank.

continues

TABLE 11-3 (continued)

PROPERTY	DESCRIPTION
Link	Allows you to override the UserProfile template URL defined in the Workarea. You can embed the following two tokens: * {0} - Represents the User's ID * {1} - Represents the User's Name to create a URL such as this: * /UserProfile.aspx?gid={0}&gn={1}
MaxResults	The maximum number of items to return.

Another noteworthy section of the previous snippet is found at the top of the GetGroupProfile method, where you can see the CommunityGroupAPI being used to programmatically retrieve group information by the group's ID. This information gathers data that is passed as an XSLT argument into the XSLT transformation. At the bottom of the GetGroupProfile method, you can see that the result of this transformation is rendered to the page using an ASP.NET Literal Server Control.

> The register statements at the top of the GroupProfile.ascx include the following user controls:
> - ./Accordion/Blog.ascx
> - ./Accordion/Calendar.ascx
> - ./Accordion/Dashboard.User.ascx
> - ./Accordion/Documents.ascx
> - ./Accordion/Favorites.ascx
> - ./Accordion/Groups.ascx
> - ./Accordion/Photos.ascx
> - ./Accordion/User.ascx
>
> Each of these files contains code that can be repurposed for use in your own user profile. Make sure to explore these files further.

Under the Hood

To further your understanding of the Community Framework APIs relevant for Community Groups and the group profile, this section continues to look through the list of ASHX handlers listed earlier in the chapter. In the ProcessRequest method in ~/Profile/Handlers/profile.members.ashx, you'll find the following snippet

```
public void ProcessRequest(HttpContext context)
{
```

```
//set header info
context.Response.ContentType = "application/json";
context.Response.Cache.SetNoStore();
context.Response.Cache.SetRevalidation(
  HttpCacheRevalidation.AllCaches);

GetRequestParams();

switch (this.Action)
{
    case RequestAction.AcceptInvitation:
        long userAccepting = 0;
        if (this.MemberId > 0) {
            userAccepting = this.MemberId;
        } else {
            userAccepting = this.contentApi.UserId;
        }
        this.groupApi.AcceptGroupInvite(userAccepting, this.GroupId);
        this.response = @"{""Status"":""OK""}";
        break;
    case RequestAction.AddMember:
        this.groupApi.AddUserToCommunityGroup(this.GroupId,
                                              this.MemberId);
        this.response = @"{""Status"":""OK""}";
        break;
    case RequestAction.ApproveMember:
        this.groupApi.ApprovePendingGroupUser(this.MemberId,
                                              this.GroupId);
        this.response = @"{""Status"":""OK""}";
        break;
    case RequestAction.DeclineInvitation:
        long userDeclining = 0;
        if (this.MemberId > 0) {
            userDeclining = this.MemberId;
        } else {
            userDeclining = this.contentApi.UserId;
        }
        this.groupApi.DeclineGroupInvite(userDeclining, this.GroupId);
        this.response = @"{""Status"":""OK""}";
        break;
    case RequestAction.DeleteMember:
        if (this.IsPending) {
            this.groupApi.DeletePendingGroupUser(this.MemberId,
                                                  this.GroupId);
        } else {
            this.groupApi.RemoveUserFromCommunityGroup(this.GroupId,
                                                       this.MemberId);
        }
        this.response = @"{""Status"":""OK""}";
        break;
    case RequestAction.JoinGroup:
        this.groupApi.AddUserToCommunityGroup(this.GroupId,
                                              this.MemberId);
        if (this.contentApi.IsAdmin()) {
```

```
                this.groupApi.ApprovePendingGroupUser(this.UserId,
                                                    this.GroupId);
            }
            break;
        case RequestAction.LeaveGroup:
            long idToLeave = 0;
            if (this.MemberId > 0) {
                idToLeave = this.MemberId;
            } else {
                idToLeave = this.UserId;
            }
            this.groupApi.RemoveUserFromCommunityGroup(this.GroupId,
                                                        idToLeave);
            this.response = @"{""Status"":""OK""}";
            break;
        case RequestAction.CancelJoinRequest:
            this.groupApi.CancelJoinRequestForCommunityGroup(this.GroupId,
                                                            this.UserId);
            break;
    }
}
```

This method defines the business rules executed when various actions occur. The current action is evaluated in a `switch` statement and processed accordingly. The group-related actions handled in this method are AcceptInvitation, AddMember, ApproveMember, DeclineInvitation, DeleteMember, JoinGroup, and LeaveGroup.

Looking through these action handlers, it is clear that the bulk of the work is performed through the Community Group API that was instantiated earlier in the file through the following code:

```
groupApi = new Ektron.Cms.Community.CommunityGroupAPI();
```

This API provides the following methods that are used to implement these action handlers.

```
groupApi.AcceptGroupInvite(userAccepting, GroupId);
groupApi.AddUserToCommunityGroup(GroupId, MemberId);
groupApi.ApprovePendingGroupUser(MemberId, GroupId);
groupApi.CancelJoinRequestForCommunityGroup(GroupId, UserId);
groupApi.DeclineGroupInvite(userDeclining, GroupId);
groupApi.RemoveUserFromCommunityGroup(GroupId);
```

The Framework API has the ability to retrieve a list of groups using the GetList/Criteria pattern described earlier

 The Framework API is covered as well in Appendix B. See this appendix for more information about the Framework API, including cookbook style code snippets.

```
    Ektron.Cms.API.Community.CommunityGroup groupApi = new
Ektron.Cms.API.Community.CommunityGroup();

    Criteria<Ektron.Cms.CommunityGroupProperty> criteria = new
```

```
Criteria<Ektron.Cms.CommunityGroupProperty>();
        criteria.AddFilter(Ektron.Cms.CommunityGroupProperty.GroupName,
CriteriaFilterOperator.StartsWith, "H");
        List<Ektron.Cms.CommunityGroupData> groupList = groupApi.GetList(criteria);

        gvCommunitGroups.DataSource = groupList;
        gvCommunitGroups.DataBind();
```

The results set returned from the Framework API's GetList method is data-bound to a data-bindable control (in this case the ASP.NET GridView Server Control), which gives developers and designers fine-grained control over the markup that is produced.

DASHBOARDS

Ektron's Dashboards allow site visitors to create personalized portals of information, aggregating data from various sources, simplifying the decision-making process by gathering information into one single location. These portals can be personalized for an individual based on their interests, or for an entire group of people based on the collective purpose of that group. For example, as an individual member of the marketing department, you might have a dashboard filled with various types of Web analytics information as well as a list of tasks waiting for your attention.

Sites like iGoogle have made it possible to create such dashboards centered around the Search textbox. As an iGoogle user, any time you launch your browser to perform a Google search, you're presented your iGoogle gadgets keeping you informed of any changes to the information in which you're interested, such as stocks, or the weather.

As a developer using Ektron, you have access to its dashboard feature which means you can easily implement dashboards on your website, allowing your visitors to create personalized portals of widgets to aggregate information and to keep people on the site from switching to other applications.

Site visitors using this feature can drag widgets into their personalized dashboard to display e-mail, events, syndication feeds, and Web analytics, as well as perform tasks related to their roles (see Figure 11-10). As a content author, you can make edits to content right from the dashboard. As a human resources manager, you can add new posts to the list of available jobs, without having to navigate to the Workarea or to the jobs section of a website.

What's on the Dashboard?

A dashboard consists of multiple pages, each containing a number of tabs, with each tab containing a number of columns, and each column a number of widgets. A group dashboard is used by group members to set up a portal page that addresses that group's unique needs. Any group member can view and create or edit the page's content.

Tabs can be made public or private. A private tab is available for viewing and editing only by its creator. This means that on a private group dashboard, only group members can view and create or edit it. If a tab is public, anyone can view the tab and its widgets, but authentication is often required because viewing some types of content requires content permissions and valid credentials. So, If the tab is public, anyone can view it but only the group members can create and edit the content.

Because widgets are just user controls, you can create your widgets and expose them through the Widget Tray, or extend the ones already shipped with the product, or extend the ones that are already there. Personalization lets a membership user or community group member customize a single page on the site for their own use. A PageBuilder page, on the other hand, lets an Ektron user create pages on the actual website.

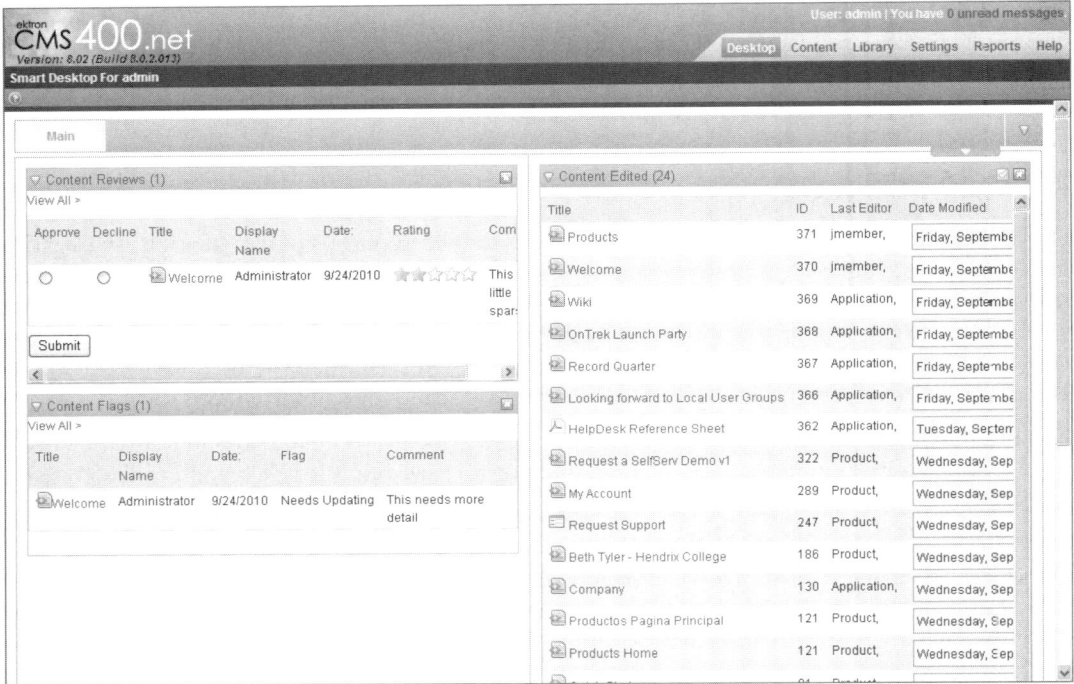

FIGURE 11-10

Using the Dashbard Components and Widget Spaces

The OnTrek user and group profile pages each include a dashboard component. The dashboard component is a personalization control that requires a few configuration steps. Before opening Visual Studio, you must first go to the Workarea to create a new widget space. A *widget space* is simply a collection of widgets that you can use to present to members to populate their dashboards. You can create multiple widget spaces. For example, one group of users could only be allowed to create dashboards with Sales and Marketing Widgets, whereas another group might only be able to select from Engineering and Support Widgets. The process of creating a widget space also assigns it a widget space ID.

To create a widget space:

1. Go to the Workarea ➪ Settings ➪ Configuration ➪ Personalization ➪ Widget Space screen.
2. Click the Add button.
3. Enter a title for the widget space. This title is a descriptive name that is used only in the Workarea.

4. Select the Group Space checkbox if you'll use this widget space for a Community Group Dashboard. Leave it deselected if you intend to use it for a User Group Dashboard. See Figure 11-11.

5. Select the widgets to include in the widget space. The widgets included here are available to site visitors and appear in the dashboard's Widget Tray.

6. Click the Save button and take note of the ID of the widget space.

The dashboard implementation for OnTrek can be found in ~/Profile/Accordion/Dashboard.ascx and in Listing 11-3. The source code is extremely simple, as it registers the personalization user control that is shipped by Ektron in the Workarea, which handles the bulk of the work.

LISTING 11-3 Dasboard.ascx: The User Profile Dashboard

```
<%@ Control Language="C#" AutoEventWireup="true"
  CodeFile="Dashboard.User.ascx.cs"
  Inherits="UserControls_Profile_Dashboard_User" %>
<%@ Register TagName="Personalization"
  Src="~/Workarea/Personalization/personalization.ascx"
  TagPrefix="ucEktron" %>
<div class="dashboard">
    <asp:PlaceHolder ID="ph1" runat="server" />
</div>
```

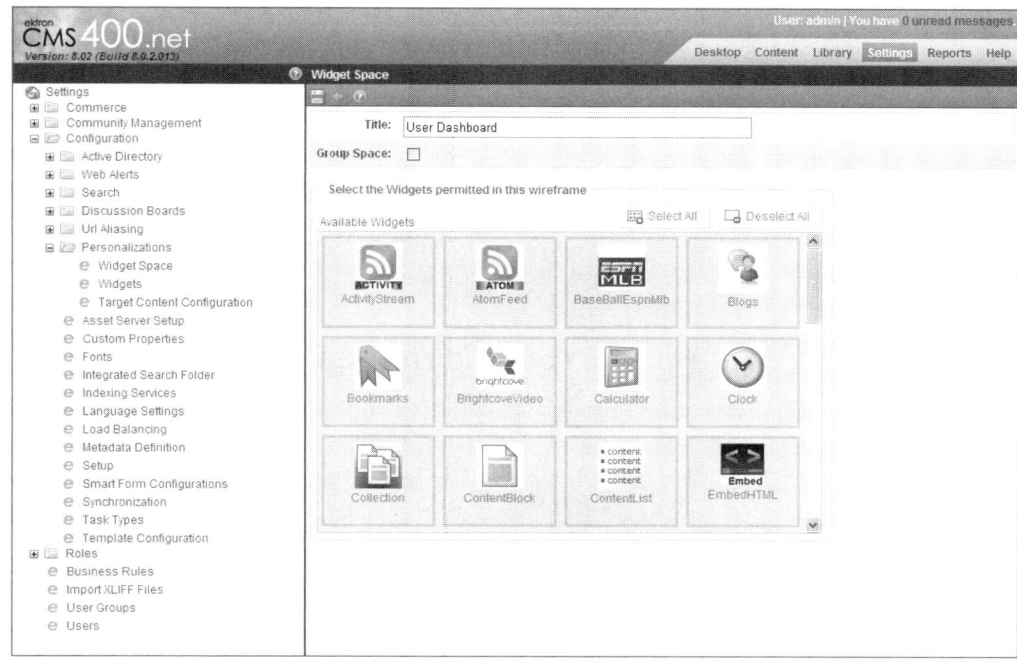

FIGURE 11-11

To implement the dashboard user control on your own page, follow these steps.

1. Open Visual Studio and create a new Web form.
2. From the toolbox, drag-and-drop a Script Manager from the AJAX extensions on the Toolbox. You might need to download the Microsoft AJAX Library if this item is not available on the Toolbox.
3. In Visual Studio's folder browser, navigate to the following folder: workarea/personalization/.
4. Drag-and-drop a personalization user control (personalization.ascx).
5. In the User Control's property box, specify the widget space ID that you created earlier.

ACTIVITY STREAMS

An activity stream is a list of tasks or actions that a person performs and that friends and colleagues read to keep informed about that person. The feature was first popularized on social networking sites like Facebook so users could share pictures with friends, comment on a friend's activities, register for events, or exchange contact information with another friend. Ektron sees the power of such lists in other contexts as well. On the eIntranet, Ektron's intranet product, Ektron uses activity streams to keep employees informed of business activities. On public-facing sites, activity streams are more than for informing friends of new photos, as demonstrated in the OnTrek website; they can notify members when knowledge-based articles are published or when product blog posts are written.

Activity streams are also useful in helping people find information in two new ways:

➤ **Through timeline navigation:** Often times, you publish documents only to discover you need to make edits soon after. Timeline navigation allows you to find a document through your personal activity stream, providing an alternative to searching for it or navigating to it through a folder or menu structure.

➤ **Through social navigation:** Activity streams mean users can "share" activities, which is in effect a way of providing a "vote" for the activity. This causes popular activities to bubble to the top of the activity stream, and when items are repeatedly shared, they remain at the top longer, thus giving greater visibility to popular items.

Using Activity Streams to Your Advantage

Like most technologies, the many benefits of activity streams may blind you to the importance of building a strategy to take full advantage of streams. When social networks are active, activity streams grow quickly, which increases the possibility that a useful activity message will be lost in the noise. In this section, you'll learn the key concepts needed to get working with activity streams and learn ways to implement them to improve their "signal to noise" ratio. In the Activity Streams "Under the Hood" section you'll dive into the underlying Notification Framework used by the activity streams, and learn how to extend that framework to support custom notification agents and activity types.

Why would you want to use activity streams on your community site? Here are six reasons:

➤ **Discovery:** Activity streams give community members the ability to find and navigate to relevant and timely information as it is created in real time.

> **Awareness:** Activity streams give members insight into the public events and workplace activities that may impact their goals.

> **Collaboration:** With greater awareness comes more involvement with and contribution of ideas to projects that would otherwise remain unnoticed.

> **Notification:** You can send your members notification of time sensitive events delivered through text and e-mail messages.

> **Stickiness:** As notifications drive people back to the site, and streams give greater awareness of info available on it, now site visitors have more reasons to visit the site and engage with its members.

> **SEO:** Think of the activity stream as a dynamic "sitemap" pointing to the latest active content, giving search crawlers a window into the most up-to-date content, and increasing the possibility of finding information through search results.

Using the ActivityStream Widget to Manage Streams

To understand how to use an activity stream, look at the ActivityStream Widget illustrated in Figure 11-12. By default, this widget is configured to show all the activities from the current user's social network. When users log in and view this widget, they see all their colleagues' activities plus those activities that occur within the community groups to which the users belong. This activity stream also considers content and community group permissions; so for example, if a colleague posts a document to a private group that you do not belong to, you do not see it in your activity stream. Likewise, if you update private content that only you can see, none of your colleagues are notified of this event.

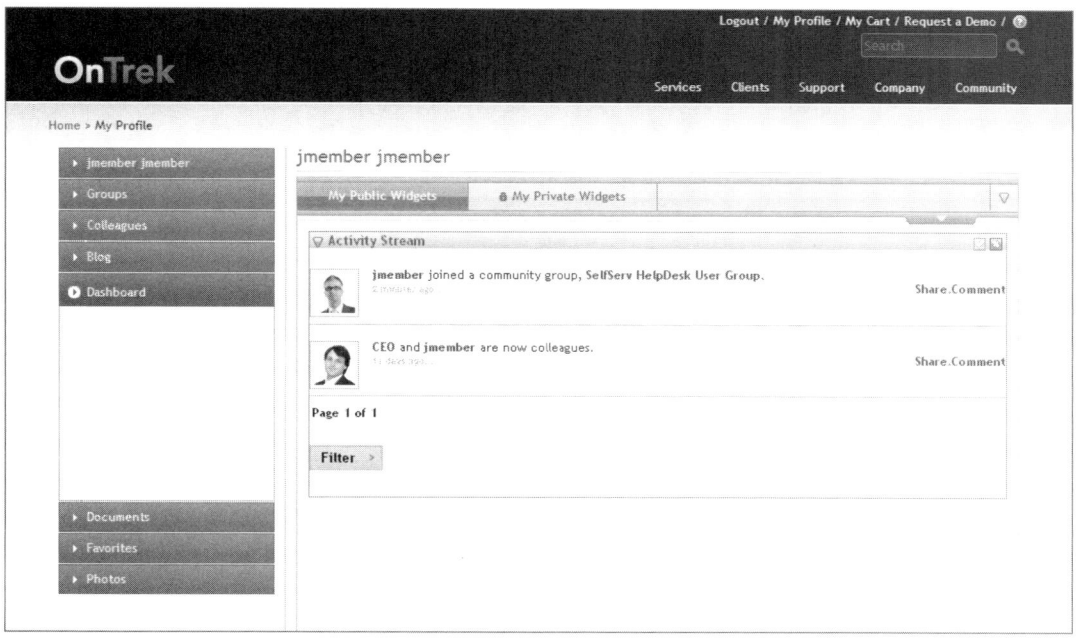

FIGURE 11-12

Users of the ActivityStream Widget can filter the activities by clicking the Filter button. Doing so opens a textbox that accepts the names of users and community groups and updates the widget's display to include the activities from only those names. The filtering defined on the widget persists in the widget storage (see Chapter 9). Therefore, you can use multiple ActivityStream Widgets on a PageBuilder Page or dashboard, with each instance of the widget having its own filter criteria. Users can also populate their dashboards with these widgets filtered in such a way as to improve the "signal to noise" ratio. For example, on an intranet, a marketing manager might filter the widget to display only activities from his direct reports. On a public website like OnTrek, site visitors might include only activities from OnTrek employees or other product experts.

A site visitor can also globally control what displays in the activity stream by managing activity preferences either through the site's membership profile settings or the Workarea (if they have Workarea permissions). Figure 11-13 shows the Activities settings screen, which has three sections:

- **Colleagues:** Allows users to control what type of user displays by default in controls like the ActivityStream Widget. Any filtering done at the widget level filters off of this information.

- **Community Groups:** Allows users to control what type of community group activities displays by default in controls. Any filtering done at the widget level filters off of this information.

- **My Activities:** Here, users can control which of their activities are published into the activity stream.

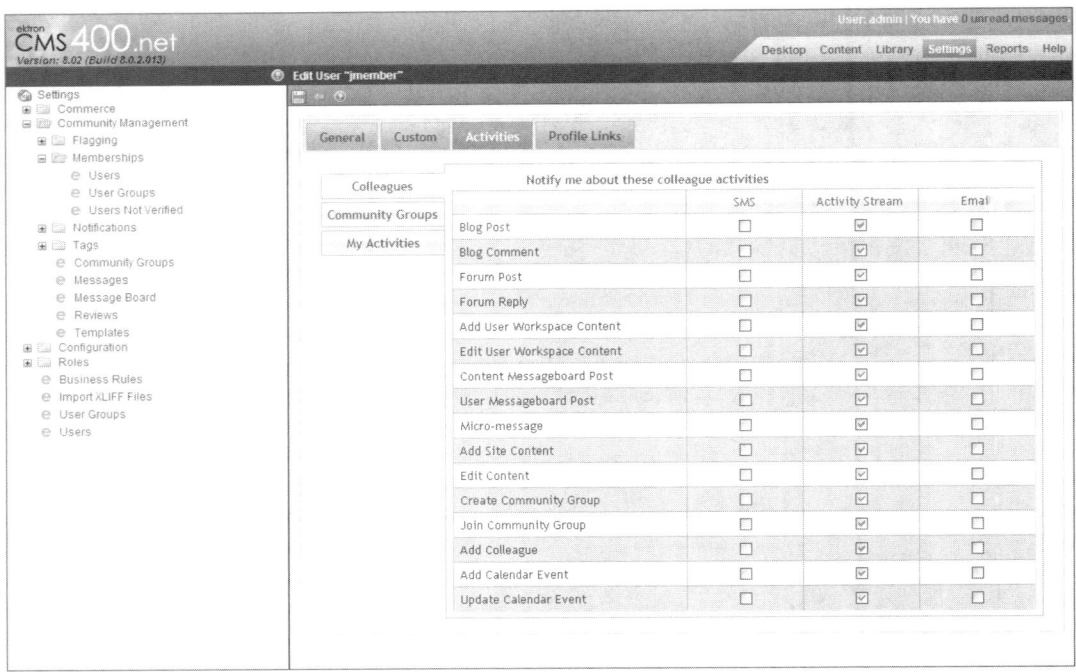

FIGURE 11-13

In Figure 11-13 you'll also notice that, in addition to the Activity Stream column, there are two additional columns, SMS and Email, which you use to configure notification of activities on your mobile device or through your e-mail account. As you might have guessed from this screen, the activity stream system sits on top of a larger Notification Framework. This topic's "Under the Hood" section covers the Notification Framework and demonstrates its extensibility by showing how to create custom Notification Agents and custom Activity Types.

Using the Server Control to Manage Streams

In addition to the ActivityStream Widget, there is a server control and APIs for working with and displaying activities. Much like its widget counterpart, the ActivityStream Server Control displays activities from the current user's social network of colleagues and community groups per their activity notification settings. The server control, however, does not provide the same type of user-driven filtering through the GUI as does the widget. Instead, you can programmatically control the ActivityStream Server Control through its API in codebehind; you must do any filtering using code like this:

```
// You can exclude the current user from the stream
activityStreamCtrl.ExcludeUserIds.Add(CurrentUserID);

// You can also choose to exclude certain groups
activityStreamCtrl.ExcludeGroupIds.Add(GroupId1);
activityStreamCtrl.ExcludeGroupIds.Add(GroupId2);
```

The control has a number of properties that modify its behavior, including displaying a particular community group or user's activities, or a set of users' activities. If you want to display the activity stream associated with a particular group instead of the logged-in user's activity stream, set the control's `ObjectType` property to `User` or `Group` to specify that the control is associated with a community group. Then set its `DefaultObjectID` property to the community group ID for the particular community group. The important point to note here is that once this configuration is made, the user who views this page will see the activities of this particular group, regardless if they're a member of the group or not.

This brings up a very important attribute of the activity and notification system. Although, by default, only those activities to which a user has permission to see will appear for them, developers can override this and force the server control to display activities from the global activities, which might not fall within the activities the logged-in user has specified in their settings. The ActivityStream API also has the same ability, that is to either retrieve activities and filter them according to community group, content permissions and configuration settings, or to allow a developer to define the logic that governs which activities display. A partial list of properties is listed in Table 11-4.

TABLE 11-4 Selected Properties from the Activity Stream Server Control

PROPERTY	DESCRIPTION
CacheInterval	Sets the amount of time, in seconds, that the server control's data is cached. The default value is 0.
DefaultObjectID	The ID of the object whose activity stream is to display. If you want to display a user's activities, set the ObjectType property to User and set DefaultObjectID to the user's ID.

continues

TABLE 11-4 *(continued)*

PROPERTY	DESCRIPTION
DisplayXSLT	Defines the XSLT that customizes the markup presented by the control.
MaxResults	The maximum number of activities to display in the activity stream.
ObjectType	Activity streams can be displayed for a user or a group. This property lets you define which to display. Then use the DefaultObjectID to specify the ID of the user or group.

Looking through Table 11-4, you can see that you control the activity stream markup using XSLT by setting the DisplayXSLT property, just as you would for most Ektron server controls. Providing your own XSLT overrides the default presentation and allows you to customize how the activity stream displays. Keep in mind that any of the default functionality provided by the server control will be overridden as well, so you'll have to implement your own paging.

Querying the Activity Stream Using the Activity Stream API

Another approach to customizing the activity stream markup is to query the activity stream using the Activity Stream API and then data-bind the results to a templatable server control like the ASP .NET ListView or Repeater Server Controls. This approach uses standard ASP.NET data binding and templating functionality and therefore means that your markup is controlled in an ASPX template or ASCX User Control. Listing 11-4 shows an ASPX template hosting an ASP.NET ListView Server Control to render a list of activities with custom markup.

LISTING 11-4: CustomStreamDisplay.aspx

Available for download on Wrox.com

```
<body>
   <form id="form1">
   <div>
     <h1>Activity Stream</h1>

     <asp:ListView ID="listViewActivityStream" runat="server">
        <LayoutTemplate>
           <div id="ActivityList">
              <asp:PlaceHolder ID="itemPlaceHolder" runat="server">
           </div>
        </LayoutTemplate>

        <ItemTemplate>
           <div id="ActivityMessage">
              <img class="ActivityAvatar" alt="Avatar"
                  src="<% #Eval("ActionUser.Avatar") %>"/>
              <span class="ActivityDisplayName">
                 <%#Eval("ActionUser.DisplayName") %>
              </span>
              <div class="date"><%#Eval("Date") %></div>
              <div><%#Eval("Message") %></div>
           </div>
```

```
            </ItemTemplate>

            <EmptyDataTemplate>
                <h3>No activities have been posted yet.</h3>
            </EmptyDataTemplate>
        </asp:ListView>

    </div>
    </form>
</body>
```

In Listing 11-5, you find the code that retrieves the activity list using the ActivityStream API. In this example, the `GetUserActivityStream` (long) method retrieves the activities from a particular user's social network. You can also use this API to retrieve a specific user's activities, or the activities for one or more community groups. Once you retrieve the activity list, the ASP.NET ListView's `DataBind()` method data-binds the activity list to the ListView Server Control.

LISTING 11-5 CustomStreamDisplay.aspx.cs

Available for download on Wrox.com

```
Using Ektron.Cms;
using Ektron.Cms.Framework;
using Ektron.Cms.Activity;
using ActivityStreamApi = Ektron.CMS.Framework.Activity;

public partial class Developer_ActivityStream_CustomStreamDisplay :
    System.Web.UI.Page
{
    protected void Page_Load(object sender, EventArgs e)
    {
        DisplayActivityStream();
    }

    private void DisplayActivityStream()
    {
        PagingInfo pageInfo = new PagingInfo();
        pageInfo.TotalRecords = 10;

        ActivityStreamApi activityStreamApi = new ActivityStreamApi();
        long userId = activityStreamApi.RequestInformation.UserId;

        List<ActivityData> listActivities =
          activityStreamApi.GetUserActivityStream(userId);

        listViewActivityStream.DataSource = listActivities;
        listViewActivityStream.DataBind();
    }
}
```

Using the Activity Stream on the Community Homepage

The OnTrek site uses activity streams primarily to give site visitors a way to find the information being contributed (discovery), to give a greater understanding of what is happening within the community (awareness), and to allow site visitors to be notified of time-sensitive information, such as product security patches (notification). This is done through the activity stream integration on the community homepage, through the use of the ActivityStream Server Control. The implementation for this is very straightforward since it uses the standard ActivityStream Server Control with no customizations.

1. In Visual Studio, open ~\OnTrek\Pages\Community.aspx.
2. Drag-and-drop the ActivityStream Server Control onto the page template.

The OnTrek website has implemented this feature on the ~\OnTrek\Pages\Community.aspx template.

Under the Hood

There are a few items which can be customized to allow for a greater degree of flexibility when working with activity streams. In this section you'll be exposed to customizing the messages published when activities occur, as well as adding new activity types to your implementation.

Enabling the Notifications and Activity Streams

Although the activity stream framework is installed and enabled by default on all new installations of Ektron, upgrades from installations prior to version 8.0 have this feature disabled. The reason for this is that in order to enable the feature on upgrades, you must run a script that updates each user's default activity preference settings, which in some databases represents a very large number of records and could increase the time it takes to upgrade the site. For this reason, administrators wanting to use this feature must enable the feature manually once the upgrade process is complete. This is done in the Workarea by navigating to Settings ➪ Community Management ➪ Notifications ➪ Settings and clicking Publish Notifications. This will update the appropriate records in the database, and after a short wait your notifications will begin functioning.

Customizing Activity Messages

The messages that display in activity streams, although specific to the activity that has occurred (for example, "Derek is now friends with Gerson"), follow a general format that you define by following these steps:

1. Go to the Workarea in Settings ➪ Community Management ➪ Notifications ➪ Messages. This screen lists all the notification message templates that the notification architecture uses, activity streams included.
2. Modify a template by clicking the title of a particular notification message template then clicking Edit. Figure 11-14 shows the screen where you edit notification message templates.
3. In Figure 11-14, there are two key areas to keep in mind:

    ➤ **Tokens:** Lists all of the Notification Message Template Tokens that are applicable to this particular message. You can place these anywhere in the Text or Plain Text fields.

➤ **Text and Plain Text:** These fields define the actual text of the message, once the tokens have been processed by the notification engine. For example, once the site user named Derek updates a content titled "My Weekly Status," the tokens in the string "@SubjectUser.DisplayName@ updated content '@content.Title@'" would be replaced, yielding a final output of "Derek updated content 'My Weekly Status'."

On this screen you can copy the tokens you want to display from the Tokens field and paste them into the Text and Plain Text fields so they are rendered into the final output.

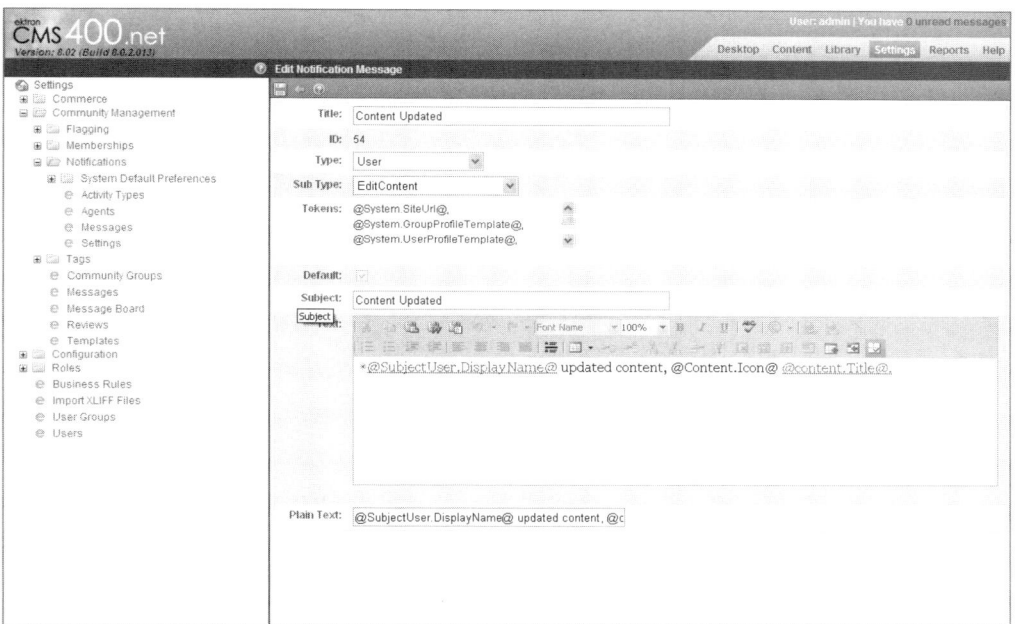

FIGURE 11-14

4. Once you have filled in the fields, click Save, and from that point forward the defined message will be used in notifications when the specified activity occurs.

Creating a Custom Activity Type

The notification framework makes it possible to define custom activity types, which means that you can tailor the activities in an activity stream to the types of activities that are happening on that site. For example, on a website for stock traders, the activity stream could include messages such as "Bill rated the stock NAOC positively" or "Bill put the stock NNEJ on his favorites list." On an intranet, the activity stream could include a message such as "John logged in." Creating and raising a custom activity is a two-step process. The rest of this section walks through how to create a custom activity type that will be raised when a user logs into the site.

First, you must add a new Custom Activity definition in the Workarea.

1. Go to Settings ➪ Notifications ➪ Activity Types, which lists all of the system's currently configured activities. See Figure 11-15.

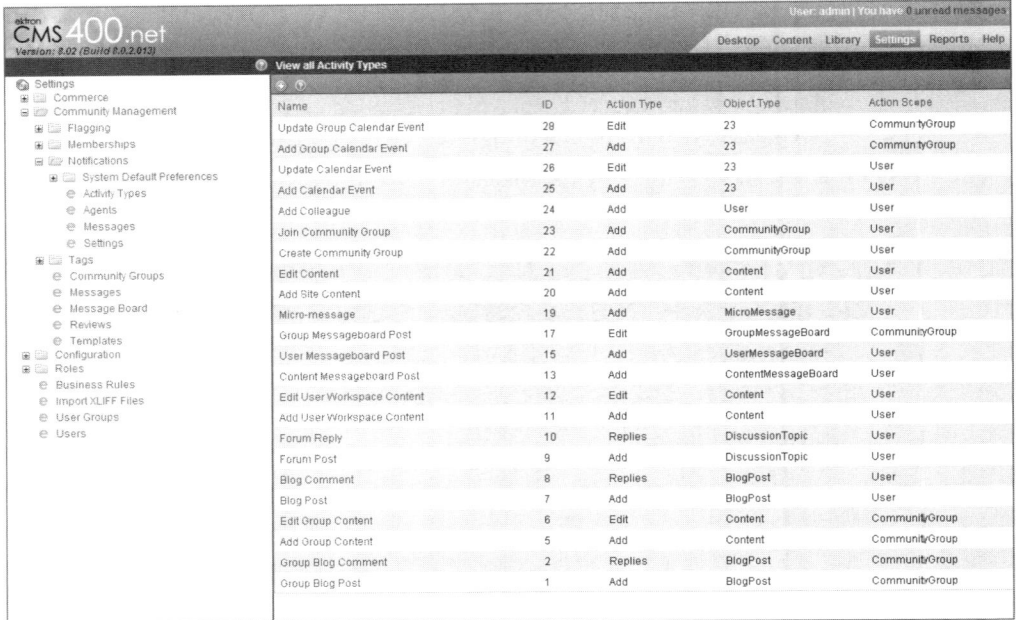

FIGURE 11-15

2. Click the Add icon ( ).

3. Type **User Logged In** for the name of the custom activity type name.

4. **Specify the action scope.** The action scope is the context in which the activity is raised. There are two types of activities:

    ➤ **Community Group:** Those raised by a user from within a community group.

    ➤ **User:** All other activities.

    The User Log In activity is raised outside of a community group, so you should select User.

5. Now that the activity type has been registered, take note of its Activity Type ID, as displayed in the list shown in Figure 11-16. The activity ID in this development environment is ID 1001.

Now, users must modify their preferences to define how they want to be notified when the User Logged In activity occurs. As shown earlier, this is controlled on the Users Activities preferences screen shown in Figure 11-17. Make sure to select the User Logged In checkbox on the Colleagues and My Activities sections.

Writing the code to raise a custom activity is a straightforward three-step process:

1. Using the ActivityAPI, create an instance of the ActivityData object and specify the ActivityTypeId of your newly created custom activity as defined in the Workarea (mine was 1001).

2. Raise the activity using the ActivityAPI's `Publish()` method.

3. Encapsulate this code into a method and call this method in the code from which you want the activity to be raised.

Activity Streams | **431**

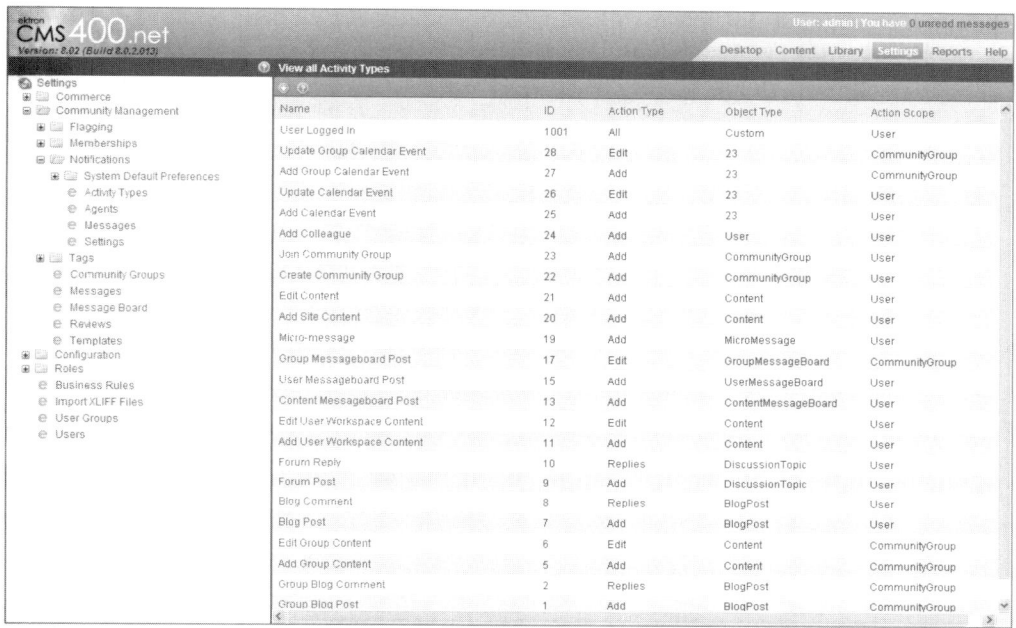

FIGURE 11-16

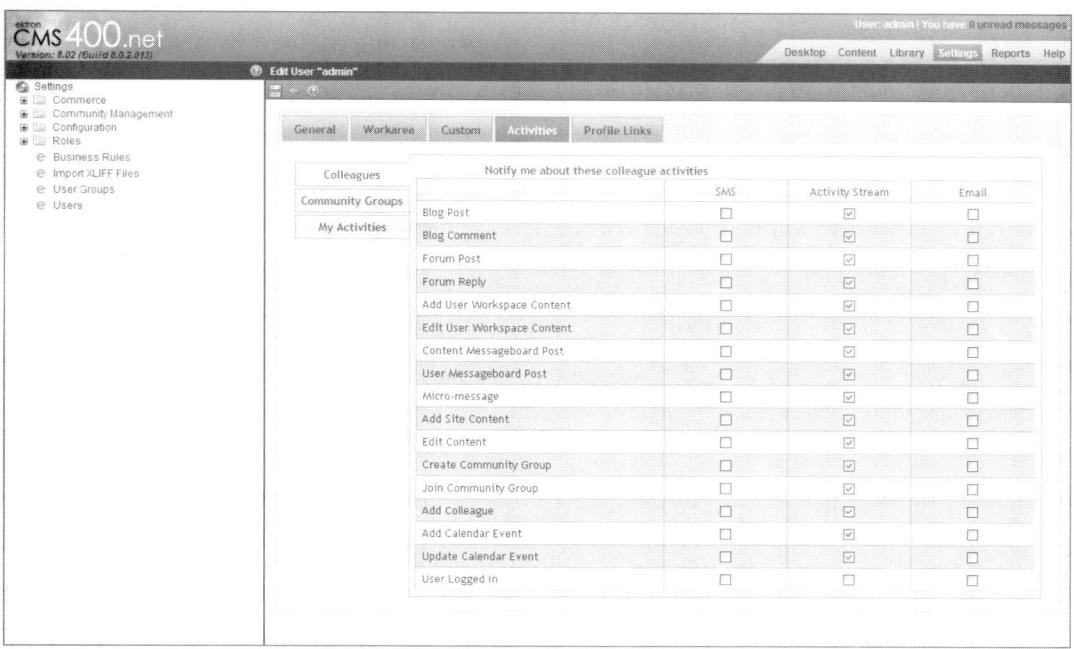

FIGURE 11-17

You can see an example of this in the following code snippet, which defines the `RaisedLoggedInActivity()` and encapsulates the code that defines the `ActivityData` object and then raises it. Because you want the custom activity to be raised anytime a site visitor logs in, you must insert a reference to the custom `RaisedLoggedInActivity()` method wherever your login processing logic is defined.

```
private void RaiseLoggedInActivity()
{
    // The user is now logged in, get their ID
    Ektron.Cms.Framework.Activity.Activity activityApi =
      new Ektron.Cms.Framework.Activity.ActivityApi();
    ActivityUserInfo activityUser = new ActivityUserInfo();
    activityUser.Id = activityApi.UserId;

    // Define the "User Logged In" activity
    ActivityData activityData = new ActivityData();

    // Reference to the user that raised the activity
    activityData.ActionUser = activityUser;

    // Our activity type ID as defined in the Workarea
    activityData.ActivityTypeId = 1001;

    // The activity message that is put in the Activity Stream
    activityData.Message = "<p>I logged in</p>";

    // The language ID of this particular message
    activityData.LanguageId = 1033;

    // Raise the "User Logged In" activity
    activityApi.Publish(activityData);
}
```

It is also worth noting that the activity message for custom activities does not use the activity message template to define the message format. Instead, the message is defined by setting the Message attribute of the ActivityData object as is done in the previous code snippet. One benefit of this approach is that these messages could be defined as XML, which implies that you can add any custom metadata to the message and keep the message data separate from its presentation.

For more information on activity streams, take a look at the Ektron Developer screencast titled "Getting Activity Streams on Your Website," which includes a video walkthrough of some of these concepts and pointers to a Notification Architecture diagram as well as a document describing how to troubleshoot the notification system. See http://dev.ektron.com/getting-activity-streams-on-your-website/.

MICRO-MESSAGING

It took the general Web population some time to make heads or tails out of Twitter-style micro-messaging after its arrival in 2006. Over the years, micro-messaging has become an extremely important communication tool and one that you need to consider when planning your website's community strategy.

What niche does micro-messaging fill that made it so popular? Prior to micro-messaging, there was no way to deliver quick and frequent bursts of information to a large audience — something that combined the brevity of instant messaging with the public nature of blogging. What originally started off as a means for primarily updating personal status has evolved into a marketing platform — a way to solicit feedback from customers, a means for promoting events, and an opportunity to build relationships. This mode of communication has its place on both third-party sites like Twitter and on your own website. While there are significant business benefits to participating in micro-messaging in both places, this section focuses on why you might want to use micro-messaging on your site and how to best integrate it there.

Micro-Messaging Strategies

Use cases for micro-messaging on a public-facing site differ somewhat from those on an internal one. The OnTrek site uses micro-messaging within the context of the OnTrek community to engage members in a conversation with OnTrek employees and other members of the community. This allows the marketing group to have an authentic and public conversation with the community, share information that they've found, and publically send stuff to their friends.

On an intranet such as Ektron's eIntranet, micro-messaging becomes a way to give employees a greater awareness of what's happening around them. In either scenario, micro-messaging facilitates building a tighter knit community by allowing members to share what they're thinking, what they're doing, and what is capturing their attention.

Ektron provides two ways to display and post micro-messages on a website: the MicroMessage Server Control and the Community APIs. By default, the MicroMessaging Server Control shows posts (also sometimes called status updates) from members of the visitor's social network of colleagues. A single micro-message post consists of the name of the user posting the message, the micro-message post itself, and the age of the post. The control's DisplayMode property can control the displayed micro-messages. The four DisplayModes are shown in Table 11-5.

TABLE 11-5: MicroMessage Server Control DisplayMode Options

DISPLAYMODE	DESCRIPTION	USE CASE
User	Micro-messages from a specific user	Use this mode when you want to provide a list of messages for a particular user. For example, the user profile might contain a list of a particular individual's micro-messages.

continues

TABLE 11-5 *(continued)*

DISPLAYMODE	DESCRIPTION	USE CASE
Colleagues	Micro-messages from a specific user's social network of colleagues	Use this mode when you want to display micro-messages from the colleagues of a particular user. For example, a community homepage might use this mode so users can see what micro-messages their colleagues have posted.
TimeLine	Micro-messages for all users that have marked their profiles as "public"	Use this mode when you want to display all messages marked as public, including messages from those users that are outside of a user's social network of colleagues.
Message	A single micro-message	Use this mode when you want to have a page that displays a single micro-message. This is useful as it gives site visitors a permanent link to a single message.

> *Micro-messages are a type of activity in the notification framework (see the section entitled "Activity Streams" earlier in this chapter) which indicate that visitors can choose to be notified of micro-messages via SMS, e-mail, and other custom notification agents that may have been optionally created. It also means that micro-messages will appear in the activity stream through the ActivityStream Widget, Server Control, and APIs.*

The MicroMessage Server Control also displays a Search tab when the micro-message search feature is enabled, which allows users to search through micro-messages published by the logged-in user, their colleagues, and all members whose profiles are public. The results are filtered to include only those messages that contain each of the search terms entered by the users. Exact matching is achieved by surrounding phrases with quotes. It's important to note that this feature does not use the larger search architecture (see Chapter 7) used by the system for searching managed items like content, documents, and so on. If this feature is not enabled, and you want to offer your site visitors the ability to search micro-messages, you need to do the following:

1. Install the Full Text Search component of the Microsoft SQL Server. To do this, insert the SQL Server Installation disc and select Full Text Search from the installation options. This allows you to enable and add the Full Text Search component to an existing SQL Server installation.

2. Run the FullTextIndex.sql script on your database. You can find this script in: Program Files\Ektron\CMS400v80\Utilities\SiteSetup\Database\FullTextIndex.sql.

3. Verify that the Full Text Index is configured properly by viewing an ASPX template containing the MicroMessaging Server Control. The Search tab appears on the control once the system is configured properly.

The properties of the MicroMessaging Server Control are similar to many Ektron Server Controls and allow you to customize its behavior in a number of significant ways. Table 11-6 lists the significant server control properties.

TABLE 11-6: Properties on the MicroMessaging Server Control

PROPERTY	DESCRIPTION
CacheInterval	Sets the amount of time, in seconds, that the server control's data is cached. The default value is 0.
DefaultObjectId	In cases where you're displaying a user's micro-messaging stream, this value represents the user ID.
DisplayXSLT	Defines the XSLT that customizes the markup presented by the control.
DynamicObjectParameter	Defines the name of the parameter that is evaluated to read an object ID dynamically. By default, its value is id. If you want to override this to a value such as UserId, specify that here.
MaxResults	The maximum number of messages to return. 0 signifies that an unlimited number of results should be returned.

Adding Micro-Messaging to the User Profile

Micro-messaging is included in the OnTrek website through the user's profile. Following Ektron's general best practices, its implementation is encapsulated into a custom user control and is found in ~/Profile/Accordion/User.ascx.

Given the Wireframe for the user profile on the OnTrek site, it is required that the textbox that accepts the user input for micro-messages is visually separated from the list of existing micro-messages, as shown in Figure 11-18. This indicates that the MicroMessaging Server Control's default presentation cannot be used because it displays the textbox vertically stacked above the list of micro-messages. For this reason, an external textbox captures the visitor's text input and a server control renders the micro-messages separately. When the Submit button is clicked, the micro-message is programmatically submitted using the MicroMessaging API, and the list of micro-messages is updated.

To examine the code that brings these pieces together, and see an example of how to use an external textbox to post micro-messages, follow the steps below.

1. Open the user control found at ~/Profile/Accordion/User.ascx. This user profile page has five tabs, including one for My Activity, which is the label used for micro-messages and activity notifications. Look through the source code and notice how it uses an ASP.NET MultiView Server Control for controlling which view to present based on the selected tab.

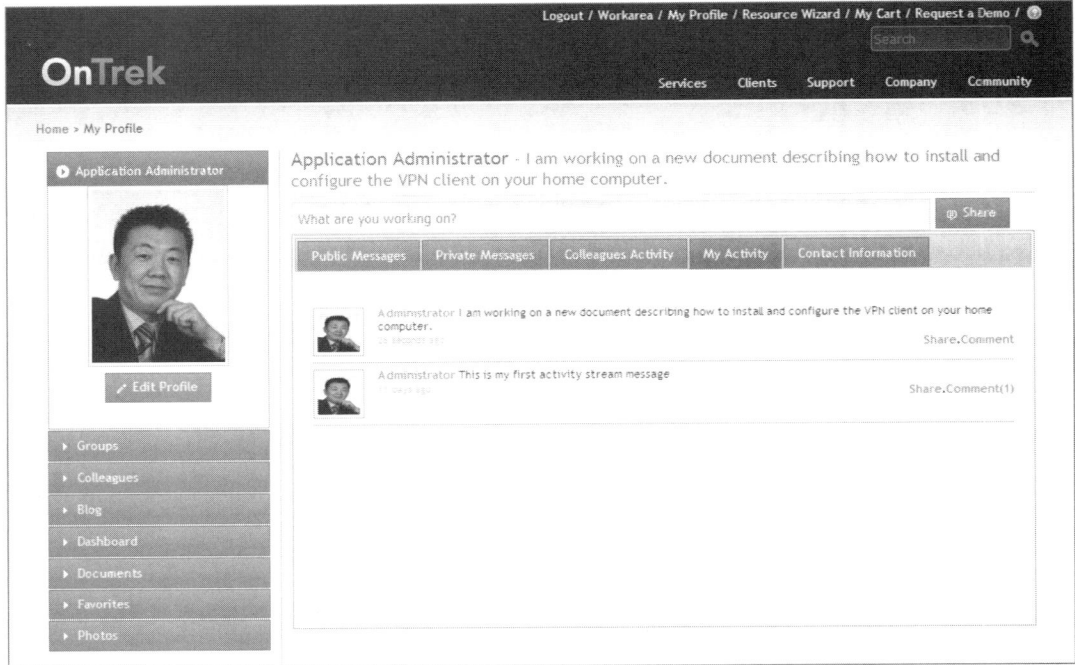

FIGURE 11-18

2. Towards the top of the server control, you will notice the following snippet of code for rendering the textbox for posting micro-messages and the "Share" button:

```
<div id="uxStatusWrapper" runat="server" class="clearfix setStatus">
    <asp:TextBox ID="uxStatus" runat="server" CssClass="status"
              Columns="30" Text="What are you working on?"></asp:TextBox>
    <p class="setStatus">
        <asp:LinkButton ID="uxSetStatus" runat="server" OnClick="uxSetStatus_Click" />
        <span class="ui-button ui-widget ui-state-default
              ui-corner-all ui-button-text-icon setStatusButton" >
          <span class="ui-button-icon-primary ui-icon ui-icon-comment"></span>
          <span class="ui-button-text">Share</span>
        </span>
    </p>
</div>
```

3. On the LinkButton, notice the `OnClick` attribute. This references the `uxSetStatus_Click` event handler which has the following implementation:

```
protected void uxSetStatus_Click(object sender, EventArgs e)
{
    //set status
```

```
                Ektron.Cms.Framework.SocialNetworking.MicroMessage statusApi =
new MicroMessage();
                Ektron.Cms.MicroMessageData statusData = new MicroMessageData();
                statusData.UserId = this.contentApi.UserId;
                statusData.MessageText = uxStatus.Text;
                statusApi.Add(statusData);

                //render ui
                this.ProfileData.SetStatus("- " + uxStatus.Text);
                uxStatus.Text = "What are you working on?";
                uxSetStatus.Visible = true;

                //reload activity stream (colleagues)
                cmsActivityStream.ExcludeUserIds.Add(this.ProfileId);
                cmsActivityStream.Fill();

                //reload activity stream (me)
                LoadMyActivityStream();
        }
```

This event handler uses the MicroMessage API and `MicroMessageData` class for defining and adding the message to the user's list of micro-messages. The ActivityStream Server Control, which displays a list of all the user's activities including all posted micro-messages, is used to render the list.

You may wonder why the ActivityStream Server Control was used in place of the MicroMessaging Server Control. This is simply because OnTrek's requirements specified that all activities for a user must be displayed and not just micro-messages. If the requirements specified that only micro-messages should be displayed, you could replace this implementation with the MicroMessaging Server Control.

Under the Hood

Micro-messages have the potential to reach a very wide audience; this makes micro-messaging an attractive target for spam and related abuse by ill-intentioned community members. Developers and administrators can use the spam-filtering capabilities of the micro-message system to filter out spam prior to it being added to the system. The system-defined spam filters are available when you use the MicroMessage Server control. Enabling the filters is perfomed through the use of the SpamControlType and SpamTimeSpan properties. These properties allow you to implement the following rules:

➤ Block a message when the same message has been posted within a single calendar day.

➤ Block a message when the same message has been posted within a specified time period, relative to the time of the first post.

➤ Block a message when the same message has been posted within a specified time period. The rule is specified using the SpamControlType property of the server control, and each of the three rules corresponds to a particular value:

   ➤ SameUserMessageDay
   ➤ SameUserTimeDelay
   ➤ SameMessageTimeDelay

Spam control is turned off by default.

In cases where you need to define your own spam-filtering rules, you can implement your own filter by setting `SpamControlType` to Custom and overriding the server control's `CustomSpamMethod` in codebehind. Listing 11-6 shows an example of blocking messages that contain the word "spam."

LISTING 11-6: ~/CMS400Developer/Developer/MicroMessaging/CustomSpam.aspx.vb

Available for download on Wrox.com

```vb
Imports System
Imports Ektron.Cms
Imports Ektron.Cms.Framework
Partial Class Developer_MicroMessaging_CustomSpam
    Inherits System.Web.UI.Page

    Protected Sub Page_Load(ByVal sender As Object, ByVal e As System.EventArgs) _
        Handles Me.Load
            Me.MicroMessaging1.CustomSpamMethod(AddressOf SpamHandler)
    End Sub
    Private Function SpamHandler(ByVal data As MicroMessageData) As Boolean
        If data.MessageText.IndexOf("spam", _
StringComparison.CurrentCultureIgnoreCase) > -1 Then
            Return True
        End If
    End Function
End Class
```

TAKE HOME POINTS

This chapter discussed core components of a social networking site built using the Ektron Community Framework. It explains how the Community Framework contains APIs and Server Controls that can be used to implement the Web 2.0 type features discussed in Chapter 10 to facilitate community generated content through blogs, wikis, and discussion boards. It also covers how social networking features allow users to create and benefit from social connections between community members.

The key features of social networking are as follows:

- **Ektron's friending infrastructure:** Of all the social networking functionality discussed in this chapter, none is more important than the ability for community members to establish links between one another. Through Ektron's friending infrastructure, community members can establish such connections and use the resulting "social graph" (the network of connections that form between users) to further discover information, stay on top of the news, and share content. You learned about user profiles and saw how they can be used to display much of the information created and shared by users using the UserProfile Server Control. The OnTrek implementation was also covered, and it showed how APIs were used to present a highly customized presentation.

- **Community groups:** In this chapter, you learned how community members form community groups. Discovery of community groups primarily happens either through the community group search functionality, which allows members to search for groups by name or tag, or by navigating through the list of most active, most popular, or most recently added groups. Community groups allow members to come together to discuss and collaborate on particular topics.

- **Activity streams:** Once users are connected to a social graph and belong to community groups, it's important to have some way to know what has happened in these circles since the last visit. This is where activity streams are useful. Activity streams provide the list of activities for a user, a social network, a community group, or some combination of them. Most community-related events flow through the notification system, which allows users to be notified through the activity stream, but Ektron can also use SMS, e-mail, and potentially other custom notification agents.

- **Micro-messages:** Another way to keep members of a social network informed of the events that have the potential to impact them in some way is through the use of micro-messaging. Community members post short micro-messages that typically include some type of status information (for example, "I'm currently working on the Q2 sales projections"), buzz-worthy content such as a link worth sharing, information about an upcoming event, and so on. Micro-messages are also an activity type, which means they also raise events in the notification system and are then made available through SMS, e-mail, and other gateways.

Creating the Catalog of Products for the eCommerce Storefront

> ➤ How do you configure product, payment, and shipping for eCommerce?
>
> ➤ How do you create catalogs and products for a storefront?
>
> ➤ How do you enable marketing incentives using coupons?
>
> ➤ What's the best way to work with product reports and order management?

The eCommerce feature of Ektron is one of the largest new features in the product. It supports the entire lifecycle of commerce transactions, with a rich suite of features to enable complex processes. In this chapter and the next, you will be working through the process of implementing the eCommerce feature on the OnTrek website. In this chapter, you approach things from the Workarea side, so it's more about configuring your site to enable eCommerce, and then creating the catalog of products. You will also work with reports, and move products through the fulfillment process. The next chapter approaches the subject from a more technical viewpoint, covering how to implement the server controls necessary to create a seamless shopping experience for site visitors.

In this chapter, you spend your time configuring the basic options of eCommerce, including tax structures and shipping options. You'll work with currencies and payment options and learn about notifications. You will go through the process of creating product types and learn about the various capabilities of each class of product type. You'll create a catalog in parallel with the existing catalogs on the OnTrek site, and a sample product as well, learning about the options available at each step. You'll also explore how coupons can support the user experience by offering a wide array of discount structures.

Finally, you'll examine the capabilities of the reporting subsystem and order workflow system. You'll learn how to extend the workflow process, and how to move items through it. You will also walk through the various steps in completing purchases, and see how the historical data is managed.

USE CASE

Now that the infrastructure of the community, support, and marketing portions of the OnTrek website have been constructed, you are left with the eCommerce functionality of the website. The eCommerce piece is a fairly large portion to chew off, so the OnTrek implementation team has decided to break it into two pieces, the first of which is the fundamental act of creating the infrastructure of shipping, tax, coupons, and product inventory so that customers can order goods directly from OnTrek through the website.

> ### ADDING ECOMMERCE FUNCTIONALITY
>
> This use case introduces the primary actor Dan, a site administrator and developer, who has been charged with populating the OnTrek website with the catalog of goods that OnTrek offers to its clientele. It describes the expected scenario and defines the desired outcome.
>
> #### Wireframe
>
> The example Wireframe for this chapter, shown in Figure 12-1, is the eCommerce landing page, which lists out some selected products from the OnTrek catalog, and invites the user to add them to their cart or browse for further products.
>
> #### Description
>
> This use case defines the process Dan must follow to build up the underlying infrastructure in order to create a fully functioning eCommerce solution on the OnTrek website. It will walk through basic configuration, and creation of the catalog of products, so that the developer, Ted, has the necessary content to develop the front-facing portion of the codebase to support the actual purchasing process.
>
> #### Actor
>
> Dan is a member of the marketing team at OnTrek. Through feedback on the site, his manager has determined that users browsing the OnTrek site would be much more likely to convert to customers if they could do so online rather than having to deal with the sales team during what is mostly a manual process at this point. Armed with his convictions, the manager has tasked Dan with managing the process of creating an online shopping experience using the Ektron Framework. Dan will then hand off the completed foundation to the IT team for development of the front end of the shopping cart experience.
>
> #### Scenario
>
> In this scenario, Dan:
>
> ➤ Configures the underlying options for supported regions and currencies

- Configures higher level options, such as taxes and shipping support
- Connects the site with an online payment gateway to accept funds from customers
- Creates the notification messages that customers will receive
- Creates a set of product types that will support the various categories of goods that OnTrek wants to sell
- Creates the catalog structure to store the inventory
- Creates the set of products that OnTrek sells

Outcome

The OnTrek marketing team is now prepared to hand off the site to a dedicated developer to build out the eCommerce functionality supporting the online purchasing of goods by OnTrek customers.

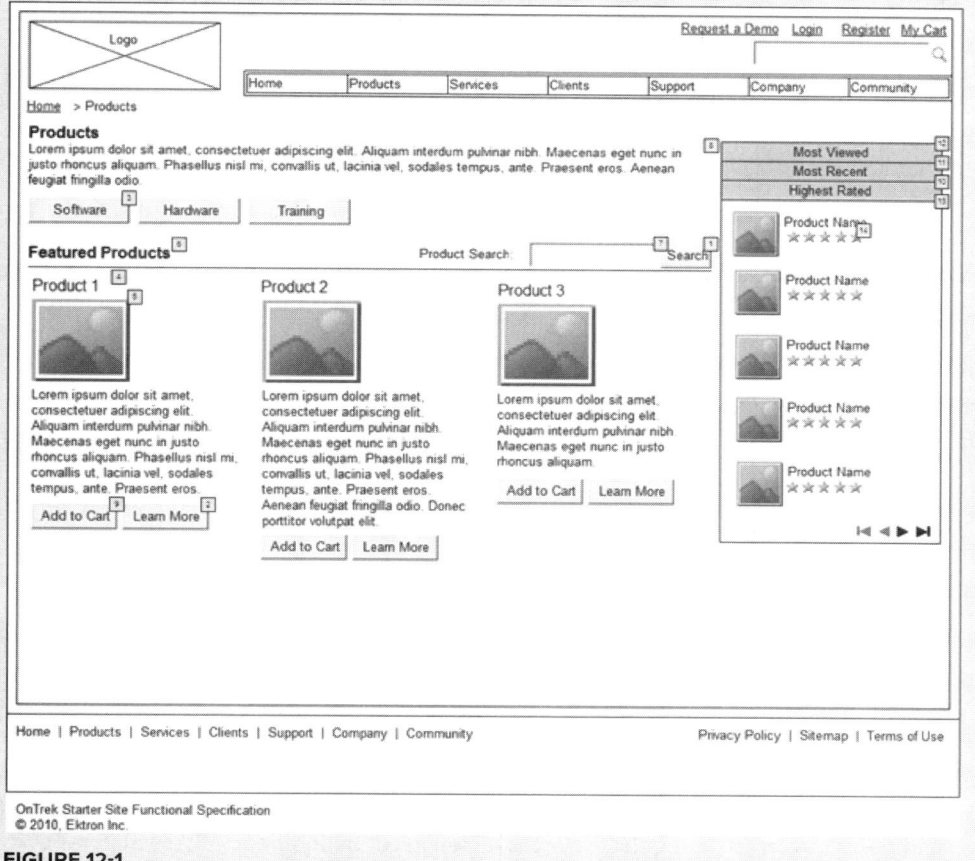

FIGURE 12-1

UNDERSTANDING THE TECHNOLOGY

In this chapter, you will cover the underlying requirements in the build out of an eCommerce feature for an existing website. This chapter doesn't cover the code development side, which is instead reserved for the next chapter, but will spend a lot of time covering all the various options that can impact how the eCommerce feature of your site works.

For the configuration of the site options, you'll delve into the shipment providers and payment gateway providers. The ability to modify these providers in the Ektron Framework allows you a large amount of flexibility in matching the capabilities your site provides to your business model. You'll also learn how to build custom providers in the next chapter. You'll explore how taxes are configured, as well as currencies, regions, and types of payments. These features make it easy to participate in the global marketplace, without needing customizations. You'll also take an in-depth look at how e-mail notification messages are constructed.

Once that has been completed, you'll examine product types and classes and how to build them. The eCommerce feature allows for the specification of Smart Form-like product configurations, allowing you to easily capture the relevant data for each class of product, ensuring consistency for users browsing your site. This chapter will discuss some best practices and things to keep in mind when building these types, and will discuss how to manage them going forward.

The chapter will then cover coupons, including how to create them, how they are applied, and the variety of ways they can affect your customers' orders. Coupons also can be limited in their application; this creates a safety net by limiting your exposure to discounts.

Armed with the product types, you'll explore how to create actual catalogs of goods, and then dive into creating products and groups of products. Working with the catalogs and products is similar to working with content, allowing you to leverage the knowledge you've already gained about the Ektron Framework. The chapter will also discuss the reporting options available, including order workflows and how to extend them. The chapter will end with a discussion on the states of orders, and how to manage orders as they move through the workflow. There will be further discussion of customizing the default workflow behavior in Chapter 13, however the default workflow the eCommerce feature ships with will cover the needs of most developers.

CONFIGURING ECOMMERCE

In a production environment, eCommerce has a couple of key requirements to be enabled for use. First and foremost, it requires a license. Like a few other features in the Ektron Framework, the eCommerce feature is not included in the standard license, but can be added to a standard or professional license through the use of a module license. The eCommerce feature is included with an enterprise license, however. When working in a keyless environment, as is the norm for developers building code on a Localhost site, the feature will also be enabled. In this situation, the server is only accessible through the loopback interface, so users will not be able to visit the site via a host name.

In the OnTrek environment, if the license is not enabled, any pages that interact with the eCommerce feature will return an error stating the feature is not enabled. In addition, any menu items that point to a page that has an eCommerce item on it will be hidden. If you can't see any eCommerce links in your installation, or when you follow an eCommerce link you receive an error, please speak with your Ektron sales representative.

Once the eCommerce feature is enabled on your site, you must enter the Workarea to set up the appropriate configuration options in order for your server controls to render properly. In this section, you learn how to configure the basic aspects of the eCommerce feature. In the next section, you work with some products in the workflow and some supporting features. For the configuration aspect, this section specifically covers the following areas:

➤   Managing major configuration options
➤   Configuring the settings for shipping and taxes
➤   Configuring payment methods and currencies
➤   Creating product types

Managing Major Configuration Options

The majority of the configuration for eCommerce takes place in the Settings tab in the Workarea. To get to the eCommerce configuration section follow these steps:

1. Log into the Workarea now as admin and switch to the Settings tab.
2. Directly under the Settings entry in the Settings tree, there should be a node for Commerce. If there isn't, please speak to an Ektron sales representative about getting a trial license with the eCommerce feature.
3. To enter the new license key, go to Workarea ➪ Settings ➪ Settings Tree ➪ Configuration ➪ Setup.
4. Under the eCommerce node, there are six major groups of items. The first area covered in this section is the Configuration node. Open this now, and you'll see six items underneath it, as shown in Figure 12-2.

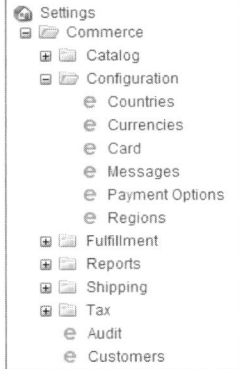

FIGURE 12-2

These items manage settings that act system wide, and control availability of catalogs in the site among other things. The following list enumerates each item and describes what it is used for. After covering the items from a high level, the subsequent sections will dive a little deeper into each item.

- **Countries:** Allows you to manage the list of countries usable throughout the system. This populates the list of options in areas throughout the eCommerce feature, for example, tax management and warehouse management.

- **Currencies:** The eCommerce system allows use of all currencies throughout the world. In this item, you can choose which currencies should be supported on your site, as well as manage exchange rates.

- **Card:** This node supports creating new payment options and managing existing payment options. For instance, you may want to allow for gift cards that act like credit cards in the payment options on your site. You can use this area to create the definition so that the option appears in the payment type dropdown presented to customers when they check out.

- **Messages:** Customers of your site will be accustomed to receiving e-mail notifications at several events during the order fulfillment lifecycle. This section is used to manage the form letters sent when those events take place.

- **Payment Options:** This area allows you to configure gateways used to collect payment on orders. There are several gateways with re-built connectors that can be used out-of-the-box. In addition, the eCommerce feature is built in an extensible way so that you can build additional providers for further gateways painlessly.

- **Regions:** While the eCommerce Framework comes with a list of predefined countries and regions, these may change over time or be inadequate for your needs. The Regions area allows you to update the regions of each country as needed. For instance, in the United States, each state is a region.

Countries

The Countries pane, shown in Figure 12-3, contains the list of countries throughout the world. It stores numeric ISO code, as well as the long and short ISO abbreviations. This list is used in two main ways:

- **To define country level taxes:** These can optionally be overridden with regional settings. For instance, in the U.S., there is no sales tax if the sale crosses state borders. This means that the country tax for a company based in Massachusetts would be 0, whereas orders shipping to Massachusetts would have the sales tax applied; in this case it is 6.25 percent.

- **To determine shipping costs.** The country list allows you to enable or disable appropriate countries as shipping destinations. The shipping provider then uses the country code to correctly determine the cost of shipping to that location.

To enable or disable a country for customer locations, follow these steps:

1. Go to Workarea ➪ Settings ➪ Settings Tree ➪ Commerce ➪ Configuration ➪ Countries, and select the country from the Countries pane, as shown in Figure 12-3.

    This brings you into the details pane for the country you selected. At this point, you see the same details as in the list, including the full name of the country, the numeric ISO code along with the short and long ISO abbreviation for the country, and an indicator of whether the country is enabled.

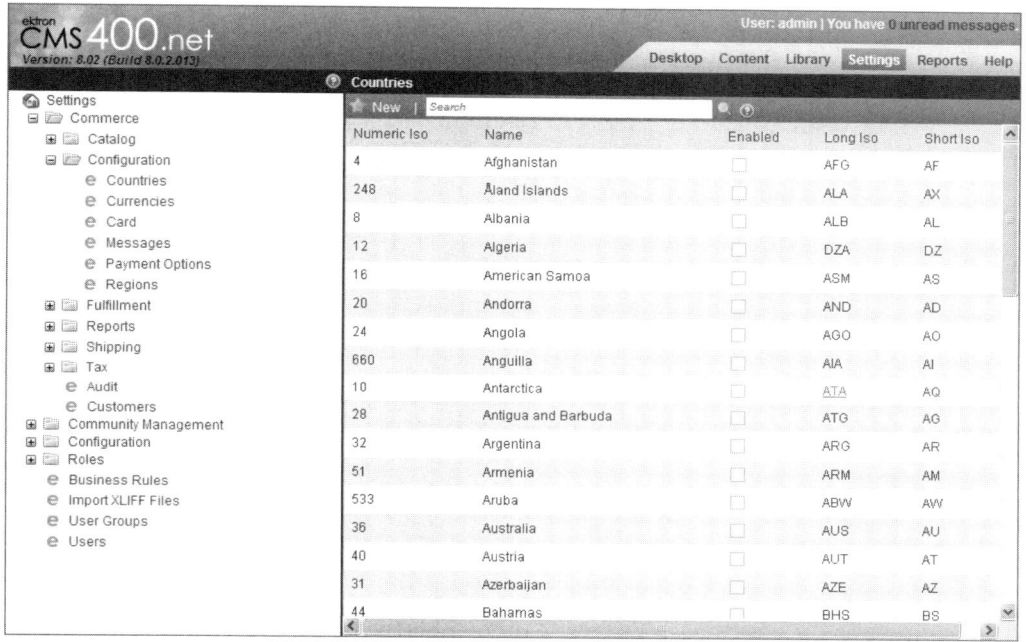

FIGURE 12-3

2. Click Edit the toolbar to edit these settings now, and you will see the Edit Country screen as shown in Figure 12-4.

3. On the Edit Country screen you can enable or disable the country at will. Enabled countries will appear on dropdowns of customer locations and shipping destinations.

Currencies

The Currencies pane allows you to manage the list of supported currencies. There are no internal limitations in the eCommerce engine restricting the use of currencies. The system comes preloaded with all currencies defined in the ISO 4217 name list. Each currency is stored with a name, the numeric ISO code, the ISO abbreviated name, and the exchange rate.

Currencies are switched on the site by using the Currency Select Server Control, which operates very similarly to the Language Select Server Control, allowing the end users to select the currency for the item being priced. A default currency can be selected for the site by setting the value of the ek_ecom_DefaultCurrencyId tag in the web.config file at the root of your site.

 Remember not to change the ek_ecom_DefaultCurrencyId tag after creating products, as it can corrupt the pricing of those products on the site.

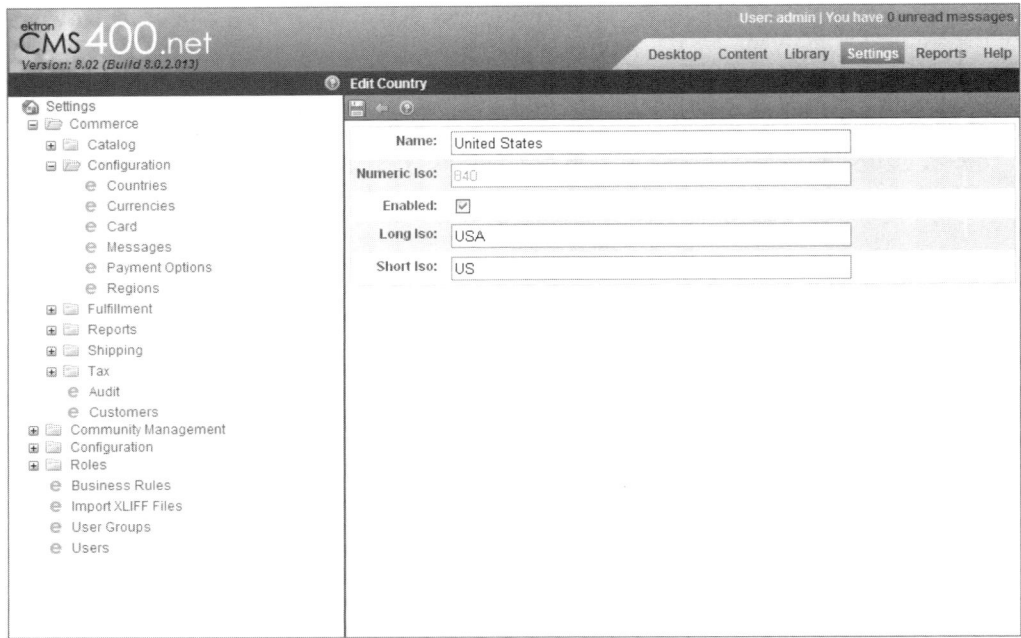

FIGURE 12-4

While pricing on a per-currency basis can be performed for each item individually, you also have the option of having the Ektron Framework automatically calculate the appropriate price for each product by using the exchange rate defined for that currency. The exchange rate calculation is performed against the default currency. For example, out-of-the-box, the default currency is U.S. dollars. Each additional enabled currency then can have its own exchange rate that would be calculated against the dollar in this case. So let's say you kept the USD as the default currency, and enabled GBP as an alternate currency with an exchange rate of 1 USD = .65 GBP. If you were to then create a product with a price of 100 USD, site visitors could use the Currency Select Server Control to switch currencies to GBP, in which case they would see the price automatically calculated as 65 GBP. These calculations are performed as needed, so if you were to then modify the exchange rate for GBP, the price would reflect the change on the site immediately.

To manage the currencies for your site, follow these steps:

1. Go to Workarea ➪ Settings➪ Settings Tree ➪ Commerce ➪ Configuration ➪ Currencies. This will bring up the Currencies pane, as shown in Figure 12-5.

2. You can filter the list of currencies using the Search box on the toolbar. A currency can be edited by selecting the currency from the list. This brings up a modal window that allows you to edit the details of that currency, as shown in Figure 12-6. This modal allows you to modify the name, whether or not the currency is enabled, and the exchange rate versus the default currency.

Configuring eCommerce | **449**

FIGURE 12-5

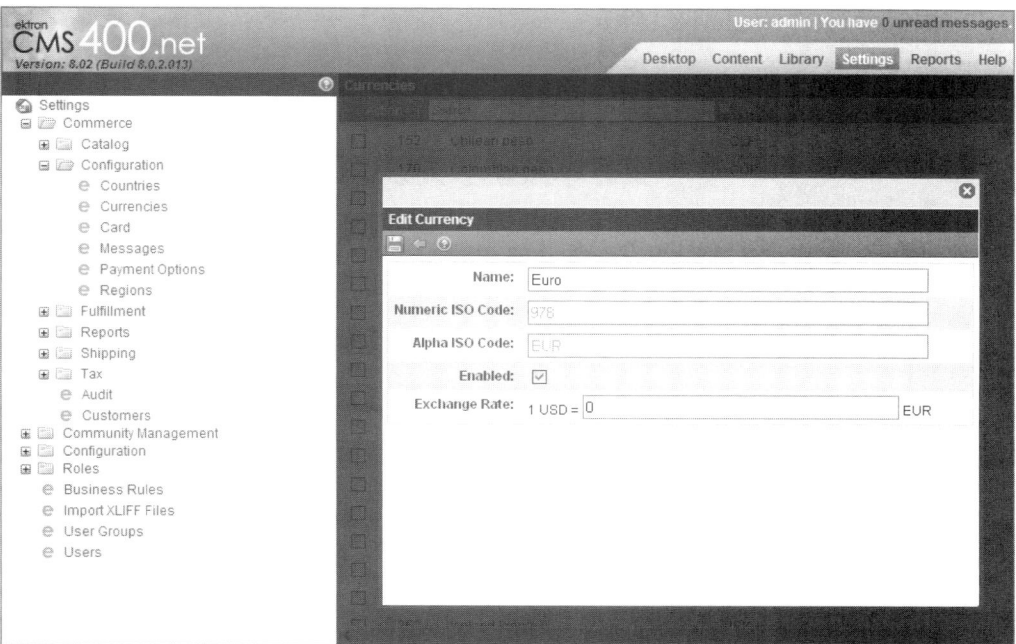

FIGURE 12-6

3. You can also update the exchange rates for all the enabled currencies from a single screen. From the Currencies pane, select Action ➪ Edit Exchange Rates. This brings up a modal listing each of the active currencies, with a textbox showing the current exchange rate where you can enter a new exchange rate, or disable any of the active exchange rates. This modal is shown in Figure 12-7.

4. When you are finished editing, select Action ➪ Update to save your edits.

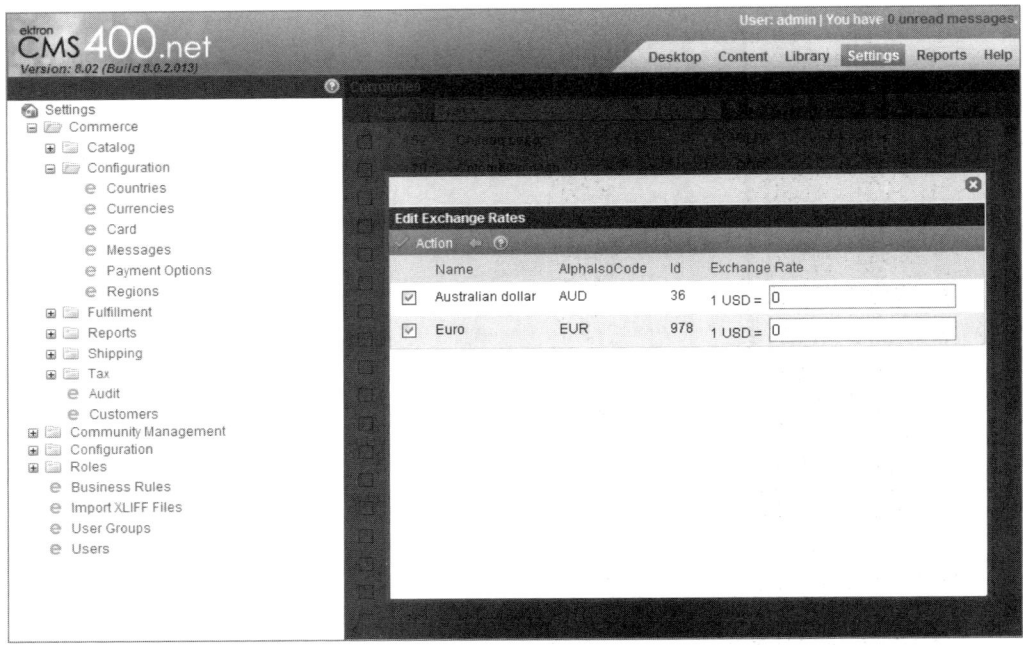

FIGURE 12-7

The currency exchange rates can also be programmatically manipulated through the `Ektron.Cms.Commerce.ExchangeRateApi`. This API can be used to keep your stored exchange rates up-to-date with market conditions if desired. This operation is more advanced, however, and is beyond the scope of this book.

Card

The Ektron eCommerce feature comes with five predefined credit card types: American Express, Diners Club, Discover, MasterCard, and Visa. These card types are used to populate the credit card type dropdown in the checkout process. Each card specification can be updated with custom naming, icons, and regular expressions for early validation of that card type.

There are two main actions available in this area. New cards can be added, and current cards can be updated. To perform either of these actions, go to Workarea ➪ Settings ➪ Settings Tree ➪

Commerce ➪ Configuration ➪ Card. This brings you to the Card Types pane, pictured in Figure 12-8. This pane contains a list of the currently defined card types, and shows whether each type will be available on the site.

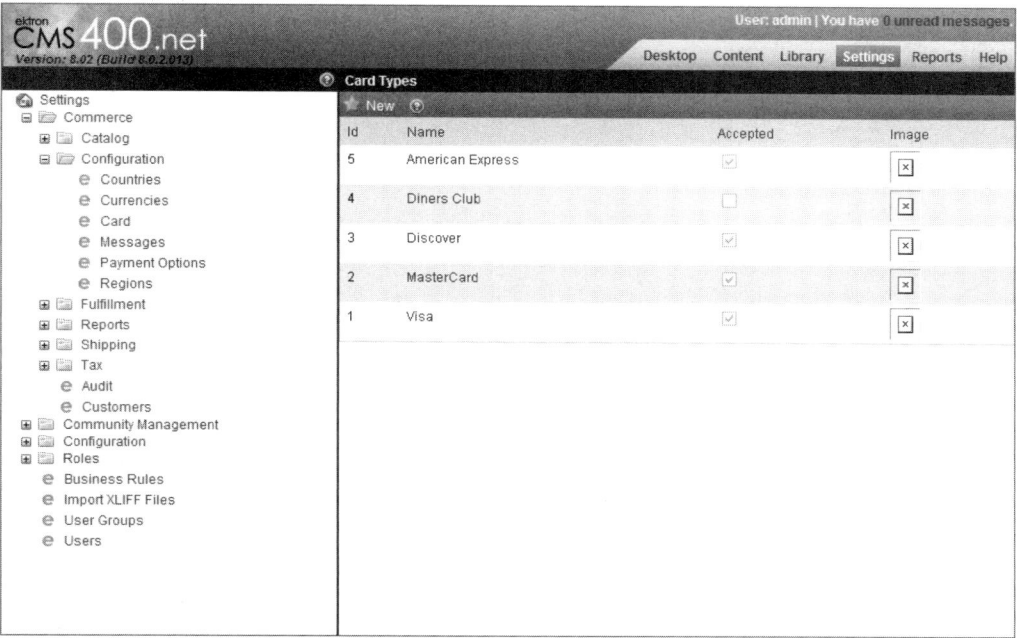

FIGURE 12-8

- ➤ **To add a new card type:** Select New ➪ Card Type from the toolbar menu of the Card Types pane. This brings up the editing interface for cards, allowing you to enter a name, an image to use as an icon, a regular expression to provide early validation, and a checkbox to mark the new card as accepted. Only cards marked as accepted show up in the card type dropdown.

- ➤ **To edit the existing cards:** Simply select the card from the list, which brings up the same interface used for new cards but is pre-populated with the current options. The Edit Card Type pane is shown in Figure 12-9.

Messages

There are several occasions during the order and fulfillment process when notifications are typically sent to the ordering party. The messages center allows you to define the format used in the e-mails that are sent when these events occur. The events and the associated message type are described in Table 12-1.

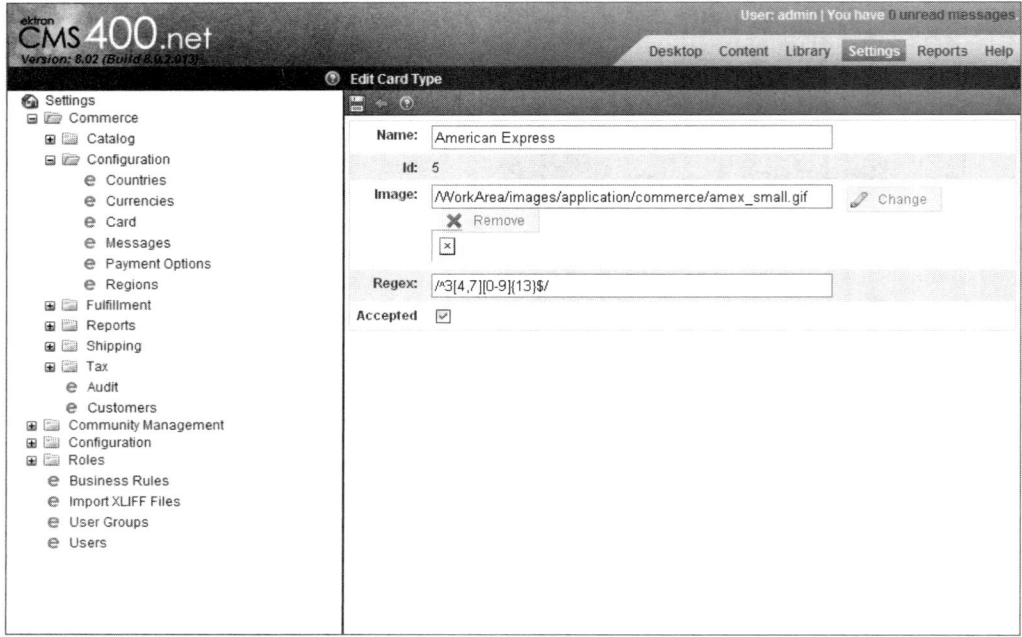

FIGURE 12-9

TABLE 12-1: eCommerce Message Types

EVENT	MESSAGE TYPE	DESCRIPTION
Order Submission	OrderReceived	Occurs when an order is placed on the website.
Order Cancellation	OrderCancelled	Occurs when an order is cancelled.
Order Shipped	OrderShipped	Occurs when an order is shipped from the warehouse.
Order Completed	OrderCompleted	Occurs when an order is closed out and completed.

The messages used in eCommerce follow the same token string replacement method employed in other messages throughout the system. The acceptable tokens are listed in Table 12-2.

TABLE 12-2: eCommerce Message Tokens

TOKEN STRING	DESCRIPTION
@CustomerFirstName@	First name of the customer.
@CustomerLastName@	Last name of the customer.

TOKEN STRING	DESCRIPTION
@OrderId@	ID of the order.
@OrderSubTotal@	Total cost of the order excluding taxes, shipping, and coupons.
@OrderTotal@	Total cost of the order to be charged to the customer.
@OrderShippingTotal@	Cost of shipping the order.
@OrderCouponTotal@	Value of coupons applied to the order.
@OrderTaxTotal@	Total tax applied to the order.
@OrderItemTitle@	The title of an individual item on the order. This token must be used within the @OrderItemStart@ and @OrderItemEnd@ loop markers.
@OrderItemSalePrice@	Sale price of an individual item on the order. This token must be used within the @OrderItemStart@ and @OrderItemEnd@ loop markers.
@OrderItemQuantity@	Quantity for a given line item on the order. This token must be used within the @OrderItemStart@ and @OrderItemEnd@ loop markers.
@OrderItemTotal@	The total cost of a given line item. Excludes taxes and shipping; is calculated by multiplying the item quantity by the item sale price. This token must be used within the @OrderItemStart@ and @OrderItemEnd@ loop markers.
@OrderItemStart@ and @OrderItemEnd@	These markers are used to specify the start and end location of the text to repeat for each line item in the order.
@TrackingUrl@	Replaced with the URL for the order shipment tracking page.

The eCommerce messaging system uses the same underlying technology as the content notification system. This means that for these e-mails to be sent, the CDOSYS SMTP and relay information must be configured properly in the web.config, as well as in IIS.

> *For more information on this process, see "Configuring E-Mail for Tasks and Content" in Chapter 1 of the CMS400 manual, installed with the Ektron Framework on your system.*

To create or modify the messages for your eCommerce system, follow these steps:

1. Go to Workarea ➪ Settings ➪ Settings Tree ➪ Commerce ➪ Configuration ➪ Messages. This will bring up the list of predefined messages, as shown in Figure 12-10.

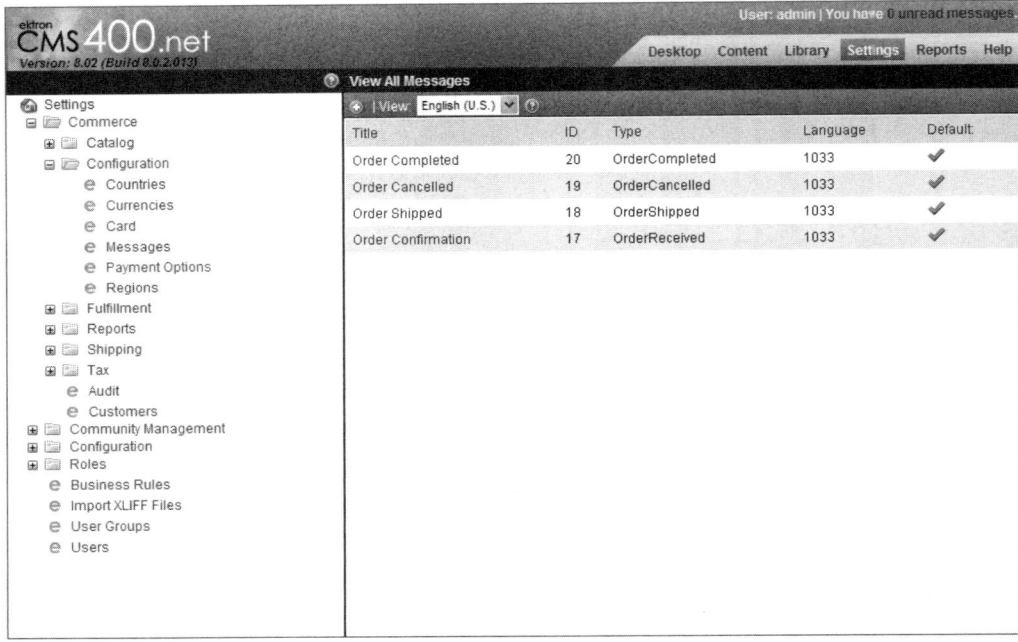

FIGURE 12-10

2. From there you can either select an existing message to edit, or you can create a new message by selecting the Add icon from the toolbar. Additionally, you can create messages for each language enabled on your site by selecting the appropriate language in the dropdown on the Messages pane toolbar. When the system generates the e-mail for a specific event, it uses the message template in that user's language.

3. Select the Order Confirmation message now, and select Edit on the resulting pane. The view updates with the edit screen, as shown in Figure 12-11. As is shown in the screenshot, the editing interface is a rich HTML editor, meaning you can easily create detailed attractive message formats. This message also shows a relatively complex e-mail format.

Payment Options

There are two types of payment options available in the eCommerce subsystem. The first type is PayPal, which is commonly accepted on many sites. The second type is to use a payment gateway, which allows you to hook up a merchant account directly to your website for immediate payment processing.

Setting Up PayPal

Using PayPal is frequently a less complicated way of enabling payment on your site but requires that the user be handed off to the PayPal website to complete the payment process. As this happens via a customized page you can still maintain some level of custom branding on the destination page. This is in contrast to a payment gateway, however, where the users never leave your site to complete their purchases.

Configuring eCommerce | **455**

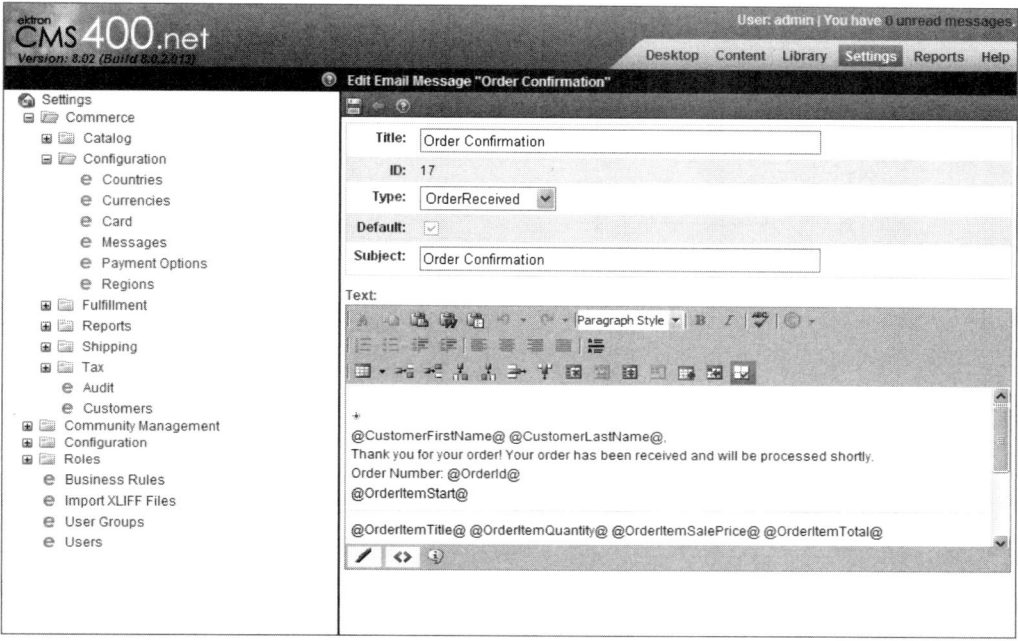

FIGURE 12-11

There are two ways for the customer to use PayPal during the checkout process.

➤ **If the customer selects PayPal from the Shopping Cart screen, the process proceeds as follows, and is illustrated in Figure 12-12.**

   1. The customer starts on the cart screen.

   2. The customer selects PayPal as the payment method.

   3. The PayPal website comes up, requiring the customer to log into their PayPal account.

   4. The customer selects the payment and address information from their PayPal stored data.

   5. The information is passed back to the eCommerce system, pre-populating the addresses for shipment and billing.

   6. Shipping and billing information is presented to the user for modifications.

   7. Additional costs, such as shipping and taxes, are determined based on the addresses.

   8. The customer confirms the order.

   9. The customer returns to PayPal to finish checking out.

➤ **If the customers do not click the PayPal button on the Shopping Cart screen, they follow a slightly different process.** They manually enter the addresses rather than having them be pre-populated from the PayPal account. The rest of the process, however, is exactly the same.

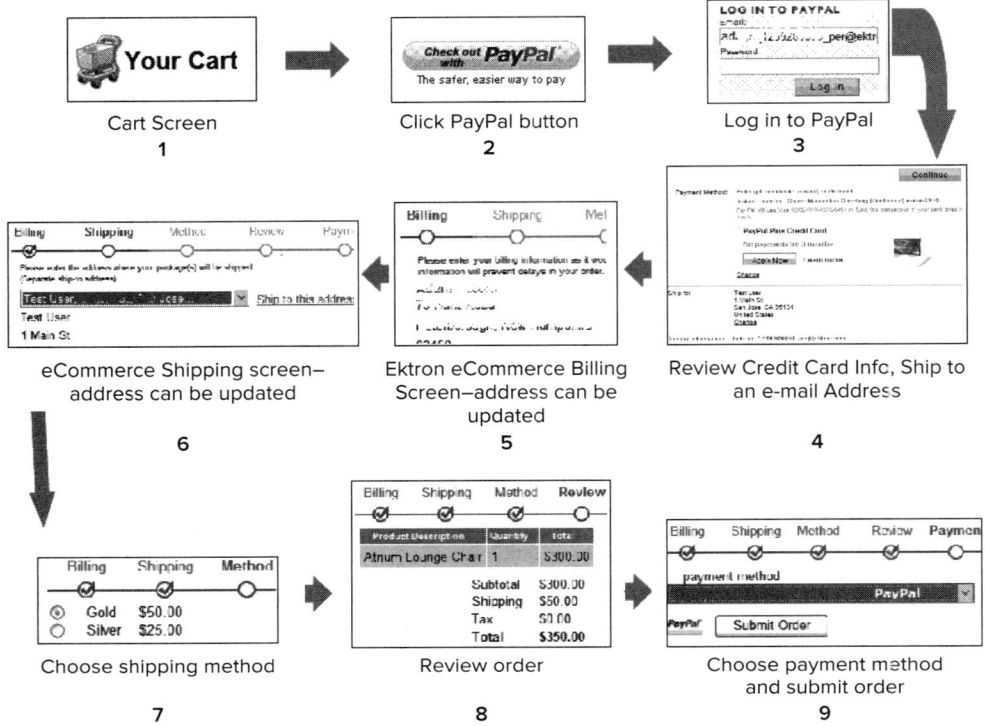

FIGURE 12-12

To enable PayPal support, follow these steps:

1. Create an account on PayPal as a seller.
2. Update the PayPalUser, PayPalPwd, and PayPalSignature keys in your web.config with the API username, password, and signature exposed by PayPal for that account.
3. Enable PayPal as a valid option in the Workarea.
4. You can customize the PayPal payment page to match your site more closely. These steps are covered in depth in "Enabling PayPal Support" in Chapter 17 of the CMS400 manual, installed with the Ektron Framework on your machine.

To enable PayPal in the Workarea, follow these steps:

1. Go to Workarea ➪ Settings ➪ Settings Tree ➪ Commerce ➪ Configuration ➪ Payment Options. This will bring you to the Payment Options pane, which lists in two tabs all the available payment methods on your site. This is shown in Figure 12-13.
2. From the toolbar, select Action ➪ Edit Payment Options, which brings you to the Edit Payment Options pane.
3. Check PayPal, and click Save to enable PayPal as a valid option on your site.

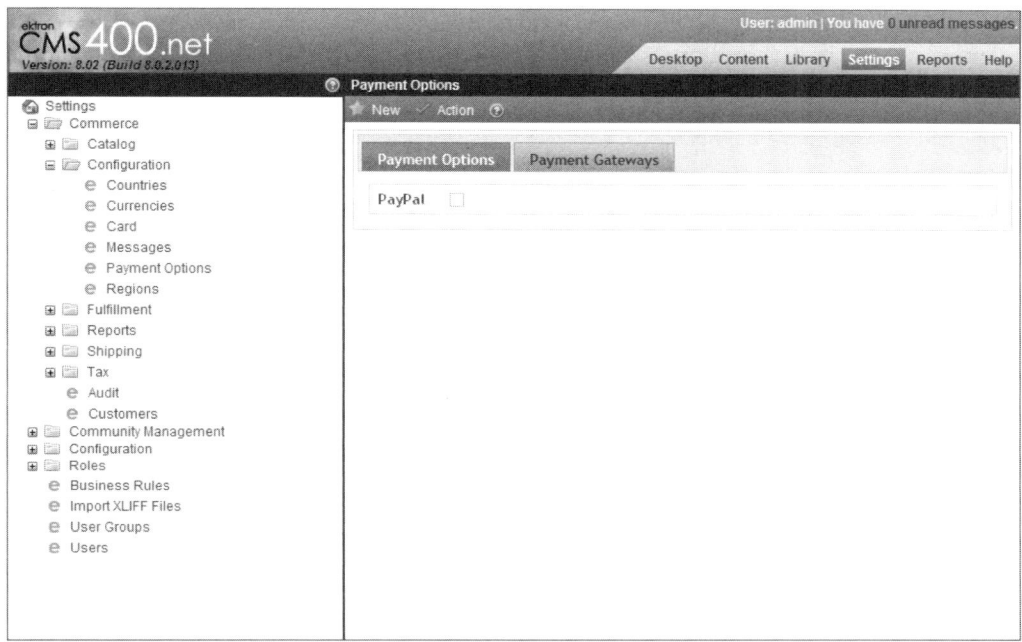

FIGURE 12-13

Setting Up a Payment Gateway

The other option for accepting payments on your website is to use a payment gateway. A payment gateway is a service that accepts credit card payments on behalf of your website, through a back channel. From the customer's point of view, the experience appears to take place exclusively on your site.

The Ektron Framework ships with three payment gateway modules, supporting Authorize.Net, PayFlow, as well as a manual gateway that allows you to use an offline payment service. You can use this service, for instance, if you don't have a Web-enabled merchant account, but instead manually run credit cards at a physical location. In addition, the gateway system follows a provider model, allowing you to extend the system by creating custom gateway software to hook into other merchant account companies.

Gateways allow you to process payments other than credit cards as well; for instance, it is possible to accept payment by check through a gateway. Depending on the type of payment, the processing method may vary. The process for credit cards is outlined here:

1. The gateway provider on your site must first send the transaction information, such as the credit card number and amount, to a merchant account processor.

2. The merchant account processing system then passes the information to the Credit Card Interchange, which then passes the information to the credit card issuer.

3. The credit card issuer approves or declines the transaction and passes the appropriate funds back through the Credit Card Interchange.

4. The Credit Card Interchange passes the results back to the merchant account processor, which sends the received funds to your account, and the result of the transaction to the gateway provider on your site.

5. Finally, the gateway provider saves the results of the transaction to the database.

Notice that the gateway provider does not save the credit card information in that process. For security purposes, customer account information is never stored, only transaction results are.

In order to accept gateway transactions, you must first create a relationship with a payment gateway provider. As mentioned earlier, the eCommerce system supports Authorize.Net and PayFlow out-of-the-box, so if you do not yet have a merchant account, it is recommended that you choose one of these providers to minimize implementation time.

The eCommerce system supports entries for multiple gateways, but will only ever use one gateway at a time. In the Workarea, one gateway is marked as the primary gateway, and that gateway is used for all transactions. That gateway cannot be deleted unless another gateway is marked as default.

Managing gateways takes place in the Workarea, at Workarea ➪ Settings ➪ Settings Tree ➪ Commerce ➪ Configuration ➪ Payment Options. The second tab in this screen, as shown in Figure 12-14, lists the gateway providers currently defined in the system. From here, you can edit the settings of the existing gateway, or create a new gateway definition.

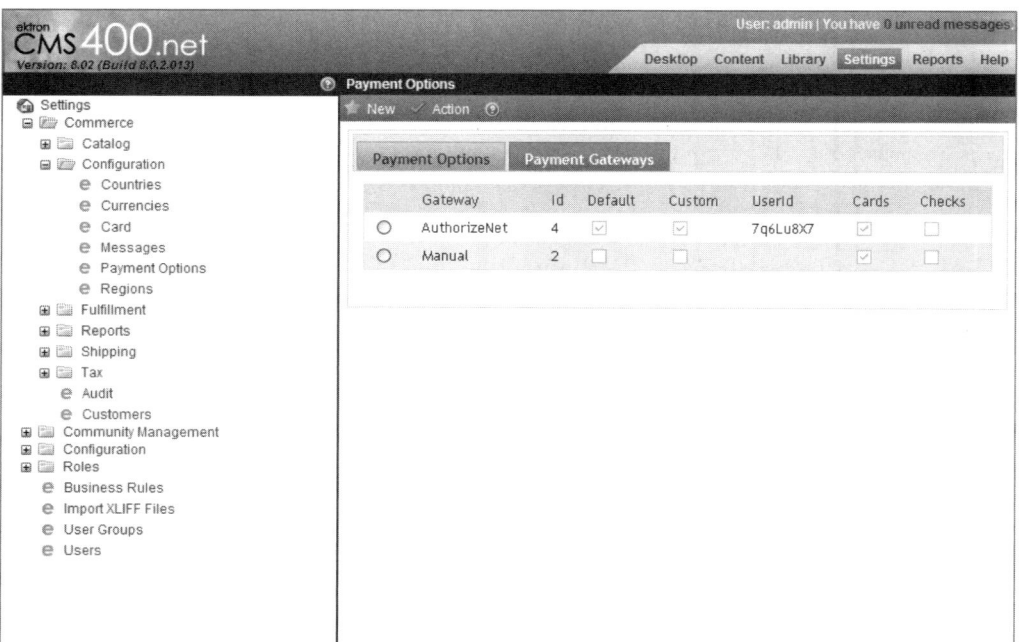

FIGURE 12-14

To modify an existing gateway definition, click the name in the list of gateways. Click the Edit button to modify the values shown to you. Table 12-3 lists and explains each field.

TABLE 12-3: Payment Gateway Form Fields

FIELD	DESCRIPTION
Name	The name of the payment gateway provider. This list is generated from the installed provider modules on your site.
Default	This field specifies whether this gateway is the default provider. Only the default provider is used to process payments.
User ID	This is your user ID with the gateway provider. It identifies your account to ensure the payment goes to the correct account.
Password	The password for your gateway provider account.
Custom Values	Some providers require additional details; for instance, PayFlow requires a vendor and partner string to be specified. These additional values are put into the Custom Values fields.
Credit Cards	Specifies whether the gateway supports credit cards.
Checks	Specifies whether the gateway supports checks.

Adding a gateway definition to the system takes place through the same form. From the Payment Options pane, select New ⇨ Payment Gateway. This brings up the same form, but with no default values, as shown in Figure 12-15.

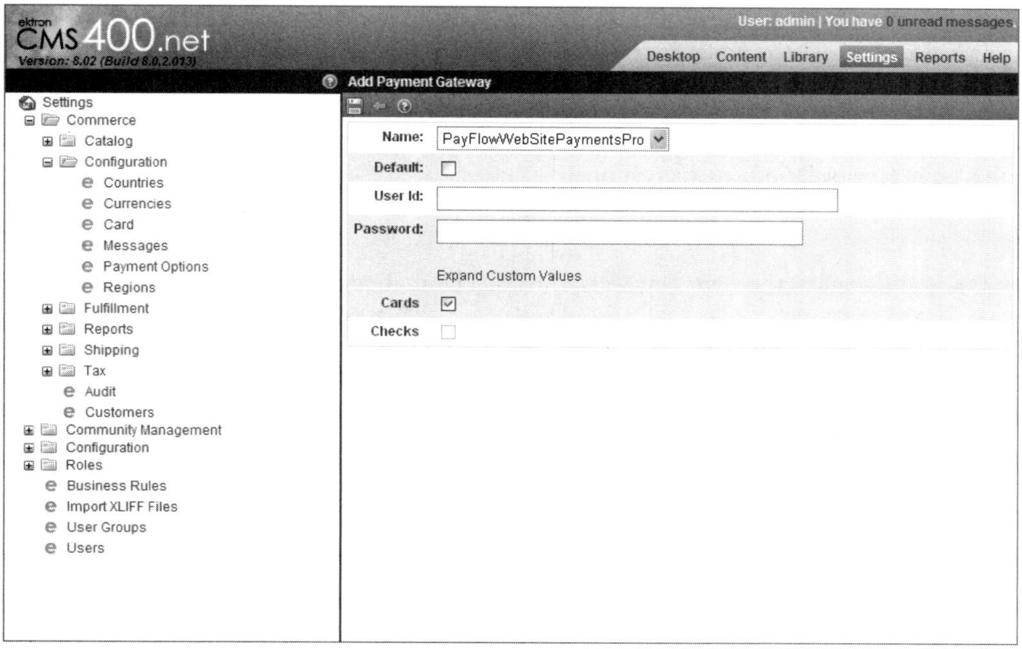

FIGURE 12-15

Checks are a special case in the eCommerce system. If supported by your gateway, checks are listed in the Payment Method dropdown on the payment screen during the checkout process. The customer is then asked to specify their bank name, account number, and routing number, as shown in Figure 12-16.

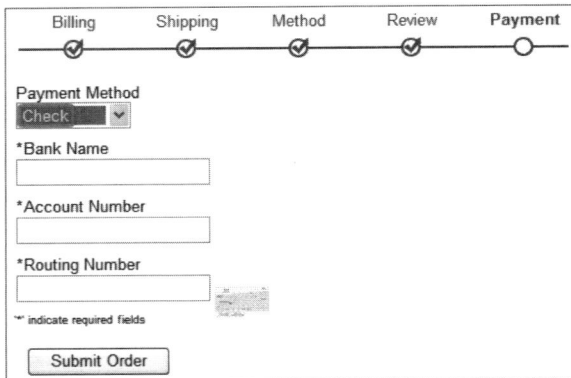

FIGURE 12-16

The process by which check payments are processed also differs slightly from the normal process. The process for processing these payments is as follows.

1. The eCommerce CMS user goes to the View Payment screen on the order, and selects Action ➪ Capture, which starts the payment collection process by submitting the information to the customer's bank.

2. After a few days, the funds are transferred to the merchant account, at which point the eCommerce CMS user updates the order by selecting Action ➪ Mark as Settled on the View Payment screen for the order.

From this point, the order processing continues as normal.

Regions

Regions are used in much the same way as countries. They define a list of geographic areas within a country for the purposes of taxes. The list of regions is displayed as part of the checkout process when collecting address information for billing and shipping. These regions' definitions vary from country to country — for instance, in the United States, each region is a state, as that is the variance for tax structures.

By default, the regions defined in the eCommerce system are the 50 U.S. states, the District of Columbia, and 9 Canadian Provinces. To add further regions for other countries, follow these steps:

1. Go to Workarea ➪ Settings ➪ Settings Tree ➪ Commerce ➪ Configuration ➪ Regions. This displays the Regions pane, as shown in Figure 12-17.

2. From this screen, select New ➪ Region. This brings up the Add Region form. The elements of this form are listed and described in Table 12-4.

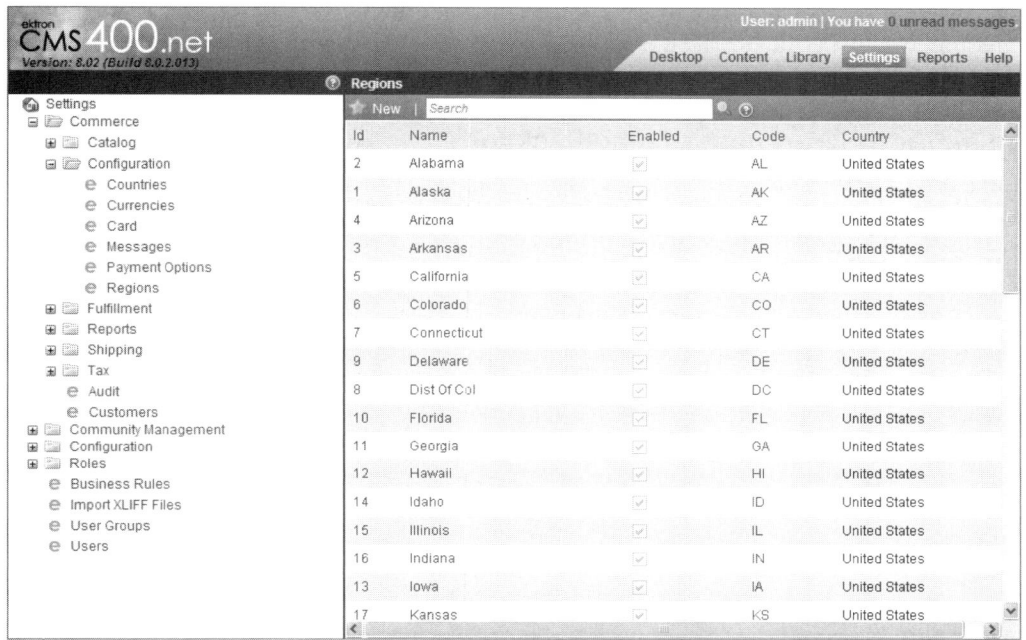

FIGURE 12-17

TABLE 12-4: Add Region Form Fields

FIELD	DESCRIPTION
Name	The name of the region.
Code	An abbreviation for the region.
Country	The country this region belongs to. This list is generated from the list of enabled countries; if the country you want is not shown, go to Workarea ⇨ Settings ⇨ Settings Tree ⇨ Commerce ⇨ Configuration ⇨ Countries and enable the country if it exists or create it if it doesn't.
Enabled	This controls whether the region is displayed in the region dropdown in the Checkout Server Control.
Add another region to this country?	If checked, the form reloads after adding the region, allowing you to quickly add another region.

3. To enable the region for use, check the Enabled checkbox. Click the save icon to save the item.

Configuring the Settings for Shipping and Taxes

Now that you have set up the major configuration options, you're ready to move into the shipping and taxes sections. The shipping section allows the configuration of shipping options available to the customers on the site, and enables you to hook into external systems so that you can provide accurate shipping cost estimates. The taxes section gives you the ability to define tax rates based on geographic locations so that customers do not overpay or underpay taxes on their goods.

Shipping Methods, Warehouses, and Packages

Much like the payment model, the shipping system follows a provider model, so that you can create plug-ins that allow for shipping through methods not supported out-of-the-box. The eCommerce system ships with providers for FedEx and UPS out-of-the-box, along with a Flat rate provider that charges a fixed cost.

The providers available for the system are defined in the shipment.config file at the root of your site. This file contains the type data needed to instantiate your provider. You'll notice that it has an entry for each of the three shipment providers the system ships with. The FedEx and UPS entries are incomplete in a new installation. In order to use these in a production environment, you need to contact the appropriate company to obtain the following information:

➤   Sservice URL

➤   Key

➤   Password

➤   Account number

➤   Meter number

➤   Transaction ID.

This information must then be entered into the shipment.config file.

> Because the shipment provider is read in from the shipment.config file, and this file exists at the root of the site, in a multisite environment you must ensure that each multisite contains an exact copy of this file.

While any number of shipping providers can be defined in the shipment.config file, only one provider can be active in the system at a time. The default shipment provider is selected through the attribute `defaultProvider` on the `shipmentProvider` tag in the shipment.config file. If the new shipping method does not match the desired provider's offerings, you should ensure that the default is set correctly.

Your inventory can also be managed through the eCommerce Framework, relying on the concept of warehouses. The system supports multiple warehouses, but only calculates cost for shipping from the default warehouse.

The final piece of the shipment puzzle is to define packages. Packages allow you to specify standard box sizes along with weight restrictions. The shipping calculator built into the eCommerce Framework uses the box definitions along with the list of products to be shipped to the destination to approximate the best fit into the smallest-sized and fewest number of packages. This minimized number of boxes is then passed into the shipment provider for cost estimation. If the ordered item exceeds the size of the largest defined package, the dimensions of that item are passed directly to the shipment provider instead.

To add a shipping method, managing your warehouse and defining packages, follow these steps:

1. Go to Workarea ➪ Settings ➪ Settings Tree ➪ Commerce ➪ Shipping ➪ Methods. This brings up the Shipping Methods pane, which lists the currently defined methods. These are shown in Figure 12-18.

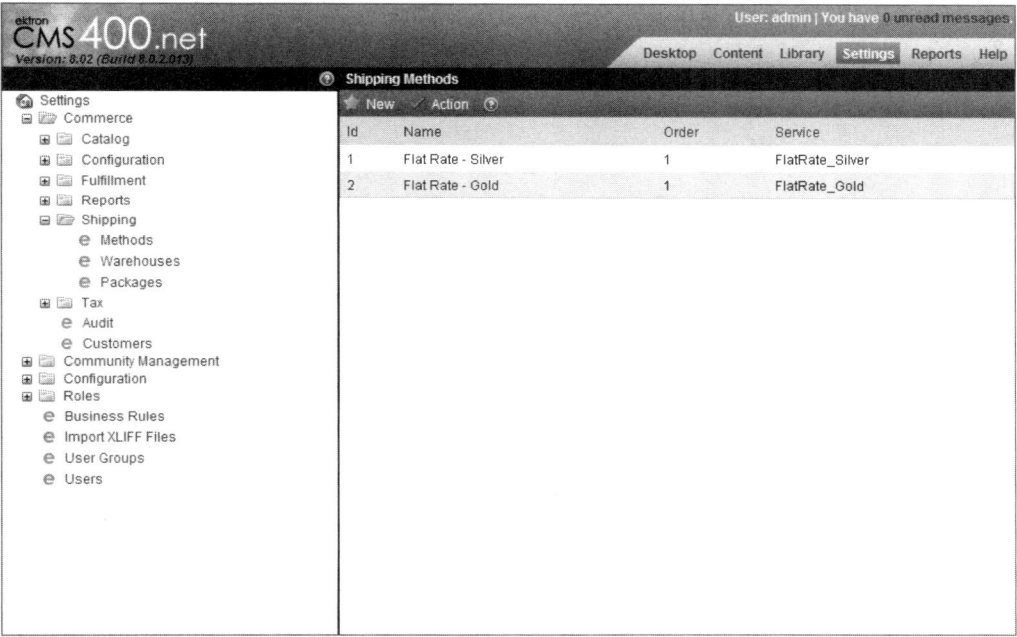

FIGURE 12-18

2. Select New ➪ Shipping Method. This brings up the Add Shipping Method pane. This has three main fields, as described in Table 12-5.

TABLE 12-5: Add Shipping Method Form Fields

FIELD	DESCRIPTION
Name	The name for the level of service that displays to the users as part of the checkout process in the Checkout Server Control.
Active	Specifies whether the specified service level is available as a choice on the checkout form.
Provider Service	The internal name for the level of service. Clicking View Options shows a drop-down displaying valid options gathered from the shipment provider. Selecting one of the dropdown options fills in this field with the appropriate value.

3. The management of warehouses takes place in the Workarea at Workarea ➪ Settings ➪ Settings Tree ➪ Commerce ➪ Shipping ➪ Warehouses.

> *One of the requirements for the eCommerce platform to work correctly is that at least one warehouse be defined in the system. This is required even if you are not managing inventory online, or are dealing exclusively in online products.*

4. To create a warehouse, go to the Warehouses pane at Workarea ➪ Settings ➪ Settings Tree ➪ Commerce ➪ Shipping ➪ Warehouses, and select New ➪ Warehouse from the toolbar menu. This brings up the Add Warehouse form, shown in Figure 12-19.

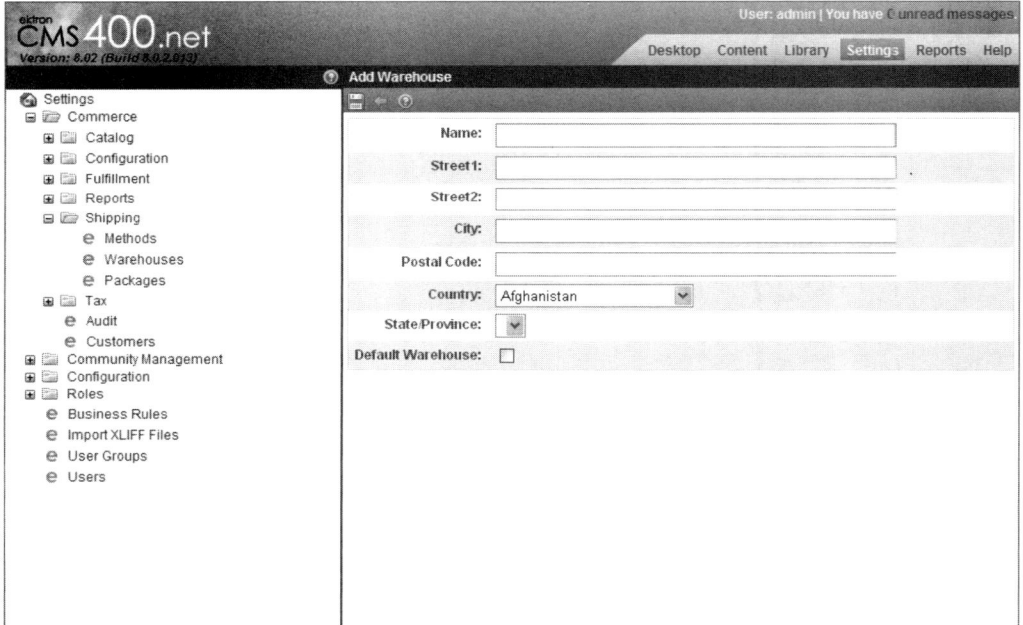

FIGURE 12-19

The fields on this form are mainly designed to capture the location of the warehouse, which is then passed to the shipment provider to calculate the shipping cost for each order so that the customers can be charged appropriately. The fields are described in Table 12-6.

TABLE 12-6: Create Warehouse Form Fields

FIELD	DESCRIPTION
Name	Name of the warehouse.
Street1, Street2	The street address of the warehouse.
City	The city of the warehouse.

FIELD	DESCRIPTION
Postal Code	The postal code of the warehouse.
Country	The country of the warehouse.
State/Province	The state or province of the warehouse.
Default Warehouse	Specifies whether this warehouse should be used in cost calculations. If default, this is the only warehouse used in calculations.

5. Package management takes place through the Packages pane at Workarea ➪ Settings ➪ Settings Tree ➪ Commerce ➪ Shipping ➪ Packages. This pane lists the predefined packages in the system, and allows you to create new packages or edit existing packages. This is shown in Figure 12-20.

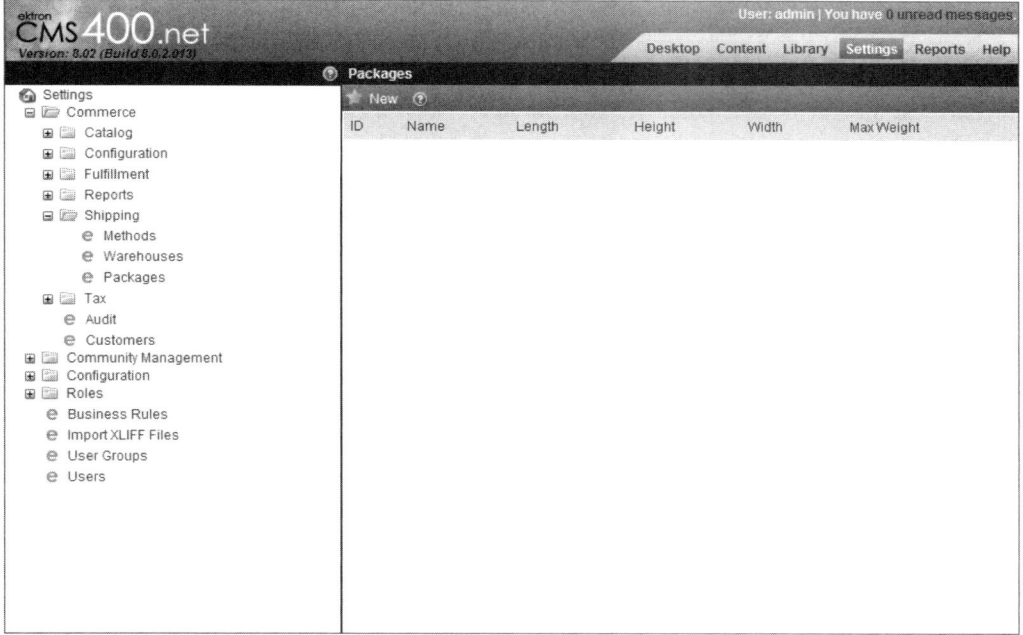

FIGURE 12-20

6. To add a new package, select New ➪ Package. This brings up the New Package form, which is the same form used when editing existing packages. The fields for this form are listed in Table 12-7.

TABLE 12-7: New Package Form Fields

FIELD	DESCRIPTION
Name	The name you choose to use for this package size.
Length	Length of the packages. The unit you use should match the unit that appears to the right of the field, either inches or centimeters.

continues

TABLE 12-7 *(continued)*

FIELD	DESCRIPTION
Height	Height of the package in the correct unit.
Width	Width of the package in the correct unit.
Max Weight	The maximum weight this package can support, with the units matching the units on the field — pounds or kilograms.

Taxes

The Ektron eCommerce package supports a fairly complex tax structure, allowing you to create classes of goods that are taxed at different rates, as well as variances of those rates based on destination locations. Management of these rates takes place through the Workarea in the Workarea ➪ Settings ➪ Settings Tree ➪ Commerce ➪ Taxes section. The first step in setting up the tax rates is creating the classes of goods you plan to sell.

The eCommerce feature comes preloaded with four tax classes: alcohol, goods, services, and tobacco. You can add, update, or delete these classes at any time. This list populates the Tax Class field when editing catalog entries, so that each product is categorized correctly. To manage these tax classes, follow these steps:

1. Go to Workarea ➪ Settings ➪ Settings Tree ➪ Commerce ➪ Tax ➪ Classes. This brings up the list of existing categories, as shown in Figure 12-21.

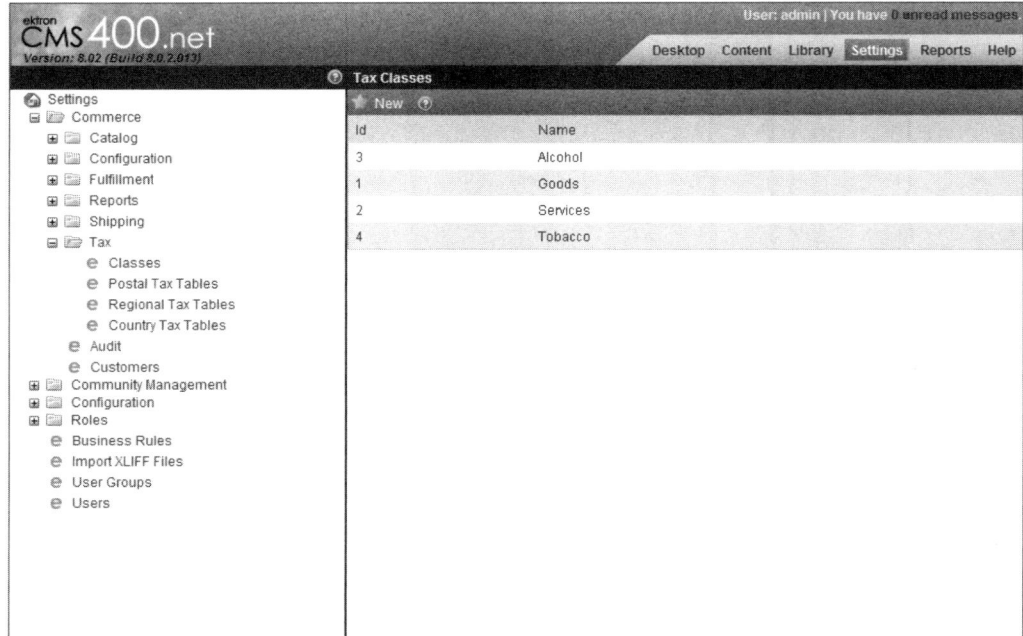

FIGURE 12-21

2. To edit one of the existing categories, click its name.

3. To add a new category, select New ⇨ Tax Class. This brings up the Add Tax Class form, which contains a single field for Name. The actual administration of the tax rates takes place elsewhere, since the tax rates are dependent on geographic location.

Taxes are applied to the order through a waterfall method. For each item in the order, the tax class of that item is found, and then the eCommerce engine tries to find a matching tuple that defines the tax code for the shipping destinations postal code and tax class. If it finds a match, it applies that rate and stops. If there is no matching tuple, the engine then looks at the regional tax rate for the destination and tax class. Again, if it finds a match, it applies the match and quits; otherwise the engine then checks the country rate.

If for a given destination you must apply multiple levels of taxes, you should build the combined rates into the smallest applicable geographic area. For instance, if in your postal code you must pay a 5 percent sales tax, and in your state you must pay a 4 percent sales tax, you should enter a 9 percent sales tax for your postal code, and 4 percent at the state level.

The three remaining screens in the Tax section on the Settings tree are for managing the rates at each geographic level. The Postal tax table allows you to enter rates for the postal code level, Regional at the regional level, among other levels.

As an example of managing the rates, this section explores how to set up the rates for a given state. Assume you have a company based out of Massachusetts. The state sales tax in Massachusetts is 6.25 percent. This means that for orders going to Massachusetts, you need to charge the appropriate tax. For orders going outside the state, there is no tax. To set up the rates for a given state, follow these steps:

1. Open the Regional tax table, by going to Workarea ⇨ Settings ⇨ Settings Tree ⇨ Commerce ⇨ Tax ⇨ Regional Tax Tables. The Regions Tax Table pane comes up with a list of all the regions defined in the system.

2. Click a region name. The display updates to show you the tax rates for that region. Find Massachusetts in the list, and click it. The stored tax rates are 0 percent across the board, as shown in Figure 12-22.

3. Click the link "Click here to edit the tax rates," and the display updates to show the detail view of that region.

4. Click Edit on the toolbar, and then select the Tax Rates.

5. Update the Goods category to reflect the 6.25 percent tax, and click the save icon on the toolbar.

CREATING A CATALOG AND PRODUCT

Now that the fundamentals of your eCommerce site have been set up, you are ready to create the products. Before you can jump into the products themselves though, you need to configure your product types. Once you have defined the types, you need to create a catalog to house the products. Finally, you can then create the products themselves. In this section, you look at those items in that order.

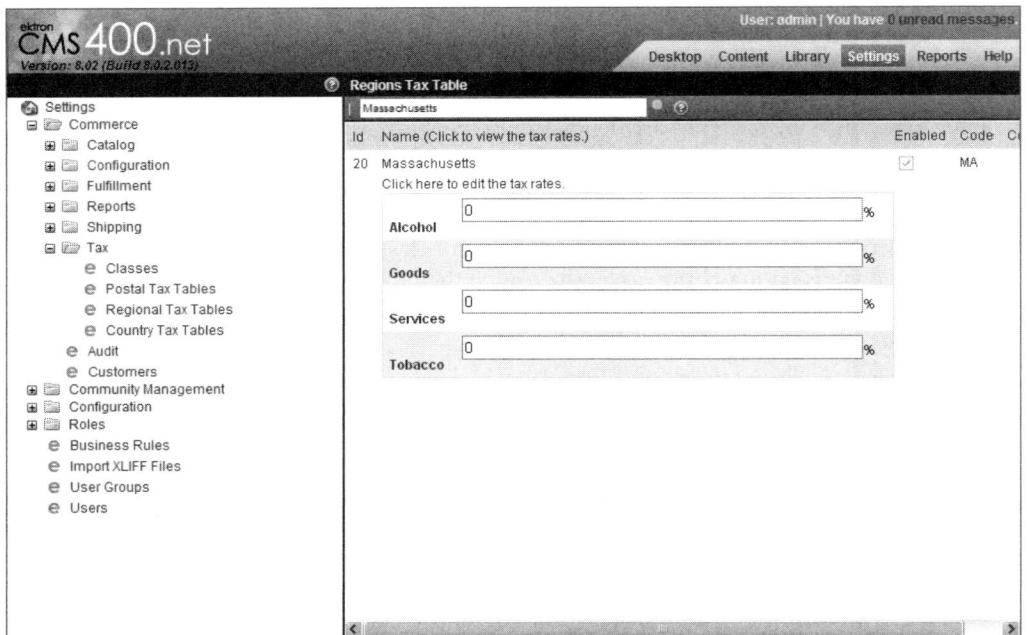

FIGURE 12-22

Creating Product Types

Product types are used to define the different categories of products you sell on your site. A type definition allows you to specify the type of information you capture about each product belonging to that type. For instance, you might have a product type for books, in which you can specify the title, author, synopsis, ISBN, and page count. You may also want to carry movies on your site, which have a series of other properties to capture, such as the title, year, lead actors, synopsis, and several reviews. Having a product type for each line of goods allows you to require the relevant details so your customers can easily understand the product, and your catalog managers can ensure that relevant details are captured.

In addition to the field definition, called the content page, the other main detail to note in a product type is the class of the type. There are four classes of product types. The class of a type affects both the management of the products based on that type as well as the process of purchasing products of that type. The classes are outlined in Table 12-8.

TABLE 12-8: Product Classes

CLASS	DESCRIPTION
Kit	A type of product that contains a list of free text options. The options can affect the overall price of the product. For instance, a laptop's price will go up or down based on the amount of memory in it, as well as the hard drive size.

CLASS	DESCRIPTION
Bundle	A single item that consists of other items from the catalog. It has its own price and images separate from the underlying product entries. For instance, when buying a desktop computer, you may want a bundle consisting of a monitor, a keyboard, and a mouse, with a discounted overall price.
Product	Products can be a simple product, which is a single entry, or a complex product. A complex product is similar to a bundle in that it takes several simple products and groups them together, but unlike a bundle it maintains each simple product's price and details, and the customer interacts with them as separate products. The benefit is that on the Product List or Product Search, only the complex product is displayed. It's only when the users get to the product details that they choose a specific variant of the product with its own price. For instance, you may have Kingston Value RAM, available in different speeds, at different prices. By grouping them into a complex product, you create less overhead when people are trying to decide on the type of memory they should get, only presenting them with a choice of speed after they've made the choice of brand.
Subscription	A subscription is fundamentally different from other types of products in that it allows for recurring billing. In addition, it adds purchasers into a specified membership group, allowing you to manage the group's access to private content.

Product types are used when creating a catalog, in much the same way that Smart Forms are used when creating content folders. They dictate the types of products that you can add to each catalog. Let's investigate creating a new product type now. You'll create a type for training videos on OnTrek:

1. Go to Workarea ➪ Settings ➪ Settings Tree ➪ Commerce ➪ Catalog ➪ Product Types to see the list of currently defined product types in the system. The View Product Types pane comes up, showing you the title and class of each product type in the system. This is shown in Figure 12-23.

2. To create a new product type, select New ➪ Product Type from the toolbar. This brings up the Add Product Type pane, with three tabs. The fields and their descriptions are listed in Table 12-9.

TABLE 12-9: Add Product Type Form Fields

TAB	FIELD	DESCRIPTION
Properties	Title	The title of the type. It displays under the new menu in catalogs it is assigned to.
	Description	A description of the product type.
	Class	The class of the product type, selected from Product, Kit, Bundle, or Subscription.

continues

TABLE 12-9 *(continued)*

TAB	FIELD	DESCRIPTION
Attributes	Attributes	Used to manage secondary information about the product. The types of data are limited to free text, dates, numeric, and Boolean values. You can compare attributes to metadata on a Smart Form versus the content stored inside the Smart Form itself.
Media Defaults	Thumbnails	Allows you to specify a set of thumbnail sizes to generate. These are generated from the main image associated with products based on this type, and are usable in the display page for products, as well as on product lists.

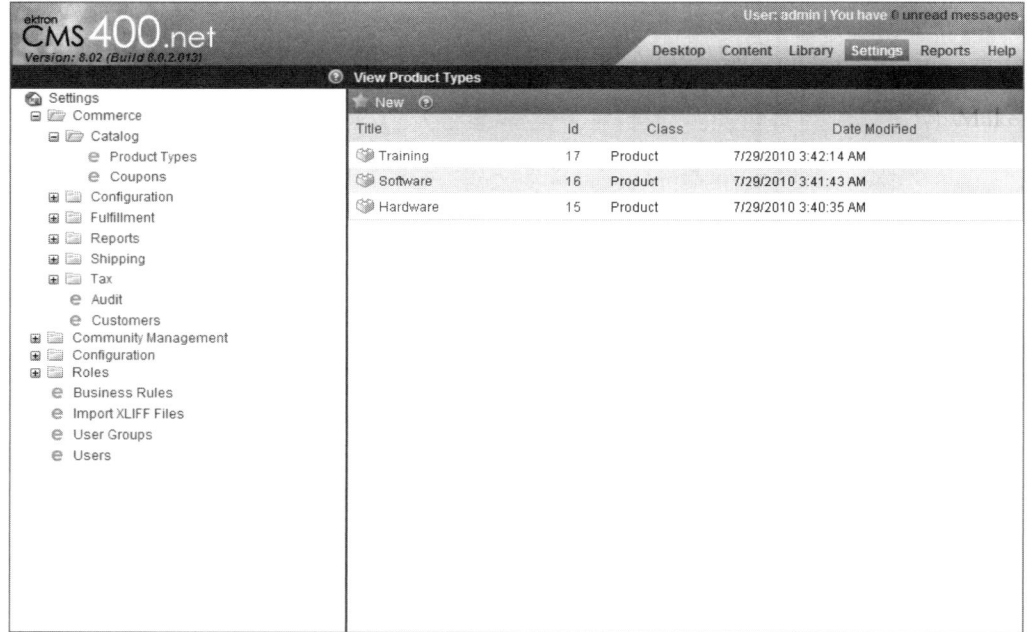

FIGURE 12-23

3. For the training video product type, enter **Training Video** for the title and description, and select Product as the class.

4. On the Media Defaults tab, add two entries, one called large at 150 x 125 pixels, and one called small at 70 x 58 pixels.

5. Click Save, and move to the second stage of type creation, which is to create the content page (similar to a Smart Form) for the product type.

6. Add three text fields with titles to this form: title, description, and running time. Set the description field to be multi-line.

This example is simple, but when you are designing product types for your catalog, spend time to make sure you're getting the information you'll need going forward. Also remember that much like Smart Forms, products based on a type are not automatically updated or flagged when the underlying type is modified. This means that doing updates to the product type's content page after products have been entered based on the type may break those products. Spend time up front designing these pages so you don't find yourself struggling with a poor design later.

7. The final content page is shown in Figure 12-24. Click Save and return to the overview of the new product type.

Now that you have a product type to work with, you can create a catalog to contain your training videos.

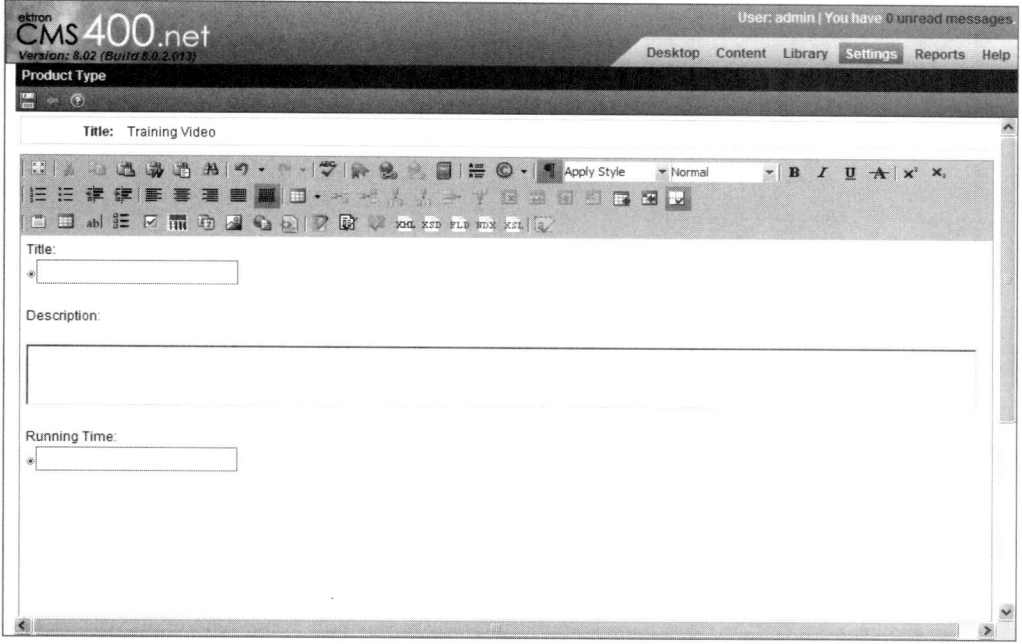

FIGURE 12-24

Creating a Catalog

Catalogs are the method by which products are organized, and they serve as the storage location in the Content Tree for those products. They function just like content folders, and are required in order to create products. Creating a catalog is very similar to creating a content folder. Instead of picking Smart Forms, however, you pick product types. Create a catalog now by following these steps:

1. Go to Workarea ⇨ Content ⇨ Folder Tree ⇨ MainSite ⇨ Content ⇨ Store.
2. Select New ⇨ Catalog from the toolbar.
3. Name the new catalog **Videos**, and then switch to the Product Types tab. The tab is shown in Figure 12-25. This tab is very similar to the Smart Form tab in a normal folder.

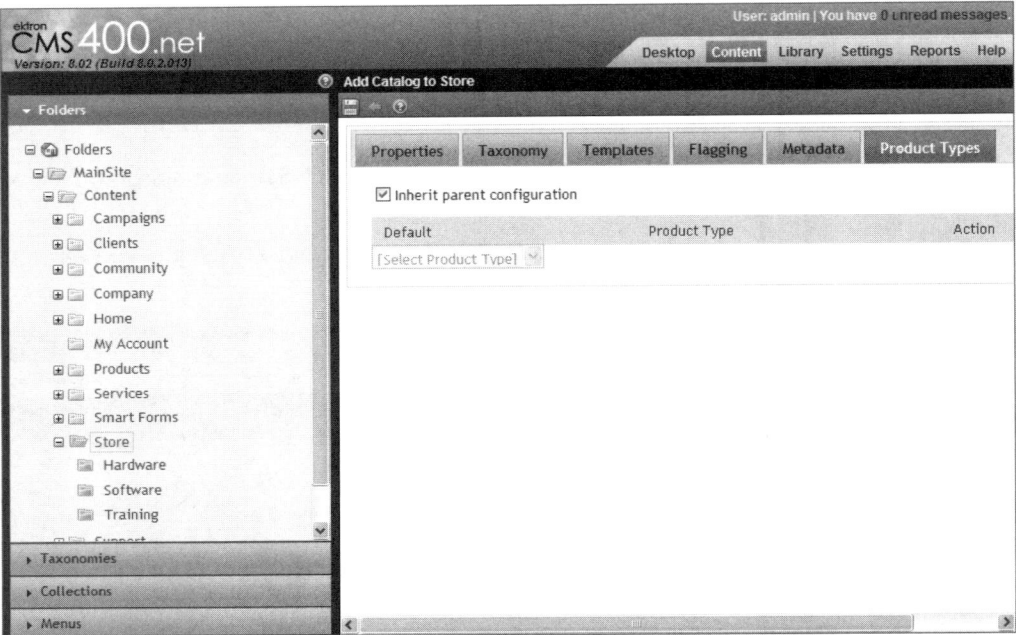

FIGURE 12-25

4. Deselect the Inherit parent configuration checkbox, and add Training Video from the drop-down to the list.
5. Click Save — you are returned to the Store catalog.
6. Select the new Videos catalog from the folder tree, and the view is updated with the list of products currently in the folder.

As is visible from the catalog view shown in Figure 12-26, the interface is almost the same as a folder. For instance, catalogs are language specific, meaning that you can create translations for each product in the catalog. One of the only differences is that under the View menu, the options for filtering the view are catalog-centric — having to do with the class of product. You can filter the view by All Types, Products, Kits, Bundles, or Subscriptions.

Now that you have the catalog created, you need to create a training video product.

Creating a Catalog and Product | **473**

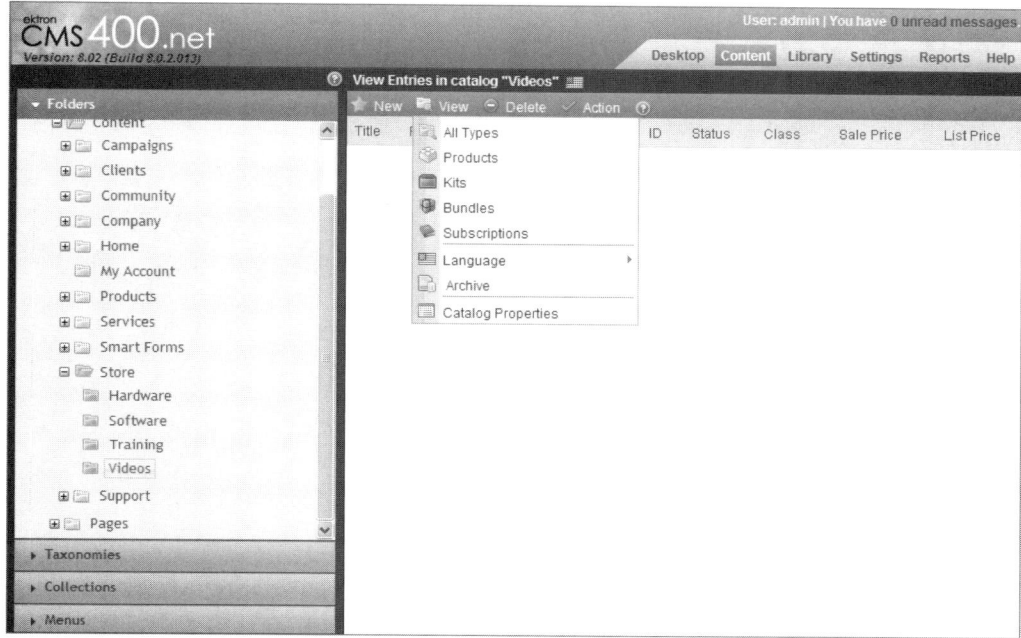

FIGURE 12-26

Creating a Product

As we discussed, the goal of the new catalog is to house a series of training videos available for purchase. We have the catalog in place, so now we will add our first training video for sale.

The SmartForm Content Tabs

To view the SmartForm content tabs, select New ➪ Training Video. This brings up an interface similar to adding Smart Form based content, The following list explains the various SmartForm content tabs from left to right.

➤ **Content:** This is the same tab (see Figure 12-27) you see when working with Smart Forms. You'll recognize the Smart Form design from when you put together the product type design.

➤ **Summary:** The Summary is displayed in search results, and in the ProductList Server Control as shown in Figure 12-28.

➤ **Properties:** Shown in Figure 12-29, you use this to manage system-level product properties that are required. By default this includes the SKU, how many items are in a single purchase (such as 2 DIMMS of memory in a single order of dual channel RAM), tax class, whether the item is purchasable, the dimensions, and inventory data for the item.

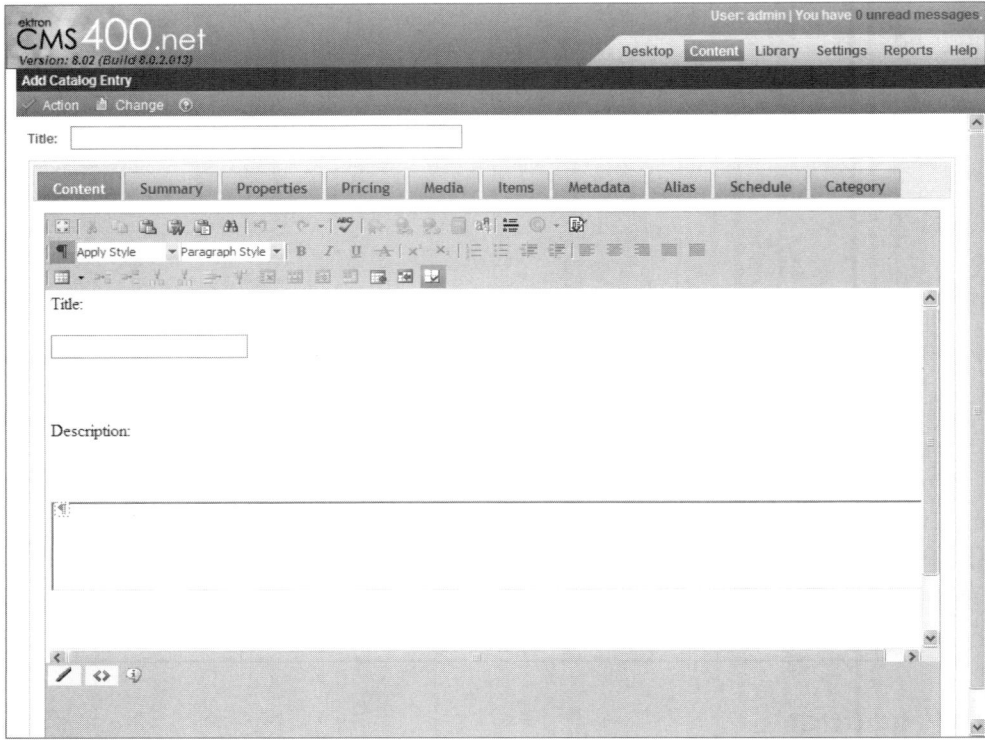

FIGURE 12-27

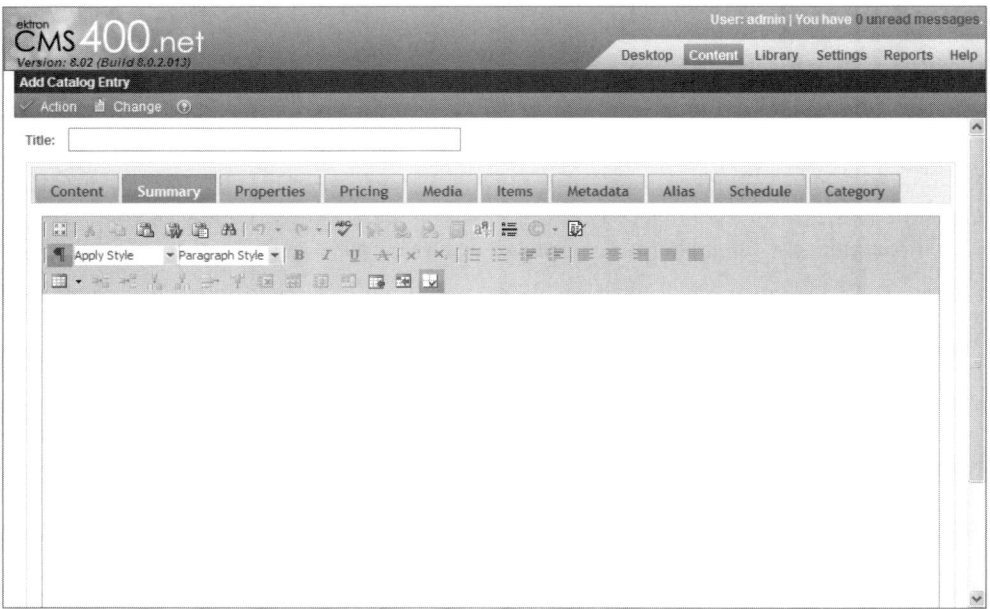

FIGURE 12-28

FIGURE 12-29

- **Pricing:** Shown in Figure 12-30, this allows you to enter pricing details about the product. The list price usually displays the original price, or the manufacturer's suggested retail price for the product. The sales price below that is what you are actually selling the product for. Additionally, beneath the standard pricing you can add tier pricing; for instance you may want to sell a $20 item for $15 as long as the customer orders more than 10 of them. Finally, you may notice that in the top-right side of the interface you can select other currencies. You can manually set the price in a foreign currency here. If you don't set the price manually, the price in the foreign currency is calculated based on the exchange rates defined in the Currency screen in the Settings tab.

- **Attributes:** Shown in Figure 12-31, this manages any custom properties that were created as part of the product type definition. If no custom properties were defined, this tab won't show up.

- **Media:** Shown in Figure 12-32, this allows you to specify the images to display for a product on the site. You can add an image from the library or upload one. Adding an image automatically creates the thumbnails of the original based on the thumbnail definitions in the product type specification. Once an image is added, you can specify details about it, such as the title, alt text, and whether to show it in the product gallery. You can also choose one of the uploaded images to use as the product icon. All the images are available in XSLTs on the Product Server Controls, allowing you to specify what size to use in which scenarios (except for the Product Search Server Control, which always uses the full-size version of the default product icon).

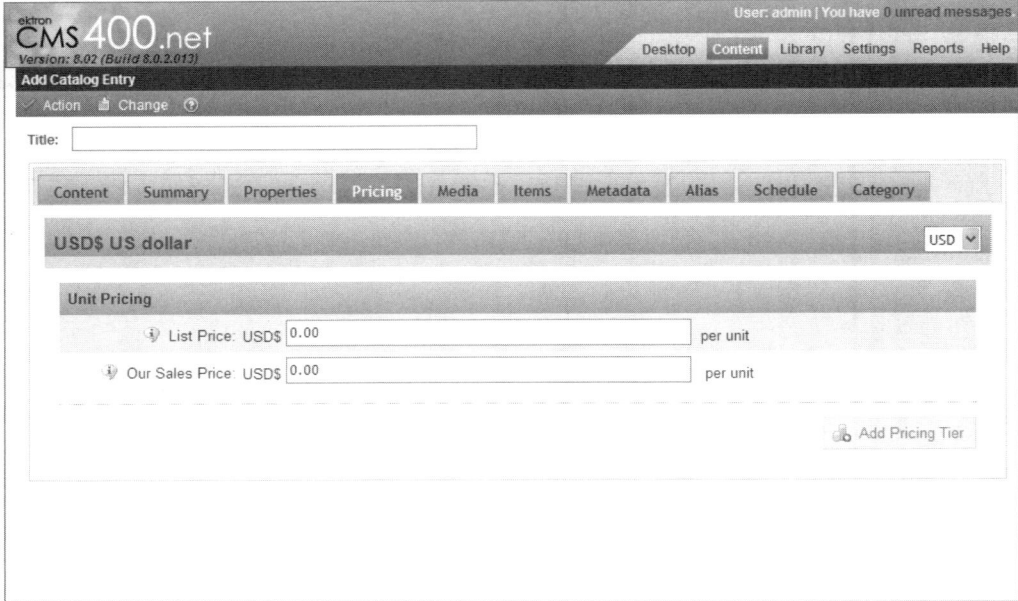

FIGURE 12-30

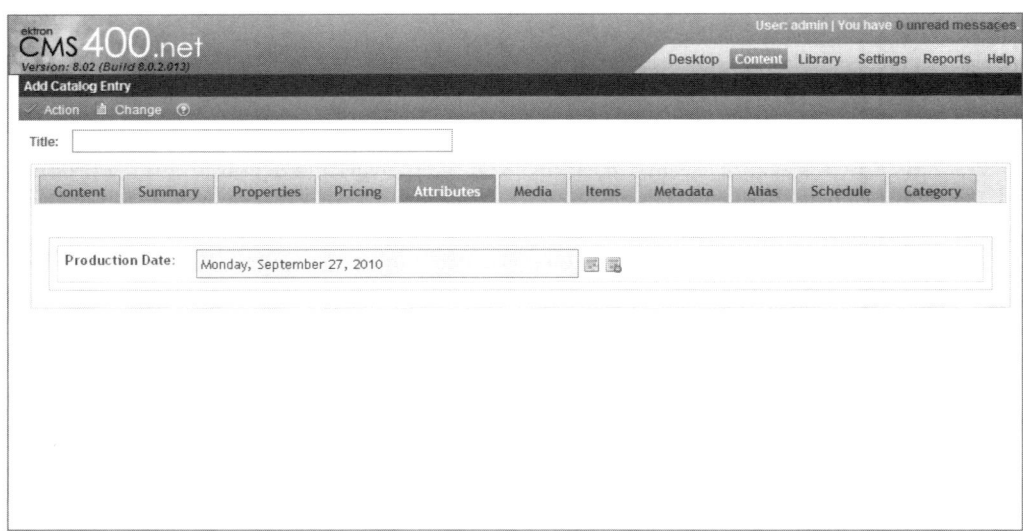

FIGURE 12-31

➤ **Items:** As shown in Figure 12-33, you use this for all product classes, but in different ways. For simple products, when you use it to select additional products, it turns the simple product into a complex product, allowing grouping of common products. When working with:

➤ **A bundle class product type:** You can select the other products that combine to make this bundle.

➤ **Kit class product types:** You can work with the groups of options that make up the kit, and specify how they modify the price.

➤ **A subscription class type:** You can select the membership group where purchasers should be added.

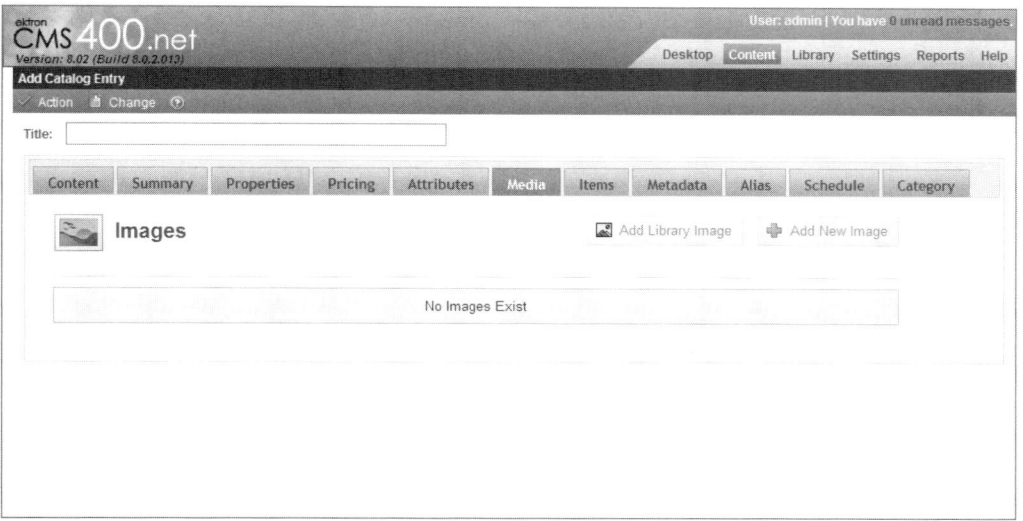

FIGURE 12-32

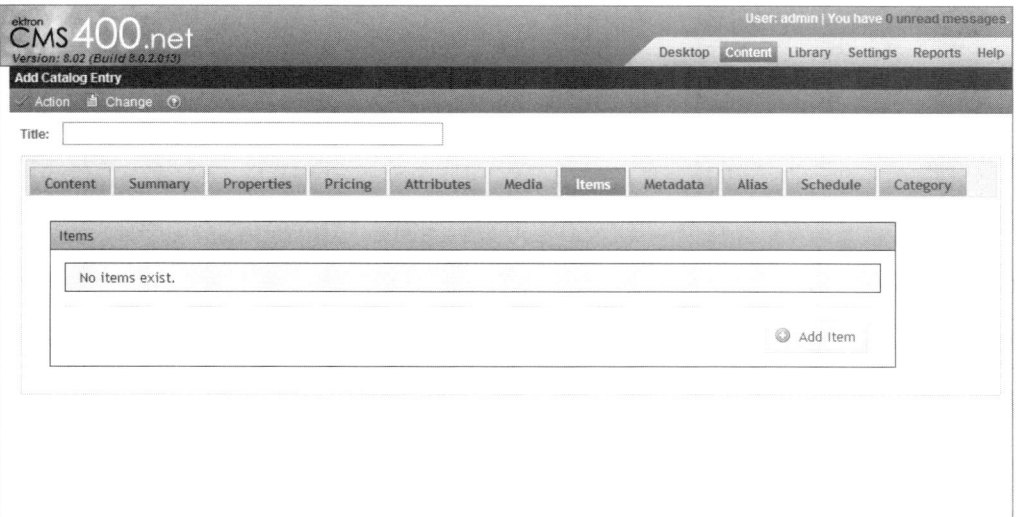

FIGURE 12-33

➤ **Metadata:** The Metadata tab (shown in Figure 12-34) is the same as for normal content.

➤ **Alias:** Aliases (shown in Figure 12-35) also work the same way as normal content, and can be a useful way of managing SEO for your product catalogs.

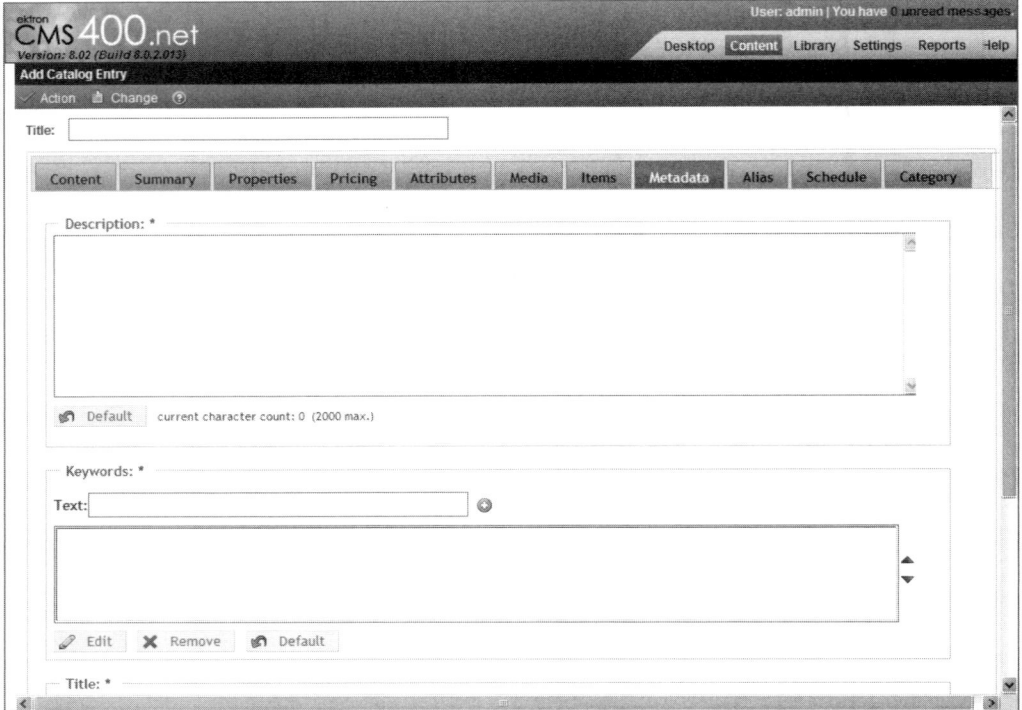

FIGURE 12-34

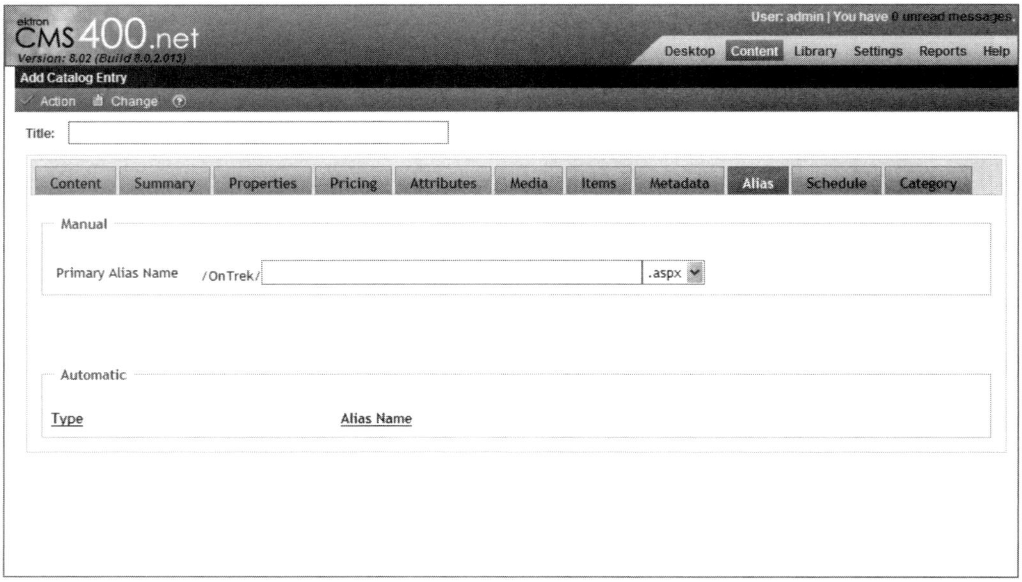

FIGURE 12-35

➤ **Schedule:** Just like normal content, you can schedule a go-live date and set expiration dates for products in your catalog.

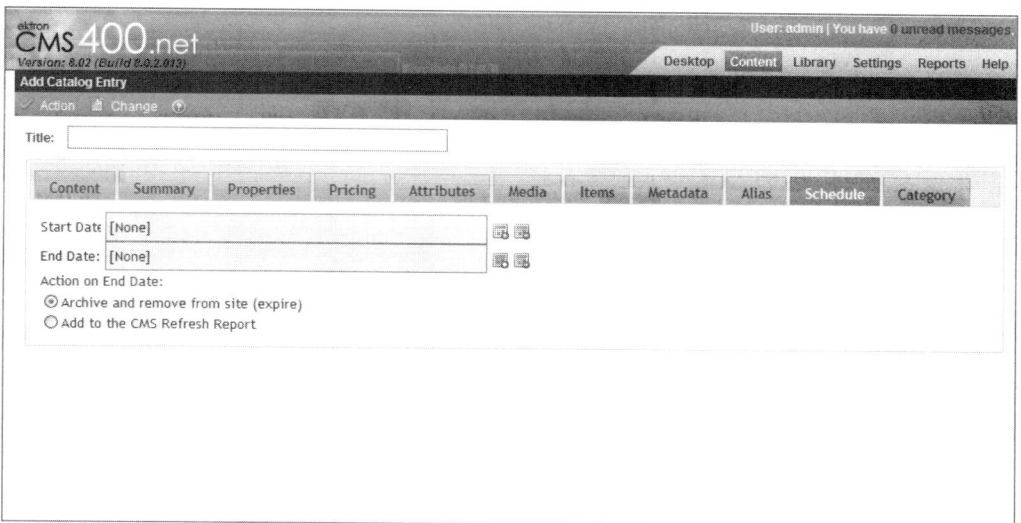

FIGURE 12-36

➤ **Category:** You also have the ability to use taxonomy to categorize your catalog items (see Figure 12-37).

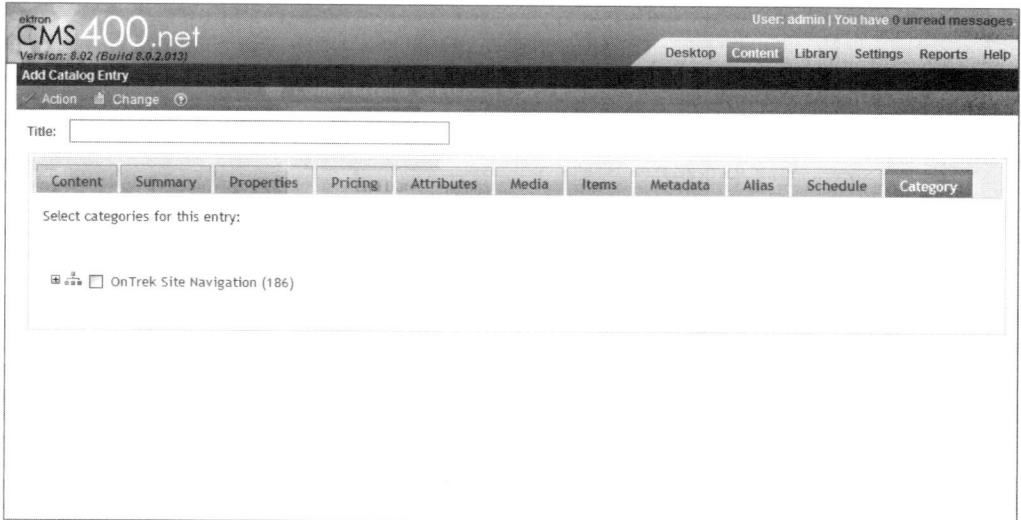

FIGURE 12-37

Creating a New Product in a Video Catalog

Now that you know what all the tabs are all about, follow these steps to create a new product in the Videos catalog:

1. Select New ➪ Training Video. This brings up an interface similar to adding Smart Form based content, as shown in Figure 12-38.

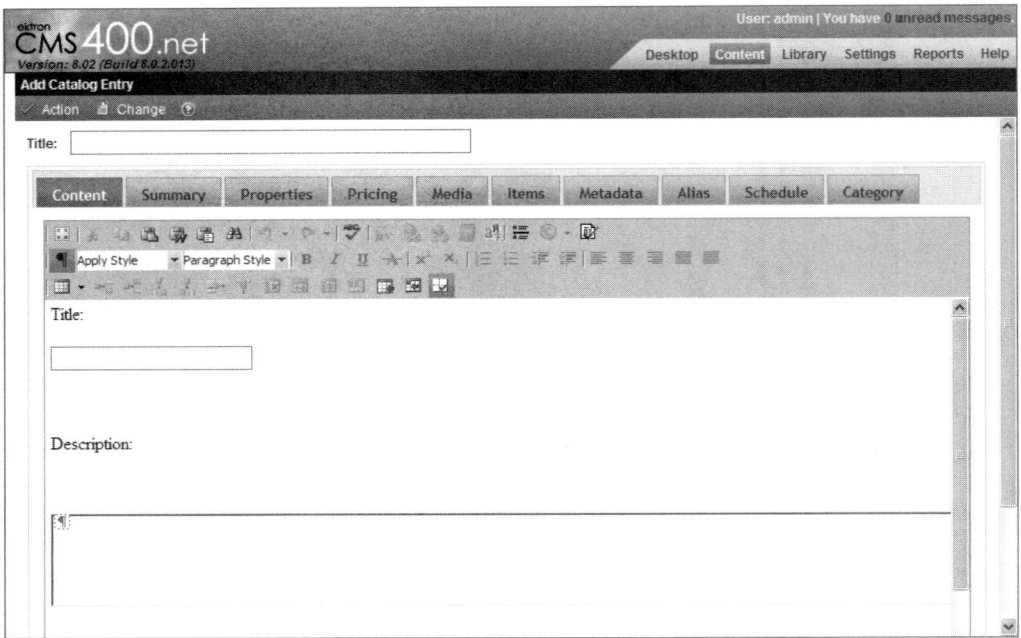

FIGURE 12-38

2. Enter **Administrator Training Video** for the title.

3. Switch to the Content tab, and in the title field on the custom form, enter "Administrator Training Video," and "See step by step directions on the included DVD for administering your OnTrek Software" for the description. Enter "6 hours" for the running time.

4. Switch to the Pricing tab and enter in a list price of $800, and a sales price of $750.

5. Fill out any required fields on the Metadata and Category tabs.

6. Select Action from the toolbar, and click Submit.

In addition to the familiar interface of editing items through the Workarea, you can also manage most of the properties on catalog items through the front end of your site, through the editor's menu. You can look at the options that are new when viewing an existing product in the Workarea. Browse to Workarea ➪ Content ➪ Folder Tree ➪ MainSite ➪ Content ➪ Store ➪ Hardware, and select the Basic Wireless Router product.

You'll notice, as shown in Figure 12-39, that the toolbar has some additional items on it that are not on regular content. Specifically, the View menu has two new items, Cross Sell and Up Sell. You can use these items to drive additional sales by presenting customers with additional options as they shop on your site.

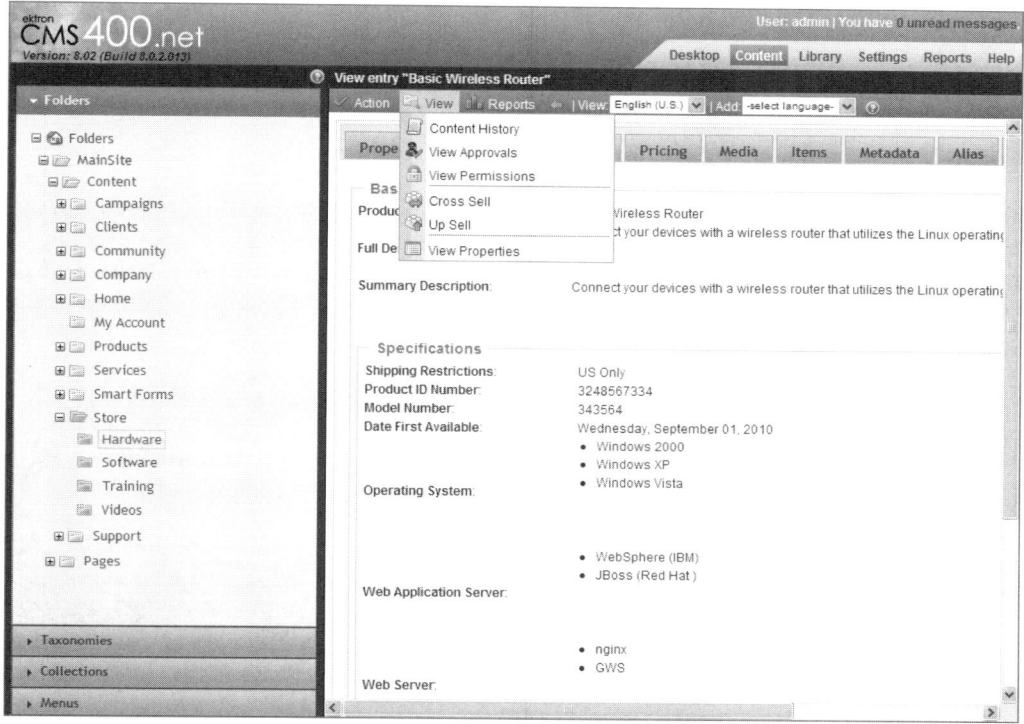

FIGURE 12-39

> **Cross Sell:** Offers items that are related to the product in question. For instance, a monitor and a laptop bag would both be good cross sell items for a customer buying a laptop.

> **Up Sell:** Is a higher end, more expensive laptop than the one the customer is currently looking at.

The interfaces for adding cross sell and up sell items are the same, simply displaying a list of items, and allowing you to add more by browsing the catalog in a modal window to find the target product.

COUPONS

Coupons are one of the features that can easily be overlooked in the eCommerce product. They are rich in their capabilities, and are useful tools in aiding marketing efforts. The capabilities of coupons include discounting by a dollar amount or by a percentage. If you discount by a percentage, you specify a maximum dollar value of the discount. You have a wide range of options to restrict usage including:

> Applying coupons to specific products

> Applying to the most or least expensive item in a shopping cart

> Specifying that a customer can only use a coupon once

➤ Limiting a coupon so it's only applied when other coupons are not applied

➤ Specifying a date range the coupon is valid for

➤ Specifying a maximum number of redemptions for a given coupon

➤ Specifying a minimum order value before a coupon can be used

This rich set of capabilities means that you can create a coupon to fit any situation you run into. Let's explore the process of creating coupons now. Creating a coupon is a four-step process, with the first step being to specify the type of coupon. Next is setting up the discount, followed by setting up the scope of the coupon. Finally, you can specify the catalog items the coupon can be applied to.

To create a coupon, follow these steps:

1. Go to Workarea ➪ Settings ➪ Settings Tree ➪ Commerce ➪ Catalog ➪ Coupons. This brings up the Coupons pane, as shown in Figure 12-40. This pane lists all the coupons defined in the system, and allows you to add new coupons.

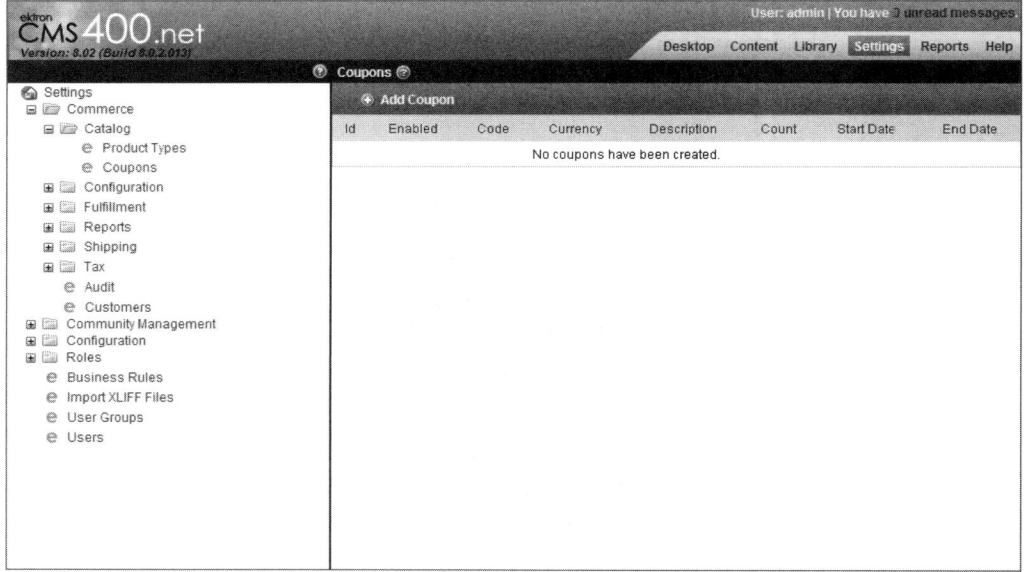

FIGURE 12-40

2. Click Add Coupon now, and you will see the Add Coupon pane. It consists of a Wizard.

3. Fill in the first window of the Wizard:

   a. Specify the type, as shown in Figure 12-41.

   The coupon type step allows you to specify the fundamental elements of the coupon. Table 12-10 lists the fields in this form along with a description of each field.

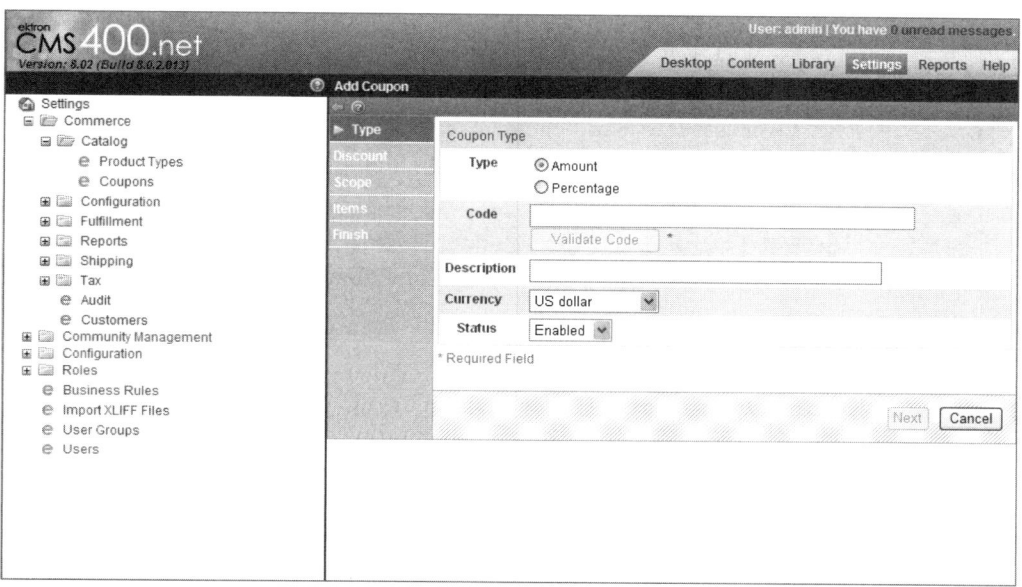

FIGURE 12-41

TABLE 12-10: Add Coupon Type Step Fields

FIELD	DESCRIPTION
Type	Can be set to Amount or Percentage and dictates the type of the discount.
Code	The code the users must enter to activate the coupon in their carts. Because it does not make sense to have two coupons with the same code, the Validate Code button next to the field allows you to check if the code you want for the coupon is available.
Description	Allows you to specify a description for the coupon.
Currency	Allows you to specify currency this coupon can be used with. A coupon can be used with a single currency only if it is a numeric discount, and is rejected if the user is browsing the site with a different currency. If the coupon is a percentage discount, it can be used with any currency.
Status	Set to Enable to allow users to use this coupon provided the other conditions for the coupon are met.

   b. Specify the discount amount. If, on the first step (specifying the type), you selected Amount for the type, you can specify exactly what that discount should be. If instead, you specified that this should be a percentage discount, in this step you specify what that percentage should be, along with a maximum amount for the discount. If the maximum is left at 0, there is no maximum. If you specify a maximum amount and the percentage would result in a discount larger than that amount, the discount still applies, but is whatever you specified as the maximum rather than the percentage calculation.

c. The Scope screen allows you to limit the coupon's usability. It is shown in Figure 12-42, and Table 12-11 lists the fields and descriptions found on the Scope pane.

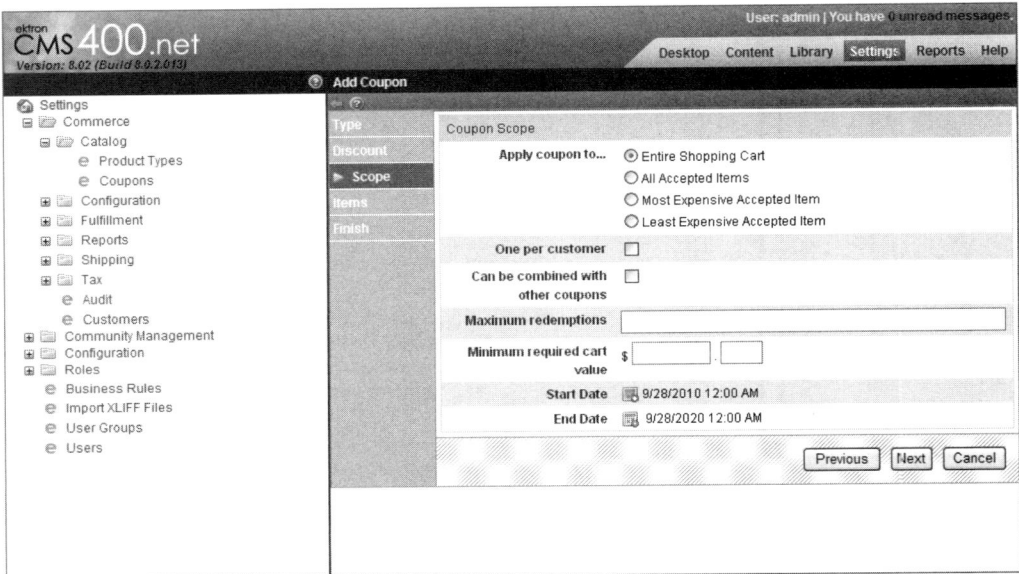

FIGURE 12-42

TABLE 12-11: Add Coupon Scope Step Fields

FIELD	DESCRIPTION
Apply Coupon To	Sets how coupons can be applied. Can be set to Entire shopping cart, items that have been approved for use with the coupon, just the most expensive accepted item in the cart, or just the least expensive item in the cart.
One per Customer	Whether a customer can reuse the same coupon.
Can be combined with other coupons	A flag to set whether the coupon should only be applied singly or whether it can be applied in conjunction with other coupons.
Maximum redemptions	The number of times the coupon can be redeemed before it expires and is invalid.
Minimum required cart value	The value the cart must contain before the coupon can be applied.

FIELD	DESCRIPTION
Start Date	The beginning of the period that the coupon can be redeemed.
End Date	The end of the period the coupon is valid.

    d. You can modify Items only if the Apply Coupon To field has been set to something other than the entire shopping cart. If set to All Accepted Items instead, you have the opportunity on this screen to specify the list of included items, and the list of excluded items. If an item satisfies conditions on both lists, it is excluded. This means that, depending on whether you have a large list of items you want the coupon to be accepted for, or a small list to accept it for, you can approach the list from either direction.

4. Click Finish to return to the list of coupons.

PRODUCT REPORTS AND ORDER MANAGEMENT

At this point you have all the administrative areas of your eCommerce solution set up. What remains is the processing of reports, and actually running orders through the system. This section first covers the various reports that can be run to get snapshots of how many orders and which orders are in various states of fulfillment, and then covers the process by which orders are pushed through from the initial receipt of an order to the fulfillment of that order.

Reports

The eCommerce reports are accessible through two locations in the Workarea. These locations are:

➤ Workarea ➪ Settings ➪ Settings Tree ➪ Commerce ➪ Reports

➤ Workarea ➪ Reports ➪ Reports Tree ➪ Commerce

The same set of reports are in both locations, but depending on the roles the eCommerce user is assigned to, they may not be able to access the reports through the Settings tab. Additionally, these reports are all available as widgets so that you can add them to the Desktop in the Workarea.

Report Types

There are five reports the eCommerce system provides.

➤ **Customer Reports:** Summarizes the top customers in several categories. It displays the name of the customer, the number of orders the customer has submitted, the total dollar amount the customer has purchased, and the date the person first became a customer.

The report can be run against several types of data: by selecting the most recent link, a dropdown displays, allowing you to report against the most recent customers, the most valuable customers, and the most active customers.

- **Key Performance Indicators:** Lets you compare sales and orders from two time periods. You can set the time periods to compare by clicking the This Month link in the period column. It displays a dropdown containing many options for time periods, ranging from today and yesterday to comparing whole years. Set the current period and previous period, and then click the refresh button to update the report.

- **Payment Reports:** This lists the received payments within a given time period. You can use it to reconcile financial statements with the ordering system. It displays the date the payment was captured, the last four digits of the credit card, the type of payment, the transaction ID, the amount of the transaction, and how much of the transaction, if any, was voided.

    A report can be run by using the calendar icons to specify a start and end date for the report, and then clicking the Set New Dates link to update the report.

- **Sales Trends:** Generates a line graph of order volume versus date. The X-axis of the graph can be set to daily or monthly by selecting the period link at the top of the report.

- **Top Products:** Displays the most successful products on your site. It is ordered by the quantity sold, and can be run by selecting the period and the number of records to display, and then clicking the Update button.

Using the eCommerce Order Workflow

In addition to these high-level reports, you can run reports against fulfillment criteria, which is useful in pushing orders through the order workflow. Before you look at those reports, take a moment and look at how orders move through the eCommerce system.

The eCommerce system supports creating custom workflows through the Windows Workflow Foundation. For more information on this, see Chapter 13 of this book. For most cases, the default workflow will be capable of supporting your needs.

The built-in order processing workflow is as follows:

1. **Submission of an order on the site.** At this point the payment is processed for authorization, but has not yet been captured.

2. **The order goes into a queue.** Once in the queue, it awaits interaction by an eCommerce CMS user, and it can be marked as fraudulent, or it can be captured, in which case the transaction actually takes place.

3. The order is updated and has the following status:

    - **Complete:** With the default workflow, this happens as soon as the order is shipped but with custom workflows it could represent some post-sale activity as having been completed.

    - **Cancelled:** The order was cancelled either by the customer or by a site eCommerce administrator.

➤ **InProcess:** The state an order is in after it has been submitted, but when payment has not yet been captured for it.

The process is simplified for intangible goods, and is almost completely automated in that scenario. The workflow map is shown in Figure 12-43.

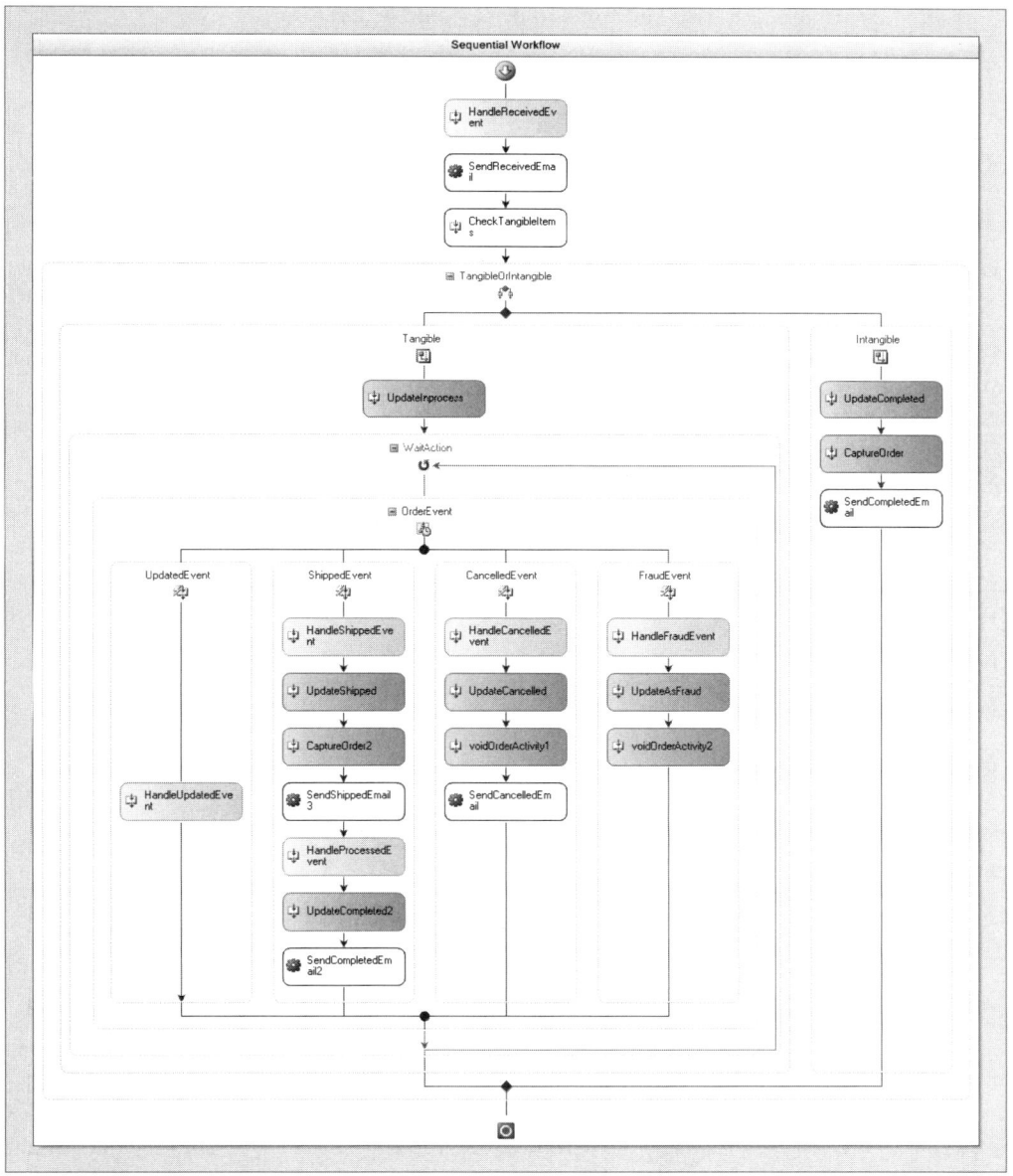

FIGURE 12-43

Using the Manual Workflow

The manual state transitions in that workflow take place through the View Order screen, which you can open by accessing individual orders through the Orders report:

1. Access the Orders report by navigating to Workarea ⇨ Settings ⇨ Settings Tree ⇨ Commerce ⇨ Fulfillment ⇨ Orders. This pane displays a list of the orders in the system, ordered by submission date and time, in descending order.
2. Select orders by the date range, the customer, or the catalog item.
3. When you have found an order that requires processing, click the order to enter the View Order screen.

Order Management

The View Order screen, shown in Figure 12-44, has a list of tabs that contain information about the order. When an order is placed, the information about the items, coupons, and so on is all copied out of the original locations into a permanent location in the database so that the order details are never lost, even if the details of the original items change. The tabs display that copied data, so the View Order screen always shows the correct data for that order.

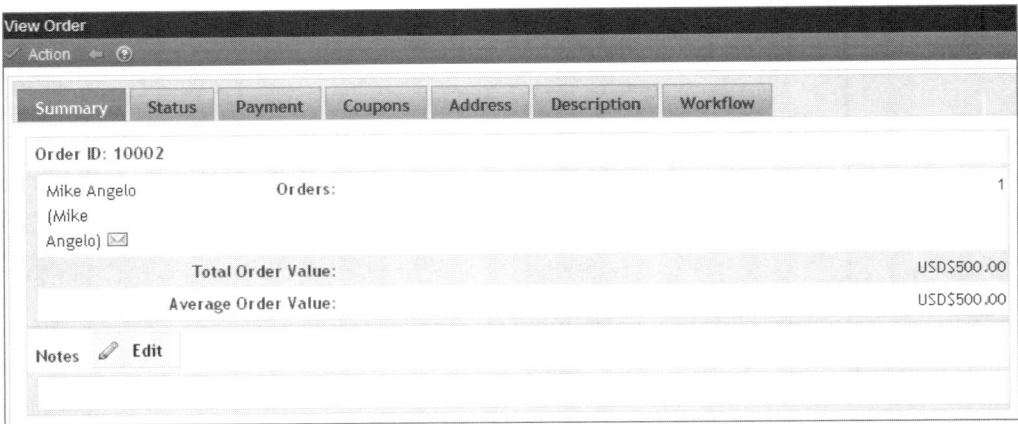

FIGURE 12-44

In order from left to right, the tabs display the following information.

> **Summary:** Shows the order ID, the person who placed the order, and the order value. It also allows you to capture notes about the order.

> **Status:** The Status tab shows the current status of the order, as well as the status history.

> **Payment:** Displays the list of payments applied to this order. By clicking a payment you can retrieve the details of that payment, including the transaction ID, the gateway, the type of payment, the last four digits of the card number, the amount received, and the date of authorization and capture.

- ➤ **Coupons:** Displays any coupons that were applied to the order, and the effect of those coupons.
- ➤ **Address:** Displays the billing and shipping addresses associated with the order, and allows you to edit them. In addition, it displays the tracking method and number if one has been entered.
- ➤ **Description:** Displays the items that are in the order, allowing you to fulfill the order and ship the items.
- ➤ **Workflow:** Displays a log of the actions the order workflow engine has applied to the order up to this point.

Most of the interaction that takes place with orders is done through this screen, by selecting appropriate entries on the Action menu. When an order is received, you want to capture the order, then track it:

1. Selecting Action ➪ Capture causes the order to be captured, meaning that the payment gateway provider submits a conversion order to the payment gateway system, requesting that the authorization it approved earlier be converted to a payment. At this time, the customer's card is deducted the amount, and your account is credited the amount.
2. Once the order ships, next update the tracking number for the order. Select Action ➪ Edit Tracking Number to enter the details, and mark the order as shipped. At this point, the customer receives an e-mail containing the tracking number.

You can also mark the order as fraud and cancel the order. If your organization deems an order to be fraudulent, select Action ➪ Mark as Fraud. The order is not completed from this point. Selecting Action ➪ Cancel Order changes the order's status to cancelled and ceases operation at that point. The built-in order workflow has no activities defined for either of these end conditions, but you can modify and extend these to perform actions necessary to your business, if required.

TAKE HOME POINTS

This chapter covered a large subset of the activities required to get the eCommerce feature functioning on your site, including the following:

- ➤ The basic configuration of geographic locations, such as countries and regions.
- ➤ The currencies in use at each location and how to manage exchange rates for those currencies.
- ➤ How to manage the card types defined in the system as well as the payment options.
- ➤ How to manage the messages defined in the system.
- ➤ Some of the settings that rely on the lower order settings, such as tax structures. This included how those tax structures are used to calculate the correct taxes on each order, as well as how to set them based on geographic shipping destination.

- How to manage the shipping options, including the way goods are packaged, the providers you can specify as handlers for your shipping needs, and the warehouses your goods are stored in.
- How it all comes together to calculate the correct cost for shipping the order.
- Creating product types, which you learned are basically an extension of Smart Forms.
- Creating a catalog, which was a lot like working with folders
- Creating a simple item.
- The other item classes, and how they can be used to fulfill complex needs in your inventory.
- Coupons, and how you can use them to support marketing needs.
- About the different types of coupons, how you can manage the reusability of those coupons, and how you can extract the most value out of making coupons available to customers.
- The overall process of handling and processing orders. You learned how to run reports to find out the success rate of your store, and how to fulfill orders from start to finish.
- The actions available to you on a per-order basis.
- How to create a successful strategy for approaching the fulfillment of orders.

13

Constructing the Online Storefront with eCommerce

- ➤ What are the eCommerce server controls and how do you implement with them?
- ➤ How do you create a custom order workflow?
- ➤ How do you build a payment gateway provider?

The last chapter closely investigated the eCommerce feature and how it relates to the Workarea. It dealt with configuring the basic setup for eCommerce, and you learned how to create catalogs and products. What you didn't do at all in that chapter was work with the eCommerce feature from a developer's perspective. That's what you'll approach in this chapter.

The eCommerce Framework is exciting due to the way it addresses the developer experience in one of the most open portions of the Ektron Framework. While at a high level it closely resembles working with the rest of the framework, with a set of easily deployable server controls and out-of-the-box functionality, it also provides a large number of programmatic hooks so you can customize the capabilities to a large degree.

This chapter starts by looking in depth at the server control set that the eCommerce feature provides, exploring each control's capabilities and customizability. You will learn when they are used, and how to use them. You then take a close look at how the eCommerce experience was developed for the OnTrek site, looking specifically at the product browsing experience and the ordering experience. You'll find that the out-of-the-box implementation is sufficient for most of these needs.

You will then spend the remainder of this chapter looking at a couple of ways that the eCommerce capability set can be easily extended. First you'll look at creating custom order workflows. The stock Ektron eCommerce workflow is generally sufficient for most customer needs, but many businesses have complex business processes. Leveraging the Windows Workflow Foundation allows Ektron to expose a key part of the business process to developers, creating the capability to incorporate those complex business processes directly into their websites. You will look at using the CMS400 SDK as a base to develop these custom workflows.

Second, you will dig into the process of building a custom payment gateway provider for use on your site. While Ektron ships with support for PayPal, Payflow, and Authorize.Net, among other payment gateways, and if you already have a merchant account, it is not unlikely that it might be with a different company than those. This will give you some insight into how to build a provider so that you can continue to use your current merchant account provider, while leveraging the capabilities of the Ektron eCommerce solution.

USE CASE

As the OnTrek development team continues their buildout of the eCommerce capabilities of their website, they enter into the actual development phase for the website. The website needs to support customers coming to the site, finding a product they are interested in, and purchasing the product all through the commerce engine.

This buildout includes the ability to seek out products, read reviews of those products, add them to a shopping cart, and finally check out of the site by purchasing their goods via credit card payment.

> ### SETTING UP AN ESTORE
>
> This Use Case introduces the primary actor Derek, a site visitor who went through the research process for OnTrek's wares, and has decided to purchase those goods on the website. It describes the expected scenario and defines the desired outcome.
>
> ### Wireframe
>
> The example Wireframe for this chapter, shown in Figure 13-1, is the eCommerce landing page, which lists out some selected products from the OnTrek catalog, and invites the user to add them to their cart or browse for further products.
>
> ### Description
>
> The implementation of this section will culminate in the ability for Derek to purchase goods on the OnTrek website. At the completion of this exercise, he will be able to search for goods on the website, read descriptions of those goods, purchase the goods, and effectively maintain his account and order history. In the backend, the team will also be developing a custom Payment Gateway Provider to allow them to maintain their existing merchant account, and they will be also be addressing the needs of the post-sales support team by modifying the default order workflow used by the eCommerce engine.

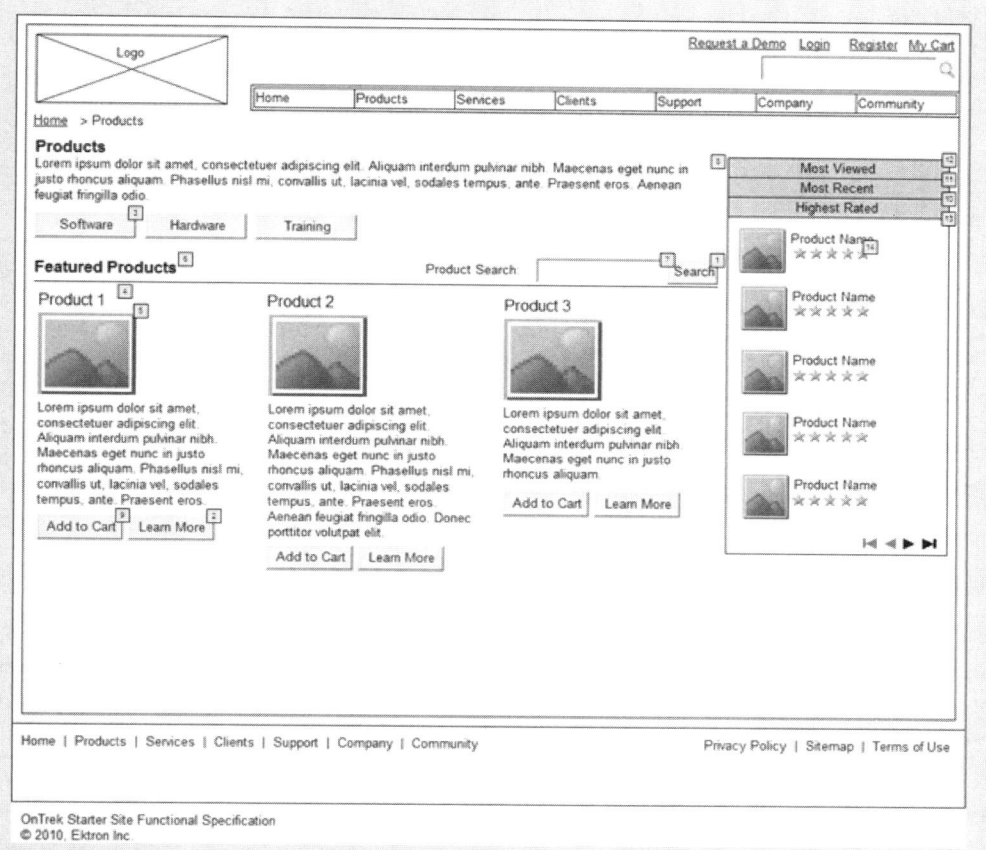

FIGURE 13-1

Actor

Derek is an employee at Acme Inc. Having researched OnTrek's product offering thoroughly, he is now ready to take the plunge and purchase their hardware. He wants to use the website for the entire transaction, rather than dealing with smarmy salespeople.

Scenario

In this scenario, Derek:

➤ Connects to the OnTrek site looking for a way to purchase OnTrek's hardware offerings.

➤ Comes to the store landing page, where he scans through the top rated hardware.

➤ Finds a link to the hardware he is interested in, and then continues on to the product detail page.

continues

> (continued)
>
> ➤ From the product detail page, he adds the item to his cart.
>
> ➤ Proceeds to check out, entering in his payment and shipping details, and completing the purchase.
>
> ➤ Returns to the site to view his order history and check the status of his order, at a later time.
>
> **Outcome**
>
> By implementing the eCommerce functionality on their website, the OnTrek team attracts millions of users just like Derek, and sells out of their goods in a week. They are bought out by Microsoft the following week, and everybody gets stock options valued in the millions. Each member of the team buys a private island in Dubai, and retires in the lap of luxury.

ECOMMERCE SERVER CONTROLS AND IMPLEMENTATION

Just like working with the rest of your website in the Ektron Framework, eCommerce has two major steps to implementation. The first step, creating the catalog and products, you completed in the last chapter. In this section, you'll work on understanding the server controls available as part of the eCommerce suite, and then look at the methodology for implementation followed in OnTrek.

There are nine server controls related to eCommerce functionality. These can be broken into two groups, the first group being those controls that relate to the browsing experience. These controls are:

- ➤ CurrencySelect Server Control
- ➤ ProductSearch Server Control
- ➤ ProductList Server Control
- ➤ Product Server Control
- ➤ Recommendation Server Control

In addition to these controls, there are another four controls that allow the users to manage the rest of the purchase experience. These controls revolve around account maintenance, and the order process. They are listed here:

- ➤ MyAccount Server Control
- ➤ OrderList Server Control
- ➤ Cart Server Control
- ➤ Checkout Server Control

This section explores each of these controls, briefly covering the functionality of the browsing experience controls. You'll then learn about the purchase of experience controls, with additional time spent on the Cart Server Control and the Checkout Server Control as you explore the information flow of those controls.

Finally, you will examine some sample pages from the OnTrek site to understand how these pieces all fit together to create a functioning eCommerce implementation. To cover this collection of information, this section contains the following elements:

➤ Browsing experience controls

➤ Purchase and maintenance controls

➤ OnTrek eCommerce implementation

Browsing Experience Controls

Of the nine eCommerce controls, five controls relate to the catalog browsing experience users go through on the site. These will become the heart of the purchasing process in your implementation. The controls are defined as follows:

➤ **CurrencySelect Server Control:** Much like the Language Server Control, this Control displays a list of available currencies on your site. When a user selects a different language from the dropdown, all the prices displayed by the other eCommerce controls are converted to the new currency.

➤ **ProductSearch Server Control:** This is based on the WebSearch Server Control, but is designed to only search for products listed in the catalog. It has two interfaces for searching, which are displayed on two tabs when it renders. The first interface is a basic textual search, whereas the second allows for advanced searching — it allows the users to specify filters such as price below, and price above. Additionally, the ProductSearch control allows the users to optionally filter the products shown by taxonomy categories.

➤ **ProductList Server Control:** This is similar to a ListSummary in that it displays a list of catalog items. The interface is a little more complex than a standard ListSummary, allowing for sorting of the items, and displaying the thumbnail and price as well as the link to the product. It also has a richer set of capabilities in the backend developer experience, allowing for many different types of sources to generate the list of products to display. For instance, it can use one or more catalogs or taxonomy nodes to determine which products to show. It can also be set to a collection, or a specific list of products.

➤ **Product Server Control:** This is used to display the details of any given product type. It relates to the ContentBlock Server Control, but is specifically designed to display catalog items. The default output of the Product Server Control includes the image and gallery of additional images, along with the title, description, and price for the particular product being shown. It also displays an Add to Cart button to allow your visitors to purchase the product. In the case of Bundle, Complex, or Kit products, the server control also displays the variants and allows the users to select options, if appropriate.

➤ **Recommendation Server Control:** This hooks into the list of CrossSell and UpSell products associated with the specified item, and displays them on the website as a list of items under the title, "You might also like." In addition to displaying a list of items with links to view more details about the products, it can also display an Add to Cart button to allow users to purchase the item with a minimum number of clicks.

CurrencySelect Server Control

The CurrencySelect Server Control, pictured in Figure 13-2, retrieves the list of enabled currencies for the site and displays that list in a dropdown so that site visitors can easily switch the currency that prices are displayed in. The currency that the user selects is not stored in the user profile, but instead in a cookie. If the user clears their cookies, the currency needs to be reselected.

FIGURE 13-2

There are no properties that need to be configured for the CurrencySelect Server Control to operate. To implement it, simply place the following code snippet in your page.

```
<CMS:CurrencySelect ID="CurrencySelect1" runat="server" />
```

ProductSearch Server Control

The ProductSearch Server Control is divided into two interfaces, with the basic interface shown in Figure 13-3. The Basic Search is a purely textual search, and finds products that are published, active, and searchable. The products must also be contained in the catalog specified in the CatalogId property, and they must contain the text either in the description or in associated metadata. The user must also have read permission or the product must be public.

FIGURE 13-3

The advanced interface allows for more directed searching, and is shown in Figure 13-4. The text can be divided into words that must be contained in the item, phrases that must be contained, a set of which at least one member must be contained, and a list of words that must not appear in the item or metadata. Additionally, the user can specify filters for the minimum price, maximum price, and product SKU. The price filters compare to the product's sale price, not the list price.

FIGURE 13-4

In addition to searching by text, the results displayed can be filtered by category. If the developer sets the ShowCategories property to true, a Filter by Category link appears below the Search box. When this link is clicked, a tree containing the available nodes appears, and the user can select which nodes to include products from.

You can customize the search results display format via XSLT, but by default they contain the thumbnail, name of the product, product SKU, description, list price, sale price, and an Add to Cart button if the product is available for purchase. The default search results interface is shown in Figure 13-5.

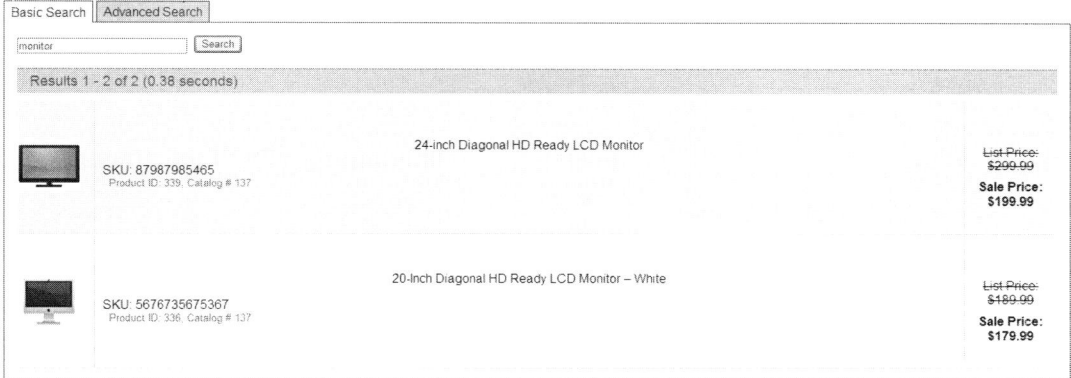

FIGURE 13-5

The properties used to modify the functioning or display of the ProductSearch Server Control are listed in Table 13-1.

TABLE 13-1: ProductSearch Server Control Properties

PROPERTY	DESCRIPTION
`ButtonImgSrc`	The path to an image to use for the submit button.
`ButtonText`	The string to use for the submit button if an image is not specified, or as the `ALT` text if an image is specified.
`CatalogId`	The catalog to search within. If the Recursive property is False, the search only returns products directly in this folder.
`CustomOrderBy`	This property supersedes the OrderBy property if set, and allows you to specify the result ordering by a property's friendly name in the indexing service.
`CustomXml`	By populating this property with an XML snippet, the snippet appended to the end of the XML output of the control prior to being processed by the XSLT. This allows you to send additional information to the XSLT.

continues

TABLE 13-1 *(continued)*

PROPERTY	DESCRIPTION
DisplayXslt	Allows you to specify the path to a custom XSLT for rendering. The default XSLT is located at ~\Workarea\Xslt\Commerce\ProductSearch.xsl.
DynamicProductParameter	Specifies the query string parameter to include the link generated to take users from the search results to the product details page.
EnableAdvancedLink	Controls whether the Advanced tab is displayed on the search interface.
LinkTarget	Specifies the value of the target attribute for links generated for product details.
LoadingImage	The image that is displayed while search results are being loaded via AJAX.
MaxTeaserLength	If the DisplayXslt property is set to ecmteaser, and the ShowCustomSummary property is set to false, this property can be set to an integer value, and the item teaser is truncated to that length. Under other conditions, this property is ignored.
OrderBy	Sets the field by which the results are ordered. Has a large number of preset options, including FolderName, Title, and DateModified. If the CustomOrderBy property is set, this property is ignored.
OrderDirection	Determines whether the sort order is used to display the results. Can be set to Ascending or Descending.
Recursive	Determines whether the catalog specified in CatalogId is searched, or that catalog, plus all subfolders.
ResultsPageSize	Determines the maximum number of results per page.
ResultTagId	Specifies the tag that should be used to display the search results. This allows you to display the search interface at one location in the page, and display the results in a completely different location on the same page.
ShowCategories	Boolean that determines whether to display the Filter by Category Link. If you want to show the link, ShowSearchBoxAlways must also be set to true.
ShowCustomSummary	If you set this to true, the item's summary is retrieved and displayed rather than the search characterization for that item. Defaults to false.

PROPERTY	DESCRIPTION
ShowSearchBoxAlways	If you set this to false, the search box is not displayed when results are shown.
TaxonomyOperator	Specifies the operator used when a user selects multiple categories in the taxonomy filter. If set to And, products are only shown that appear in all the categories selected. Or it requires only that the product appear in one of the selected categories.
TemplateCart	This must be set for the Add to Cart button to appear. Can be set to a relative or absolute path to the template containing the Cart Server Control.
TemplateProduct	The relative or absolute path to the template containing the Product Server Control. This is used to build the link to the product detail page.

An example implementation of a ProductSearch Server Control might look something like the following code snippet.

```
<CMS:ProductSearch ID="ProductSearch" runat="server"
ButtonText="Search" CatalogId="136" OrderBy="Title"
OrderDirection="Ascending" ResultsPageSize="20"
ShowCategories="True" ShowCustomSummary="True"
TaxonomyOperator="or" TemplateCart="Cart.aspx"
TemplateProduct="ProductDetail.aspx" Recursive="true" />
```

This code would output a display as depicted in Figure 13-6.

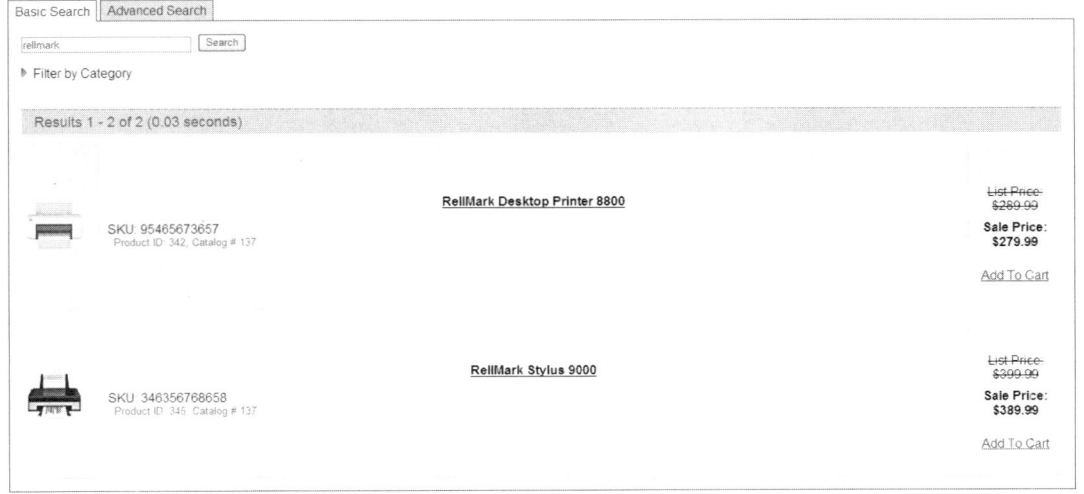

FIGURE 13-6

ProductList Server Control

The ProductList Server Control is most easily compared with the ListSummary Server Control. However, unlike the ListSummary Server Control, the ProductList Server Control has the ability to display products not just from a given catalog or folder, but also from a collection or taxonomy category. It can also display a list of hardcoded products. This makes it more like a combination of the ListSummary Server Control, the Collection Server Control, the ContentList Server Control, and the Directory Server Control. The default output of the ProductList Server Control is shown in Figure 13-7.

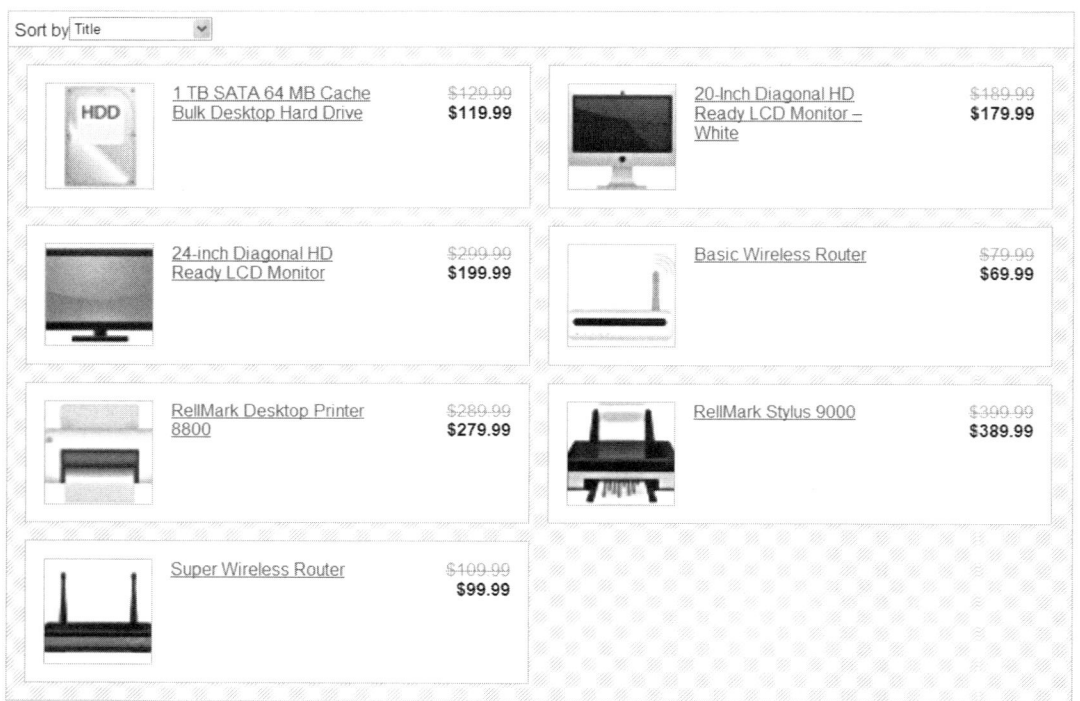

FIGURE 13-7

The ProductList Server Control's default display shows the product thumbnail, the title, the list price, and the sale price. Additionally, it contains a dropdown allowing the users to specify the sort order. The list can be sorted by Title, SKU, Price ascending or descending, Rating ascending or descending, and number of ratings.

Table 13-2 contains the list of properties available for the ProductList Server Control. It may be unclear at first how to set up the sources for the product list — this is done by setting the SourceType to Catalog, CatalogList, Taxonomy, TaxonomyList, Collection, or IdList. If you are setting the source type to one of the options supporting a list setting (CatalogList, TaxonomyList, or IdList), you can specify the list as a comma-separated string containing the specific IDs in the IdList property. Otherwise, the ID of the object should be placed in the SourceId property.

TABLE 13-2: ProductList Server Control Properties

PROPERTY	DESCRIPTION
`CustomXml`	Allows you to specify additional XML to be inserted into the generated XML before transformation by the XSLT takes place. This allows you to pass parameters or extra details into your custom XSLT easily.
`DisplayXslt`	Path to a custom XSLT to use to render the results. The default XSLT is located at ~\Workarea\Xslt\Commerce\ProductList.xsl.
`DynamicParameter`	Sets the query string parameter to use for the Source ID. This does not operate with the IdList property, only with the SourceId property.
`GetAnalyticsData`	If set to true, the display for a given product in the list is updated to include the average rating for the product along with the number of ratings that product has received.
`IdList`	A comma-separated list of IDs corresponding to the type set in SourceType. Only used when SourceType is set to IdList, TaxonomyList, or CatalogList.
`LoadingImage`	The image that is displayed while the product list is retrieving results.
`OrderBy`	This allows for more granularity in how results are sorted. If you want to use one of the modes listed here, you must set SortMode to None, which also prevents users on the site from switching the sort order. Available options are: `AverageRating`, `CatalogId`, `CollItemsDisplayOrder` (usable when the source is a collection,) `ContentStatus`, `CurrencyId`, `EndDate`, `EntryType`, `GoLive`, `Html`, `Id`, `IsArchived`, `IsBuyable`, `IsPublished`, `LanguageId`, `LastEditDate`, `LastEditorFirstName`, `LastEditorLastName`, `ListPrice`, `Media`, `NumberRated`, `ProductTypeId`, `SalesPrice`, `Sku`, `Status`, `Summary`, `TaxClassId`, `TaxItemsDisplayOrder` (usable when the source is a taxonomy,) `Title`, and `ViewCount`.
`PageSize`	The number of items to show per page.
`PageSpan`	In the paging display, this controls how many page links are shown before and after the current page. For instance, if there are five pages of results, the user is on page three, and this is set to 1, then the paging links are First... 3 4 5 ...Last.
`SortMode`	Sets the default item selected in the Sort By dropdown. Can be set to Title, SKU, Price Descending, Price Ascending, Highest rated, Lowest rated, and Most rated.
`SourceId`	The ID of the source to use. This value is only read when the SourceType is set to Catalog, Collection, or Taxonomy.

continues

TABLE 13-2 *(continued)*

PROPERTY	DESCRIPTION
SourceType	Has two types of sources available to read products from. The Catalog, Taxonomy, and Collection options allow you to choose a specific item to retrieve the products from. The CatalogList, TaxonomyList, and IdList options allow you to choose a list of products or sources to retrieve products from. If specifying a single source, set the SourceId with that value. When specifying a list of items or sources, set the IdList property with a comma separated list containing the IDs.
TaxonomyDepth	When the source is either Taxonomy or TaxonomyList, this determines how far beneath the given category to retrieve. The default is 1, and it is recommended to keep the value 1, as recursively retrieving taxonomy categories can become computationally expensive.
TemplateProduct	The relative or absolute path to the template containing the Product Server Control.

An example implementation of a ProductList Server Control might look something like the following code snippet.

```
<CMS:ProductList ID="ProductList" runat="server"
  GetAnalyticsData="True" PageSize="10" PageSpan="2"
  SortMode="HighestRated" SourceType="CatalogList"
  IdList="137,138,139" />
```

This code would output a display exemplified in Figure 13-8.

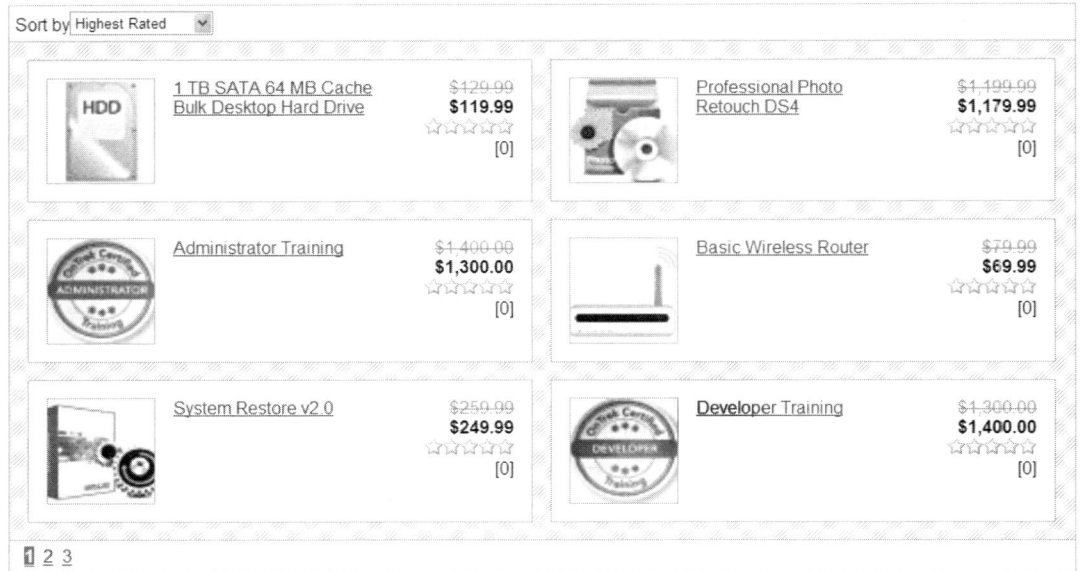

FIGURE 13-8

Product Server Control

The Product Server Control is closely related to the ContentBlock Server Control. It displays all the information about a given catalog entry, including the title, description, image and associated secondary images, the sale price, and a link to add the item to the cart. This is shown in Figure 13-9.

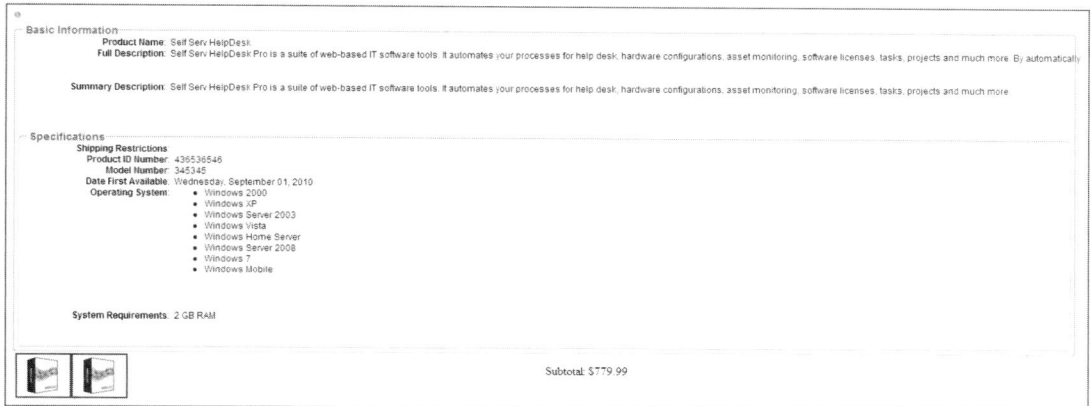

FIGURE 13-9

Additionally, the Product Server Control has the smarts to display the relevant information for product types other than Simple Product. For example, when working with a Bundled Product, the Product Server Control displays an additional area beginning with "This Bundle Includes" and then lists the items contained in the bundle along with their thumbnails and details. For Complex Products, the section is shown beginning with the text "Variants" and then listing the thumbnail, details, and price for each option. Kits are similar to Complex Products, with the section starting with "Options" and then listing each type of option with radio buttons for the selections available for that option, along with the uplift for choosing that option. Figure 13-10 shows a screenshot of the output of the Product Server Control for a kit product.

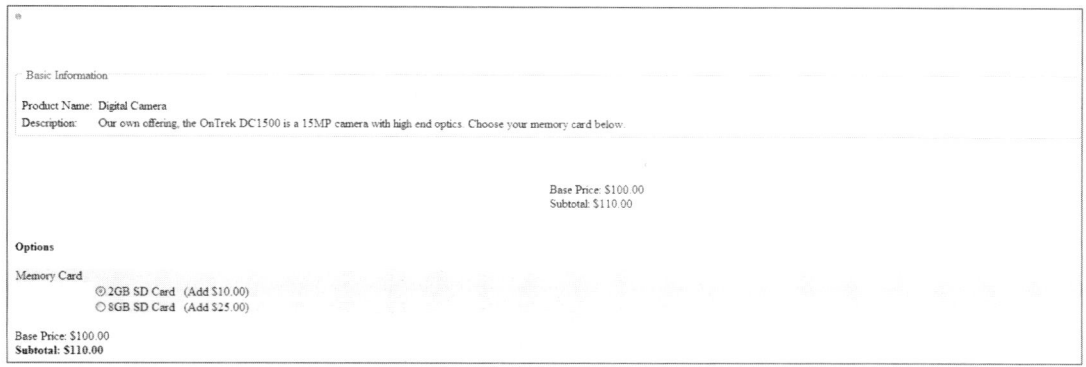

FIGURE 13-10

Table 13-3 lists the available properties for the Product Server Control.

TABLE 13-3: Product Server Control Properties

PROPERTY	DESCRIPTION
CustomXml	Specifies additional XML to append to the generated XML before it is passed to the XSLT for final transformation.
DefaultProductID	Specify the Product ID here if you want to hardcode it.
DisplayXslt	Specifies the XSLT to use to display the product. The default XSLT is located at ~\Workarea\Xslt\Commerce\product.xsl.
DynamicParameter	Specifies that the Product Server Control should read the product ID from the query string parameter.
ImageGallery	If this is set to List, the list of images specified on the media tab for the product are shown beneath the primary image. If a user clicks one of the thumbnails, the full image is shown. If set to None, the gallery is not displayed.
OverrideXslt	Like all Smart Forms, products have up to four XSLTs that you can specify for the display layer. When managing the product configuration, there is a packaged XSLT, as well as three additional XSLTs that the path can specify. You can set this property to 0, 1, 2, or 3. If set to 0, the packaged XSLT displays the product. Otherwise, the XSLT files specified as additional display XSLTs is used. If the DisplayXslt property is set, this property is ignored.
ShowAddToCart	Controls whether the Add to Cart button appears on the Product Server Control. The link will not be shown regardless of this value if the Buyable checkbox is unchecked for a given product.
TemplateCart	The relative or absolute path to the template containing the Cart Server Control. This is used to generate the links for the Add to Cart button.

An example implementation of a Product Server Control might look something like the following code snippet.

```
<CMS:Product ID="Product" runat="server"
  DynamicParameter="id" ImageGallery="List" ShowAddToCart="true"  />
```

This code would output a display as exemplified in Figure 13-11.

Recommendation Server Control

The Recommendation Server Control allows you to display the CrossSell and UpSell opportunities you defined in the product options. Typically displayed alongside the Product Server Control, it shows the product thumbnail, title, price, and optionally an Add to Cart button. This can be useful in getting the most bang out of your eCommerce implementation, by steering customers to a more expensive variant of the product they are currently looking at, or by prompting them to purchase an additional item that might also be interesting to them. The Recommendation Server Control is shown in Figure 13-12.

FIGURE 13-11

FIGURE 13-12

The properties available on the Recommendation Server Control are listed in Table 13-4.

TABLE 13-4: Recommendation Server Control Properties

PROPERTY	DESCRIPTION
CustomXml	Allows you to specify a string containing custom XML that you want to inject into the XML generated by the control. This injection will occur prior to transformation by the XSLT.
DefaultProductID	Specify this if you do not want the control to act dynamically based on the query string.
DisplayXslt	Allows you to specify a custom XSLT file to use when rendering results. The default file used is "\Workarea\Xslt\Commerce\Recommendation.xsl.

continues

TABLE 13-4 *(continued)*

PROPERTY	DESCRIPTION
`DynamicCartParameter`	Specifies the query string parameter that should be used to pass the product ID to the Cart Server Control. This is used when building the URL used in the Add To Cart link.
`DynamicProductParameter`	Specifies the query string parameter that should be used to pass the product ID to the Product Server Control. This is used when building the URL used in the details link.
`PageSize`	Specifies the number of items to show per page.
`RecommendationType`	Can be set to CrossSell or UpSell, and determines which group of associated products are shown in the Recommendation Server Control.
`TemplateCart`	Specifies the relative or absolute path to the template containing the Cart Server Control. Used to generate the Add to Cart links.
`TemplateProduct`	Specifies the relative or absolute path to the template containing the Product Server Control. Used to generate the detail links.

An example implementation of a Recommendation Server Control might look something like the following code snippet.

```
<CMS:Recommendation ID="Recommendation" runat="server"
  DynamicCartParameter="product" DynamicProductParameter="id"
  RecommendationType="CrossSell" TemplateCart="cart.aspx"
  TemplateProduct="product.aspx" />
```

This code would output a display as shown in Figure 13-13.

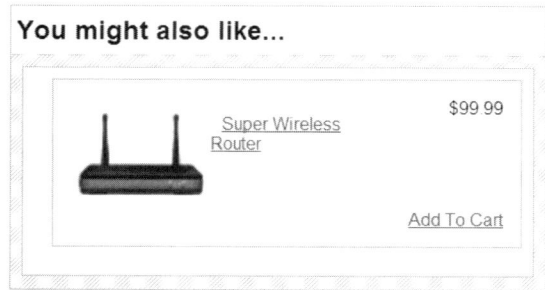

FIGURE 13-13

Purchase and Maintenance Controls

Now that you have explored the controls relating to the catalog browsing experience, you'll explore the last four controls, which relate to account maintenance and the actual purchasing process. The controls are described as follows:

➤ **MyAccount Server Control:** The area where the customers can manage their user details, including their names, e-mail addresses, passwords, billing addresses, and a list of shipping addresses. Remember that the Ektron Framework does not store credit card information, so customers cannot manage that information from this control.

➤ **OrderList Server Control:** Allows customers to view the list of past orders associated with that account. It displays the order date and number, along with the current status of the order. They can also examine the past orders in detail, viewing what items they ordered and the status of those individual items, the shipping and billing addresses associated with the order, and the pricing details of the order.

➤ **Cart Server Control:** Allows the customers to view the items they have currently selected to purchase, and manage quantities of those purchases. They can view the pricing details, and apply coupons to these items as well. Additionally, the Cart Server Control allows them to save carts containing items they are interested in, and recall those carts at any time.

➤ **Checkout Server Control:** Takes the customers through the process of purchasing their goods. This is a multistep process, starting with collecting the billing and shipping information, reviewing the order, supplying the payment information, and finally receiving notification of the successful order placement. It supports checking out both registered and unregistered users, and allows unregistered users to create accounts as part of the checkout process.

MyAccount Server Control

The MyAccount Server Control is a counterpart to the Profile Server Control. It allows users to manage some items that are not available in the Profile Server Control, notably the billing and shipping addresses that the customer wishes to use.

It behaves differently based on the user viewing it. If users visit the page when they are not logged in, they are redirected to the URL specified in the web.config at the key "ek_RedirectToLoginURL." Alternatively, if users view the control but are missing information that is required for their account, they are required to enter that information before moving on.

The fields that the MyAccount Server Control captures are the first name, last name, e-mail address, and password. These are all required values in the system. For the billing and shipping addresses, customers can enter their names, company, address, city, state, postal code, country, and phone number. For each address stored, the only field not required is the company. Additionally, the control is capable of capturing additional data specified through Custom User Properties, by specifying the properties to capture through the CustomerPropertyID property.

The properties available to the MyAccount Server Control are listed in Table 13-5.

TABLE 13-5: MyAccount Server Control Properties

PROPERTY	DESCRIPTION
CustomerPropertyID	A comma-separated list of Custom User Properties to capture on the user properties pane. These properties can be modified in the Workarea at Settings ⇨ Configuration ⇨ Custom Properties.

continues

TABLE 13-5 *(continued)*

PROPERTY	DESCRIPTION
CustomXML	Allows you to inject XML into the generated XML before it is passed to the XSLT for transformation.
DefaultCountryID	The Country ID to select by default when customers are entering new addresses. The IDs can be found in the Workarea at Settings ➪ Commerce ➪ Configuration ➪ Countries.
DisplayXslt	Allows you to specify a custom XSLT document to use to render the output of the control. The default XSLT is at "\Workarea\Xslt\Commerce\MyAccount.xsl.
LoadingImage	The image that is shown while the control is performing an AJAX fetch of data.
RedirectUrl	The relative or absolute path to a page containing the login control. If this is not set, the web.config key "ek_RedirectToLoginURL" is checked for a value.

An example implementation of a MyAccount Server Control might look something like the following code snippet.

```
<CMS:MyAccount ID="MyAccount" runat="server"
   CustomPropertyID="240" DefaultCountryId="840" RedirectUrl="Login.aspx" />
```

This code would output a display as depicted in Figure 13-14.

FIGURE 13-14

OrderList Server Control

The OrderList Server Control is generally used in conjunction with the MyAccount Server Control. It allows users to look through their past orders and get status updates on orders still in progress. It is shown in Figure 13-15.

Users can also dive into the details of a particular order by selecting that order from the list. The display updates to show the overall status of the order, along with the date it was placed and the ID of the order. It displays the Ship To and the Bill To names and addresses associated with the order, along with a list of the items in the order and their individual prices. It also displays the order subtotal, coupon total, taxes applied, shipping cost, and total amount that was or will be charged to the customer. This view is shown in Figure 13-16.

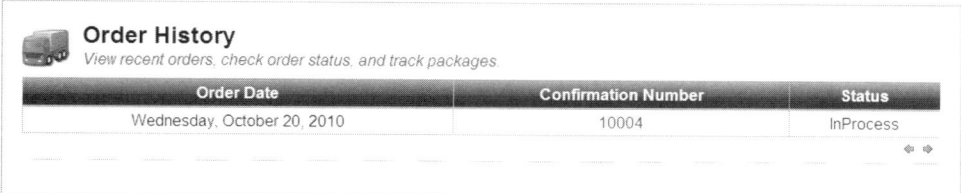

FIGURE 13-15

FIGURE 13-16

The properties available to the MyAccount Server Control are listed in Table 13-6.

TABLE 13-6: OrderList Server Control Properties

PROPERTY	DESCRIPTION
CustomXML	Allows you to inject XML into the generated XML before it is passed to the XSLT for transformation.
DefaultUserID	The User ID whose orders will be displayed. If this is not set, the current user's orders are shown instead.

continues

TABLE 13-6 *(continued)*

PROPERTY	DESCRIPTION
`DisplayXslt`	Allows you to specify a custom XSLT document to use to render the output of the control. The default XSLT is at ~\Workarea\Xslt\Commerce\OrderList.xsl.
`DynamicProductParameter`	The query string parameter to fill with the product ID when building a link to the product detail page.
`DynamicOrderParameter`	The query string parameter to read when displaying a particular order.
`GuestOrderView`	If set to true, guest accounts can view their orders by entering the particular order number as well as their e-mail addresses.
`MaxResults`	Specifies the maximum number of orders to display before switching to the paged interface.
`PageSize`	Specifies the number of orders to show per page.
`TemplateProduct`	An absolute or relative path to a template containing the Product Server Control. If this is set, the title of a product inside an order becomes a link to view the details of that product.

An example implementation of an OrderList Server Control might look something like the following code snippet.

```
<CMS:OrderList ID="OrderList" runat="server"
DynamicOrderParameter="OID" DynamicProductParameter="id"
TemplateProduct="Product.aspx" />
```

This code would output a display as shown in Figure 13-17.

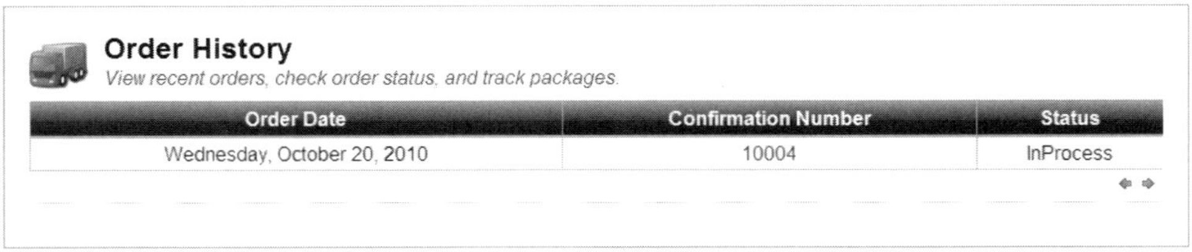

Order History
View recent orders, check order status, and track packages.

Order Date	Confirmation Number	Status
Wednesday, October 20, 2010	10004	InProcess

FIGURE 13-17

Cart Server Control

The Cart Server Control allows users to manage multiple carts containing items of interest to them. They can save a currently selected list of items for long-term decision-making by giving the cart a name, or restore old carts by selecting them. They can also manage the items in a given cart by deleting them, or modifying the quantities in the cart. It is shown in Figure 13-18.

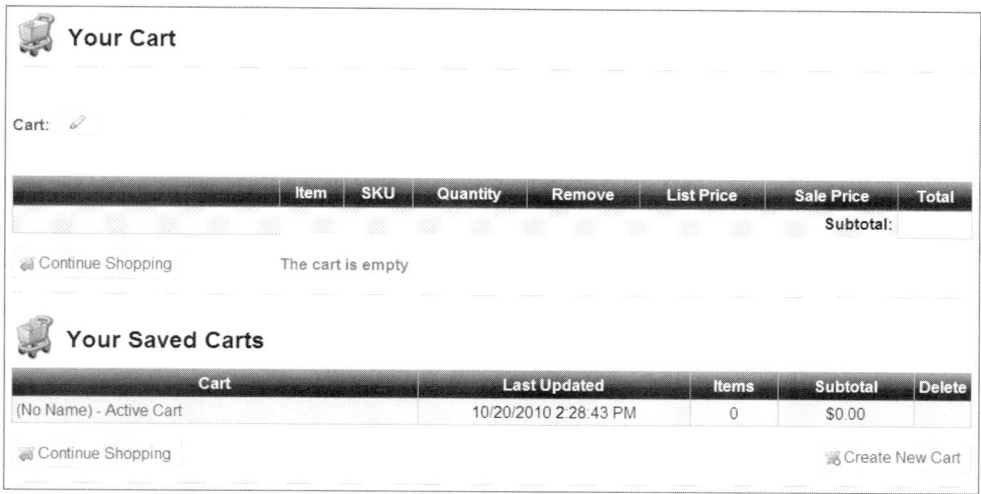

FIGURE 13-18

In addition to the basics of cart management, users can also apply coupons to the cart or items in a cart, before moving on to the checkout process. The properties available to the Cart Server Control are listed in Table 13-7.

TABLE 13-7: Cart Server Control Properties

PROPERTY	DESCRIPTION
CustomXML	Allows you to inject XML into the generated XML before it is passed to the XSLT for transformation.
DisplayXslt	Allows you to specify a custom XSLT document to use to render the output of the control. The default XSLT is at ~\Workarea\Xslt\Commerce\Cart.xsl.
DynamicProductParameter	The query string parameter to fill with the product ID when building a link to the product detail page.
EnableCoupons	If this is set to false, the Apply Coupon button is hidden.
LoadingImage	The image to display when the cart performs an AJAX fetch of data from the server.
TemplateCheckout	An absolute or relative path to a template containing the Checkout Server Control. This is used to build the link to the checkout page.
TemplateProduct	An absolute or relative path to a template containing the Product Server Control. If this is not set, the QuickLink for the product is used for the Details link.
TemplateShopping	This is the URL to continue to when the user selects the Continue Shopping link.

An example implementation of a Cart Server Control might look something like the following code snippet.

```
<CMS:Cart ID="Cart" runat="server"
  DynamicProductParameter="id" EnableCoupons="true"
  EnableImages="true" TemplateCheckout="Checkout.aspx"
  TemplateProduct="Product.aspx" TemplateShopping="Store.aspx" />
```

This code would output a display as depicted in Figure 13-19.

FIGURE 13-19

Checkout Server Control

The Checkout Server Control is the final control that users interact with as part of their shopping experience on your site. It takes them from having a cart full of items, to actually purchasing those items by selecting the billing and shipping addresses to use, and providing payment details. This control has the most hooks into the rest of the system, relying on tax providers, shipping providers, and payment gateways to complete its task. It is shown in Figure 13-20.

The control acts differently depending on whether the customer currently checking out is logged in. If the user has not yet logged in, he's invited to do so, but he's also presented with the option of creating a profile in line with the checkout procedure, or of checking out without creating a profile. This choice is shown in Figure 13-21. The steps for the checkout process are as follows:

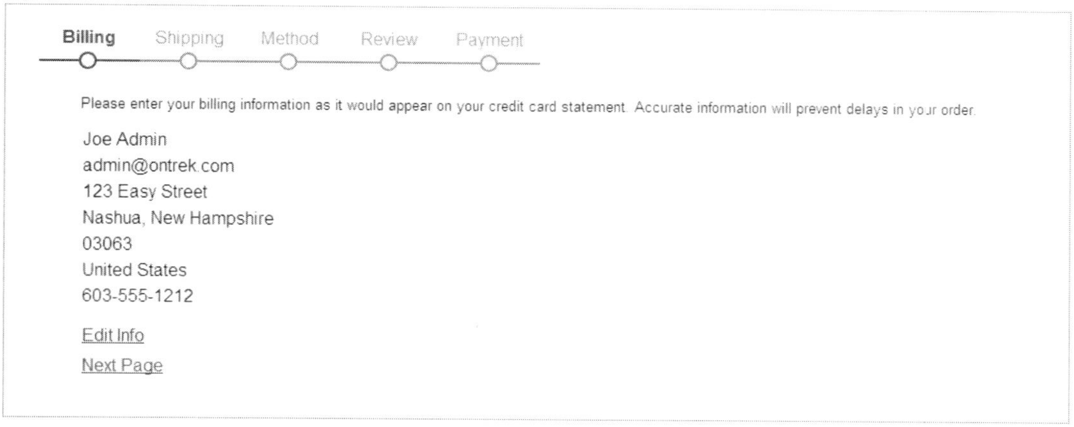

FIGURE 13-20

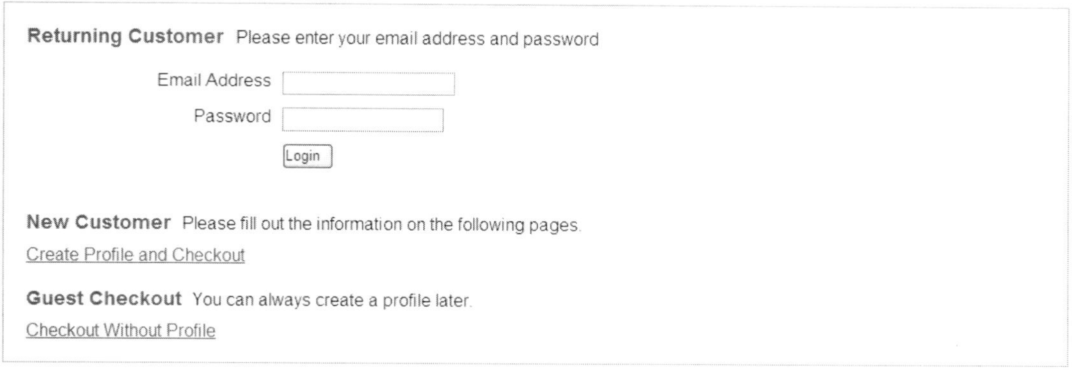

FIGURE 13-21

1. **Billing information:** When users are logged in, this is pre-populated with their saved data.

2. **Shipping information:** The shipping address defaults to the billing address, unless they have saved addresses, in which case the list of addresses currently saved to the account are shown, along with the option of editing or deleting those addresses, or adding a new address. This is shown in Figure 13-22.

3. **Shipping method:** This screen displays the options available, along with the estimated cost of each method. These methods are read from the available methods in the Workarea, which are configured through the use of a shipping provider.

4. **Order review:** The user will then have the opportunity to review the order, which shows them all the updated associated charges, such as taxes and shipping costs. They also have the ability to edit their carts at this point.

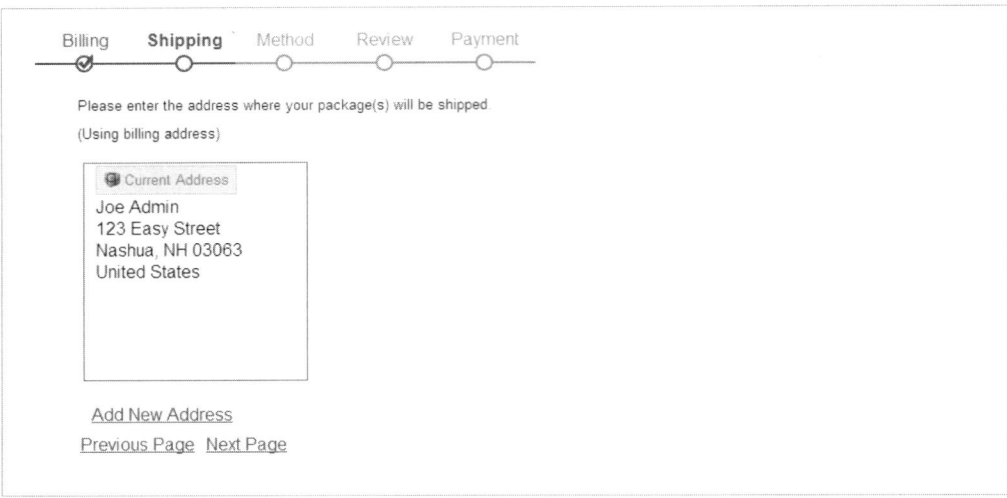

FIGURE 13-22

5. **Order submission:** Finally, the next step allows users to submit the order. It is on this screen that they have the option of selecting a payment method and entering the details of their payment option, as shown in Figure 13-23.

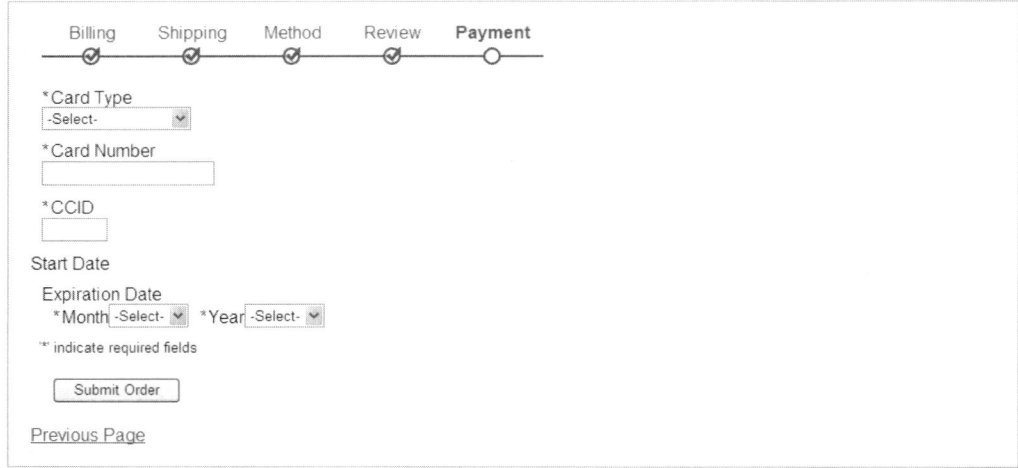

FIGURE 13-23

6. **Thank you message:** These options, like the shipping options, are read in from the settings defined in the Workarea at the Payment Options screen. Once the users submit their information on this page, the charge is sent to the payment gateway, and the order is recorded in the database. Users are then presented with a thank you message.

The properties available to the Checkout Server Control are listed in Table 13-8.

TABLE 13-8: Checkout Server Control Properties

PROPERTY	DESCRIPTION
CurrentPhase	Allows you to jump the users to specific phases in the checkout process by modifying the value in codebehind. The available phases are: Login, BillingInfo, BillingInfoEntry, ShippingInfo, ShippingInfoEntry, ShippingMethodSelect, ReviewOrder, SubmitOrder, Complete, Error_EmptyBasket, and Error_UnhandledException. For example, you might want to offer the users the ability to jump back to the ShippingMethodSelect phase from the ReviewOrder phase.
CustomXML	Allows you to inject XML into the generated XML before it is passed to the XSLT for transformation.
DefaultCountryId	The default country shown in the billing and shipping address dropdown.
DynamicPhaseParameter	The query string parameter that stores the phase ID.
DisplayXslt	Allows you to specify a custom XSLT document to use to render the output of the control. The default XSLT is at ~\Workarea\Xslt\Commerce\Checkout\Standard\Checkout.xsl.
FriendlyErrorMessage	This text is shown to the users if an unhandled error occurs.
AllowGuestCheckout	Set to true to allow guests to check out without creating an account.
IsSSLRequired	If set to true, the Checkout Server Control automatically switches the user to an SSL connection. This requires that an SSL certificate be installed to your site, and is strongly recommended for production eCommerce implementations.
LoadingImage	The image to display when the cart performs an AJAX fetch of data from the server.
TemplateCart	The path to a template that contains the Cart Server Control.
TemplateOrderHistory	The path to a template that contains the OrderList Server Control.
TemplateRecoverPassword	The path to a template that allows the users to recover their passwords.
TemplateShopping	This is the URL to continue to when the users select the Continue Shopping link.

An example implementation of a Checkout Server Control might look something like the following code snippet.

```
<CMS:Checkout ID="Checkout" runat="server"
  AllowGuestCheckout="True" DefaultCountryId="840"
```

```
        FriendlyErrorMessage="Oops, something broke!"
        TemplateCart="ShoppingCart.aspx"
        TemplateOrderHistory="OrderHistory.aspx"
        TemplateRecoverPassword="RecoverPassword.aspx"
        TemplateShopping="Store.aspx" />
```

This code would output a display as shown in Figure 13-24.

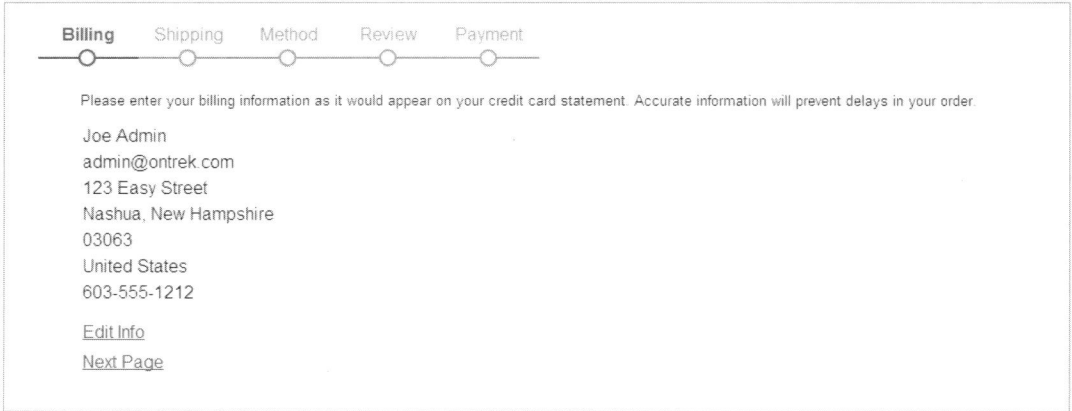

FIGURE 13-24

OnTrek eCommerce Implementation

Now that you have examined the server controls that make up the eCommerce development experience, this section takes a look at how those pieces come together in the OnTrek site to create a unified shopping experience.

Understanding the Landing Page

The OnTrek implementation of eCommerce is based around a single template that changes its presentation based on what the current view is. It presents three possible views to the users — the landing page for the commerce section, the product search view, and the product detail view. PageBuilder is used for the landing view, but the other two views are more firm in the presentation, with only the right channel being modifiable. In the case of the PageBuilder based landing page, you'll be using the default layout as installed in the OnTrek site.

This section starts by taking a look at how the product detail structure works. It's based around the products.pb.aspx Wireframe, which contains a multiview exposing the different views the page can handle. The contents of this page are reproduced in Listing 13-1.

LISTING 13-1: ~/products.pb.aspx

```
<%@ Page Language="C#"
    MasterPageFile="~/components/templates/2ColumnChannelRight.master"
    AutoEventWireup="true" CodeFile="products.pb.aspx.cs"
```

```
      Inherits="Ektron.Site.Products.Products" Title="Products" %>
<%@ Register Assembly="Ektron.Cms.Controls"
   Namespace="Ektron.Cms.Controls" TagPrefix="CMS" %>
<%@ Register Assembly="Ektron.Cms.Widget"
   Namespace="Ektron.Cms.PageBuilder" TagPrefix="PB" %>
<%@ Register Src="~/Workarea/PageBuilder/PageControls/PageHost.ascx"
   TagName="PageHost" TagPrefix="CMS" %>
<%@ Register Src="~/Workarea/PageBuilder/PageControls/DropZone.ascx"
   TagName="DropZone" TagPrefix="CMS" %>
<%@ Register
   Src="~/Components/userControls/products/products.productDescription.ascx"
   TagName="ProductDescription" TagPrefix="uc" %>
<%@ Register
   Src="~/Components/userControls/products/products.productSearch.ascx"
   TagName="ProductSearch" TagPrefix="uc" %>

<asp:Content ID="contentBody" ContentPlaceHolderID="uxContentBody" runat="Server">
   <CMS:PageHost ID="pageHost" runat="server" />
   <asp:MultiView ID="uxProductsMultiView" runat="server">
      <asp:View ID="uxProductsLandingView" runat="server">
         <CMS:DropZone ID="cmsDropZoneLanding" runat="server"
            AllowColumnResize="false" AllowAddColumn="false">
            <ColumnDefinitions>
               <PB:ColumnData columnID="1" unit="percent" width="100" />
            </ColumnDefinitions>
         </CMS:DropZone>
      </asp:View>
      <asp:View ID="uxProductSearchView" runat="server">
         <CMS:ContentBlock runat="server" ID="cmsContentProductSearch"
            DefaultContentID="122" />
         <uc:ProductSearch ID="ucProductSearch" runat="server" />
      </asp:View>
      <asp:View ID="uxProductDescriptionView" runat="server">
         <uc:ProductDescription ID="ucProductDescription" runat="server" />
      </asp:View>
   </asp:MultiView>
</asp:Content>

<asp:Content ID="channelRight" ContentPlaceHolderID="uxChannel" runat="Server">
   <asp:PlaceHolder ID="uxProductsChannelRightPlaceholder" runat="server" />
   <CMS:DropZone ID="cmsDropZoneProducts" runat="server"
      AllowColumnResize="false" AllowAddColumn="false">
      <ColumnDefinitions>
         <PB:ColumnData columnID="0" unit="percent" width="100" />
      </ColumnDefinitions>
   </CMS:DropZone>
</asp:Content>
```

The multiview in this file exposes three views: uxProductsLandingView, uxProductSearchView, and uxProductDescriptionView. Then the right side of the page is made up of a single PageBuilder DropZone, making it customizable. Let's take a look at the codebehind of this file to get a clearer picture of what is happening. Listing 13-2 contains the codebehind in products.pb.aspx.cs.

Available for download on Wrox.com

LISTING 13-2: ~\Products.pb.aspx.cs

```
using System.Web.UI;
using System.Web.UI.HtmlControls;
using System.Web.UI.WebControls;
using System.Web.UI.WebControls.WebParts;
using Ektron.Cms;
using Ektron.Cms.API;
using Ektron.Cms.PageBuilder;
using Ektron.Site;
using Ektron.OnTrek;

namespace Ektron.Site.Products
{
  [LicenseRequirement(Ektron.Cms.DataIO.LicenseManager.Feature.eCommerce)]
  public partial class Products : SitePageBuilder
  {
    protected void Page_Init(object sender, EventArgs e)
    {
      Ektron.OnTrek.Utility.Current.SiteUtility.BreadcrumbControl.DoInitFill
        = false;

      Ektron.OnTrek.Utility.Current.SiteUtility.BreadcrumbControl
        .AddContentTitleToBreadcrumb
        = true;

Ektron.OnTrek.Utility.Current.SiteUtility.BreadcrumbControl.DynamicParameter
        = "pageid";
    }
    public override void OnPageReady(object sender, EventArgs e)
    {
      SetActiveView();
    }

    #region helpers

    public override void Error(string message)
    {
      jsAlert(message);
    }
    public override void Notify(string message)
    {
      jsAlert(message);
    }
    public void jsAlert(string message)
    {
      try
      {
        Literal lit = new Literal();
        lit.Text = "<script type=\"\" language=\"\">{0}</script>";
        lit.Text = string.Format(lit.Text, "alert('" + message + "');");
        Form.Controls.Add(lit);
      }
      catch (Exception)
```

```csharp
        {
        }
    }    private void SetActiveView()
    {
        long PageID = SiteData.Current.PageBuilder.PageId;
        switch (PageID)
        {
            case 53:
                uxProductsMultiView.SetActiveView(uxProductsLandingView);
                break;
            case 82:
                uxProductsMultiView.SetActiveView(uxProductSearchView);
                break;
            default:
                if (!String.IsNullOrEmpty(Request.QueryString["id"]))
                {
    Ektron.OnTrek.Utility.Current.SiteUtility.BreadcrumbControl.DynamicParameter
            = "id";
                }
                // anything else and the user is viewing a specific product
                UserControl ucProductsCrossSell =
                    (UserControl)Page.LoadControl(SiteData.Current.Cms.SitePath +
                    "components/userControls/products/products.CrossSell.ascx");
                UserControl ucProductsUpSell =
                    (UserControl)Page.LoadControl(SiteData.Current.Cms.SitePath +
                    "components/userControls/products/products.UpSell.ascx");
                uxProductsChannelRightPlaceholder.Controls.Add(ucProductsCrossSell);
                uxProductsChannelRightPlaceholder.Controls.Add(ucProductsUpSell);
                uxProductsMultiView.SetActiveView(uxProductDescriptionView);
                break;
        }
    }
    #endregion
    }
}
```

In Listing 13-2, the key portion is the `SetActiveView` method, which is called on the page ready event. It is clear from this code that the Wireframe is designed to display two layouts in particular, layout ID 53, which is the landing page for the eCommerce section, and layout ID 82, which is the product search page. Any other page layout means that this is actually a product being displayed.

Understanding the User Controls

Now that you understand how the product page switches between the three modes — search, browsing, and product detail — you can take a look at the user controls that encapsulate those pieces of functionality to see how they work in more detail. Let's start by looking at the landing portion, contained in the `uxProductsLandingView` view. This view is highlighted in Figure 13-25.

By default, this DropZone in this view contains a ContentBlock Widget that is set to display the intro text, and two custom widgets.

➤ **Site-ProductSearch Widget:** This was custom built for the OnTrek site and contains a ProductSearch Server Control.

➤ **Site-FeaturedProduct Widget:** Contains the collection of controls that make up the featured products section.

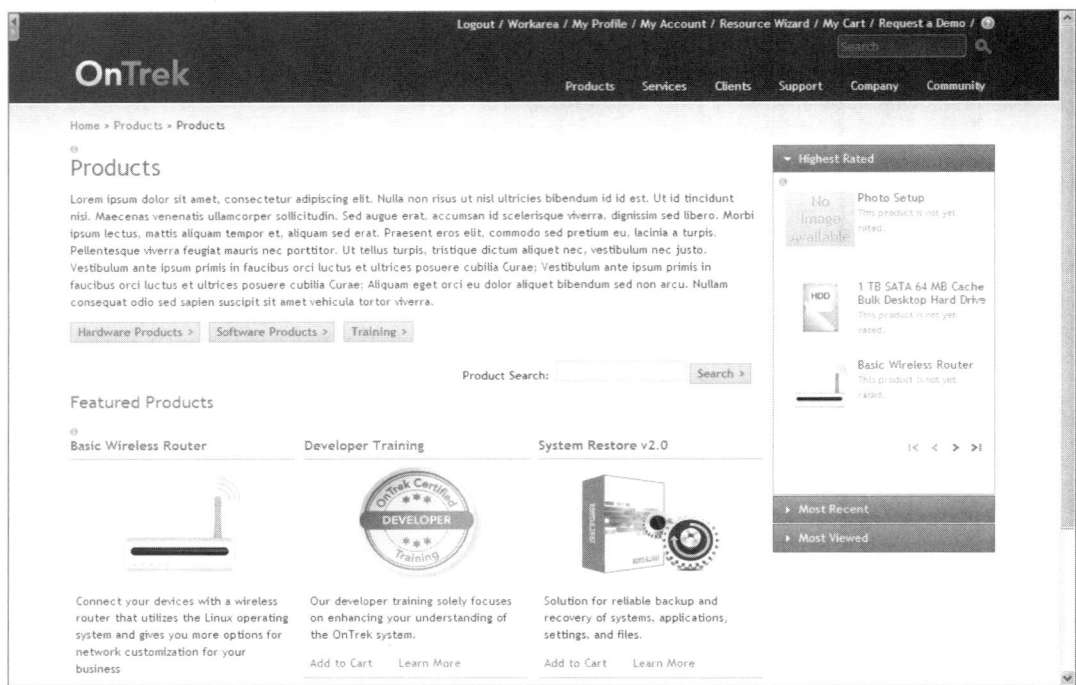

FIGURE 13-25

Let's dive into the FeaturedProduct Widget, which is located at ~/widgets/Site-FeaturedProducts .ascx, and shown in Listing 13-3.

LISTING 13-3: ~/widgets/Site-FeaturedProducts.ascx

Available for
download on
Wrox.com

```
<%@ Control Language="C#" AutoEventWireup="true"
   CodeFile="Site-FeaturedProducts.ascx.cs"
   Inherits="Ektron.Site.Widgets.FeaturedProducts" %>
<%@ Register Assembly="Ektron.Cms.Controls"
   Namespace="Ektron.Cms.Controls" TagPrefix="CMS" %>

<div>
   <h2><asp:Literal ID="uxFeaturedProductsTitle" runat="server" /></h2>
   <CMS:Collection ID="cmsFeaturedProducts"
                   Visible="false" Random="false"
                   DefaultCollectionID="4"
                   SelTaxonomyID="190" GetHtml="true"
                   runat="server" AddText="Add Featued Product"
                   class="Site-FeaturedProductCollection" />
   <CMS:ProductList ID="cmsFeaturedProductsList"
                   SortMode="None" SourceType="Collection"
```

eCommerce Server Controls and Implementation | 521

```
                SourceId="4" SuppressWrapperTags="true"
                OrderBy="CollItemsDisplayOrder" runat="server" />
</div>
```

This user control is very simple: It contains a title block, an invisible collection control, and a ProductList Server Control. The codebehind for this file only contains a few lines of interest, shown in the following code snippet.

```
cmsFeaturedProducts.Fill();
uxFeaturedProductsTitle.Text = cmsFeaturedProducts.CollectionTitle;
cmsFeaturedProductsList.DisplayXslt = Ektron.Site.SiteData.Current.Cms.SitePath +
    "widgets/Site-FeaturedProducts/Site-FeaturedProducts.xsl";
```

What happens in this user control is that the Collection Server Control is being loaded to retrieve the title, which is then populated into the Literal at the top of the user control. The actual product display is then handled exclusively by the ProductList Server Control, which simply displays collection ID 4. It uses a custom XSLT to render the results, which is stored at ~/widgets/Site-FeaturedProducts/Site-FeaturedProducts.xsl.

This shows the power of the out-of-the-box eCommerce controls, that so little modification is needed to create a rich interface.

Understanding the Product Detail Interface

Let's jump in a different direction now, and take a look at the product detail interface. When you click a product link, you are presented with the page shown in Figure 13-26 in the browser.

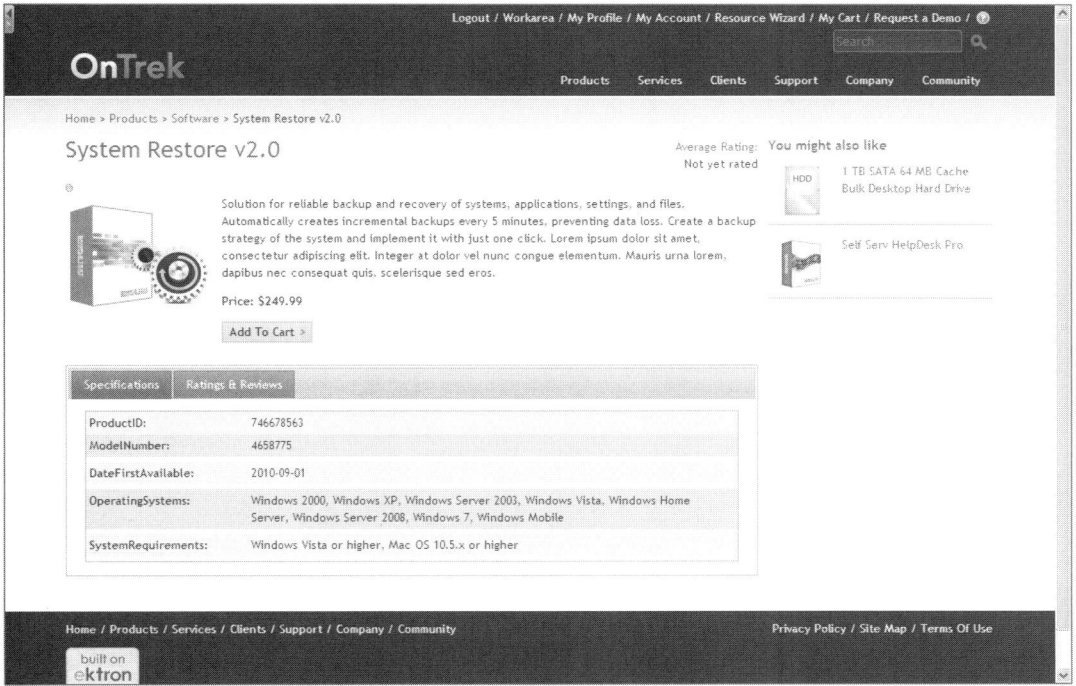

FIGURE 13-26

You know from looking at the products.pb.aspx Wireframe that the entire display layer for the product detail interface is actually handled by a single user control, which exists at ~/Components/userControls/products/products.productDescription.ascx. Let's take a look at the source and code-behind for that user control now, in Listing 13-4.

LISTING 13-4: ~/Components/userControls/products/products.productDescription.ascx

Available for download on Wrox.com

```
<%@ Control Language="C#" AutoEventWireup="true"
    CodeFile="products.productDescription.ascx.cs"
    Inherits="Ektron.Site.Products.ProductDescription" %>
<%@ Register Assembly="Ektron.Cms.Controls" Namespace="Ektron.Cms.Controls"
    TagPrefix="CMS" %>
<%@ Register Src="~/Components/userControls/rating/averageRating.ascx"
    TagName="AverageRating" TagPrefix="uc" %>

<div class="site-productDescription">
  <div class="clearfix">
    <h1 class="span-14"><asp:Literal ID="uxProductTitle" runat="server" /></h1>
    <div class="span-4 last ektron-ui-floatRight socialAndRatingsWrapper">
      <CMS:SocialBar ID="cmsSocialBar" WrapTag="div"
        CssClass="ektron-ui-floatRight" DynamicObjectParameter="id"
        ObjectType="Content" Direction="LeftToRight"
        Items="Addto,Email,Print,Twitter,FaceBook" runat="server" />
      <uc:AverageRating ID="ucAverageRating" TextAlignment="Right"
        Title="Average Rating:" runat="server" />
    </div>
  </div>
  <CMS:Product ID="cmsProductView" DynamicParameter="id" runat="server"
    CssClass="productBasicInfo" />
  <div class="site-products-productTabs">
    <ul>
      <li><a href="#Ratings">Ratings &#38; Reviews</a></li>
      <li><a href="#Specifications">Specifications</a></li>
    </ul>
    <div id="Ratings" class="clearfix">
      <cms:ContentReview ID="cmsContentReviews" WrapTag="div" runat="server"
        DynamicParameter="id" DisplayXslt="Review List"
        GetReviews="content" />
      <cms:ContentReview ID="cmsContentRatings" WrapTag="div" runat="server"
        DynamicParameter="id" />
    </div>
    <div id="Specifications">
      <asp:Xml ID="uxSpecificationsXml" runat="server" />
    </div>
  </div>
</div>
```

In the code, you can see that the key parts of this user control are the SocialBar and ContentReview Server Controls, with the product itself being displayed by the Product Server Control. The Product Server Control itself has very few properties set in the declarative side, and only two properties set in the codebehind, as shown in the following snippet.

```
// set product view params
cmsProductView.TemplateCart = SiteData.Current.Cms.SitePath + "cart.aspx";
```

```
cmsProductView.DisplayXslt = SiteData.Current.Cms.SitePath +
  "components/usercontrols/products/products.productDescription.xsl";
cmsProductView.Fill();
```

As with the ProductList Server Control, you are dealing with a near stock eCommerce Server Control, with a customized XSLT to provide the styling needed for the site.

Understanding the Server Controls

Having looked at how some of the product interaction works, you can take a look at some of the more complex server controls, like the Cart Server Control and the Checkout Server Control. On one of the product pages, click the Add to Cart button to see the cart.aspx page, as shown in Figure 13-27.

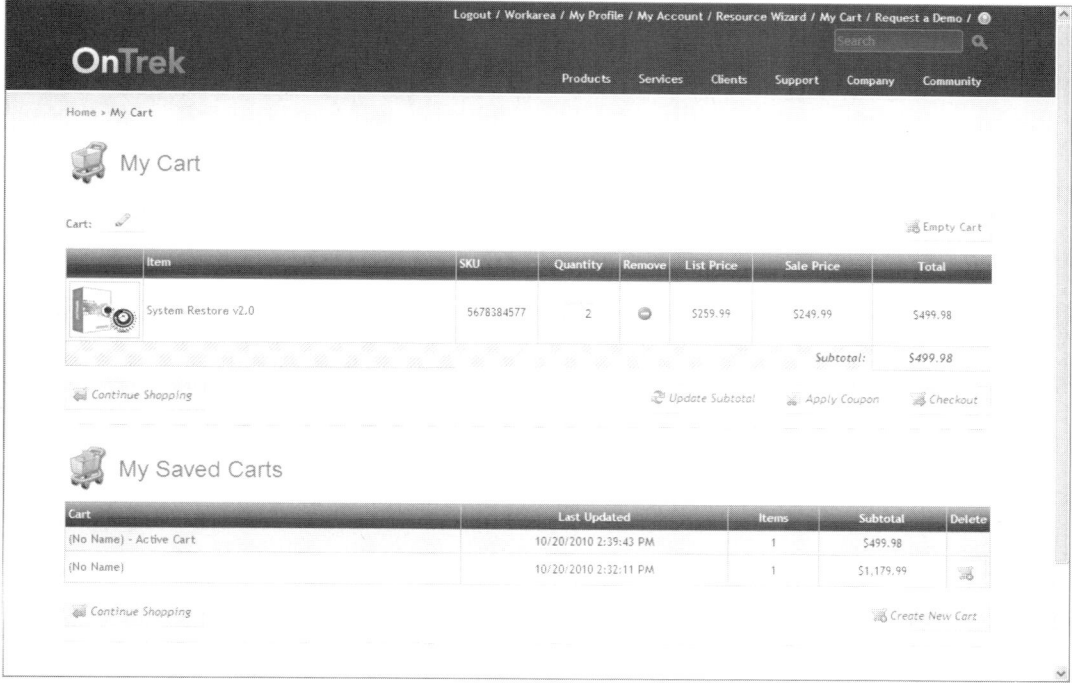

FIGURE 13-27

All the interaction with the cart takes place on the Cart.aspx page, so let's look at the code for that, as shown in Listing 13-5.

LISTING 13-5: ~\Cart.aspx

Available for download on Wrox.com

```
<%@ Page Language="C#" MasterPageFile="~/components/templates/Full.master"
    AutoEventWireup="true" CodeFile="cart.aspx.cs"
    Inherits="Ektron.Site.Cart" Title="My Cart" %>

<%@ Register Assembly="Ektron.Cms.Controls" Namespace="Ektron.Cms.Controls"
```

continues

LISTING 13-5 *(continued)*

```
    TagPrefix="CMS" %>

<asp:Content ID="contentBody" ContentPlaceHolderID="uxContentBody" Runat="Server">
    <CMS:Cart ID="cmsCart" EnableCoupons="true" EnableImages="true" runat="server" />
</asp:Content>
```

This file is exceedingly simple. Containing a lone Cart Server Control, it is a straightforward example of implementing the shopping cart portion of your eCommerce site. The codebehind is no more complex, with the relevant lines shown in the following snippet.

```
cmsCart.TemplateCheckout = SiteData.Current.Cms.SitePath + "checkout.aspx";
cmsCart.TemplateShopping = SiteData.Current.Cms.SitePath + "Products";
cmsCart.DisplayXslt = SiteData.Current.Cms.SitePath + "XmlFiles/cart.xsl";
```

This codebehind is adding pointers to the correct URLs when a customer is ready to check out or wants to continue shopping. This example uses a slightly customized XSL on this server control. Let's now continue with the Checkout Server Control.

When you click checkout on the cart page, you are brought to the checkout.aspx page, which is shown in Figure 13-28. This page is also very straightforward, with only the one item being displayed.

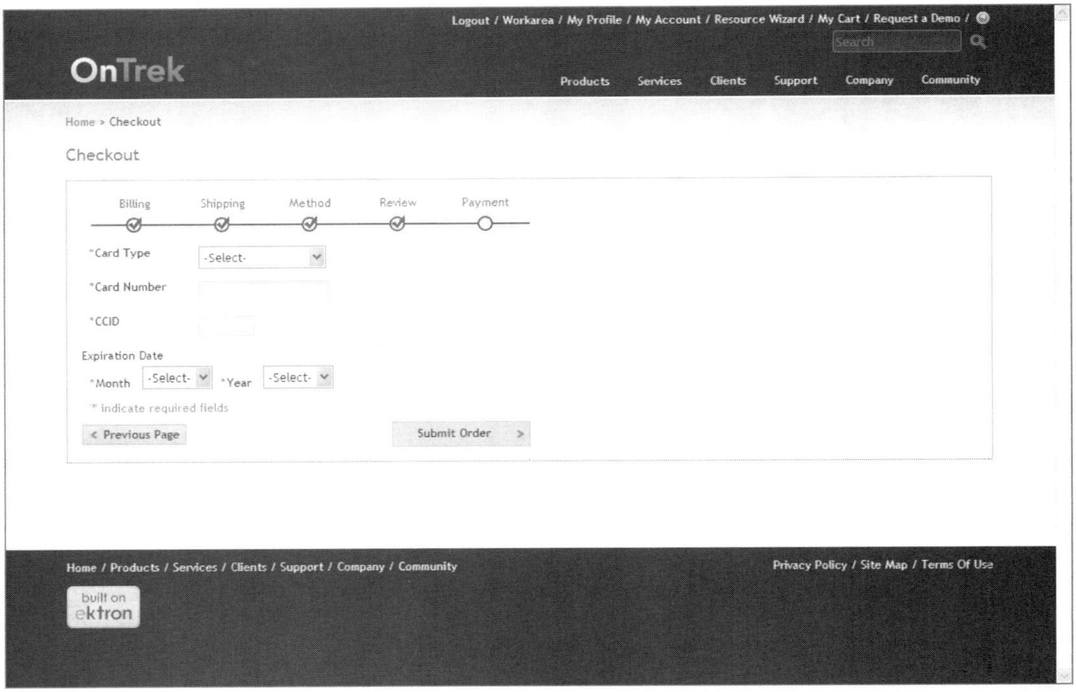

FIGURE 13-28

Looking at the code for the checkout.aspx page, you can see that just like the cart.aspx page, this is a nearly stock control. This is shown in Listing 13-6.

LISTING 13-6: ~\Checkout.aspx

Available for download on Wrox.com

```
<%@ Page Language="C#" MasterPageFile="~/components/templates/Full.master"
    AutoEventWireup="true" CodeFile="checkout.aspx.cs"
    Inherits="Ektron.Site.Checkout" Title="OnTrek: Checkout" %>
<%@ Register Assembly="Ektron.Cms.Controls" Namespace="Ektron.Cms.Controls"
    TagPrefix="CMS" %>

<asp:Content ID="contentBody" ContentPlaceHolderID="uxContentBody" Runat="Server">
    <h2>Checkout</h2>
    <CMS:Checkout ID="cmsCheckout" Stylesheet="css/ektron.site.checkout.css"
      IsSSLRequired="false" runat="server" />
</asp:Content>
```

And again like the cart.aspx page, the codebehind is very simple. It simply sets up the CSS stylesheet and sets some file pointers to allow for link construction.

```
cmsCheckout.Stylesheet = SiteData.Current.Cms.SitePath
    + "css/ektron.site.checkout.css";
cmsCheckout.TemplateCart = SiteData.Current.Cms.SitePath
    + "cart.aspx";
cmsCheckout.TemplateOrderHistory = SiteData.Current.Cms.SitePath
    + "account.orderHistory.aspx";
cmsCheckout.TemplateShopping = SiteData.Current.Cms.SitePath
    + "Products";
```

Having looked through some key elements of the eCommerce implementation on the OnTrek site, you should now have some ideas about how to implement the functionality on your own site.

CUSTOM ORDER WORKFLOW

One of the huge strengths of the Ektron eCommerce package is the many extension points available in the infrastructure. One example of these points is the ability to create new order workflows from whole cloth. This section explores this process and shows a step-by-step process for building a new workflow engine.

The order workflow engine in the eCommerce feature is built around the Windows Workflow Foundation, which is Microsoft's framework for building complex workflow implementations. It allows developers to construct these workflow patterns by chaining together predefined pieces of functionality, called activities. These activities consist of anything from conditional blocks to custom code.

This section requires that you install CMS400 SDK to your system. Additionally, you must install the Visual Studio 2005 extensions for Windows Workflow Foundation if you are running Visual Studio 2005. Visual Studio 2008 already has this tool integrated. The Visual Studio 2005 extensions can be downloaded at:

```
http://www.microsoft.com/downloads/en/details
.aspx?FamilyId=5D61409E-1FA3-48CF-8023-E8F38E709BA6&displaylang=en
```

This section looks at Ektron's predefined activities, builds a new activity, and then builds a custom workflow that utilizes that activity. You will then incorporate the new workflow into OnTrek. The sections are as follows:

- Windows Workflow Foundation basics
- Creating a custom activity
- Building a workflow
- Using a custom workflow in an Ektron site

Windows Workflow Foundation Basics

The Windows Workflow Foundation is designed to be incorporated into a variety of applications, and to be the basic engine for providing workflow technology across Windows applications. It's built around handling both system and human workflows as well as both simple sequential workflows and complex state machine workflows that can handle outside events.

There are six major components used in the workflow engine.

- **Activity:** The basic unit of work. There is a list of basic activities provided as part of the toolbox, similar to the basic server controls provided to an ASP.NET developer. These activities are chained together, with the output of one activity being the input of the next activity. This allows for complex operations to take place.
- **Workflow:** The combination of many activities that implement a subset or the entirety of a business process.
- **Windows Workflow Foundation designer:** A tool integrated with Visual Studio. It allows you, as a developer, to construct a workflow to solve your business needs.
- **Windows Workflow Foundation base activity library:** This is analogous to the toolbox used in .NET development, containing basic chunks of capabilities that you can combine in novel ways to address your specific needs. They may not cover all the scenarios, which is why you are also able to build custom activities.
- **Windows Workflow Foundation runtime engine:** Provides the basic platform required to execute a workflow. This handles communication with the outside world, such as Web services and event mechanisms. This is, for the most part, invisible to the developer, just like the ASP.NET worker process.
- **Host process:** In this case, the Ektron Framework provides the supporting functionality required to manage the workflow. Functionality includes persisting workflow state, handling transactions, and any other capabilities the developers need to expose.

Most of these components can be safely shelved for now, so you can focus on the two most important parts — activities and workflows. Workflows, as mentioned, are made up of a series of activities. These activities generally take one of two forms: blocks that control the flow of events, and blocks that execute functionality. Table 13-9 contains some of the activities exposed as part of the base activity library:

TABLE 13-9: Activities Exposed as Part of the Base Activity Library

ACTIVITY	DESCRIPTION
`IfElse`	Conditionally switches the workflow between two or more paths, based on a custom rule.
`While`	Loops through one or more activities, checking a condition before each execution loop.
`Sequence`	Executes many activities, one at a time, waiting to start the next activity until the previous has completed.
`Parallel`	Branches the workflow into two separate processes, and ensures that both sides have completed execution before continuing to the next activity in the flow.
`Code`	Executes a piece of custom code.
`Listen`	Allows you to bind to an event, and begins running the activities attached to it when that event is raised.
`Delay`	Allows you to suspend execution of a workflow for a set amount of time.
`InvokeMethod`	Executes a method in the application.
`EventSink`	Acts as a target to be called from outside the workflow, but inside the application.
`InvokeWorkflow`	Begins execution on another workflow.
`InvokeWebService`	Calls a Web service method.
`Terminate`	Ends the current workflow.

Using these activities will allow you to build up the basis of your new workflow, but if you need to go beyond these basic abilities, it can sometimes be useful to build custom activities.

Creating a Custom Activity

Let's assume that you'll need to publish a new piece of content whenever an item is purchased from the store. You can follow these steps:

1. Start by opening Visual Studio and selecting File ➪ New ➪ Project.
2. Under Project Types, select Visual C# ➪ Workflow, and then under Templates, select Workflow Activity Library.
3. Name the project OnTrek.Activities and select OK. This takes you to the design view of the Activity1 activity, as shown in Figure 13-29.
4. Ensure that the name of your activity reflects what it does. In the Solution Explorer, right-click Activity1.cs, select Rename, and enter the new name **AddContentActivity**. This renames the file as well as the class contained in it.

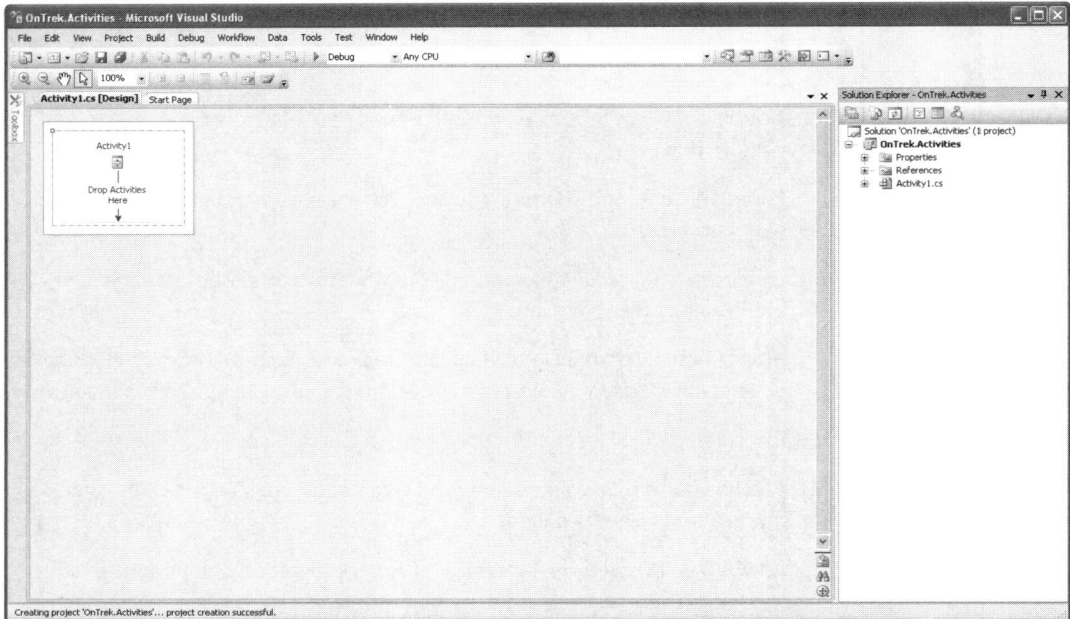

FIGURE 13-29

5. Update the code to add content. Right-click the file AddContentActivity.cs in the Solution Explorer, and select View Code.

6. Ensure that the class defined in the file inherits from System.Workflow.ComponentModel .Activity, as this is the base class for all activities in the workflow engine.

There are a few other skeletal items needed to define the activity as well.

7. The first piece of code to insert is the descriptors for the properties you will use. You first need to set up `DependencyPropertys` for each property, and register them with the workflow engine. This informs the engine which properties are available to be set from outside the activity so that the activity can perform its function. Once you have the `DependencyPropertys` defined, you create the actual properties, which retrieve and set the values via the base class. This section of code looks like the following snippet.

```
public static DependencyProperty ContentTitleProperty =
  DependencyProperty.Register("ContentTitle", typeof(string),
    typeof(AddContentActivity));
public static DependencyProperty FolderIdProperty =
  DependencyProperty.Register("FolderId", typeof(long),
    typeof(AddContentActivity));

public string ContentTitle
{
  get
  {
    return Convert.ToString(base.GetValue(ContentTitleProperty));
```

```
      }
      set
      {
        base.SetValue(ContentTitleProperty, value);
      }
    }

    public long FolderId
    {
      get
      {
        return Convert.ToInt64(base.GetValue(FolderIdProperty));
      }

      set
      {
        base.SetValue(FolderIdProperty, value);
      }
    }
```

8. Create a constructor that applies the name of the activity to the base class, as shown in the following snippet.

    ```
    public AddContentActivity()
    {
      base.Name = "AddContentToCMS";
    }
    ```

9. The final section is to actually execute the unit of work this activity handles, which is done by overriding the Execute method. To add the content, you need to get access to the Ektron DLLs, so right-click the OnTrek.Activities project in the Solution Explorer and select Add Reference. In the window that comes up, select the Browse tab, and browse to your site location, which is by default C:\Inetpub\wwwroot\OnTrek\bin. Select the files Ektron.Cms.ObjectFactory.dll, Ektron.Cms.BusinessApi.dll, Ektron.Cms.Common.dll, and Ektron.Cms.Framework.dll.

10. Click OK.

11. Once you have your references added, you can add the code that will add content to the site. This code looks like the following snippet.

    ```
    protected override ActivityExecutionStatus Execute(
       ActivityExecutionContext executionContext)
    {
      ActivityExecutionStatus status = ActivityExecutionStatus.Closed;

      try
      {
        Ektron.Cms.Framework.Core.Content.Content frameworkContentApi
          = new Ektron.Cms.Framework.Core.Content.Content(
              Ektron.Cms.Framework.ApiAccessMode.Admin);

        Ektron.Cms.ContentData newContent = new Ektron.Cms.ContentData();
        newContent.FolderId = FolderId;
    ```

```
            newContent.Html = "Product Purchased!";
            newContent.Title = ContentTitle;

            frameworkContentApi.Add(newContent);
        }
        catch (Exception ex)
        {
           status = ActivityExecutionStatus.Faulting;
        }
        return status;
    }
```

Putting all these elements together nets you a file that defines an activity that adds a piece of content to the CMS. You can now use this activity in any workflow. The complete file is reproduced in Listing 13-7.

LISTING 13-7: AddContentActivity.cs

Available for
download on
Wrox.com

```
using System;
using System.ComponentModel;
using System.ComponentModel.Design;
using System.Collections;
using System.Drawing;
using System.Linq;
using System.Workflow.ComponentModel.Compiler;
using System.Workflow.ComponentModel.Serialization;
using System.Workflow.ComponentModel;
using System.Workflow.ComponentModel.Design;
using System.Workflow.Runtime;
using System.Workflow.Activities;
using System.Workflow.Activities.Rules;

namespace OnTrek.Activities
{
  public partial class AddContentActivity : System.Workflow.ComponentModel.Activity
  {
    public static DependencyProperty ContentTitleProperty =
      DependencyProperty.Register("ContentTitle", typeof(string),
        typeof(AddContentActivity));
    public static DependencyProperty FolderIdProperty =
      DependencyProperty.Register("FolderId", typeof(long),
        typeof(AddContentActivity));

    public string ContentTitle
    {
      get
      {
        return Convert.ToString(base.GetValue(ContentTitleProperty));
      }
      set
      {
        base.SetValue(ContentTitleProperty, value);
      }
```

```csharp
    }

    public long FolderId
    {
      get
      {
        return Convert.ToInt64(base.GetValue(FolderIdProperty));
      }
      set
      {
        base.SetValue(FolderIdProperty, value);
      }
    }


    protected override ActivityExecutionStatus Execute(
        ActivityExecutionContext executionContext)
    {
      ActivityExecutionStatus status = ActivityExecutionStatus.Closed;

      try
      {
        Ektron.Cms.Framework.Core.Content.Content frameworkContentApi
          = new Ektron.Cms.Framework.Core.Content.Content(
              Ektron.Cms.Framework.ApiAccessMode.Admin);

        Ektron.Cms.ContentData newContent = new Ektron.Cms.ContentData();
        newContent.FolderId = FolderId;
        newContent.Html = "Product Purchased!";
        newContent.Title = ContentTitle;

        frameworkContentApi.Add(newContent);
      }
      catch (Exception ex)
      {
        status = ActivityExecutionStatus.Faulting;
      }
      return status;
    }
  }
}
```

Building a Workflow

With your newly created activity, you are now ready to create a complete workflow to handle orders as they come in. Rather than build the workflow from scratch, in this example you will use the stock Ektron workflow and add your element to it. To do so, follow these steps:

1. In the Solution Explorer, right-click the OnTrek.Activities Solution and select Add ⇨ New Project.

2. Select Visual C#⇨ Workflow under Project types, and under templates select Ektron Ordering Sequential Workflow.

If the Ektron Ordering Sequential Workflow template does not appear in your Add Project window, make sure to copy the "Ektron Ordering Sequential Flow .zip" file from C:\Program File\Ektron\CMS400SDK\Commerce\Workflow\ Templates\VS2008 to C:\Documents and Settings\~user name~\My Documents\ Visual Studio 2008\Templates\ProjectTemplates\Visual C#\Workflow.

3. Name the project OnTrekWorkflow and select OK. This creates a workflow project with the default Ektron workflow in it.

4. Double-click the Workflow1.cs file, and you are presented with the design view of the workflow, as shown in Figure 13-30.

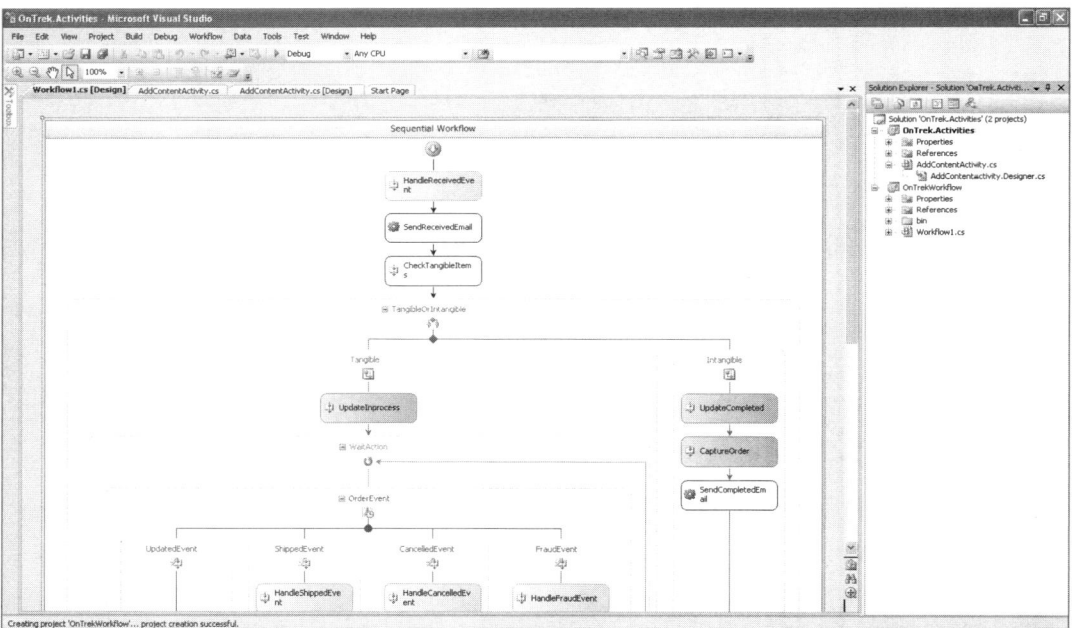

FIGURE 13-30

5. Open the toolbox, and you are presented with a list of activities that can be used in the workflow. The existing workflow also has a whole list of activities used, beginning with `HandleReceivedEvent`, which responds to an order event, and moving through a decision tree based on whether the order is Tangible or Intangible, and so on.

Ektron also provides a series of activities, which you can add to the toolbox

1. Right-click inside the toolbox and select Choose Items.

2. In the dialog box that comes up, under .NET Framework Components, select Browse, and browse to your bin folder of your site, by default at C:\inetpub\wwwroot\OnTrek\ bin. Select the Ektron.Workflow.dll file.

3. You are returned to the Choose Toolbox Items display, where you should click OK.

This process adds the activities, shown in Table 13-10, to your toolbox:

TABLE 13-10: Activities that the Workflow Process Adds to the Toolbox

ACTIVITY	DESCRIPTION
AdvancedEmailActivity	Sends a specified type of e-mail for the current order.
BasicEmailActivity	Sends a generic e-mail.
CaptureOrderActivity	Submits the order information to the payment gateway.
CheckDelayedPaymentTypeActivity	Checks whether the payment type is a delayed payment, such as a check.
CheckStockActivity	Checks whether the item is in stock.
CheckTangibleItemsActivity	Checks whether the item is a tangible item that needs to be shipped or is a virtual item such as an article or download.
MakePaymentSettledActivity	Updates the order to be settled.
OrderCancelledEventActivity	Triggers when an order is cancelled.
OrderCapturedEventActivity	Triggers when an order is captured.
OrderFraudEventActivity	Triggers when an order is marked as fraudulent.
OrderProcessedEventActivity	Triggers when an order is being processed.
OrderReceivedEventActivity	Triggers when an order is marked received.
OrderShippedEventActivity	Triggers when an order is marked shipped.
OrderUpdatedEventActivity	Triggers when an order is updated.
UpdateOrderActivity	Updates the order records.

6. Add your custom-built add content activity to the workflow after the SendReceivedEmail activity. First you need to add the activity to the toolbox. Because the project is in the same solution, simply right-click the OnTrek.Activities project in the Solution Explorer, and select Build. This should add the AddContentActivity item to your toolbox, as shown in Figure 13-31.

7. Return to the Workflow1.cs file if you don't already have it up, and drag the AddContentActivity onto the green arrow between the SendReceivedEmail and CheckTangibleItems activities at the top of the workflow. Your workflow is updated, as shown in Figure 13-32.

8. Set the FolderId property to 0, and the ContentTitle property to "Activity" on the AddContentActivity in the Properties pane, and the workflow is done.

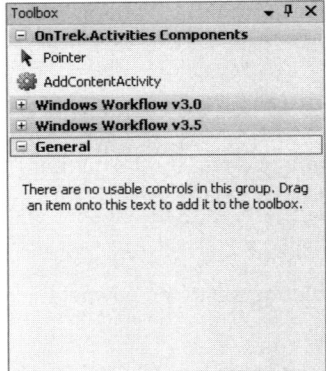

FIGURE 13-31

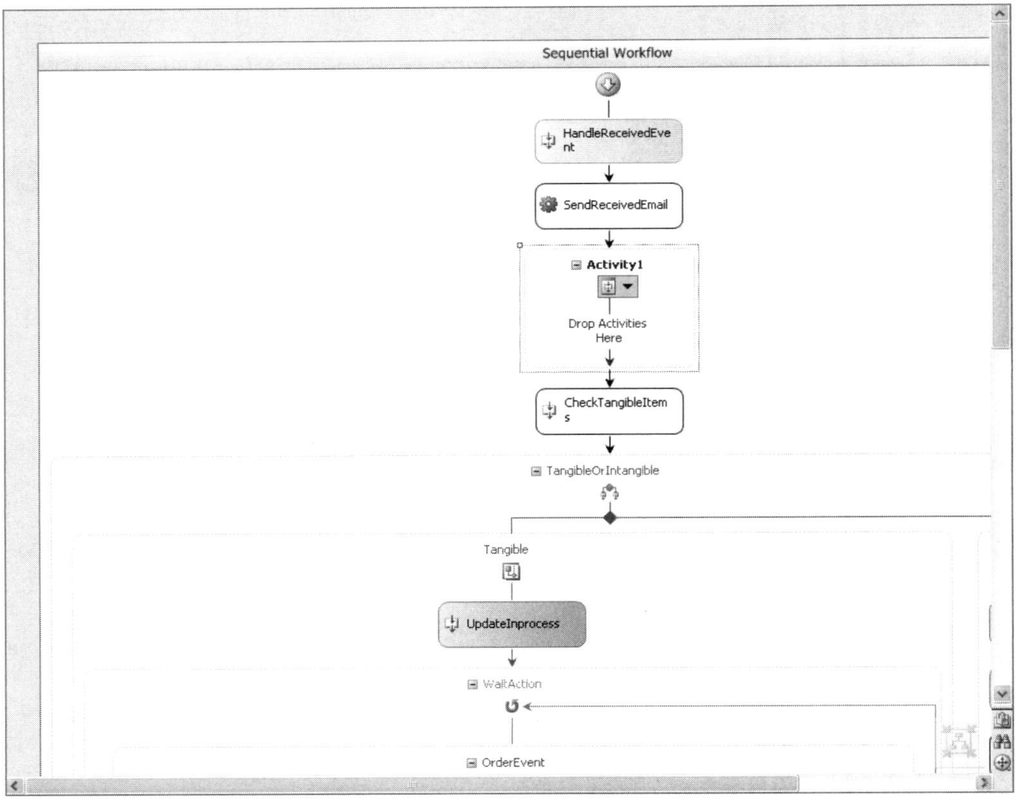

FIGURE 13-32

Using a Custom Workflow in an Ektron Site

Now that the workflow has been created, you need to build it, and then configure the site to use it rather than the pre-built workflow. To do so, follow these steps:

1. Right-click the workflow in the Solution Explorer, and select Build. This constructs the DLL containing the new workflow.

2. Copy the DLL you just built into the bin directory of the website by opening the project directory for your workflow in Windows Explorer and browsing down two levels into bin/debug or bin/release (depending on what your target was during the build process). In that folder, you will find a workflow DLL corresponding to your project. Copy this file into your site bin directory, which is at C:\inetpub\wwwroot\ontrek\bin by default.

3. Launch the Workarea for the site logged in as the admin user. In the Workarea, browse to Settings ➪ Commerce ➪ Fulfillment ➪ Order Workflow, and you will be taken to the Order Workflow pane. This pane contains a dropdown that's dynamically loaded from all the available workflows. You should see your new workflow in the dropdown, as shown in Figure 13-33.

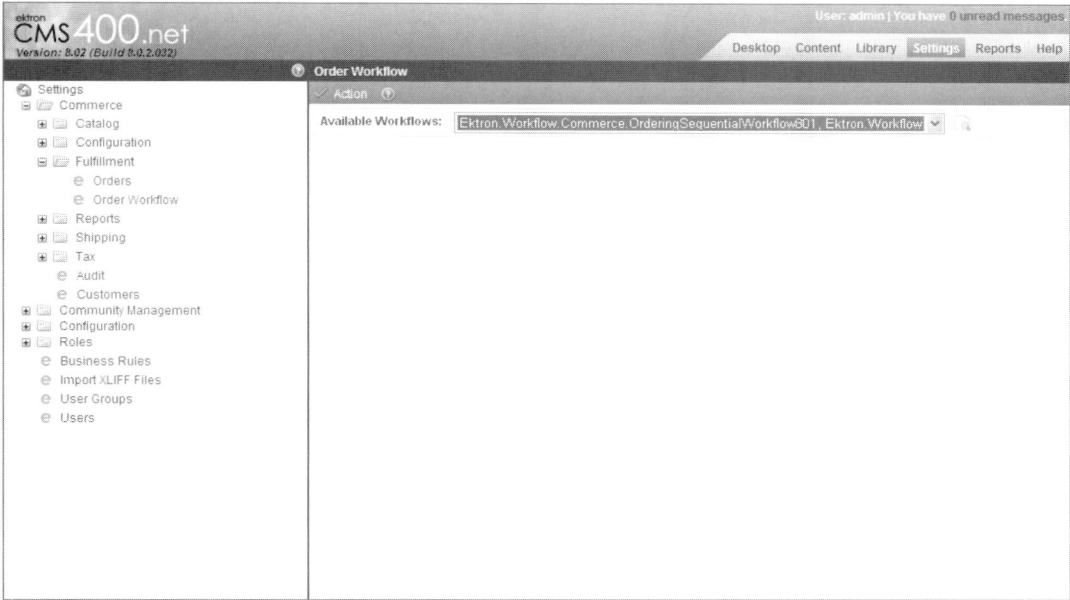

FIGURE 13-33

4. Select your new workflow, and then select Action ➪ Save. By default, your new workflow will be used rather than any of the existing workflows.

> If your workflow is not showing up in the dropdown, you may need to update the references to the Ektron DLL's in your workflow project. Delete the existing references and add references to the same DLL's in your site bin directory. Once the workflow has been installed, you can click the magnifying glass next to the dropdown to see a visual representation of the workflow, as shown in Figure 13-34.

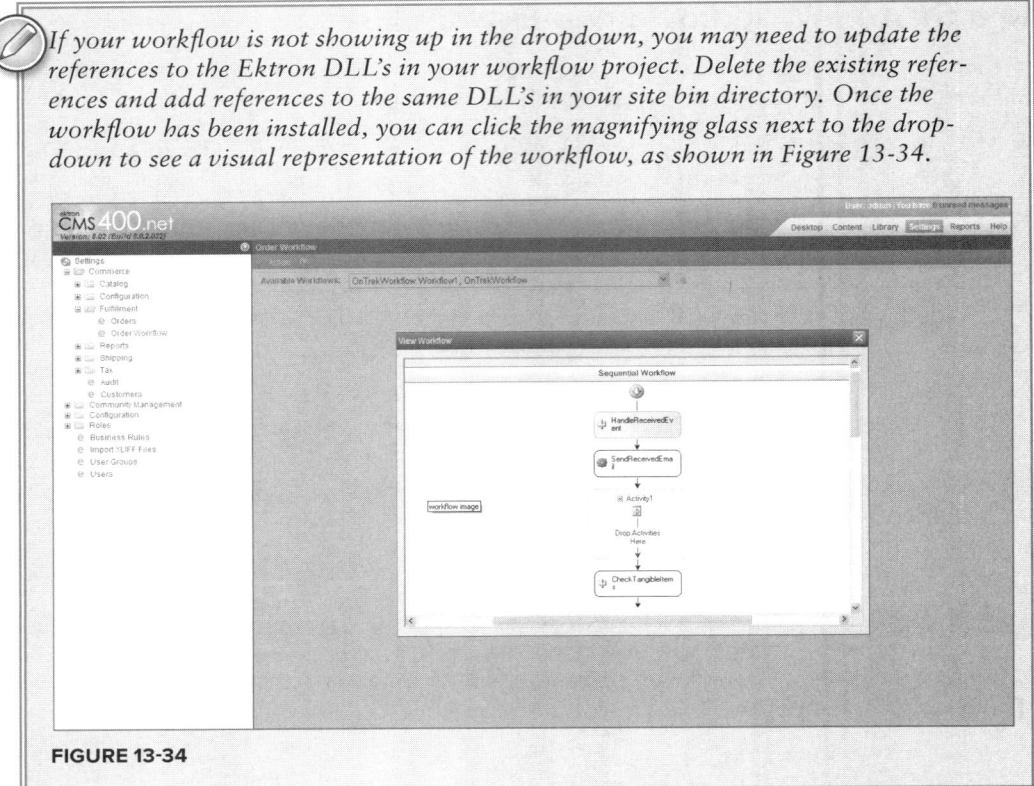

FIGURE 13-34

BUILDING A PAYMENT GATEWAY PROVIDER

Like order workflows, the ability to create custom payment gateways is a powerful way of customizing your eCommerce installation. While the Ektron eCommerce feature set ships with two prebuilt gateways, one for PayFlow, and one for Authorize.net, there are many other gateway providers out there, and if you already have an eCommerce setup that you are rebuilding using the Ektron Framework, it is quite possible you're using a gateway that is unsupported out-of-the-box.

In this section, you'll create a gateway provider that doesn't actually connect to anywhere or authorize anything, but it provides a starting example for how to connect to an external gateway. In this section you will:

➤ Learn about payment gateways.

➤ Create a gateway provider.

➤ Install the gateway provider into the OnTrek website.

Brief Overview of Payment Gateways

A payment gateway is typically a Web service of some type that authorizes payments in real time for eCommerce websites. It performs an action that is the same as that performed by credit card readers at physical stores, collecting the details about the payment type, authorizing the charge, and then performing the actual exchange of funds.

Payment gateways differ in the way they operate depending on the type of payment, but as an example, for most credit card gateways, the order of operations to complete a charge is as follows:

1. The customer places the order on the website.
2. The website passes the payment information to the payment gateway.
3. The payment gateway passes the information to the payment processor.
4. The payment processor passes the information to the credit card association (Visa or MasterCard).
5. The credit card association passes the information to the bank servicing the card.
6. The bank approves or declines the transaction, and sends the result back to the association.
7. The association passes the result to the payment processor.
8. The payment processor passes the result to the payment gateway.
9. The payment gateway passes the result to the website.

The transaction of funds then takes place separately, with batch processing of the various transactions that have taken place.

In the Ektron implementation, the details on how to connect to the payment gateway from the website is all contained within a payment gateway provider, which is what you will be building in this section.

As an example of the type of transaction that takes place between the payment gateway provider and the payment gateway, for Authorize.Net, the data in Table 13-11 is posted to the Web service URL `https://test.authorize.net/gateway/transact.dll`.

TABLE 13-11: Authorize.Net Sample Post Data

POST FIELD	EXAMPLE DATA	DESCRIPTION
x_login	API_LOGIN_ID	The login for your authorize.net account.
x_tran_key	TRANSACTION_KEY	The transaction key for your authorize.net account.
x_delim_data	TRUE	Specifies whether the response should be delimited.
x_delim_char			The delimiter character to use for the response.

continues

TABLE 13-11 *(continued)*

POST FIELD	EXAMPLE DATA	DESCRIPTION
x_relay_response	FALSE	Routes the result to your Web server using an out-of-band connection.
x_type	AUTH_CAPTURE	The type of card transaction.
x_method	CC	The method of payment.
x_card_num	4111111111111111	The credit card number.
x_exp_date	0115	The expiration date of the card.
x_amount	19.99	The transaction amount.
x_description	Sample Transaction	A description of the transaction.
x_first_name	John	First name of the customer.
x_last_name	Doe	Last name of the customer.
x_address	1234 Street	Address of the customer.
x_state	WA	State of the customer.
x_zip	95004	ZIP code of the customer.

Each gateway has a different set of requirements for the data to be sent, and has differing methods of attaching that data to the request, but the general formula is very similar from gateway to gateway.

Creating a Gateway Provider

The gateway providers the Ektron Framework ships with are open source. The source for them is installed at C:\Program Files\Ektron\CMS400SDK\Commerce\Providers\Commerce.Providers\PaymentGateways by default, and they can be used as a launching point for new provider implementations.

Creating a New Provider from Scratch

In this case, you will create a new provider from scratch, by following these steps:

1. Open Visual Studio and go to File ➪ New ➪ Project.
2. In the New Project window, select C# under Project Types, and select Class Library under templates.
3. Name the project **OnTrek.Commerce.Provider** and select OK.
4. Once the project comes up, you must first add a reference to the provider base class DLL, so right-click the project in the Solution Explorer and select Add Reference.

5. In the resulting window, switch to the Browse tab, and navigate to your website's bin directory, which is at C:\Inetpub\wwwroot\ontrek\bin by default.
6. Select the files Ektron.Cms.Commerce.dll, Ektron.Cms.Common.dll, Ektron.Cms.ObjectFactory.dll, Ektron.Cms.Instrumentation.dll, and System.Configuration.dll and select OK.
7. Now that you have your references set up, you need to rename your class to something more suitable than Class1. Right-click Class1.cs in the Solution Explorer and select Rename. Rename the class to **SamplePaymentGatewayProvider.cs**, and when Visual Studio asks if you'd like to update the references, select OK.
8. The final step in this initial portion of the process is to set the provider to inherit from the class Ektron.Cms.Commerce.PaymentGatewayProvider. Once you have set the inheritance, right-click the PaymentGatewayProvider class name and select Implement Abstract Class. Your code should now look like the following code snippet.

```
using System;
using System.Collections.Generic;
using System.Linq;
using System.Text;

namespace Ontrek.Commerce.Provider
{
  public class SamplePaymentGatewayProvider:
      Ektron.Cms.Commerce.PaymentGatewayProvider
  {
    public override string Authorize()
    {
      throw new NotImplementedException();
    }

    public override string AuthorizeAndCapture()
    {
      throw new NotImplementedException();
    }

    public override string CapturePreauthorization(string transactionId)
    {
      throw new NotImplementedException();
    }

    public override string VoidPreAuthorization(string transactionId)
    {
      throw new NotImplementedException();
    }
  }
}
```

Implementing the abstract method creates four methods that you can customize in order to support transaction management through the gateway. These methods and their purposes are outlined here:

➤ **Authorize()**: Preauthorizes a transaction — in other words, ensures that payment can be collected at a later date. This simply checks to make sure the funds are available.

➤ **AuthorizeAndCapture()**: Combines the authorization and capture of funds into one step. When a payment is captured, the funds are removed from the account holder.

➤ **CapturePreauthorization()**: Allows you to capture payment on a transaction that was previously preauthorized.

➤ **VoidPreAuthorization()**: Cancels a preauthorization hold on an account, thus cancelling the transaction altogether.

As each method is called, the base class exposes several fields containing information about the current transaction. A subset of these fields is listed in Table 13-12.

TABLE 13-12: Fields in the PaymentGatewayProvider Class

FIELD	DESCRIPTION
Amount	Amount for the transaction.
Authorization	Contains the details about the authorization.
Basket	Contains information about the basket for the current order.
BillingAddress	The billing address for this order.
CurrencyId	The currency used for the order.
CustomerId	The ID of the current user.
IsSubmissionSuccess	Flag indicating whether the submission was successful.
Order	All the information about the current order.
OrderId	The ID of the current order.
PaymentMethod	The payment method selected.
SubmissionError	Description for when there is an error submitting.
SupportsCheckPayments	Flag to indicate whether this gateway supports checks.
SupportsCreditCardPayments	Flag to indicate whether this gateway supports credit cards.
SupportsRecurringPayments	Flag to indicate whether this gateway supports recurring payments.

Each method implemented in the provider would normally connect with an external gateway, and then update a set of fields in these objects. In this example, you will skip the first step of connecting externally. The following sections list the updated code for each method, and then walk through what the method achieves.

The Authorize Method

The Authorize method is shown in the following code snippet.

```csharp
public override string Authorize()
{
  if (PaymentMethod.GetType() != typeof(Ektron.Cms.Commerce.CreditCardPayment))
  {
    throw new Ektron.Cms.Commerce.Exceptions.AuthorizationException(
      "Invalid Payment Type");
  }
  Ektron.Cms.Commerce.CreditCardPayment creditCard =
    (Ektron.Cms.Commerce.CreditCardPayment)this.PaymentMethod;
  if (creditCard.ExpirationDate.IsExpired())
  {
    throw new Ektron.Cms.Commerce.Exceptions.Payment.CreditCard
      .CardExpiredException(
      "Card Is Expired");
  }
  IsSubmissionSuccess = true;
  Authorization.AuthorizedOn = DateTime.Now;
  Authorization.TransactionId = new Guid().ToString();
  return Authorization.TransactionId;
}
```

This code does the following:

➤ It ensures that the payment type is a credit card.

➤ Once the payment type is confirmed, it casts the payment method information into a credit card payment, and checks if the card has been expired.

➤ It updates the submission success flag and saves the authorization information. In a real gateway provider, you would connect to the gateway after the expiration check and potentially a few other basic sanity checks, and actually collect the information of whether the transaction was successful, and store the actual details.

The AuthorizeAndCapture Method

The next method, AuthorizeAndCapture, is similarly simple. It is listed in the following snippet.

```csharp
public override string AuthorizeAndCapture()
{
  IsSubmissionSuccess = true;
  Authorization.AuthorizedOn = DateTime.Now;
  Authorization.CapturedOn = DateTime.Now;
  Authorization.TransactionId = new Guid().ToString();
  return Authorization.TransactionId;
}
```

Just like authorize, you skip the actual communication piece, and instead directly update the transaction with some made up information. This is the information required to move the payment forward in the system, however. CapturePreauthorization and VoidPreAuthorization are also straightforward, merely updating the details locally. When you combine the whole file, you get Listing 13-8.

Available for download on Wrox.com

LISTING 13-8: SamplePaymentGatewayProvider.cs

```csharp
using System;
using System.Collections.Generic;
using System.Linq;
using System.Text;

namespace Ontrek.Commerce.Provider
{
  public class SamplePaymentGatewayProvider :
      Ektron.Cms.Commerce.PaymentGatewayProvider
  {
    public override string Authorize()
    {
      if (PaymentMethod.GetType() != typeof(Ektron.Cms.Commerce.CreditCardPayment))
      {
        throw new Ektron.Cms.Commerce.Exceptions.AuthorizationException(
          "Invalid Payment Type");
      }
      Ektron.Cms.Commerce.CreditCardPayment creditCard =
        (Ektron.Cms.Commerce.CreditCardPayment)this.PaymentMethod;
      if (creditCard.ExpirationDate.IsExpired())
      {
        throw new
          Ektron.Cms.Commerce.Exceptions.Payment.CreditCard.CardExpiredException(
          "Card Is Expired");
      }
      IsSubmissionSuccess = true;
      Authorization.AuthorizedOn = DateTime.Now;
      Authorization.TransactionId = new Guid().ToString();
      return Authorization.TransactionId;
    }

    public override string AuthorizeAndCapture()
    {
      IsSubmissionSuccess = true;
      Authorization.AuthorizedOn = DateTime.Now;
      Authorization.CapturedOn = DateTime.Now;
      Authorization.TransactionId = new Guid().ToString();
      return Authorization.TransactionId;
    }

    public override string CapturePreauthorization(string transactionId)
    {
      IsSubmissionSuccess = true;
      Authorization.CapturedOn = DateTime.Now;
      return Authorization.TransactionId;
    }

    public override string VoidPreAuthorization(string transactionId)
    {
      IsSubmissionSuccess = true;
      Authorization.VoidedOn = DateTime.Now;
      return Authorization.TransactionId;
    }
  }
}
```

Installing the Gateway Provider into the OnTrek Website

Now that you have your provider built out, you need to install it to the site. You can do so by following these steps:

1. Right-click the OnTrek.Commerce.Provider project in the Solution Explorer and selecting Build.

2. Once the build has completed, navigate to the bin folder in Windows Explorer and copy the OnTrek.Commerce.Provider.dll file into your site bin directory, normally at C:\inetpub\wwwroot\ontrek\bin.

3. Register the provider in the web.config for your site. Open the web.config, and navigate to the EktronPaymentGateway section. First add a new key under the provider's tag with the name SamplePaymentGatewayProvider, and the type Ontrek.Commerce.Provider.SamplePaymentGatewayProvider. Then update the defaultProvider attribute on the EktronPaymentGateway tag to reflect the name of the new provider, in this case SamplePaymentGatewayProvider. The section should now look like the following code snippet.

```
<EktronPaymentGateway defaultProvider="SamplePaymentGatewayProvider">
  <providers>
    <add name="Manual"
      type="Ektron.Cms.Commerce.Providers.Payment.ManualPayment" />
    <add name="PayFlow"
      type="Ektron.Cms.Commerce.Providers.Payment.PayFlowPayment" />
    <add name="AuthorizeNet"
      type="Ektron.Cms.Commerce.Providers.Payment.AuthorizeNetPayment" />
    <add name="PayPal"
      type="Ektron.Cms.Commerce.Providers.Payment.PayPalGateway"
      AuthValuesEncrypted="false" PayPalUser=""
      PayPalPwd="" PayPalSignature=""
      CheckoutUrl="https://www.sandbox.paypal.com/cgi-bin/webscr"
      CheckoutTestUrl="https://www.sandbox.paypal.com/cgi-bin/webscr"
      NVPUrl="https://api-3t.sandbox.paypal.com/nvp"
      NVPTestUrl="https://api-3t.sandbox.paypal.com/nvp"
      PayPalVersion="53.0"
      apiparamHDRIMG="https://ektron.com/images/homepage-logo-small.jpg" />
    <add name="SagePay"
      type="Ektron.Cms.Commerce.Providers.Payment.SagePayGateway"
      SagePayVersion="2.23" SimulatorMode="false"
      Description="Ektron CMS Order" />
    <add name="PayFlowWebSitePaymentsPro"
   type="Ektron.Cms.Commerce.Providers.Payment.PayFlowWebSitePaymentsProPayment"
      />
    <add name="SamplePaymentGatewayProvider"
      type="Ontrek.Commerce.Provider.SamplePaymentGatewayProvider" />
  </providers>
</EktronPaymentGateway>
```

4. Save the web.config file and open the Workarea.

5. In the Workarea, navigate to Settings ➪ Commerce ➪ Configuration ➪ Payment Options.

6. In the Payment Options pane, select New ➪ Payment Gateway.
7. From the New Payment Gateway screen, select SamplePaymentGatewayProvider, and check the Cards checkbox, then click Save.

Your site will now use the custom provider you just created.

TAKE HOME POINTS

This chapter was devoted to gaining a deeper understanding of the developer experience surrounding the eCommerce feature set. Continuing on the education path started in the last chapter, which covered Workarea-based configuration and product management exercises, this chapter focused on how to implement the front-end user experience necessary to allow customers to hand you their money. Discussions included:

- The controls that allow users to browse to specific products and gather information about them:
  - CurrencySelect Server Control
  - ProductSearch Server Control
  - ProductList Server Control
  - Product Server Control
  - Recommendation Server Control
- The controls that manipulate the actual purchasing experience:
  - MyAccount Server Control
  - OrderList Server Control
  - Cart Server Control
  - Checkout Server Control
- Implementing a full eCommerce experience using the server controls, specifically the model followed by the OnTrek team.
- Creating a custom order workflow, built on the Windows Workflow Foundation. You also learned about creating custom activities, and how to install your completed order workflow.
- Creating a custom payment gateway, allowing you more flexibility in choosing your merchant account provider.

The combination of development exercises covered in this chapter should give you the confidence needed to address whatever business needs your company presents you with when it comes to eCommerce implementations.

PART III
Deploying the TechPoint Site

- **CHAPTER 14:** Deploying Your Website
- **CHAPTER 15:** Maintaining Your Website
- **CHAPTER 16:** Next Steps

14

Deploying Your Website

- ➤ How do you meet the pre-conditions for a successful deployment?
- ➤ What are the different deployment scenarios?
- ➤ What are the final stages of deployment?

It's late at night. Project managers, developers, and QA engineers are pacing around in nervous anticipation with little to do besides hover and wait. There's a feeling of excitement tinged with anxiety. In the end, it boils down to a few final clicks of a mouse and the words "it's live" and everyone holds their breath to see what happens next...

Does the website launch succeed? Does it fail? Success and failure are usually determined by one factor — preparation. What sort of preparation was done leading up to the launch? Oftentimes the answer is, unfortunately, very little. Too frequently engineers, managers, and operations folk pour blood, sweat, and tears into the development and testing of a website only to have it fall apart during the "final push" into the production environment. If you've been involved with any number of Web deployments, it's a safe bet to say you've experienced this at some level at some point in time.

A number of the problems that are commonly experienced during Web deployments stem from the misconception that there is a single "silver bullet" deployment configuration applicable to most every organization, and even worse, that this "silver bullet" configuration can be deployed, at the push of a button, at the bottom of the ninth inning. To understand why there is no single applicable configuration, let's start by asking just three of the many questions that you need to think through during deployment planning:

- ➤ How does content flow through your website's production environment?
- ➤ What are the performance requirements for the site?
- ➤ What is the budget for hardware?

As you can imagine, every organization will have different answers for these questions. As such, there are many production configurations possible, but this is often forgotten when it comes time to move the website from development into its home in the production environment.

So what can be done to ensure a successful deployment? The good news is, there's quite a bit that can and must be done. This chapter defines what is needed to ensure your website has a successful deployment into a live production environment and will help to replace the jitters surrounding your release with a confident excitement.

PRE-CONDITIONS FOR A SUCCESSFUL DEPLOYMENT

This section covers everything that you need to consider and complete before deployment can begin. In other books you might find the term "pre-deployment" used, but this is not a preferred label because it gives the impression that there is a dedicated "pre-deployment" phase where all these items are completed. In fact, there is no such phase. Instead, we favor the phrase "pre-conditions" for deployment because it implies that there are tasks that are hard prerequisites for a successful deployment, without implying that there's a dedicated time for completing them

These pre-conditions are items that must be considered and occur well before deployment — during discovery, development, and testing. Chances are, the later these items are considered, the greater the chance that something will be overlooked or neglected due to time constraints. The goal of formulating this into a list is to help you start thinking of these items well before the actual talk of deployment begins. Read through each of the following sections and their corresponding bullet points and be careful not to make assumptions about what's included. There are valuable tips that were tough lessons learned by someone else.

Creating the Discovery Collateral

The discovery process is an extremely important part of the overall website delivery process, as it is the period where requirements are gathered, defined, documented, and shared with members of the project team. From a deployment standpoint, this process is important because these collateral documents are pivotal for each of the subsequent development phases, and in particular, for the Final User Acceptance Testing phase (Final UAT).

Final UAT is the period in which the key stakeholders and end users are given an opportunity to verify first hand that the website meets their expectations as expressed in the requirements documents. Having a well-written set of requirements makes the process of Final UAT much more effective and gives everyone a common reference point when questions and potential disagreements arise around expected behavior.

In addition to Final UAT, the requirements documents also include the performance expectations of the site, which details how many site visitors will be expected to use the site over time, page load time expectations, and availability expectations. This information is critical to have in order to perform effective load testing that proves the website can sustain these expected loads.

Call to action:

- ➤ I have written requirements that capture the expected behavior of the website.
- ➤ I have written requirements that capture the website's performance requirements.

Completion of the Development Process

The development process is a phase during which the requirements are implemented and functional testing is performed. Saying this is a pre-condition for deployment might sound obvious, however, we have seen many situations where people begin the process of deployment while changes are still being made to the codebase. To "save time," some project managers or team leads succumb to the false idea of performing development and deployment-related activities in parallel. The problem this has on deployment is simple — without having finalized code in place, one of the most critical components of the deployment process, namely the source code, is a moving target as you're trying to install it. Trying to deploy an incomplete codebase inevitably leads to patches being pushed, servers being upgraded, and source code and software versions being out of sync across servers in the deployment. There will be a number of moving parts during the deployment process — but the source code should not be among them.

Another situation that underscores the importance of finishing development before starting the deployment process is the case in which well-intentioned network and operations folks, eager to prepare for deployment, begin the process of installing the pre-requisite software components onto the production hardware and configure it many weeks or months in advance of code completion. This might sound like a good idea; why not get a good head start?

The problem this presents, however, is that the actual version of the components used in development may end up changing during the development process, which could result in the need to upgrade, re-install, or re-configure the software components in the production environment. For example, imagine that the developers are building on version 8.0.1 at the start of the project. The Net Ops folks might reasonably assume that version 8.0.1 is what will be deployed, so they install the same base software configuration in production in anticipation of the eventual release.

However, developers continue to upgrade their environments with incremental updates during the development process, so by the time the release makes its way to production, its base version is out of sync with the software previously installed. This means that the production environment needs to be upgraded and reconfigured. It's best to wait until the software version is locked and configuration options have been finalized.

Call to action:

➤ I have verified that the website source code is code-complete.

➤ I have determined the version of the software.

➤ I have ensured the source code is managed through a source control system, such as Subversion (SVN) or Perforce.

➤ I have a permanent development environment established for making code-level changes to the website.

Creating the Staging Environment

A staging environment is an important part of the overall deployment architecture. In some cases, organizations choose to use a staging environment to approve content changes or other modifications to the website such as changes to graphic design, look and feel, or code files. In environments such as these, code changes are made in a local development environment and then propagated to the staged environment. Content changes are made in the staged environment as it serves as an internal replica of the website deployed in the production environment.

However, even in cases in which the organization's final deployment scenario does not include an "official" staging environment used as described here (that is, to approve content or code modifications), an internal staging environment is important to have for other reasons.

One important reason is that a staged environment that mirrors the production environment can be used in the event a problem arises in production that requires troubleshooting. Consider a scenario in which your organization has no formal staging server after your website is deployed. A few months after a successful launch, you're starting to notice some type of unexpected behavior on the website — let's say that an error is occasionally displaying and you need some assistance in troubleshooting and diagnosing the issue, so you give a call to Ektron support.

Without being able to access a staged environment, Ektron Support may request a copy of your production database, its code templates or error log, and then take all of this and re-build a staged environment on Ektron's support servers. All of this can take hours or even days, which may add unnecessary lag time in critical situations where each hour feels like an eternity. You can mitigate this possibility by keeping an internal staged server in sync with your production environment. In such a scenario, the support department could perform a good number of troubleshooting steps on the staged server and potentially resolve the issue without needing to create a replicated environment. If possible, the hardware of the server hosting the staging environment should mirror the hardware of a machine in the production environment. Similar machines allow for more accurate diagnosis and troubleshooting and also provide a good environment for stress and load testing before the website is put into the final production environment.

Call to action:

➤ I have a staged environment on an internal server that contains the final source code and final versions of software components.

➤ I have a staged environment that mirrors the performance of a machine in my production environment.

Content Is in a Staged Environment

Final User Acceptance Testing occurs in the staged environment, and in order for it to be truly effective, the website needs to be filled with real-world content. How many times have you seen other developers test with "asdf" finger-rolls as input to textboxes or use single letter characters for first names and last names, failing to observe how the application behaves with real content?

Content migration must happen before deployment so that User Acceptance Testing efforts are not wasted testing the website without actual data. Additionally, performance and load testing results are more meaningful when the website has a realistic volume of content. Lastly, because the deployment process ultimately leads to customers, employees, and prospects visiting your website, you need to make sure approved content is available, loaded, and ready to go once the final push to production occurs.

There are two ways Ektron recommends migrating content into Ektron from an external repository:

- Using the Ektron content and metadata APIs
- Manually entering content using the Workarea user interface

Using the Ektron APIs, you can create applications that write and import content into the staging environment. When doing so, you must consider how the metadata associated with existing content items map to the metadata available in Ektron, create the associated metadata types, and import both the content and the associated metadata. Likewise, it's important to consider permission, workflow, folder hierarchies, and all the related items surrounding content.

In cases where you're working with a system that does not work with a CMS or RDBMS (such as a site build using static HTML files or content hard coded into ASPX templates), you can use scraping scripts to pull content from the site and then use the Ektron APIs to import that content into the system. Alternatively, if the volume of content is somewhat small, it might be easier to manually import the content. There are many companies that offer manual content migration services at hourly rates.

Call to action:

- I have verified that the content has been approved by the editorial team.
- I have verified that the final content has been migrated into the staged environment.

Completion of System Testing

For someone unfamiliar with the testing process, the idea that there are several distinct types of testing can sometimes come as a surprise. These tests include:

- Functional testing
- Final User Acceptance testing
- Performance testing
- Load testing
- Stress testing
- Security testing

Ensuring that everyone on the project is aware of the various types of testing and their importance can be as important as the tests themselves, because without this awareness, some choose to artificially meet deadlines by removing or short-changing the testing process.

Functional Testing

This type of testing is performed by a developer and QA engineer during the development process. Developers need to test their code according to the use cases and functional requirements as defined during the discovery process. Ektron encourages its developers to perform what is called "pair testing" during the development process, which consists of a developer and a QA engineer sitting side-by-side testing the software to ensure it properly implements the use cases by performing black box testing and negative testing, among other tests. Having a QA Engineer sit down and work with a developer helps the developer to gain or improve their knowledge of software testing, and gives the QA engineer a better understanding of how the application functions and was built. The ultimate purpose of developer level functional testing is to catch the obvious bugs. Nothing slows down final User Acceptance Testing and weakens confidence in the website like the repeated discovery of obvious defects.

Final User Acceptance Testing

Once the staged environment has been properly set up, filled with final content, and has seen its source code go through functional testing, it is time to perform Final User Acceptance Testing with the key stakeholders and site users on a staged machine in a controlled test environment. The purpose of this is to make sure that each member of the testing team has the ability to voice any concerns and have them cross checked with the requirements documents as a sanity check. The ultimate goal is to give the team confidence that the site meets the overall project objectives and, in the event that there are last-minute issues or concerns, they are addressed before the deployment of the website.

Many studies have shown that the cost of finding a defect increases by orders of magnitude the later it is found in the website development pipeline. If a defect is found and fixed while the website is in development, the fix involves a single person (the developer). If the defect is found in QA and fixed by a developer, it involves two people. If it is found in the field by a customer, reported by a technical support engineer, fixed by a developer, and verified by a QA engineer, it involves (at least) four people. This model obviously doesn't take into account the negative financial effects that defects can have, due to the loss of an existing or potential customer. Suffice it to say the earlier in the chain that defects are found; the less costly they are to fix.

Call to action:

➤ I have gone through the process of Final User Acceptance Testing with my stakeholders and key website end users.

Performance Testing

Some developers use the terms performance testing, load testing, and stress testing interchangeably. However, because there are important and significant differences among them, this chapter discusses each and highlights why they should be covered. The goal of performance testing is to identify and eliminate bottlenecks during the development and testing process. This is not to test how the site performs under any real-world type of load — that is covered during load and stress testing. Instead, performance testing is about identifying potential bottlenecks in an application, database reads, disk writes, network activity, and memory consumption, and establishing a baseline of performance for future performance tests. This helps developers to understand whether certain changes are increasing or decreasing these baselines. Because there is no production level load or stress placed on the system, performance testing is typically done during the development process on the developer's machine.

Checklist:

➤ I have established a set of performance baselines for at least the homepage and key interior content pages.

Load Testing

Wikipedia defines *load testing* as "the process of putting demand on a system or device and measuring its response." The first goal of load testing is to find bugs that show themselves only when the system is under a reasonable load. The bugs that show up here are typically memory leaks and resource management bugs, for example, not closing SQL connections. These are difficult bugs to find when you are a single developer testing on a single machine, but they show up pretty quickly when you are using a tool to simulate real traffic.

The second goal is to ensure that the application meets the performance baseline over time. Because the staged environment ideally mirrors the hardware of a production machine, real-world load tests can be run against it. In cases in which the hardware configuration of the staging machine is significantly different than the hardware configuration of the production machines, it may be necessary to temporarily "borrow" the production machine hardware for the load test. If your website configuration has multiple machines behind a load balancer, consider taking one machine from the cluster over the weekend.

The load test operates at the highest load the system can accept while still performing as expected. It is important to note that the goal of load testing is not to cause the system to fail. It should try to keep the system working at its peak capacity, but no more. The system should behave well during load tests because this load should represent the maximum number of users that the site should reasonably be able to handle.

Call to action:

➤ I have performed a load test on at least the homepage and key interior content pages. The system was able to perform at a level that indicates it can handle the expected peak traffic load of the production website.

Stress Testing

Stress testing tries to cause the system to fail by overwhelming its resources to surface issues that are more easily noticed when the system is pushed to its limits. During stress testing, take note of how the system fails and determine what can be done to either prevent the scenario or recover from it, should it happen in a production environment.

Call to action:

➤ I have performed a battery of stress tests on at least the homepage and key interior content pages to observe how the system behaves under a traffic stress that is greater than the expected traffic level to ensure the desired recovery from failure.

Security Testing

The purpose of security testing is to find and eliminate any issues with the application that compromise your application, the system, or its data. It's smart to begin security testing in the discovery phase by establishing your security goals for the website. Some goals will be different, depending on whether you're running a marketing campaign page or an online store and need to ensure compliance with PCI Data Security Standard (PCI DSS). Some goals will be the same, for example, does the application prevent cross site scripting or SQL Injection attacks? Once goals have been established, make sure that developers are aware of them and are educated on ways to prevent them during the development process. Security isn't a feature that can be bolted on at the end of a project. After the development process is complete, testing tools can be useful in automating the process of probing the site for vulnerabilities. Tools might uncover a number of weaknesses, but manual testing is often needed to uncover the more insidious bugs.

Call to action:

- ➤ I have verified that the site has gone through security testing and have responded to any issues that surfaced during the process.

UNDERSTANDING THE DIFFERENT DEPLOYMENT SCENARIOS

Up to this point, this chapter has focused on pre-conditions for deployment. Keep in mind that all the pre-conditions discussed so far hold true regardless of which deployment configuration is decided upon. This section will outline different types of configuration possibilities and highlight the things you need to consider while trying to decide upon your own.

Understanding the Basic Terminology

Although deployment scenarios differ from organization to organization based on a project's goals and requirements, they will each be comprised of the same basic building blocks. Most everyone is familiar with the concept of a development environment, and has a general understanding of what a staging environment is for, but for the sake of completeness, it is worth taking a few paragraphs to explain their generally accepted purpose.

- ➤ **Development environment:** This environment typically has a complete working version of the website, but will not always have the content that is visible on the public site. Developers might occasionally pull down content from the production website if it helps to debug a problem, develop a new feature, or design a new layout. However, typically the content in the development environment is not in sync with the content on the website. Source code is often not in sync with the website either, because the development environment is the location where developers modify the source code to build new features and fix defects.

- ➤ **Source Control repository:** This Source Control Management System (SCMS) such as SVN or Perforce is used by developers to store the source code files of the website. The SCMS does not typically store anything other than the website's source code. The website's documents and assets are excluded from the SCMS and instead are stored within the Ektron content management system. Although Ektron is used to synchronize source control files across machines in the deployment scenario, it should not be used in place of an SCMS. You still need to keep your source code in an SCMS.

- ➤ **Staging environment:** The staging environment is the location that is used to test new features or verify content before it makes its way to the production website. The staging environment usually matches the production environment in terms of its source code and content, except in cases when content has been modified by an editor or a new feature has been added by a developer through an update to its source code from the development environment. The staging environment is less volatile than the development environment as the only changes being made are those that have made it through the development process and are in finished form awaiting final approval.

➤ **Pre-Staging environment:** Some organizations choose to have a pre-staging environment that is used by QA engineers and developers to vet technical changes made to the website's source code and keep the staging environment as a place to moderate content changes. This scenario is not too common but it is seen in organizations with large editorial and Web development teams as a way to prevent people from stepping on toes and to minimize the volatility of any one single environment.

➤ **Production environment:** The production environment serves the live traffic to the website. This may represent a single physical machine or a cluster of machines sitting behind a load balancer. In the cases of a public website, this sits outside of the corporate network.

➤ **Deployment environment:** The deployment environment represents the manner in which each of the previously mentioned environments connects and enforces such things as content authoring policies, workflow and approval processes, and changes to source code. It is sometimes also referred to as the deployment plan, the deployment scenario, the deployment architecture, or Web deployment.

Determining the Content Flow

One of the first concepts to consider when you are determining how to architect your deployment environment is the content flow — how does the content move throughout the entire production system, from content creation on the staging machine to content delivery in the production environment? Looking at all deployment scenarios from this perspective, you will find that they all fall at some place along a spectrum; where one end of the spectrum represents websites where content is authored exclusively by the community, sites such as Wikipedia; and at the other end you have the editorially driven "one way push" websites, such as brochure-ware and marketing micro-sites. Both ends of the spectrum represent a one-way flow of information, but in different directions.

But there are few purely community-driven sites such as Wikipedia. The number of old corporate "brochure-ware-style" websites is also dwindling. Most modern websites fall somewhere in the middle of these two points of the spectrum — sites that have both editorially-driven and community-driven content — and this is where it gets interesting. It is where you'll find various scenarios supporting the flow of content back and forth between the production environment and the staging environment. Figure 14-1 shows different deployment scenarios, focusing in on the movement of content within the deployment content flow. Consider where your deployment architecture fits on this spectrum; where is your content authoring taking place? Who is authoring it?

The next point to consider is what sort of approval process will be used with content authoring? Even when you are supporting community driven content, it might be the case that you want to put an approval process around it. For example, it is not uncommon to have an approval process around community authored content, as you frequently see with blog comments. Another real-world example is the case of a software company using community-generated content to augment its online technical documentation. Using an approval process that includes the organization's technical writers benefits community-authored content, with editorial correction and approval. Figure 14-2 presents a diagram showing how such an approval process flow might look on a single-production environment.

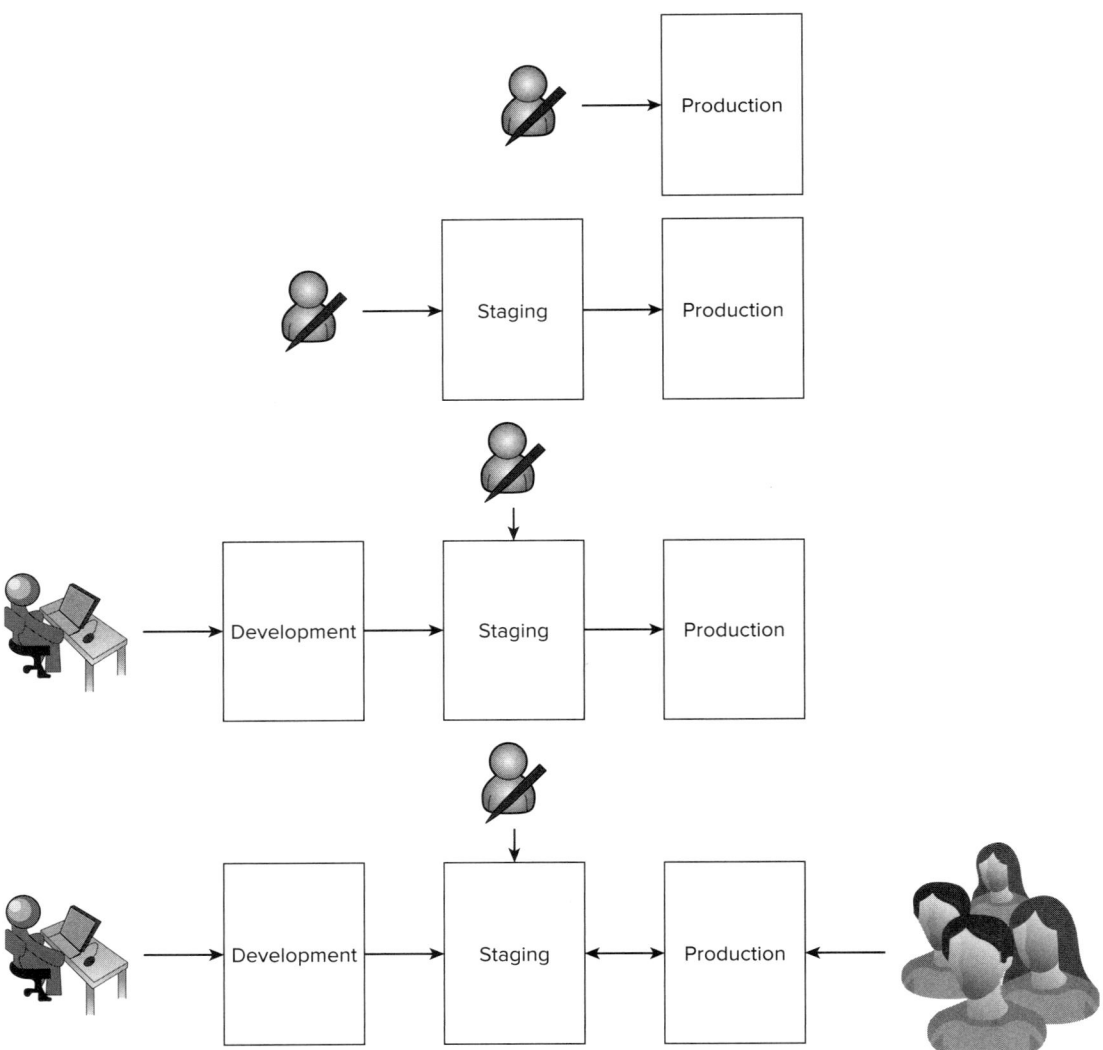

FIGURE 14-1

Understanding the flow of content is not only important for planning the overall pattern of your deployment scenario, but is also critical in determining the performance requirements of content-authoring environments. In cases where the public website is the content-authoring environment, your performance assessment is usually well thought out. But most websites have some element of editorially-authored content, which means you need to ask yourself how many content authors will be producing and managing content. In a situation where you have a significant number of content authors, you might need to consider having content authoring occur on a dedicated staging environment with multiple machines to handle the load that can occur when content producers are logged-in and authoring simultaneously. Even if you don't have the number of authors requiring this type of authoring environment, you might still benefit from having a formal staging server in your deployment architecture production environment, as it gives them a single place to make edits without having to touch the production server. In this case, the content authors will make content changes in a staged environment and push those content changes to the production environment. Figure 14-3 shows a diagram with a formal staging and production environment.

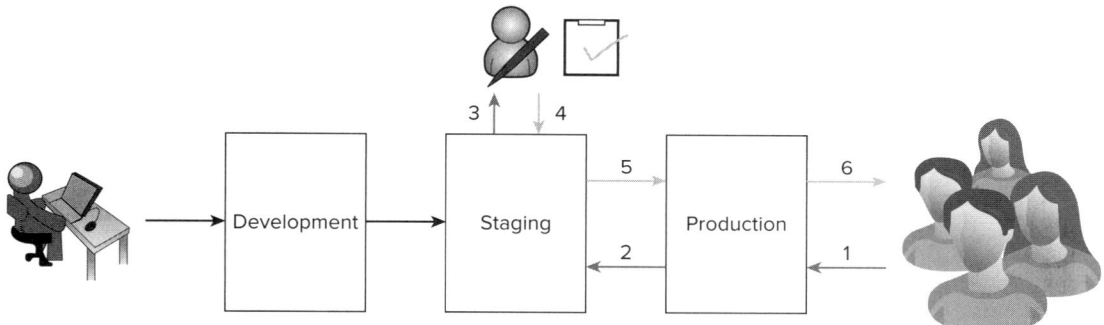

FIGURE 14-2

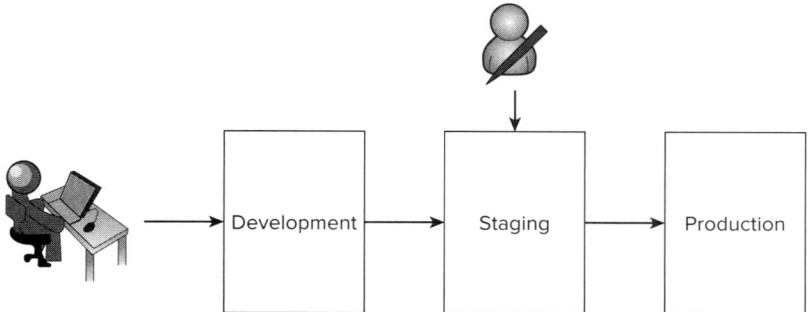

FIGURE 14-3

Call to action:

➤ I understand how content will flow throughout my deployment environment. Whether it is authored in production by the community, in staging by an editorial staff and then pushed to production, some combination of these, or something else entirely, the flow of it has been defined. The purpose of this call-to-action is to establish how many environments your production environment will have, such as dev, staging, pre-production, and production.

➤ A content production process has been established and everyone in my organization understands what workflows and content approval processes are in place.

➤ I know how many content producers will be authoring and managing content and where they will be doing so. This information is needed to determine whether a dedicated staging environment is needed and what type of hardware is needed for it.

Now that you've worked through the process of establishing what your content flow looks like and have an understanding of how many different environments you have in your deployment architecture, the chapter will move onto the options available for moving content and source code from one environment to the next.

MOVING CONTENT WITH OR WITHOUT ESYNC

Moving content through environments of a deployment scenario has historically been a challenge for organizations. Even today the problem is often solved through the use of time-consuming manual processes that are wrought with the potential for human error. How many times have you been asked to upload something on a website or to make a "quick change" on some current content? Without the right plan and the supporting technology in place to facilitate the desired movement of content through your deployment architecture, these types of scenarios will inevitably become accepted practice.

The previous section looked to define a pattern that describes how content moves through your deployment architecture. This section assumes that you've got a handle on this and are now looking to decide on the right technology for supporting the deployment architecture. Depending on what you determined to be your requirements here, different options present themselves. This section discusses these options, focusing on how to support the flow of content with and without Ektron's eSync.

Moving Content with eSync

Ektron's eSync was designed to solve the challenges of moving content from one environment to another. This sounds like a simple and straightforward problem. Information from one database is moved to a different database. Simple enough, right? If you've ever tried to solve this problem yourself, either manually or in some automated fashion, you understand the complexities that are involved with data synchronization and can appreciate what Ektron's eSync brings to the table. For anyone who does not understand the complexities surrounding this, it is important to be aware of them because in doing so, you will understand why certain deployment environments fundamentally require the use of eSync.

Let's begin by looking at typical data transactions that occur in any normal Web deployment that has at least a staging and a production environment. In such a scenario, you will eventually ask some of the following questions:

- How do I move a single content change from my staging environment to my production environment without affecting the availability of my website? Without pushing other content changes that are not ready?

- How can I update my staging environment with the data from my production environment so that I have a local copy of all data, including the content authored by the community? And do it without destroying the new content I've been authoring in staging?

- How can I quickly push through a correction for a typo that I found on the website that originates in a code file? Without having to involve a small army of IT people?

Ektron's eSync solves the technology challenges that are associated with these questions. On a website without Ektron eSync, moving a single content item in the ways described here is a difficult and usually manual process. Also, moving code files from one environment to the next usually requires the availability of a developer, access to the servers, IT folks with the proper passwords and access, and perhaps a formal QA cycle: ultimately adding up to a good amount of time and creating a lot of risk.

Ektron's eSync solves these problems by providing a bi-directional synchronization technology that allows for incremental and full synchronization of both content and website templates between two servers in a deployment. This means that select changes can be sent to the production environment, without having to send over the entire database or file structure. Figure 14-4 shows a deployment architecture with staging and production Environments that uses eSync to keep information in sync.

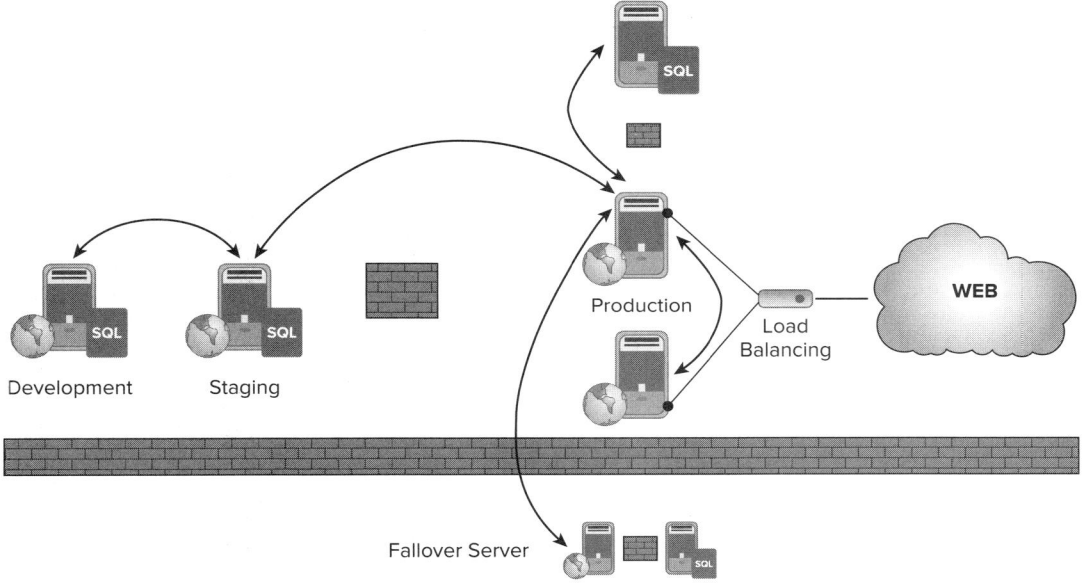

FIGURE 14-4

eSync solves very real content deployment pains with its sophisticated synchronization technology and the benefits of using eSync are clear. So why wouldn't it be used in all cases? One reason may be its licensing cost is prohibitive for your organization — the project's budget simply won't allow it. Additionally, while there are some deployment scenarios that have a hard requirement of eSync, there are others where it is merely a recommendation. To understand when it is a requirement, and when it is a recommendation, see Table 14-1.

TABLE 14-1: Deployment Scenario Data Flows and Process

PLAN	DATA FLOW	PROCESS
1	Data moves in one direction from staging to production.	eSync
2	Data moves in both directions between production and staging.	eSync

continues

TABLE 14-1 *(continued)*

PLAN	DATA FLOW	PROCESS
3	Templates move in both directions between staging and production.	eSync
4	Data moves in one direction from production to staging.	eSync/Other
5	Templates move in one direction from staging to production.	eSync/Other
6	Templates move in one direction from production to staging.	eSync/Other
7	Data is authored just in production.	Other

Table 14-2 describes each scenario above, explaining how eSync satisfies the requirements of that particular deployment plan. To summarize, however, you can apply the following rule of thumb: If you need to do incremental content updates (for example, push a single content item change) or want content to flow in two directions, you need eSync.

TABLE 14-2: Deployment Plan Descriptions

PLAN	DESCRIPTION
1	Requires eSync because content flows from staging to production. Without eSync, developers need to come up with a homegrown synchronization process, or resort to a database backup and restore that has the seriously negative side effect of taking the website offline.
2	Requires eSync because content flows in both directions. Any bidirectional synchronization needs to take into account situations where one repository has information that the other does not, and it needs to have a strategy for moving content and handling conflicts when the same content has changed on both sides. These problems are solved by eSync.
3	Requires eSync because website templates move in both directions. This plan was included for completeness, but it is not common because modifying templates on both staging and production is not a best practice.
4	Recommends eSync but does not require it in all scenarios. It is required in any situation where individual content items are moving from production to staging. It is not required otherwise, because it is possible to use a database backup and restore to move production content into your staging environment. This also has the negative side effect of taking your staging environment offline while the database restore completes.
5 and 6	Recommend eSync but do not require it. It is not required because there are many common file transfer tools that can be used to push templates in one direction. eSync is recommended, however, because it provides additional capabilities such as scheduled synchronization.
7	Does not require or recommend eSync because no data is moving toward or away from the production environment. This deployment plan is discussed in the next section, "Moving Content without eSync."

If your deployment plan falls into any of the scenarios where eSync is recommended but not required, make sure to look down the road and consider future requirements as well. One major pitfall that developers and network operation engineers have run into in the past is trying to "bolt" eSync after deployment into a deployment scenario that hasn't been designed with eSync in mind. Similarly, if your scenario does require eSync, it is extremely important to not expect to "tack" at the end without considering everything discussed in this chapter so far. Both of these pitfalls have been encountered when eSync is installed into a production environment with little definition of how the data will move, resulting in repeated configuration changes as this extremely significant detail is worked out. Save yourself the headache and make sure that the people processes such as content flow, approval processes, and content workflows are well understood before you try to put technology processes in place.

> *The purpose of discussing eSync in this chapter is limited to understanding how you use it in a deployment configuration. Configuring eSync is beyond the scope of this book. There is documentation available online and good material on configuring eSync in the Ektron Reference Manual. Please see these resources for more information about setting up, configuring, and managing eSync.*

Moving Content without eSync

When eSync is not an option, you'll need to consider how to architect your website and your deployment scenario in a way that supports the desired flow of your content. The following section discusses these configurations and makes recommendations about technologies other than eSync that you can use.

Content Authoring in Production: Virtual Staging

In Deployment Plan #6, you read that eSync was not required nor recommended because no data moves to or away from the production environment. In this scenario, the recommendation is virtual staging. Virtual staging is a configuration where editorially created content is authored on the same server that the website visitors access. For example, if your website is accessible to your site visitors through the URL www.mysite.com/, your content authors would also create new content through the URL www.mysite.com/. Because no physical staged environment exists, content authors can publish this information into a "virtual" staging environment using the system's content preview capabilities to see how the content would appear to site visitors, without having to publish it publically. When a content author is authenticated with the system, a "Preview" button appears on pages that use the Login Server Control. The output of this server control is shown in Figure 14-5.

FIGURE 14-5

When you click on the Preview button, all server controls know to display the website as if the checked-in content were published. You can additionally use the workflow approval processes to ensure that content is first viewed and approved by other members of the editorial staff to prevent accidental publishing of content directly onto the website. Virtual staging is created by the combination of using content preview along with the content approval process.

If you are using the content APIs on your website and want to use virtual staging, keep in mind that you will need to set the preview state on the Content API. The following snippet shows how this is specified in the GetContentMetadataList method. Look at the API's documentation or IntelliSense to know where to specify this property. All server controls handle this automatically.

```
ContentAPI api = new ContentAPI();
bool InPreviewMode = Convert.ToBoolean(api.SitePreview);
CustomAttributeList ContentMeta =
    api.GetContentMetadataList(ContentBlock1.EkItem.Id, InPreviewMode);
```

Why would you choose to use Virtual Staging? It is an effective deployment configuration when both the number of content editors and the volume of content changes are minimal, and your site does not have any of the data synchronization requirements previously described.

Moving Data and/or Templates from Production to Staging

If your production environment does not require data to flow back and forth between staging and production (bi-directional movement of data and templates) and instead enforces that data flow from production to staging in one single direction, you have the option to:

➤ Pull the templates from production to staging using a file transfer protocol such as FTP or RSYNC, among others.

➤ Pull the database from production to staging using a method such as backup/restore, keeping in mind that this will cause your staging server to be unavailable while the database restore process completes.

Figure 14-6 shows a diagram depicting this configuration.

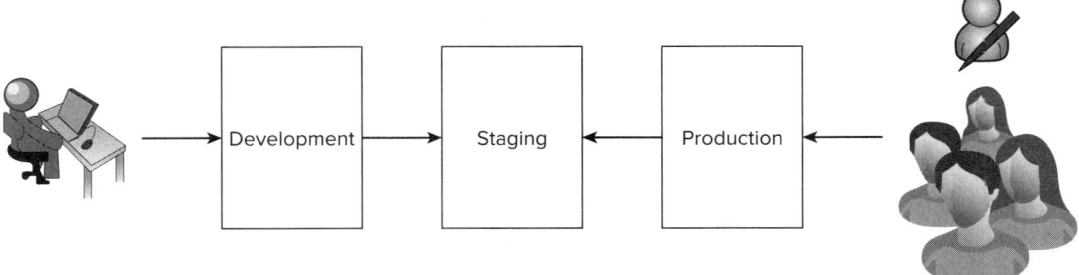

FIGURE 14-6

While eSync is not a requirement for this configuration, it is recommended because it allows for the possibilities of transferring select content items, which is not possible without eSync. Also, transferring a database using backup restore is a brute force process that transfers all or nothing. Although it can be automated, it is typically a manual process and is therefore prone to human error. The advantage of eSync is its ability to move both data and templates from production to staging in an automated fashion, removing the potential for the problems associated with backing up and restoring a database.

Templates Move from Staging to Production

If your staging environment is exclusively used to test and verify changes to templates and code and not to verify content changes to push to production, you have the option to:

> Push the templates and code files from staging to production using any file transfer protocol using FTP or RSYNC, among others.

Again, eSync has the added benefit that it can be used to schedule items and is available in the event that future requirements ask that content items be synchronized as well. For example:

Call to action:

> I understand what technology will be used to support the content flow and move content and templates between environments of my deployment architecture.

THE DEPLOYMENT

At this point in the process, you've got a good understanding of how your deployment architecture is organized. Now is the time to peel back a few layers and put the pieces of the architecture in place.

Installing Your Website on Another Server

Before installing your website onto another server, it is important to verify that the new environment meets the hardware and software requirements outlined in Table 1-2 in Chapter 1. Once you've verified this, installing Ektron on another environment begins with the process outlined in Chapter 4 (it uses the CMS400Min.exe). Replicating the CMS400Min.exe installation processes is not recommended because the installer performs many functions, including modifying the IIS metabase, installing Windows services, and updating the Windows Registry. You should expect these things to happen in a particular order. Additionally, the installer offers logging and reporting on the status of the install.

Once you have done this, you have two possible ways to continue installing your site into the production environment for the first time:

- Manually copying your website
- Using the Package and Deploy Wizard

As you can imagine, although possible (and even common), manually copying your website, involves performing a number of steps that are simplified through automation with the Package and Deploy Wizard.

Manually Deploying Your Website

Although it is highly advised that you do not try to manually install Ektron, it is common for developers to manually install an existing website onto the server once the website is developed, tested, and ready to be deployed. The following check list of items should be followed in order.

1. **Install the CMS400Min onto the production server.** Make sure that all of the servers in your deployment scenario are using the version with which the site was developed.

2. **Back up and restore the database.** Before you begin the process of performing the backup and restore, make sure you first clean the database and remove references to development and staging servers. To do so:

   ➤ Delete all entries from the following tables: AssetServerTable, perform_action, and failed_action.

   ➤ Perform a database backup for full recovery model, which ensures that all information is included.

   ➤ Transfer the backup file to the database server in the production environment and run through the process of performing a standard database restore.

3. **Import the templates, Wireframes, and Widgets:**

   ➤ Export the templates, Wireframes, widgets, and other site resource files (such as JavaScript and CSS) from the source control system and compress them into a single ZIP file, making sure that the file structure aligns with the production website.

   ➤ Move the ZIP file to the production server and unzip it into the root of the site.

4. **Export the Asset library:**

   ➤ Move folders and files that were most likely not in source control to the proper location on the production server. This may include files in the DMS Assets, PrivateAssets, and UploadedFiles.

   ➤ Navigate to the AssetLibrary folder using Windows Explorer. By default, the AssetLibrary folder is created on the server's C drive.

   To find where this is located on your server, you can do the following:

   ➤ Navigate to your site's AssetLibrary folder, open the AssetManagement.config file, and check the StorageLocation path.

   ➤ Navigate to the folder specified in the StorageLocation path and copy it. Next, move it to AssetLibrary folder on the production server, open the AssetManagement .config file on the production server, and update the StorageLocation path with the new folder name.

5. **Update the web.config file:**

   ➤ The web.config file holds configuration information for the site. Copy the web.config file from the production server to the development or staging server. Compare the files and manually merge any changes required by the custom implementation.

   ➤ Move the updated file back to the production site.

   ➤ Update the database connection string with the new database name, username, and password.

Using the Package and Deploy Tool

You use the Package and Deploy tool packaging your site and deploying it to a remote server. This tool performs all of the steps that a manual deployment performs. You can find the PackageSite.exe utility in Ektron's application directory (typically C:\Program Files\Ektron\CMS400v80\Utilities\PackageSite\PackageSite.exe). It packages your site, database, AssetLibrary, and site files for easy deployment to your production server.

This tool is also useful if you need to set up a new development or staging environment. To get started with this, do the following:

1. Launch the Package Site utility by double-clicking PackageSite.exe.
2. From the pull-down menu (shown in Figure 14-7), select the site you want to package, and click Next.

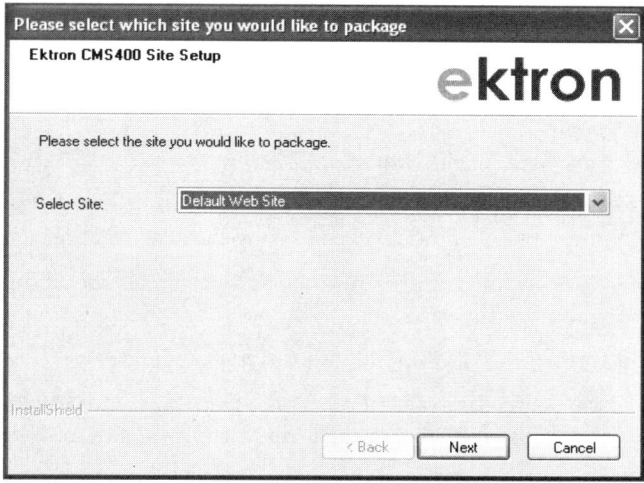

FIGURE 14-7

3. Browse to the directory where this site is located (for example, c:\inetpub\wwwroot).
4. Browse to the path where you want the package to be created and saved. This can be in any location. Select your path and then click Next.
5. Enter the name of the package and click Next.
6. Enter the name of your database server, username, and password. For trusted connections, you can leave the username and password blank.
7. Once you've provided this information, click Next. The installer will now copy all the templates, CSS, assets, and so on, including any subfolders.

If you are using Subversion or another source control system, you may have a number of .svn folders in your site tree. You should delete them from the output folder after you package the site. To strip .svn folders using TortoiseSVN you can export a folder to itself or you can recursively delete folders from a command prompt with this command:

```
FOR /r %f IN (.svn) DO RD /s /q "%f"
```

If your database connection test passes, the utility starts packaging the site. You will see the status window displaying percentages complete. If your database is large, this step can take a long time. It uses Ektron's SQL Generator to turn all the data in your database into a text file named cms400_data.sql with a large number of SQL INSERT statements.

8. After the site is packaged, a new window opens with instructions on how to restore the site on a production server.

Your site has now been packaged and is ready to be deployed. To begin the deployment process:

1. Navigate to the folder where the site package was saved. It should contain the following folders:
    - assetlibrary
    - content
    - setup
2. Move the entire packaged site folder to the production server.
3. On your production machine, double-click CMS400Base.exe (if not installed already). Make sure that all machines in your deployment scenario are using the same version.
4. When the Site Setup Installation automatically runs, stop it by clicking Cancel on the site setup utility for now; you will rerun this later.
5. Copy the packaged folder to the Ektron\CMS400v80\startersites folder.
6. Run the Site Setup utility by clicking Start ➪ AllPrograms ➪ Ektron ➪ CMS400 v80 ➪ Utilities ➪ CMS400 Site Setup. When you get to the dropdown list of sites to install, choose your packaged site name.
7. Follow the prompts and finish the install.

Congratulations, you've now installed your website onto the production server.

After the Installation

Now that you've installed your website, here's a list of things to perform or verify, prior to the final launch of your website.

1. Verify that everything has been deleted from the AssetServerTable.
2. Verify that everything has been deleted from the Perform_Action table.
3. Verify that everything has been deleted from the failed_action table.
4. Consider purging content history. This is done through the folder properties in the Workarea's content folder tree.
5. Delete any test content, users, or folders from the Workarea.
6. Designers often use "Lorem Ipsum" as a placeholder for actual content; verify that it has all been removed by searching for "Ipsum."

Securing the Server

Securing an Ektron system involves reviewing the permission structure on your website, renaming or removing a Web services file, and changing the default passwords for superusers, as shown next.

ServerControlWS.asmx is the Web service that permits the server controls to communicate with the system from Visual Studio for design-time display purposes (it is not used by the server controls at runtime on the website). The path is coded in the web.config file and appears in the following way:

```
<!-- Web Service URL for Server Controls design time -->
<add key="WSPath"
     value="http://localhost/CMS400Developer/Workarea/ServerControlWS.asmx" />
```

It is strongly advised to remove or change the name of this file and update the web.config value accordingly. Failing to do so exposes your site to vulnerabilities that could allow someone to access or modify the content of your website.

There are two default super user accounts in Ektron. Because these default users also have default passwords, failing to change these passwords means that anyone with knowledge of Ektron can log into your system and make administrator level changes. To change the Admin password, do the following:

1. In the Workarea, navigate to Settings ⇨ Users.
2. Click the Admin user.
3. Click the Edit Users button.
4. In the Password field enter a new password.
5. In the Confirm Password field, confirm the new password.
6. Click Save.

The Builtin user is an account that can be used to modify system settings. This account is not shown in the user screen, so you need to change its password by following these steps:

1. In the Workarea, navigate to Settings ⇨ Configurations ⇨ Setup.
2. Click the Edit button.
3. Find the Built in User field.
4. In the Password and Confirm Password fields, enter the new password.
5. Click the Update button.

Lastly, by this point in the deployment process, you should feel comfortable with the permission structure of your content tree, but it is worth taking a second look through it to make sure that all the permissions look correct and do not grant elevated or undesired access to users in your system. When the system is first installed, the Everyone group has all permissions. This is most likely already removed, but checking to verify this is the safe thing to do.

TAKE HOME POINTS

This chapter covered the deployment process and what it takes to ensure a successful deployment. It started by discussing the pre-conditions for a successful deployment. The pre-conditions are things that must be done before the point of deployment, and a checklist was provided summarizing each of them. If you have met each of the pre-conditions, you now have a code complete website that is properly installed in a staged environment and has been thoroughly tested. The following list aggregates each of the bullet points outlined earlier:

- I have written requirements that capture the expected behavior of the website.
- I have written requirements that capture the website's performance requirements.
- I have verified that the website source code is code-complete.
- I have determined the version of the software.
- I have ensured the source code is managed through a source control system, such as SVN or Perforce.
- I have a permanent development environment established for making code-level changes to the website.
- I have a staged environment on an internal server that contains the final source code and final versions of software components.
- I have a staged environment that mirrors the performance of a machine in my production environment.
- I have verified that the final content for the site has either been newly created or migrated from an existing repository into the staged environment
- I have gone through the process of Final User Acceptance Testing with my stakeholders and key website end users.
- I have an established a set of performance baselines for at least the homepage and key interior content pages.
- I have performed a load test on at least the homepage and key interior content pages. The system was able to perform at a level that indicates it can handle the expected peak traffic load of the production website.
- I have performed a battery of stress tests on at least the homepage and key interior content pages to observe how the system behaves under a traffic stress that is greater than the expected traffic level to ensure the desired recoverability from failure.
- I have verified that the site has gone through security testing, and Final User Acceptance Testing.

The chapter then discussed deployment scenarios, by defining terminology and helping to understand which scenario makes the most sense by focusing on the flow of content in the deployment. The availability of eSync, which offers powerful synchronization capabilities, depends on the chosen configuration. This section outlined different ways to move website content and templates between environments within your website's deployment architecture. Table 14-1 can be used to help determine what options are available for particular scenarios. In many cases, specifically any time content flows from a staging environment to a production environment, eSync needs to be used to move information. When content exclusively flows in the other direction, eSync is a recommended best practice but not a requirement.

Finally, this chapter discussed the technical aspects of deployment, which includes a discussion of moving your website to a staged and production environment, the steps required to secure it, and best practices for verifying that the configuration is set up as you intended.

15

Maintaining Your Website

- ➤ What are the essentials for creating an effective maintenance plan?
- ➤ How do you maintain content freshness?
- ➤ How do you ensure that your site is available?
- ➤ What do you need to do to increase your site's performance?
- ➤ What are the basics for a user friendly site?
- ➤ How do you drive traffic to your site?
- ➤ What do you need to have in place to avert disaster?

Your website is live and has been up-and-running with no issues for some time now. With a seemingly functional website, happy site visitors, and no complaints from management, you decide that the website project was a success. With one solid success under your belt, it's time to move on to new projects and new challenges…that is until your phone starts ringing because your manager suddenly realized Web sales are far from her expectations, or the intermittent errors that have gone undetected by you have not gone unnoticed by customers, among other problems.

CREATING AN EFFECTIVE MAINTENANCE PLAN

Every website requires maintenance and having a website maintenance plan in effect can help prevent these types of issues by defining what success looks like, monitoring for success (or the lack there of), and taking actions that lead you in the right direction. It's unrealistic to think that a website, even one that was an initial success, will remain successful without some level of active and ongoing maintenance.

This chapter describes the activities that are needed to ensure the long-term success of your website. In general, all maintenance-related activities can be generalized into the following process or methodology. You will need to:

- **Capture** data such as site usage, server performance, and Web metrics that describe the activity on the website and the behaviors of its site visitors.
- **Analyze** the data to understand how it compares to the desired outcomes as defined by the Key Performance Indicators (KPIs).
- **Act** upon this data to improve the overall website experience.

Some of the items that you might think about tracking so that you can solve for issues using the methodology outlined previously are:

- Number of visitors to your site
- Number of members on your site
- Average page load speed
- Advertising revenue generated
- Feedback from users on your content
- Type and frequency of server errors

Capturing Data

The first part of creating your maintenance plan is determining which data needs to be captured. Some of the data points you collect will be the same regardless of the purpose of your website, be it a content website or an eCommerce one. These include statistics server errors and page load speeds Other metrics will be custom tailored to capture the information relevant to your site's unique *Key Performance Indicators* (*KPIs*). For instance, a shoe store might need to capture the volume of transactions related to a certain type of shoe (for example, "number of sales of the cross training running sneaker") while an xyz website may add more value by tracking abc (for example "hij"). Ensuring that all the proper information is being logged is extremely important. You don't want to be in a situation where you are trying to answer a specific question only to realize that the data you need to analyze is not being captured. Once you've done this, you can take the next step, which is to analyze that data.

Analyzing Data

To perform meaningful analysis and provide meaningful answers, you need to ask meaningful questions. The type of analysis you perform on your data needs to be guided by the success criteria for your website. Some success criteria are driven by KPIs that are unique to your site. A good question is driven by desired outcomes. Some critical success metrics relevant to all websites are those around a website's physical performance. Here are some examples:

- How quickly does my website respond to my visitors interactions?
- What level of availability does my website have?

Based on the questions you've asked, you can now look to your data to find the answer. Sometimes finding the right data might be easy. For example, a question such as "how many visible errors have appeared on my website" might be answered by simply looking in a particular log file. However, in other cases, finding the answer might not be so straightforward and requires you to dig into multiple datasets to determine a good answer. A question such as "are my site searches yielding relevant results" can be challenging to answer. In cases where you're dealing with a difficult question, make sure the right question is being asked before you start looking. A sign of a good question is that it focuses on the business and important business outcomes.

Acting upon Data

Once you've asked the right questions and analyzed the data, it's time to compare the results to the expected outcome. If you've reached the desired outcome, briefly congratulate yourself and then prepare for a new set of desired outcomes (for example, higher revenues)! If you've missed the mark, put together an action plan that can bring you to your goal. Actions might include:

➤ Replacing or scaling hardware to handle the increasing website traffic demands

➤ Updating your product roadmap to reflect the evolving requirements of your site visitor

➤ Strategizing on ways to grow the size of your site's visitors through the use of social media marketing, search engine optimization, or search engine marketing

If you repeat this process at regular intervals and add automation whenever possible you will not only avoid the chicken-little "sky is falling" disaster scenarios described earlier but you will also have your website on track for long-term success.

Understanding the desired outcomes for your website is an important task and one that needs to be understood before you put together a maintenance plan. If you don't know what the longer term business goals are for your website, involve someone that does.

This chapter provides you with some insight into things you'll need to keep in mind while formulating your maintenance plan. You'll also read about lessons learned, pitfalls to avoid, useful tools, and tips and tricks.

MAINTAINING CONTENT FRESHNESS

How often have you come across a website with blatantly stale information? Websites seem to forget that one of the primary reasons people visit them is to gather some type of information. This information needs to be timely and relevant. Small details like an old copyright notice at the bottom of the page can leave your site visitors with the impression that the website has been abandoned or neglected. Here are some points to consider in setting up or reviewing to help keep your content fresh.

➤ Run content reports.

➤ Perform content "spot checks."

Running Content Reports

The Refresh Reminder Report can prompt you to review content that may have become stale and in need of editorial review. As you learned earlier in Chapter 5, every managed content item in the system has the ability to specify an end date. This date can be set by an author while creating or editing content. Depending on which option is chosen by the content author, the content item can either be archived and removed from the site, or remain on the site but added to the Refresh Report, once the date has passed.

To set the end date for a content item:

1. Open the Workarea ⇨ Content screen.
2. Open a content item to edit.
3. From the content edit screen, select the Schedule tab.
4. Set the start date. Setting this has the effect of publishing content at the specified point in the future.
5. Set the end date.
6. Specify what you want to happen once the end date has passed. As you can see in Figure 15-1, your three options are:
    ➤ Archive and remove from the site (expire)
    ➤ Archive and remain on the site
    ➤ Add to the CMS Refresh Report
7. Select Add to the CMS Refresh Report to have this content item included once the date has passed.

Alternatively, if you are certain that content is no longer relevant after a certain date, you should select the Archive and Remove from the Site (Expire) option. An example of content that might need to expire on a particular date could be a time-sensitive marketing promotion that needs to be removed from the site once the marketing campaign ends. Using this option has the effect of not only removing the content from the website once the end date has passed, but also causes the content item to appear on the Expired Content Report.

In cases where you're looking to see what content is pending expiration, use the Content to Expire Report. This report lists all content whose end date occurs between today and a number of days that you specify and gives you the opportunity to modify the end date if needed.

Another useful content report to help determine the freshness of the content on your website and identify any items worthy of an editorial review is the Site Update Activity Report. This report, as shown in Figure 15-2, lists how many content items were published within a time span that you provide. This report can be used while trying to answer questions like:

➤ How much information has the editorial team created and published to the website?
➤ How does the freshness of content relate to average length of time on the website?

Maintaining Content Freshness | **575**

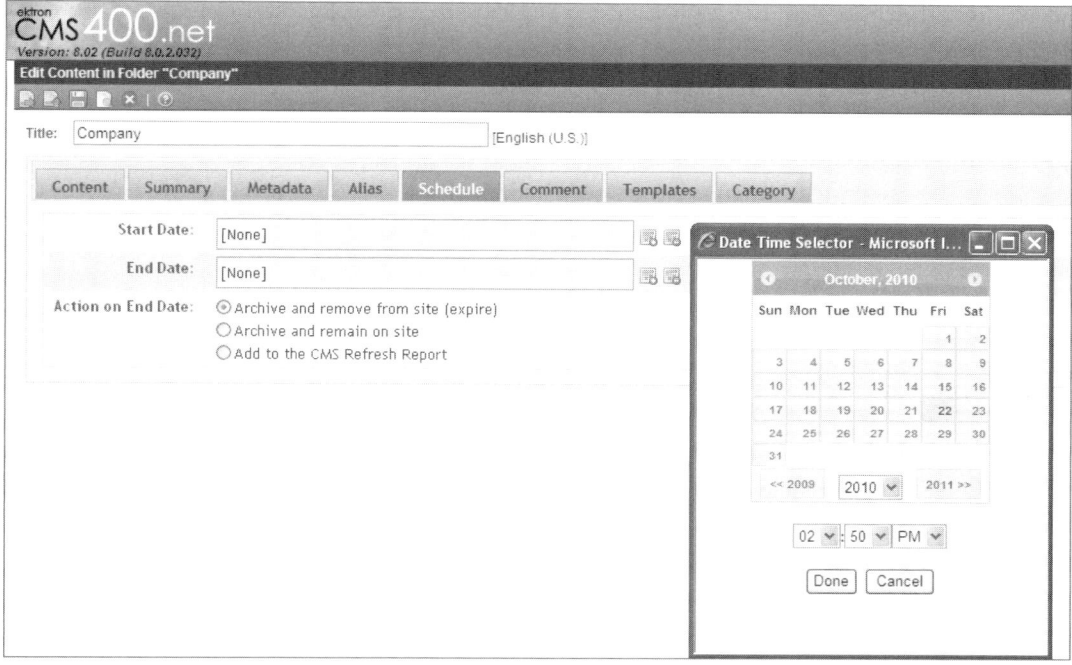

FIGURE 15-1

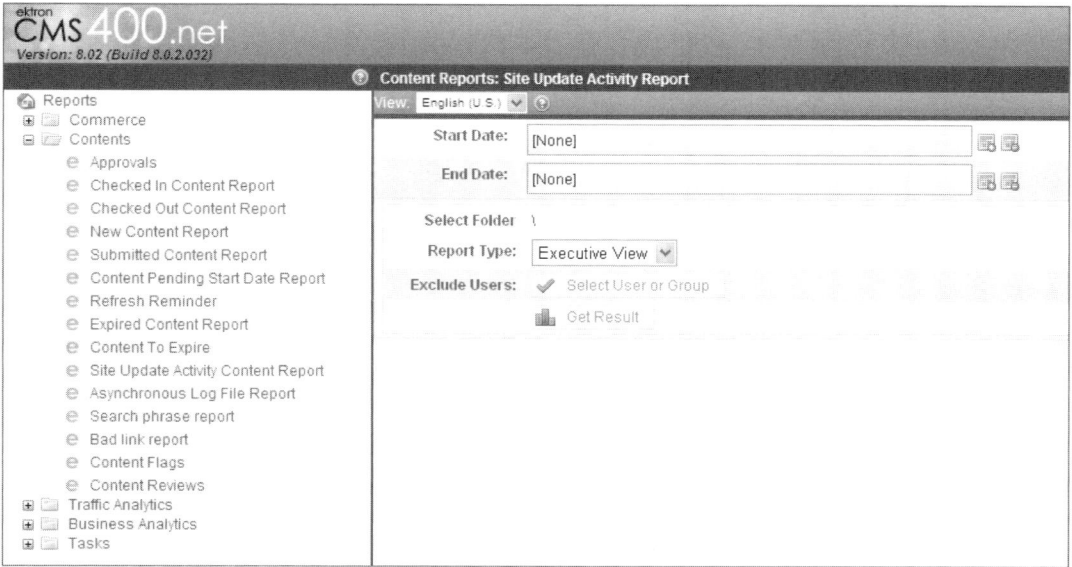

FIGURE 15-2

Each of the content reports discussed here can be found in the Workarea's Report section in the following way:

1. Open the Workarea and navigate to Reports.
2. Expand the Report tree to find the following:

    ➤ Reports ⇨ Contents ⇨ Refresh Reminder
    ➤ Reports ⇨ Contents ⇨ Expired Content
    ➤ Reports ⇨ Contents ⇨ Content to Expire
    ➤ Reports ⇨ Contents ⇨ Site Update Activity

Performing "Spot Checks"

As mentioned earlier, it's important to remember that reports can only tell you so much. It's better to turn to a report only after you've formulated some meaningful business question and are using the report as a data point in discovering an answer. Also keep in mind that there might be content on your website that is unmanaged and this information will not appear in the report. For this reason, it's worth conducting a "spot check" content review every once in a while looking for signs of stale, unmanaged content. Good places to check are the website's images, such as logos and banners, and any information that appears in the header and footer.

While you're performing a manual content scan, consider checking other items that might be out-of-date, yet may not be managed content and not listed in these content reports. Has your company changed locations? Opened a new office? Changed its 1-800 number? Check the privacy policy — has there been a change in the way your company handles customer information, such as e-mail addresses, that should be reflected there?

All businesses naturally experience some rate of attrition, which, from a maintenance perspective, means that any templates that list employee information, such as a "management team" page or a community hub, should be checked occasionally for references to employees who no longer work for the company. For those active employees, take a moment to verify that their contact information is correct — checking items such as phone numbers, e-mail addresses, and social media handles.

In addition to content being affected by the changes in personnel, you need to make sure that your website's content permissions and approval processes are revisited to keep track of how they're affected by changes in roles, hiring, and attrition. Key questions to ask here include the following:

➤ Have the right people been included in the content approval process?
➤ Are the current approval processes out-of-date?
➤ Are there new employees that should be included?
➤ Are there ex-employees with permission to access the system?

Another item to check related to changing employees are HTML forms — many forms trigger some type of notification activity such as an e-mail notification prompting an individual to take some type of next-action step. When employees change roles, e-mails may potentially be dropped or ignored, which can cost the loss of a sale or create an aggravated customer. Schedule time to review the HTML forms on the site and make sure that they are being sent to the proper individuals. On a related note, spam has been known to render useless any e-mail accounts listed on a public website. This also holds true for group e-mail addresses (such as "sales@mycompany.com"), which should also be checked to make sure they are still active.

MAINTAINING AVAILABILITY

Any period of time where your website is unavailable can cause a number of serious issues, ranging from the obvious issues when site visitors are unable to complete sales transactions to the less-considered ones such as search engine spiders being unavailable to update search results. Large scale outages occur less frequently but are highly visible and certainly more dramatic. These larger outages can be detected easily enough through the use of networking and application monitoring tools such as What's Up Gold (by Ipswitch, Inc) or Nagios. These tools monitor your website and network for issues and alert employees when things go wrong. Brief outages, on the other hand, occur more frequently but often fly right under the radar, going unnoticed, yet still negatively impacting online transactions. It is important to monitor both the large outages and the small hiccups to maintain a successful, well-functioning website.

Any fault-tolerant website should be designed to continue to function in spite of system errors. In most cases, these errors are not visible to the end user and are instead logged. Ensuring that your Web application is logging errors is critical in being able to answer questions around availability. This section outlines places that you can review to find information to provide answers and identify potential issues requiring attention.

By default, Ektron logs any application errors to the server's Event Viewer, as shown in Figure 15-3.

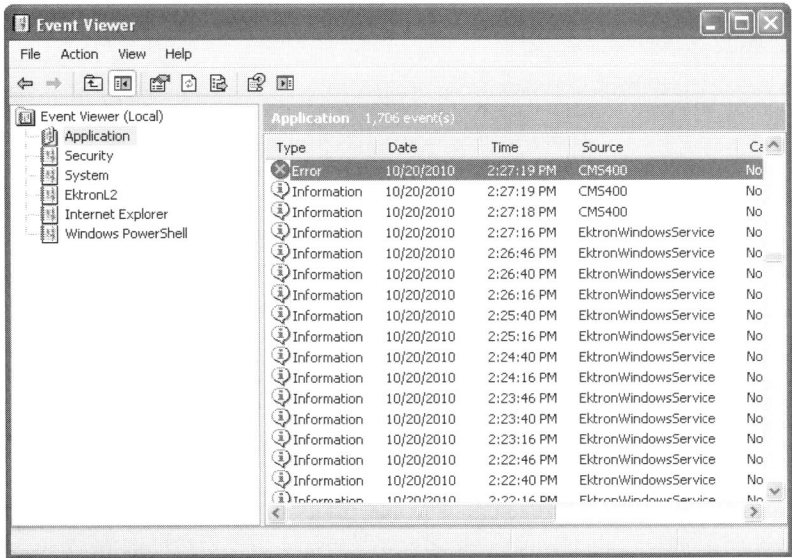

FIGURE 15-3

MAINTAINING YOUR WEBSITE

...y this behavior to have system warning and diagnostic messages included as well.
...configured in the web.config file, which has a setting to define the type of information logged into the Event Viewer. To modify this, open the web.config file and change the LogLevel value shown in the following snippet to the integer that corresponds to the level of the message to log.

```
<system.diagnostics>
    <switches>
      <!-- Determines the level of messages that are logged
        1 = Error:   Only Errors are logged.
        2 = Warning: Only warnings and Errors are logged.
        3 = Information: Only Informationals, Warnings, and Errors are logged.
        4 = Verbose: Everything is logged.
      -->
      <add name="LogLevel" value="1" />
    </switches>
```

Ektron uses the Microsoft Logging Application Block internally to log these system messages. This means you have the ability to control a number of characteristics through the application .config file also located in the website's root directory. You can control these characteristics in three easy steps:

1. Specify where these messages are physically stored. If you don't want to log to the Event Viewer, you can configure your system to log to a SQL Server database, or other data store.

2. Specify different locations for each type of message. A practical use case here would be to log all error messages to the Event Viewer, so they're picked up through system error monitoring tools, but log everything else into a database for an external log file.

3. Choose to be notified of messages through e-mail or another way.

For more information on these configurations, http://msdn.microsoft.com/en-us/library/cc309506.aspx.

Beyond application errors, there are other undesirable events that you want to keep an eye out for, such as issues with your hyperlinks. Broken links not only give the impression that your site is unavailable, but it is a source of serious frustration to visitors. Your maintenance plan should include the use of Ektron's "Bad Link Report," which scans your website for broken links. This report includes only content that is managed by the system and it does not spider all pages on the website.

In addition to using the Bad Link Report, consider reviewing your HTTP logs regularly. This may seem redundant, but the Web servers' HTTP logs need to be reviewed frequently, looking for any HTTP 4xx Client Errors or 5xx Server Errors. This is important to check for HTTP 404 File Not Found errors, in addition to the Bad Link Report, since it will include HTTP 404 errors for unmanaged resources such as CSS, JavaScript files, and images.

Log Parser is another log processing tool that is extremely powerful and available free from Microsoft's website. If the idea of being able to query the Event View, HTTP Log Files, and so on, using a SQL-like syntax is appealing, this is the power tool for you. Since you can run it from the command line as well as through a GUI, scheduling report generation is simple through the use of Windows Scheduler.

The last point to mention here is to review your domain names. Make sure to keep a list of the domain names that you own and when they expire. Many individuals (and organizations) quickly grab expired domain names soon after their expiration date has passed, which can result in your company losing an important asset. This risk can be mitigated by renewing your domain name for a longer period of time, keeping up-to-date on when it expires, and keeping the registration and contact information correct.

Automate as many of these processes as possible. It's a bad idea to put too much faith in the memory of any individual to remember to check for issues, especially considering they are highly amenable to automation.

MAINTAINING PERFORMANCE

A website's throughput, or the average rate of successful responses it elicits, is a function of four characteristics: the traffic load, the hardware configuration, the software design and configuration, and the volume of data stored in the system. This means that if you change one of these variables in some way, you affect, either negatively or positively, the performance of the website. It's important to keep this in mind as you log, analyze, and act on data related to performance, since there is no single dial to turn to in order to "improve performance." Answering performance-related questions can often require looking into multiple sources of data for answers.

The best way to keep tabs on performance is through constant and automated monitoring of key metrics. From a hardware perspective, these metrics indicate the server's health and include such items as memory, CPU, hard disk, and network utilization. PerfMon is a server tool that collects data on potentially hundreds of data points, including those previously listed as well as more granular data points related to ASP.NET, IIS, SQL Server, and the .NET CLR. Figure 15-4 shows a picture of PerfMon capturing and logging CPU utilization. Running PerfMon takes resources itself, as does the overhead of sampling the dataset too frequently. Therefore, when using PerfMon for ongoing analysis, it is best to keep the sampling rate low.

Depending on your website's implementation, the amount of data in a system may affect your system's performance. It is therefore a good idea to remain aware of how much of the website's code scales relative to the size of some dataset such as the number users, the amount of content, the number of folders, and the nodes in a taxonomy, among others. In general, the point is to understand how the architecture of your website scales according to the growth of data, and to keep track of the amount of this data when relevant.

Ektron also gives you the ability to delete historical versions of content in a folder using the Purge History option, shown in Figure 15-5. This is useful when you have a large number of content or document revisions that are no longer necessary.

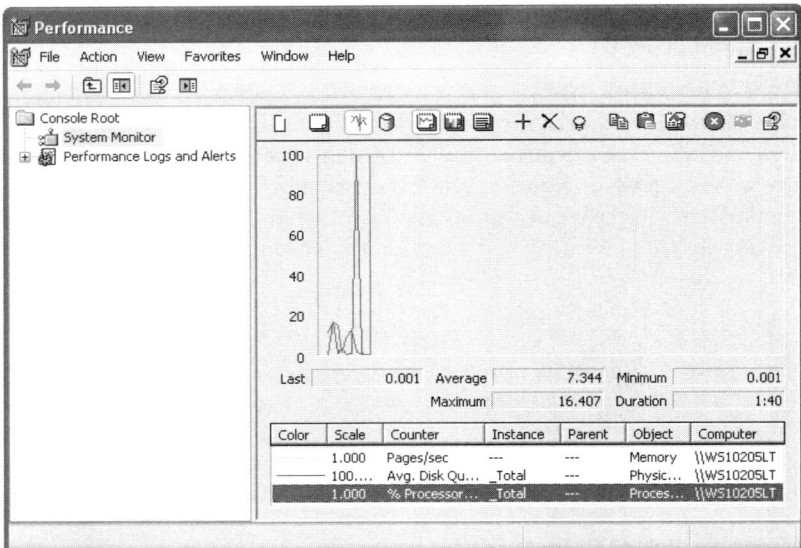

FIGURE 15-4

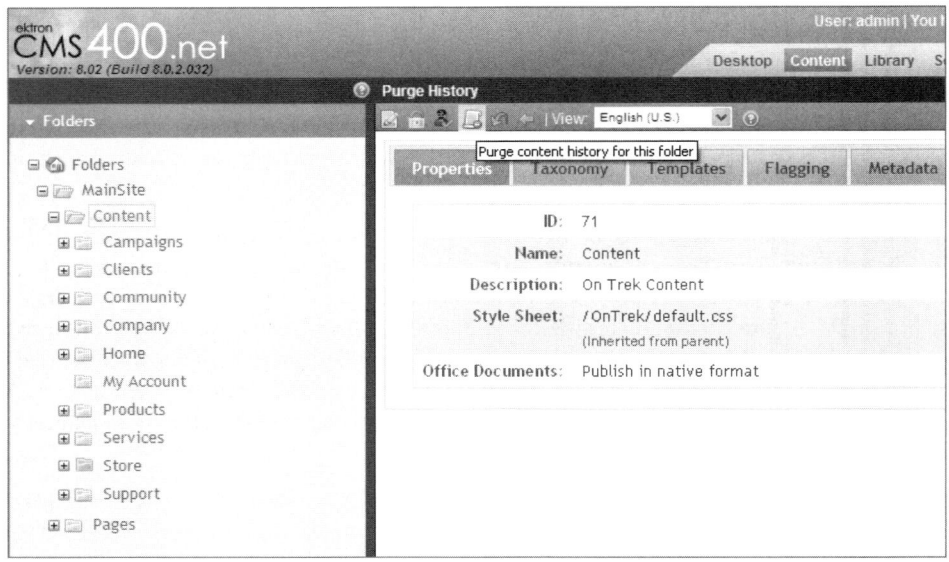

FIGURE 15-5

In the case of managed content, each revision occupies a record in the content table. In the case of a managed document, it additionally keeps a document for each saved version. If you have a large number of sizable documents, you might want to run through the process of purging history to free up disk or database space. To run purge history, do the following:

1. Open the Workarea ⇨ Content folder tree.
2. Select the folder whose history you want to purge.
3. Access the folder's Properties screen.
4. On this screen you have the ability to specify various purge options, including whether you want to purge recursively and the time frame that you want to purge, among other options.
5. Click the Purge History button and then OK to continue.

Website throughput is measured in a number of ways, including pages per second and requests per second. The performance and load testing performed during staging and deployment should have given you a solid sense of the average throughput for your website under normal and above-average traffic conditions. Using this as a baseline, you can then turn to throughput monitoring solutions, such as Keynote, to track ongoing throughput relative to the baselines you established during your controlled tests. Services such as Keynote are nice because they give you an understanding of your website's actual throughput experienced by site visitors, without the need to take servers out of production for a dedicated load test. Figure 15-6 shows a sample report provided by Keynote.

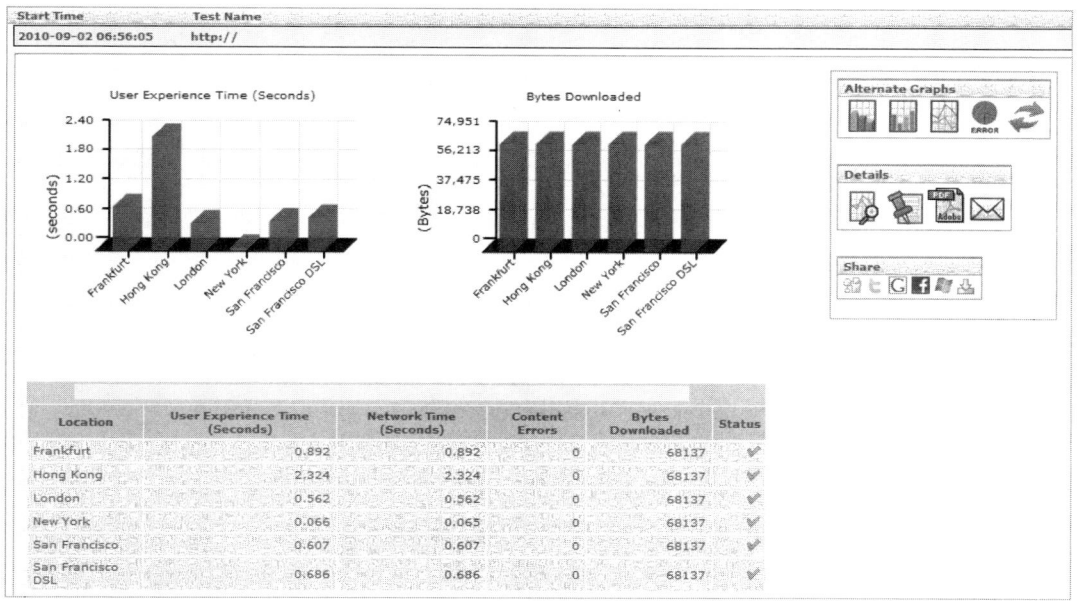

FIGURE 15-6

MAINTAINING USABILITY

If you are doing your job, your website will undoubtedly continue to change long after the initial launch date. Small incremental changes might not seem substantial enough to warrant usability testing, but over time they can add up to significant changes to the overall user experience.

Given this, it's worth conducting a usability study once in a while to make sure that website visitors are still able to find what they're looking for and accomplish their goals. If you conducted usability studies during discovery or development, consider repeating portions of the usability study that cover the areas that have changed. A usability study does not need to be elaborate and formal. While it's a good idea to get a cross-section of your customer base, a lot of information can be gleaned by pulling in an existing employee to run through a quick study and gut-check usability assertions.

It's also a good idea to make sure that your documentation team is made aware of these small incremental changes as they occur so they can update the website's help guide or reference manual if there's one associated with the website. Small changes in text, labels, and navigation can greatly affect procedural steps found in most help manuals and ultimately further confuse the site visitors looking to the help manual for guidance.

Graphic design also plays an important part in the overall perception of the website. Take note of how your website's design compares to other websites. Does your website's design feel outdated? Have incremental changes been made to the design and it's no longer accurately reflecting the branding efforts of the marketing department? This last question might be difficult to answer yourself, so if you're unsure, ask a design or marketing colleague for help.

MAINTAINING (AND BUILDING) REACH

This section is not intended to offer a one-size-fits-all roadmap for building the traffic to your website. Instead, it will offer you points to consider as you create your maintenance plan:

- What questions should you ask?
- What data should you log?
- What analysis should you perform?

Before you can think about increasing your website's traffic, start by asking good questions and making sure the data is available for meaningful analysis. Some of these questions may include:

- Do you have a good understanding of who is currently using your website?
- Do you know what they like about it?
- What problems do they have?

If you artificially gain traffic without understanding your current base of site visitors, you stand the risk of putting a ton of effort into simply having an increase in unhappy site visitors.

Chapter 9 covered Ektron's approach to Web Analytics through the support of integration with Web Analytics providers such as Google Analytics and Omniture. Through these Web Analytics providers, you have the ability to capture and analyze most any statistic related to the activities on your website.

A long-term strategy will offer no single way to increase traffic to your website. Maintaining and building your website's online presence requires a holistic look at your website's traffic from many different angles. Such a strategy will most likely involve some elements of:

- Search engine marketing
- Search engine optimization
- Social media strategy
- Online advertising
- Print advertising

Not all organizations can afford to have a full-time employee focused on SEO to ensure your position in the search engines. Out of the items listed here, this one often falls on the shoulders of a Web developer. If this is a responsibility that you will have, it's important to make sure you're setting SEO-related goals and are therefore capturing, analyzing, and taking action on data related to the position of your website in the search indexes.

Once content-related SEO considerations have been addressed (such as content relevance, metadata, and keywords), your attention should turn to how many inbound links you have pointing to your website. This is a very important metric since each link is, in effect, a "vote" for your website and its content. Imagine trying to determine the best place to get pizza in your town and being able to query the phone records to see which one gets the most phone calls. The one that gets more phone orders might give an indication as to which is more popular, and therefore, could be inferred as having better pizza. Similarly, search engines use the number and quality of links pointing to your website as a metric to determine rank.

How many inbound links are pointing to your site? You can use the advanced search syntax of Google to show you the number of inbound links pointing to your website. For example, the following query shows all links pointing to mysite.com that do not originate from the domain mysite.com:

```
link:mysite.com -site:mysite.com
```

Understanding, measuring, and tracking key SEO metrics is important in improving your search engine standing. It has been said that "what is tracked, improves." How does your search engine ranking compare to when you first launched? After six months? After a year?

Ektron provides an SEO tool that is helpful in gathering tracking information like this. The tool analyzes your website for W3C compliance, Alexa rankings, image ALT text, keyword density, and metadata, and also gives you an indication of your website's score for these metrics. Figure 15-7 shows a screenshot of the SEO tool.

If SEO concepts like these sound foreign, consider talking with someone who understands SEO and is willing to offer some advice. Additionally, there are many good authoritative blogs on the subject. Investing a little time to learn about search engines and how they rank Web pages can yield big rewards in terms of your website's search traffic.

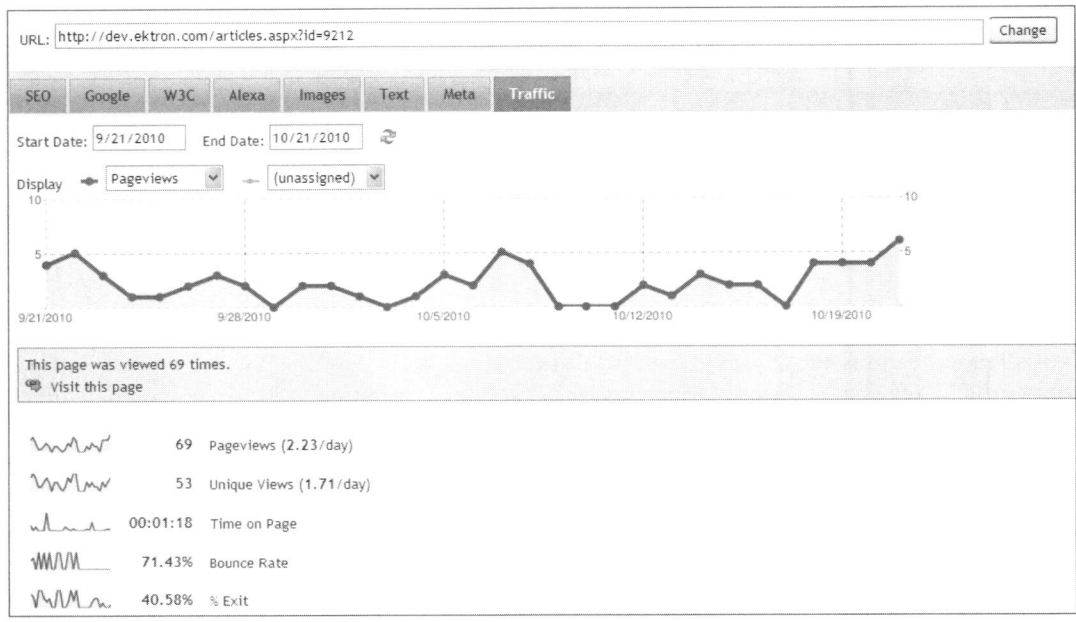

FIGURE 15-7

MAINTAINING CALM DURING DISASTER RECOVERY

"By failing to prepare, you are preparing to fail," said Benjamin Franklin. Although a crisis situation may never happen, it's important to consider the points of failure in your system, to have a plan in place if something were to go wrong, and to have practiced this plan to verify that there are no chinks in the armor. If you've followed along and have gone through the process of putting together a maintenance plan according to the guidance provided here, you will be in a good position to dodge most bullets because you are proactively dealing with potential hiccups rather than reactively dealing with a crisis situation.

But in the event that a crisis situation does occur, what can you do to prepare for it? How can you mitigate the disruption caused by it?

The first step is understanding the constraints of your deployment architecture and what it means for recovery, failover, and general availability. What happens if the hard drive fails in production? Have you built redundancy into all of your hardware? At what level of availability are you striving for? Availability is typically expressed in terms of the uptime for a given year.

- 99 percent ("two nines") is equivalent to 3.65 days of downtime per year
- 99.9 percent ("three nines") is equivalent to 8.76 hours of downtime per year
- 99.99 percent ("four nines") is equivalent to 8.76 hours of downtime per year

The point here is not to push you to "four nines" but for you to set the expectations of your deployment scenarios and to organize your disaster recovery plans correspondingly.

The most important things to have backed up are:

- Source code (including templates, JavaScript, CSS, codebehind, and so on)
- Content (including database and assets stored on the filesystem)
- Software (including installation and configuration options)

Source code should already be managed in a Source Control Management System and in sync with your production environment. Content found in databases needs to be configured for automatic backups with backup storage living on a network separate from your production server. Software licenses and installation executables need to be backed up.

Once your plan is in place, it is important to perform a disaster recovery dry-run to make sure that you have all the information in place to recover from a crisis situation. It's one thing to know you have daily backups of your database, but how useful are database backups when you're trying to hunt down software, licenses, and passwords to get the backup restored? Having periodic dry-runs will give you a level of confidence in your disaster recovery plans.

TAKE HOME POINTS

The success of your website is ultimately gauged on its ability to deliver on longer term goals. Failing to have a plan in place for maintaining your website inevitably results in a website that at best, appears abandoned and at worst, becomes unusable.

This chapter provided:

- A general process for creating an effective maintenance plan using business goals and KPIs to drive what data is monitored and analyzed.
- A discussion showing that once your plan is in place, you greatly reduce the chances of needing to reactively deal with a problem because you are proactively tuning your website for success.

16

Next Steps

- What have you learned thus far?
- Why should you engage with the Ektron developer community?
- What Professional Services does Ektron offer?
- What online resource does Ektron Offer?

In past chapters, you learned all about Ektron, its Framework, tools, features, and community. This chapter not only reviews what you've learned so far, but also gives you some guidance on what to do with your newly gained knowledge, including a full list of webinars available to you.

REVIEWING WHAT YOU LEARNED

In the first three chapters, you gained a high-level understanding of the Ektron Framework, its architecture, and major components; you learned about the services and solutions offered by Ektron's professional services division; and you were introduced to the Web project methodology followed by Ektron's own Best Practice and Professional Services teams.

In the 10 chapters that followed, you learned how to set up an Ektron development environment and build a complete website using the Ektron Framework. Each chapter focused on a specific area of the OnTrek website and walked through the process of understanding its implementation by focusing on the key concepts of the technology used, a review of the implementation, and a look "Under the Hood" to gain a deeper understanding of the inner workings of the particular technology.

In the final two chapters, you read about the deployment process, including considerations for designing your deployment architecture, pre-conditions for deployment, and steps for physically deploying your website. You also learned about the maintenance process and a systematic approach to understanding which data to capture, analyze, and act upon for a comprehensive and holistic approach to website maintenance.

This chapter details the various available resources as you continue to work with Ektron. A primary resource is the Ektron online community. It also explains how to reach out to Ektron technical support when you need more information than the online community can provide. Finally, this chapter lists developer resources — including screencasts and webinars — designed to help you further build on your knowledge of the Ektron product.

CONNECTING WITH EKTRON AND THE ONLINE COMMUNITY

At any point during your Web projects, it's important to know that there is a great amount of help literally available at your fingers. The Ektron developer community has a large presence on social networking sites such as Twitter and Facebook. On Twitter, Ektron regularly watches and responds to the stream of Twitter posts that contain the word Ektron (or #ektron). Public conversations between Ektron employees, developers, and community members are very common on Twitter. Engaging with the Ektron community on social networking sites such as these is something Ektron looks at as an opportunity to assist customers through hurdles, connect them with the resources to ensure a projects success, and engage in conversation. Twitter has shown to be a very powerful way for Ektron employees to connect with Ektron developers and customers alike.

Ektron also uses both Twitter and Facebook as a way to share information such as product webinars, technical screencasts, as well as the Web projects completed by Ektron's partners and customers. Joining Ektron's Facebook group is a good idea as it provides another opportunity for you to engage Ektron in a conversation. Ektron's tagline, "What do you want your website to do?," is more than just empty marketing jargon — it captures the importance of customer feedback to Ektron for the growth of the company and its products. By joining these communities you can participate in discussions that have the potential to impact the future direction of the company and even see one of your feature ideas go from concept, to conversation, to product release and ultimately to influencing the direction of the product.

In addition to Twitter and Facebook, Ektron has its own Developer Community hub, called the Ektron Dev Center (`http://dev.ektron.com`), which serves as a centralized location for developers to communicate with one another and with Ektron's own technical engineer staff. The discussion boards are very active on the Dev Center and contributions to them come from both the Ektron Developer Community and Ektron's own engineering teams. These discussion boards are a great place to post questions, request feedback, and seek help when troubleshooting.

In cases when you need more support than what's offered through the online community, keep in mind that Ektron offers full technical support to all customers with active maintenance, as well as access to all product downloads, including all new software releases. Maintenance needs to be renewed yearly; once the one year anniversary of the purchase date passes, your maintenance expires. To prevent this from happening, you must renew your maintenance agreement with your account manager in advance of your maintenance expiration date.

A Quick Review of Ektron's Technical Support

Chapter 1 covered the four ways to contact technical support, but it's worth repeating so I'll summarize it here (for more information on this, see Chapter 1):

- **Phone Support:** Phone calls are answered immediately by a Technical Support Engineer (TSE), who triages your issue, gathers information, and creates a case. A TSE is then assigned to the case and must return the call within two hours. When you have a critical issue needing attention, use phone support.
    - **United States:** 1-866-4-EKTRON x7002
    - **United Kingdom:** +44-1628-509-040
    - **Australia:** +61-2-9248-7222
- **Web Form Support:** Technical support cases initiated using the Web form (http://dev.ektron.com/requestsupport) will receive a call from a TSE responding to the customer within four to six hours.
- **E-mail Support:** Technical support cases initiated by sending e-mail to support@ektron.com will receive a response from a TSE within 24 hours. This is a good option for lower-priority issues that still require a resolution.
- **Chat Support:** Basic questions can be answered through live chat on the Ektron website from 8:30 a.m. to 5:30 p.m. EST (http://ektron.com/support/).

You may have noticed that the Dev Center and social networking sites like Twitter and Facebook are not listed as ways to engage Ektron Support for assistance. Don't infer from this they shouldn't be used or are not taken seriously. They're not listed simply because Ektron does not offer a Service Level Agreement (SLA) around this type of community-driven support. Given that responses on these social media outlets come primarily from the community as opposed to official Ektron representatives, predicting and guaranteeing the time it will take to receive a response from the community is not possible. In some cases it may take as little as an hour, other times a day or more. It's also entirely possible that a question posted on the Dev Center might not get a response all together.

In cases like this, it's important to keep in mind Ektron's technical support team. If you have an issue that needs a response, and you are not getting the response you need from the Ektron community, contact Ektron Support using one of the four ways outlined earlier. Which of the four methods you use to contact support depends on how quickly you need resolution to the issue. Keeping these options in mind and using the right support channel will help you to avoid unnecessary waits and get you a quick resolution.

Don't Forget Your Account Manager

Don't forget the fact that once you purchase a license you also have access to a dedicated Account Manager. Oftentimes customers misunderstand the role of the account manager and as a result, miss out on an opportunity to tap into a valuable resource that is freely available to every Ektron customer. At the most basic level, the Account Manager is the customer relations point of contact — someone who you work with when you purchase or renew your license, or need to discuss upgrading to access new features. More importantly, however, the Account Manager serves as your advocate within the Ektron organization. This is helpful when you need an Ektron contact to act as a champion for such things as a feature request and escalating support issues to the management team. Keeping your maintenance agreement plan active gives you access to your Account Manager and to Ektron support.

UTILIZING EKTRON'S PROFESSIONAL SERVICES AND TRAINING PACKAGES

Ektron offers a full range of services that can be leveraged in a number of different ways at various points during the lifecycle of your Web project. These include:

- Best Practice
- Application Engineering
- Training packages

Both Best Practice and Application Engineering offer services that can help your project when needed by bringing in Ektron application engineers and project managers experienced in building, deploying, and managing Ektron projects. Additionally, Ektron's training services pay an important role in the process of education for many different types of people involved in your Web project. The Application Engineering department is filled with seasoned Web project managers, business analysts, CMS Architects, developers, and QA testers who know how to take a project from the discovery phase to the delivery and deployment phase. They can be leveraged to complete entire Web projects or used to augment your own-in house development efforts.

The Best Practices department can support your Web project by giving you access to a best practice solution engineer. This resource serves as an advanced support system — giving you greater access and availability to the specific individual assigned to your project who can provide you with help for items such as architectural guidance, deployment configuration recommendations, and experienced troubleshooting.

Ektron offers a number of different training packages so you can receive raining based on the requirements of your Web project and the roles of the individuals needing training. Training sessions include Administrator Training, Developer Training, Advanced Developer Training, and Customized Training. There are facilities at which this training takes place available throughout the world. Additionally, Ektron offers personalized training that allows you to define a customized training plan tailored to the needs of your organization.

LEVERAGING ONLINE DEVELOPER RESOURCES

Ektron regularly produces webinars and screencasts that offer developer guidance on new and existing technologies. The following sections features a sampling of some of the more popular webinars and screencasts that can help you continue to learn about the Ektron Framework and give you ideas about ways to further integrate this technology into your Web projects.

The Ektron Exchange (`http://dev.ektron.com/exchange/`) is another excellent resource where you can find code submitted by both Ektron Engineers and members of the Ektron developer community available for reuse in your own Web projects. The most popular type of code currently available through the Ektron Exchange are PageBuilder Widgets; you can find widgets readily available for features like rotating banners, taxonomy driven menus, integration with bit.ly for URL shortening, and many others.

The Framework API

`http://dev.ektron.com/FrameworkAPI/`

Webinar description: The Framework API represents a new API for Ektron officially launched in its 8.0 release. The design goals of this API are to provide an API that offers discoverability, consistency, and simplicity.

CMS Extensions

`http://dev.ektron.com/ExtensionFramework/`

Webinar description: The CMS Extension Framework is the new extensibility architecture released in version 8.0. This screencast discusses the benefits it provides over the plug-in architecture, including:

➤ **Context:** You have direct access to the Web application from within the extension, including, HTTP Context, Session, Cache, and all of Ektron's CMS APIs.

➤ **Easier to debug:** You can attach Visual Studio directly to IIS and set breakpoints just as you would when debugging any Web application.

➤ **Performance:** Previously, you had to use Web services to access the Web application context. Since you have direct access with CMS Extensions, you no longer have to issue Web service calls.

➤ **No Windows service:** Since CMS Extensions run within the context of the Web application, no Windows service is needed.

Integrating Ektron with a Content Delivery Network

`www.ektron.com/Resources/Webinars/Integrating-Ektron-with-a-Content-Delivery-Network/`

Webinar description: A content delivery network (CDN) is a powerful infrastructure of servers made available to maximize bandwidth for access to your Web data, reducing page load times and improving user experience. The webinar discusses:

➤ What a CDN is as well as its technical benefits

➤ Other services available through CDN providers, such as Akamai

➤ How to integrate with Akamai via a CMS extensions (plug-ins) for forward caching capabilities

Building Your First Ektron eCommerce Site

www.ektron.com/Resources/Webinars/Building-Your-First-Ektron-eCommerce-Site/

Webinar description: As part of Ektron, you can have a single application running both your website and online marketplace, which allows you to manage both from the same interface. Jason Arden takes you through the initial steps to get your store up-and-running.

During this webinar, you learn how to:
- Utilize the eCommerce server controls.
- Create a Landing page for your products.
- Create a Product Detail page.
- Create a Product Search page.
- Create a Checkout process.
- Create a My Account page for previous shoppers.

Utilizing the Ektron eCommerce APIs

www.ektron.com/Resources/Webinars/Utilizing-the-Ektron-eCommerce-APIs/

Webinar description: Covers working with eCommerce functionality and utilizing the API layer. Developers gain an understanding of how to access, add, update, and delete data programmatically around:

- Customers and customer information
- Products and product catalogs
- Baskets and coupons

Introduction to the Ektron eCommerce Workflow Engine

www.ektron.com/Resources/Webinars/eCommerce-Workflow-Engine.aspx

Webinar description: Covers creating and customizing an eCommerce workflow utilizing the Windows Workflow Foundation (WF) available within .NET 3.0. Workflows are composed of activities and each activity represents a portion of your business processes. Covers how to work with different types of activities and how to create your own. The webinar wraps up by adding the new workflow to the Ektron CMS and walking you through the purchase process.

Agenda:
- Introduction to the Windows Workflow Foundation
- Creating a workflow from a workflow template
- Working with the Ektron activities
- Creating your own activities
- Adding a new workflow to the CMS

Creating Your Own eCommerce Payment Gateway Provider

www.ektron.com/Resources/Webinars/Creating-Your-Own-Payment-Gateway-Provider/

Webinar description: A payment gateway provider is a pluggable component that is integrated into Ektron's eCommerce module. A payment provider handles eCommerce customer payments by utilizing third-party payment gateways. Ektron comes with several payment providers, including Authorize.NET and PayFlow. This webinar covers how to create your own payment gateway provider for use within your own Ektron-powered website.

Hands On with the Content Targeting Widget

www.ektron.com/Resources/Webinars/Hands-on-with-the-Content-Targeting-Widget/

Webinar description: The Content Targeting Widget in PageBuilder can be one of the most important elements in your developer toolkit. Learn how to use targeting technology to build better user experiences.

Agenda:

- How the Targeting Widget is architected
- Out-of-the-box Conditions Rulesets such as Referral URLs, Cookies, User Properties, User Groups, and query string Parameters
- How to add new Condition Rulesets
- How to use the underlying framework of the Targeting Widget to provide a customized user experience

Introduction to Ektron eSync

www.ektron.com/Resources/Webinars/eSync-Revolutionize-the-way-you-build-deploy-and-maintain-your-Web-site/

Webinar description: eSync was designed specifically to meet the needs of enterprise-level websites. It is the next generation in advanced Web synchronization technology and this webinar shows how it can revolutionize the way you build, deploy, and maintain your website.

Agenda:

- Bi-directionally manage content changes and membership information.
- Deploy your first, second, or tenth revision of your website with zero site downtime.
- Move only the changes you want to move, from single pieces of content and specific functionality to entire sites.
- Manage multiple servers across a server farm, the globe, or in a load balancing environment.
- Strategically schedule synchronization.
- Build out complete development environments in minutes.

Introduction to the Ektron Marketing Optimization Suite

www.ektron.com/Resources/Webinars/Ektron-Marketing-Optimization-Suite/

Webinar description: An agile marketing department needs the ability to gain real-time insight into the behavior of website visitors and optimize the Web experience to drive business results.

Agenda:

- Create marketing campaigns and landing pages without the need for Web developers.
- Deliver personalized content in real time to all your site visitors and customer segments.
- Test different combinations of copy, images, and page layout to drive site visitors to take action.
- Make your Google, Omniture, and Webtrends data-actionable.
- Enforce Search Engine Optimization best practices and identify areas for SEO improvement.
- Score site visitors and prospects based on their activities on your website.

Ektron Widgets in Version 8

www.ektron.com/Resources/Webinars/Building-Widgets/

Webinar description: With the release of PageBuilder, Ektron revolutionized how websites are built and maintained. An important part of this strategy was the separation of functionality from display that was created through the use of widgets.

Writing an RIA Application with Ektron

www.ektron.com/Resources/Webinars/Writing-An-RIA-Application-On-Top-Of-The-Ektron-Platform/

Webinar description: Building an RIA on top of the Ektron platform. Code and concepts covered are relevant to any developer building RIAs with Flash, Flex, or Silverlight.

This webinar covers basic concepts, such as how to pull data out of the CMS for display within an RIA. It also demonstrates best practices for data manipulation within the CMS.

In this webinar, you learn how to:

- Display HTML/XML managed content in an RIA
- Add data to the CMS
- Create a mini app for data manipulation

TAKE HOME POINTS

Ektron is a very transparent company that is actively involved in online social media communities. Its transparency gives you the an opportunity to connect with Ektron employees to ask questions, voice your thoughts, and provide feedback on the platform, support, services, or overall experience with Ektron in general. To recap:

- Ektron offers formal methods for receiving assistance through dedicated Support and Professional Services. You can use these services any time you need official support from Ektron to support the success of your Web project.
- Ektron Training is available for those customers who need custom, developer, administrator, or onsite training courses.
- The Training department is committed to creating online video training collateral for access by the general user community. This comes at no cost via the Ektron homepage, educational screencasts and webinars.

PART IV
Appendixes

- ▶ **APPENDIX A:** CMS Extensions
- ▶ **APPENDIX B:** Framework API
- ▶ **APPENDIX C:** Performance Checklist

CMS Extensions

One of the strengths of the Ektron Framework is the ability to hook into events in the system and run custom code against them. You experimented with some of the methods for running custom code against system events through the eCommerce Workflow engine and eCommerce Provider interfaces in Chapter 13. In this appendix, you will look at working with content and user oriented events using the CMS Extension system.

BENEFITS OF EKTRON FRAMEWORK, VERSION 8

Prior to version 8 of the Ektron Framework, the methodology for running custom code on certain events was to use plug-in extensions; however, with version 8 and the addition of CMS Extensions, several benefits are brought into play over the old system.

- **The handler executes in the context of the request.** Executing in the context of the request means that your code will have access to the user session, the different caches, and the HTTP Context of the request. In previous versions, when working with the plug-in architecture, the custom code was executed outside of the request, which meant that only some of the additional information was exposed to the custom code, limiting the ability of the developer to understand the action that was taking place. With CMS Extensions, however, your code runs in the same reference frame as the Ektron Framework itself, so all the features you have in a page are available from your extension also.

- **Extensions perform better than plug-ins.** Since plug-ins ran outside of the context of the CMS, in order to interact with the CMS itself through API calls, you first had to connect via a Web service. Since extensions run in the same context, there is no overhead when executing system calls.

- **It is easier to construct more complex system interactions.** Without the added overhead of building Web services for your CMS interaction, you can easily build up rich functionality in the same manner you would when using API calls on the page directly. This means less code, which leads directly to less development time and easier maintenance. Additionally, debugging your code is also simplified, since you are able to simply attach a debugger in the same manner as you would on a page.

BUILDING YOUR EXTENSION

This appendix constructs a sample extension that operates on every piece of content as it is being published and appends a link to search Google for similar Web pages. The link uses the title of the content being published for the search terms. This is a simple example, but the steps show how you can connect your custom code to the events, and even modify the item currently being operated on.

1. To start building your extension, open Visual Studio and select File ➪ New ➪ Project. This will bring up the New Project screen. Under Project Types, select Visual C#, and under templates select Class Library. Name the project GoogleExtension, and click OK.

2. The new solution and project will be created, and it will contain a single class file to begin with, called Class1.cs. Rename the file CustomContentStrategy.cs by right-clicking the file in the Solution Explorer and selecting Rename.

3. Next you need to add some project references so that you can properly hook into the Ektron Framework. Right-click on the GoogleExtension project in the Solution Explorer, and select Add Reference. Switch to the Browse tab, and navigate to your site bin folder, which in this instance is located at C:\inetpub\wwwroot\OnTrek\bin. Select the following two files: Ektron .Cms.Common.dll and Ektron.Cms.ObjectFactory.dll. Click OK.

4. Now that the fundamentals are in place, you are ready to construct the code for your extension. Open the CustomContentStrategy.cs file and start by adding the following lines to the top of the file after the existing `using` statements.

```
using Ektron.Cms;
using Ektron.Cms.Common;
using Ektron.Cms.Extensibility;
using Ektron.Cms.Extensibility.Content;
```

5. Next you need to set the `CustomContentStrategy` class to inherit from the `Ektron.Cms .Extensibility.ContentStrategy` class as shown in the following snippet. This class contains the default behaviors for events that happen to content as it moves through the workflow, and provides a set of overrides that can be used to extend the default behavior.

```
public class CustomContentStrategy : Ektron.Cms.Extensibility.ContentStrategy
```

Available Strategies and Overrides

There are a large number of strategy classes to base your custom class on, and each strategy class contains a number of override functions for which you can write custom code. Table A-1 contains a list of the available strategies and overrides.

TABLE A-1: Strategy Classes and Events

STRATEGY	EVENT SIGNATURE
ContentStrategy	OnBeforeAddContent(ContentData, CmsEventArgs)
	OnAfterAddContent(ContentData, CmsEventArgs)

STRATEGY	EVENT SIGNATURE
	OnBeforeDeleteContent(long, CmsEventArgs)
	OnAfterDeleteContent(long, CmsEventArgs)
	OnBeforePublishContent(ContentData, CmsEventArgs)
	OnAfterPublishContent(ContentData, CmsEventArgs)
	OnBeforeUpdateContent(ContentData, CmsEventArgs)
	OnAfterUpdateContent(ContentData, CmsEventArgs)
CommunityGroupStrategy	OnAdd(CommunityGroupData, CmsEventArgs)
	OnAfterUserAdd(long, long, CmsEventArgs)
	OnAfterUserDelete(long, long, CmsEventArgs)
	OnDelete(long, CmsEventArgs)
	OnUpdate(CommunityGroupData, CmsEventArgs)
FolderStrategy	OnBeforeAddFolder(FolderData, CmsEventArgs)
	OnAfterAddFolder(FolderData, CmsEventArgs)
	OnBeforeDeleteFolder(long, CmsEventArgs)
	OnAfterDeleteFolder(long, CmsEventArgs)
	OnBeforeUpdateFolder(FolderData, CmsEventArgs)
	OnAfterUpdateFolder(FolderData, CmsEventArgs)
MessageBoardStrategy	OnAdd(MessageBoardData, CmsEventArgs)
	OnAfterReplyAdd(MessageBoardData, CmsEventArgs)
	OnDelete(long, CmsEventArgs)
	OnMessageApprove(MessageBoardData, CmsEventArgs)
	OnUpdate(MessageBoardData, CmsEventArgs)
MicroMessageStrategy	OnBeforeAdd(MicroMessageData, CmsEventArgs)
	OnAfterAdd(MicroMessageData, CmsEventArgs)
	OnBeforeDelete(long, CmsEventArgs)
	OnAfterDelete(long, CmsEventArgs)
TagStrategy	OnAdd(TagData, CmsEventArgs)
	OnDelete(long, CmsEventArgs)
	OnUpdate(TagData, CmsEventArgs)
TaxonomyStrategy	OnBeforeAdd(TaxonomyData, CmsEventArgs)
	OnAfterAdd(TaxonomyData, CmsEventArgs)
	OnBeforeAssignItem(TaxonomyRequest, CmsEventArgs)

continues

TABLE A-1 *(continued)*

STRATEGY	EVENT SIGNATURE
	OnAfterAssignItem(TaxonomyRequest, CmsEventArgs)
	OnBeforeDelete(long, CmsEventArgs)
	OnAfterDelete(long, CmsEventArgs)
	OnBeforeUpdate(TaxonomyData, CmsEventArgs)
	OnAfterUpdate(TaxonomyData, CmsEventArgs)
UserStrategy	OnBeforeAddUser(UserData, CmsEventArgs)
	OnAfterAddUser(UserData, CmsEventArgs)
	OnAfterColleagueRequest(ActionRequestData, CmsEventArgs)
	OnAfterAddColleague(long, long, CmsEventArgs)
	OnBeforeDeleteUser(long, CmsEventArgs)
	OnAfterDeleteUser(long, CmsEventArgs)
	OnBeforeLogin(UserData, CmsEventArgs)
	OnAfterLogin(UserData, CmsEventArgs)
	OnBeforeUpdateUser(UserData, CmsEventArgs)
	OnAfterUpdateUser(UserData, CmsEventArgs)
WebEventStrategy	OnBeforeAdd(WebEventData, CmsEventArgs)
	OnAfterAdd(WebEventData, CmsEventArgs)
	OnBeforeAddVariance(WebEventData, CmsEventArgs)
	OnAfterAddVariance(WebEventData, CmsEventArgs)
	OnBeforeCancelOccurrence(WebEventData, CmsEventArgs)
	OnAfterCancelOccurrence(WebEventData, CmsEventArgs)
	OnBeforeDelete(long, CmsEventArgs)
	OnAfterDelete(long, CmsEventArgs)
	OnBeforePublish(WebEventData, CmsEventArgs)
	OnAfterPublish(WebEventData, CmsEventArgs)
	OnBeforeUpdate(WebEventData, CmsEventArgs)
	OnAfterUpdate(WebEventData, CmsEventArgs)

The Completed Extension

Selecting from the available events in the ContentStrategy class, you will be updating the content before it gets published, so you will use the OnBeforePublishContent event. Adding the method override to your CustomContentStrategy class, and populating the method with the code to append the link to Google will yield the finished file, as shown in Listing A-1.

Available for download on Wrox.com

LISTING A-1: CustomContentStrategy.cs

```csharp
using System;
using System.Collections.Generic;
using System.Linq;
using System.Text;
using Ektron.Cms;
using Ektron.Cms.Common;
using Ektron.Cms.Extensibility;
using Ektron.Cms.Extensibility.Content;

namespace GoogleExtension
{
  public class CustomContentStrategy : Ektron.Cms.Extensibility.ContentStrategy
  {
    public override void OnBeforePublishContent(Ektron.Cms.ContentData contentData,
                                      CmsEventArgs eventArgs)
    {
      string searchPhrase = contentData.Title.Replace(" ", "+");
      string searchLink = "";
      searchLink += "<a href='http://www.google.com/search?q=";
      searchLink += searchPhrase + "'>";
      searchLink += "Search Google for similar content";
      searchLink += "</a>";
      contentData.Html = contentData.Title + "<br />" + searchLink;

      base.OnBeforePublishContent(contentData, eventArgs);
    }
  }
}
```

Registering Your Extension

Now that you have your extension completed, build the assembly and then copy the GoogleExtension .dll file from the bin directory of your project into the bin directory of your website. All that remains is to make the ObjectFactory in the Ektron Framework aware of the new strategy.

Extensions must be registered by modifying the ObjectFactory.config file in the root of your website:

1. Open the file now and browse to the <strategies> node in the <add name="Content"> section in the file.

2. Add a new key in the format shown in the following snippet. For this format, the type consists of the namespace and class name, followed by a comma, followed by the assembly name. Unless you modify it, the assembly name is the same as your project name.

   ```xml
   <add name="GoogleExtension"
       type="GoogleExtension.CustomContentStrategy, GoogleExtension"/>
   ```

Table A-2 lists the valid set of names for use with extensions on children of the `<objectStrategies>` node.

TABLE A-2: Valid Names in the objectStrategies Section of the objectFactory.config File

Content	MessageBoard	Taxonomy
CommunityGroup	MicroMessage	User
Folder	Tag	WebEvent

Your extension should now be up-and-running, and any events that are overridden will fire at the appropriate times.

Framework API

The Framework API is the newest member of the API set that Ektron includes with CMS400 .NET. It was added to promote discoverability and consistency. *Discoverability* means that a developer should be able to guess the namespace, object name, and method to use without having to read through huge amounts of documentation. With a well designed API, users should be able to intuit their way through a situation using context clues delivered by the naming of objects and IntelliSense.

For *consistency*, the goal was to make the API work in similar ways for similar functions. Therefore, it should be easy to understand how to work with a given object because it works in the same way as other objects you have already used. The final goal was to make the API simple to use. It should make easy things easy to do, while steering developers down the path of having easily maintainable code that follows best practices, without needing to keep a large number of rules in mind.

This appendix discusses some of the overall themes of the Framework API, and then jumps into a few snippets demonstrating how to achieve some typical simple goals.

WORKING WITH THE FRAMEWORK API

There are two points to understand before you can effectively work with the Framework API. The first is how the API interacts with the underlying permission model, and the second is the overall construction of the API. For the Framework API, the permissions flag is set when the API objects are initially created, by specifying a switch in the constructor for the object.

Framework Object Constructors

When creating a new Framework object to perform actions, the constructor has an optional parameter to specify the access mode for that object. For instance, when creating a new Content object, the code will look like the following snippet.

```
Ektron.Cms.Framework.Core.Content.Content content
  = new Ektron.Cms.Framework.Core.Content.Content(
        Ektron.Cms.Framework.ApiAccessMode.Admin);
```

This snippet contains the optional parameter specifying the access mode, which in this case is set to `Admin`. The two valid options in the enumeration are:

- `Ektron.Cms.Framework.ApiAccessMode.Admin`: The Admin mode specifies that permissions should be ignored for all actions undertaken via this object.
- `Ektron.Cms.Framework.ApiAccessMode.LoggedInUser`: When set to `LoggedInUser`, the object will query and work within the permissions set for the current user.

There is no way to set the objects to work as a different user than the current logged-in user or an administrative user. However, this ability to switch between the two options allows you to easily circumvent the permissions model when you run into a task that requires it.

You can also skip this parameter, in which case the default behavior is to act as the currently logged in user. When objects are created as the current user, the system will properly maintain user attributions in the history for the item.

Where to Find the Framework API

The Framework API lives in the namespace `Ektron.Cms.Framework`. The namespace then contains a series of further namespaces, each of which contains objects for dealing with a particular data type in the CMS.

- `Ektron.Cms.Framework.Activity`: The activity namespace contains objects needed to manage user and group activity streams.
- `Ektron.Cms.Framework.Analytics`: The analytics namespace contains the object needed to manage business analytics, and reporting services that expose data about site visitors.
- `Ektron.Cms.Framework.Calendar`: The calendar namespace is used to manage calendars and events on the WebCalendar stack.
- `Ektron.Cms.Framework.Core`: The core namespace contains objects to manage content and folders, as well as custom properties, which allow you to add programmatically maintained data to any CMS object.
- `Ektron.Cms.Framework.Messaging`: The messaging namespace is used to work with e-mail message definitions.
- `Ektron.Cms.Framework.Notifications`: The notifications namespace is used to work with the notifications engine, which allows the sending of messages through a variety of mediums, including e-mail and SMS messages.
- `Ektron.Cms.Framework.SocialNetworking`: The social networking namespace contains tools to work with the social networking feature, including MicroMessaging.
- `Ektron.Cms.Framework.Users`: The users framework, appropriately, allows you to perform operations on users in the system.

Each namespace may contain one or more objects to work with data in a given area. The Framework API, as the newest member of the APIs made available to developers, will continue to expand and should be the first stop for people developing against the Ektron Framework.

CRUD OPERATIONS ON CONTENT

Now that you have looked at a high level at what is available in the Framework API, let's dive in for a deeper look at how to perform CRUD (create, retrieve, update, and delete) operations using the API. These examples work with content, but the methodology is the same across all the objects that the Framework API exposes.

Create

The creation methods in the framework API are called `Add()`. In each case the `Add()` method will take in a data object and store the data in the database. In the Content object, the data object is of type `Ektron.Cms.ContentData`, and is passed in by reference, which means the appropriate fields are updated in place after the content has been added to the system. The following snippet adds a new piece of content to the root folder with the language set to English.

```
//create the Content object set to observe permissions
Ektron.Cms.Framework.Core.Content.Content ContentAPI =
    new Ektron.Cms.Framework.Core.Content.Content();

//set up the contentdata object
Ektron.Cms.ContentData newContent = new Ektron.Cms.ContentData();
newContent.LanguageId = 1033;
newContent.FolderId = 0;
newContent.Title = "Content Added through the Framework API";
newContent.Teaser = "The summary for my content";
newContent.Html = "<p>The HTML for programmatically added content</p>";

//add the content
ContentAPI.Add(newContent);

//output the new content ID
Response.Write(newContent.Id.ToString());
```

Retrieve

Retrieving content is equally simple. The method used for retrieving a single item is called `GetItem()`, and is named that way across the entire Framework API. It will return a data object, in this case an instance of `Ektron.Cms.ContentData`. The following snippet retrieves the content item with ID 30, in the current language. Remember that this will respect the permissions of the logged-in user, so if they don't have permission to the content, the object returned will be empty unless you instantiate the object in `ApiAccessMode.Admin`.

```
//create the Content object set to observe permissions
Ektron.Cms.Framework.Core.Content.Content ContentAPI =
    new Ektron.Cms.Framework.Core.Content.Content();

//retrieve the content
Ektron.Cms.ContentData contentData;
contentData = ContentAPI.GetItem(30);

//output the retrieved item's content
Response.Write(contentData.Html);
```

Retrieving a List of Data

In addition to retrieving single pieces of data, sometimes you'll need to retrieve a list of items matching a constraint. In the framework API, this is done through the use of Criteria objects. Every API object in the Framework API provides a method called GetList(), which accepts a Criteria object. Criteria objects in turn accept items from an appropriate enumeration containing fields to search against, along with an operator and operand. The method to add these tuples is called AddFilter().

There are several additional properties on the Criteria object that allow you to define output parameters. These properties are listed here:

- Filters: Allows you to examine or modify the filters currently applied.
- OrderByField: The resulting list is sorted by the field specified in this property.
- OrderByDirection: Specifies whether to sort the output in ascending or descending order.
- PagingInfo: Contains properties allowing for control over paging of the results.

The following code snippet shows how you might retrieve a list of content from the root folder that is published. It also specifies a filter to retrieve items only with the word "TitleSearch" in the title of the content.

```
//create the Content object set to observe permissions
Ektron.Cms.Framework.Core.Content.Content ContentAPI
    = new Ektron.Cms.Framework.Core.Content.Content();

//create the criteria object
Ektron.Cms.Common.Criteria<Ektron.Cms.Common.ContentProperty> myCriteria
    = new Ektron.Cms.Common.Criteria<Ektron.Cms.Common.ContentProperty>();

//add a filter to specify the root folder
myCriteria.AddFilter(
    Ektron.Cms.Common.ContentProperty.FolderId,
    Ektron.Cms.Common.CriteriaFilterOperator.EqualTo,
    0);

//add a filter to only retrieve published items
myCriteria.AddFilter(
    Ektron.Cms.Common.ContentProperty.IsPublished,
    Ektron.Cms.Common.CriteriaFilterOperator.EqualTo,
    true);

//add a filter to only retrieve items that contain the word "TitleSearch"
//in the title
myCriteria.AddFilter(
    Ektron.Cms.Common.ContentProperty.Title,
    Ektron.Cms.Common.CriteriaFilterOperator.Contains,
    "TitleSearch");

//create the output object
List<Ektron.Cms.ContentData> resultList;

//retrieve the results
resultList = ContentAPI.GetList(myCriteria);
```

Update

Updating is, as one would expect, done through the `Update()` method. This method takes in the data item and updates the database with the modified fields. This action requires that the developer first retrieve the existing item, and then they can call the `Update()` method after modifying some properties. The following example retrieves the content item with ID 30 and updates the `Title` property before saving it back to the database.

```
//create the Content object set to observe permissions
Ektron.Cms.Framework.Core.Content.Content ContentAPI =
    new Ektron.Cms.Framework.Core.Content.Content();

//get the content item
Ektron.Cms.ContentData myContent;
myContent = ContentAPI.GetItem(30);

//update a field on the content item
myContent.Title = "This was updated";

//save the updates
ContentAPI.Update(myContent);
```

Delete

The final piece of CRUD operations is to delete an item from the database. The method used when deleting items is called `Delete()`, and just like the rest of the methods in the Framework API, it will respect the logged-in user's permissions unless the API object was instantiated in `Admin` mode. The following snippet deletes the item with ID 30.

```
//create the Content object set to observe permissions
Ektron.Cms.Framework.Core.Content.Content ContentAPI =
    new Ektron.Cms.Framework.Core.Content.Content();

//delete the content item
ContentAPI.Delete(30);
```

TAKE HOME POINTS

There are cases where the Framework API will not perform the exact function you need in a particular instance. In those cases, you will need to look at some of the other APIs exposed by Ektron. However, if you can perform a given function with the Framework API, that should always be your first stop.

Performance Checklist

Chapters 14 and 15 briefly discussed some of the things to keep an eye on when deploying and maintaining your website. Some of the items covered included performance monitoring, and tracking availability and uptime. This appendix provides a checklist of items that should be addressed and kept in mind while developing and maintaining your website to maximize performance.

The items in the checklist require involvement from many roles in your organization, ranging from the developer to the hardware experts and administrators. By addressing these issues, you will be able to provide a highly available and efficient site that is able to serve your expanding business needs.

HARDWARE REQUIREMENTS

As mentioned in Chapter 1, the minimum recommended hardware requirements to run the Ektron Framework are a Core 2 processor or greater with 4GB of RAM, and a RAID Array for storage. The requirements will scale with your usage metrics, however. The benchmark for your running website requires that the server load should nominally be less than 75% CPU usage, with spikes remaining below 85% utilization. Your memory usage should be below 50% of the system memory. The reasoning behind keeping the usage well below maximum capacity is that if the load increases enough to overwhelm the server, requests will begin timing out and returning errors, and the server may not get a chance to catch up to the request cycle. This downward spiral can bring a server to its knees, so it's best to be on the safe side.

APPROPRIATE SQL SERVER DEPLOYMENT

It is strongly recommended that your SQL Server instance exist on a separate machine from the Web server. This is for two primary reasons.

- **Security:** As the Web server must, by definition, be accessible to potentially public users, this means that the server is also exposed to the outside world. To minimize risk, it is recommended that the database backing your site be located elsewhere in the network, behind a firewall. You can then configure the firewall to accept connections only from the Web server, substantially decreasing the ability for intruders to access and modify the data.

- **Performance:** By separating the roles of Web server and database server, you will better be able to manage the hardware requirements of each capability, fine-tuning the machines to serve their given function.

APPROPRIATE AND JUDICIOUS CACHING

Caching different aspects of your site can be one of the most powerful ways to increase the performance you can achieve from given hardware. By minimizing the amount of back and forth between the database server, and reducing the amount of time running complex code on your pages, you can drastically increase the number of pages a server can produce. Caching in the Ektron Framework falls into three main categories.

- **Data caching:** This method is usually the first thing that developers should ensure is in use. This type of caching includes setting the CacheInterval property on the built-in server controls, which will store the data for a given set of properties in the application cache. It also includes storing relevant data, especially data that is costly to produce, in either the application cache, or the session state. By storing this data, you reduce the amount of time the server spends retrieving the data from the database or analyzing the data. The server still needs to go through the render cycle to produce markup suitable for sending to the client.

- **Fragment caching:** Fragment caching is the next step after data caching. By wrapping costly elements of your page into a user control and setting directives for fragment caching on those, the server will cache the actual HTML output for that piece of the page, allowing it to skip the render cycle for those sections of the page. This method can allow you to avoid repetitive code at low cost, while keeping dynamic elements of the page configured to render the results fresh for each page load. For instance, a list of recent messages to a user would not be a suitable candidate for fragment caching, but the menu system for the site might be.

- **Output caching:** Output caching is like fragment caching on steroids. It performs the same basic functionality, but instead of caching the markup for a small portion of the page, the ASP.NET worker process will cache the entire rendered version of the page. This eliminates the majority of code that must be run in order to produce the markup, but at the cost of dynamic elements not being run every time. This can affect elements like tracking code or user profiles, where each render should show individualized output for the specific user browsing the site. Output caching can be configured to cache multiple versions of the same page, through the VaryByParam, VaryByHeader, VaryByControl, and VaryByCustom attributes, which can frequently give you the flexibility you need to create an efficient and functional caching approach.

For more information on data caching when working with the Ektron Server Controls, see Chapter 26 in the Ektron CMS400 Manual, installed with the framework on your system. For information on ASP.NET caching methods, see http://msdn.microsoft.com/en-us/library/xsbfdd8c%28v=VS.85%29.aspx.

CODE PROFILING

Using a tool like the Redgate's ANTS Performance Profiler will allow you to connect to your development server instance in real time and analyze the slow portions of your code. Attaching to your server and requesting the more popular pages on your site a few times will allow you to iteratively rework the code to maximize the throughput and eliminate wasteful code, sometimes with extremely large performance gains. This can be a very powerful tool and should not be underestimated.

COMPILED SITE

Compiling your site ensures that every page has been built, eliminating lengthy just-in-time compilation. It also will alert you to errors and warnings that your code may throw when visitors browse your site. It serves as a sanity check for your code as well a performance boost over uncompiled sites. There are many tools available to help automate this process, such as NANT and Cruise Control.

EVENT ERROR MAINTENANCE

When errors occur on your website, they are entered into the Event Log in Windows. This is costly for two reasons: The errors themselves mean that something went wrong on your website, and that visitors are not receiving the functionality you intended. Additionally, the process of generating and logging each error causes additional overhead that can easily be avoided through analysis and debugging.

GZIP RESPONSE COMPRESSION

In the hierarchy of round trip time for a Web request, typically the slowest part of retrieving information is the time that the server spends actually constructing the response. This is followed by the length of time it takes to send the response through the network. Enabling response compression minimizes this time by reducing the amount of information that needs to be funneled through the pipe, at a slight processor cost. IIS can be configured to do this automatically, and is a recommended procedure.

EXTERNALIZE RESOURCES AND USE CDNS WHERE APPLICABLE

Using content delivery networks (CDNs) helps your website's performance by reducing the number of requests to your server. In a typical page load, in addition to the actual HTML being displayed by the browser, there may be as many as 10 to 30 times as much data being retrieved through separate responses that are needed to display the final page. This additional data includes JavaScript, CSS, images, videos, and any other resources that do not change from page load to page load, but can represent a large fraction of the overall traffic that the Web server must support. Each of these requests, in addition to utilizing available network bandwidth and IO throughput, also requires that IIS utilize one of the available threads to service it. By offloading these requests to an external highly developed network, not only can you reduce the load on your server, thus increasing the capability to generate and serve pages, you might also be able to reduce your costs by using the less expensive bandwidth and storage made available by CDN companies such as Akamai or Amazon.

REQUEST MINIMIZATION

Going hand-in-hand with the CDN recommendation, the number of requests a browser must make in order to display a page can dramatically increase the rendering time of that page. You should seek to reduce the number of requests required to retrieve all the pieces of a page by combining separate files into single requests. A typical site may have many disparate CSS and JavaScript files — while this aids in maintainability of the codebase, if the files are kept separate it means many more round trips to the server, increasing render time and server load as the server has to respond many more times. There are two approaches to minimizing the number of requests: One is to compile these disparate CSS and JavaScript files into a smaller number of files pre-deployment by copying the separate contents into a common file or set of files and updating the references to these files throughout the site.

The alternative method is to use the `Ektron.Cms.API.JS.RegisterJs` and `Ektron.Cms.API.Css.RegisterCss` functions. These functions will attempt to automatically aggregate multiple files into a single request, no matter what control includes them. This method requires that you include your CSS and JavaScript from codebehind, but it is the method that Ektron uses internally, as it allows for higher performing code without additional development work.

GLOSSARY

The following is a list of terms defined in this book. *Italicized words* refer to other glossary terms.

activity streams   On both user profiles and group profiles, this is a list of activities related to the group or member.

Agile methodologies   Instead of defining all aspects of the project requirements up front, this defines requirements while the development effort is ongoing. The project is broken into a series of sprints, at the end of which customers are presented with results, and requirements are refined based on their feedback. As feedback is incorporated into subsequent sprints, the website increasingly nears a final format.

All-in-One   Provides all features and functionality "out-of-the-box" without requiring integration with other third-party systems.

ambiguous queries   Searches resulting in two sets of results, each with completely different meanings.

API Namespace   A namespace provides a way of categorizing classes.

Application Engineering Professional Services   Designed to fill in the blanks on your project, this option is useful when you need either a turn-key solution, or when you've hit a rough spot and your deadlines are looming.

Application Search   A programmatic search that does not just deliver results based on a site visitor's query but rather based on criteria that includes queries on text, metadata, properties, and more.

Approval chains   Similar to *permissions* in that they restrict publishing rights to a given piece of content. In Ektron, these refer to a linear workflow, with each approval simply moving the content to the inbox of the next approver.

Best Practice Services   Giving you access to a dedicated on-call solution engineer at low cost, this is the king of advanced support systems, where you might need faster turnaround times than normal support can provide, or where you want the assurance of having someone who knows your project and has been involved with it to be available at any time.

Best-of-Breed   Specialized tools useful for a singular purpose. What Best-of-Breed systems lack in breadth, they make up for in depth.

Blogs   Allow for a simple interface to post content, keeping customers and clients in the loop on key issues.

Board   A type of folder that can only contain other folders of the forum type.

Breadcrumbs   Navigational cues showing the hierarchy of content, which allow site visitors to easily discover the information architecture on a site.

Business Analytics   Collects and provides reports on data pertaining to visitor activities and viewing habits. This differs from Site Analytics in that it usually refers to performance on items like conversions in the sales cycle.

catalog   In the context of eCommerce, this is a folder that contains a collection of products or services for sale on a site.

Certified Developer Training   In depth, hands-on, technical training covering best practices, development, deployment, and methodology.

Certified System Administrator Training   A training from which any Webmaster, Web administrator, or IT staff responsible for the ongoing website management and maintenance benefits.

CMS implementation guide   This is a document that defines server controls and API calls, Elements of customization must meet the business, user experience, and technical requirements for the project. Typically, a technical developer who is already familiar with the Ektron Server Controls and APIs develops the CMS implementation guide.

CMS Namespace   The home for all of Ektron's APIs, both the internal ones and the public ones. If you're looking to programmatically access the CMS and cannot find an API to use either in the Framework Namespace or the API Namespace, the CMS Namespace gives you what you need.

colleagues   In terms of social networking, this is a list of users who are colleagues of a particular community member.

collection   A static list of managed content items, similar in concept to a playlist in a music player such as Apple iTunes in that the list is manually defined.

Community aliasing   Allows you to assign an alias for community groups or users so that a site visitor can enter a simple URL to find them.

Community Documents   Every user in a social network (both CMS and membership users) has a personal content repository associated with his account. This repository can be accessed and managed using the CommunityDocuments Server Control.

Community folders   Content in these folders can be generated either by the CMS author or by membership users. This allows for synchronization between staging and production servers.

community group   Individual members who unite around a common purpose or share information on a specific subject.

complex product   Similar to a bundle in that it takes several simple products and groups them together, but unlike a bundle it maintains each simple product's price and details, and the customer interacts with them as separate products.

Content Block Server Control   This reads content items from the database and displays them on the website. It can be hardcoded to a specific content item, it can be configured to read the content ID from the query string, or the ID of the content to display can be set programmatically at runtime.

content flow   How content moves throughout an entire production system, from content creation on the staging machine to content delivery in the production environment.

Content localization features   Helps you expose your website's content to a global audience by managing multilingual versions of a content item.

Content tab   Where users interact with the primary elements of the CMS.

coupons   In the context of eCommerce, these are customer incentives that allow users to discount a percentage of a product they are purchasing.

customer reports   Reports generated by the eCommerce subsystem on recent and top customers.

Dashboards   Ektron's Dashboards allow site visitors to create personalized portals of information, aggregating data from various sources into one location and thus simplifying the decision-making process.

Deployment Environment   This is the location that has the live site installed.

Dev Center   A peer-to peer support area for clients to assist one another with problems and ask general questions, with input from Ektron technical support and engineering staff.

Development Environment: This environment typically has a complete working version of the website, but will not always have the content that is visible on the public site.

Discovery phase   In website development, this phase is designed to capture the detail level view of requirements from the perspective of business, creative, and technical stakeholders. Fundamentally, the discovery phase is focused on answering the question: "What do you want your website to do?"

DropZones   Regions of the page that can be populated with widgets. Part of the PageBuilder infrastructure.

EKML   An Ektron created language that handles basic XML to XHTML transformations through simple looping and string replacement of tokens.

Ekron PageBuilder   Provides the framework on which the Ektron Widgets and Wireframes are created.

Ektron   A global Web solutions leader, providing Web content management, marketing optimization, and a social software platform; founded in 1998 and headquartered in Nashua, New Hampshire.

Ektron Exchange (http://dev.ektron.com/exchange)   Providing over 30 ready-to-use widgets, this community-based website lets developers upload and share code with the Ektron developer community.

Ektron Framework   A collection of features and technologies installed as an application on a website. Its primary function is Web content management, but it also has features supporting diverse needs like eCommerce and analytics.

Ektron Smart Form   An ideal way to handle content that follows a very structured format, such as Press releases. The data is stored internally as XML, and the definition contains information necessary to create forms for easy data entry.

End User Training   While the other training types are geared toward people who administer your site, the end user training is geared to help your users understand the system and to facilitate end user adoption.

eSync   An Ektron feature designed to solve the challenges of moving content from one environment to another.

Exchange Community   An extension of the *Dev Center*, this community is where Developers can upload and showcase their code, add-ons, and widgets with others.

Final User Acceptance Testing (Final UAT)   The period of time in which the key stakeholders and end users are given an opportunity to verify firsthand that the website meets their expectations as expressed in the requirements documents.

Flex Menu   A server control used to render menus in the Ektron Framework. It supports richer interfaces and complex configurations.

Folder aliasing   Similar to taxonomy aliasing, with the difference that folder aliases use the folder structure of the content tree to derive their URL aliases. This is useful when you have a meaningful and logical structure to your content tree and want to expose content using this folder structure.

Forums   Allow for easy management of threaded discussions, centered around a given theme. They are the evolutionary descendant of dial-up bulletin board systems.

Framework API   The newest member of the Ektron API, it was designed in response to feedback received from developers that the legacy APIs could be cumbersome.

friending (friended)   A process in which a member establishes a connection with another member.

full factorial   The method used to generate the list of possible combinations that can be displayed in a multivariate experiment. The combination list is created by taking every single possible combination of columns from each Multivariate Section.

functional requirements document   Using the feedback captured during the business stakeholder interviews and any subsequent prioritization sessions, this documents the specific functional and business requirements of the website.

functional requirements guide   Captures, from a business perspective, how the site should operate.

HTML forms   Allow you to build traditional HTML forms containing standard input elements such as textboxes and option lists, with the added ability to define client-side form validation rules, enable spell checking, and more, all using the WYSIWYG authoring environment.

IFilters   Components that understand how to handle a specific file format, such as Microsoft Word, Office documents, text documents, Shockwave Flash files, and PDF documents.

Implementation phase   In Web development, this phase is where you start building to the specifications you have been developing.

information architecture guide   This document defines the types of information you'll find on the site, as well as the structure of the information and how the content items relate to one another through *metadata* and *taxonomy*.

key performance indicator report   Lets you compare sales and orders from two time periods.

Language Export feature   Helps you export content items as a single zip file. These bundles are compressed and then delivered to a translation company where the information is translated and returned in the same bundle, which is then imported back into the system.

Page Layout   An XML serialized package which stores all the necessary information to recreate a PageBuilder page, including the width of each column, and the widgets as well as the data that displays in each column.

ListSummaries   Display a list of the content in a folder, and optionally recursively down the child folders.

Load balancing   A feature of the Ektron Framework that allows multiple servers to keep assets including library items and search summaries synchronized. If load balancing is not set up, any assets uploaded are not copied to the other sites.

load testing   The process of putting demand on a system or device and measuring its response.

Lock model   The method used to manage content in the Ektron Framework. Very similar to a source control model, in this model, when one user is editing content, no other user can edit at the same time.

Machine translation   Refers to the process of using language translation algorithms to translate text. Websites such as Babelfish and Google Translate, as well as the slew of translation plug-ins for Web browsers such as Firefox, have made the use of machine translation fairly commonplace.

Manual aliasing   Offers content editors tight control over URL aliases assigned to content items. You use this when a URL falls outside of the patterns defined by the other types of aliasing or when you need to override automatically generated URLs.

Manual translation   This is great to use in situations where editors are translating a small amount of content, under a dozen content items or so. This is performed by CMS users and is performed through the content editing interface of the Workarea.

Message Boards   Allows community members to publically author comments about a user, community group or content item.

Metadata   Additional information associated to the content.

micro blogging   See *micro messaging*.

micro messaging   A method of communicating where members publish very short messages, share status updates, and post relevant URLs and other interesting bits of information.

navigation indicators Guides in a website that help users determine their current position in the overall information architecture.

overly general search terms Searches that do not produce meaningful results. You can use Ektron's Suggested Results feature to force certain results to the top of the search in these circumstances.

PageBuilder A feature that takes the concept of ASP.Net User Controls and moves it one step further by providing controls that allow non-developers to add components to pages, and modify component settings. It eschews the need for a developer to intervene, and entirely drops the requirement for Visual Studio from the page layout update cycle.

PageBuilder Wireframes In contrast to traditional CMS templates, these define specific zones where content and widgets are placed. With this basic framework in place, content authors can drag-and-drop pre-built pieces of functionality or content into the zones defined by the PageBuilder Wireframe.

payment report Lists the received payments within a given time period.

performance testing Testing for the purpose of identifying and eliminating bottlenecks during the development and testing process of a website.

Permissions A structure that controls whether a given user has access to perform a given action on a given object.

Pre-Staging Environment Some organizations choose to have this specifically for use by QA engineers and developers to vet technical changes made to the website's source code and keep the staging environment as a place to moderate content changes.

Private messaging The Messaging Server Control allows community members to send and receive private messages. This is an important feature, as it offers a way for community members to communicate information that should not or cannot be shared publically on the website.

product bundle A single item that consists of other items from the catalog. It has its own price and images separate from the underlying product entries. For instance, when buying a desktop computer, you may want a bundle consisting of a monitor, a keyboard, and a mouse, with a discounted overall price.

product kit A type of product that contains a list of free text options. The options can affect the overall price of the product. For instance, a laptop's price will go up or down based on the amount of memory in it, as well as the hard drive size.

product reports Snapshots of how many orders users have made on a site as well as the various states of the orders' fulfillment.

product subscription A product type that allows for recurring billing.

Production Environment Serves the live website to users. This may represent a single physical machine or a cluster of machines sitting behind a load balancer. In the cases of a public website, this frequently sits outside of the corporate network.

Quality Assurance phase The testing phase of the project methodology, this phase is intended to capture and resolve any issues, bugs, or problems with the website.

Quick Start Consulting A fast-paced training that covers the essentials to get you up to speed and running with Ektron.

RegEx aliasing Useful when your website contains URLs that follow a certain predictable pattern, such as the URLs for blog posts. When enabled, the Ektron Framework will try to match requested URLs with those patterns defined in the RegEx alias settings.

Report tab The area of the Workarea where users can generate reports.

RIAs Stands for "Rich Internet Applications and is a Web application with many characteristics similar to a desktop application and which a browser or plug-in delivers.

sales trends report Generates a line graph of order volume versus date using data from the eCommerce system.

Search APIs See *Application Search*.

security testing Testing specifically for finding and eliminating any issues with the application that compromise your application, the system, or its data.

Settings tab Where non–content oriented options are managed. This includes system wide configuration options like license keys, user and community management, as well as eCommerce management.

simple product The basic product type that allows you to store information about a single item. The other product types, including kits and bundles, allow for alteration of components of the item, simple products do not.

Sitemap A list of key content items and pages in your site. Useful for indexing content by third-party search engines because they are designed to follow links to find other pages.

Smart Form Design Package All the elements that comprise a Smart Form Design are encapsulated into this XML entity.

Smart Form Designs *Smart Forms* definitions, which you create using the WYSIWYG form builder called Smart Form Designer.

Smart Forms From a developer's perspective, these provide structured content modeling and authoring as well as a mechanism for creating strongly typed content definitions used for content authoring.

Source Control Repository A software package, such as SVN or Perforce, that is used by developers to store the source code files of the website. Typically this will also provide versioning of the source files, allowing for comparison between revisions, and rollback of changes.

Staging Environment The location that is used to test new features or verify content before it makes its way to the production website.

stress testing Testing that tries to cause a system to fail by overwhelming its resources for the purpose of locating weak points.

Structured content Information or content made up of elements which are individually defined. Structured content often refers to information that has been classified using XML, but can also relate to information classified using other standard or proprietary forms of metadata.

synonym search A set of searches that contain possible misspellings of a name, product, or object. These result in incorrectly spelled search terms yielding correctly spelled names results.

Taxonomy A content-categorization system authors use to organize information into meaningful hierarchies. These category structures can then be used to create navigation structures, such as menus and directories, which guide users to the information they're looking for.

Taxonomy aliasing Uses the site's information architecture defined by a taxonomy to create URLs that follow the same structure, thus allowing aliases to be automatically created based on a taxonomy that is already in use.

Tidy process A process that cleans up non standard HTML. All content is run through this process as it is being published.

Top Level Domain (TLD) The last part of the domain name of a site. In the US, common TLDs are .COM, .EDU, .ORG, and .NET, but the country signifier is also a TLD; for instance .CA, or .UK.

top products report Displays the most successful products on your site.

Traffic Analytics Encompasses capturing and reporting of metrics related to all aspects of Web traffic, including where site visitors come from, what they click on, what pages they visit, how they respond to the content presented, covering all activities down to the page level.

URL Aliasing feature A powerful engine that lets you turn undescriptive URLs into meaningful resource identifiers. The URL Aliasing feature is also called URL mapping, URL redirection and URL rewriting.

Waterfall-based methodologies With this approach, the project begins with a comprehensive discovery effort, consisting of stakeholder interviews, functional requirements gathering, technical solution development, and the creation of user experience components. This is all used as a base-line to measure the progress of the project.

Widget Space A collection of widgets that you present to users of a social network so they can populate Dashboards. See also: *Dashboards*.

Widgets Extended .NET User Controls that encapsulate site functionality and the user interface in a reusable way.

Wireframe This is a mockup of a final page that allows stakeholders and developers to understand the desired functionality. Differs from PageBuilder Wireframe.

Workarea Almost all content management activities in the Ektron Framework happen here. The Workarea provides an interface to manage your folder structure, content, menu system and metadata, and system setup.

XML Configurations The old term for *Smart Forms*. Although this terminology has been removed from Ektron's Workarea, documentation, and website, you might run across references to this terminology on the Ektron Dev Center in older forum posts.

XSL Transforms A complete language designed to transform XML from one format to another. Within the Ektron Framework, XSL transforms are typically used to convert XML into XHTML for display on the website.

INDEX

A

accordion functionality, 414–416
Account Manager at Ektron, 589–590
ActiveTopics Server Control, 353
Activities, 424
    User Logged In, 430–431
activities (Windows Workflow Foundation), custom, 527–531
Activity Stream API, 426–427
activity streams, 439
    advantages, 422–428
    community homepage, 427–428
    enabling, 428
    Facebook, 422
    filtering, 424
    message customization, 428–429
    queries, 426–427
    social navigation, 422
    timeline navigation, 422
activity types, 429–432
ActivityStream Server Control, 425–426
ActivityStream Widget, 423–425
Add Blog form, 355
Add Files permission, 102
Add Folder Interface, 88
    Breadcrumbs tab, 89
    Flagging tab, 89
    Metadata tab, 89
    Properties tab, 89
    Smart Forms tab, 89
    Taxonomy tab, 89
    Templates tab, 89
    Web Alerts tab, 89
Add Folders permission, 102
Add Hyperlinks permission, 102
Add Images permission, 102
Add permission, 102
AddContentActivity.cs, 530–531
Admin, 54
AdRotator.cs, 156–157
agile methodologies, 18
Alias-Admin built-in role, 103
Alias-Edit built-in role, 103
aliases

manual aliasing, 109
query string parameters, 134
RegEx aliasing engine, 136
URL aliasing, 109, 130
    community aliasing, 132
    enabling, 133–135
    folder based, 132
    manual aliasing, 132
    parameter resolution logic, 134–135
    RegEx based, 132
    taxonomy based, 131–132, 135–136
aliasing, 130–131
All-In-One approach, 8–9
AllowAnonymousPost property, 348
Analytics Viewer built-in role, 103
AnalyticsDataProvider tag, 327
API Namespace, 11
APIs (Application Programming Interface)
    Activity Stream API, 426–427
    folders and, 95
    forums, 353
    Framework, 591
    Tidy process, 123
Application Engineering, 6, 590
approval chains, 96
    language, 103
    setup, 98–100
    users in twice, 103
ASHX handler, 405
ASP.NET Master Page, 196–197
.ASPX templates, 24
    Wireframes, 268
associating Wireframes to folders, 286, 305–307
authentication, Facebook, 220–223
Authorize method, 540–541
AuthorizeAndCapture method, 541–542
availability, 577–579

B

backups, 585
Bad Link Report, 578
Best-of-Breed approach, 9
Best Practice Services, 6, 590

best practices, implementation guide creation, 42–43
Blog folder, 87
Blog Server Control, 335, 353
    properties, 359–360
    templates, 358–363
Blog Server Sub-controls, 360–361
blogs, 334–335
    commenting system, 361–363
    folders, 353
    Google Blog, 334
    trackback URLs, 356
    use case, 336–338
    Workarea, creating, 354–358
`BoardID` property, 348
boards, 339
Boiko, Bob, *Content Management Bible*, 111
Breadcrumb feature, 151
BreadCrumb Server Control, 209, 224
    FolderBreadcrumb Server Control, 212–213
    implementing, 212–213
    properties, 213
breadcrumbs, 209, 224
    click trail, 209
    creating, Products folder, 210–212
    forums, 344
    parent folders, 211
Breadcrumbs tab (Add Folder interface), 89
BrightCove PageBuilder Widget, 257
broken links, 578
browsers, language and, 142
built-in roles
    Alias-Admin, 103
    Alias-Edit, 103
    Analytics Viewer, 103
    Business Rule Editor, 103
    Collection and Menu Admin, 104
    Collection Approver, 104
    Commerce Admin, 104
    Community, 104
    Community Group Admin, 104
    Community Group Create, 104
    Folder User Admin, 104
    Master Layout Create, 104
    Message Board Admin, 104
    Metadata Admin, 104
    Move or Copy, 104
    Search Admin, 104
    Smart Forms Admin, 104
    Synchronization Admin, 104
    Task Create, 104
    Task Delete, 104
    Task Redirect, 104
    Taxonomy Administrator, 104
    Template Configuration, 104
    User Admin, 104
    XLIFF Admin, 104

Builtin, 54
Business Analytics, Traffic Analytics and, 324–325
business case, 18–19
business requirements, stakeholder interviews, 20–21
Business Rule Editor built-in role, 103
`bxSlider` library, 161

C

caching engine, 136
    TTL (Time To Live), 136
CALENDAR.ASPX, 255
CALENDAR.ASPX.CS, 255–256
CalendarDataSource, properties, 248
calendars, 225, 228
    community groups, 245
    creation, 263
    displaying, 263
    event list
        cancellations, 243
        new events, 242–243
    events, 263
        upcoming, 253–256
    group, creating, 243–245
    managing, 263
    recurrences, 241–242
    system, creating, 240–243
    Telerik Scheduler, 239
    updates, 239
    user, creating, 243–245
    Workarea, 239
Calendars.aspx, 246
campaign effectiveness, measuring, 328–329
campaign landing page. *See* OnTrek Campaign Landing Page
capturing data, 572
Card Types pane, eCommerce configuration, 450–451
Cart Server Control, 507, 510–512, 522–525
Cart.aspx, 523–524
catalog (eCommerce), 467–468, 471–472
    video, 479–481
CDN (content delivery network), 591
CEOBlog.aspx, 358
chat support, 6
Checkout Server Control, 507, 512–516
child nodes
    handlers, 172–181
    rendering, 170–172
    retrieving, JavaScript, 181–183
classes
    as `DataContract`, 172
    `DataContractJsonSerializer`, 172
    definitions, serialization and, 173
    `DropZoneData`, 296
    PaymentGatewayProvider, 540
    products, 468–469

RequestItem, 173
TaxonomyItem, 174
XML Schema Definition tool, 117–118
client side scripts, registering, 161
CMS Extension Framework, 591
CMS implementation guide, 23, 31–32
    document formatting
        object tables, 32
        page layouts, 31–32
        sitemap, 31
        widget listing, 32
    OnTrek implementation guide and, 32
CMS Menu, 189
    customization examples, 195
CMS Menu Server Control, 187
    samples, 189
CMS menus, 186
CMS Namespace, 11
CMS Refresh Report, 67–68
CMS400Min site, 54
code, setting to use XSLT, 166–169
code listings
    /Widgets/Collection.ascx, 276–278
    /Widgets/MyTestControl.ascx, 300–301
    /Widgets/MyTestControl.ascx.cs, 299, 302
    AddContentActivity.cs, 530–531
    AdRotator.cs, 156–157
    CALENDAR.ASPX, 255
    CALENDAR.ASPX.CS, 255–256
    Calendars.aspx, 246
    Cart.aspx, 523–524
    CEOBlog.aspx, 358
    CustomStreamDisplay.aspx, 426–427
    CustomStreamDisplay.aspx.cs, 427
    Dashboard.ascx, 421–422
    Friends.ascx, 401–404
    HomePageBannerSerialization.aspx, 158–159
    HomePageBannerSerialization.aspx.cs, 159–160
    HomePageBanner.xsd, 154–156
    Invite.aspx, 376–377
    Membership.aspx, 216
    SamplePaymentGatewayProvider.cs, 542
    SearchResults.aspx.cs, 203–204
    SetOutput( ) method from /Widgets/Collection.ascx.cs, 278–279
    SimpleHandler.aspx, 183–185
    SocialBar.ascx, 372–373
    socialbar.ascx, 380–381, 382–383
    TaxonomyExampleService.ashx, 177–181
    UnorderedListSummary.ekml, 238–239
    UnorderedListSummary.xslt, 235
    UserGroupForum.aspx, 348
Collection and Menu Admin built-in role, 104
Collection Approver built-in role, 104
collection data model, 280
Collection Server Control, properties, 279–280
Collection Widget
    implementation, 298
    implementation file, 276–278
    presentation, 275–280
collections
    adding to, 272–273
    assigned content items, 281
    Collection Server Control, 270
    Collection Widget, 270
    creating, 270, 271–272
    definition, 270
    displaying, 270
    on landing page, 273–274
    language, 270
Collections menu, 270
Collections permission, 102
Collections Server Control, 268
Collections Widget, 269
commenting system in blog, 361–363
Commerce Admin built-in role, 104
community aliasing, 132
Community built-in role, 104
Community folder, 87
community folders (Wikis), 363
Community Framework, 390
    activity streams, 390
    alerts, 392
    APIs, 396
    colleagues, 392
    community group, 390
    Community Groups, 392
    Framework API, retrieving friends, 407–408
    friending, 392–393
    friending infrastructure, 439
    Friends Server Control, 401–404
    importance of, 390–391
    members, 390, 392
        dashboard, 391–392
        templates, 396–397
    micro-blogging, 391
    micro-messaging, 391, 392
    notifications, 392
    searches, 199
    taxonomy and, 406–407
    user profiles, 391, 393–396
        Colleagues, 395
        Community Documents, 395
        Community Groups, 395
        Message Boards, 395
        Private Messaging, 395
        tiers, 396
    UserProfile Server Control, 394, 397–404
    users, 392
Community Group Admin built-in role, 104
Community Group Create built-in role, 104
Community Group Profile Server Control, 392
community groups, 408–409, 439
    activity streams, 409

enabling, 428
calendars, 245
creating, 409–411
intranets, 408
membership user groups comparison, 409–410
notifications, enabling, 428
templates, 411–412
user discovery, 409
community homepage, activity stream, 427–428
CommunityGroupBrowser Server Control, 409
CommunityGroupList Server Control, 409
CommunityGroupMembers Server Control, 403
    properties, 415–416
CommunityGroupProfile Server Control, 408
CommunitySearch Server Control, 409
company background, 3–4
configuration, 24
    eCommerce, 444–445
        licensing, 444
        packages, 462–466
        Settings tab, 445–461
        shipping, 461–467
        shipping methods, 462–466
        taxes, 461, 466–467
        warehouses, 462–466
    menus, 189–191
    taxonomy, folder assignment, 128
contact information form, 312–315
contact methods, 6
containers, list containers, 136
content
    authors, 54
    collections, 281
    creating items, 64
    displayed language, 141–142
    DMS menu, 79
    editing, toolbar options and, 74–79
    exporting, 109
    flagging, definition setup, 378–379
    flow, deployment, 555–558
    folder tree, permissions, 125
    full factorial, 317
    historical versions, 579
    language-specific editions, 140
    localization features, 109
    lock model, 63–64
    migration, 25–26
    multilingual sites, 139
        enabling support, 143–144
    organization, taxonomy, 124
    process, 62
    reports, 574–576
    searches, excluding, 198
    spot checks, 576–577
    states, 63
    status, 62–64
    storage, 62–64
    structured, 110
    taxonomy, 128–129
    tree, associating to Smart Form Designs, 121–123
    unstructured, 110
    website needs, 107
Content Block Server Control, 79
    event display, 250–253
    implementing, 82–84
    Smart Forms, 251
    Tidy process, 123
    Wikis, 364
    XSLT, overriding, 112–113
Content HTML field, 123
Content Management Bible (Boiko), 111
`Content Management Bible` (Boiko), 111
content managers, Workarea, 54
Content pane toolbar, 69
Content tab (Workarea), 60–61
Content Targeting Widget Webinar, 593
ContentBlock Widget, 519
ContentFlagging Server Control, 333
    implementing, 379–383
    properties, 380
ContentReview Server Control, 333, 378
    implementing, 379–383
    properties, 381–382
Countries pane, eCommerce configuration, 446–447
coupons (eCommerce), 481–482
    scope, 484–485
    types, 483–484
crawling
    full, 206
    incremental, 206
    Search Framework, 205–207
Credit Card Interchange, 458
CSS (Cascading Style Sheets), 10
    Firebug, 10
    Flex menu, 188–189
Currencies pane, eCommerce configuration, 447–450
CurrencySelect Server Control, 495, 496
custom role creation, 100–101
customer testimonials, 257–263
customers
    blogs, 334–335
    forums and, 334
    Wikis, 335
CustomStreamDisplay.aspx, 426–427
CustomStreamDisplay.aspx.cs, 427

D

dashboard page, OnTrek implementation guide, 39–42
    object table, 40–41
Dashboard.ascx, 421–422

dashboards, 60, 419
    Activities, 424
    activity streams, filtering, 424
    components, 420–422
    contents, 419–420
    personalized, 419
    tabs, public/private, 419
    user controls, implementing, 422
    widget spaces, 420–422
    widgets, 59
    Workarea, 56
data analysis, maintenance and, 572–573
data capture, 572
Data Designer, Smart Form Designs, 111
data storage, 13
data structures, taxonomy and, 125
data synchronization, Ektron Framework, installation, 47–48
DataBinding, 10
databinding, Image Rotator, 153–161
`DataContract`, 172
`DataContractJsonSerializer` class, 172
debugging
    Flex Menu Server Control, 188
    XSLT, Visual Studio, 165–166
`DefaultObjectID` property, 348
Delete Folders permission, 102
Delete permission, 102
deliverables, Discovery Phase
    CMS implementation guide, 23, 31
    functional requirements document, 23, 31
    information architecture document, 23, 31
deployment
    content moving, 561–563
        eSync, 558–561
        production to staging, 562
        staging to production, 563
    manual, 563–564
    Package and Deploy tool, 564–566
    plan descriptions, 560
    scenarios, 554
        content flow, 555–558
        data flows and process, 559–560
        Deployment Environment, 555
        Development Environment, 554
        Pre-Staging Environment, 555
        Production Environment, 555
        Source Control Repository, 554
        Staging Environment, 554–555
        virtual staging, 561–562
    server security, 567
Dev Center, 4
    forums, 334
Developer Community hub, 588
Developers, 30
development process, 549

development scenarios, 47
DHTML Menu Server Control, 189
Did You Mean search widget, 202
Directory Server Control, 170
Disable Language Awareness property, 134
disaster recovery
    backups, 585
    uptime and, 584
discovery collateral, 548
Discovery Phase, 19–20
    deliverables
        CMS implementation guide, 23, 31
        functional requirements document, 23, 31
        information architecture document, 23, 31
    kickoff, 20
    project manager, selection, 20
    project plan, developing, 20–23
Discussion Board, folder, 87
discussion board, creating, 340–343
DMS, objects, adding, 257–259
DMS menu, 79
    Content Block Server Control and, 79
domain names, 579
DropZone User Control, 282
    properties, 295
`DropZoneData` class, 296
DropZones, 268, 282
    ContentBlock Widget, 519
`DynamicForumParameter` property, 348
`DynamicGroupParameter` property, 348
`DynamicParameter` property, 348
`DynamicThreadParameter` property, 348

E

e-mail message tokens, 376
e-mail support, 5
eCommerce, 441
    browsing experience, controls, 495–506
    card types, 450–451
    Cart Server Control, 507, 510–512
    Cart.aspx, 523–524
    catalog, 467–468, 471–472
    Checkout Server Control, 507, 512–516
    configuration, 444–445
        licensing, 444
        packages, 462–466
        Settings tab, 445–461
        shipping, 461–467
        shipping methods, 462–466
        taxes, 461, 466–467
        warehouses, 462–466
    countries, 446–447
    coupons, 481–482
        scope, 484–485

types, 483–484
currencies, 447–450
CurrencySelect Server Control, 495, 496
implementation, 516–525
landing page, 516–519
maintenance controls, 506–516
messages, 451
    creating, 453–454
    modifying, 453–454
    tokens, 452–453
    types, 452
MyAccount Server Control, 507–508
order management, 488–489
order workflow, 486–487
OrderList Server Control, 507, 508–510
payment
    gateway, 457–459, 536–544
    PayPal, 454–460
product detail interface, 521–523
Product Server Control, 495, 503–504
ProductList Server Control, 495, 500–502
products, 467–468
    classes, 468–469
    reports, 485–488
    SmartForm content tabs, 473–479
    types, 468–471
    video catalog, 479–481
ProductSearch Server Control, 495, 496–498
purchase controls, 506–516
Recommendation Server Control, 495, 504–506
regions, 459–461
use case, 442–443
Webinar, 592
eCommerce APIs Webinar, 592
eCommerce Catalog folder, 87
eCommerce payment gateway provider webinar, 593
eCommerce site build Webinar, 592
eCommerce Workflow Engine Webinar, 592
Edit Folders permission, 102
Edit In Context, 79–80
    Add Library Item option, 81
    Add/Remove Hyperlink option, 81
    Bold/Italic option, 81
    Cancel option, 81
    Save option, 81
    Spell Check option, 81
edit interface for widgets, 300–301
Edit permission, 102
`EditButtonClicked` event, 303
editing screen for widgets, 298
`EditorCSS` property, 349
`EditorToolbar` property, 349
EKML (Ektron Markup Language), 10, 263
    ListSummary Server Control, 236–239
    tokens, 237–238
    tags, 236
    UnorderedListSummary.ekml, 238–239

Ektron
    Application Engineering, 6, 590
    Best Practice Services, 6, 590
    company background, 3–4
    configuration, 24
    contact methods, 6
    Hosting Solutions, 7
    online community, 4, 588
        Account Manager, 589–590
        Developer Community hub, 588
        Facebook, 588
    technical support, 589
    training, 7
    users, 15–16
    Webinars, 590–591
        CDN (content delivery network) integration, 591
        CMS Extension Framework, 591
        Content Targeting Widget, 593
        eCommerce APIs, 592
        eCommerce payment gateway provider, 593
        eCommerce site build, 592
        eCommerce Workflow Engine, 592
        eSync, 593
        Framework API, 591
        Marketing Optimization Suite, 594
        Widgets in Version 8, 594
        Writing RIA Application, 594
Ektron Certified Developer Training, 7
Ektron Certified System Administrator Training, 7
Ektron Collections, 268
Ektron Custom End User or Administrator Training, 7
Ektron End User Training, 7
Ektron Exchange Community, 4, 591
Ektron Framework, 16
    alternatives, 262–263
    background, 7
    Ektron.CMS, 11
    Ektron.CMS.API, 11
    Ektron.CMS.Framework, 11
    installation, 46–47
        data synchronization, 47–48
        development scenarios, 47
        license key, 46
        source control, 47
    Server Controls, 9
        functionality, 10
    special groups, 55
    special users, 54–55
Ektron Menus, 185
Ektron Ordering Sequential Workflow, 532
Ektron Quick Start Consulting, 7
Ektron Reference Manual, menus, 187
Ektron Smart Form, 26, 145
EkXml object, 160
`EnableForumQuickSelect` property, 349
`EnableThreadRating` property, 349
    Forum Server Control, 339

eSync, 24
    moving content, 558–561
    Webinar, 593
event list (calendar)
    new events, 242–243
    upcoming, 253–256
Event Viewer, 577–578
events
    `EditButtonClicked`, 303
    `Page_Load`, 160
    Smart Forms, 251
    WebCalendar Server Control, 246
    WidgetHost, 308
    `WidgetHost.Edit`, 302
    widgets, 299–300
experiments
    creating, 319–320
    parameters, 322–323
    results, 322–323
Expired Content Report, 574
extensions
    files, 94
    images, 94

F

Facebook, 4
    activity streams, 422
    authentication, 220–223
    Ektron presence, 588
    FacebookLogin Server Control, 220–223
FacebookLogin Server Control, 224
FAST Enterprise Search, 205
fields
    Add Discussion Forum form, 347
    product types, 469–470
    taxonomy, 127–128
    XML, structured searches, 199
files
    extensions, 94
        URL aliasing and, 131
    library, 92
    upload path, 94
`Fill` method, 84
Final UAT (Final User Acceptance), 548
    testing, 552
Firebug
    CSS and, 10
    HTML and, 10
flagging and review data, 383–387
flagging definitions, setup, 378–379
Flagging tab, 386
    Add Folder interface, 89
Flash settings in Work area, 260–261
Flex Menu
    CSS, 188–189

customization examples, 195
master page, 192–194
presentation, 188–189
Reference Manual, 187
rules, 187
Flex Menu Server Control, 187
    debug mode, 188
    logging feature, 188
    properties
        `AutoCollapseBranches`, 188
        `CacheInterval`, 188
        `DefaultMenuID`, 188
        `DisplayXslt`, 188
        `EnableMouseOverPopup`, 188
        `EnableSmartOpen`, 188
        `IncludeJS`, 188
        `SuppressAddEdit`, 188
    XSLT to modify markup, 189
Folder Admin Role, 96
folder based URL aliasing, 132
folder-specific roles, 103
Folder User Admin built-in role, 104
FolderBreadcrumb Server Control, 212–213, 224
folders
    adding, 85–95
    APIs and, 95
    Blog, 87
    blogs, 353
    boards, 339
    Community, 87
    community folders (Wikis), 363
    creating, 85
    data types stored, 85
    Discussion Board, 87
    eCommerce Catalog, 87
    forums, 338
    inheritance, 85
    Multisite, 87
    navigating, 86–87
    permissions, restricting to, 97–98
    Products, breadcrumbs, 210–212
    properties, 85
        modifying, 91
    Root, 87
        folder creation, 87–91
    searches, Integrated Search, 199
    Standard, 87
    taxonomy configuration, 128
    types, 85, 87
    WebCalendar, 87
    Wireframe associating, 286
FormBlock Server Control properties, 311
forms
    HTML
        capabilities, 269
        contact information, 312–315
        creating, 310–311

displaying, 310–311
form data model, 315–317
Request a Demo, 311–315
library, 92
Forum Server Control
    `EnableThreadRating,` 339
    implementation, 347–351
    interactions, 350–353
    properties, 348–349
forums, 334, 338–339
    Add Discussion Forum form, 347
    APIs, 353
    breadcrumbs, 344
    creation flow, 339–340
    Dev Center, 334
    display
        Messaging, 352
        Notification, 353
        Profile, 353
        Quick Link, 352
    folders and, 338
    ListSummary Server Control, 339
    properties, 343–345
    server controls, 334
    subjects, 344
    taxonomy, 344
    templates, 344
    Terms & Conditions, 344
    use case, 336–338
    viewing, 350–351
    Workarea, 339
        creating, 346–347
        discussion board, 340–343
Framework API, 11, 591
    retrieving friends, 407–408
friending infrastructure, 439
friends in Community Framework, 392–393
Friends Server Control, 401–404
Friends.ascx, 401–404
Front-End Widgets, 299
full factorial, 317
functional requirements document, 23
functional testing, 551–552

G

gateway provider, 538–542
    installation, 543–544
Generic Handler template, 172
`GetBannerSlides` method, 160
`GetChildren` method, 175–176
`GetRolePermissionSystem` system call, 104
`GetUserActivityStream` method, 427
global search accessibility, 203–205
Google Blog, 334
graphics, rotating, 150

serialization, 153–161
group calendar, creating, 243–245
Group Profile User Control, 412–416
    source code, 413–414
groups, special groups, 55

H

handlers, child nodes, 172–181
history, Purge History, 579–581
Home Page Banner, 153
homepage, 147
    interactions, types, 151–153
    menus, 185
    navigation
        links, 150–151
        search, 150–151
    navigation indicators, 151
    rotating graphics, 150
        serialization, 153–161
        XSLT, 162–165
    server, returning to, 152
    static displays, 152
    use case, 148–149
HomePageBannerSerialization.aspx, 157–159
HomePageBannerSerialization.aspx.cs, 159–160
HomePageBanner.xsd, 154–156
Hosting Solutions, 7
HTML form data model, 315–317
HTML Form Wizard, 310–311
HTML (HyperText Markup Language)
    Firebug, 10
    forms
        capabilities, 269
        compared to Smart Forms, 110
        contact information, 312–315
        creating, 310–311
        displaying, 310–311
        Request a Demo, 311–315
    ListSummaries, XSLT and, 232–236
hyperlinks
    broken, 578
    library, 92

I

IA (information architecture), 22
iCal, feed output, 256–257
IFilters, 207
Image Rotator
    creating, 153–161
    XSLT
        custom, 162–165
        debugging, 165–166
        setting code to use, 166–169

images
    extensions, 94
    library, 92
    upload path, 94
implementation, 19
    Collection Widget, 276–278
    phases, 19
implementation guides, best practices, 42–43
Implementation Phase, 19
    content migration, 25–26
    development, 24–25
in-context editing, Content Block Server Control, 79
indexing
    IFilters, 207
    Search Framework, 205–207
information architecture document, 23
inheritance, folders, 85
installation, Ektron Framework, 46–47
    data synchronization, 47–48
    development scenarios, 47
    license key, 46
    source control, 47
instances, data storage, 301–302
Integrated Search, folders, 199
interactions, types, 151–153
interfaces
    Add Discussion Board, 340
    Add Folder, 88
    `IWidget`, 298
    product detail, 521–523
InternalAdmin, 54
intranets, community groups, 408
Invite Server Control, 374
    e-mail message tokens, 376
    properties, 375
Invite.aspx, 376–377
IP address location services, 142
`IsARoleMember` system call, 104
`IWidget` interface, 298

J

JavaScript, children, retrieving, 181–183
`JavaScriptEditorHeight` property, 349
`JavaScriptEditorWidth` property, 349
jQuery
    Image Rotator, 153–161
    images, rotating, 150

K

kickoff meeting, 20
KPIs (Key Performance Indicators), 324
    metrics, 572

L

LanguageSelect Server Control, 141
language
    approval chains, 103
    collections, 270
    Disable Language Awareness property, 134
    language-specific editions of content, 140
    menus, 187
    multilingual sites
        APIs, 142
        browser locale, 142
        default, 144
        designing, 137–138
        editions, 138, 140
        enabling support, 144–145
        forcing viewing, 142
        IP address location services, 142
        managing displayed, 141–142
        user interface, 142
    taxonomy, 125
    translation
        machine, 140
        manual, 140
Language Export, 109, 141
Language toolbar, 78
LanguageAPI Server Control, 142
layout, 282
    compared to Wireframes, 293–295
    creating, based on Wireframe, 286–292
    full factorial, 317
library, 85
    adding items, 92–93
    `bxSlider`, 161
    files, 92
    folders, searching, 93–95
    forms, 92
    hyperlinks, 92
    images, 92
    navigating, 91–92
    QuickLinks, 85, 92
Library Read Only permission, 102
license key, 46
    Workarea and, content authors, 54
licensing, eCommerce, 444
Link Searches, 94
links
    homepage, 150–151
    Wikis, 367–369
list containers, 136
ListSummaries, 228
    `DisplayXslt` property, 231
    implementing, 229–232
    server control properties, 229–230
    UnorderedListSummary.ekml, 238–239
    UnorderedListSummary.xslt, 235

XSLTs, 228
    HTML markup and, 232–236
ListSummary Server Control, 263
    appearance, 231
    EKML, 236–239
        tokens, 237–238
    event display, 250
    forums, 339
    Wikis, 364
    XML output, 232–235
load testing, 553
localization of text, 139–140
lock model, 63–64
log in, OnTrek site, 55–56
Log Parser, 578–579
Logging Application Block (Microsoft), 578
loops, permissions, 96

M

machine translation of language, 140
maintenance
    availability, 577–579
    content freshness, 573
    content reports, 574–576
    data analysis, 572–573
    data capture, 572
    disaster recovery, 584–585
    performance, 579–581
    planning, 571–573
    reach, 582–584
    usability, 581–582
managed objects, 259–261
    displaying, 261–262
manual aliasing, 109, 132
manual translation of language, 140
Marketing Optimization Suite Webinar, 594
Master Layout Create built-in role, 104
Master menu, 196–197
master page
    ASP.NET, 196–197
    Flex Menu, 192–194
membership, capabilities, 215
Membership control, 216
Membership Server Control, 215–218, 224
membership user groups, community group comparison, 409–410
membership users, 54, 215
    server controls, 215
Membership.aspx, 216
menus, 223
    Add/Edit Menu screen fields, 190–191
    CMS Menu, 189
    CMS Menu Server Control, 187
    Collections, 270
    configuration, 189–191

creating, phases, 186
displaying, 187
DMS, 79
Flex Menu Server Control, 187
items, adding, 191–192
language, 187
Master, 196–197
navigation, 185
Slave, 196–197
Menus tab, new items, 191–192
Message Board Admin built-in role, 104
MessageBoard Server Control, 251
messages
    activity streams, 428–429
    eCommerce, 451
        creating, 453–454
        modifying, 453–454
        tokens, 452–453
        types, 452
    micro-messaging, 433
Messaging Experts, 30
Metadata Admin built-in role, 104
Metadata tab (Add Folder interface), 89
methodologies
    agile, 18
    waterfall-based, 18
methods
    Authorize, 540–541
    AuthorizeAndCapture, 541–542
    `Fill`, 84
    `GetBannerSlides`, 160
    `GetChildren`, 175–176
    `GetUserActivityStream`, 427
    `Page_Load`, 304
    `ProcessRequest`, 176–177, 405
    `RaisedLoggedInActivity( )`, 432
    `SerializeList`, 174
    `updateDisplay`, 183
micro-messaging, 392, 433, 439
    user profile, 435–437
MicroMessage Server Control, 433–435
    properties, 435
Microsoft Logging Application Block, 573
misspellings in searches, 201–202
Modify Preapproval permission, 103
Move or Copy built-in role, 104
multilingual sites
    browser locale, 142
    content, 139
        enabling support, 143–144
        forcing language, 142
    default language, 144
    designing, 137–138
    editions, 138
        language-specific editions, 140
    IP address location services, 142
    languages, enabling support, 144–145

user interface, 142
Multisite folder, 87
Multivariate Experiment Widget, 317, 318
Multivariate Section Widget, 317–318
    content modification, 320–322
Multivariate Target Widget, 317, 318
multivariate testing, 317–323
Multivariate Testing and Web Analytics, 265
Multivariate use example, 319
MyAccount Server Control, 507–508

N

navigating
    folders, 86–87
    homepage
        links, 150–151
        search, 150–151
    library, 91–92
    searches for, 197–198
navigation, menus, 185
navigation indicators, 151
.NET ASCX User controls, 268
.NET Classes, generating from Smart Form Design, 116
.NET Framework, 116–118
    Smart Form Designs, 116
nodes, child
    handlers, 172–181
    rendering, 170–172
notifications, enabling, 428

O

object tables, OnTrek implementation guide
    dashboard page, 40–41
    homepage, 34–35
    Product Cross Sell Widget, 38–39
    product page, 37–38
    What Customers Are Saying Widget, 35
objects
    EkXml, 160
    managed, 259–261
        displaying, 261–262
ObjectType property, 349
onclick property, 203
online community (Ektron), 4
    Account Manager, 589–590
    Dev Center, 4
    Developer Community hub, 588
    Ektron Exchange Community, 4
    Facebook, 4, 588
    Twitter, 588
    web addresses, 4
    Webinars, 590–591
    CDN (Content Delivery Network), 591
    CMS Extension Framework, 591
    Content Targeting Widget, 593
    eCommerce APIs, 592
    eCommerce payment gateway provider, 593
    eCommerce site build, 592
    eCommerce Workflow Engine, 592
    eSync, 593
    Framework API, 591
    Marketing Optimization Suite, 594
    Widgets in Version 8, 594
    Writing RIA Application, 594
online presence, 582–584
OnTrek Campaign Landing Page, 266–268
    collection, 273–274
OnTrek implementation guide, 29
    CMS implementation guide and, 32
    dashboard page, 39–42
        object table, 40–41
    homepage, 33–35
        object tables, 34–35
        What Customers Are Saying Widget, 35
    product page, 35–36
        object tables, 37–38
        Product Cross Sell Widget, 38–39
OnTrek Information Architecture, taxonomy and, 126
OnTrek site
    eCommerce and, licensing, 444–445
    Group Profile User Control, 412–416
    launching, 148
    log in, 55–56
    testimonials, 257
order workflow (eCommerce), 486–487
    Ektron Site, 535–536
    Windows Workflow Foundation, 525–527
        activities in toolbox, 533
        activity creation, 527–531
        building workflow, 531–534
OrderList Server Control, 507, 508–510
Overwrite Library permission, 102

P

Package and Deploy tool, 564–566
Page Host User Controls, 282
    properties, 294–295
PageBuilder, 12–13
    Smart Forms and, 293
    structure, 292–293
    user controls, 30
    Widgets, 265, 268, 282
    Wikis, 365–367
    Wireframes, 26, 265, 268, 282
        creating, 282
PageHost, 282
Page_Load event, 160

`Page_Load` method, property updates, 304
parameters
 experiments, 322–323
 parameter resolution logic, 134–135
parent folders, breadcrumbs, 211
passwords
 resetting, 219–220
 special users, 55
payment gateway, 457–458, 536–537
 form fields, 459
 gateway provider, creating, 538–542
 provider, installation, 543–544
PaymentGatewayProvider class, 540
PayPal for eCommerce, setup, 454–457
performance
 metrics monitoring, 579
 PerfMon, 579
 testing, 552
permissions, 95–96
 Add, 102
 Add Files, 102
 Add Folders, 102
 Add Hyperlinks, 102
 Add Images, 102
 Collections, 102
 content folder tree, 125
 Delete, 102
 Delete Folders, 102
 Edit, 102
 Edit Folders, 102
 Library Read Only, 102
 Modify Preapproval, 103
 Overwrite Library, 102
 Read Only, 102
 Restore, 102
 restricting to folders, 97–98
 roles, 96
 Search Framework API, 209
 Traverse Folders, 103
phases of menu creation, 186
phone support, 5
popular search terms, 202
PostHistory Server Control, 353
presence online, 582–584
`ProcessRequest` method, 176–177, 405
product detail interface, 521–523
Product Server Control, 495, 503
 properties, 504
ProductList Server Control, 495, 500–502
products (eCommerce), 467–468
 classes, 468–469
 reports, types, 485–486
 SmartForm content tabs, 473–479
 types, 468–471
 video catalog, 479–481
Products folder, breadcrumbs, 210–212

ProductSearch Server Control, 495, 496–497
 properties, 497–499
`ProfileLink` property, 349
project manager, selection, 20
project plan
 business requirements, stakeholder interviews, 20–21
 Discovery Phase deliverables, 23
 technical requirements, 21–22
 user experience requirements, 22–23
properties
 ActivityStream Server Control, 425–426
 Add Blog form, 355
 Blog Server Control, 359–360
 BreadCrumb Server Control, 213
 CalendarDataSource, 248
 Cart Server Control, 510–512
 Checkout Server Control, 515
 Collection Server Control, 279–280
 CommunityGroupMembers Server Control, 415–416
 ContentFlagging Server Control, 330
 ContentReview Server Control, 381–382
 Disable Language Awareness, 134
 DropZone User Control, 295
 `EnableThreadRating`, 339
 folders, 85
  modifying, 91
 FormBlock Server Control, 311
 Forum Server Control, 348–349
 forums, 343–345
 Invite Server Control, 375
 ListSummaries, 229–230
 MicroMessage Server Control, 435
 MyAccount Server Control, 507–508
 `onclick`, 203
 OrderList Server Control, 509–510
 Page Host User Controls, 294–295
 `Page_Load` method, 304
 Product Server Control, 504
 ProductList Server Control, 501–502
 ProductSearch Server Control, 497–499
 Query String Action, 134
 Recommendation Server Control, 505–506
 SiteMap Server Control, 214
 SocialBar Server Control, 370–371
 users, modifying, 218–219
 WebCalendar Server Control, 246–247
 WidgetHost, 308
 `Widgets`, 295
 `Zones`, 295
Properties tab (Add Folder interface), 89
Provider Model Design Pattern, 325
Public-Facing Widgets, 299
Purge History, 579–581

Q

Quality Assurance Phase, 19
    system testing, 26–27
    user acceptance testing, 27–28
queries, activity streams, 426–427
queries in searches
    ambiguous, 200
    architecture, 207
    Search Framework, 205–207
    Search Server, 207
Query String Action property, 134
query string parameters, aliases and, 134
QuickLinks, library, 85, 92

R

`RaisedLoggedInActivity( )` method, 432
RDBMS (Relation Databases Management systems), 110–111
Read Only permission, 102
Recommendation Server Control, 495, 504–505
    properties, 505–506
recovery, 584–585
Refresh Reminder Report, 574
RegEx aliasing engine, 136
RegEx based URL aliasing, 132
registration, 224
    membership users, 215–218
Reporting pane, 384
reports
    Bad Link Report, 578
    content reports, 574–576
        Expired Content Report, 574
        Refresh Reminder Report, 574
    eCommerce
        Customer Reports, 485
        Key Performance Indicators, 486
        Payment, 486
        Top Products, 486
    Reports tab (Workarea), 62
    Reports tree, 384
    Search Phrase Report, 199–200
    Web Analytics, 325–326
Request a Demo form, 311–315
`RequestAction.AddFolder`, 405–406
`RequestItem` class, 173
requirements, software, 45–46
resetting passwords, 219–220
RESTful interface, 116
RESTful services, 152, 223
Restore permission, 102
restricting permissions to folders, 97–98
results
    experiments, 322–323
    from searches, none, 201
reusable templates, 181
RIAs (Rich Internet Applications), 151, 223
    writing, Webinar, 594
Rogers, Bill, 3
Rogers, Ed, 3
roles, 96
    custom, creating, 100–101
    Folder Admin Role, 96
    folder-specific, 103
    system-wide, 103
Root folder, folder creation, 87–91
root folder, 87
Rotating Ad Smart Form, 153
rotating graphics, 150
    serialization, 153–161
rules, Flex Menu, 187

S

SamplePaymentGatewayProvider.cs, 542
scripts, client side, registering, 161
Search Admin built-in role, 104
Search Framework, 205
    crawling, 205–207
    indexing, 205–207
    querying, 205–207
    Search Framework API, 208–209
        permissions, 209
Search Phrase Report, 199–200
    insufficient search terms, 200
Search Server, queries, 207
Search Server 2008, 205
Search Server 2010, 205
Search Server Express 2008, 205
Search Server Express 2010, 205
searches, 224
    content, excluding, 198
    Did You Mean Widget, 202
    folders, Integrated Search, 199
    general terms, 202
    global accessibility, 203–205
    homepage, 150–151
    library, 93–95
        Link Searches, 94
    misspellings, 201–202
    navigation, 197–198
    no results, 201
    popular terms, 202
    queries, ambiguous, 200
    SiteSearch, strategy, 198–202
    SiteSearch Server Controls, 203–205
    SiteSearchInput Server Dontrol, 205
    social networking, 199
    Suggested Results feature, 202

synonym search, 201–202
technologies supported, 205
tracking, 199–200
XML fields, 199
SearchResults.aspx.cs, 203–204
securing server, 567
security testing, 553–554
SEO (search engine optimization)
online presence and, 583–584
URL aliasing and, 131
serialization
class definitions, 173
`DataContractJson-Serializer`, 172
`EkXml` object, 160
rotating graphics, 153–161
`Serialization.JavaScriptSerializer`, 172
`Serialization.JavaScriptSerializer` object, 172
`SerializeList` method, 174
server
returning to, 152
security, 567
server controls, 9
ActiveTopics Server Control, 353
ActivityStream Server Control, 425–426
Blog Server Control, 335, 353
BreadCrumb Server Control, 209
Cart Server Control, 507, 510–512, 522–525
Checkout Server Control, 507, 512–516
CMS Menu Server Control, 187
Collection Server Control, 279–280
Collections Server Control, 268
Community Group Profile Server Control, 392
CommunityGroupBrowser Server Control, 409
CommunityGroupList Server Control, 409
CommunityGroupMembers Server Control, 403
CommunityGroupProfile Server Control, 408
CommunitySearch Server Control, 409
Content Block Server Control, 79
ContentFlagging Server Control, 333, 379–383
ContentReview Server Control, 378, 379–383
CSS, 10
CurrencySelect Server Control, 495, 496
DataBinding, 10
DHTML Menu Server Control, 189
EkML, 10
FacebookLogin Server Control, 224
Flex Menu Server Control, 187
FolderBreadcrumb Server Control, 212–213
FormBlock Server Control, 311
Forum Server Control, 347–351
forums, 334
Friends Server Control, 401–404
functionality, 10
Invite Server Control, 374
properties, 375
LangageSelect Server Control, 141
LanguageAPI Server Control, 142
ListSummary Server Control, 263
membership management, 215
Membership Server Control, 215–218
MessageBoard Server Control, 251
MicroMessage Server Control, 433–435
MyAccount Server Control, 507–508
OrderList Server Control, 507, 508–510
PostHistory Server Control, 353
Product Server Control, 495, 503
properties, 504
ProductList Server Control, 495, 500–502
ProductSearch Server Control, 495, 496–498
properties, 497–499
Recommendation Server Control, 495, 504–505
properties, 505–506
SiteMap Server Control, 213–214
SiteSearch Server Controls, 203–205
SiteSearchInput Server Control, 205
SocialBar Server Control, 333, 369–370
properties, 370–371
SocialBar.ascx, 372–373
User Profile Server Control, 391
UserProfile Server Control, 394
WebCalendar Server Control, 239
XSLT, 10
ServerControlWS.asmx, 567
Settings tab (Workarea), 62
eCommerce, 445–446
Countries pane, 446–447
Currencies pane, 447–450
messages, 451–454
Regions pane, 459–461
shipping (eCommerce), 461–467
`ShowCategories` property, 349
SimpleHandler.aspx, 170–172, 183–185
Site-FeaturedProduct Widget, 520
Site-ProductSearch Widget, 519
SiteMap, 151, 213–214, 224
SiteMap Server Control, 213–214
properties, 214
sitemaps, 209
SiteSearch, 198–202
SiteSearch Server Controls, 203–205
SiteSearchInput Server Control, 205
Slave menu, 196–197
Smart Desktop, 59. *See also* Dashboard
Smart Form Data, creating, 123
Smart Form Design Package, 123–124
Smart Form Designer, 108
Smart Form Designs, 108, 110–111
content trees, associating to, 121–123
creating, 111–112, 118–121
Data Entry XSLT, 124
form elements, 124
.NET Classes, generating, 116

.NET Framework, 116
XML content, default, 124
XML Schema, 111, 124
XSLT, default display, 124
Smart Forms, 108, 109–110
    built-in role, 104
    compared to HTML forms, 110
    Content Block Server Control, 251
    events, 251
    Home Page Banner, 153
    Image Rotator, serialization, 153–161
    PageBuilder and, 293
    products, 473–479
    Rotating Ad, 153
Smart Forms tab (Add Folder interface), 89
social media, uses, 389
social navigation, activity streams, 422
social networking. *See* Community Framework
SocialBar Server Control, 333
    e-mail, message tokens, 376
    Invite Server Control, 374
    `Items` property options, 371–372
    overview, 369–370
    properties, 370–371
    SocialBar.ascx, 372–373
    widget implementation, 370–377
SocialBar.ascx, 372–373, 380–381, 382–383
software requirements, 45–46
source control, 47
Source Control Management System, 585
special groups, 55
special users, 54–55
splash pages, usability and, 152
spot checks, 576–577
sprints, 18
SQL (Structured Query Language), 13
staging environment, 549–550
    content, 550–551
stakeholder interviews for business plan, 20–21
static displays, 152
storage, 295
    instance data, 301–302
stored procedures, 13
storefront, use case, 492–494
storing content, 62
stress testing, 553
StringBuilder, 116
structured content, 110
structured data, Content Block Server Control, 112–116
Suggested Results feature in searches, 202
`SuppressBeacon` element, 327–328
Synchronization Admin built-in role, 104
synonym search, 201–202
system calendar
    creating, 240–243
    recurrences, 241–242

system calls
    `GetRolePermissionSystem`, 104
    `IsARoleMember`, 104
system requirements, 13–14
system testing, 26–27
    Final UAT testing, 552
    functional testing, 551–552
    load testing, 553
    performance testing, 552
    security testing, 553–554
    stress testing, 553
system-wide roles, 103

T

tags, unclosed, 123
Task Create built-in role, 104
Task Delete built-in role, 104
Task Redirect built-in role, 104
taxes (eCommerce), 461–467
taxonomy, 109, 145
    browsing by category, 125
    Community Framework and, 406–407
    configuration, folder assignment, 128
    content, adding, 128–129
    content organization and, 124
    creating, 126–128
    data structures and, 125
    fields, 127–128
    forums, 344
    language awareness, 125
    site rendering, 139
    taxonomy based URL aliasing, 131–132
        configuring, 135–136
    taxonomy tree, 125
    use cases, 125
    Wikis, 363
Taxonomy Administrator built-in role, 104
Taxonomy data object, 129
Taxonomy ID, 129
Taxonomy tab (Add Folder interface), 89
TaxonomyExampleService.ashx, 177–181
`TaxonomyItem` class, 174
technical requirements, 21–22
technical support, 16, 589
    chat support, 6
    contact methods, 6
    e-mail support, 5
    phone, 5
    Web form, 5
Telerik Scheduler, 239
    WebCalendar Server Control, 246
Template Configuration built-in role, 104
templates, 109
    .ASPX, 24

Blog Server Control, 358–363
community groups, 411–412
forums, 344
Generic Handler, 172
reusable, 181
XHTML, 24–25
Templates tab (Add Folder interface), 89
testimonials, 257–263
text localization, 139–140
Theme property, 349
Tidy process, 123
timeline navigation, activity streams, 422
TLD (Top Level Domain), 142
tokens, e-mail messages, 376
toolbar
    Add Task button, 76
    Analytics button, 78
    Content Reports button, 76–77
    Delete button, 75
    Edit button, 74
    Edit Properties button, 78
    Export for Translation button, 78
    History button, 74
    Language toolbar, 78
    Link Search button, 76
    View Approvals button, 76
    View Diff button, 75
    View Permissions button, 75
    View Publish button, 75
trackback URL, 356
tracking searches, 199–200
Traditional Ektron content block, 26
Traffic Analytics
    Business Analytics and, 324–325
    campaign effectiveness, 328–329
    site wide, 326–328
training, 7, 16
translating content
    Heartstone Translation Studio, 141
    language export, 141
    machine, 140
    manual, 140
    SDL Trados, 141
Traverse Folders permission, 103
TTL (Time To Live), 136
Twitter presence, 588

U

UnorderedListSummary.ekml, 238–239
UnorderedListSummary.xslt, 235
unstructured content, 110
updateDisplay method, 183
uptime, 584
URLs

aliasing, 109, 130, 145–146
    community aliasing, 132
    Disable Language Awareness property, 134
    enabling, 133–135
    file extensions and, 131
    folder based, 132
    manual aliasing, 132
    parameter resolution logic, 134–135
    Query String Action property, 134
    RegEx based, 132
    SEO and, 131
    taxonomy based, 131–132
        configuring, 135–136
    trackback URLs, 356
    usability for humans, 131
usability, 582
use cases
    blogs, 336–338
    connecting to clients, 226–227
    eCommerce, 442–443
    forums, 336–338
    homepage, 148–149
    OnTrek Campaign Landing Page, 266–268
    storefront, 492–494
    Wikis, 336–338
user acceptance testing, 27–28
User Admin built-in role, 104
user calendar, creating, 243–245
user controls
    dashboards, implementing, 422
    PageBuilder, 30
    widgets, 268, 298
user experience requirements, 22–23
User Logged In activity, 430–431
User Profile Server Control, 391
user profiles, micro-messaging, 435–437
UserGroupForum.aspx, 348
UserProfile Server Control, 394, 397–404
users
    community group discovery, 409
    content authors, 54
    Developer, 30
    membership, 54, 215
    Messaging Expert, 30
    properties, modifying, 218–219
    registering, allowing, 215–218
    special users, 54–55
    Web Production Manager, 30

V

Variance-Cancelled Occurrence events (calandar), 242
Variance-Extra Occurrence events (calandar), 242
video, 225, 227–228
    customer testimonials, 257–263

video catalog (eCommerce), 479–481
videos, 263
virtual staging, 561–562
Visual Studio, XSLT, debugging, 165–166
Vs, 54

W

waterfall-based methodologies, 18
    taxes on sales, 467
WCMS (Web content management system), 7
Web Alerts tab (Add Folder interface), 89
Web Analytics, 324
    reach and, 582–583
    reports, 325–326
    Traffic Analytics
        Business Analytics and, 324–325
        site wide, 326–328
Web form support, 5
Web Production Managers, 30
Web services, 152
    consumption, 169–170
    creation, 169–170
WebCalendar, folder, 87
WebCalendar Server Control, 239
    displaying events, 246–250
    properties, 246–247
    Telerik Scheduler, 246
WebEventData, 254
Webinars, 590–591
    CDN (Content Delivery Network), 591
    CMS Extension Framework, 591
    Content Targeting Widget, 593
    eCommerce APIs, 592
    eCommerce payment gateway provider, 593
    eCommerce site build, 592
    eCommerce Workflow Engine, 592
    eSync, 593
    Framework API, 591
    Marketing Optimization Suite, 594
    Widgets in Version 8, 594
    Writing RIA Application, 594
websites
    audience, 108
    business case, 18–19
    content needs, 107
    deploying
        development process, 549
        discovery collateral, 548
        pre-conditions, 548–554
        staging environment, 549–551
        system testing, 551–554
    multilingual, designing, 137–138
    navigation cues, 108
    organization, 108

    project startup, 18
    structural definition, 108
    templates, 109
    validation definition, 108
Widget Settings, 282
widget spaces, 420–422
Widget Sync button, 305
Widget Tray, 420
WidgetDataMember attribute, 302
WidgetHost, 299, 307
    events
        Close, 308
        Create, 308
        Edit, 308
        Maximize, 308
        Minimize, 308
    properties, 308
WidgetHost.Edit event, 302
widgets, 12, 297–298
    ActivityStream, 423–425
    BrightCove PageBuilder Widget, 257
    Collection Widget, 270
    Collections Widget, 269
    ContentBlock Widget, 519
    creating, 299–307
    Did You Mean, 202
    DropZones, 268
    edit interface, 300–301
    editing screen, 298
    events, 299–300
    Front-End Widgets, 299
    instantiation, 307
    Multivariate Experiment Widget, 317, 318
    Multivariate Section Widget, 317–318
        content modification, 320–322
    Multivariate Target Widget, 317, 318
    PageBuilder, 282
    PageBuilder Widgets, 265
    preloaded, 59
    Public-Facing, 299
    Site-FeaturedProduct Widget, 520
    Site-ProductSearch Widget, 519
    SocialBar, implementing, 370–377
    user controls and, 268, 298
    Widget Tray, 420
Widgets in Version 8 Webinar, 594
Widgets property, 295
wiki feature, 364–365
Wikis, 335
    community folders, 363
    Content Block Server Control, 364
    creating, 364
    editing existing content, 369
    links, 367–369
    ListSummary Server Control, 364
    PageBuilder page, 365–367

taxonomy and, 363
use case, 336–338
using, 367–369
Windows Service, crawls, 206
Windows Workflow Foundation, 525
    activities, 526
        base activity library, 527
        custom, 527–531
        toolbox, 533
    base activity library, 526, 527
    designer, 526
    Host process, 526
    overview, 526–527
    runtime engine, 526
    workflow, 526
        building, 531–534
Wireframes, 22, 26, 148
    ASPX templates, 268
    associating, 305–307
    compared to layouts, 293–295
    creating, 282, 283–286
    folder associations, 286
    layout creation, 286–292
    PageBuilder, 282
wizards, HTML Form Wizard, 310–311
Workarea
    Activities, 424
    blogs, creating, 354–358
    calendars, 239
    community groups, creating, 410–411
    content, viewing, 69–73
    content authors, license key, 54
    content managers, 54
    Content pane toolbar, 69
    Content tab, 59, 60–61
        Alias tab, 66
        Category tab, 67
        Comment tab, 67
        Metadata tab, 65
        Schedule tab, 66–67
        Summary tab, 65
        Templates tab, 67
    Dashboard, 56, 60
    Data Designer, Smart Form Designs, 111
    Flash settings, 260–261
    folders, boards, 339
    forums, 339
        creating, 346–347
        creation flow, 339–340
        discussion board, 340–343
        Discussion Forum, 346
        properties, 343–345
        Replace Word, 346
        Restricted IP, 346
        Subject, 346
        User Rank, 346
        viewing, 350–351
    launching, 56
    Library tab, 59
    PayPal, 456–457
    Report section, 576
    Reports tab, 59, 62
    Settings tab, 59, 62
    Smart Desktop, 59
    View Content Screen
        Alias, 71
        Category, 71
        Comment, 71
        Content, 69
        Metadata, 71
        Properties, 69
        Summary, 69
        Tasks, 71
    Wikis, creating, 364
Writing RIA Application Webinar, 594

X

XHTML templates, 24–25
XLIFF Admin built-in role, 104
XML (eXtensible Markup Language)
    fields, structured searches, 199
    Widget Settings, 282
XML Schema, Smart Form Designs, 111
XML Schema Definition file, 116
XML Schema Definition tool, 116–117
    classes, 117–118
XPath, 116
.XSD file, 116
XSL Transforms, 263
XSLT (XML Stylesheet Language for Transformations), 10
    benefits, 115
    Flex Menu Server Control markup, 189
    Image Rotator
        custom XSLT, 162–165
        debugging, 165–166
        setting code to use, 166–169
    Knowledge Base articles, 115
    ListSummaries, 228
        HTML markup and, 232–236
    overriding, Content Block Server Control, 112–113
XsltArgumentList object, 404

Z

Zones property, 295